Visual Basic Programmer's Guide to the .NET Framework Class Library

Lars Powers and Mike Snell

201 West 103rd St., Indianapolis, Indiana 46290 USA

ASSOCIATE PUBLISHER
Linda Engelman

ACQUISITIONS EDITOR
Sondra Scott

DEVELOPMENT EDITOR
Karen Wachs

MANAGING EDITOR
Charlotte Clapp

PROJECT EDITOR
Tony Reitz

COPY EDITOR
Barbara Hacha

INDEXER
Rebecca Salerno

TECHNICAL EDITORS
Jawahar Puvvala
Dan Suceava

TEAM COORDINATOR
Lynne Williams

INTERIOR DESIGNER
Gary Adair

COVER DESIGNER
Aren Howell

PAGE LAYOUT
Julie Swenson

Overview

Contents

Foreword

It's been said that change is "the constant, the signal for rebirth, the egg of the phoenix." In today's dynamic operating environment, change and rebirth are not only constants, but also essential elements to the survival of any successful business.

As individuals, our computing experience has continued to evolve rapidly, most noticeably in recent years. In fact, if we take a step back in time, we can see how far things have really come in this short period. In 1990, just over 10 years ago, I owned an NEC Powermate 286—a machine, that at the time, fulfilled the vast majority of my computing needs quite nicely. After all, it cranked along at a steady 8MHz, it included not only a 5.25" floppy drive, but also 20MB hard disk that I knew I would *never* fill, and of course, that 640KB of RAM on board was *all I would ever need.* When it came time to "surf" for information, I'd simply fire up my 2400bps modem and do *what*? No, not dial into my Internet Service Provider—I would make a direct phone call to my local Bulletin Board System (BBS) in order to view page after page of flashing, colored ANSI text across my screen. Yes, it all sounds so innocent today, and yet it was just over 10 years ago.

During the past decade, we've undeniably witnessed a revolution in the computing industry. Moore's Law, stating that computing power doubles approximately every 18 months, has been an important agent in the corporate success of many of our companies. In addition, the prolif-eration of mobile devices, the rapidly decreasing costs and increasing bandwidth of online con-nectivity, as well as the penetration of standards such as XML and SOAP into the Internet, have all been major contributing factors to the computing revolution that we continue to expe-rience today. But what is the net effect of these radical industry changes on us *as developers*? The computing revolution of the past decade has not only significantly expanded our range of programming possibilities, but has also presented us with larger, more complex challenges than we have ever before faced.

In 1991, a new developer tool emerged that would not only address the development chal-lenges of the time, but would also fundamentally change the way that we build applications. Like the computing climate of the past decade, Microsoft Visual Basic 1.0 was revolutionary—it enabled both professional and casual developers to quickly and effectively build Windows applications—a task that, at the time, was anything but trivial. Visual Basic introduced the con-cept of RAD (Rapid Application Development) by providing an entirely graphical environment to build Windows applications. Not only did this cause an upsurge in the number of Windows applications being developed, but it also gave birth to a new market of third-party control vendors. Together, these acted as a major driving force in the rapid adoption of the Windows platform.

While more and more of us were jumping on the quickly growing RAD VB trend, the computing landscape and the development needs of our corporations were evolving. At each step of the way, the Visual Basic language and tool evolved to meet these ever-changing needs. Sometimes the changes introduced in a new version were relatively minor (Visual Basic 2.0), sometimes they introduced more radical changes (Visual Basic 4.0), but the overall outcome remained consistent—a developer tool agile enough to adapt to the changing needs of the industry and radical enough to play a major part in the adoption of the platform. This not only applied to Windows-based development with the release of VB 1.0, but also to client-server programming with VB 2 and 3, 32-programming and the world of Windows 95 with VB 4, and component development with Visual Basic 5.0.

Yet while each subsequent version of Visual Basic played a crucial role in driving platform adoption, it has ironically always remained separate from the platform itself. The VB runtime, while "protecting" us from the underlying complexities of the Win32 APIs and COM programming, also served to obstruct us from new platform features until they were wrapped and made available to us in our runtime DLL—VBRUNxxx.dll or MSVBVMxx.dll. This somewhat unnatural separation from the platform has not only caused headaches, but has also been the source of Visual Basic being disregarded as a second-class language—not suitable for true enterprise-level development.

Now, as we enter a new era of challenges, highlighted by the need to build highly scalable, secure enterprise-critical software and Web services powered by XML, a new version of Visual Basic, Visual Basic .NET, is once again poised to revolutionize the way we build applications. However, unlike previous versions of Visual Basic, Visual Basic .NET finally achieves that integration with the underlying platform—the .NET Framework—that will empower VB developers to accomplish tasks never before possible.

The effects of the new .NET Framework, Visual Basic .NET, and the integration between them are both exciting and far-reaching. Because Visual Basic .NET was built from the ground-up to be a first-class player on the .NET Framework, it neither impedes VB developers from directly accessing the rich feature set available in the Framework libraries nor carries with it antiquated nonstructured programming constructs of our father's BASIC. It provides a streamlined, modernized language that promotes both highly efficient and well-structured programming. Combine that with the .NET Framework's provisions for disconnected data access, multi-threading, code access security, and a full set of object-oriented concepts, and you've got a Visual Basic with unprecedented levels of both power and productivity.

However, with so many new features there comes an inevitable associated cost—that of learning the new concepts. This is precisely why I'm so excited about Lars' and Mike's book, *Visual Basic Programmer's Guide to the .NET Framework Class Library*. In addition to making the large, hierarchical structure of the .NET Framework highly digestible, Lars and Mike do so in a way that enables developers to learn the concepts as they directly relate to common programming tasks. They cover everything from the organizational structure of the extensive class library to the various namespaces for building UI, working with XML data, and accomplishing common network-based programming tasks. In addition, the book aptly discusses techniques for accessing existing COM+ services and mapping existing skills from the Win32 APIs to their equivalents in the world of .NET.

As the application development landscape continues to evolve and reinvent itself, it will be crucial that we as VB developers continue to evolve in concert. Visual Basic .NET and the .NET Framework provide the springboard we need to take our next big evolutionary step. And with this book, you're already well on your way to understanding and applying the new concepts and programming constructs that will propel us into the next 10 years of RAD Visual Basic application development.

Ari Bixhorn
Product Manager
Visual Basic .NET
Microsoft Corporation

Preface

.NET is not simply a new set of developer tools to be unleashed in late 2001 or early 2002. It is a multilevel strategy that will be realized over years, not months. Its impact to computing will be broad and long lasting. Let's take a look at where .NET came from.

.NET was made public at the Professional Developers Conference (PDC) in Orlando, July 2000. We were both lucky enough to be in attendance. What a shocker. We watched with nodding heads and jaws agape as speaker after speaker illuminated solutions and described new paradigms in computing. We furiously took notes and couldn't wait to get our hands on the .NET bits. We installed Beta 1 in our hotel rooms. We were bitten. It was obvious Microsoft had done it right and had taken our favorite programming language, Visual Basic, to new heights. One of the questions that we have since asked ourselves is, "Why did Microsoft decide to tackle such a vision?" and "Where was .NET (or this vision) before Orlando?"

The .NET Vision

Bill Gates relates that the vision for .NET could actually be traced back as far as 1990. In his Forum 2000 keynote address he stated, "I'd even go back to the vision efforts like the Information at Your Fingertips work that we did back in 1990." He also referred to the "the investments [Microsoft] made in basic research over the intervening years" and stated that .NET is the result of the billions of dollars Microsoft has poured into research and development over the years. He states, "almost every one of these new capabilities I'm talking about benefits from work that took many, many years and was off in that research environment being pulled together without a particular schedule in mind."

.NET did not evolve out of Microsoft's existing DNA architecture or strategy. It is nearly a total rewrite around delivering a distributed infrastructure. In fact, what's interesting is that the phrase, "software as a service" is actually credited to two of Microsoft's chief competitors. A recent whitepaper by the Gartner Group grades .NET after its first six months. It says it best in the following:

> The software-as-a-service phrase originated around 1997 with Oracle's CEO Larry Ellison and Sun Microsystems' CEO Scott McNealy, during the age of network computer hype. Oracle and Sun never really delivered on this concept, and their vision was more of centralized-only resources. However, to any software company listening—and Microsoft certainly listens—Ellison and McNealy's remarks indicated that a big change in the software market was about to happen. .NET is Microsoft's attempt to define this change and the rate at which it will occur.
>
> This definition of .NET—i.e., a shift to a software-as-a-service paradigm—is the one best understood by most users. Gartner believes Microsoft is now providing more vision and influence regarding this shift than any other vendor.

We start to get a picture of how .NET evolved out of the research laboratory and into Microsoft's products. As for the question, "Why .NET and not something else?" we can only speculate. A quick look at some of Microsoft's goals for .NET is the basis for our speculation.

- Open standards without compromising intellectual property
- Answer the requests of developers for stronger OOP support
- Answer the requests of businesses to build a scalable, robust platform
- Solve the problems of interoperability
- Integrate all Microsoft products and services

These are some ambitious goals by any standard and are by no means the only goals of Microsoft's .NET strategy. However, this subset allows you to see how .NET became a bet-the-company strategy. In the end, however, Microsoft knew it was the right strategy, saw a chance to make it happen, and boldly went for it. With the .NET Framework, Microsoft has made a concerted effort to go back to the drawing boards and fix the fundamental problems that exist for many developers working with the current crop of Windows DNA/COM/Win32 technologies. Ground zero for .NET is its prolific set of namespaces.

The Vision of This Book

This book's genesis can be traced back to the recognition of a simple fact: The .NET Framework Class Library is a universal starting point for developers. This includes those transitioning from older versions of Visual Basic and developers just entering the .NET realm—regardless of their chosen language.

As we started to dig more and more into .NET, we recognized the need for an all-encompassing book that would take the class library, split it into digestible pieces, and then feed those pieces to developers as they relate to a typical programming task. This book, we figured, would need to teach developers how to execute common programming tasks using the .NET namespace classes and components while retaining a reference aspect that would document and explain many of the various elements that developers would interact with in their code.

Thankfully, a few individuals at Sams Publishing shared in our vision and suggested that we go ahead and write the book! In a way, this book plays a similar role to the book, *VB Programmers Guide to the Win32 API*, that we all know and love. It attempts to demystify what is essentially a large and complex code library (thankfully, the developers at Microsoft have made this code library one that is actually a pleasure to deal with). When VB .NET developers first set out to create applications for .NET, it will be crucial for them to have a base understanding of the capabilities of the intrinsic .NET technologies. They will need to comprehend the capabilities of the existing namespaces in .NET and how they can then be leveraged by extension or reference to create applications ranging from the simple to the complex. This book is for them.

In this book, we try to answer some very fundamental questions in regard to each unique technology, such as the following:

- What does the .NET Class Library provide in terms of reusable code?
- Are .NET structures available that I can use to accomplish a specific task?
- How do I go about interfacing with the .NET Framework through my code?

In short, what we hope we have delivered is a definitive guide to the capabilities of the .NET Framework Class Library. We have tried to provide an appropriate mix of introductory text (to ease developers into a specific technology that they may not have worked with in the past, such as XML or Directory Services), combined with task-driven code samples and detailed reference information.

Our hope is that you get as much joy discovering .NET through our eyes as we did discovering .NET at the PDC in Orlando, but with a lot less frustration.

About the Authors

Lars Powers (lars@brilliantSTORM.com)

Lars is a Microsoft Certified Solutions Developer (MCSD) with more than 10 years of experience analyzing business problems and developing software solutions. Most of his experience centers on leading development teams and writing software in Microsoft development environments.

Mike Snell (mike@brilliantSTORM.com)

Mike is also a MCSD with more than 10 years of experience writing and designing software. His experience centers on creating enterprise-level, Web-based systems using the Microsoft platform.

Lars and Mike

Lars and Mike have been working together at four separate companies for more than six years. In doing so, they've built a wealth of knowledge about executing successful projects and delivering enterprise-level systems.

Together, they have formed brilliantStorm (http://www.brilliantstorm.com): a partnership focused on providing developers with .NET productivity tools, information, and training.

About the Technical Editors

Dan Suceava is currently a Senior Programmer for Vitrix, Inc., a time and attendance software company located in Tempe, Arizona. He has been developing desktop and *n*-tiered applications in Visual Basic since 1996. He has recently completed work on an ASP solution that offers timekeeping over the Web to other businesses. He holds a Master's Degree in Computer Science from Arizona State University.

Jawahar (JP) Puvvala is currently working as a senior developer. He has extensive experience with Microsoft and Java technologies, having designed and developed several enterprise systems. He has two Master's Degrees, and currently holds MCSD, MCSE, and MCDBA certifications. JP also has research experience and has published several conference and journal papers.

Dedication

Lars

To my wife, Cheryl, and my daughter, Kelsey, who unfortunately bore the brunt of my absence from all things social as my world closed down to just a computer screen and various builds of .NET. Their simple contribution of understanding and patience helped in ways too numerous to mention.

Mike

To my wife, Carrie, whose continuous support made this possible (I hope I can return the gesture), and to my daughter, Allie, and my son, Benjamin, who shouted their encouragement (and let me know when it was time to eat or sleep) into the ventilation ducts that carried their messages down to me in the basement...I can come up now.

Acknowledgments

We have been involved with many software projects on many levels, and, without exception, they have all involved a concerted team effort. This project was no different.

We would like to thank all the hard-working professionals at Sams Publishing for helping us deliver what you see before you. We would especially like to thank Sondra Scott for believing in us from the start, Karen Wachs for her editorial determination and patience, and JP and Dan, our technical editors, who found errors both big and small.

Finally, we would like to thank the hardworking folks at Microsoft for having the courage and talent to deliver such a monumental piece of technology; it has been many years since we have been this energized and excited about what the future holds.

Tell Us What You Think!

As the reader of this book, *you* are our most important critic and commentator. We value your opinion and want to know what we're doing right, what we could do better, what areas you'd like to see us publish in, and any other words of wisdom you're willing to pass our way.

As an Associate Publisher for Sams Publishing, I welcome your comments. You can fax, e-mail, or write me directly to let me know what you did or didn't like about this book—as well as what we can do to make our books stronger.

Please note that I cannot help you with technical problems related to the topic of this book, and that because of the high volume of mail I receive, I might not be able to reply to every message.

When you write, please be sure to include this book's title and author as well as your name and phone or fax number. I will carefully review your comments and share them with the author and editors who worked on the book.

Fax: (317) 581-4770

E-mail: feedback@samspublishing.com

Mail: Linda Engelman
          Associate Publisher
          Sams Publishing
          201 West 103rd Street
          Indianapolis, IN 46290 USA

Introduction

It's not often you get to take over a franchise. Through hard work and dedication, Dan Appleman has built his *Visual Basic Programmer's Guide* series of API books into some of the most recognized and best selling Visual Basic books of all time. Those books are the inspiration for this one.

When Dan was approached to do a similar book for the .NET Framework, he felt he needed to pursue other directions and other titles. The paradigm shifts brought on by .NET were also causing authors and editors to rethink their titles and opportunities. .NET meant a total rewrite of nearly every title and completely different approaches. Well, as Dan moved in another direction, we were talking with Sams Publishing about doing a book on the .NET namespaces. The *Programmer's Guide* concept was presented to us; we saw the opportunity and pounced.

We want to thank Dan for the groundwork he has laid for us as Visual Basic developers and authors. By applying the approach he pioneered with the Win32 API to the world of .NET, we hope to continue to bring this member of the Sams *Programmer's Guide* series honor and distinction amongst the sea of technical books.

What Is the Purpose of This Book?

Our intention is to provide developers a roadmap to the .NET Framework Class Library. Chapters are designed to teach you how to use the .NET namespaces to solve your specific business problems. This book attempts to educate current Visual Basic 6 programmers and new VB .NET programmers on the core .NET namespaces and their uses.

Potential buyers should view this book as a reference and guide to the new API exposed by the .NET Framework through its many namespaces, classes, and data types. We realize that when you first set out to create applications using .NET, it is crucial to have a basic understanding of the capabilities of the .NET technologies. You need to comprehend the capabilities of the existing namespaces in .NET and how they can then be leveraged by extension or reference to create applications ranging from the simple to the complex.

Bottom line: We want to get you writing useful, production-ready code utilizing .NET.

Who Should Read This Book?

.NET developers should read this book. We've set our sights directly on the intermediate to advanced VB developer transitioning to .NET. Those ready to see what the class library can do to make their coding day more productive will benefit most from this title. That said, although there are not many facets to this book targeted at the novice or beginning VB developer, the book will be a useful resource to them as well. It will assist in teaching the promise of .NET and serve as a great how-to reference for the namespace functionality.

The namespaces themselves are language neutral. All languages in .NET derive from the same Framework Class Library. Nearly every section in this book can be applied outside of VB. Of course, all the source code (and there is a lot of source code) is written in VB syntax. However, we provide liberal comments in the code to ease understanding and help with porting.

After finishing the book, you should have a solid understanding of the functionality available in the .NET Framework Class Library. You should be able to intelligently use and inherit this functionality to accomplish a wide variety of common and not-so-common programming tasks. In addition, you will walk away with a firm grasp of how the different pieces of .NET relate to one another and work together to provide a fully realized system for software development.

What Is This Book Not?

This book is not a comprehensive reference to the .NET Framework, although there is a great deal of useful reference information included. The size of the Framework Class Library forced us to take a different approach. There are more than 3,000 classes (and growing) in the namespace. It would be a daunting task to reference all this information, and the value of duplicating material easily available from MSDN would be questionable. Additionally, this reference information is now exposed to you directly in the IDE.

Instead of a reference, this book stresses the "guide" in its title. We provide a roadmap to the various namespaces, and teach you how to write code using the classes. From there, you should have no problem finding and using that specific enumeration value or just the right overload to a method.

This book is not *Teach Yourself VB .NET Programming in 24 Hours* or *The Complete Idiot's Guide to VB .NET*. Those titles are certainly useful in their own right but we expect readers to have a degree of proficiency with VB and programming in general. If you do not, we suggest you get a quality beginner-level book and return to this as a how-to reference for various namespaces.

What Is in This Book?

This book is divided into three parts. Part I, "An Introduction to .NET," is designed to give readers a solid footing with regard to .NET, object-oriented programming, and the Framework Class Library. Part II, "Working with the .NET Namespaces," walks readers through specific programming tasks using the namespaces. Part III, "Real-World .NET Programming," is where we get into some of the more advanced issues related to .NET development. We position the lessons learned in Part II within the context of real projects and present some of the more advanced concepts in the library.

How to Read This Book

We encourage readers to read the book from front to back. We also know this is often not practical due to time pressures and the length of this title. Therefore, if you are familiar with .NET (have been using the betas) and are fairly comfortable with OOP, just skim the first section. You can always go back, right?

For Part II, we suggest readers examine the table of contents and peruse the actual content in order to become familiar with what is available to you. Then, pick a topic that you need to know for a project or intend to use and read the associated chapter. This will give you a flavor for the other Part II chapters. Now, you can go back and get the information as needed.

We believe Part III is a must-read. Developers need to be concerned with the issues presented to help make their project more successful.

What Is on the Web Site?

There is a companion Web site to this title. On this site you will find full source code available for download. This should save you the time of retyping and allow us to provide you with the most up-to-date information. Any corrections or known issues with the source code or text in the book will be noted. Additionally, we provide you with a means to communicate thoughts, comments, and suggestions directly to us. We will be sure to post as many comments as we can.

To visit the companion Web site, visit Sams Publishing at www.samspublishing.com.

Or, you can visit the author's Web site at http://www.brilliantStorm.com. This site contains the book's source and related information. Plus, it will contain links to other .NET resources, tips, and articles.

An Introduction to .NET

Part I of this book focuses on introducing developers to .NET as a whole, delineating and defining the pieces of .NET, and explaining the general format, structure, and intent of the Framework Class Library. This section positions Microsoft's .NET strategy within the context of previous Microsoft technologies and environments. Focus will be given to how .NET affects you, the developer.

Part I explores

- What .NET is and why .NET is important
- The evolution of VB .NET
- The object-oriented characteristics of VB .NET
- The structure of the Framework Class Library

After reading this section, you should be well equipped for the content on the Framework Class Library that follows in Part II.

Evolution of .NET

IN THIS CHAPTER

We start this book by describing Microsoft's .NET strategy and its relevance to the industry. We first present .NET's overall timetable and provide a description of the various components that comprise .NET. We then detail the ramifications and relevance of .NET. Finally, we end the chapter by defining the parts of the .NET Framework and detailing the benefits they provide our application development efforts.

After reading this chapter, you should

- Understand Microsoft's .NET initiative, its components, and its timeline
- See the .NET initiative in the context of its relevance to specific audiences
- Have a solid understanding of the .NET Framework including the Common Language Runtime (CLR) and Framework Class Library (FCL)
- Understand the benefits of the .NET Framework for you as a developer
- Begin to see the various programming paradigm shifts necessary to transition from VB6/Win32 development to .NET

The Composition of .NET

Simply stated, Microsoft is reinventing its company around the concept of delivering software as a service across the Internet. Its ambition is to connect islands of information and functionality into a collaborative, rich, and coherent experience for users.

In order to realize this vision, Microsoft is recreating its development tools, server software, operating systems, user applications, and Web browser. It is creating new tools and applications and helping to define new Internet standards. This all revolves around the concept of providing software as a service.

It all starts with the development platform. That is the core of the .NET platform and the focus of this book.

But what *are* the physical pieces that make up .NET? This is a difficult question to answer. For instance, try your luck with the following multiple-choice question:

Microsoft .NET is a

    a. Point of view advocating software as a service

    b. Series of software development tools

    c. Set of server products (like Windows 2000)

    d. Marketing and branding strategy initiated by Microsoft

    e. Evolution of Microsoft's recommended way to design and build software

The answer? All of the above! Now you can begin to understand the problem with identifying all of the different pieces of .NET. Generally speaking, Microsoft considers the pieces of .NET to focus on three different areas:

1. Tools and languages for .NET-based software development

2. Building block services products for programmers and non-programmers

3. Third-party developed services

Right now, the major pieces to consider fall under the first two categories: software development tools and so-called building block services. Third-party services will be in more evidence after .NET has been broadly adopted.

Microsoft .NET Timeline

Table 1.1 outlines the products and parts that make up Microsoft's .NET initiative.

TABLE 1.1   .NET Timetable

	2000	*2001*	*2002+*
Experiences		Windows XP	Additional .NET Experiences
		bCentral	
		MSN	
Clients	Windows CE	Windows XP	Tablet PC
	Windows NT Embedded	Windows XP Embedded	Other smart devices
	Windows 2000	Talisker	
		Stinger	
		XBox	
Services		Hailstorm	Additional Services
Tools	Visual Studio .NET Beta 1	Visual Studio .NET	
	SOAP Toolkit Beta	.NET Framework	
	MSDN Online	.NET Compact Framework	
Servers	Windows 2000 Server	Mobile Information Server	Additional Servers
	SQL Server 2000		Whistler Server Embedded
	BizTalk Server 2000		Whistler Server

Tools and Languages

Most of the visible thrust of .NET has been concentrated on the .NET development tools. In order to accomplish the vision of creating software as a service, programmers must first have tools that directly support that vision. .NET offers a suite of tools and technologies that will help you write distributed software.

The .NET Framework

The .NET Framework represents the actual plumbing of .NET; it is a set of services and pre-built classes that you can use to access core operating system functionality such as sending e-mail or output to the printer. That is, in fact, the focus of this book: the .NET Framework Class Library. This runtime environment allows us to write robust code more quickly, efficiently, and to manage and deploy the code more easily.

Along with these classes, the framework includes such things as the Common Type System (CTS), Common Language Runtime (CLR), and the Common Type Specification (CTS). These items will be explained in detail later in this chapter.

The framework can be broken down to the following definition: The .NET Framework is the base structure necessary to write .NET applications. Without it, there is no .NET and no .NET applications.

One of key aspects of the .NET Framework is that it is language agnostic. The way you program with it does not change depending on the .NET language you are using. This is a huge productivity benefit for programmers and finally creates a level playing field for all Windows developers.

Visual Studio .NET

Visual Studio .NET is the flagship IDE for .NET development. Finally, all Microsoft development shares a single IDE! No more VB for this, InterDev for that; .NET consolidates design, development, and debugging into one cohesive environment. Of course the IDE is fully customizable and extensible. Look for third parties to offer extensions or versions of the IDE. And of course, the object model is exposed for you to write custom extensions.

Another powerful technology is .NET enterprise templates. These templates allow team leaders to control features and access portions of the IDE. For example, you can restrict certain team members to only be able to create forms or do UI design. At the same time, other developers might only be able to create components using a specific language. .NET enterprise templates give managers control over the capabilities of specific team members.

Microsoft ASP.NET

Since the introduction of IIS (Internet Information Server) in late 1997, ASP (Active Server Pages) has been the principal technology for Microsoft developers to deliver Web content. As we all know, ASP forced developers to embed script and logic inside of UI (HTML) code. While this was simple enough and relatively easy to use for basic tasks, it quickly became cumbersome to program against and support as applications grew in scale and complexity.

The .NET version of Microsoft's ASP finally separates user interface (HTML) from script. ASP.NET implements a feature that Microsoft calls *code-behind*. This feature allows you to write HTML and code into separate files; the HTML file simply maintains a link to its associated code file. Sounds simple enough, and it is; it is remarkable how much easier it makes life for developers. The paradigm is equivalent to the win-forms paradigm (in fact, it is called Web Forms) where developers create a form using drag-and-drop and write code behind the various controls. Additionally, the code behind Web Forms can be written in any .NET language.

Another problem from which ASP suffered is slow performance due to the scripting code being processed at runtime. ASP.NET automatically compiles code files when deployed or first accessed. There is no longer a performance difference between a script class and one written and compiled into a DLL! However, ASP.NET does not take away your ability to promote code simply by copying over a file in a directory. Thanks to the JIT (just-in-time) compiler, a file can be replaced and it will simply be recompiled by the system as need be.

> **NOTE**
>
> ASP developers of old, don't fret; both the Response and the Request objects are still available.

ASP.NET allows programmers to quickly infuse Web sites with dynamic content and functionality. It represents a serious step forward for the ASP technology.

Microsoft Visual Basic .NET

After 10 years, VB is finally moving from a cool technology with which to build applications to an actual, first-class programming language. Visual Basic .NET represents a complete overhaul of the previous Visual Basic products from Microsoft. While introducing new components that make .NET programming easier than ever, it faithfully adheres to its past goals of allowing developers to build quality programs quickly. Chapter 2, "Evolution of VB .NET," will further explore the new Visual Basic language.

Microsoft-Managed Extensions for Visual C++

The latest incarnation of Microsoft's acclaimed C++ development environment, Visual C++ .NET differs from the other .NET languages: It is the only language in which you can write unmanaged code. Unmanaged code does not run inside the .NET runtime, whereas .NET code is "managed" by the runtime.

Microsoft C#

Microsoft decided to launch .NET with a new language—C#. There were multiple reasons for creating C#. For one, the language keeps the syntax of a typical C++ application while providing some of the simplicity of Visual Basic. Microsoft's hope is that C# will become the language of choice for those developers hooked on C++. Secondly, C# provides developers with a Java-like alternative. It is no secret that the .NET architecture shares some of Java's design concepts; C# is the Java of .NET. Of course, .NET will have a Java story (Rational and others will make sure of that) but Microsoft hopes that C# is compelling enough to lure Java developers over to the .NET camp. Finally, Microsoft wrote most of the .NET Framework code using C# thus solidifying it as the language of .NET.

Building Block Services

One of the many benefits of .NET is the ease with which you can integrate legacy applications and software written on disparate systems. The software industry still struggles with this concept; a concept that other industries have down to a science. For instance, a newly built home may be assembled from a complete, modular staircase made by a company in Canada, a deck composed of pre-assembled timber from a company in Minnesota, and front and side frames from a company in Illinois. It is a rare occasion when a builder or architect doesn't leverage work done by another firm or company when it comes to actually raising the walls of a house.

It is just such a business model that the software industry has been pursuing: one where companies are free to build the "blocks" that they have the most experience and expertise with, and then sell them (as a service) multiple times, creating a commodity item.

Traditionally, this has been difficult to do with software because the process of taking someone else's code and making it work inside of, or in conjunction with, your own was a technically challenging and risky proposition. It is definitely not as easy as integrating that staircase you brought from Canada in your house: A few nails, some sweat, and you have a structurally sound set of stairs! Software integration typically involves data format incompatibilities as well as discrepancies in architecture and design.

Some of these building block services that have already been announced are listed next.

Identity Services

These include such things as login and password verification and electronic wallets. These services represent a secure and safe way to verify someone's identity and then act accordingly.

Notification and Messaging Services

Building on technology already employed for things like Hotmail (Microsoft's free e-mail service) and Microsoft Instant Messenger (Microsoft's free messaging software), these services aim to provide e-mail, fax, and voicemail to and from almost any device from a PC to a handheld device.

Personalization Services

Targeted squarely at companies that are interested in catering to the individual, these services manage the rules and preferences necessary to show people only what they want to see on a Web site or other computer system.

Calendar Services

Calendar services allow for the integration and management of personal, work, and home calendars. They allow people to track their time and appointments intelligently, and collaborate with others doing the same.

Directory and Search Services

Directory and search services are a means of cataloging and then searching a variety of things (people, places, and so on). They expose a virtual "yellow pages" of information that can be queried for specific, relevant information.

.NET Enterprise Server and Office Products

To accelerate the introduction, development, and propagation of service-based software, Microsoft is rapidly infusing its core product lines with .NET technology, positioning it as yet another building block layer of helper services, all with the same goal of easing development of software as a service.

Application Center 2000

Application Center 2000 is a management tool designed to simplify the management of groups of servers. Using Application Center makes it much easier to administer and maintain Web applications that span multiple machines. How? This product lets you treat a group of servers as one server.

BizTalk Server 2000

When different companies have to exchange data between their systems, problems inevitably arise. Most of the issues revolve around the fact that, typically, different companies will store their data in different formats. A typical scenario involves trading partner hubs—companies passing invoices, purchase orders, and inventory information back and forth. Because it is unrealistic to expect every company involved in such an exchange to change their data format to some common, central format, the solution is data mapping. Quite simply, data mapping is the processing of mapping one piece of data to another. What one company calls a SKU, another company might call an inventory control number; one company may allow alphanumeric SKUs, while another allows only numeric control numbers. To help companies map their data and overcome these obstacles, BizTalk implements a simple drag-and-drop interface.

Microsoft is also customizing BizTalk specifically for certain vertical industries.

Commerce Server 2000

Commerce Server provides all of the things necessary to build and deploy an e-commerce Web site. It aims to reduce the complexity of publishing products onto the Web for sale. It is a comprehensive solution that covers business to business (businesses selling or buying from other businesses) or business to consumer (the traditional retail model of commerce—customers buy products) models.

Exchange Server 2000

Exchange Server is Microsoft's premiere collaboration and messaging tool. It gives a company the ability to store and easily share information through e-mail and other mediums such as real-time conferencing, workflow, and instant messaging.

Host Integration Server

One of the premises that .NET applications are built on is the capability to "talk" between software applications—even if they reside on different types of machines. Host Integration Server is Microsoft's product to enable just that. This is a substantial revision of its prior product, Microsoft SNA Server. It provides a gateway for talking to many different varieties of systems, both mainframe and PC based.

Internet Security and Accelerator Server

The Internet has been a great vehicle for progress, enabling unprecedented communication between individuals and companies. This same ease of communication, however, comes with a downside: It is all too easy for predators to maliciously destroy information, steal identities, and, in general, make life a mess for those on the receiving end of a hacker's attack. Internet Security and Accelerator Server is a software-based "firewall": It sits between a company's machines and the Internet to guard against intrusion and criminal activity. This server also offers another benefit: By storing copies of Web pages, images, and other data, it can substantially speed up Web surfing.

Mobile Information Server

One of the big goals of .NET is to bring software services to all sorts of devices: personal computers, hand-held computers, even cell phones! Mobile Information Server helps to extend

1

the reach of software and data to mobile devices. It enables users to access their personal data (e-mail, faxes, appointments, tasks, and so on) in real-time wherever they happen to be. This is a key enabler for "wireless" applications in the .NET world.

Office .NET

Office .NET is an example of a .NET product that starts to extend services right onto a user's personal desktop. Details of this product are still sketchy because it hasn't been released yet. It is expected that Microsoft will finally make its popular Office products such as Excel, Word, and PowerPoint available as a service for a monthly fee instead of as shrink-wrapped software. It is important to note that Microsoft does not see this method of distributing Office as the only method; this will become just another option or choice for consumers on how they want to pay for and use typical functionality like word processing and spreadsheet management.

SQL Server 2000

SQL Server 2000 is a complete database and data management package. One of its key .NET characteristics is its ability to support "queries"—requests for data—across the Internet in a variety of different formats, including XML. SQL Server is designed to be "self-tuning;" that is, it can monitor its own performance and functions and make changes on its own without human interaction.

Windows 2000 Server, Advanced Server, and Data Center Server

Last, but certainly not least, is the Windows 2000 family of operating systems. These are multipurpose operating systems for businesses of all sizes. These operating systems are responsible for implementing services that computer users usually take for granted: sharing files, printing, hosting Web sites, and running applications like Office .NET. As part of the .NET strategy, Windows 2000 was built with all of the technologies to enable software as a service to become reality. Windows XP will continue this trend even further.

 # Suggestions for Further Exploration

⊃ For the definitive resource on .NET, check out http://www.microsoft.com/net

⊃ Visit MSDN® Online for .NET information at http://msdn.microsoft.com/net

⊃ For more information on Visual Studio .NET check out
   http://msdn.microsoft.com/vstudio/nextgen

⊃ For more information on SOAP go to http://msdn.microsoft.com/soap

⊃ Check out the ASP.NET site at http://www.asp.net

⊃ GotDotNet is Microsoft's community .NET site: http://www.gotdotnet.com

⊃ To read about .NET Enterprise Servers: http://www.microsoft.com/servers/net

.NET's Relevance

.NET intends to change the way we develop, access, and interact with Internet applications. Given this, it's easy to see its importance. Of course, .NET changes the way you write software, but it is important to know that anyone who accesses information electronically will feel the effects of .NET. Because .NET's reach is so great, its relevance is defined differently for different audiences. This section explores each audience and outlines the ramifications and relevance of .NET to the given audience.

Developers

Of course, as developers, you are our primary audience for this book. We believe you are also Microsoft's primary target for .NET. Nothing happens without the code. You are needed to evangelize, upgrade, learn, design, and develop .NET software. You are in control of .NET's future. The nice thing? .NET makes it an easy decision and migration path.

The .NET Framework gives you control. It allows you to choose your language and project paradigm; even the development environment is completely customizable. We are no longer forced to compromise or make trade-offs in lieu of productivity. In the past, if you chose an easy-to-use syntax like Visual Basic you compromised features and speed; if you chose C++, you compromised ease, manageability, and productivity. No more. In .NET, all languages are created equal.

.NET allows us to build applications. The vast majority of today's business application development has some Internet component. Currently, to do routine tasks and ensure things like security and scalability, many programmer cycles are wasted writing repetitive plumbing code. With .NET, these things are built in. You can construct your application from .NET code libraries (the focus of this book). You are free to refocus your efforts on solving business problems (or going home before midnight) and not working on the plumbing of your system.

.NET is done right. As application developers first and authors second, we have first-hand knowledge of the tools. The .NET tools and environment are a joy. Developers will see increased productivity and enhanced capabilities. It takes a few hours to get used to, but once you do, we think you will find that .NET and the new Visual Studio are like a finely refined cockpit; nearly everything is in its right place and works just the way you think it should.

System Architects

.NET further closes the gap between design and code for the system architects. There is no longer a need for the architects to have one software license like Visio Enterprise and the development team another. How many times has a developer wanted to open and change a model only to be told he or she needed to buy another license? What typically happens is that the models go unupdated and often unexamined past the architecture phase. Developers get heads-down on code and the models become secondary. Visual Stuido.NET has built-in support for UML. That's right, now your models can co-exist with your code! Architects can write some code and developers can help keep the models updated. Additionally, Microsoft hopes to further extend the capabilities of the Visual Studio IDE through its partners in the Visual Studio Integrator Program (VSIP). Companies like Rational will offer its products as both versions and extensions of the Visual Studio .NET IDE.

Of course, .NET's strong OOP capabilities no longer force architects into workarounds for specific languages. When designing Visual Basic components before, for example, architects where not free to design with inheritance. The constraints of the Visual Basic language just did not support this design. With .NET, architects can model the right way and know that any language that the developer chooses to implement will work just fine.

Project Managers

We consider project managers to be anyone who has to answer to both users and upper management on the state, status, or feature set of a piece of software. We know this often includes a lot of developers. When was the last time you were free to focus on writing code and not sitting in meetings or pushing paper? If you are on the front line of software development, you are the one who faces a transfer or gets fired when the project goes a year off track and a million dollars over budget.

.NET promises to help change this. Applications can be delivered in shorter time frames due to increased productivity and more focus on business issues. Projects can be delivered at lower costs. Development teams can again focus on solving real business problems and know, at the end of the day, things like scalability, reliability, and robustness are baked in by .NET. In short, those on the front line can once again become the hero. .NET helps ensure successful projects, time and again.

Companies

The .NET platform fundamentally changes the way companies interact internally, with customers, and with partners over the Internet. .NET promises a higher degree of communication, connectivity, and productivity. It connects employee to employee, employee to partner, and most importantly, employee to customer. Internet applications evolve from simple user forms to rich, interactive collaboration. .NET frees the Internet from the PC. It Internet-enables and connects cell phones, televisions, and other appliances.

.NET allows companies to explore new business models. Just like the Internet created new markets and sales channels, Microsoft intends software services to evolve existing business models. For example, think of a company that today gathers auto insurance rate information for its customers. It collects this data, and helps its customers make informed decisions. It may even expose this information on the Internet. With .NET, this company can wrap this information into a software service that can be embedded into hundreds of applications. They still collect the data; they in fact change very little. However, they now have new revenue-generating market opportunity.

.NET opens new partnering opportunities for business. As the prior example illustrated, companies can now draw on each other's expertise to make a richer offer to potential customers. For example, if I sell used cars on the Internet, I know my customers will need insurance. I am not in the business of offering insurance nor do I want to be. With .NET I can find, grab, and use the insurance service to make a more compelling offer to my customers. If there is a bank loan rate service I'll grab that too. In the end, I've increased my sales by making it easier for customers to transact.

.NET allows companies to focus on the future without throwing out the past. Time and again companies are told that in order to realize their new business model they must rewrite their legacy systems. .NET is designed to extend and interoperate with those legacy systems. Companies are encouraged to use .NET to leverage their current investments and at the same time, plan for the future with built-in standards like XML.

End Users

We are often asked, "Will end users ever actually feel the effect of .NET?" Our answer, "You'd better believe it." .NET puts users in control of their information. How frustrating is it that we have to enter our address and credit card details time and again on site after site. We have to trust that each site secures our data properly and doesn't sell it off to list brokers. .NET promises centralized services. Imagine only one company knowing your private information. Imagine never re-typing your ship-to or bill-to address. You authorize access to your information and a service executes secure transactions on your behalf. Imagine being notified via an alert on your cell phone that the Father's Day gift you ordered is out of stock—and never giving out your cell phone number!

Ultimately, the end user may never hear of .NET. Although knowing the marketing might of Microsoft, this is probably unlikely. However, it is likely end users will never fully grasp that when they pick up the TV changer they will be accessing a myriad of .NET services and servers, or that when they order movie tickets from their cell phone while stuck in traffic, they are communicating with .NET components. .NET promises to empower users to communicate on their terms.

The .NET Framework: Under the Hood

This section lifts the hood of the .NET Framework and shows you what's underneath. In doing so, we present each topic, describe its importance, and relate applicable or intended application development benefits.

The .NET platform did not evolve out of Microsoft's DNA architecture. It is an entirely new platform and set of technologies. As a result, it requires that you bring an open mind to your development. The pitfalls of the past are gone and typically, there is a new way to do everything. This book is going to explore and teach you how to accomplish these tasks with .NET.

The term, .NET Framework, refers to Microsoft's new programming platform, which has been highly optimized for distributed application development. It encapsulates the runtime, classes, interfaces, and type system, designed to speed and streamline the development process. There are two principal pieces to the .NET Framework: the Common Language Runtime (CLR) and the Framework Class Library (FCL).

The CLR is the foundation of the Framework. It provides the services and code execution environment for .NET development. It is made up of a number of additional sub-components, like the Common Type System (CTS) and the Just-In-Time (JIT) compiler, all of which we will discuss in detail.

The other piece to the .NET Framework puzzle, the Framework Class Library (FCL), represents a collection of reusable classes that can be used to execute most common Windows programming tasks. Of course, it is also the focus of this book.

Common Language Runtime (CLR)

The Common Language Runtime (CLR) is the basis for all code in .NET. It is the execution engine designed to manage and control our code. It provides a number of services for our application (most are discussed in detail in the coming paragraphs). The CLR

- Manages memory and provides isolation and garbage collection

- Provides and enforces Code Access Security (CAS)

- Ensures type safety through the Common Type System (CTS)

- Provides a Just-In-Time (JIT) compiler for converting Intermediate Language (IL) code into actual native code

- Supplies developer services including profiling and debugging

- Grants support for an unlimited number of languages via its Common Language Specification (CLS)

- Provides versioning and deployment support

These services provide a number of direct benefits to our application development efforts and code execution. Some of these direct benefits are listed next:

- One of the biggest benefits to .NET development is that the CLR does not restrict the syntax in which code is written. If a compiler exists for a given language, you can write .NET code using its syntax. Some of the many languages currently being offered include Visual Basic, C#, C++, Perl, COBOL, and even Java.

- Real, cross-language development is now possible thanks to the CLS. We can write code in various languages and ensure that we can inherit from one component to the other, debug across language boundaries, and even handle exceptions raised from one language to the next.

- .NET does not force us to throw out the old. There is full support for interoperating with COM/COM+ services. .NET code can access COM code of old; there is even support for COM code accessing code written with .NET.

- We are now freed from the registry and all its pitfalls. Code written for .NET includes *metadata*, or descriptive information about the code itself, including its dependencies. With metadata, your code is said to be self-describing, thus rendering the registry, type libraries, and Interface Definition Language (IDL) obsolete. It also makes the task of installation and removal much more trivial.

- Our code will execute much faster due to performance gains with the platform, the use of more compiled code (VB, ASP), and managed services.

- We now have full support for all object-oriented features from within VB, including implementation inheritance!

- .NET should make memory leaks and reference counting things of the past thanks to its garbage collector (GC).

- There is now the potential to compile once (to MSIL) and run on any platform! This is the real Holy Grail of .NET. If a platform supports the runtime, your code will execute on it.

Common Language Specification (CLS)

The Common Language Specification (CLS) is a group of rules that provide language and compiler authors a guide when creating or porting a language targeted at the .NET Framework CLR. The CLS defines the basic set of features that each language must implement for it to be considered .NET compliant. Thanks to the CLS, and the architects of .NET, it is possible to ensure true language-to-language interoperability. Languages might be syntactically different, but their strict adherence to the CLS ensures their cross-language compatibility.

That said, it is still quite possible (and very likely) for both language and library authors to implement non-CLS–compliant features. A language author may target the CLR, but may also need to create specific features that are not understood by other .NET languages. The key is that any code you write using a language or library must only use CLS features in the API that it exposes. If you stay true to this rule, your code is guaranteed to be accessible from all programming languages that support the CLS. All non-compliant features are marked as such in the language definition and usually have a good reason for their non-compliance.

For example, nearly every member of the .NET Framework Class Library is CLS-compliant. This ensures their access and use from every .NET language. However, some members provide support for features that are not defined by the CLS. All non-conforming members are identified in the documentation, and in all cases, a CLS-compliant alternative has been made available.

We are the big benefactors of the CLS. Developers currently can choose from more than 20 different languages when writing .NET code! And the best thing? Every class that you learn to use by reading this book works the exact same way from all these other languages. We are no longer constrained by syntax, but instead, are free to choose the language with which we are most productive—and we only have to learn one API!

Common Type System (CTS)

The Common Type System (CTS) is a set of rich types that are built directly into the CLR. It is the rule system that all languages (and developers) must adhere to when defining types. The system enforces how types are used (type safety) and managed within the runtime.

The CTS is one of the key components to ensuring language-to-language interaction. For instance, you can be assured that an integer in VB is the same size in C#. Thanks to the CTS, we are now afforded language interoperation not just at runtime, but also during development.

Microsoft Intermediate Language (MSIL)

The Microsoft Intermediate Language (MSIL or simply IL) is the language into which code written with the Framework gets precompiled. The point of MSIL is to provide a CPU-independent instruction set. This way, code can be deployed on a varying number of platforms (in the form of MSIL) and efficiently converted to native code for the given platform by the runtime. Yes, it seems the future of .NET lies beyond simply the WINTEL platform.

Along with the MSIL, compilers create the metadata that describes the types, members, and code references for the given compiled code. This metadata helps the runtime do things like enforce security, locate and load class, and generally describes the code's interaction with the runtime. The MSIL and metadata are combined in one file called a Portable Executable (PE) file. Again, thanks to metadata, code written for the runtime is self-describing and eliminates the need for the registry, type libraries, and IDL.

It is the responsibility of the Just-In-Time (JIT) compiler to convert the MSIL (using the meta-data) into native code. It is important to note that MSIL is not interpreted by the runtime. It is, in fact, compiled natively as a method is requested. Compiling one method at a time saves the runtime the overhead of compiling the entire library when it only needs one method. Additionally, methods that are never requested don't need compiling. Of course, subsequent calls to the method do not require a recompile. The native code is stored in memory, which is used to process the additional requests.

> **NOTE**
>
> If you just can't stand knowing that you are deploying IL code, Microsoft has shipped a pre-JIT compiler. This allows you to JIT compile your code and store it on disk at deployment. The pre-JIT compiler is called ngen.exe.

Managed Code

Code written specifically for the CLR is said to be *managed code*. The term, managed, refers to the runtime's services executing against your code. For instance, .NET's memory manager and garbage collector (GC) manage the memory used for a class you write. The advantage: You are no longer responsible for reference counting or controlling memory leaks. Or course, the runtime offers a number of other managed services in addition to memory management.

All code written with VB .NET is managed code by default. On the other hand, code written with C++ is unmanaged by default. To write managed code with C++ you must throw a compiler switch and mark code as managed with a keyword inside of the managed extensions for C++. Similarly, C# can mark data as unmanaged by using a keyword.

The benefit of managed code is that it can take advantage of the .NET runtime. Cross language interoperability, code access security, and garbage collection are available only to managed code. One drawback is that managed classes created to target the CLR can only inherit from one base class.

> **NOTE**
>
> The .NET Framework provides the System.Runtime.InteropServices namespace to facilitate access to native operating system services and other unmanaged code. The namespace exposes a set of types for working with unmanaged code.

Assemblies

An assembly represents a group of functionality that is deployed as a single, logical unit. Assemblies represent the code we write and can include other resources such as images or other binary files associated with our applications. Assemblies are typically the bricks of our .NET solution. They group functionality, which forms a boundary around code access security, type, reference scope, version, and deployment unit.

All .NET applications must contain one or more assemblies. Assemblies have what are called *manifests*. Assembly manifests represent the metadata that describes the assembly. The manifest contains information on the exposed portions of the assembly, its references to other assemblies, its version, name, and the files that make up the assembly.

One direct benefit of the .NET assembly model is that it is the end of DLL hell. Assembly versioning and referencing allows specific reference to versions of a component. This means multiple versions of a single component can now execute side-by-side.

Another benefit of assemblies is easier installation and deployment. Assemblies will make zero impact and XCOPY installs possible.

Global Assembly Cache (GAC)

Most assemblies are created to be private to our applications. That is, the assemblies are consumed by one another and not shared outside of the application. Private assemblies are installed into the application's directory. This is the preferred method unless sharing an assembly is required.

Shared assemblies are those building blocks that need to be referenced by more than one application. To do so, you must load the assembly into the Global Assembly Cache (GAC). The GAC is a machine-wide cache designed for the purpose of sharing assemblies. GAC assemblies must have *strong names*. That is, their names must be unique via the use of cryptographic key pairs. This ensures versioning and security for your assembly in the deployment environment.

> **NOTE**
>
> To add, remove, or view assemblies in the GAC, Microsoft provides a developer tool called the Global Assembly Tool (gacutil.exe). Alternatively, you can drag-and-drop components into the GAC using Windows Explorer since the GAC is also represented as a directory.

Assemblies stored in the GAC often exhibit better runtime performance. Thanks to the key-pairs, the CLR does not have to recheck the assembly's security, and thus, tends to locate these bits faster.

NOTE

There is no need to install assemblies into the GAC in order to make them accessible to COM or unmanaged code.

Garbage Collector (GC)

Garbage collection is a feature built into the CLR that detects and cleans up (de-allocates memory) managed objects that are no longer accessible. As VB developers, we are somewhat familiar with this concept, as we've been relying on COM/COM+ services to handle this operation.

However, if you are accustomed to using the `Terminate` event for code clean-up routines then you will need some slight restructuring of your component design. While the runtime does call the `Dispose` method when de-allocating your object, you cannot rely on when this method will be called. It is better to move this `Terminate` code into another close method that can be explicitly called by users of your component as is necessary.

The benefits of a garbage collector include:

- The elimination of persisted objects in memory due to circular references
- Faster object de-allocation and memory reclamation
- Never having to worry about memory leaks or reference counting

Namespace

The term namespace is nothing more than a design-time, logical naming scheme for .NET types. Types are organized in a namespace based on hierarchy indicated by a dot (`.`). For example, in the namespace, `System.IO`, the dot separation indicates that `IO` is under the hierarchy of `System`. There can only be one `System` at that level and only one `IO` under the `System` level. Of course, there could be an `IO.System` or even a `System.System`.

> **NOTE**
>
> The System namespace is the root namespace in the .NET Framework. Classes in this namespace represent the data types used in our applications. Types include: Object (the root of all that is .NET), Byte, Char, Array, String, Int16, and so on. Typically, these types correspond directly to the data types used in the .NET languages. For instance, the Integer keyword in VB corresponds (and derives from) .NET's Int32 type.

As developers, we can create and control our own namespaces. To do so, we simply use the Namespace keyword. This allows us to organize our types under a hierarchy. It's important to note, however, that namespaces are only a design-time convenience. As we've discussed, at runtime, names scope is controlled by the assembly.

> **NOTE**
>
> The Imports keyword allows you to treat the contents of a namespace as part of your own namespace. It does not actually import anything. It simply provides you the convenience of refering to members of the namespace as if they were part and parcel to your own. For example, the call Dim q as System.Messaging.MessageQueue can be shortened to Dim q as MessageQueue provided that your application has the line Imports System.Messaging at the the top.

Framework Class Library (FCL)

The Framework Class Library is a set of Window's utility classes designed around providing developers prebuilt code for executing common programming tasks. The library is, of course, organized around a namespace hierarchy. Classes include functionality for file I/O, printing, font management, security, data access, threading, Web services, string manipulation, messaging, Windows Forms, and the list goes on and on.

All classes are designed to be object-oriented and are tightly integrated with the CLR. Often, you can derive functionality directly from the library into your own managed code. And, of course, the principal benefit to developers is that you only have to learn one library; the FCL works the same across languages. You no longer have to know the details of the Win32 API, ATL, and MFC—one library for all languages.

Should you need to access the Win32API, however, it is still there. It is simply no longer needed as often thanks to the rich set of classes inside the framework. These libraries replace the majority of its functionality, and often, actually derive their features from the API themselves.

> **NOTE**
>
> To access the Win32 API, you use P/Invoke. This is explained in detail in Appendix A, "Calling the Win32 API from Managed Code."

Interoperability

The CLR provides true language-to-language interoperability, both at design and runtime. Thanks to the CLS and CTS, you can inherit, debug, and raise exceptions across languages. COM promised developers interoperation, and it worked, but only at runtime. A component written with VB could be called from C++ and vice versa, but this only worked at the binary level. There was no support for true, design-time, cross-language development.

Of course .NET supports calling the raft of existing COM objects; any existing COM component can be called from managed code. Microsoft knows you cannot (and should not have to) re-create all your existing code for .NET. Instead, it provides the Runtime Callable Wrapper (RCW) inside the Framework. The RCW acts as a proxy that translates COM interfaces into those of .NET. With the RCW, your managed code thinks it is calling other .NET code.

.NET also supports the calling of COM components directly from managed code. To do so, you must create a COM Callable Wrapper (CCW). COM does limit the .NET constructs of which your application can take advantage. Things like parameterized constructors and static methods are not supported.

One drawback, as you may have guessed, is performance. While it is possible—and often a very good idea—to communicate between COM and .NET, all of this cross marshaling will have a performance impact. This is a trade-off you will have to make when deciding when to rewrite for .NET or interoperate.

Security

.NET provides us with a host of security options. Security in .NET is grouped into the following basic set of services:

- **ASP.NET Web Application Security** is a model that allows you to authenticate users of a site against the NT file system permissions or an XML file that lists users and their roles.

- **Code Access Security (CAS)** defines to what resources your code has access. This model allows you to build distributed components that can be easily trusted due to their access permissions.

- **Role-based security** makes decisions on what the user can do or access based on his or her identity and role membership. This is similar to the security model of MTS/COM+.

NOTE

For more information on Security in .NET, read Appendix C, ".NET Security Models."

 ## Suggestions for Further Exploration

⊃ For a great comparison of .NET languages, their constructs, types, and so on, check out MSDN: Visual Studio .NET/Developing with Visual Studio .NET/Reference/Language Equivalents.

⊃ For more detailed information on the inner workings of the .NET Framework, including using the CTS to create your own value types from VB, details on the makeup of assemblies, and description of the CLS in relation to languages and compilers, visit MSDN: Visual Studio .NET/.NET Framework/Inside the .NET Framework.

⊃ For a great source on language-to-language interoperation, read MSDN: The MSDN Library/.NET Development (General)/Technical Articles/Handling Language Interoperability with the Microsoft .NET Framework.

Summary

In this chapter we presented Microsoft's .NET strategy and discussed its makeup and importance relative to various target audiences. We then took a quick look under the hood of .NET. This information helped position the benefits of .NET to our application development. It will also serve as a basis for discussion in the coming chapters.

The following is a summary of some of the key points presented in this chapter:

- .NET is Microsoft's initiative to deliver software as a service.

- .NET is more than a set of developer tools. It includes services, server products, operating systems, and so on.

- The .NET timeline spans years, not months.

- .NET is important to anybody who accesses, stores, or interacts with data electronically.

- Code in .NET is compiled into MSIL and metadata, stored in PE files, and JIT compiled natively for a specific platform and hardware.

- Code written in one .NET language can be easily used by any other .NET language thanks to the CLS and the CTS.

- The Framework Class Library provides basic programming functions and works the same from all .NET languages.
- You can call COM objects from .NET and .NET objects from COM.
- Security in .NET is accomplished through Web Application Security, Code Access Security (CAS), and role-based security.

Evolution of VB .NET

IN THIS CHAPTER

The evolution of Visual Basic, over time, has led to inconsistencies and redundancy. VB .NET did not evolve out of VB6; it is not VB7. VB .NET exists to clean up the language and promote it to equal footing with other modern languages.

This chapter walks readers through some of the profound changes and productivity enhancements that VB .NET and the new tool, Visual Studio .NET, provide. Developers can expect nearly every aspect of the way they write code today to be altered in some manner. For the most part, these changes are intuitive and logical—you should not have trouble picking up and adapting them.

First, we illustrate the prime drivers and goals behind the new language and tools. We then walk through a number of key new language concepts. Finally, we present some of the enhancements the new tools provide.

After reading this chapter you should

- Understand the direction Microsoft has taken the VB language and for what reasons
- Appreciate how traditional VB language constructs have changed
- Begin to use the new VB and .NET language constructs
- Understand and work with some of the key new tools and enhancements VS .NET provides

Design Goals

VB developers represent a very vocal, loyal, and large Microsoft customer base. These developers (of which we count ourselves) want to hold on to VB's ease of use and its hiding of complexities. At the same time, we desire the power and access that other language developers have. Microsoft had to walk this tightrope when redefining VB for .NET.

To meet these demands, VB clearly had to move from a language of features (or a technology) to an actual programming language. In this section, we present some of the principles that were adhered to when VB was extended for .NET. This should help put in perspective the sweeping changes that the language has undergone.

Where We Came From

The latest versions of VB were created to handle client/server, database-driven development. You need to look no further than the existence of Visual InderDev and Active Server Pages (ASP) to understand this. VB .NET, on the other hand, was created in response to a full-blown shift to highly distributed and loosely coupled application development.

Ideals

VB .NET had to adhere to some of the ideals of past incarnations of VB. Additionally, it had to make sure that new features that VB developers have been requesting for years were supported. Some of the VB ideals include the following:

- The language should be simple and consistent.
- Code written in VB .NET should be easy to read, maintain, and understand.
- Applications should be easy to error proof and debug.
- Developers should be relieved of writing plumbing or redundant code.
- The language should allow for rapid application development.

Some of the new features developers requested and received include the following:

- The capability to execute programming tasks, access servers, write tasks, and so on without leaving the IDE.
- Full support for OO development, including inheritance, constructors, and the like.
- Performance should not be compromised for choosing VB .NET over another language.

When designing .NET, the architects of Visual Basic knew that major changes were in store in order to support the Common Language Runtime (CLR) and adhere to the Common Language Specification (CLS). The broad scope of the required changes allowed for a major overhaul and cleanup of the language. Thankfully, they did not divert and create a crippled .NET language in favor of ease of use, but instead elevated Visual Basic to a first-class language for .NET.

New Language Concepts

The changes reflected in Visual Basic .NET are in direct relation to many of the changes brought about by the evolution of Windows programming to .NET. The CLR and adherence to the CLS, coupled with the goals set out for the language, required a great deal of change. The Framework Class Library (FCL) resulted in many Visual Basic functions being replaced or augmented by methods inside of a class. Together, these factors ensured that the changes to the Visual Basic language and the underpinning technology would be far reaching and numerous.

That said, the new and very much improved language is intuitive and, as a result, makes for an easy transition. This section details some of the major changes to the Visual Basic language brought about by .NET.

> **NOTE**
>
> The largest impact to the language involves VB .NET's new object-oriented (OO) support. This includes inheritance, constructors, overriding, delegates, interfaces, and the like. The changes are so many, in fact, that we devoted Chapter 3, "Object-Oriented Concepts in .NET," to the subject. Similar in impact, the topic of multithreading is covered in Chapter 12, "Working with Threads," and exception handling is covered in Chapter 20, "Profiling, Debugging, and Exception Handling." For a complete list of data type changes, see Appendix D, ".NET Framework Base Data Types." A number of the items presented next are also explained in further detail throughout the book.

Declaring Variables and Data Types

This section details a number of the changes within VB .NET regarding the manner in which variables are declared and scoped. In nearly all cases, the developer is left with more control as poor or outdated parts of the VB language have been eliminated or replaced.

Syntax

A number of syntactical changes affect dimensioning variables. Variables declared on one line separated by a comma, for instance, all result in the same data type. In VB6, a declaration such as Dim x, y, z as Integer resulted in x and y being declared as Variants and z as an Integer. With .NET, all three variables would be of type Integer. You can still, of course, declare two variable types on the same line, such as Dim x as Integer, y as String.

The syntax for creating objects at the time of declaration is also slightly altered by VB .NET. You can now use the following to create new instances of objects during a Dim statement:

```
'not syntactically dissimilar to VB6
Dim myObject As New SomeObject()

'equivalent to above, but more explicit
Dim myObject As SomeObject = New SomeObject()

'create an object and set constructor parameters
Dim myObject As SomeObject = New SomeObject(New SomeOtherObject(), x)
```

Note that the caveats that applied to dimensioning objects As New in VB6 no longer apply with VB .NET. In previous versions of Visual Basic, if a variable was declared As New, it was often impossible to destroy; simply accessing it added a reference count. This practice often led to lost reference counts, and Dim As New was considered taboo. In VB .NET, however, no implicit object creation exists; this, along with garbage collection, should remove the As New construct from the "bad form" list.

Arrays

A number of changes were made to the way .NET handles array declarations. The first is that the `Option Base` statement is gone from VB .NET. `Option Base` allowed you to set the lower bound value for all arrays declared in your code. With .NET, all arrays have a lower bound value of zero (`0`).

Additionally, the support for creating arrays with a range of boundaries is also gone with .NET. VB6 developers could set an array with elements 2 through 5 with the following syntax:

```
Dim myArray(2 to 5)
```

> **NOTE**
>
> You can still call the keywords `UBound` and `LBound` to return the upper and lower limits of a given array. However, arrays created in .NET derive from the Array class. As such, they expose the methods like GetUpperBound and GetLowerBound. Each takes a value indicating the dimension of which you want to determine the bound. For example, you can write code that looks like the following:
>
> ```
> For i = 0 To myArray.GetUpperBound(0)
> ```

Contrary to early beta releases, the number of elements in a VB .NET array is unchanged from VB6. The statement, `Dim MyArray(5)`, for instance, still contains six items (0–5).

Finally, .NET offers a couple of new ways to dimension arrays. `Dim MyArray() as Integer = New Integer(5)` is equivalent to `Dim MyArray(5) as Integer`. The first example simply explicitly creates the Integer object. Additionally, you can now initialize the items in an array at the time of dimensioning. The following code creates a five-item array, each with an initial value:

```
Dim myArray(5) as Integer = {1, 2, 3, 4, 5}
```

Note that `Redim` and `Redim Preserve` are still supported by VB .NET.

Strings

With .NET, you no longer need to dimension a string variable with a given length. For instance, the VB6 syntax, `Dim myString as String * 50`, is no longer supported. VB .NET manages strings differently and allocates memory based on the size of the actual string at the time of assignment.

In fact, the String data type in .NET is said to be immutable. *Immutable* refers to the fact that after it is created, the contents of the string cannot be changed. Consider the following example:

```
Dim myString as String = "This value cannot change"
myString = "Changed Value"
```

The code executes without issue (an example of Visual Basic easing complexities and maintaining backward compatibility). However, .NET actually has to create two separate strings to handle this code. The first is created (and memory allocated) when the variable is declared. The second line of code actually causes a new set of memory to be allocated and referenced by the variable myString.

The same immutable nature of strings holds true for concatenation. The line, myString = myString & " some more text", will execute fine, but .NET is required to create and destroy memory accordingly. For this reason, .NET provides the System.Text.StringBuilder class. This class is optimized for heavy string concatenation and should be used when performing a lot of string concatenations. Its syntax is simple: myStringBuilder.Append(" some more text"). After it is concatenated, you can convert the object into a string value by calling myStringBuilder.ToString. Of course, the class has a number of other properties, methods, and parameters that you are encouraged to explore.

Scope

For the most part, variable scoping remains the same with VB .NET with the exception of block scope. *Block scope* dictates that variables dimensioned within a code block are available only for the term of the given code block. This enables you to dimension variables that are not actually allocated unless the code falls into the block. A code block is defined as the section of code contained in the constructs If ... Then, For ... Next, Select ... Case, and Do ... Loop.

The following code illustrates block scope. Notice that as you nest blocks, you simply narrow the possible scope. However, variables declared inside a parent block are available within the child blocks. In this case, this means the z that is declared within the For ... Next loop is accessible inside the nested If ... Then block, but y is not accessible to the For ... Next block.

```
Sub Main()

    'available for the sub
    Dim x As Int16

    For x = 1 To 10

        'available inside the loop and all narrower
        Dim z As Int16

        If x = 2 Then

            z = 3
```

```
                'only available inside the if block
                Dim y As Int16

                y = 5

            End If

        Next

    End Sub
```

Note that if you exit a code block and re-enter during the same call, the variable's value is still maintained for the life of the object; it is simply available only inside the block.

Integers

The Integer data type in VB .NET is compliant with both the CLS and CTS, (and therefore other .NET languages). Unfortunately, an Integer in VB6 is no longer an Integer in VB .NET, but rather a Short. The following table describes the changes:

VB6	VB .NET	CLS/CTS
Integer	Short	Int16 (16 bits)
Long	Integer	Int32 (32 bits)
None	Long	Int64 (64 bits)

Given the confusion this might cause, we suggest declaring your types explicitly using the CLS/CTS types (Int16, Int32, Int64). This way, you will know what size type you are creating and non-VB programmers, when reading your code, will also know!

NOTE

One nice effect of this change is that Integers in VB .NET are now the equivalent of Integers of the SQL data type.

Variant

The Variant data type is gone from .NET. Its replacement is the Object data type.

Currency

The Currency data type is absent from VB .NET. Its replacement is the Decimal type.

FCL Classes That Replace/Augment VB6 Elements

Thanks to the FCL, a number of functions that were inherent to the Visual Basic language are now abstracted to class library methods. The helps ensure that C# and VB .NET objects can communicate with one another, because they both use the same library. Table 2.1 indicates a number of these changes.

TABLE 2.1 FCL Classes to VB6 Elements Cross Reference

Namespace	VB6 Programming Element
System.Drawing	Circle, Line
System.Math	Atn, Sgn, Sqr, Rnd, Round
System.Diagnostics	Debug.Pring, Debug.Assert
System.String	LSet, RSet, and string functions like Replace, Split, Trim, and so on
System.Windows.Forms.MessageBox	MsgBox
DateTime Structure	Now, Date, Time, Date$, Time$
System.Globalization	Calendar

> **NOTE**
>
> The Microsoft.VisualBasic namespace is imported by default with any VB .NET project created within the IDE.

Behavioral Changes

VB6 developers need to be aware of a number of behavioral changes. For instance, VB .NET sometimes completely reverses VB6 defaults. All changes were made for a good reason, however, and developers should be able to easily adapt to them. This section indicates a number of key changes that the language, and its support for the CLR and CLS, dictates.

Destroying Objects

VB6 COM objects relied on reference counting (and the set myObj = nothing construct) to destroy objects and free resources. VB .NET, however, uses the CLR's garbage collection (GC) service to clean up and destroy objects. The result of this change is that you no longer have to worry about cleaning up your objects.

In exchange for this feature, however, the Class_Terminate event is no longer supported. In its place is a Finalize method that can be overridden to provide similar support. This method will be called by the GC service when freeing your object. Developers should, however, not rely on this method to destroy key system resources such as database connections and the like. The nature of GC is such that its time of execution cannot be reliably predicted. Waiting for the GC to call `Finalize` on your object to free these resources can impact and limit the scalability of your system.

Instead of a `Finalize`, developers are encouraged to implement a `Dispose` method on all their objects that require cleanup code at the time of destruction. Cleanup code should be placed directly inside this `Dispose` method. It is important to note, however, that unlike `Finalize` (and `Class_Terminate`), `Dispose` is not automatically called by the runtime. This standard construct should be called explicitly by all clients of an object. In fact, .NET provides the interface `IDisposable` that should be implemented to ensure a standard construct for all objects. The following is a simple example:

```
Public Class SomeClass

    Implements System.IDisposable

    Public Sub Dispose() Implements IDisposable.Dispose
        'clean up and free resources
    End Sub

End Class
```

Parameter Usage

By default, parameters are now passed by value (`ByVal`) rather than by reference (`ByRef`), which was the default in VB6. We suggest that you still explicitly indicate `ByVal` and `ByRef` to make your code readable and easily understood.

One key change developers will quickly appreciate is the standardization of parentheses inside parameterized calls to methods, objects, and the like. In VB6, if you expected a return value, you used parameters around your call:

```
myVar = MyObject.MyMethod(myOtherVar)
```

When not expecting a return, you omitted the parameters, unless you used the `Call` keyword, in which case you used the parentheses.

VB .NET makes it simple: Parentheses are always required.

Another change to parameters is the use of optional parameters in VB .NET. All optional parameters must have an explicitly defined default value. This eliminates the need for the `IsMissing` function. VB .NET optional parameters look like the following:

```
Private Sub myOptions(ByVal somOtherParam As Integer, _
    Optional ByVal someParam As Boolean = True)
```

Notice that optional parameters still must be defined at the end of the function signature.

Property Declarations

VB .NET unifies, and renders obsolete, the `Property Get` and `Property Set` statements with the `Property` declaration statement. The following is an example of the VB .NET method for defining a property:

```
Public Class SomeOtherObject

    Dim myLocalValue

    Public Property SomeProperty()

        Get
            Return myLocalValue
        End Get

        Set(ByVal Value)
            myLocalValue = Value
        End Set

    End Property

End Class
```

VB6 supported the concept of default properties on objects. This required you to use the `Set` statement when executing an object assignment instead of accessing the default property. It also had the effect of making code difficult to read and developers were therefore encouraged to be explicit. For instance, code that "assigned" an object to a string variable required a developer to look up the object and determine its default property before being able to work with it.

VB .NET does not allow for default properties without parameters. Now, developers must be explicit when executing an object assignment or accessing a property. The new syntax eliminates the need for the `Set` and `Let` statements. The compiler is no longer confused by the call `myObject = SomeObject`—it is clearly a reference assignment.

.NET does support default properties that take arguments. This seems contradictory at first glance. However, calls to these properties are not ambiguous and therefore are supported. Primarily, default properties should be reserved to collection classes. It is apparent to the compiler and the developer that a call to `myVar = myCollection(1)` is accessing a default property (most likely, an `Item` property). To declare a default property, you use the `Default` keyword.

Short Circuiting

One of the key changes to Visual Basic's behavior inside of .NET is the new support for short circuiting. *Short circuiting* states that items evaluated in an expression are not evaluated unless accessed.

To support this new feature and at the same time maintain compatibility with existing code, VB .NET introduces the short circuiting operators OrElse and AndAlso. When you want to have your expressions short circuit, you use OrElse as a replacement for the Or operator and AndAlso for the And operator. For example, when two items in an expression are separated by an OrElse operator, if the first item in the expression evaluates to True, the second item is never evaluated by the runtime. Instead, the code short circuits. In VB6 (and with the Or operator in VB .NET) the entire expression (both conditions) is evaluated before execution—this often resulted in errors or had the effect of limiting developers. The following code presents an example.

```
Dim x As Object 'Variant for VB6
Dim y As Int16


x = "Hello World"
y = 2


'the second expression is not allowed but it never gets evaluated
If y = 2 OrElse x / y = 10 Then

    Console.WriteLine(y)

End If
```

 ## Suggestions for Further Exploration

⊃ For more information on what is new within VB .NET, check out MSDN: Visual Studio .NET, Visual Basic and C#, Getting Started, What's New in Visual Basic and C#.

Interactive Development Environment (IDE)

The goal in designing the new IDE was simple: developers should not have to go outside of their development environment to execute programming tasks. The result is a powerful set of tools, with very intuitive access to their features. The VS .NET IDE will change the way in which you write your VB .NET code. This section provides exposure to some of the tools and editing enhancements that VS .NET offers. It is not meant to be a complete or detailed reference, but it will make you aware of what is available to you.

New Tools

The IDE offers a number of new tools as well as improvements on nearly all previous tools. In the following section, we will walk through some of the key productivity enhancing tools inside of the VS .NET IDE.

Solutions, Projects, and Source Files

The Visual Studio .NET Solution Explorer enables you to manage the various files that make up and relate to your application. The tool is not a radical departure from the VB6. In fact, if you are familiar with Visual InterDev, the revised Solution Explorer should be very familiar. The biggest difference, which is a great productivity enhancer, is that the Solution Explorer and IDE now handle all Microsoft source files in one place. This simple concept allows you to work on an XML file, an ASP.NET form, a VB class, a C# class, and so on—without switching tools or even opening and closing projects!

Files are grouped by two containers. The solution container (.sln) enables you to group a number of projects under one solution. This is similar to VB6's group (.vbg) file. Grouping projects in this way allows you to compile, run, and debug the group as a whole. The project container (.vbproj) is similar to VB6's project file (.vbp). This file contains the source files that make up a given project. A project's source is compiled directly into DLLs, EXEs, and the like.

> **NOTE**
>
> To change the project that starts when you click the Run button inside a project group, you simply right-click the project file and choose Set as Startup Project. Similarly, in an ASP.NET project, you can right-click a page and choose Set as Start Page.

The Solution Explorer is also used to manage the various files that relate to an application. All VB .NET files have the same extension, .vb. These are equivalent to VB6's class files (.cls), forms (.frm), modules (.mod), and so on. Additionally, you can work with and link to related files directly within the Explorer. Support exists for miscellaneous files, similar to VB6's related documents, and solution items—even projects of different sources can be mixed within the solution. Figure 2.1 captures a shot of the Solution Explorer.

FIGURE 2.1

VS .NET Solution Explorer.

Class View

The counterpart to the Solution Explorer is the Class View. In Class View, you work with a code-centric view of your source files. As with the Object Browser or other object-oriented (OO) views of your code, each class, method, property, and so on is represented in a hierarchical view. Additionally, each OO type has its own graphical icon. Each icon is altered slightly with a padlock when a given member is private. Overall, this view provides fast and easy access to the key areas within your source files without forcing you to scroll through .vb files in search of the property or method you want to work with. Figure 2.2 illustrates the Class View tool.

FIGURE 2.2
VS .NET Class View.

Server Explorer

Perhaps one of the biggest gains in ease of use is the embedded Server Explorer. This tool provides developers with access to all servers and associated tools and services that a given server might publish. This simple concept should save you time switching between and launching the various server-management applications. For instance, if your component logs to the event log on your development server and you want to check a bug, you do not have to leave the IDE to view that server's events. Additionally, when programming against a database, you can view the tables, procedures, and so on from within your source editor. The Server Explorer allows you to watch messaging queues and manage server services. The Server Explorer tool also allows you to view and use XML Web services that a given server might expose. Figure 2.3 is a screenshot of this tool.

Clipboard Ring

The Clipboard Ring is one of those tools that, after using it for a day or two, you will wonder how you got along without it. The tool is simple: It keeps track of the items that you cut or copy. It caches each item in the Clipboard, up to a total of 15 items. The last item copied becomes the first item in the ring. After 15 items, the old items start dropping off the list.

You can access items from the ring in two ways: The easiest way is a shortcut key, Ctrl+Shift+V. Repeatedly pressing the V key when you're holding down Ctrl and Shift cycles through the ring within the text editor. Additionally, you can access the items in the ring from the toolbox; Figure 2.4 illustrates this concept.

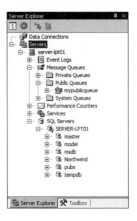

FIGURE 2.3

The Server Explorer.

FIGURE 2.4

The Clipboard Ring.

Command Window

The Command Window inside the IDE is a new concept for VB .NET developers. The basic premise is that it enables you to execute Visual Studio commands by typing them command style directly into a Command Window embedded inside the IDE. Commands range from those that enable you to manage files, projects, and source code to those that execute builds, list threads, and view the stack contents. Figure 2.5 captures a shot of the Command Window. Notice the Intellisense and AutoCompletion support for the commands.

2

EVOLUTION OF
VB .NET

FIGURE 2.5

The Command Window.

Incremental Search

Incremental Search is another one of those tools that you'll wonder how you ever did without. The tool enables you to easily find items within your source code from within the editor. Like most good tools, it is simple in concept and simple to use. Inside a source file, press Ctrl+I (Edit, Advanced, Incremental, and Search). Your cursor will change to the binocular icon and an arrow indicating the direction in which the search is being performed. As you enter text, the cursor will find and highlight the nearest occurrence of the complete text entered. For instance, typing **c** might take you to the first occurrence of a class declaration, but adding the letters **an** could take you to your defined property, `CanImport`. To remove a letter from your search, press the Backspace key. To find the next occurrence of a search string, press Ctrl+I again. To change search directions, press Ctrl+Shift+I.

Printing Code

Finally, developers have control over the printing of their source code! From VS .NET, you can print all source code, in color. VB developers have been clamoring for this for a long time, usually resorting to some third-party application or tool to allow the printing of their code. This may seem basic, but it is another example of IDE enhancements to your productivity. Figure 2.6 captures the Page Setup dialog box for managing how your code is output; note the check box for line numbers.

Code Editor

The code editor is typically where developers live, breath, and create. VS .NET incorporates a number of new features that make editing source code less painful, without being overly intrusive.

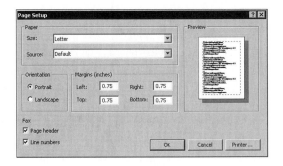

FIGURE 2.6

The Page Setup dialog box.

Task List

The Task List embedded in the IDE is both a new tool for VB developers and a code-editing enhancement. The tool provides task-based management that directly relates to and tightly integrates with your source code. Developers can add tasks directly within the task pane; no more going out to other applications such as Outlook to manage your development tasks. But the biggest benefit is the automated tasks. These are tasks that the IDE writes directly into the list when an error occurs while you're editing code or building a project. These tasks are tracked by the IDE. You can double-click one and be taken directly to the hot spot in your code that pertains to the task. As a problem is fixed, the task automatically disappears.

Additionally, using special comment tokens, you type your own tasks within your code as comments. The default tokens are TODO, UNDONE, and HACK. VB .NET developers simply type a standard comment followed by the token and a colon. The IDE automatically picks up the token and creates a task in the list with the appropriate category, source file, and line number reference. You can even create your own custom tokens. To do so, from within the IDE, choose Tools, Options, Environment, and Task List. Figure 2.7 shows the Task List in action.

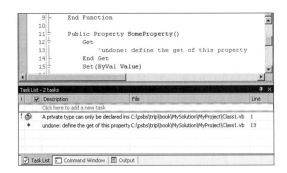

FIGURE 2.7

Task List.

Dynamic Help

Another tool that works with the text editor is the context-based help system. Again, keeping with the theme of staying in the IDE to execute development tasks, VS .NET embeds a help system that links directly to the code you are in the process of writing. In past incarnations, if you had a question about a particular object or method that Intellisense (what did we do before Intellisense?) can't answer, you had to launch MSDN and start searching the index or browsing the content tree. Now, as you code, the help system updates itself with relevant information based on your keystrokes. For example, take a look at Figure 2.8. Here the cursor is positioned on a line that dimensions a variable of the type EventLog. Notice the Dynamic Help pane. We have access to the Dim statement, the EventLog class, its members, and other associated topics.

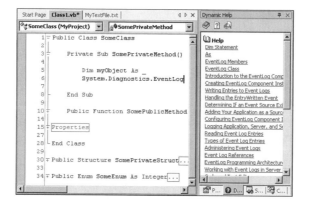

FIGURE 2.8
Dynamic Help.

Outlining Code

The text editor with VS .NET supports code outlining. Code outlining automatically arranges your code in hierarchical, tree-like blocks. A block might be a class or property definition. Code inside a block can be hidden and expanded per your preferences. This makes it easier to work with long source files. You can hide the blocks that you have finished with or are not working on and view them only as needed. To turn outlining off and on, you use either a shortcut key or access the associated menu from Edit, Outlining.

Additionally, VB developers have the #Region directive available. This enables you to define outlined blocks (or regions) of code independent of the editor. To do so, you simply time #Region "RegionName" and end the region with #End Region, where RegionName is a string used to name your region. Figure 2.9 shows a number of outlined blocks. Notice the collapsed block "Properties." This is a custom-defined region we created to block all our property statements together.

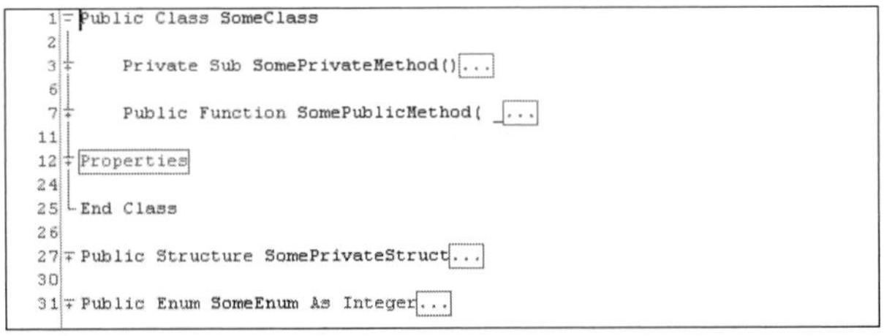

```
 1 ┌ Public Class SomeClass
 2 │
 3 ┤     Private Sub SomePrivateMethod()...
 6 │
 7 ┤     Public Function SomePublicMethod( ...
11 │
12 ┤ Properties
24 │
25 └ End Class
26
27 ┬ Public Structure SomePrivateStruct...
30 │
31 ┬ Public Enum SomeEnum As Integer...
```

FIGURE 2.9

Outlined code.

Line Numbering

As you've undoubtedly noticed from some of the previous screenshots, VS .NET supports line numbering. Developers can quickly scan and find code based on error reports that indicate line numbers. To turn line numbering on and off, you navigate to Tools, Options, Text Editor.

Hyperlinked Comments

Hyperlinked comments represent another small but important enhancement. Developers can embed hyperlinks to more information directly within their source code. One use for this would be to embed author details within the source code. This way, if the original developer changes jobs, moves, and so on, she can update her credentials on a Web site, and all those maintaining her code can have up-to-date access information for her. To create a URL inside a comment, simply type **http**. Figure 2.10 illustrates a URL embedded in a comment.

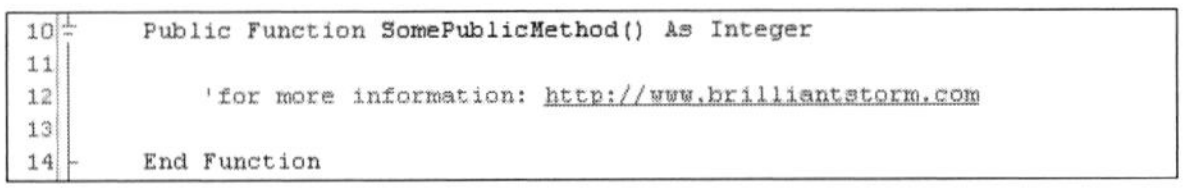

```
10 ┬     Public Function SomePublicMethod() As Integer
11 │
12 │         'for more information: http://www.brilliantstorm.com
13 │
14 ┴     End Function
```

FIGURE 2.10

Hyperlinked code comment.

Brace Matching

Brace matching is another small, elegant productivity enhancement. When you're typing code using braces { [(, the editor highlights the opening and closing active set of braces. This is very useful when writing long statements that contain braces embedded inside of braces; how many times in VB6 have you sat counting and matching closing and ending braces?

Because VS .NET represents such a sweeping overhaul of the tools, languages, and environments, a number of additional new tools and enhancements are available for you to explore. These include but are not limited to the following:

- Start page
- Application templates
- Object Browser
- XML editor
- HTML editor
- Style Builder for cascading style sheets

Summary

VB .NET takes the language that we all know and love to its destined height. The transition, although not easy, should be intuitive—and worth the effort.

The following are key points presented in this chapter:

- VB .NET is not VB7. Instead, it moves the language away from being a technology toward being an actual language.
- VB .NET changes a number of programming constructs such as scope, array declaration, integer, data type, and the like.
- The .NET FCL replaces a number of VB6 functions with classes and associated methods.
- VS .NET intends to embed all necessary tools to realize the goal of allowing developers to stay within the IDE to execute all programming-related tasks.

Object-Oriented Concepts in .NET

IN THIS CHAPTER

Starting with the release of Visual Basic 4.0, the capability to create classes has been intrinsic to the Visual Basic language. Some might say that Microsoft's move to support this was the true beginning of VB's evolution into an object-oriented language. Whenever it started, and whatever you thought of Visual Basic's prior ability (or inability) to support object-oriented (OO) concepts, .NET brings Visual Basic up to speed with all of the basic properties of an object-oriented programming language. The deep object support in Visual Basic .NET, and the .NET Framework in general, is certainly one of the most compelling changes offered in this new environment.

This chapter will focus on defining the concepts of object orientation as they relate to software development in general. In Chapter 4, "Introduction to the .NET Framework Class Library," we will also examine their specific manifestations in the .NET Framework.

There have been more than a few books written on object-oriented programming, so this chapter will not attempt to deliver a full treatise on a subject well deserving of hundreds of pages. Instead, we will cover only the ground that we need to cover so that programmers new to object-oriented programming and programmers with no OO experience at all will have a good backdrop of knowledge for exploring the .NET Framework Class Library.

We'll start by reviewing all of the pertinent characteristics of object-oriented languages—an obvious first step when you consider that the classes and other pieces of the Framework Class Library are all object-oriented in nature. Then we'll examine how these concepts have been brought to life inside of .NET and Visual Basic .NET, hopefully arming you with a solid-enough understanding of these concepts to make your programming experiences with the Framework Class Library more productive.

In years past, many developers have debated whether Visual Basic was an object-oriented language. Instead of investigating any of these prior claims, arguments, or discussions, let's focus instead on the here and now. Visual Basic .NET supports the major traits of an object-oriented language, including the capability to:

- Wrap data and behavior together into packages called classes (this is a trait known as *encapsulation*)
- Define classes in terms of other classes (a trait known as *inheritance*)
- Override the behavior of a class with a substitute behavior (a trait known as *polymorphism*)

We'll examine each one of these traits in detail. We'll also examine ways in which you will see these concepts at work inside of the .NET Framework. Chapter 4 will continue this thread by specifically examining the nature of the Framework Class Library and attempting to relate these object-oriented concepts directly to the Framework Class Library.

Classes—*Wrapping Data and Behavior Together*

Classes are blueprints or specifications for actual objects that we will create in our code. They define a standard set of attributes and behaviors. Because classes only define a structure or intent, they are virtual in nature. For instance, a class cannot hold data, it can't receive a message, and in fact can't do any processing at all. This is because classes are only meant to be object factories. Just like real engineering blueprints of a building, they only exist to construct something else. When we program, this "something else" we are trying to construct is an object. An object *can* hold data, *can* receive messages, and *can* actually carry out processing.

While you don't typically use the term class in your everyday (non-programming) life, we are all certainly familiar with the concept of objects. These are the things that surround us day in and day out; they are the nouns in our universe. We are used to interacting with objects. For example, you place a plate on your table for dinner. The plate has food on it—a few different types of food, in fact. We can see that all of these things have distinct properties: The plate is white with a faint flower pattern, and the food has a particular texture, taste, and smell. We also expect that objects will allow us to interact with them in different ways.

Just like in the real world, code objects (we also call them instances) are actual physical manifestations of classes.

Classes as Approximations

If we discuss classes in the context of programming, we say that they establish a template for objects by defining a common set of possible *procedures* and *data*. Procedures are used to imbue the class with a set of behaviors; when implemented in a class they are called *methods*. Classes maintain data inside of *properties* (which may or may not be visible to other classes). Behaviors are the verbs of classes, and properties are the nouns. A car, for instance, will accelerate in a prescribed fashion. This would be a behavior. A car will also have a specific weight, color, length, and so on. These are properties. From a technical, implementation point of view, there is actually no difference between the way that methods and properties are implemented. They both have function signatures, and both execute some body of code. In addition, both of them can accept parameters and return values.

> **NOTE**
>
> There are some general guidelines for when to use properties versus methods (and vice versa), but probably the best advice is to just be consistent. Most of the time, these rules will help steer you to the correct decision:
>
> *continues*

- Use a method if you are going to be passing in more than a few parameters.
- If you find yourself writing a method called GetXXX or SetYYY, chances are good this should be a property instead.
- Methods are more appropriate than properties if there will be many object instantiations or inter-object communication inside of the function.
- Properties, when implemented, should be stateless with respect to one another. In other words, a property should not require that another property be set before or after it is set. If you find this kind of dependency inside of a property, it should probably be a method instead.

Classes are typically constructed to mimic, or approximate, real-world physical structures or concepts. By using classes in your code, you can simplify both your architecture and your understanding of the code; this is due to the inherent approachability of objects—your mind is used to deal with objects. For example, which do you suppose would make more intuitive sense to you?

You are writing code to move an icon from the left side of the screen to the right side of the screen. The procedural programming way would probably have you calling some API function (maybe it's called SystemDskRsrcBlit) and passing parameters into the function call. But, what if you were free to do this:

- Create an icon object
- Tell it to MoveLeft

The object-oriented way just seems to make more sense to us—it seems to appeal to the way that our minds are wired.

NOTE

The difference between the system that we are programming and the real-world process that we are modeling is often referred to as the *semantic gap*. You could summarize some of what we have been talking about here by saying that object-oriented programming aims to reduce the semantic gap between programming and the real world.

Of course, just because the basic premises of objected-oriented programming are simple to understand doesn't mean that the actual programming of object-oriented systems is trivial. Once you can work your way through the syntax and condition yourself to think in an object-like fashion while actually designing your applications, some of the perceived complexity associated with software development will begin to fade.

Talking Between Classes

We have said that classes define a set of behaviors. These behaviors would be useless to us unless we had a way to actually stimulate or initiate a particular behavior. Therefore, we have the concept of *messaging*. A message is nothing more than a request, from one object to another, to perform some sort of action. The receiving object may choose to ignore the action (especially if it doesn't have a behavior defined that would map to the requested action) or it may perform a specific action that could, in turn, send messages to other objects.

A core tenet of object-oriented systems is that classes think for themselves. A particular class knows how it should react to an incoming message; the calling class isn't forced to understand how or why the receiving class behaves the way that it does. This is the essence of *information hiding*. In information hiding, an object hides its internal machinations from other objects (see Figure 3.1). Information hiding is important because it helps reduce the overall design complexity of an application. In other words, if Class A doesn't have to implement code to understand how Class B operates, we have just reduced the complexity of the code.

As programmers, we initiate a message from one class to another by calling a method or property on the target class. Part of this message that we send encapsulates any parameters or data needed by the receiving class to execute the action.

Thus, we have classes in an object-oriented programming environment. A physical manifestation of a class in the programming world consists of code that defines these attributes and behaviors through property and method routines.

In this book, our focus on the Framework Class Library will introduce you to new classes in each chapter. They will exhibit all of the traits and characteristics of the classes that we have just defined.

Now, let's move on and discuss the next OO trait of Visual Basic .NET—inheritance.

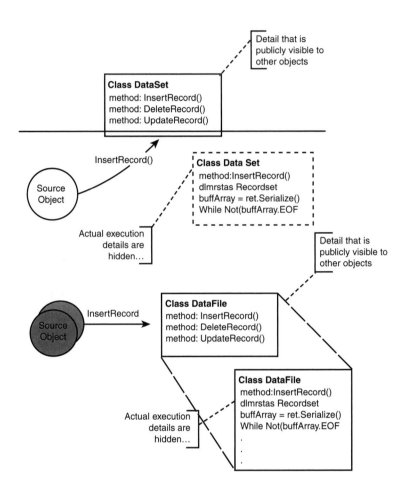

FIGURE 3.1

Messaging and information hiding.

Inheritance—*Defining Classes in Terms of One Another*

Inheritance is the capability for one class to inherit or take on the traits of another class. Typically, this happens in a hierarchical fashion. Consider the following simple example to see how this inheritance results in a natural hierarchy of classes. Figure 3.2 shows three classes: HR Employee, IT Employee, and Warehouse Employee. Each of these is shown with some of their properties and methods.

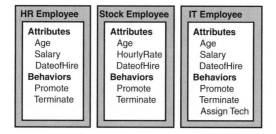

FIGURE 3.2

Three classes—no parent class.

By looking at them, it quickly becomes clear that we could hierarchically structure these classes by abstracting their common traits into a parent class. These three classes would then be *child classes* of that one *parent class*. Figure 3.3 shows how this results in a tree structure for our classes. Another way to think about this is called sub-typing. Children classes can often be thought of as different "types" of the parent class (an HR employee is a type of Employee, and so on).

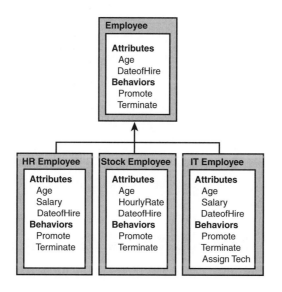

FIGURE 3.3

Introduction of a parent class.

This hierarchical structure is typical of well-engineered class libraries—the Framework Class Library is organized in just such a way.

NOTE

If you examine Figure 3.3, you will see that our arrows point from the child classes to the parent class. This may not seem intuitive to you; after all, aren't we creating a child class *from* a parent class? This notation is advocated because it shows that the child knows about the parent, but the parent does not (necessarily) know about the child.

Inheritance by Natural Relationship

One of the nice things about inheritance is that it often simply realizes a relationship that we already make in our minds. That is, it is often just a recognition of real-world relationships. We can tell that a dog or a cat is a type of an animal—the inheritance between the concept of an animal class and a dog or cat class is obvious. Again, this is a good thing as it helps to reduce the semantic gap that we talked about earlier and helps you make your code organization easier to understand. Organizing your code is only one benefit of inheritance—code reuse is another.

We have said that a class can inherit the traits of another class. We have also said that the traits of a class are implemented as property and method routines. When these routines are inherited between classes, it obviously means we are assuming the actual source code of one class into another. Thus, we have code reuse.

If we look back at Figure 3.3 we can see how each line of code that was written to implement the parent class methods can be reused by each of the child classes. Code reuse in this fashion becomes a powerful rapid application development enabler. If we needed to change some lines of code in one of the parent class methods, the change would be immediately realized in its children classes. This also allows us to build up complexity in a child class by inheriting from potentially simple base classes.

NOTE

There are many different ways to express the inheritance relationship: parent to child, super-class to sub-class, ancestor class to descendant class, generalized class to specialized class, and so on. In this book, anytime we use these terms you should know that we are just referring back to this basic concept of inheritance relationship.

Figure 3.4 shows class nomenclature, in ancestor/descendant terms, against a class tree.

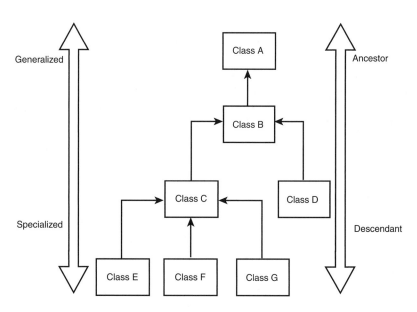

FIGURE 3.4

Inheritance nomenclature examples.

We now know that identifying logical relationships between objects will help us out in the area of code reuse. But the examples we have talked about so far have been based on relationships between objects—an appraisal of one object being a type of another object. If, however, you approach inheritance by first looking at its end result, you'll find that you can end up with an entirely different perspective. Let's look at an example: Let's say that we have a class that defines operations for a specific type of printer. We'll call this class `InkJet`. Intuitively, we sense a parent class that would most likely be called `Printer`. Introducing a `Printer` parent class produces the inheritance that we see in Figure 3.5.

Inheriting from the `Printer` class is a good solution for us because it already defines some basic operations (line feed, paper out, and so on) that we can use as building blocks for our `InkJet` class. At the same time, we will add some of our own behaviors that are specific to inkjet printers. But what if we had the requirement for some low-level communication code that would send an error signal across a parallel port? Also, what if that code was already available to us in yet another class?

Figure 3.6 shows how we could inherit from a fictional `ParallelPort` object to leverage the `SendErrorSignal` code that we need.

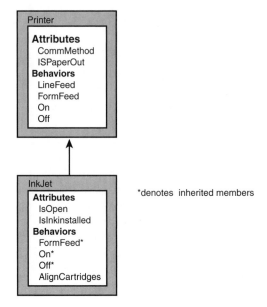

*denotes inherited members

FIGURE 3.5

Inheritance based on relationship.

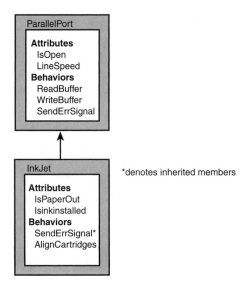

*denotes inherited members

FIGURE 3.6

Inheritance strictly for code reuse.

This is subtly different from what we were doing before because it is very difficult to envision a logical relationship between a parallel port object and an inkjet object. After all, an inkjet printer is not a type of a parallel port—there is no obvious hierarchical relationship to draw between the two. In this case, we would be implementing inheritance to get at raw code reuse. This doesn't do anything for us in terms of making our code easier to understand—it does not reinforce a relationship between abstract classes and real-world objects.

> **NOTE**
>
> Inheriting for pure code reuse in the absence of a sub-type relationship is certainly something that you *can* do with classes, but isn't always the best approach. You gain code reuse at the expense of increased complexity in your system (and therefore, a corresponding increase in the effort required to understand your system). In .NET, we advocate implementing an interface instead of using class inheritance to represent this relationship; you still get the desired code reuse without complicating your class relationships (more on interfaces in Chapter 4).

What if you decided to proceed ahead with class inheritance, and decided to inherit from both the `Printer` *and* the `ParallelPort` class? This is called *multiple inheritance* (see Figure 3.7). Multiple inheritance is not supported by the .NET runtime.

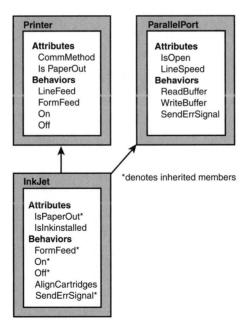

FIGURE 3.7

An example of multiple inheritance.

Polymorphism—*Overriding One Class Method with Another*

The next OO trait we will discuss is polymorphism. Unlike inheritance, polymorphism is concerned with how a class presents itself to the outside world. Polymorphism roughly means "many forms," and alludes to the fact that a specific named behavior can be implemented in different ways by different classes.

In other words, classes can reuse behavior names but implement them differently.

Overriding

One of the common examples used to demonstrate this concept involves a class library that describes geometric shapes. One of the behaviors that we would like to imbue into our shape classes is the capability to draw themselves. Using our basic knowledge of geometry, we know that each shape will require different parameters and use different operations to actually accomplish the draw operations (pi may be used when drawing circles, squares will need to know a side length, and so on). Because a procedural programming language doesn't allow us to reuse behavior names (think methods), we would end up with a different routine for each shape type such as DrawCircle, DrawTriangle, and so on. Because we can reuse method names with polymorphism, we can simplify the programming model considerably by reusing one method called Draw; each shape class would implement this in a slightly different fashion. This is called *overriding* and specific manifestations of this in the Framework Class Library are discussed in Chapter 4.

Overriding further promotes the concept of information hiding that we talked about earlier: Each class knows internally how to implement its behaviors, but calling classes don't know and don't care. We just send a message saying, "Draw," and the target class worries about how to carry it out. You will often see overriding with inheritance. A child class may override a parent class's methods to implement specific functionality not relevant to the parent class.

Overloading

A class may also override its own methods based on parameter lists. Consider the class shown in Figure 3.8.

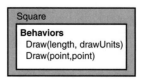

FIGURE 3.8

Method overloading.

It represents a class, Square, and its draw methods. The implementation of the draw behavior differs based on the information that is passed into the Draw method. This is a special case of overriding called *overloading*. In our example here, we want to avoid implementing methods called DrawFromLength and DrawFromCoords; we simplify our class architecture by implementing just one method, Draw, and let it determine which implementation of Draw to use based on the function signature. In this way, both of the following would be valid method calls:

```
mySquare.Draw(10,"inches")
mySquare.Draw(topLeftPoint, bottomRightPoint)
```

Polymorphism is really all about keeping interfaces between classes the same while allowing actual implementations to differ. This encourages loosely coupled object designs and hopefully clarifies system architecture and reduces complexity.

Summary

In this chapter, we introduced the major object-oriented concepts that you will need to understand to get the most out of programming against the Framework Class Library.

We have seen how:

- Classes are used as templates for objects, defining how they behave and the types of information they need to store.
- Inheritance is used to implement class hierarchies and reuse code from a parent class in its children classes.
- Polymorphism allows classes to take on many different forms of behaviors, depending on the particular circumstances.

As we explore the class library in Part II of this book, you will see ample evidence of these concepts in action. In the next chapter, we will show how many of these OO concepts physically manifest themselves in the .NET Class Library.

Introduction to the .NET
Framework Class Library

IN THIS CHAPTER

The Framework Class Library is a vast tapestry; it will take a while before you are familiar enough with it to immediately identify its possible uses in a given situation. This chapter will introduce you to the class library that ships with the .NET Framework. We will examine its organization, and look at exactly how the classes operate as a reusable layer of functional building blocks for .NET developers. You should walk away from this chapter understanding, in principle, what position in the larger .NET initiative that the Framework Class Library holds, and how it is really designed with the end developer in mind. You should also be primed and ready to look at actual code examples in the chapters that follow in Part II, "Working with the .NET Namespaces," of this book.

This chapter will specifically

- Describe the organization of the class library namespaces.
- Illustrate how the class library implements the core concepts of classes, enumerations, delegates, interfaces, and structures.
- Identify the key productivity enhancements offered by programming against the class library.

So, before getting in to the actual makeup of the .NET base classes, we will examine a few basic aspects of the namespaces that constitute the class library.

Introducing the Framework Class Library

As you have probably figured out from its name, the class library is merely a collection of classes and related structures that can be leveraged as base building blocks for application development. As such, it is safe to think of this collection of classes as an API: They are a boundary interface between our applications and the operating system. This concept, of course, is really nothing new to Visual Basic developers: the ADO library, the Win32 API, the COM+ services library—all of these constructs have allowed us to reference and use pre-existing code in our applications. The class library is a massive library of pre-existing code that you can use as a foundation for your application features.

> **NOTE**
>
> Referencing pre-existing libraries of code has traditionally been pretty easy with Visual Basic. One of the main issues, however, was that many times these code libraries weren't initially consumable by Visual Basic developers. If you were a C++ programmer, the world was open to you in terms of functionality. VB programmers had to wait for Microsoft or some other entity to make a wrapper or interface available that we could use from VB. Documentation also tended to be a problem.

Organization—The Namespace Hierarchy

The primary units of organization for the class library are *namespaces*. A namespace is just a bucket for functionality: It describes a grouping of like-focused classes and constructs. You can liken the concept of a namespace to that of a file system folder—they both attempt to implement organization across objects with parent and child relationships. Just as a folder can contain other folders and actual documents, a namespace can contain other namespaces or actual classes, delegates, and so on.

All namespaces stem from a common root: the `System` namespace. The `System` namespace is the one and only common root for all other namespaces.

The `System` namespace, for instance, contains the actual structures that define the common data types used in .NET such as `Boolean`, `DateTime`, and `Int32`. It also contains the most important data type of all, `Object`, which is the base object inherited by all other .NET objects.

Walking the Tree

The first level of children namespaces under the System namespace represents the high-level functionality groupings exposed by the API. Table 4.1 shows these high-level namespaces, with a brief description of their focus. Remember that each one of these high-level namespaces can (and likely will) have other children namespaces that further decompose and organize the functionality and focus of the parent namespace. A good example of this is the `System.XML` namespace, which parents the `System.XML.Schema`, the `System.XML.Serialization`, the `System.XML.XPath`, and the `System.XML.XSL` namespaces.

TABLE 4.1   Primary Namespaces Under the System Root

Name	*Focus*
CodeDOM	Source code document structure and manipulation (including compilation).
Collections	Collections of objects including arrays, hash tables, and dictionaries.
ComponentModel	Runtime and design-time behavior of components and controls.
Configuration	Configuration settings management for the Framework.
Data	Data access and management (essentially defines the ADO.NET technology).
Diagnostics	Application debugging and execution tracing. Also included in this namespace are classes related to event log manipulation and performance monitoring.
DirectoryServices	Access to the Active Directory.
Drawing	Graphics and drawing, including printing.

TABLE 4.1   Continued

Name	Focus
EnterpriseServices	COM interactions and settings.
Globalization	Definition of culture-specific settings.
IO	Synchronous and asynchronous access to files and streams.
Management	Access to WMI functionality.
Messaging	Message creation and transmission in addition to management of message queues.
Net	Network communications and protocols.
Reflection	Examination and on-the-fly creation of types, methods, and fields.
Resources	Management of culture-specific resources.
Runtime	Access to low-level runtime functions, including compilation and interop services.
Security	General runtime security including policies, permissions, and credential resolution.
ServiceProcess	Creation and installation of Windows services.
Text	Conversion and formatting of text.
Threading	Explicit thread creation and management.
Timers	Server-based timers.
Web	Browser/server communication over HTTP.
Windows	Form-based Windows creation.
XML	XML processing.

You should know that the Framework Class Library can be extended, but that the system root namespace will always contain classes that are universally useful to applications. Companies may introduce their own libraries that will co-exist with the System namespace and that will, in fact, operate under their own root namespace. Microsoft, for instance, has already shown us an example of this by including several language-focused namespaces under a root Microsoft namespace. Thus, we have Microsoft.Csharp, Microsoft.VisualBasic, and so on.

Enhancing Developer Productivity

An important design goal of the Framework Class Library is to enhance developer productivity.

It may surprise you to know that the class library primarily targets the goal of enhanced productivity not by introducing new functionality but by repackaging functionality in an object-oriented way. That is to say that, while the Framework Class Library does introduce some new features, much of the functionality exposed by the namespaces was previously available to us through the Win32 API, ActiveX controls, COM-based DLLs, and so on. Now, however, it is wrapped in a way that allows us to program at an abstracted level where we don't have to deal with the complexities and granular pieces of data required by the Win32 API. As a direct result, we only have to deal with one over-arching design pattern in our applications: one that uses and promotes components in an object-oriented environment. Moreover, the functionality is available across all of the CLR-targeted languages!

> **NOTE**
>
> In case you were wondering, the Framework Class Library does not replace the Win32 API. The class library still relies on the actual Win32 API classes to talk directly to the Win32 API to execute code through something called a P/invoke (platform invoke). We'll talk more about this process when we dig into the details of calling the Win32 API from your code in Appendix A, "Calling the Win32 API from Managed Code." Of course, if the .NET Framework is ported to another environment, the P/invoke code will be calling into that environment's native API.

Finding the Code That You Need

If we start to examine the ways that the class library helps to make for a more productive development experience, we can see a few things immediately. For one, the class library allows you to easily find the functionality for which you are looking. While the size of the class library may seem daunting at first, its logical presentation inside of the namespaces allows functionality to be discovered in a straightforward fashion. For instance, the `System.Drawing` namespace contains classes that will provide you with drawing functions. The `System.IO` namespace exposes classes for basic input/output operations, and so on. And inside the `System.Drawing` namespace, we find objects that would be familiar to any Windows graphics programmer: the `Pen` object, the `Brush` object, and so on.

With any sufficiently sized API, the task of actually locating the code or function that you need for a given task is not an inconsiderable issue. Contrast the organization of the namespaces that we have talked about thus far with the organization of the flat, monolithic namespace offered up by the Win32 API. The Win32 API has given us such gems as FindClosePrinterChangeNotification (which doesn't find anything; it closes a resource). The problem is that, as the Win32 API has grown at its core, its developers have had to be more and more creative with their function names. The ability to look at a function name and know without some research what its purpose is has started to deteriorate. To be fair, it is possible to be productive using the Win32 API from Visual Basic. It just takes some determination and a lot of reference information. The Framework Class Library is a more approachable API: Things are where you expect them to be. It appeals to the OO programmer in all of us who, after all, is just interested in simplifying software by using objects.

> **NOTE**
>
> We call any code that runs under the control of the .NET runtime *managed code*. *Unmanaged code* is any code that runs outside of the .NET runtime, such as the Win32 API, COM components, and ActiveX controls. Currently, the only development tool available from Microsoft for writing unmanaged code is Visual C++.

Using the Class Library

Finding the class you need is the first step; after you have found it, the Framework Class Library also makes utilizing it easy. By exposing functionality through properties and methods, we have straightforward access to features that are extremely complicated under the hood. In the true spirit of data hiding and encapsulation, we are dealing with black boxes—we neither know nor care what takes place in the box. What we do care about is that we talk to the black box in a standard and predictable way.

This element of productivity is not insignificant. Again consider the effort required to work directly with the Win32 API. Because Visual Basic was talking to an API that had a different type system, there was not a clear, one-to-one mapping between API calls and actual Visual Basic syntax. Now, due to the integral role that the Common Type System plays, all languages talk to runtime components through the same data types. This ensures that the classes in the Framework Class Library can be consumed evenly by any of the .NET languages. For the first time, Visual Basic developers have the full range of framework functionality open to them with no corresponding drop in productivity.

There is little to no disjoint when a programmer hops between language-intrinsic functions and the class library. In other words, Visual Basic developers are finally free to accomplish their application programming without jumping in and out of different coding paradigms (such as moving from procedural Win32API patterns to VB component patterns). Design patterns can remain consistent throughout your code regardless of the actual type of component being con-sumed. This is because the entire library was built to support object and component-based pro-gramming intrinsically—these concepts are "built-in" and not bolted on. What's more, the class library usage follows familiar design patterns for VB developers. There is no esoteric syntax required; instead, you reference the component, instantiate it, and then use its methods and properties.

Because the Framework Class Library is written in managed code that runs on top of the .NET Common Language Runtime, it reaps all of the benefits of any other piece of managed code, such as:

- Freedom from GUIDS, hResults, and so on
- Automatic garbage collection of unused resources and memory
- Support for structured exception handling

Code Reuse

The holy grail of all object-oriented development, code reuse is a large part of the value of the Framework Class Library. As all code libraries are intended to do, the intent with the class library is to provide developers with a foundation for application development. If you recall the concepts of inheritance that we talked about in Chapter 3, "Object-Oriented Concepts in .NET," VB .NET programmers are free to derive any of their classes from a base class defined in one of the system namespaces (assuming, of course, that the class has not been marked as sealed—see our note on sealed classes later). These classes don't behave any differently than a class that you would write in Visual Basic .NET. In VB .NET, the `Inherits` keyword is all that is needed. The following code snippet shows a program inheriting from the `XMLDocument` class in the `System.Xml` namespace:

```
Public Class MyDOM
    Inherits System.Xml.XmlDocument
    .
    .
    .
End Class
```

In addition to using the Framework classes for inheritance, you can also simply instantiate an object directly from one of these classes, and use it—you simply reference the namespace that you need, and then dimension and instantiate an object from one of the classes in that namespace. Object instantiation will look familiar to VB developers, because this is similar to what you have done with type libraries and COM DLLs.

This code snippet shows how you can use the `Imports` keyword to reference a specific namespace in the class library. The DNS class contained in the `System.Net.Sockets` namespace is then used to instantiate an object. The code is clear and simple to read.

```
Imports System.Net.Sockets


Public Class TargetServer
    Sub Main()
        Dim resolver As DNS = New DNS()
```

4

```
          .
          .
          .
    End Sub
End Class
```

> **NOTE**
>
> You should know that there are classes that don't allow you to inherit from them. Conversely, there are also classes that *require* you to inherit from them. These classes are called *sealed* and *abstract,* respectively, and are discussed in more detail in the following section.

The end result is a universal, free, logical, and component-based API that can be easily consumed by any of the .NET languages without loss of functionality.

The Elements of a Namespace

Each namespace can define its own set of classes, structures, delegates, interfaces, and enumerations. And, as we have seen with the System namespace, they can also sometimes contain value types. Let's examine each one of these in turn.

Classes

As we discussed in Chapter 3, a class is a template or blueprint for an object. It defines how an object should look and behave. It does this principally through methods, properties, and events.

If you have read on from the last chapter or have some experience with object-oriented programming, you should be familiar by now with the concepts of classes. You should note, however, that the .NET runtime supports some class attributes that you may *not* be familiar with. These attributes are summarized in Table 4.2.

TABLE 4.2   .NET Class Attributes

Class Attribute	Description
Sealed	Specifies that you cannot inherit from this class. A good example of a sealed class in the Framework Class Library is the String class. In Visual Basic .NET you can create your own sealed classes by using the NotInheritable keyword.

TABLE 4.2 Continued

Class Attribute	Description
Implements	Specifies the interfaces implemented by a particular class. For instance, the Array Class implements the Ilist interface, imbuing Arrays with the capability to add members and retrieve the index of a member.
Abstract	Indicates that the class cannot be directly instantiated. They typically exist as a means of organizing lower-level derived classes, or as a convenient virtual class that is used solely as a template for other classes instead of instances. Examples of abstract classes include the XMLWriter class in the System.XML namespace, and the Image class in the System.Drawing namespace.
Inherits	Identifies the base class that the current class inherits from. As an example, the ColorDialog Class inherits from the CommonDialog class—an acknowledgment of the fact that it is a type of common dialog.
Exported/Not Exported	Indicates whether a class is visible outside of its defining assembly. Exported classes are those visible outside of the assembly in which they are defined.

Classes typically define a *constructor*; this is a specialized behavior of a class that is called whenever a new instance is created from that class. In Visual Basic .NET, you will define your constructors using the Sub New routine. Class_Initialize and Class_Terminate events are no longer supported. Classes may also implement *destructors* that will be called when the object is being destroyed.

Object destruction in .NET works a little bit differently than you have come to expect. .NET implements something called a *garbage collector*. The garbage collector continually examines a "reference tree;" if it finds an object that doesn't have any more branches on the reference tree, it calls the destructor of that object. It is no longer necessary to explicitly destroy managed objects; the garbage collector will take care of it for you.

4

NOTE

If your class uses resources that are unmanaged in nature, you should implement a Finalize method. This method, which is not public, will be called by the garbage collector as it destroys unneeded objects. If you need to provide a public method for freeing resources (such as a Close method for your class), you should implement the IDisposable interface.

All objects in the .NET Framework inherit from the System.Object class. System.Object is the ultimate superclass in the Framework Class Library.

Structures

Structures are the .NET version of user-defined types from prior versions of Visual Basic. User Defined Type (or UDT) syntax in Visual Basic, versions 6 and earlier, looked something like this:

```
Type InventoryItem
        SKU As String * 50
        Price As Single
        Name As String * 25
        Count As Integer
End Type
```

The metamorphosis into structures means the Type...End Type syntax is no longer supported. It has been replaced with Structure...End Structure:

```
Structure InventoryItem
        Public SKU As String
        Private Price As Single
        Public Name As String
        Private Count As Integer
End Structure
```

Note that with structures, each structure element can have its own scope modifier (for example, can be public, private, and so on). This was not previously possible with UDTs.

And that's not all that has changed. Structures in .NET behave a lot like classes. They support most of the constructs of a class including properties, methods, and events. Table 4.3 summarizes some of the key similarities and differences between classes and structures.

TABLE 4.3 Structures versus Classes

	Class	Structure
Allows parameter-less constructors?	Yes	No
Supports properties, methods, and events?	Yes	Yes
Can be inherited from?	Yes	No
Can implement interfaces?	Yes	Yes
Support for destructors?	Yes	No

In the class library, structures are used to represent value types such as integers (Int16, Int32, Int64). In fact, the actual structure object inherits directly from the class ValueType in the root System namespace.

Delegates

Delegates may be an unfamiliar concept to the average Visual Basic developer. In essence, delegates are function pointers: They encapsulate method calls to other objects. Delegates are described by the parameters they accept and the value type they return. In other words, you can declare a delegate that will map to a method call that takes an integer and a single and returns a string:

```
public delegate myDelegate(value1 As Integer, value2 As Single) As String
```

To use the delegate, you would declare a variable that references the delegate like this:

```
Dim myCallback As myDelegate = New myDelegate(obj.SomeMethod)
```

If the SomeMethod method that you reference has a function signature that matches the definition of myDelegate, you are home free, otherwise an error will be raised.

One of the powerful capabilities of a delegate is its ability to perform its function pointing in a late bound fashion. You can use the preceding delegate to map to any method that follows the parameter and return type signature; you don't need to explicitly make a tie between the delegate and a specific function at design time.

Delegates are defined throughout the Framework Class Library namespaces and fulfill a variety of different tasks, most associated with implementing designs regarding callbacks and event processing.

Interfaces

An interface is most commonly described as a contract. If you implement an interface, you are essentially entering into a contract with all other components that exist that says, "I agree to provide the following functionality in the following manner forever and ever...." Interfaces can have methods and properties just like classes.

You can implement interfaces defined in the Framework Class Library by using the Implements keyword:

```
Public Class Class1
    Implements IDisposable

    Public Sub Finalize() Implements IDisposable.Dispose
        .
        .
        .
    End Sub
End Class
```

This code snippet shows a class implementing the IDisposable interface.

Back when we talked about inheritance and code reuse in Chapter 3, we said that interfaces provide a good structure for implementing code belonging to a class that isn't necessarily "logically" related to our core class.

This kind of code reuse keeps our class hierarchies from becoming cluttered with seemingly random inheritance relationships.

> **NOTE**
>
> There are some design considerations to think about when deciding between class inheritance and interface implementation. For instance, because interfaces are meant to be binding and perpetual contracts, they can't (or shouldn't) be changed. Implementing code in an interface that is likely to change, such as business rules, leads to a very brittle architecture. You don't have this concern with class inheritance because methods and properties can always be added to a base class without "breaking" its descendant classes.

Enumerations

An enumeration is essentially a named constant—it is an aid to developer productivity because it allows you to reference values using a recognizable name. Using enumerations greatly improves code readability and speeds up coding because they provide a way to name or reference a value that maps to one of the underlying data types defined by the CTS. Visual Basic developers should be familiar with the concept of "enums"—the syntax has not changed moving into Visual Basic .NET. The .NET runtime allows enumerations to evaluate to any of the signed or unsigned integer data types that are defined (such as `Int32`, `Int64`, and so on).

As far as the Framework class library is concerned, enumerations are in many of the namespaces. One example of an enumeration in the class library is `Appearance`, contained in the `System.Windows.Forms` namespace.

To use an enumeration from your code, simply reference the enumeration's name and the value name that you want to use:

```
myButton.Appearance=Appearance.Button
```

In the preceding code, we use the Appearance enumeration to specify that the button control we are using should take on the "Button" appearance.

Enumerations are derived from the `System.Enum` class, which means you can reference enumerations in some very cool ways. For instance, you can call the `GetValues()` method to get an array of all values defined by an enumeration. You can also call the `GetNames()` method to get an array of all names for the values defined by an enumeration.

Programming with the Framework Class Library

Because the Framework Class Library contains classes in the true object-oriented spirit of that word, there are two primary ways you will find yourself using these base classes:

- Black boxes that you can call into
- Classes that you can inherit from and extend to craft your own functionality

Instantiating Objects from the Class Library

The use of base classes as a black box is probably the primary path for most developers. In this mode, your code will be treating the class library as a simple API to get at core functions on your particular operating system.

Using the class library classes in this manner does not represent a departure from the programming model that Visual Basic developers are used to. As an example, if you have programmed Visual Basic applications that have made use of the ADO library, you probably did the following:

1. You set a reference to the code library through the VB IDE.
2. You Dim'd a container for one of the ADO objects.
3. After you had a container object, you instantiated a version of an ADO object into it.
4. After that, you simply invoked its methods and properties as needed.

With Visual Basic .NET, your consumption of Framework classes will follow the exact same pattern.

> **NOTE**
>
> Not all classes in the Framework class library allow you to create instances just by using the New operator—some force you to go through a class factory method to get your initial instance of the class. The WebRequest class is one example: In order to create a new WebRequest object, you have to use the WebRequest.Create method. You should also be aware that some classes have static methods and properties. Static methods apply to classes and not instances. That means that you don't have to create an instance of the class in order to use the method. The WebRequest.Create method is an example of a static method: We simply call it using the class reference without an actual instance having been created.

Inheriting from the Framework Class Library

With the exception of those classes marked as sealed, you are free to build your own classes on any of the base classes in the class library using the inheritance model in .NET.

As you explore the Framework Class Library, you will see many instances of inherited classes that override and overload class members (both of these concepts were discussed in the previous chapter). In the documentation for a specific class, you may see a method defined as Overrides:

```
Overrides Public Function GetYear(ByVal time As DateTime) As Integer
```

This example shows the method prototype for the GetYear method on the JulianCalendarClass. It shows us that this function is overridden from its base class (in this case, from the Calendar class).

Overloading is a form of overriding by providing multiple method instances that differ only in their parameter list.

As with overriding, when you explore the Framework Class Library you will notice plenty of examples of overloading. Many class constructors are overloaded to give developers the maximum choice of instantiation based on the available data.

Consider the following constructors for the TCPClient class:

```
Overloads Public Sub New()
Overloads Public Sub New(ByVal localEP As IPEndPoint)
Overloads Public Sub New(ByVal hostname As String, port As Integer)
```

These constructors give you the choice of how you want to instantiate a TCPClient object.

NOTE

If you have been paying attention, you will have noticed by now that both Visual Basic .NET and the Framework Class Library define base data types. In other words, you have the Int32 data type defined in the System root namespace, and the Integer data type defined in Visual Basic. From a best-practice perspective, you may be asking yourself, which is the preferred method: declaring things using VB .NET intrinsics, or their actual System types?

To illustrate, both of the following lines of code are valid:

```
Dim SomeVar As Integer
Dim AnotherVar As System.Int32
```

We suggest you pick whatever comes more naturally to you, and use it consistently. Using the actual Framework data types has some attraction if you are programming across multiple languages; you don't have to shift gears. On the other hand, dimensioning a variable as `Integer` will come much more naturally to Visual Basic developers. And of course, you don't have to worry about the repercussions of your choice: The CLR ensures that all of your code is mapped to the correct underlying data type.

Exception Handling

Exception Handling is the process of managing errors that may be encountered during the execution of your code. The .NET runtime, and the .NET languages, supports the concept of Structured Exception Handling (SEH). These exception handlers follow a standard format that defines a `Try` block, a `Catch` block, and a `Finally` block.

Writing an exception handler requires you to place the code that could possibly generate an error into the `Try` block. In the `Catch` block, you place your code that deals with the error. The `Finally` block is where you place operations that should be performed regardless of whether an error was raised or not. The following code snippet shows a simple routine that implements its code inside of an exception handler.

```
Sub DoCalc(ByVal num1 As Integer, ByVal num2 As Integer) As Integer
    'The exception handler is initiated with the 'try' block
    Try
        DoCalc = num1 / num2
    Catch appError As Exception
        'handle the error; here, we just alert the user
        'through a message box. To get more detailed
        'debugging level info, we could use the
        'Exception.StackTrace property...
        MsgBox("Error:" & appError.Message)

    Finally

        Beep()

    End Try
End Sub
```

Notice that the `Catch` statement syntax allows you to deal with the exception as an object. The class library defines an actual `Exception` class that allows the runtime to treat pass exceptions through as instances of the `Exception` class. The `Exception` base class is, in turn, used to derive more specialized exception classes such as the `ApplicationException` and `SystemException` classes (both defined in the `System` root namespace) and the `WebException` class (defined in the `System.Net` namespace). In fact, there is a fairly deep class hierarchy built from the `Exception` class base (see Figure 4.1).

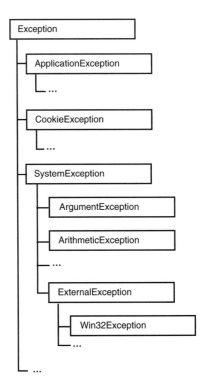

FIGURE 4.1

Partial snapshot of the Exception Class Hierarchy.

As you examine the Exception class descendants, you will see that they offer methods and properties specific to a given coding scenario. They often, for instance, override the ErrorCode property to provide specific error codes for their particular scope. An exception handler with multiple catch blocks looks like this:

```
'The exception handler is initiated with the 'try' block
Try
     'code that could raise an exception goes here
Catch appError As Exception
    'handle the generic error

Catch win32Error As Win32Exception
    'handle win32 error

Catch sockError As SocketException
    'handle network socket error

Finally
```

```
          'code to run regardless of exception or not

    End Try
```

You can use the appropriate level (generalized or specialized) of exception object that is appropriate to your specific piece of code. You will often find yourself using multiple catch blocks in your code to deal with exceptions raised across different levels of the exception class hierarchy.

As we talk in-depth about the Framework classes in the chapters to come, we'll devote time to talking about these specialized exception classes in the namespaces, and the additional properties that they offer.

Summary

In this chapter, we have seen how the .NET Framework Class Library employs the basic OO concepts of classes, inheritance, and polymorphism to provide developers with a rich API for managed code.

We also investigated:

- The various pieces of a namespace including classes, delegates, interfaces, structures, and so on

- How the Framework Class Library is designed to make it easy for developers to find and then consume functionality exposed by its classes

- How to use the class library as an API and as a bed for class inheritance

Now that the anatomy of the class library has been exposed, the next part of this book will concentrate on visiting, in-depth, some of these namespaces. We'll explore their classes and figure out how to write code against them.

4

INTRODUCTION TO
THE .NET
FRAMEWORK
CLASS LIBRARY

Working with the .NET Namespaces

Part II of this book focuses on an in-depth examination of select Framework Class Library namespaces. The structure of Part II is developer task–based. It presents you with an overview of how to accomplish a given task, leads you through detailed examples (written in VB .NET), and finally, provides detailed reference information on select namespace classes, delegates, structures, and interfaces.

Part II explores

- Which classes and namespace elements to use for a given programming task
- Design patterns and best practices for using a namespace
- Sample applications to cement the concepts covered in each chapter
- Reference information on specific namespace elements to help you become immediately productive with the class library

This section can be read in sequence, but most readers will want to skip around as needed. It is organized around common programming tasks and designed to get you producing quality code with a given namespace.

Forms, Menus, and Controls

IN THIS CHAPTER

Visual Basic has always excelled at forms-based application development. It has made the art of crafting user interfaces with graphical windows a quick and easy job, involving drag-and-drop controls and simple event coding. Visual Basic .NET continues that tradition, aligning itself squarely with rapid forms development. Today, Visual Studio .NET and the .NET Framework itself have become key enablers for graphical user interface (GUI) development. With the .NET Framework, access to Windows Forms constructs is provided through the `System.Windows.Forms` namespace (and its descendants). This means that all languages that leverage the .NET runtime and its Framework can take advantage of these powerful classes to provide forms capabilities.

In this chapter, we will start our exploration of the `Forms` namespace by investigating how it allows you to create and manipulate Windows Forms. Then, we'll cover adding menus to forms and working with menu events. We'll wrap up with a discussion of controls and how to create custom controls from the `UserControl` class. We *will not* cover the design of Windows Forms using Visual Studio itself; instead, we will focus explicitly on those items strictly from a class library perspective. We will also not examine the multitude of controls available with Visual Studio.

After reading this chapter, you should be able to

- Create forms and alter their appearance programmatically
- Control the interaction of multiple-document interface (MDI) parent and child forms
- Add menus to forms and respond to their events
- Add controls to a form programmatically and create your own controls

Key Classes Related to Windows Forms

In the .NET Framework, the visual design of applications starts at the class library level, and a number of classes are dedicated to providing Windows Forms functionality. Table 5.1 lists the classes that are discussed in this chapter.

TABLE 5.1   Key Classes of the `System.Windows.Forms` Namespace

Class	Description
AxHost	This class provides a way to wrap ActiveX controls so that they can be used as Windows Forms controls.
Clipboard	This class is used to interact with the Windows Clipboard.
ContainerControl	This class encapsulates all controls that can act as containers for other controls.
ContextMenu	This class represents a shortcut menu.

TABLE 5.1 Continued

Class	Description
Control	This class is the parent class for all control inheritance.
Cursor	This class controls the visual representation of the mouse pointer on the screen.
Cursors	This class is a collection class that can be populated with Cursor class objects.
DataFormats	This class is used in conjunction with the Clipboard class to specify a format for data that is to be interchanged with the Clipboard.
DataFormats.Format	Just as with the DataFormats class, the DataFormats.Format class is used in conjunction with the Clipboard class. It provides ID/name pair access to a specific data format.
DataObject	This class provides a way to transfer data in a format-independent fashion.
FileDialog	This class can be used to programmatically show a file selection dialog box to the user and then process the user's selection.
FontDialog	This class can be used to programmatically show a dialog box that lists all the fonts that are installed on the system.
Form	This class represents a Windows Form.
Form.ControlCollection	This class provides access to all the controls associated with a given form.
IWin32Window Interface	This class allows programmatic access to Windows HWnd handles.
MainMenu	This class is used to add the initial menu structure to a form.
Menu	This is the base class from which all other menu classes derive.
Menu.MenuItemCollection	This class is used to manage collections of MenuItem instances.
MenuItem	This class encapsulates specific items in a menu.
Message Structure	This class is used to wrap Windows messages.
OpenFileDialog	This class is used to provide access to the Windows file open dialog box.
PageSetupDialog	This class is a representation of the page setup dialog box, which is common to forms that allow printing.

5

TABLE 5.1   Continued

Class	Description
PrintDialog	This class can be used to provide common printing options (including printer selection) for a forms-based application.
PrintPreviewDialog	This class is used to display a print preview dialog box for printing-enabled forms applications.
SaveFileDialog	This class is used to display a dialog box for specifying save options for a file.
Screen	This class represents the actual display screen for the current system. It is commonly used to retrieve the display bounds of the screen.
SendKeys	This class is used to send keystrokes to a specified application.
SystemInformation	This class is used to examine operating system information.

Creating Forms

A *form* is a design-time version of a window. That is, when executed, a form appears as a window. In the design-time environment, however, a form functions as a canvas with which programmers can interact. Programmers can place code behind a form, and they can add controls, menus, and other items to the form; they can customize the way the form looks and behaves. Users and programmers alike are familiar with forms and their properties for a good reason: They are the graphical, visual manifestations of programs. They are how consumers of program functionality interact with programs to balance bank accounts, manage inventory, calculate taxes, write books, and complete many other tasks.

Introducing the Form Class

In the .NET Framework, the Form class is the primary object that you use to create and manipulate forms. It is a representation of any type of window that you might need to display in an application, from dialog boxes to resizable windows to MDI windows. You interact with the Form class as you do any other class in the .NET Framework; there is nothing inherently special or different about it. This means you don't have to alter your approach to development just to deal with forms (as developers have had to do in the past).

As .NET base classes go, the Form class is a fairly large class. We'll touch on its most important members in this chapter; you can explore the rest of the Form class members on your own.

Using the Windows Form Designer

Every forms-based .NET application, regardless of whether it is crafted inside the Visual Studio Integrated Development Environment (IDE), ends up inheriting from the Form class in one way or another. For instance, you could choose to inherit directly from the Form class, or you could inherit from another form that you have created (which in turn probably inherits from the Form class). When you add a form to an application, Visual Studio auto-generates some code that is educational. The Visual Studio template for forms-based applications shows up in the New Project dialog box as Windows Application. Selecting File, New gets you to the New Project dialog box (see Figures 5.1 and 5.2).

FIGURE 5.1

Creating a new project.

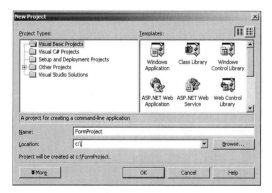

FIGURE 5.2

The New Project dialog box.

Note that because forms are objects in the .NET Framework, there is no magic that happens inside the Visual Studio .NET IDE to make them work. The IDE is a convenient shell for forms development because it allows for drag-and-drop form building through the Windows Form Designer, which takes much of the grunt work out of creating forms and controls. You could write these windows applications by using Notepad or any other simple text editor, but it would be an arduous undertaking—there would be no syntax checking, auto-completion, or even common formatting.

If you double-click on a form, you see the code behind the form. By default, the code you see should look like this:

```
Public Class Form1
    Inherits System.Windows.Forms.Form

#Region " Windows Form Designer generated code "

    Private Sub Form1_Load(ByVal sender As System.Object, ByVal e As _
    System.EventArgs) Handles MyBase.Load


    End Sub
End Class
```

Let's examine this line by line. First, a class declaration defines a class called Form1:

```
Public Class Form1
    Inherits System.Windows.Forms.Form
```

This declaration shows that this class will inherit from System.Windows.Forms.Form; that is, it will inherit from the Form class in the System.Windows.Forms namespace. This simple declaration is where all the action takes place. In one fell swoop, the IDE has created some code that is poised to take advantage of all the inherent functionality of the Framework-defined Form class, and as you will see, there is quite a lot of functionality there to be consumed.

The next line might look peculiar to someone who is new to the Visual Studio .NET IDE because the concept of code regions is new to Visual Studio .NET:

```
#Region " Windows Form Designer generated code "
```

The #Region directive is a new element in the Visual Basic language. It tells the IDE to collapse and hide sections of code. In the IDE, as shown in Figure 5.3, this directive is preceded by a plus or minus box that you can click on to selectively reveal or hide the code bracketed by the #Region directive.

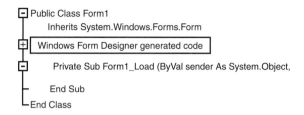

FIGURE 5.3

A collapsed code region in the IDE.

The collapsed code region in Figure 5.3 is given a name—Windows Form Designer generated code—to let users know who put it there and what it contains. By default, Visual Studio assumes that you won't want to be bothered by all the code, so it is hidden. However, this is where all the meat of the form creation code sits. If you expanding the collapsed code region, the following code is displayed:

```
#Region " Windows Form Designer generated code "

    Public Sub New()
        MyBase.New()

        'This call is required by the Windows Form Designer.
        InitializeComponent()

        'Add any initialization after the InitializeComponent() call

    End Sub

    'Form overrides dispose to clean up the component list.
    Protected Overloads Overrides Sub Dispose(ByVal disposing As Boolean)
        If disposing Then
            If Not (components Is Nothing) Then
                components.Dispose()
            End If
        End If
        MyBase.Dispose(disposing)
    End Sub

    'Required by the Windows Form Designer
    Private components As System.ComponentModel.Container
```

5

FORMS, MENUS,
AND CONTROLS

```
'NOTE: The following procedure is required by the Windows Form Designer
'It can be modified using the Windows Form Designer.
'Do not modify it using the code editor.
<System.Diagnostics.DebuggerStepThrough()> Private Sub _
InitializeComponent()
    '
    'Form1
    '
    Me.AutoScaleBaseSize = New System.Drawing.Size(5, 13)
    Me.ClientSize = New System.Drawing.Size(292, 273)
    Me.Name = "Form1"
    Me.Text = "Form1"

End Sub

#End Region
```

As you can see, most of this code is commented with warnings such as "Do not modify it using the code editor" and "Required by the Windows Form Designer." In other words, if you use the Form Designer, as a rule it is not a good idea to change the code it has written. To be on the safe side, if you need to change something, you should do it through the Form Designer itself instead of through brute-force code editing; this is yet another reason this region is hidden by default.

Working with the Form Class Constructor

The New subroutine is the constructor for the Form1 object. The first thing the New constructor does is call MyBase.New(). This is standard operating procedure for implementing inheritance through a class hierarchy. The MyBase keyword is a reference to the parent class from which the current class is inheriting. In this case, MyBase returns a reference to a generic Form class. The Form class, in its constructor, does the same thing, its parent class does the same thing, and so on. The net result is a series of cascading New calls back up through the class hierarchy tree. Thus, the most basic class has its constructor code execute first, followed by each of its children in turn, until you finally arrive at the ultimate root class, Form1. This allows you to place any specialized code that you might want in the Form1 constructor, and you are assured that all the inherited constructor code has already run.

Normally, the New constructor is where you would place any initialization code for variables, object references, and so on. Because we haven't touched any of the code yet, the only code block currently in the New constructor is a call to InitializeComponent, which the Form Designer has automatically added.

The InitializeComponent subroutine is a block of housekeeping code that the Form Designer uses to set initial form property values. You can see that it is setting the form's ClientSize property (that is, the size of the client area of the form), `AutoScaleBaseSize` property (that is, a value used to determine how much to scale the form if auto-scaling is used), `Name` property (that is, the name used to reference the form in code), and `Text` property (that is, the text displayed on the title bar of the form).

The `Dispose` routine is the polar opposite of the `New` constructor: It is where you place code to dereference objects, close files, zero out variables, and basically take care of anything important that you opened or initialized in the constructor. The Form Designer uses the `Dispose` routine to clean up any components that it has used in conjunction with the form.

Instantiating a Form Object

All the code up to this point in the chapter has been needed to define the form. To actually create a form object based on the `Form1` class, you need to use the following code:

```
Dim frmMain As Form1 = New Form1()
```

As you can see, this is no different from instantiating other objects from classes. It gives you a base form to work with, and from here, you need to decide what style of form should actually manifest itself when it is shown. We'll cover these form characteristics when we continue our discussion about the properties and methods of the `Form` class later in this chapter. Before we do that, though, let's take some time to examine the inheritance hierarchy that culminates in the custom `Form1` class.

The Form Class Hierarchy

Figure 5.4 shows how the `Form` class (and the `UserControl` class) is inherited from the generic `Control` class.

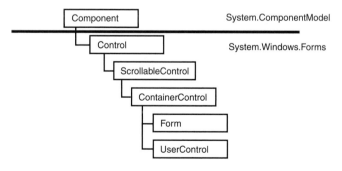

FIGURE 5.4

An inheritance tree for the `Form` and `UserControl` classes.

The `Control` class inherits from the `Component` class in the `System.ComponentModel` namespace. This is why you see references to components in `Form1`'s constructor.

The `Control` Class

The `Control` class represents components that have a visual aspect, such as buttons, check boxes, and treeviews. Because the `Control` class is the first level in the class hierarchy that specializes in visible structures, it is also the first class to start exposing visual attributes such as `ForeColor`, `BackColor`, `Height`, `Width`, and `Cursor`. The `Control` class also implements support for such user interface conventions as mouse and keyboard events.

The `ScrollableControl` Class

The `ScrollableControl` class provides functionality for objects that need the capability to scroll, either horizontally or vertically. It includes only a few properties that aren't inherited from Control that are related to determining whether scrollbars are visible and how to handle auto-scrolling. There is generally not much reason to directly inherit from the `ScrollableControl` class alone.

The `ContainerControl` Class

Container controls are controls that can function as containers for other controls. A form is a good example of this because forms typically contain many other controls. The `ContainerControl` class provides the entire code infrastructure necessary to manage focus on controls. For instance, the `ActiveControl` property returns (or sets) a reference to the currently active control inside the container. The `ContainerControl` class also implements support for parent and child form referencing: The `ParentForm` property gets or sets the form that the container belongs to.

Visual Characteristics of Forms

When you add a form to a project, you will likely want to stipulate how the form will look to the end user. This section examines the various ways you can alter and affect a form's appearance.

Figure 5.5 shows the different pieces of a form or window that are discussed in this section.

Setting Form Modality

A *modal form* is a form that requires the user to close it before continuing to interact with the rest of the application. A *modeless form,* on the other hand, allows the user to continue interacting with any of the other windows that the application is currently displaying while the form is open.

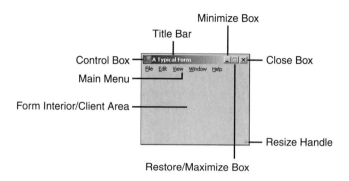

FIGURE 5.5

The parts of a form.

With prior versions of Visual Basic, forms were modeless by default. However, you could display a modal form by using an enumeration passed into the Show method of the form object, like this:

```
frmAbout.Show vbModal
```

The Visual Basic–defined constant vbModal tells the runtime to display the form modally. The Form class in the .NET Framework provides two different types of Show methods: ShowDialog and Show. You display a form modally by calling the ShowDialog method, as in the following example:

```
aboutBox.ShowDialog()
```

You can pass an owner to the ShowDialog method in the following manner:

```
aboutBox.ShowDialog(mainForm)
```

This tells the runtime that the dialog box is a child form to the window, represented by an instance called mainForm. The owner parameter is optional; if you don't provide it in the call to ShowDialog, the resulting dialog box is automatically assigned to the currently active window as its parent/owner.

You display a modeless form by using the Show method:

```
mainForm.Show()
```

Creating MDI Forms

A typical design consideration involves the concepts of single-document interface (SDI) versus MDI applications. An SDI application supports one document at a time, whereas an MDI application can support multiple open documents at a time. As shown in Table 5.2, a few properties that are exposed on the Form class can be used to manage MDI applications.

TABLE 5.2   Form Properties for MDI Management

Property	Description
IsMdiChild	A Boolean value that indicates whether the form is a child to a parent MDI form.
IsMdiContainer	A Boolean value that indicates whether the form is the parent form in an MDI application.
MdiChildren	An array of individual form references, each of which is a child form to the current MDI parent form.
MdiParent	A form reference that indicates the MDI parent form of the current form.

To initially configure an MDI application, you set the IsMdiContainer property to true for the parent form. Then, when you create each child form, you set its IsMdiChild property to true. Listing 5.1 illustrates this concept by setting up Form1 as the MDI container (or parent form) and then creating three child forms.

LISTING 5.1   An Example of an MDI Application

```
Public Class Form1
    Inherits System.Windows.Forms.Form

    Private childForm1 As Form
    Private childForm2 As Form
    Private childForm3 As Form

#Region " Windows Form Designer generated code "

    Public Sub New()
        MyBase.New()

        'This call is required by the Windows Form Designer.
        InitializeComponent()

        'Add any initialization after the InitializeComponent() call

        'Indicate that this form will function as the MDI parent form
        Me.IsMdiContainer = True

        'Create three new forms; each one will have its MdiParent
        'property set to the current form. This means they will
        'be contained inside of Form1 as children forms
        childForm1 = New Form()
```

LISTING 5.1 Continued

```
    childForm1.MdiParent = Me
    childForm1.Text = "Child Form #1"
    childForm2 = New Form()
    childForm2.MdiParent = Me
    childForm2.Text = "Child Form #2"
    childForm3 = New Form()
    childForm3.MdiParent = Me
    childForm3.Text = "Child Form #3"

    'All of our MDI props have been set; go ahead and
    'display the forms.
    childForm1.Show()
    childForm2.Show()
    childForm3.Show()

End Sub


'Form overrides dispose to clean up the component list.
Protected Overloads Overrides Sub Dispose(ByVal disposing As Boolean)
    If disposing Then
        If Not (components Is Nothing) Then
            components.Dispose()
        End If
    End If
    MyBase.Dispose(disposing)
End Sub


'Required by the Windows Form Designer
Private components As System.ComponentModel.Container


'NOTE: The following procedure is required by the Windows Form Designer
'It can be modified using the Windows Form Designer.
'Do not modify it using the code editor.
<System.Diagnostics.DebuggerStepThrough()> _
    Private Sub InitializeComponent()
    '
    'Form1
    '
    Me.AutoScaleBaseSize = New System.Drawing.Size(5, 13)
    Me.ClientSize = New System.Drawing.Size(512, 445)
    Me.Controls.AddRange(New System.Windows.Forms.Control() _
        {New System.Windows.Forms.MdiClient()})
    Me.IsMdiContainer = True
    Me.Name = "Form1"
    Me.Text = "MDI Form Demo"
```

LISTING 5.1   Continued

```
    End Sub

#End Region


End Class
```

Figure 5.6 shows how the application in Listing 5.1 looks when it is run.

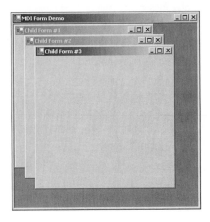

FIGURE 5.6

An example of an MDI application.

You can visually organize MDI child forms by using the `Form.LayoutMdi` method. The `Form.LayoutMdi` method accepts an `MdiLayout` enumeration value (see Table 5.3) and can cascade the forms (as shown in Figure 5.6), tile them vertically, tile them horizontally, or arrange their icons if they are minimized. Typically, MDI applications allow users access to these organizational functions through a Windows menu on the parent MDI container form.

TABLE 5.3   The `MdiLayout` Enumeration

Name	Description
ArrangeIcons	Arranges all the child form icons inside the MDI parent form.
Cascade	Cascades all the child forms inside the MDI parent form.
TileHorizontal	Horizontally tiles all the child forms inside the MDI parent form.
TileVertical	Vertically tiles all the child forms inside the MDI parent form.

Controlling Form Position and State

When you create a form, you have a few options for how to position the form. You use the `FormStartPosition` property to specify where you want the form displayed. Typically, you would set this property after instantiating the form but before displaying it. This property accepts the `FormStartPosition` enumeration shown in Table 5.4.

TABLE 5.4 The `FormStartPosition` Enumeration

Name	Description
CenterParent	Centers the form within the parent form.
CenterScreen	Centers the form on the screen.
Manual	Positions the form based on its current location and size.
WindowsDefaultBounds	Positions the form in accordance with the Windows defaults for location and bounds.
WindowsDefaultLocation	Positions the form in accordance with the Windows default location.

When you create a form, you can also specify the state of the form. By default, all forms are created in the `Normal` state. A form in a `Normal` state displays with its default size (as specified in the `Form` object's `Height`, `Left`, `Top`, and `Width` properties). You can also cause a form to maximize itself (that is, consume all available screen real estate) or minimize itself (that is, shrink down to an icon). The form's state is controlled through the `Form.WindowState` property, which is used in conjunction with the `FormWindowState` enumeration. The `FormWindowState` enumeration is described in Table 5.5.

TABLE 5.5 The `FormWindowState` Enumeration

Name	Description
Maximized	Resizes the form to a maximized window.
Minimized	Resizes the form to a minimized window.
Normal	Resizes the form to its default size, based on its `Size` property values.

Changing Border Style

The `Form` class exposes its border style through the property `FormBorderStyle`. This property is used in conjunction with the `FormBorderStyle` enumeration to customize the way a form's borders are displayed. For example, the following code line:

```
myForm.FormBorderStyle = System.WinForms.FormBorderStyle.Sizable
```

shows all the members of the `FormBorderStyle` enumeration (see Table 5.6). Note that changing the border style also affects the visual aspects of the title bar.

TABLE 5.6   The `FormBorderStyle` Enumeration

Name	Description
Fixed3D	Creates a thick 3D border on all four edges of the window. The border appears beveled on the inside of the form as well as on the outside. The window is not resizable.
FixedDialog	Creates a thick 3D border on all four edges of the window. There is no beveling on the inside of the form. In other words, the border seems to sit at the same level as the interior area of the form. The window is not resizable.
FixedSingle	Creates a thin border on all four edges of the window that is flat in aspect. The window is not resizable.
FixedToolWindow	Creates a tool window border on all four edges of the window. Tool windows have smaller title bars than normal windows, and they do not support Minimize or Maximize buttons. The window is not resizable.
None	Creates a borderless window.
Sizable	Creates a resizable window with normal borders on all four edges.
SizableToolWindow	Creates a resizable tool window border on all four edges of the window.

Creating Minimize, Maximize, and Restore Buttons

Each window or form can have a minimize box, maximize box, restore box, and control box. You specify whether to include these boxes in your form's title bar by using the `ControlBox`, `MaximizeBox`, and `MinimizeBox` properties. Each of these properties is a Boolean value used to set or query for a form's behavior with regard to these boxes. The restore box appears automatically any time either `MaximizeBox` or `MinimizeBox` is set to `true`. Setting `ControlBox` to `true` displays the control box as well as a close box.

NOTE

The control box shows up as an icon in the left-hand side of the form's title bar. Right- or left-clicking on the icon displays the Control Box menu, which usually features the commands Restore, Move, Size, Minimize, Maximize, and Close.

Controlling Opacity

One of the intriguing visual changes you can make to a form is to alter its opacity by using the Opacity property. This property has an effect only on windows that are displayed on machines running Windows 2000 or higher, and it can be used to achieve some interesting effects. For instance, you could slowly alter this property so that you slowly phase a form into view when launched and then slowly fade it out of view when closed. Setting Opacity to 1.0 (that is, 100%) displays an entirely opaque form, and setting it to 0 displays an entirely transparent form. Note that these settings also affect any controls on the form.

To test the Opacity property, start a new project and add a form to it. Drag a TrackBar control onto the form. The TrackBar control should show up in your control toolbox in Visual Studio .NET. It looks like this:

Set the TrackBar control's Maximum property to 100 and its Minimum property to 0. Double-click on the control to get to the TrackBar1 change event, and set the form's opacity to the trackbar's current value multiplied by .01. Run the application, and play around with the way different opacities look by moving the slider on the trackbar. Here's the code to alter the Opacity value based on trackbar scroll movements:

```
Public Class Form1
    Inherits System.Windows.Forms.Form

#Region " Windows Form Designer generated code "

    Private Sub TrackBar1_Scroll(ByVal sender As System.Object, _
    ByVal e As System.EventArgs) Handles TrackBar1.Scroll
        Me.Opacity = TrackBar1.Value * .01
        Me.Text = TrackBar1.Value
        Me.Refresh()
    End Sub
End Class
```

Suggestions for Further Exploration

⊃ The Form object can automatically scale its size based on the font assigned to it. You can investigate the AutoScale and AutoScaleBaseSize properties to learn more; these properties can be particularly useful if you want to allow users to change the font used on a form. Changing to a larger font might result in titles not fitting on the title bar or other examples of overflow.

Using the Clipboard

The System.Windows.Forms namespace provides Clipboard functionality—that is, the traditional cut, copy, and paste functions. The Clipboard class abstracts this functionality via two methods: GetDataObject and SetDataObject. Here are their declarations:

```
Public Shared Function GetDataObject() As IdataObject

'SetDataObject is overloaded:
'version 1
Overloads Public Shared Sub SetDataObject(ByVal data As Object)

'version 2
Overloads Public Shared Sub SetDataObject(ByVal data As Object, _
ByVal copy As Boolean)
```

Pushing Data onto the Clipboard

The SetDataObject method allows you to place data onto the Clipboard. There are two different implementations of this method. The second overloaded version allows you to specify, through a Boolean value, whether the data copied onto the Clipboard should remain on the Clipboard even after the application that placed it there has exited. A true value tells the Clipboard to keep the data around until it is explicitly flushed or cleared from the Clipboard. A value of false indicates that the data will be removed from the Clipboard as soon as the calling application has finished. The first overloaded version does not give you the option of persisting data onto the Clipboard past the lifetime of the calling application; the data placed through that method is always cleared upon termination of the application.

You can easily copy the text selected in a text box to the Clipboard, as in the following example:

```
Clipboard.SetDataObject(myTextBox.SelectedText)
```

This section discusses how to interact directly with the Clipboard. As you start to develop applications that use Clipboard functionality, you should keep in mind that many controls support Clipboard commands directly. For example, to copy selected text from a textbox, you could either use the Clipboard.SetDataObject method or the TextBox.Copy method.

Reading Data from the Clipboard

After items are placed on the Clipboard, you use the GetDataObject method to retrieve them. The data is returned as an instance of IDataObject. IDataObject is an interface, defined in the System.Windows.Forms namespace, that allows applications to store data in many different formats. This is an essential attribute for a global, universal concept like the Clipboard, which has to talk to many different applications, each potentially with its own format and understanding of data.

You need to first check to see if the data on the Clipboard can be massaged into a format that is appropriate for a particular situation. For example, if you wanted to take data from the Clipboard and set a text box's `Text` property equal to that data, you would first determine whether the data could be expressed as a string. The class `DataFormats` comes to the rescue here. The `DataFormats` class provides a number of shared properties that are used to identify the format of data stored in an `IDataObject` object. In this respect, its use resembles that of an enumeration. Table 5.7 shows the different shared properties exposed by `DataFormats`.

TABLE 5.7   Shared Properties of the `DataFormats` Class

Property	Description
Bitmap	Specifies Windows bitmap format.
CommaSeparatedValue	Specifies comma-separated values format.
Dib	Specifies Windows device-independent bitmap format.
Dif	Specifies Windows data interchange format.
EnhancedMetafile	Specifies Windows enhanced metafile format.
FileDrop	Specifies Windows file drop format.
Html	Specifies HTML text format.
Locale	Specifies locale format (that is, Windows culture).
MetafilePict	Specifies the Windows metafile format.
OemText	Specifies original equipment manufacturer (OEM) text format.
Palette	Specifies Windows palette format.
PenData	Specifies pen data format (that is, pen strokes delivered from handwriting software).
Riff	Specifies the audio format resource interchange file format.
Rtf	Specifies rich text format.
Serializable	Specifies serializable Windows Forms format.
StringFormat	Specifies string format.
SymbolicLink	Specifies Windows symbolic link format.
Text	Specifies ANSI standard text format.
Tiff	Specifies tagged image file format.
UnicodeText	Specifies Windows Unicode text format.
WaveAudio	Specifies wave audio format.

The following code references one of the GetDataPresent methods of the IDataObject interface; it inspects the data in the Clipboard and tells whether it matches the specifications:

```
Dim clipData As IDataObject = Clipboard.GetDataObject()

'DataFormats.Text specifies that we are interested in text data
'This is used in conjunction with the GetDataPresent to determine
'if the clipboard data matches our expectations (text)
If iData.GetDataPresent(DataFormats.Text) Then
    'If it does, we can copy it into our text box's Text property
    textBox2.Text = iData.GetData(DataFormats.Text)
End If
```

The GetDataPresent method accepts one of the fields from the DataFormats class as a parameter, and it returns a true or false value, indicating whether the data in the IDataObject object is amenable to conversion to that format. If the method indicates that the data is in fact in text form, you have one more step to go through: You need to get the data out of IDataObject and assign it to the TextBox.Text property. IDataObject.GetData does this. You again have to pass a field from the DataFormats class to tell the GetData method how to receive the data. From there, it is a straight assignment to the TextBox.Text property.

This might seem like a lot of work, but notice that only four lines of code have allowed you to use a very powerful, generic object that can share and store heterogeneous data across different applications.

NOTE

The real beauty of the DataFormats class is that it allows you to create new data formats and add them to the list of items that it understands. In this way, the Clipboard and other objects that rely on the DataFormats class are infinitely extensible and applicable to items that the .NET Framework runtime might not know about up front.

Suggestions for Further Exploration

⊃ Research the DataFormats and DataFormats.Format classes to see how you would describe a new data format to the Clipboard class. Like most things in the .NET Framework, the ability to use the Clipboard is restricted based on security policies. It is turned on by default. For more information, see the .NET Framework Software Development Kit documentation on the default security policy.

Creating Menus

Like forms, menus are objects in their own right in the .NET Framework. When you set out to create menus for an application, you are either creating a *main menu* that appears below the title bar, or you are creating a *context menu* that is displayed when the user right-clicks over an area of the form. (Context menus are often called *pop-up menus*.) Menus have become an established part of user interface design. This section covers the menu-related classes in the .NET Framework and shows you how to imbue your forms with menu-based functionality.

Adding a Main Menu to a Form

Before you associate a main menu with a form, you first have to create an object instance of the menu. The code to do this is straightforward:

```
Dim appMenu As MainMenu = New MainMenu()
```

The `MainMenu` class is the menu that you will see directly on the form. Some standard items that would appear on a main menu include File, Edit, View, Window, and Help, among others, but you can place whatever you want on your main menu. Each item on the main menu is, in .NET Framework terms, a *menu item* represented by the `MenuItem` class. To add a File element to a main menu, you could write code like the following:

```
Dim fileMenu As MenuItem = appMenu.MenuItems.Add("&File")
```

From this code snippet, you can see that each `MainMenu` instance has a collection, called `MenuItems`, that can contain instances of the `MenuItem` class. Membership in this collection determines what the main menu actually contains. To add something to the main menu, you simply add a menu item to this collection.

NOTE

There is a `Menu` class in the forms library. For the most part, you will never need to deal with it directly; your primary interaction with menus is likely to be through the `MainMenu`, `ContextMenu`, and `MenuItem` classes. However, it is important to know that all these classes—and many others that are associated with menus—inherit directly from the `Menu` class. For more information, see the .NET Framework documentation on the `Menu` class.

A menu item can be thought of as any selectable item that appears on *any* menu, not just on the main menu. This means that in order to add a selection to the File menu—such as an Open item—you would access the collection of MenuItems, only this time you would reference the fileMenu object instead of the appMenu object:

```
fileMenu.MenuItems.Add("&Open")

'or, if we needed a reference to the Open item...
Dim openMenuItem As MenuItem = fileMenu.MenuItems.Add("&Open")
```

The ampersand (&) included in the string "&Open" tells the Form Designer that it should assign a mnemonic, in this case the letter O, to the menu item you are adding. A *mnemonic* is used to access the menu from the keyboard: You hold down the Alt key and then press the mnemonic of the menu or menu item you want to access. In this way, you can quickly select the corresponding menu. You can programmatically determine the mnemonic for any menu item by looking at the MenuItem.Mnemonic property, which is read-only. The mnemonic is set during the construction of the menu item (for example, through the Add method on the MenuItems collection).

An important point is that the MenuItems collection is actually just a property on the Menu class (and thus the MainMenu, MenuItem, and ContextMenu classes that inherit from the Menu class). The MenuItems property returns the data type Menu.MenuItemCollection. Note the distinction that MenuItems is a property that returns an instance of MenuItemsCollection, which is a class.

NOTE

A particular instance of a MenuItem class can be contained in only a single menu at a time. It also cannot be added more than once to the same menu. If you need to duplicate a menu item from one menu to another, you use the MenuItem.CloneMenu method, as follows:

```
menu2.MenuItems.Add(myMenuItem.CloneMenu())
```

In this way, you can essentially copy an existing menu item into a new menu.

You now have all the base code elements you need to create a simple main menu and use it on a form. At this point, however, all you have done is created a MainMenu instance and added some menu items to it. If you were to run a form project with just that code, you still wouldn't see a menu on the form because you now need to associate the MainMenu instance to the form. This is not done automatically for you; you must set the reference in your code by using the Form.Menu property:

```
Form1.Menu = appMenu
```

Listing 5.2 shows a standard main menu implemented on a form. Figure 5.7 shows what the generated menu and form look like.

LISTING 5.2   Creating a Simple Main Menu

```
Public Class Form1
    Inherits System.Windows.Forms.Form

    Private appMenu As MainMenu
    Private fileMenu As MenuItem
    Private editMenu As MenuItem
    Private windowMenu As MenuItem
    Private helpMenu As MenuItem

#Region " Windows Form Designer generated code "

    Public Sub New()
        MyBase.New()

        'This call is required by the Windows Form Designer.
        InitializeComponent()

        'Add any initialization after the InitializeComponent() call
        appMenu = New MainMenu()

        With appMenu
            fileMenu = .MenuItems.Add("&File")
            editMenu = .MenuItems.Add("&Edit")
            windowMenu = .MenuItems.Add("&Window")
            helpMenu = .MenuItems.Add("&Help")
        End With

        Me.Menu = appMenu
    End Sub

    'Form overrides dispose to clean up the component list.
    Protected Overloads Overrides Sub Dispose(ByVal disposing As Boolean)
        If disposing Then
            If Not (components Is Nothing) Then
                components.Dispose()
            End If
        End If
        MyBase.Dispose(disposing)
    End Sub

    'Required by the Windows Form Designer
    Private components As System.ComponentModel.Container
```

Listing 5.2 Continued

```
'NOTE: The following procedure is required by the Windows Form Designer
'It can be modified using the Windows Form Designer.
'Do not modify it using the code editor.
<System.Diagnostics.DebuggerStepThrough()> _
    Private Sub InitializeComponent()
    '

    'Form1
    '

    Me.AutoScaleBaseSize = New System.Drawing.Size(5, 13)
    Me.ClientSize = New System.Drawing.Size(294, 183)
    Me.FormBorderStyle = System.Windows.Forms.FormBorderStyle.FixedDialog
    Me.MaximizeBox = False
    Me.MinimizeBox = False
    Me.Name = "Form1"
    Me.Text = "Form1"


    End Sub

#End Region

    Private Sub Form1_Load(ByVal sender As System.Object, _
        ByVal e As System.EventArgs) Handles MyBase.Load


    End Sub
End Class
```

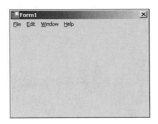

Figure 5.7

A form and its main menu.

Listing 5.2 expands the Windows Form Designer region because that is where all the initialization code for the menu appears. You first declare the menu objects that you need—one
MainMenu and three MenuItem instances—and then in the constructor you actually create the
main menu object and add items to it.

Creating Context Menus

Context, or pop-up, menus are used to display menu items that are specific to a certain form element. You access a context menu by-right clicking on an object such as a text box or the client area of a form. For example, most users expect to be able to right-click on a text box to access the cut, copy, and paste commands that are typically found in an Edit menu. Context menus allow programmers to target specific menu-based functionality and then deliver that functionality when and where the user expects it. This can be a powerful way to make an application more intuitive and make users more productive.

Access to context menus is provided through the `ContextMenu` class, which is similar in structure to the `MainMenu` class described in the preceding section. To create a context menu, dimension a new `ContextMenu` object, as follows:

```
Dim formContextMenu as New ContextMenu()
```

Similarly to the way you assign a main menu to a form, you assign the context menu to a form by using the `ContextMenu` property. The following snippet assumes that Me refers to a form:

```
Me.ContextMenu = formContextMenu
```

Unlike the `MainMenu` property, the `ContextMenu` property is first implemented way back in the class hierarchy with the `Control` class. This is because context menus are useful across any type of control, not just forms. To set up a context menu for a text box control, for instance, you can use this code:

```
Dim ctrlContextMenu As New ContextMenu()
myTextBox.ContextMenu = ctrlContextMenu
```

To see an example of a context menu, look ahead to Figure 5.13.

Managing MDI Applications and Menus

A few pieces of functionality are exposed on the `MenuItem` class, expressly for the purpose of managing menus in an MDI-based application. There are a few established standards for displaying menus in MDI applications. First, MDI applications usually display a Window menu on the main form. The Window menu usually contains a list of the currently open child forms, allowing a user to select one of them from the menu to make it active. This menu usually also provides commands for arranging the child forms (see the discussion of the `MdiLayout` enumeration earlier in this chapter, in the section "Creating MDI Forms"). The `MenuItem` class provides intrinsic support for these lists of child forms, with the `MdiList` property. `MdiList` is a Boolean property, and setting it to `true` causes that particular menu item to automatically display a list of all child forms that are declared within the application.

> **NOTE**
>
> If an application has more than nine child forms, the window list itemizes only the first nine and then displays the More Windows item. Selecting the More Items item launches a dialog box that has a complete list of all the child windows.

Another common menu feature of MDI applications is the consolidated menu. The parent MDI window's menus may contain items that are specific to the currently displayed child window. Users can select functionality that may be specific or relevant only to the child window from the parent window's menus, allowing more flexibility and ease of use. The .NET Framework runtime automatically merges a child form's menu onto the parent form's menus in an MDI application. You can use the `MergeMenu` method in code to make this happen. We'll investigate using this method in the next section.

Working with Menu Items

When a top-level menu is in place, you can start adding submenus or items to it. You create submenus by using the same process you use to add items to a main menu. After creating submenus, you can worry about their various visual decorations such as separator lines and check marks.

Adding Submenus

To demonstrate how to add submenus, in this section we will expand on the File menu from the previous section. To add the contents of the File menu, you need to add a few new items to the `MenuItems` collection of the file menu:

```
With appMenu
    fileMenu = .MenuItems.Add("&File")
    fileMenu.MenuItems.Add("&Open...")
    fileMenu.MenuItems.Add("&Save")
    fileMenu.MenuItems.Add("Save As...")
    fileMenu.MenuItems.Add("View As Web Pa&ge")
    fileMenu.MenuItems.Add("&Close")
    fileMenu.MenuItems.Add("E&xit")
    editMenu = .MenuItems.Add("&Edit")
    windowMenu = .MenuItems.Add("&Window")
    helpMenu = .MenuItems.Add("&Help")
End With
```

The File menu constructed in this code example is shown in Figure 5.8. The main menu consists of several menu items, and each of these menu items is itself a submenu that contains items that the user can select. This nested relationship might seem confusing, but it is actually quite simple. After creating the main menu, you have the choice of implementing submenus (which show lists of commands) or items (which are commands).

FIGURE 5.8
File menu items.

If you were to nest even more items under one of the File menu items, you would end up with a cascading, or *fly-out,* menu. For example, you can add a menu item to the existing Close item, which means Close becomes a way of showing another menu:

```
Dim fileCloseMenu As MenuItem

With appMenu
    fileMenu = .MenuItems.Add("&File")
    fileMenu.MenuItems.Add("&Open...")
    fileMenu.MenuItems.Add("&Save")
    fileMenu.MenuItems.Add("Save As...")
    fileCloseMenu = fileMenu.MenuItems.Add("&Close")
    fileCloseMenu.MenuItems.Add("Now")
    fileMenu.MenuItems.Add("E&xit")
    editMenu = .MenuItems.Add("&Edit")
    windowMenu = .MenuItems.Add("&Window")
    helpMenu = .MenuItems.Add("&Help")
End With
```

Figure 5.9 shows a cascading menu in action.

You can continue nesting menus in this fashion until you decide to create the bottom of the menu tree, where the user-selectable commands are. Obviously, for usability reasons, you should avoid nesting levels more than a few deep.

Adding Checkmarks, Shortcuts, and Separator Bars to Menus

To indicate on or off menu selections, the Windows menu system supports the ability to place checkmarks next to menu items. You can also add shortcut keys and include separator bars to help organize menus. Let's add some of these features to the File menu we've been working with in this chapter. First, let's add some separator bars to organize the menu items. You add separator bars the same way you add menu items; you just set the menu item name to a dash (" - "), like this:

```
fileMenu.MenuItems.Add("-")
```

FIGURE 5.9

A File menu with Close menu.

You want to group the Open, Save, and Save As items together. The View As Web Page item should sit in a group by itself, and the Close and Exit items should sit together in the last group. The code to make this happen looks like this:

```
With appMenu
    fileMenu = .MenuItems.Add("&File")
    fileMenu.MenuItems.Add("&Open...")
    fileMenu.MenuItems.Add("&Save")
    fileMenu.MenuItems.Add("Save As...")
    fileMenu.MenuItems.Add("-")
    fileMenu.MenuItems.Add("View As Web Pa&ge")
    fileMenu.MenuItems.Add("-")
    fileMenu.MenuItems.Add("&Close")
    fileMenu.MenuItems.Add("E&xit")
    editMenu = .MenuItems.Add("&Edit")
    windowMenu = .MenuItems.Add("&Window")
    helpMenu = .MenuItems.Add("&Help")
End With
```

You add shortcut keys and check (or uncheck) menu items through properties in the `MenuItem` class. To check a menu item, you use the `Checked` property, which is a Boolean property that you can set to `true` or `false`. To add a shortcut key to one of the menu items, you use the `Shortcut` property, which is an enumeration of type `System.Windows.Forms.Shortcut`. You use the enumeration `Shortcut` to specify the key that you want to assign as the shortcut key. Table 5.8 lists the values that are available in the `Shortcut` enumeration. The menu now looks like the one in Figure 5.10.

TABLE 5.8   Shortcut Enumeration

Name	Description
Alt0 (...Alt9)	Creates a shortcut with the key combination Alt+0. Values range from Alt+0 through Alt+9.
AltBksp	Creates a shortcut with the key combination Alt+Backspace.
AltF1 (...AltF12)	Creates a shortcut with the key combination Alt+F1. Values range from Alt+F1 through Alt+F12.
Ctrl0 (...Ctrl9)	Creates a shortcut with the key combination Ctrl+0. Values range from Ctrl+0 through Ctrl+9.
CtrlA (...CtrlZ)	Creates a shortcut with the key combination Ctrl+A. Values range from Ctrl+A through Ctrl+Z.
CtrlDel	Creates a shortcut with the key combination Ctrl+Delete.
CtrlF1 (...CtrlF12)	Creates a shortcut with the key combination Ctrl+F1. Values range from Ctrl+F1 through Ctrl+F12.
CtrlIns	Creates a shortcut with the key combination Ctrl+Insert.
CtrlShift0 (...CtrlShift9)	Creates a shortcut with the key combination Ctrl+Shift+0. Values range from Ctrl+Shift+0 through Ctrl+Shift+9.
CtrlShiftA (...CtrlShiftZ)	Creates a shortcut with the key combination Ctrl+Shift+A. Values range from Ctrl+Shift+A through Ctrl+Shift+Z.
CtrlShiftF1 (...CtrlShiftF12)	Creates a shortcut with the key combination Ctrl+Shift+F1. Values range from Ctrl+Shift+F1 through Ctrl+Shift+F12.
Del	Creates a shortcut with the key Delete.
F1 (...F12)	Creates a shortcut with the key F1. Values range from F1 through F12.
Ins	Creates a shortcut with the key Insert.
None	No shortcut key is associated with the menu item.
ShiftDel	Creates a shortcut with the key combination Shift+Delete.
ShiftF1 (...Shift12)	Creates a shortcut with the key combination Shift+F1. Values range from Shift+F1 through Shift+F12.
ShiftIns	Creates a shortcut with the key combination Shift+Insert.

5

FORMS, MENUS, AND CONTROLS

FIGURE 5.10

Setting shortcut keys and checking menu items.

NOTE

You can show or hide the shortcut keys that you have defined for a menu item. Shortcut keys are displayed by default, but you can modify them by using the property `MenuItem.ShowShortcut`. This can be useful if you want to control (or let users control) the verbosity of the menus. Not showing shortcuts can help reduce the overall image footprint of menus, perhaps for advanced users who don't need or want to be reminded of the shortcuts all the time.

Working with Radio Checks

The `MenuItem` class supports a form of mutually exclusive checking of menu items. You use this feature when presenting a group of menu items in which only one option can be selected at any time (similar to radio button controls). First, you set the `RadioChecked` property to `true` for each menu item that will participate in this mutually exclusive group. Then, when you set the `Checked` property, it shows up as a radio button graphic instead of a checkmark. The following code illustrates this concept:

```
With appMenu
    fileMenu = .MenuItems.Add("&File")
    fileMenu.MenuItems.Add("&Open...")
    fileMenu.MenuItems.Add("&Save")
    fileMenu.MenuItems(1).Shortcut = Shortcut.CtrlS
    fileMenu.MenuItems.Add("Save As...")
    fileMenu.MenuItems.Add("-")
    fileMenu.MenuItems.Add("View As Web Pa&ge")
    fileMenu.MenuItems(4).RadioCheck = True
    fileMenu.MenuItems(4).Checked = True
    fileMenu.MenuItems.Add("View As &HTML")
    fileMenu.MenuItems(4).RadioCheck = True
    fileMenu.MenuItems.Add("-")
    fileMenu.MenuItems.Add("&Close")
    fileMenu.MenuItems.Add("E&xit")
```

```
        editMenu = .MenuItems.Add("&Edit")
        windowMenu = .MenuItems.Add("&Window")
        helpMenu = .MenuItems.Add("&Help")
End With
```

The resulting radio button style, which takes care of visually displaying the radio button checkmark, is shown in Figure 5.11. You still have to write the code to enforce the mutually exclusive nature of the selection by turning the checkmark off for one menu item while turning it on for another.

FIGURE 5.11
Checking mutually exclusive menu items.

Setting Default Menu Items

You can specify a menu item as a default. This menu item shows up in bold, and if a user double-clicks a menu that has a default item defined, that item is automatically selected.

The following code sets the Save item as the default item:

```
With appMenu
    fileMenu = .MenuItems.Add("&File")
    fileMenu.MenuItems.Add("&Open...")
    fileMenu.MenuItems.Add("&Save")
    fileMenu.MenuItems(1).DefaultItem = True
    fileMenu.MenuItems(1).Shortcut = Shortcut.CtrlS
    fileMenu.MenuItems.Add("Save As...")
    fileMenu.MenuItems.Add("-")
    fileMenu.MenuItems.Add("View As Web Pa&ge")
    fileMenu.MenuItems(4).RadioCheck = True
    fileMenu.MenuItems(4).Checked = True
    fileMenu.MenuItems.Add("View As &HTML")
    fileMenu.MenuItems(4).RadioCheck = True
    fileMenu.MenuItems.Add("-")
    fileMenu.MenuItems.Add("&Close")
    fileMenu.MenuItems.Add("E&xit")
    editMenu = .MenuItems.Add("&Edit")
    windowMenu = .MenuItems.Add("&Window")
    helpMenu = .MenuItems.Add("&Help")
End With
```

Figure 5.12 shows how this code looks when it is executed.

FIGURE 5.12

Setting a default menu item.

Merging Menus

The menu items contained in one menu can be programmatically merged with the menu items in another menu. Context menus, for instance, may have items in them that are mere duplicates of items already defined inside the form's main menu. Rather than recode all those items, you can use the MenuItem class to simply merge the items from the main menu into the context menu, via the MenuItem.MergeMenu method.

There are a few types of possible merges. The MenuMerge enumeration (see Table 5.9) classifies these merges; this enumeration is used with the MenuItem.MergeType property to specify, for each menu item if needed, exactly how it should be merged when the MergeMenu method is called. To merge menus, you need to first set the MergeType property appropriately for each menu item that is supposed to take part in the merge. You can even control in what order the items are merged, through the MenuItem.MergeOrder property (an integer value). The lower the MergeOrder value, the higher up in the merge menu the item will appear.

TABLE 5.9   The MenuMerge Enumeration

Name	Description
Add	Causes the referenced MenuItem object to be added to the collection of existing MenuItem objects in a merged menu.
MergeItems	Causes all submenu items of the referenced MenuItem to be merged with those of the merged menu; the items are merged in their same positions.
Remove	Causes the referenced MenuItem to not be included in a merged menu.
Replace	Causes the referenced MenuItem object to replace an existing MenuItem object in the same position in a merged menu.

Creating `OwnerDraw` Menu Items

Normally, when a menu is selected, Windows paints it to the screen. This means that all the menus have a standard way that they are drawn in all applications and that they have a standard look and feel. If you want to draw a highly specialized or stylized menu, you can elect to draw the menu yourself. This is referred to as an *owner draw* menu item, and you can set it for individual menu items by using the `OwnerDraw` property. `OwnerDraw` is a Boolean property: If it is set to `true`, the menu, before being displayed, is routed through code that you supply to draw whatever you like for the menu; if it is set to `false`, Windows draws the menu.

The `MenuItem.DrawItem` event is fired if you have set a menu item's `OwnerDraw` property to `true`. Inside the `DrawItem` event, you can design a menu that looks any way you want it to look, subject only to the capabilities and limitations of the `Graphics` object. (See the `System.Drawing` namespace, and Chapter 9, "Drawing Functions," for more information on the Graphics object.)

Here is how the `MenuItem.DrawItem` event routine is defined:

```
Public Delegate Sub DrawItemEventHandler(ByVal sender As Object, _
   ByVal e As DrawItemEventArgs)
```

The `sender` object is not new; it is a standard object used with events, and it represents an instance of the object that fired the event. `DrawItemEventArgs` is the key here. It is a class, contained in the `Windows.Forms` namespace, that essentially encapsulates a bunch of properties that can be set to alter how the menu is drawn. Table 5.10 shows the properties exposed by the `DrawItemEventArgs` class and their description.

TABLE 5.10 Properties of the `DrawItemEventArgs` Class

Property	Description
BackColor	Specifies the background color of the menu item being drawn.
Bounds	Specifies the bounded rectangle that represents the bounds of the menu item being drawn.
Font	Specifies the font of the menu item being drawn.
ForeColor	Specifies the foreground color of the menu item being drawn.
Graphics	Specifies an instance of a graphics surface on which the menu item will be drawn.
Index	Specifies the index value of the menu item being drawn.
State	Specifies the state of the menu item being drawn. `State` is defined with the `DrawItemState` enumeration.

If you wanted to draw your own menu items, you would first write a handler for the DrawItem event for the particular MenuItem object. It would look something like this:

```
Private Sub OwnerDraw_DrawItem(ByVal sender As System.Object, _
ByVal e As DrawItemEventArgs) Handles MenuItem2.DrawItem
    Dim rect As New Rectangle(0, 0, 16, 16)
    Dim i As New Icon("sampleicon.ico")
    e.Graphics.DrawIcon(i, rect)
End Sub
```

In this example, the drawing of MenuItem2 is handled through raw code. To draw an icon onto the menu, you use an instance of the Rectangle class and the Icon class, in conjunction with the DrawItemEventArgs.Graphics class instance that is passed into the event.

> **NOTE**
>
> If you plan to create owner-drawn menus, remember that it is an all-or-nothing proposition. If you set the OwnerDraw property to true, you are telling the compiler and the runtime that you will handle *all* the drawing for that menu: background, text, colors, positioning, and so on. You do not have the ability to paint some of the menu and then let the runtime do the rest.

Suggestions for Further Exploration

- ⊃ We have talked about the use of the MergeMenu method to consolidate one menu's items onto another menu. Investigate the CloneMenu method to see what options it provides for directly copying menu items.

- ⊃ The MenuItem class has an overloaded constructor. We have only implied a parameterless constructor up to this point, but there is a constructor that actually accepts a total of eight parameters! Investigate the .NET Framework documentation and think about where it might make sense to employ the more verbose constructor.

- ⊃ Try mimicking Visual Studio .NET's menus by utilizing the owner-draw capabilities of the MenuItem class. You will need to understand how to draw graphics to the screen by using the Graphics class. You will also need to figure out a way to make mnemonics and accelerators work.

Handling Menu Events

When the basic menu structures are in place, it is time to write the code that reacts to a user selecting one of those menu items. This involves crafting event handles for the menu items previously declared and writing code to react to those events.

Menu Items and Event Handlers

There are two different ways to link menu items to a piece of code that will run when the menu item is selected. The first way is to use the click event that the MenuItem class exposes. The click event is fired whenever a menu item is selected. Note that although the event is called *click*, it is fired regardless of *how* the item is selected. For instance, a user navigating to a menu item by using the keyboard and then pressing the Enter key causes this event to fire, as does using a menu item's shortcut key, mnemonic, and so on. The click event is only fired for bottom-level menu items; that is, if the menu item is a parent to another menu, the click event is not fired.

If you are going to use the click event, you need to declare the MenuItem object by using the WithEvents keyword, like this:

```
Dim fileMenuClose WithEvents As MenuItem
```

Now, you can stub out a routine that will fire whenever the click event fires. Here is an example:

```
Protected Sub fileMenuClose_Click(ByVal sender As System.Object, _
ByVal e As System.EventArgs) Handles fileMenuClose.Click

        'Code that reacts to the popup event goes here...
        Me.Close

End Sub
```

The key to this routine is the Handles fileMenuClose.Click syntax, which informs the compiler that the routine will be the "sink", or recipient, of the click event for the particular object that is referenced—in this case, the fileMenuClose object.

The second way to react to the selection of a menu item is by supplying your own event handler. An *event handler* is a delegate or function pointer that acts as a sink for an event. In this case, the event is the selection, either by direct selection of a menu item with the keyboard or mouse or through a shortcut key or through a mnemonic.

Remember the MenuItems.Add method? In this case, you overload it to accept an event handler as well as the name of the new menu item. Where you previously used this:

```
fileMenu.MenuItems.Add("&Open...")
```

you can also write this:

```
fileMenu.MenuItems.Add("&Open...", New EventHandler(AddressOf ourEvent))
```

Assigning event handlers to menu items has the same effect as using the click event; you are simply instructing the compiler to execute a specific block of code whenever a menu item is selected. There are, of course, syntactical differences between the two. We have already seen one, with the new use of the Add method on MenuItems. The routine that handles the event has a slightly different signature as well. Because you are not shadowing a system-defined event, there is no need to use the Handles keyword. Continuing from the preceding snippet, if you wrote a routine called myEvent to handle the File, Open selection, it would look like this:

```
Protected Sub myEvent(ByVal sender As System.Object, _
    ByVal e As System.EventArgs)
        MsgBox("File->Open was selected!")
End Sub
```

For the most part, using the click event works just fine. There are a few situations, however, in which you should use your own event handler. If you need to react to a parent menu item being selected, you have to use your own event handler because the click event does not fire for those items. Also, if you want to write one routine that multiple menu items use, you can do this quite easily with the event handler by just pointing different menu items at the same block of code.

Reacting to the Popup Event

Both the ContextMenu class and the MenuItem class have a Popup event that is fired just before the menu is displayed. Any time you need to programmatically manipulate the contents or appearance of a menu just before it is displayed, you can attach code to the Popup event. The Popup event is particularly useful with context menus. Typically, you use it to customize the content of the context menu based on which control caused the menu to be displayed. Rather than create a separate object for each control that needs a context menu, you can add the appropriate items to the menu inside the Popup event, depending on which control was responsible for initiating the menu. Reacting to the Popup event is identical to attaching the click event. You first declare the context menu by using the WithEvents directive, like this:

```
Dim ctrlContextMenu WithEvents As New ContextMenu()
```

Next, you can write a simple stub routine that executes when the Popup event is fired:

```
Protected Sub PopupEventHandler(ByVal sender As System.Object, _
ByVal e As System.EventArgs) Handles appContextMenu.Popup

        'Code that reacts to the popup event goes here...

End Sub
```

You use the sender object to determine which control fired the event, and then you can react accordingly.

Say you have one text box control and one rich text box control on a form. You would like to implement a context menu with each. It makes sense to implement Cut, Copy, and Paste commands for both. For the rich text box, you want to add an additional item to the context menu that exploits the ability of RichTextBox objects to load files. In this case, you can implement some branching logic inside the Popup event to determine whether the control that launches the menu is the rich text box and, if it is, to add the special-case Load File item. Listing 5.3 shows a sample application with a text box (TextBox1) and a rich text box (RichTextBox1). In the Popup event handler, you determine which control causes the context menu to display. If it is the text box, you show a standard Edit menu, with Cut, Copy, and Paste commands. If it is the rich text box, in addition to the standard Edit menu commands, you add a Load File item. (Notice that this example leverages the Clipboard class that we talked about earlier in this chapter, to implement the code behind the Cut, Copy, and Paste menu items.)

LISTING 5.3   Using the Popup Event and the ContextMenu Class

```
Public Class Form2
    Inherits System.Windows.Forms.Form

    'Dimension the context menu
    Private WithEvents appContextMenu As New ContextMenu()

#Region " Windows Form Designer generated code "

    Public Sub New()
        MyBase.New()

        'This call is required by the Windows Form Designer.
        InitializeComponent()

        'Add any initialization after the InitializeComponent() call
        SetupContextMenu()

    End Sub

    'Form overrides dispose to clean up the component list.
    Protected Overloads Overrides Sub Dispose(ByVal disposing As Boolean)
        If disposing Then
            If Not (components Is Nothing) Then
                components.Dispose()
            End If
        End If
        MyBase.Dispose(disposing)
    End Sub
    Friend WithEvents TextBox1 As System.Windows.Forms.TextBox
    Friend WithEvents RichTextBox1 As System.Windows.Forms.RichTextBox
```

LISTING 5.3   Continued

```
    'Required by the Windows Form Designer
    Private components As System.ComponentModel.Container

    'NOTE: The following procedure is required by the Windows Form Designer
    'It can be modified using the Windows Form Designer.
    'Do not modify it using the code editor.
    <System.Diagnostics.DebuggerStepThrough()> _
    Private Sub InitializeComponent()
        Me.TextBox1 = New System.Windows.Forms.TextBox()
        Me.RichTextBox1 = New System.Windows.Forms.RichTextBox()
        Me.SuspendLayout()
        '
        'TextBox1
        '
        Me.TextBox1.Location = New System.Drawing.Point(16, 32)
        Me.TextBox1.Name = "TextBox1"
        Me.TextBox1.Size = New System.Drawing.Size(256, 20)
        Me.TextBox1.TabIndex = 0
        Me.TextBox1.Text = "TextBox1"
        '
        'RichTextBox1
        '
        Me.RichTextBox1.Location = New System.Drawing.Point(16, 72)
        Me.RichTextBox1.Name = "RichTextBox1"
        Me.RichTextBox1.Size = New System.Drawing.Size(256, 56)
        Me.RichTextBox1.TabIndex = 1
        Me.RichTextBox1.Text = "RichTextBox1"
        '
        'Form2
        '
        Me.AutoScaleBaseSize = New System.Drawing.Size(5, 13)
        Me.ClientSize = New System.Drawing.Size(292, 149)
        Me.Controls.AddRange(New System.Windows.Forms.Control() _
        {Me.TextBox1, _
            Me.RichTextBox1})
        Me.Name = "Form2"
        Me.Text = "Context Menus"
        Me.ResumeLayout(False)

    End Sub

#End Region

    Private Sub Form2_Load(ByVal sender As System.Object, _
    ByVal e As System.EventArgs) _
        Handles MyBase.Load
```

LISTING 5.3   Continued

```
End Sub

Private Sub SetupContextMenu()
    'Add any initialization after the InitializeComponent() call
    appContextMenu = New ContextMenu()

    Dim currItem As MenuItem

    TextBox1.ContextMenu = appContextMenu
    RichTextBox1.ContextMenu = appContextMenu
End Sub

Protected Sub menuCut_Click(ByVal sender As System.Object, ByVal e As _
    System.EventArgs)
    If TypeOf Me.ActiveControl Is TextBox Then
        Dim currControl As TextBox = CType(Me.ActiveControl, TextBox)
        ' Put selected text on Clipboard.
        Clipboard.SetDataObject(currControl.SelectedText)
        currControl.SelectedText = ""
    ElseIf TypeOf Me.ActiveControl Is RichTextBox Then
        Dim currControl As RichTextBox = _
        CType(Me.ActiveControl, RichTextBox)
        Clipboard.SetDataObject(currControl.SelectedText)
        currControl.SelectedText = ""
    End If

End Sub

Protected Sub menuCopy_Click(ByVal sender As System.Object, ByVal e As _
    System.EventArgs)
    If TypeOf Me.ActiveControl Is TextBox Then
        Dim currControl As TextBox = CType(Me.ActiveControl, TextBox)
        ' Put selected text on Clipboard.
        Clipboard.SetDataObject(currControl.SelectedText)
    ElseIf TypeOf Me.ActiveControl Is RichTextBox Then
        Dim currControl As RichTextBox = _
        CType(Me.ActiveControl, RichTextBox)
        Clipboard.SetDataObject(currControl.SelectedText)
    End If
End Sub

Protected Sub menuPaste_Click(ByVal sender As System.Object, ByVal e As _
    System.EventArgs)
    Dim clipData As IDataObject = Clipboard.GetDataObject()
    'DataFormats.Text specifies that we are interested in text data
```

LISTING 5.3   Continued

```
        'This is used in conjunction with the GetDataPresent to determine
        'if the clipboard data matches our expectations (text)
        If clipData.GetDataPresent(DataFormats.Text) Then
            'If it does, we can copy it into our text box's Text property
            If TypeOf Me.ActiveControl Is TextBox Then
                CType(Me.ActiveControl, TextBox).SelectedText = _
                    clipData.GetData(DataFormats.Text)
            ElseIf TypeOf Me.ActiveControl Is RichTextBox Then
                CType(Me.ActiveControl, RichTextBox).SelectedText = _
                    clipData.GetData(DataFormats.Text)
            End If
        End If
    End Sub

    Protected Sub PopupEventHandler(ByVal sender As System.Object, _
        ByVal e As _
        System.EventArgs) Handles appContextMenu.Popup
        ' Clear all previously added MenuItems.
        appContextMenu.MenuItems.Clear()

        Dim currItem As MenuItem

        With appContextMenu
            currItem = .MenuItems.Add("Cu&t", New EventHandler(AddressOf _
                menuCut_Click))
            currItem.Shortcut = Shortcut.CtrlX
            currItem = .MenuItems.Add("&Copy", New EventHandler(AddressOf _
                menuCopy_Click))
            currItem.Shortcut = Shortcut.CtrlC
            currItem = .MenuItems.Add("&Paste", New EventHandler(AddressOf _
                menuPaste_Click))
            currItem.Shortcut = Shortcut.CtrlV
        End With


        'If the context menu is being displayed by the RichTextBox control,
        'we will add a sep bar and a Load File item to the existing items
        If appContextMenu.SourceControl Is RichTextBox1 Then

            'Create a new menu item holding the Load File text,
            ' and pointing to our event handler to
            actually perform the load.
```

LISTING 5.3   Continued

```
            Dim loadItem As New MenuItem("&Load File...", _
            New EventHandler(AddressOf _
               menuLoad_Click))

            ' Add the MenuItem to display for the PictureBox.
            appContextMenu.MenuItems.Add("-")
            appContextMenu.MenuItems.Add(loadItem)

        End If
    End Sub

    Protected Sub menuLoad_Click(ByVal sender As System.Object, ByVal e As _
        System.EventArgs)
        'When selected, this command should launch a dialog to
        'allow users to navigate to, and select, a file. To do
        'this, we need to show an OpenFileDialog object
        Dim openFile As OpenFileDialog = New OpenFileDialog()

        'Because the ultimate intent here is to load the file
        'into the RichTextBox1, we will set the dialog to filter
        'out anything but rich text files (.rtf)
        openFile.Filter = "RTF files (*.rtf)|*.rtf"

        'Show the open file dialog
        openFile.ShowDialog()

        'When closed, the dialog will have the selected file name
        'and path in its FileName property
        Dim filePath As String = openFile.FileName()

        'If the FileName prop was empty (as can happen if the cancel
        'button is selected instead of the OK button), we just ignore
        'it; otherwise, the file name and path are passed into the
        'LoadFile method on the RichTextBox1 control. This should
        'load the file into the rich text box.
        If Trim(filePath) <> "" Then
            RichTextBox1.LoadFile(openFile.FileName())
        End If
    End Sub
End Class
```

Figure 5.13 shows the result of right-clicking the RichTextBox1 control.

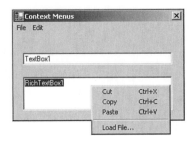

FIGURE 5.13

A dynamic context menu.

Detecting Menu Selection

A useful menu is the `Select` event, which is fired when a menu item becomes highlighted. This can happen when the user hovers the mouse over the menu item or when the user navigates to the menu item by using the keyboard. Typically, the `Select` event precedes a click event. Figure 5.14 shows the menu item Save highlighted. If the user hasn't actually clicked on Save or pressed the Enter key, the only `MenuItem` event you would expect to have fired is the `Select` event.

FIGURE 5.14

A selected menu item.

> **NOTE**
>
> One popular use of the `Select` event is to display help text in a form's status bar to indicate the exact use of the menu item that is highlighted.

An Introduction to Controls

As mentioned earlier in the chapter, we will not dig into the details of the myriad controls that ship with the .NET Framework. However, it is useful to talk about some generic control concepts that apply to a variety of programming tasks in the .NET Framework.

When working with the .NET Framework controls, such as the listbox, treeview, and button controls, programmers appreciate that they all expose a common and standard set of properties. Gone are the days of setting a label control's Caption property; if you need to alter the text on a control, whether it is a command button or label, you set the Text property.

The .NET Framework also improves on the programmer's ability to create a custom control. These user controls can inherit from the rich class tree that supports all the standard controls in the .NET Framework. This leaves the door wide open for developers to implement the controls that they want by either implementing a standard control, inheriting and extending a standard control, or implementing a control that diverges widely from existing functionality. In this section, we'll review some of the basics of programming with controls and talk about how to create your own user controls.

Common Control Properties, Methods, and Events

Most visual controls in the .NET Framework inherit directly from the Control class. Therefore, to get a good idea of the base set of properties supported by most controls, you can look back at the base Control class; examining its public instance properties gives you a good feel for the kind of default functionality provided by most controls. Table 5.11 shows a sampling of the most important properties in the Control class.

TABLE 5.11 Control Class Properties

Property	Description
AllowDrop	A Boolean property that indicates whether the control is capable of receiving context from a drag-and-drop operation.
Anchor	Specifies which sides of the control, if any, are anchored to the edges of its parent container (from the AnchorStyle enumeration).
BackColor	A color instance that indicates the background color of the control.
BackgroundImage	An image instance that indicates the background image of the control.
CausesValidation	A Boolean that indicates whether the control causes validation.
ContextMenu	Specifies a ContextMenu instance associated with the control.
Controls	A collection (Control.ControlCollection) that represents all of the controls contained within the control.
Cursor	Displays when the mouse pointer is within the bounds of the control.
Dock	A DockStyle value that indicates which sides of the parent container the control is docked to.
Enabled	A Boolean property that indicates whether the control is enabled.
HasChildren	A Boolean property that indicates whether the control has child controls.

TABLE 5.11   Continued

Property	Description
Height	An integer that specifies the height of the control.
ImeMode	Specifies the input method editor mode used by the control.
Left	Specifies the position of the control's left edge.
Name	Specifies the name of the control.
Parent	Represents the parent container of this control.
Size	Specifies the height and width of the control.
TabIndex	Specifies where in the tab order the control is located.
TabStop	A Boolean property that indicates whether the control can be given focus as the result of the Tab key being pressed.
Tag	An object instance that can be used to associate data to the control.
Text	Specifies the text associated with the control.
Top	Specifies the top edge of the control.
Visible	A Boolean property that indicates whether the control is visible.
Width	Specifies the width of the control.

Likewise, you can get a good picture of a control's functionality by examining its methods and events. Table 5.12 shows some of the most important methods available in the Control class, and Table 5.13 shows a sampling of the supported events. (To see the entire list of possible members, refer to the .NET Framework documentation on the class libraries.)

TABLE 5.12   Control Class Methods

Method	Description
BringToFront	Causes the control's z-order to change to the front.
CreateControl	Manually forces the control to be created.
CreateGraphics	Creates the Graphics object associated with the control; encapsulates the control's brush, font, foreground, and background colors.
DoDragDrop	Starts a drag-and-drop process.
FindForm	Returns an instance of the form in which the control is contained.
Focus	Places the focus on the control.
GetChildAtPoint	Given a set of coordinates, returns a control instance that represents the child control found there (if any).

TABLE 5.12   Ccontinued

Method	Description
GetContainerControl	Returns an interface (IContainerControl) that represents the parent control to this control.
GetNextControl	Returns a control instance of the next control in the tab order.
Refresh	Invalidates the control's client area, forcing a repaint of the control.
Scale	Scales the control per the specified ratio.
Select	Activates the control.
SendToBack	Causes the control's z-order to change to the back.
Show	Explicitly sets the control's Visible property to true.
Update	Forces a repaint on any invalidated areas of the control.

TABLE 5.13   Control Class Events

Event	Description
BackColorChanged	Fires when the BackColor property has been changed.
BackgroundImageChanged	Fires when the BackgroundImage property has been changed.
Click	Fires when the control is clicked.
ContextMenuChanged	Fires when the control's ContextMenu property has been changed.
ControlAdded	Fires when a new control is added.
ControlRemoved	Fires when a control is removed.
DockChanged	Fires when the control's Dock property has been changed.
DoubleClick	Fires when the control is double-clicked.
DragDrop	Fires when a drag-and-drop event is completed.
DragEnter	Fires when something is dragged into the interior of the control's region.
DragLeave	Fires when something that has been dragged into a control is subsequently dragged out of the control's region.
GotFocus	Fires when the control receives the focus.
KeyDown	Fires when a key is pressed down while the control has focus.
KeyPress	Fires when a key is pressed while the control has focus.
KeyUp	Fires when a key is released while the control has focus.
LostFocus	Fires when the focus shifts from this control to another control.

5

TABLE 5.13   Continued

Event	Description
MouseDown	Fires when a mouse button is held down while the mouse pointer is inside the control's interior.
MouseEnter	Fires when the mouse pointer enters the control's interior.
MouseLeave	Fires when the mouse pointer leaves the control's interior.
MouseUp	Fires when a mouse button is released while the mouse pointer is inside the control's interior.
MouseWheel	Fires when the mouse wheel is moved while the mouse pointer is inside the control's interior.
Move	Fires when the control is repositioned.
Paint	Fires when the control is drawn to the screen.
Resize	Fires when the control is resized.
TextChanged	Fires when the control's Text property has been changed.
Validated	Fires when the control is done validating.
Validating	Fires when the control is in the process of validating.

Handling Form Resizing

A common user interface dilemma programmers face is what to do with controls on a form if a user resizes the form. In previous versions of Visual Basic, you handled this by writing a lot of messy code in the paint and resize events to explicitly reposition each control that needed to be repositioned. Did you notice the Anchor property in Table 5.11? This represents intrinsic support for control positioning based on form resizing.

The Anchor property can be set to stick a control at a left, right, top, or bottom position (or any combination of those) during form resizing. It uses the AnchorStyle enumeration to specify the desired result (see Table 5.14).

TABLE 5.14   The AnchorStyle Enumeration

Name	Description
Bottom	Anchors the control to the bottom edge of the form.
Left	Anchors the control to the left edge of the form.
None	Removes any anchors on the control.
Right	Anchors the control to the right edge of the form.
Top	Anchors the control to the top edge of the form.

Figure 5.15 shows a simple form with two command buttons. The OK button is anchored to the top and to the left, and the Cancel button is anchored to the right and to the bottom.

FIGURE 5.15
Anchored controls before resizing a form.

After resizing the form, as shown in Figure 5.16, you can see what happens to the buttons.

FIGURE 5.16
Anchored controls after resizing a form.

Anchoring a control doesn't just cause its relative position to change; it can also change the *size* of the control. Continuing the example with the OK and Cancel buttons, if we elect to anchor the OK button to the bottom as well as to the top and left, the OK button resizes itself to remain true to its anchors, as shown in Figure 5.17.

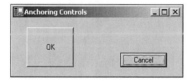

FIGURE 5.17
Control resizing based on anchors.

Here is the code to set the OK button's anchors:

```
Me.Button1.Anchor = ((System.Windows.Forms.AnchorStyles.Top Or _
System.Windows.Forms.AnchorStyles.Bottom) Or _
System.Windows.Forms.AnchorStyles.Left)
```

By using the Or operator, you can specify multiple anchors at a time with the AnchorStyles enumeration.

5

> **NOTE**
>
> Some controls won't resize, regardless of the anchors specified. The `TextBox` control, for instance, relies on its font setup to dictate the possible sizes it can change to; for instance, it does not allow partial lines of text to appear, so it must be resized in multiples of the font size.

Docking Controls

The `Control` class provides support for docking controls. Similar in concept to anchoring a control, docking a control causes it to anchor to a section of the form and then be resized to fit that section of the parent form. Docking is traditionally used with multipaned applications such as Windows Explorer. In Windows Explorer, the treeview control of files and objects appears on the left, with actual folder content on the right. This treeview control is docked to the left of the window. Toolbars are another item that is commonly docked in an application.

Figures 5.18 and 5.19 show a form with a treeview, first docked to the left and then docked to the top.

FIGURE 5.18
A treeview docked to the left.

The code to implement this is also similar to the code used with the `Anchor` property:

```
Me.TreeView1.Dock = System.Windows.Forms.DockStyle.Top
```

In the case of docking, you use the `DockStyle` enumeration, whose values are listed in Table 5.15.

FIGURE 5.19
A treeview docked to the top.

TABLE 5.15 DockStyle Enumeration

Name	Description
Bottom	Docks the control to the bottom edge of the form.
Fill	Docks the control to all sides of the form; the control expands to always fill the form's interior client area upon resizing.
Left	Docks the control to the left edge of the form.
None	Removes any docking attributes from the control.
Right	Docks the control to the right edge of the form.
Top	Docks the control to the top edge of the form.

Windows Forms and ActiveX Controls

ActiveX controls are not directly supported by Windows Forms, but there is a mechanism for making them function in the .NET Framework: the AxHost class. AxHost is a special wrapper class that is designed to encapsulate an existing ActiveX control and allow it to function completely inside the Windows Forms universe.

Essentially, the AxHost wrapper communicates with the hosted ActiveX control, and it acts as an intermediary between the Windows Form and the ActiveX control (see Figure 5.20).

The AxHost class, through its inheritance from the Control class, provides typical properties that might be used by an ActiveX control, which allows you to specify such things as the control's background color, cursor, font, and tab order. To fully leverage an ActiveX control,

5

FORMS, MENUS, AND CONTROLS

however, you have to custom-code the properties and methods that you need. This means that the typical usage for the AxHost class is as a base class from which you inherit to derive some basic operations.

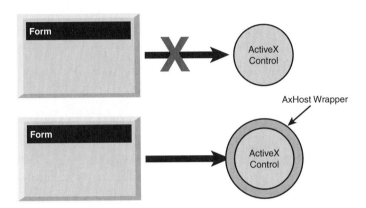

FIGURE 5.20

The AxHost wrapper.

After the wrapper assemblies have been created, you can use the ActiveX control on forms by referencing its runtime callable wrapper from the project. Microsoft has distributed a tool with the .NET Framework SDK—called Aximp.exe—that automatically creates a set of wrapper assemblies for a given ActiveX control. (Full details on the operation of Aximp.exe can be found in the .NET Framework MSDN documentation.)

Creating Your Own Controls

Although the .NET Framework and Visual Studio .NET ship with a huge assortment of user interface controls for use with Windows Forms applications, your business requirements are likely to sometimes dictate that a new control is needed—one that specifically satisfies your exact design goals. You might be able to create this control from existing control functionality, or you might need to create something entirely new.

With the .NET Framework, there are two principal ways to create a new control. One way involves custom-coding a control class that inherits directly from the System.Windows.Forms.Control class. The other way involves creating a new class that inherits from the System.Windows.Forms.UserControl class. We will distinguish between the two by calling controls created via the first method *custom controls* and controls created via the second method *composite controls* (you'll understand why we call these composite controls very shortly).

If you need a control that cannot benefit directly from any of the existing controls, you should create a completely custom control. Otherwise, inheriting from the UserControl class allows you to create a composite control; in that case, you can pick and choose from the entire control palette and select pieces of control functionality to include in your control.

Creating a Custom Control

The first step in creating a custom control is to implement the base set of properties, methods, and events that controls need to support. You do this quite simply by creating your own class and then inheriting from the Control class, like this:

```
Public Class CustomControl
    Inherits System.Windows.Forms.Control
```

From this point on, the code you write depends on exactly what you want the control to do. You implement your custom code by overriding the existing properties and methods of the control class and adding the appropriate logic to customize your control's behavior. Of course, you can also add new properties, methods, and events.

Overriding the OnPaint Event

One of the things that needs to be planned carefully is how a custom control will represent itself on the screen. Because a control is, by definition, a visual construct, you need to write logic that explicitly handles the painting of the control onto a form. You do this by overriding the OnPaint event.

The OnPaint event provides one incoming parameter—an instance of the PaintEventArgs class—which can be used to get a reference to a Graphics object. The Graphics object is the primary instrument for drawing the control to the screen. You need to provide it, along with what it should draw, how it should draw it, and where it should draw it. With the Graphics object, for instance, it is very easy to write code that draws text to the screen:

```
Protected Overrides Sub OnPaint(ByVal pe As _
    System.Windows.Forms.PaintEventArgs)

        MyBase.OnPaint(pe)

        Dim rect As RectangleF = New RectangleF(ClientRectangle.X, _
            ClientRectangle.Y, ClientRectangle.Width, _
            ClientRectangle.Height)

        'Draw the text onto the control's visible surface
        pe.Graphics.DrawString("Hello, world!", Font, _
            New SolidBrush(ForeColor), rect)

End Sub
```

This code snippet simply references the `ClientRectangle` structure (a property that is defined on the base `Control` class) to instruct the paint event to draw the words "Hello, world!" using the entire available control surface.

Adding New Properties, Methods, and Events

To add a property to a custom control, you add a private reference to a variable that will hold the property value, and then you add a property handler to the code, like this:

```
Public Class CustomControl1
    Inherits System.Windows.Forms.Control

    Private orientText As String

    .
    .
    .

    Public Property Orientation() As String

        Get
            Return orientText
        End Get

        Set(ByVal Value As String)
            orientText = Value
        End Set

    End Property

End Class
```

Adding a method is just as easy. You simply create a new public method and include logic inside it to affect the control in some way:

```
Public Sub RestoreDefault()
    orientText = "Horizontal"
End Sub
```

Adding an event is a little more involved, but it is still quite approachable. The first step is to declare the event:

```
Public Event OrientationChanged(ByVal sender As Object, _
    ByVal ev As EventArgs)
```

Then, you need to create the subroutine that handles the event (by convention, such subroutines start with `On`, as in `OnOrientationChanged`):

```
Protected Overridable Sub OnOrientationChanged(ByVal e As EventArgs)
    Invalidate()
    RaiseEvent OrientationChanged(Me, e)
End Sub
```

The final step is to actually write the code that raises the event:

```
Public Property Orientation() As String

    Get
        Return orientText
    End Get

    Set(ByVal Value As String)
        If orientText <> Value Then
            OnOrientationChanged(New EventArgs())
        End If
        orientText = Value
    End Set

End Property
```

Consuming a Custom Control

A custom control class must be compiled (into a dynamic link library [DLL]); it can then be referenced just like any other control inside a `Form` object.

First, a reference is made to the control object, somewhere in the form's declaration section:

```
Friend WithEvents TestControl As CustomControlLibrary.CustomControl
```

Next, the control is initialized and positioned on the form, inside the form's `InitializeComponents` subroutine:

```
'TextControl
Me.TestControl.Location = New System.Drawing.Point(44, 80)
Me.TestControl.Name = "TextControl1"
Me.TestControl.Size = New System.Drawing.Size(156, 20)
Me.TestControl.TabIndex = 0
```

That is all that is necessary to get the base instance of the control created and placed on a form.

Implementing a Custom Control

Listing 5.4 consolidates all the items we have talked about up to this point about custom controls. This listing includes the code fragments discussed in the preceding section, and it includes an enumeration called `OrientationMode`, to help ease get/set operations with the `Orientation` property. When this control, called `CustomControl`, is included on a form, you

5

should be able to change the orientation of the displayed text from a horizontal to a vertical position and back again. Because you are raising an OnOrientationChange event, which in turn invalidates the control and forces a repaint, the effect on the text should be immediate. After being compiled, the custom control is referenced inside the CustomControlLibrary assembly.

LISTING 5.4   Constructing a Custom Control

```
Public Class CustomControl
    Inherits System.Windows.Forms.Control

    'Sets up an event for dealing with changes
    'to the Orientation property
    Public Event OrientationChanged(ByVal sender As Object, _
        ByVal ev As EventArgs)

    Private orientText As Integer

    Public Enum OrientationMode
        Horizontal = 0
        Vertical = 1
    End Enum

    Public Sub New()
        MyBase.New()
    End Sub

    Protected Overrides Sub OnPaint(ByVal pe As _
        System.Windows.Forms.PaintEventArgs)
        MyBase.OnPaint(pe)

        'Dim a SizeF struct to hold the size of the control region
        Dim size As SizeF

        'Here is the text we want to display
        Const TEXT_STRING As String = "Hello, World!"

        'To avoid clipping the text, we get its exact size in
        'a SizeF struct
        size = pe.Graphics.MeasureString(TEXT_STRING, Font)

        'Based on the orientation mode in orientText, we either display
        'the text horizontally or vertically
        Select Case orientText
            Case OrientationMode.Horizontal
```

LISTING 5.4   Continued

```
                'We create our clipping rectangle here using
                'the overall position
                'of the control and the exact height and width necessary to
                'accommodate the text
                Dim rect As RectangleF = New RectangleF(ClientRectangle.X, _
                    ClientRectangle.Y, _
                    size.Width, size.Height)

                'Paint the Text property on the control; since we have not
                'specified a vertical orientation in the DrawString method, it
                'will write out horizontally
                pe.Graphics.DrawString(TEXT_STRING, Font, _
                    New SolidBrush(ForeColor), rect)


            Case OrientationMode.Vertical
                Dim textDirection As StringFormat = New StringFormat()

                'This enumeration allows us to specify text direction
                'inside of the DrawString method
                textDirection.FormatFlags = _
                StringFormatFlags.DirectionVertical

                'We create our clipping rectangle here using
                'the overall position
                'of the control and the exact height and width necessary to
                'accommodate the text (note that we have flipped the height
                'and width to account for the vertical display of the text)
                Dim rect As RectangleF = New RectangleF(ClientRectangle.X, _
                    ClientRectangle.Y, _
                    size.Height, size.Width)

                'Paint the Text property on the control; note the use of the
                'textDirection instance to specify vertical text
                pe.Graphics.DrawString(TEXT_STRING, Font, _
                    New SolidBrush(ForeColor), rect, textDirection)
        End Select
    End Sub

    Public Property Orientation() As OrientationMode
        Get
            Return orientText
        End Get
```

LISTING 5.4   Continued

```
        Set(ByVal Value As OrientationMode)
            If orientText <> Value Then
                'Raise an event
                OnOrientationChanged(New EventArgs())
            End If

            orientText = Value
        End Set
    End Property

    Public Sub RestoreDefault()
        orientText = OrientationMode.Horizontal
    End Sub

    Protected Overridable Sub OnOrientationChanged(ByVal e As EventArgs)
        'When the Orientation of the control has changed, we want
        'to invalidate the control to force a repaint
        Invalidate()
        RaiseEvent OrientationChanged(Me, e)
    End Sub

End Class
```

Listing 5.5 shows the code for one possible form-based consumer of the CustomControl.

LISTING 5.5   Using a Custom Control

```
Public Class Form1
    Inherits System.Windows.Forms.Form

#Region " Windows Form Designer generated code "

    Public Sub New()
        MyBase.New()

        'This call is required by the Windows Form Designer.
        InitializeComponent()

        'Add any initialization after the InitializeComponent() call

    End Sub

    'Form overrides dispose to clean up the component list.
    Protected Overloads Overrides Sub Dispose(ByVal disposing As Boolean)
```

LISTING 5.5 Continued

```
        If disposing Then
            If Not (components Is Nothing) Then
                components.Dispose()
            End If
        End If
        MyBase.Dispose(disposing)
    End Sub
    Friend WithEvents TextControl As CustomControlLibrary.CustomControl
    Friend WithEvents RadioButton1 As System.Windows.Forms.RadioButton
    Friend WithEvents RadioButton2 As System.Windows.Forms.RadioButton
    'Friend WithEvents TextBox1 As System.Windows.Forms.TextBox

    'Required by the Windows Form Designer
    Private components As System.ComponentModel.Container

    'NOTE: The following procedure is required by the Windows Form Designer
    'It can be modified using the Windows Form Designer.
    'Do not modify it using the code editor.
    <System.Diagnostics.DebuggerStepThrough()> _
    Private Sub InitializeComponent()
        Me.RadioButton1 = New System.Windows.Forms.RadioButton()
        Me.TextControl = New CustomControlLibrary.CustomControl()
        Me.RadioButton2 = New System.Windows.Forms.RadioButton()
        Me.SuspendLayout()
        '
        'RadioButton1
        '
        Me.RadioButton1.Location = New System.Drawing.Point(204, 16)
        Me.RadioButton1.Name = "RadioButton1"
        Me.RadioButton1.Size = New System.Drawing.Size(104, 16)
        Me.RadioButton1.TabIndex = 1
        Me.RadioButton1.Text = "Horizontal"
        '
        'TextControl
        '
        Me.TextControl.Location = New System.Drawing.Point(16, 16)
        Me.TextControl.Name = "TextControl"
        Me.TextControl.Orientation = _
            CustomControlLibrary.CustomControl.OrientationMode.Horizontal
        Me.TextControl.Size = New System.Drawing.Size(156, 96)
        Me.TextControl.TabIndex = 0
        '
        'RadioButton2
        '
        Me.RadioButton2.Location = New System.Drawing.Point(204, 36)
```

LISTING 5.5   Continued

```
    Me.RadioButton2.Name = "RadioButton2"
    Me.RadioButton2.Size = New System.Drawing.Size(104, 16)
    Me.RadioButton2.TabIndex = 1
    Me.RadioButton2.Text = "Vertical"
    '
    'Form1
    '
    Me.AutoScaleBaseSize = New System.Drawing.Size(5, 13)
    Me.ClientSize = New System.Drawing.Size(322, 159)
    Me.Controls.AddRange(New System.Windows.Forms.Control() _
    {Me.RadioButton2, Me.RadioButton1, Me.TextControl})
    Me.FormBorderStyle = System.Windows.Forms.FormBorderStyle.FixedDialog
    Me.MaximizeBox = False
    Me.MinimizeBox = False
    Me.Name = "Form1"
    Me.Text = "CustomControlHost"
    Me.ResumeLayout(False)

  End Sub

#End Region

  Private Sub RadioButton1_CheckedChanged(ByVal sender As System.Object, _
    ByVal e As System.EventArgs) Handles RadioButton1.CheckedChanged
    If RadioButton1.Checked Then
        Me.TextControl.Orientation = _
          CustomControlLibrary.CustomControl.OrientationMode.Horizontal
    End If
  End Sub

  Private Sub RadioButton2_CheckedChanged(ByVal sender As System.Object, _
    ByVal e As System.EventArgs) Handles RadioButton2.CheckedChanged
    If RadioButton2.Checked Then
        Me.TextControl.Orientation = _
          CustomControlLibrary.CustomControl.OrientationMode.Vertical
    End If

  End Sub
End Class
```

Figure 5.21 shows TextControl in action.

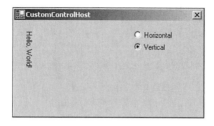

FIGURE 5.21

The TextControl *custom control.*

Creating a Composite Control

The UserControl class is a shell class that enables you to mix and match the functionality of existing .NET Framework controls to create something unique and specially suited to the work at hand.

User controls allow you to group other controls together to synthesize a new control. Consider a login form that uses a login ID textbox and a password textbox, along with a command button labeled Login. If you find yourself using these controls in this combination over and over again, it might make sense to simply compile them together as one control.

One of the benefits of creating a UserControl class is that it is fully enabled in the Visual Studio .NET IDE: It shows up in your toolbox (after you have referenced it from your project), and you can drag it from the toolbox onto a form.

To create a composite control, you first create a class that inherits from UserControl:

```
Public Class LoginControl
    Inherits System.Windows.Forms.UserControl
```

Then, for each control that will become part of the composite control, you add a reference. The following example continues with the scenario of creating a login control that is created from two textbox controls, two label controls, and a button control:

```
Friend WithEvents TextBox1 As System.Windows.Forms.TextBox
Friend WithEvents Label1 As System.Windows.Forms.Label
Friend WithEvents Label2 As System.Windows.Forms.Label
Friend WithEvents TextBox2 As System.Windows.Forms.TextBox
Friend WithEvents Button1 As System.Windows.Forms.Button
```

Next, you add these controls to the overall UserControl container by calling the AddRange method:

```
Me.Controls.AddRange(New System.Windows.Forms.Control() {Me.Button1, _
    Me.TextBox2, Me.Label2, Me.Label1, Me.TextBox1})
```

5

FORMS, MENUS,
AND CONTROLS

This takes care of adding the constituent controls to the composite control's control collection. Composite controls, at this point, start to follow the design pattern for custom controls, with code being added to handle events, properties, and methods. The sample application shown in the following section demonstrates creating and consuming a composite control.

Learning by Example: The EventLog Control

The EventLog control application demonstrates how to create a composite control and then use it in a simple form-based application. In this case, you are creating a visual control based on a label control, a listbox control, a button control, and an EventLog component. In essence, you are giving the EventLog component a visual dimension. The EventLogControl object allows you to specify an event log in its Log property; it then shows you the log entries inside the ListBox control. This section also shows the actual test application, which shows an example of consuming the EventLogControl object. You can specify a log file by selecting the File menu and then the Log menu.

Key Concepts Covered

The EventLog control application demonstrates the following:

- Creating a composite control by inheriting from the UserControl class
- Basic menu operations with MenuItem objects
- Handling custom properties, events, and methods inside a composite control
- Instantiating and working with a control on a Windows Form

To test the new control, you must first compile the composite control code (as shown in Listing 5.6) into a DLL. Then, you need to compile the code in Listing 5.7 to see how to use the previously created control. Note that you have to add a reference to the control DLL in order to use it. After you have done this, you should see the control show up in the toolbox region of your Visual Studio .NET IDE. Figure 5.22 shows the custom control in action, hosted in a Windows Forms application.

FIGURE 5.22
The EventLogControl *composite control.*

Code Walkthrough

LISTING 5.6   Code for the EventLogControl Object

All composite controls should inherit from UserControl. This gives you automatic support for all the base Control properties, events, and methods, and ensures that the new control will function seamlessly in the IDE.

Here you can see where we set up an enumeration, LogType, for specifying the event log to view. We also publish an event, LogSourceChanged, which is fired whenever the log is changed on the control.

```
Public Class EventLogControl
    Inherits System.Windows.Forms.UserControl

    'The name of the targeted log
    Private logSource As String

    'Max number of entries to hold in the listbox
    Private maxCount As Int32

    'This is the event fired when the targeted log changes
    Public Event LogSourceChanged(ByVal sender As Object, _
    ByVal ev As EventArgs)
```

LISTING 5.6 Continued

```
    'Our public enum for specifying the log to view
    Public Enum LogType
        Application = 0
        System = 1
        Security = 2
    End Enum

#Region " Windows Form Designer generated code "

    Public Sub New()
        MyBase.New()

        'This call is required by the Windows Form Designer.
        InitializeComponent()

        'Add any initialization after the InitializeComponent() call

        'Initialize the state of the control to look at the app log
        EventLog1.Log = "Application"
```

So that the new control is easy to work with in a drag-and-drop environment such as Visual Studio .NET, you anchor the listbox, button, and label controls to allow for easy, dynamic resizing at design time.

```
        'Anchor the listbox and button controls to enable easy
        'resizing
        ListEvents.Anchor = AnchorStyles.Left Or AnchorStyles.Top _
                        Or AnchorStyles.Right Or AnchorStyles.Bottom

        ButtonRefresh.Anchor = AnchorStyles.Right Or AnchorStyles.Bottom

        Label1.Anchor = AnchorStyles.Left Or AnchorStyles.Top
    End Sub

    'UserControl1 overrides dispose to clean up the component list.
    Protected Overloads Overrides Sub Dispose(ByVal disposing As Boolean)
        If disposing Then
            If Not (components Is Nothing) Then
                components.Dispose()
            End If
        End If
        MyBase.Dispose(disposing)
    End Sub
```

LISTING 5.6   Continued

```
Friend WithEvents ListEvents As System.Windows.Forms.ListBox
Friend WithEvents ButtonRefresh As System.Windows.Forms.Button
Friend WithEvents EventLog1 As System.Diagnostics.EventLog
Friend WithEvents Label1 As System.Windows.Forms.Label

'Required by the Windows Form Designer
Private components As System.ComponentModel.Container

'NOTE: The following procedure is required by the Windows Form Designer
'It can be modified using the Windows Form Designer.
'Do not modify it using the code editor.
<System.Diagnostics.DebuggerStepThrough()> _
 Private Sub InitializeComponent()
    Me.Label1 = New System.Windows.Forms.Label()
    Me.EventLog1 = New System.Diagnostics.EventLog()
    Me.ListEvents = New System.Windows.Forms.ListBox()
    Me.ButtonRefresh = New System.Windows.Forms.Button()
    CType(Me.EventLog1, _
    System.ComponentModel.ISupportInitialize).BeginInit()
    Me.SuspendLayout()
    '
    'Label1
    '
    Me.Label1.Location = New System.Drawing.Point(4, 4)
    Me.Label1.Name = "Label1"
    Me.Label1.Size = New System.Drawing.Size(128, 16)
    Me.Label1.TabIndex = 2
    Me.Label1.Text = "Application Log"
    '
    'EventLog1
    '
    Me.EventLog1.SynchronizingObject = Me
    '
    'ListEvents
    '
    Me.ListEvents.Location = New System.Drawing.Point(4, 24)
    Me.ListEvents.Name = "ListEvents"
    Me.ListEvents.Size = New System.Drawing.Size(352, 251)
    Me.ListEvents.TabIndex = 0
    '
    'ButtonRefresh
    '
    Me.ButtonRefresh.Location = New System.Drawing.Point(288, 280)
    Me.ButtonRefresh.Name = "ButtonRefresh"
```

LISTING 5.6 Continued

```
      Me.ButtonRefresh.Size = New System.Drawing.Size(68, 20)
      Me.ButtonRefresh.TabIndex = 1
      Me.ButtonRefresh.Text = "Refresh"
      '
      'EventLogControl
      '
      Me.Controls.AddRange(New System.Windows.Forms.Control() _
      {Me.Label1, Me.ButtonRefresh, Me.ListEvents})
      Me.Name = "EventLogControl"
      Me.Size = New System.Drawing.Size(364, 304)
      CType(Me.EventLog1, System.ComponentModel.ISupportInitialize).EndInit()
      Me.ResumeLayout(False)

   End Sub

#End Region
```

This is the class property, which allows users to select a log to view. Note that you raise the `LogSourceChanged` event here.

```
   Public Property Log() As LogType
      Get
         Return logSource
      End Get

      Set(ByVal Value As LogType)

         Dim logEnum As LogType
         logSource = LogType.GetName(logEnum.GetType, Value)

         'Raise an event
         OnLogSourceChanged(New EventArgs())

      End Set
   End Property

   Public Property MaxEntries() As Int32
      Get
         Return maxCount
      End Get

      Set(ByVal Value As Int32)

         Dim logEnum As LogType
         maxCount = Value
```

LISTING 5.6   Continued

```
      End Set
   End Property

   Protected Overridable Sub OnLogSourceChanged(ByVal e As EventArgs)
      'When the Orientation of the control has changed, we want
      'to invalidate the control to force a repaint
      ListEvents.Items.Clear()
      EventLog1.Log = logSource
      Label1.Text = logSource & " Log"

      ListEntries(EventLog1.Entries)

      'Invalidate()
      RaiseEvent LogSourceChanged(Me, e)
   End Sub
```

The `ListEntries` routine is used internally by the control to actually enumerate the `EventLogEntry` objects contained in the `EventLogEntryCollection` object. All this is first set up by specifying the log.

```
   Private Sub ListEntries(ByVal entriesCol As EventLogEntryCollection)
      Dim entry As EventLogEntry

      Dim count As Int32

      count = 0

      For Each entry In entriesCol
         If count > maxCount Then Exit For

         ListEvents.Items.Add(entry.TimeGenerated & ":: " & entry.Message)
         count = count + 1

      Next

   End Sub
   Private Sub EventLogControl_Load(ByVal sender As System.Object, _
   ByVal e As System.EventArgs) Handles MyBase.Load

   End Sub

   Private Sub ButtonRefresh_Click(ByVal sender As System.Object, _
   ByVal e As System.EventArgs) Handles ButtonRefresh.Click
      ListEntries(EventLog1.Entries)
   End Sub
End Class
```

Listing 5.7 shows one example of how to use `EventLogControl` on a form.

LISTING 5.7   Code for the `EventLogHost` Control

```
Public Class CompositeControlForm
    Inherits System.Windows.Forms.Form

#Region " Windows Form Designer generated code "

    Public Sub New()
        MyBase.New()

        'This call is required by the Windows Form Designer.
        InitializeComponent()

        'Add any initialization after the InitializeComponent() call

    End Sub

    'Form overrides dispose to clean up the component list.
    Protected Overloads Overrides Sub Dispose(ByVal disposing As Boolean)
        If disposing Then
            If Not (components Is Nothing) Then
                components.Dispose()
            End If
        End If
        MyBase.Dispose(disposing)
    End Sub
    Friend WithEvents appMenu As System.Windows.Forms.MainMenu
    Friend WithEvents fileMenu As System.Windows.Forms.MenuItem
    Friend WithEvents fileMenuLog As System.Windows.Forms.MenuItem
    Friend WithEvents fileMenuLogApp As System.Windows.Forms.MenuItem
    Friend WithEvents fileMenuLogSec As System.Windows.Forms.MenuItem
    Friend WithEvents fileMenuLogSys As System.Windows.Forms.MenuItem
    Friend WithEvents fileMenuExit As System.Windows.Forms.MenuItem
    Friend WithEvents GroupBox1 As System.Windows.Forms.GroupBox
    Friend WithEvents EventLogControl1 As EventLogControl.EventLogControl

    'Required by the Windows Form Designer
    Private components As System.ComponentModel.Container

    'NOTE: The following procedure is required by the Windows Form Designer
    'It can be modified using the Windows Form Designer.
    'Do not modify it using the code editor.
    <System.Diagnostics.DebuggerStepThrough()> _
        Private Sub InitializeComponent()
```

LISTING 5.7 Continued

```
Me.fileMenuLogSys = New System.Windows.Forms.MenuItem()
Me.GroupBox1 = New System.Windows.Forms.GroupBox()
Me.appMenu = New System.Windows.Forms.MainMenu()
Me.fileMenu = New System.Windows.Forms.MenuItem()
Me.fileMenuLog = New System.Windows.Forms.MenuItem()
Me.fileMenuLogApp = New System.Windows.Forms.MenuItem()
Me.fileMenuLogSec = New System.Windows.Forms.MenuItem()
Me.fileMenuExit = New System.Windows.Forms.MenuItem()
Me.EventLogControl1 = New EventLogControl.EventLogControl()
Me.GroupBox1.SuspendLayout()
Me.SuspendLayout()
'
'fileMenuLogSys
'
Me.fileMenuLogSys.Index = 2
Me.fileMenuLogSys.RadioCheck = True
Me.fileMenuLogSys.Text = "System"
'
'GroupBox1
'
Me.GroupBox1.Controls.AddRange(New System.Windows.Forms.Control() _
    {Me.EventLogControl1})
Me.GroupBox1.Location = New System.Drawing.Point(4, 12)
Me.GroupBox1.Name = "GroupBox1"
Me.GroupBox1.Size = New System.Drawing.Size(424, 380)
Me.GroupBox1.TabIndex = 0
Me.GroupBox1.TabStop = False
Me.GroupBox1.Text = "Event  Log"
'
'appMenu
'
Me.appMenu.MenuItems.AddRange(New System.Windows.Forms.MenuItem()_
{Me.fileMenu})
'
'fileMenu
'
Me.fileMenu.Index = 0
Me.fileMenu.MenuItems.AddRange(New System.Windows.Forms.MenuItem() _
{Me.fileMenuLog, Me.fileMenuExit})
Me.fileMenu.Text = "File"
'
'fileMenuLog
'
Me.fileMenuLog.Index = 0
Me.fileMenuLog.MenuItems.AddRange(New _
    System.Windows.Forms.MenuItem() _
```

LISTING 5.7 Continued

```
      {Me.fileMenuLogApp, Me.fileMenuLogSec, Me.fileMenuLogSys})
  Me.fileMenuLog.Text = "Log"
  '
  'fileMenuLogApp
  '
  Me.fileMenuLogApp.Index = 0
  Me.fileMenuLogApp.RadioCheck = True
  Me.fileMenuLogApp.Checked = True
  Me.fileMenuLogApp.Text = "Application"
  '
  'fileMenuLogSec
  '
  Me.fileMenuLogSec.Index = 1
  Me.fileMenuLogSec.RadioCheck = True
  Me.fileMenuLogSec.Text = "Security"
  '
  'fileMenuExit
  '
  Me.fileMenuExit.Index = 1
  Me.fileMenuExit.Text = "Exit"
  '
  'EventLogControl1
  '
  Me.EventLogControl1.Location = New System.Drawing.Point(8, 20)
  Me.EventLogControl1.MaxEntries = 1024
  Me.EventLogControl1.Log = _
  EventLogControl.EventLogControl.LogType.Application
  Me.EventLogControl1.Name = "EventLogControl1"
  Me.EventLogControl1.Size = New System.Drawing.Size(412, 348)
  Me.EventLogControl1.TabIndex = 0
  '
  'CompositeControlForm
  '
  Me.AutoScaleBaseSize = New System.Drawing.Size(5, 13)
  Me.ClientSize = New System.Drawing.Size(436, 397)
  Me.Controls.AddRange(New System.Windows.Forms.Control() _
  {Me.GroupBox1})
  Me.Menu = Me.appMenu
  Me.Name = "CompositeControlForm"
  Me.Text = "CompositeControl"
  Me.GroupBox1.ResumeLayout(False)
  Me.ResumeLayout(False)

End Sub
```

LISTING 5.7 Continued

```
#End Region

    Private Sub CustomControl_Load(ByVal sender As System.Object, _
        ByVal e As System.EventArgs) Handles MyBase.Load

    End Sub

    Private Sub fileMenuLogApp_Click(ByVal sender As System.Object, _
    ByVal e As System.EventArgs) Handles fileMenuLogApp.Click
        fileMenuLogApp.Checked = True
        fileMenuLogSec.Checked = False
        fileMenuLogSys.Checked = False
        EventLogControl1.Log = _
        EventLogControl.EventLogControl.LogType.Application
    End Sub

    Private Sub fileMenuLogSec_Click(ByVal sender As System.Object, _
    ByVal e As System.EventArgs) Handles fileMenuLogSec.Click
        fileMenuLogSec.Checked = True
        fileMenuLogApp.Checked = False
        fileMenuLogSys.Checked = False
        EventLogControl1.Log = _
        EventLogControl.EventLogControl.LogType.Security
    End Sub

    Private Sub fileMenuLogSys_Click(ByVal sender As System.Object, _
    ByVal e As System.EventArgs) Handles fileMenuLogSys.Click
        fileMenuLogSys.Checked = True
        fileMenuLogApp.Checked = False
        fileMenuLogSec.Checked = False
        EventLogControl1.Log = EventLogControl.EventLogControl.LogType.System
    End Sub
End Class
```

Summary

In this chapter, we have looked at the specific classes in the `System.Windows.Forms` namespace that can be used to quickly and efficiently assemble the user interface pieces of an application. By now, you should have a firm grasp of the following:

- Creating and adding forms to an application
- Adding menus and menu items to a form

- Responding to events
- Working with classes that inherit from the Control class
- Creating your own controls

The Visual Studio .NET environment automates and simplifies a lot of the programming activities discussed in this chapter. You should investigate those capabilities so that you can avoid having to write all the code yourself. This chapter should give you a much greater appreciation and understanding for the underlying classes that make the .NET Framework so useful.

Font, Text, and Printing Operations

IN THIS CHAPTER

Font, printing, and text manipulation together represent one of the more complex parts of the Windows operating system. Fortunately, the .NET Framework Class Library simplifies this for all of us. The classes presented in this chapter should give you enough insight into this technology to become very productive, very quickly.

The chapter focuses primarily on the namespaces `System.Drawing.Printing`, `System.Drawing.Text`, and to some extent on `System.Drawing`. Fonts are presented first, followed by a simple, Notepad-like sample application. We then discuss printing with the library and extend the font sample application by adding printing capabilities.

After reading this chapter, you will be able to

- Work with individual fonts and font families
- Retrieve all fonts installed on a system
- Modify text as output to the screen using the `Font` class and its associated members
- Send output to a print device
- Control printing, including paper source, page orientation, and margins
- Execute print preview functionality

Key Classes Related to Font, Text, and Printing Operations

The following details the namespaces this chapter discusses

- `System.Drawing`—Provides basic drawing functionality inside of .NET. Outside of the `Font` classes listed here, the namespace is covered in detail in Chapter 9, "Drawing Functions."
- `System.Drawing.Text`—Provides access to some advanced GDI+ typography functionality.
- `System.Drawing.Printing`—Provides functionality to manage printing functions in Windows.

Table 6.1 presents the key classes in these namespaces that you will use most often when writing printing and text-related code.

Font, Text, and Printing Operations

CHAPTER 6

155

6

FONT, TEXT, AND
PRINTING
OPERATIONS

TABLE 6.1 Key Classes in the `System.Drawing`, `System.Drawing.Text`, and `System.Drawing.Printing` Namespaces

Class	Description
Working with Fonts and Text	
System.Drawing	
Font	The Font class enables you to define a specific format for text, including the following: font face, size, and style attributes.
FontFamily	The FontFamily class abstracts a group of typefaces having a similar design but a certain variation in style.
System.Drawing.Text	
InstalledFontsCollection	With the InstalledFontsCollection, you can reference all the fonts installed on a specific system.
PrivateFontsCollection	The PrivateFontsCollection method enables you to create and add custom fonts into memory for use by your application.
Printing	
System.Drawing.Printing	
Margins	The Margins class enables you to manipulate the size of the margins (the space surrounding the text) of a printed page.
PageSettings	The PageSettings class enables you to specify print settings for one specific page.
PaperSize	The PaperSize class lets you represent the size of piece of paper.
PaperSource	The PaperSource class enables you to choose the paper tray from which the printer gets its paper for printing a given document.
PreviewPageInfo	The PreviewPageInfo class enables you to specify print preview information for a single page.
PreviewPrintController	The PreviewPrintController class enables you to display a document as a series of images prior to printing.
PrintDocument	The PrintDocument class enables you to control output to a given printer.
PrinterSettings	The PrinterSettings class enables you to set various properties of the printer and thus control how documents are printed.

Font, Text, and Printing

All text typed on a computer, a Web page, or a typewriter requires a font. The number and variety of fonts available to users is astounding. How many of us fuss with our documents, picking just the right font? I've seen programmers spend hours customizing the code windows they live in to evoke just the right feel. Take the book you are reading, for instance; a typesetter or layout artist has chosen just the right set of fonts to make the consumption of the material appetizing. The code listings are set in a monospaced font, in which all the characters in the font are of the same size. This enables you to easily compare lines of code and visually see blocks of code and nesting.

All application development requires some form of text and therefore some use of fonts. Even Web applications require developers to set a font and font size for their output. And rich-client applications often allow users to select their favorite fonts for displaying their data. The classes available through the .NET Framework Class Library provide a very powerful set of tools for managing fonts and text in your applications.

Of course, even with expensive displays and storage systems, users still like to read text from a printed page. Reading from a piece of paper is almost always easier and clearer (although technology is getting closer). On average, people read printed documents almost twice as fast as those onscreen. How many times have you been presented with a huge piece of documentation and after about a page, you hit the Print button?

Printing is a key piece of nearly all client-based application development. Users demand to be able to print and distribute their data. Again, .NET provides a rich set of tools for you to embed this functionality within your applications.

After reading this chapter, you should be well positioned to start using font and printing features in your own development.

Fonts

A font describes the way a string of text appears on a device—in most cases, a monitor or a printer. Fonts can vary in size, weight, and style. Bold fonts, for instance, are said to have a heavier weight than normal fonts. Windows automatically installs a number of standard fonts; literally thousands of fonts are available to users.

Fonts are known by their typeface name and attributes. For example, Courier Bold 12 point is a common fixed-pitch, or monospaced, font. Typically, nonscalable fonts actually demand a new font for each attribute change. For example, if you modify the point size of a font or change its characteristics to bold, italic, or underline, Windows accesses a physically different font for each version.

Font, Text, and Printing Operations

CHAPTER 6

157

6

FONT, TEXT, AND
PRINTING
OPERATIONS

In many cases, however, Windows can synthesize one font from another. For example, Windows can usually do a good job of creating an underlined font from a normal font, so you rarely need to purchase separate underlined fonts. In other cases, a significant drop in quality occurs. For example, when Windows scales a raster font from a small size to a very large one, the result can be truly ugly because slight imperfections in a letter's form become pronounced as the letter increases in size.

A font family describes a general class of font. In Windows, the term *family* is used to describe classifications of fonts, and the terms *typeface* or *facename* are used to identify a set of fonts that share a common character set and design but vary in attributes such as size, weight, slant, and so on. Every font used by Windows falls into one font-family category.

A font is really a tool that takes a character as input and enables you to determine how that character should be displayed in a given device context. The .NET `Font` and `FontFamily` classes encapsulate and simplify the use of fonts. With a few simple objects, you can write some very useful code to enable users to interact with text.

Font Attributes

When working with fonts, it is important to first understand some of the basic characteristics and dimensions of a font and to define some of the terms used in describing these attributes.

To create fonts, Windows uses various font technologies, each with different advantages and disadvantages. The following describes the three key font technologies in Windows:

- Raster fonts—A raster font is a series of character bitmaps. When a character needs to be displayed, the bitmap for the character is copied to the device. The advantage is that fonts can be optimized to look good on the device for which they are created. The disadvantage is that the font is not easily scalable.

- Vector (or stroke) fonts—Vector fonts are made up of graphical elements represented by GDI function calls. Because they are represented mathematically, they can be scaled easily with good results. For the most part, vector fonts have been replaced with TrueType fonts.

- Scalable fonts—Scalable fonts describe their characters mathematically using vectors and curves. These are the TrueType fonts built in to Windows. These fonts can be scaled to virtually any size without loss in quality. The disadvantages are at small sizes, they do not look as good as raster fonts, and they are somewhat slower to draw (not a big deal with today's horsepower).

A font's pitch can be either fixed or variable. In a fixed-pitch font, the width of each character cell is equal. In a variable-pitch font, the spacing varies depending on the character. For example, the letter "I" is narrower than the letter "W." In fact, a simple character cell actually has a great many attributes and characteristics. (It is beyond the scope of this chapter to delve much further into font dimensions, because our focus is on writing productive code.)

Font Classes

In .NET, the Font class encapsulates a font and is found in the System.Drawing namespace. At first, this sounds strange. Why would a Font class be in a drawing namespace? The answer is quite simple: Fonts, like everything else in the user interface, have to be drawn to the display. In fact, the drawing functions are used to render fonts to a device or drawing surface.

Text is defined by font face, size, and style attributes. The following is a simple example of how to manipulate the various attributes of a font at runtime. The code assumes a label control (labelExample) has been placed on a form. We then create a Font instance based on a font-family name, size, and a font style (here we use bold). Then, because .NET uses the same libraries throughout, we simply set the Font property of the label control to equal our new Font instance. The results are that the text inside the label control is now displayed using our new Font instance.

```
'create a new instance of the font object
Dim myFont as New Font(familyName:="Tahoma", emSize:=18, _
        style:=FontStyle.Bold, unit:=GraphicsUnit.Point)

'change the font of the label control
labelExample().Font = myFont
```

To create an instance of a font, we can choose from a variety of constructors in the .NET tool-box. Table 6.2 lists these constructors and provides a description of each. You can see that the table is a little long, but it does provide all the right combinations. Most of the constructors are variations on a theme.

TABLE 6.2   Font Class Constructors

New Font (ByVal prototype as Font, ByVal newStyle as FontStyle)

Prototype(Font): An existing font instance that will be used to create the new font.

NewStyle(FontStyle): A FontStyle enumeration member that will be applied to the new font instance.

Note: Use this constructor to create a new Font object from an existing Font object.

New Font (ByVal family as FontFamily, ByVal emSize as Single)

family(FontFamily): A valid FontFamily object.

emSize(Single): The size of the new font.

Note: Use this constructor to create a new Font object from a FontFamily object and a specific size. You can get a FontFamily object in a variety of ways, including straight from a string (see example code).

TABLE 6.2 Continued

6

New Font (ByVal familyName as String, ByVal emSize as Single)

familyName(String): A string that represents a FontFamily. For example, "Tahoma."

emSize(Single): The size of the new font.

Note: Use this constructor to create a new Font object directly from a FontFamily name and a specific size.

New Font (ByVal family as FontFamily, ByVal emSize as Single, Byval style as FontStyle)

family(FontFamily): A valid FontFamily object.

emSize(Single): The size of the new font.

Style(FontStyle); A valid FontStyle enumeration member (Bold, Italic, and so on).

Note: Use this constructor to create a new Font object from a FontFamily object, a specific size, and specific style. You can get FontStyle and FontFamily objects in a variety of ways, including straight from a string (see example code).

New Font (ByVal family as FontFamily, ByVal emSize as Single, ByVal unit as GraphicsUnit)

family(FontFamily): A valid FontFamily object.

emSize(Single): The size of the new font.

unit(GraphicsUnit): A valid GraphicsUnit enumeration member (Point, Pixel, Inch, and so on).

Note: Use this constructor to create a new Font object from a FontFamily object, a specific size, and a GraphicsUnit object. The GraphicsUnit value indicates how the font size is calculated.

New Font (ByVal familyName as String, ByVal emSize as Single, ByVal style as FontStyle)

familyName(String): A string that represents a FontFamily. For example, "Tahoma."

emSize(Single): The size of the new font.

Style(FontStyle): A valid FontStyle enumeration member (Bold, Italic, and so on).

Note: Use this constructor to create a new Font object directly from a FontFamily name, a specific size, and a specific style (Bold, Italics, and so on).

New Font (ByVal familyName as String, ByVal emSize as Single, ByVal unit as GraphicsUnit)

familyName(String): A string that represents a FontFamily. For example, "Tahoma."

emSize(Single): The size of the new font.

unit(GraphicsUnit): A valid GraphicsUnit enumeration member (Point, Pixel, Inch, and so on).

Note: Use this constructor to create a new Font object directly from a FontFamily name, a specific size, and a GraphicsUnit object. The GraphicsUnit value indicates how the font size is calculated.

TABLE 6.2 Continued

New Font (ByVal family as FontFamily, ByVal emSize as Single, ByVal style as FontStyle, ByVal unit as GraphicsUnit)

family(FontFamily): A valid FontFamily object.

emSize(Single): The size of the new font.

Style(FontStyle): A valid FontStyle enumeration member (Bold, Italic, and so on).

unit(GraphicsUnit): A valid GraphicsUnit enumeration member (Point, Pixel, Inch, and so on).

Note: Use this constructor to create a new Font object directly from a FontFamily, a specific size, a FontStyle, and a GraphicsUnit object.

New Font (ByVal familyName as String, ByVal emSize as Single, ByVal style as FontStyle, ByVal unit as GraphicsUnit)

familyName(String): A string that represents a FontFamily. For example, "Tahoma."

emSize(Single): The size of the new font.

Style(FontStyle): A valid FontStyle enumeration member (Bold, Italic, and so on).

unit(GraphicsUnit): A valid GraphicsUnit enumeration member (Point, Pixel, Inch, and so on).

Note: Use this constructor to create a new Font object directly from a FontFamily name, a specific size, a FontStyle, and a GraphicsUnit object.

New Font (ByVal family as FontFamily, ByVal emSize as Single, ByVal style as FontStyle, ByVal unit as GraphicsUnit, ByVal gdiCharSet as Byte)

family(FontFamily): A valid FontFamily object.

emSize(Single): The size of the new font.

Style(FontStyle): A valid FontStyle enumeration member (Bold, Italic, and so on).

unit(GraphicsUnit): A valid GraphicsUnit enumeration member (Point, Pixel, Inch, and so on).

gdiCharSet(Byte): A GDI character set value found in WinGDI.h.

Note: Use this constructor to create a new Font object directly from a FontFamily, a specific size, a FontStyle, a GraphicsUnit object, and a gdiCharSet.

New Font (ByVal familyName as String, ByVal emSize as Single, ByVal style as FontStyle, ByVal unit as GraphicsUnit, ByVal gdiCharSet as Byte)

familyName(String): A string that represents a FontFamily. For example, "Tahoma."

emSize(Single): The size of the new font.

Style(FontStyle): A valid FontStyle enumeration member (Bold, Italic, and so on).

unit(GraphicsUnit): A valid GraphicsUnit enumeration member (Point, Pixel, Inch, and so on).

TABLE 6.2   Continued

gdiCharSet(Byte): A GDI character set value found in WinGDI.h.

Note: Use this constructor to create a new Font object directly from a FontFamily name, a specific size, a FontStyle, a GraphicsUnit object, and a gdiCharSet.

New Font (ByVal family as FontFamily, ByVal emSize as Single, ByVal style as FontStyle, ByVal unit as GraphicsUnit, ByVal gdiCharSet as Byte, gdiVerticalFont as Boolean)

family(FontFamily): A valid FontFamily object.

emSize(Single): The size of the new font.

Style(FontStyle): A valid FontStyle enumeration member (Bold, Italic, and so on).

unit(GraphicsUnit): A valid GraphicsUnit enumeration member (Point, Pixel, Inch, and so on).

gdiCharSet(Byte): A GDI character set value found in WinGDI.h.

gdiVerticalFont(Boolean): Indicates if the font is derived from a GDI vertical font.

Note: Use this constructor to create a new font object directly from a FontFamily, a specific size, a FontStyle, a GraphicsUnit object, a gdiCharSet value, and a indication of gdiVerticalFont.

New Font (ByVal familyName as String, ByVal emSize as Single, ByVal style as FontStyle, ByVal unit as GraphicsUnit, ByVal gdiCharSet as Byte, gdiVerticalFont as Boolean)

familyName(String): A string that represents a FontFamily. For example, "Tahoma."

family(FontFamily): A valid FontFamily object.

emSize(Single): The size of the new font.

Style(FontStyle): A valid FontStyle enumeration member (Bold, Italic, and so on).

unit(GraphicsUnit): A valid GraphicsUnit enumeration member (Point, Pixel, Inch, and so on).

gdiCharSet(Byte): A GDI character set value found in WinGDI.h.

gdiVerticalFont(Boolean): Indicates if the font is derived from a GDI vertical font.

Note: Use this constructor to create a new font object directly from a FontFamily name, a specific size, a FontStyle, a GraphicsUnit object, a gdiCharSet value, and an indication of gdiVerticalFont.

When creating a font instance, the FontStyle enumeration allows us to indicate a standard format for the text. Table 6.3 displays the members of the FontStyle enumeration. A text example is provided alongside each enumeration member. Note that the font family used in the examples is Times New Roman.

TABLE 6.3   `System.Drawing` and `FontStyle` Enumeration Members

Member	Example	Description
Bold	**This is bold text.**	Text that has a heavier weight.
Italic	*This is italic text.*	Text that is italicized or slanted.
Regular	This is regular text.	Normal text.
Strikeout	~~This is strikeout text.~~	Text that has a line going through the middle.
Underline	<u>This is text that is underlined.</u>	Text that has a line underneath.

Font Collections

We often need to work with fonts as a group, sometimes to display all the installed fonts on a system to the user for selection or to output a document's used fonts to a dialog box. To work with groups of fonts, we use the `System.Drawing.Text` namespace. This namespace exposes to us two key classes: `InstalledFontCollection` and `PrivateFontCollection`. These classes enable us to create and use collections of fonts.

The `InstalledFontCollection` class behaves as its name indicates; it returns a collection of `FontFamily` objects that represent the fonts installed on a given system. The following code creates an instance of the collection, loops through it, and adds the font-family names to a list box control (`listBox1`).

```
'local scope
Dim myFonts As System.Drawing.Text.InstalledFontCollection
Dim i As Integer

'return the collection of installed fonts
myFonts = New System.Drawing.Text.InstalledFontCollection()

'loop through the font families and add to the list box
For i = 1 To UBound(myFonts.Families)
    listBox1().Items.Add(myFonts.Families(i).Name)
Next
```

Private Fonts

The `PrivateFontCollection` allows us to install a private version of an existing font without replacing the system version of the font. For example, we could create a private version of the Arial font in addition to the Arial font that the system uses. The `PrivateFontCollection` can also be used to install fonts that don't exist on a system. This is a temporary font installation that doesn't affect the system-installed collection. This is great when you want to use custom fonts in your application but not install them onto users' machines.

Listing 6.1 provides an example of how to load a font from a file into the private font's collection and then use that font.

LISTING 6.1 Private Fonts Collection

```
Private Sub ButtonLoadFont_Click(ByVal sender As System.Object, _
    ByVal e As System.EventArgs) Handles ButtonLoadFont.Click

    'local scope
    Dim myPrivateFonts As System.Drawing.Text.PrivateFontCollection
    Dim myFont As Font

    'instantiate a PrivateFontCollection object
    myPrivateFonts = New System.Drawing.Text.PrivateFontCollection()

    'add a font to the private fonts collection
    'NOTE: this font is stored in a file in the app's bin directory
    '      this font does NOT exist on the system
    myPrivateFonts.AddFontFile(fileName:="andalemo.ttf")

    'create of font object from the font family in the private collection
    myFont = New Font(family:=myPrivateFonts.Families(0), emSize:=12, _
        style:=FontStyle.Regular)

    'change the label's font property to use the new font
    LabelExample().Font = myFont

End Sub
```

Font Classifications

Fonts can be classified into what is called generic font families. These families are independent of the font families we've been discussing. In .NET, a generic font family represents a higher-level (or parent) category to which all fonts must belong. All fonts (or font families) belong to one generic font family. Table 6.4 lists the GenericFontFamilies enumeration members and provides a description of each.

TABLE 6.4 System.Drawing.Text and GenericFontFamilies Enumeration Members

Member	Example	Description
Monospace	This is a monospace font	Represents a generic font family that is of type Monospace. Monospace refers to the fact that each character is the exact same width.

TABLE 6.4   Continued

Member	Example	Description
Sans Serif	This is a sans serif font	Represents a generic font family that is of type Sans Serif. Sans Serif refers to the fact that each character is without (sans) serifs.
Serif	This is a serif font	Represents a generic font family that is of type serif. Serifs are the fine lines that finish off the main strokes of a character.

Hotkey Prefix

A hotkey prefix enables users to use a keyboard sequence (usually CTRL+HotKey or ALT+HotKey) to access functionality represented by text displayed on the screen. The HotKeyPrefix enumeration stores the possible values for indicating how these keys should be displayed to the user.

The HotKeyPrefix enumeration is used by the StringFormat class. The StringFormat class specifies the Windows Forms string class format, which Windows Forms uses to store string objects. Table 6.5 describes the enumeration's members.

TABLE 6.5   System.Drawing.Text and HotKeyPrefix Enumeration Members

Member	Description
Hide	Tells the application not to display a specific hotkey.
None	Indicates that there is no hotkey for a specific function.
Show	Displays the hotkey prefix.

Text Rendering

A number of options are available to you for indicating how you want .NET to draw your text to the screen. These options can be set using the TextRenderingHint enumeration. Options range from the fast-performing but low-quality SingleBitPerPixel to the clearer but slower-performing ClearType. This enumeration is used to set the TextRenderingHint property of a Graphics instance used to output text to a screen. Table 6.6 presents a visual representation of each member using a Bold, 18-point Tahoma font.

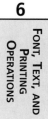

TABLE 6.6   TextRenderingHint Enumeration Members

Member	Visual Representation
AntiAlias	**AntiAlias**
AntiAliasGridFit	**AntiAliasGridFit**
ClearTypeGridFit	**ClearTypeGridFit**
SingleBitPerPixel	**SingleBitPerPixel**
SingleBitPerPixelGridFit	**SingleBitPerPixelGridFit**
SystemDefault	**SystemDefault**

 ## Suggestions for Further Exploration

⊃ Explore the ins and outs of TrueType font technology at Microsoft's Typography site: http://www.microsoft.com/typography/default.asp. Of course, there is a developer's section!

⊃ Check out Microsoft's clear type initiative. Microsoft is rewriting the way we view text to bring it inline with the printed page. In fact, the first version of this has been released with Windows XP. Information on this technology can be found inside MSDN.

Learning by Example: FontPad, a Simple Text Editor

In this example, we extend our knowledge of the font-related namespaces to create a text editor similar in design and scope to Notepad. Of course, the example concentrates on mimicking the functionality in Notepad's Font dialog box. At the end of this chapter, we will fill in the printing aspect of our application. In Chapter 7, "Stream and File Operations," we extend this sample by adding both Save and Open features.

Key Concepts Covered

The following represents the key classes and concepts demonstrated with this sample application:

• Working with the Font class to create and change the default font on a control

• Displaying all the fonts installed on a system using the InstalledFontsCollection class

• Working with font families using the FontFamily class

FontPad Main Dialog Box

The main dialog box of our application includes a menu bar and a RichTextBox control. The menu bar enables users to interact with our application through a standard set of menu items. The only functioning items in the menu are File, Exit—which exits the application—and Format, which displays the FontSelection dialog box.

For text editing, we use the RichTextBox control. This control is set to size with the form. This is done by setting its dock property to Fill.

Figure 6.1 shows an example of FontPad's main form.

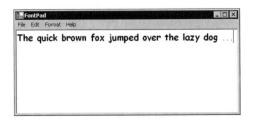

FIGURE 6.1

FontPad main form.

Code Walkthrough

The code behind the form is nearly as straightforward as the form itself. Listing 6.2 walks you through the code.

The code listing starts by defining the form and its controls.

LISTING 6.2   FontPad Main Form

```
Option Strict Off

Public Class FormMain
  Inherits System.Windows.Forms.Form

#Region " Windows Form Designer generated code "

  Public Sub New()
    MyBase.New()

    'This call is required by the Windows Form Designer.
    InitializeComponent()

    'Add any initialization after the InitializeComponent() call
```

LISTING 6.2 Continued

```
End Sub

'Form overrides dispose to clean up the component list.
Protected Overloads Overrides Sub Dispose(ByVal disposing As Boolean)
  If disposing Then
    If Not (components Is Nothing) Then
      components.Dispose()
    End If
  End If
  MyBase.Dispose(disposing)
End Sub


Private WithEvents richTextBox As System.Windows.Forms.RichTextBox
Private WithEvents button1 As System.Windows.Forms.Button
Private WithEvents button2 As System.Windows.Forms.Button
Private WithEvents button3 As System.Windows.Forms.Button
Private WithEvents mainMenu1 As System.Windows.Forms.MainMenu
Private WithEvents menuItemEdit As System.Windows.Forms.MenuItem
Private WithEvents menuItemFile As System.Windows.Forms.MenuItem
Private WithEvents menuItemHelp As System.Windows.Forms.MenuItem
Private WithEvents menuItemFormat As System.Windows.Forms.MenuItem
Private WithEvents menuItemFont As System.Windows.Forms.MenuItem
Private WithEvents menuItemWrap As System.Windows.Forms.MenuItem
Private WithEvents menuItem1 As System.Windows.Forms.MenuItem
Private WithEvents menuItemExit As System.Windows.Forms.MenuItem
Private WithEvents menuItemNew As System.Windows.Forms.MenuItem
Private WithEvents menuItem2 As System.Windows.Forms.MenuItem
Private WithEvents menuItem3 As System.Windows.Forms.MenuItem


'Required by the Windows Form Designer
Private components As System.ComponentModel.Container


'NOTE: The following procedure is required by the Windows Form Designer
'It can be modified using the Windows Form Designer.
'Do not modify it using the code editor.
<System.Diagnostics.DebuggerStepThrough()> _
Private Sub InitializeComponent()
  Me.menuItem1 = New System.Windows.Forms.MenuItem()
  Me.menuItemFont = New System.Windows.Forms.MenuItem()
  Me.menuItem2 = New System.Windows.Forms.MenuItem()
  Me.menuItem3 = New System.Windows.Forms.MenuItem()
  Me.menuItemExit = New System.Windows.Forms.MenuItem()
  Me.menuItemEdit = New System.Windows.Forms.MenuItem()
  Me.menuItemWrap = New System.Windows.Forms.MenuItem()
  Me.menuItemFile = New System.Windows.Forms.MenuItem()
```

LISTING 6.2   Continued

```
Me.richTextBox = New System.Windows.Forms.RichTextBox()
Me.menuItemHelp = New System.Windows.Forms.MenuItem()
Me.menuItemNew = New System.Windows.Forms.MenuItem()
Me.mainMenu1 = New System.Windows.Forms.MainMenu()
Me.menuItemFormat = New System.Windows.Forms.MenuItem()
Me.menuItem1.Index = 1
Me.menuItem1.Text = "-"
Me.menuItemFont.Index = 1
Me.menuItemFont.Text = "Font..."
Me.menuItem2.Index = 2
Me.menuItem2.Text = "Page Setup"
Me.menuItem3.Index = 3
Me.menuItem3.Text = "Print"
Me.menuItemExit.Index = 4
Me.menuItemExit.Text = "Exit"
Me.menuItemEdit.Index = 1
Me.menuItemEdit.Text = "Edit"
Me.menuItemWrap.Index = 0
Me.menuItemWrap.Text = "Word Wrap"
Me.menuItemFile.Index = 0
Me.menuItemFile.MenuItems.AddRange(New System.Windows.Forms.MenuItem() _
  {Me.menuItemNew, Me.menuItem1, Me.menuItem2, Me.menuItem3, _
  Me.menuItemExit})
Me.menuItemFile.Text = "File"
Me.richTextBox.AcceptsTab = True
Me.richTextBox.AutoSize = True
Me.richTextBox.AutoWordSelection = True
Me.richTextBox.Dock = System.Windows.Forms.DockStyle.Fill
Me.richTextBox.Size = New System.Drawing.Size(591, 336)
Me.richTextBox.TabIndex = 0
Me.richTextBox.Text = "richTextBox1"
Me.menuItemHelp.Index = 3
Me.menuItemHelp.Text = "Help"
Me.menuItemNew.Index = 0
Me.menuItemNew.Text = "New"
Me.mainMenu1.MenuItems.AddRange(New System.Windows.Forms.MenuItem() _
  {Me.menuItemFile, Me.menuItemEdit, Me.menuItemFormat, _
  Me.menuItemHelp})
Me.menuItemFormat.Index = 2
Me.menuItemFormat.MenuItems.AddRange(New System.Windows.Forms.MenuItem() _
  {Me.menuItemWrap, Me.menuItemFont})
Me.menuItemFormat.Text = "Format"
Me.AutoScaleBaseSize = New System.Drawing.Size(5, 13)
Me.ClientSize = New System.Drawing.Size(591, 336)
Me.Controls.AddRange(New System.Windows.Forms.Control() _
```

Font, Text, and Printing Operations

CHAPTER 6

169

6

FONT, TEXT, AND
PRINTING
OPERATIONS

LISTING 6.2 Continued

```
      {Me.richTextBox})
   Me.Menu = Me.mainMenu1
   Me.Text = "FontPad"

End Sub
```

The procedure, ResetRichTextBox, is of particular interest. In this subroutine, we create an instance of a Font class based on the global variables: g_FontFamily, g_FontStyle, and g_FontSize. We then apply this object to the RichTextBox's Font property.

This procedure gets called both when the form loads and when users apply changes to the application's font settings.

```
Public Sub resetRichTextBox()

    'purpose:   set the font properties of the rich text box

    'local scope
    Dim font As Font
    Dim fontStyle As FontStyle
    Dim fontFamily As FontFamily
    Dim styleType As System.Type

    'set a font style type
    styleType = fontStyle.GetType

    'create a font family object
    fontFamily = New FontFamily(g_FontFamily)

    'get a font style object (note: must turn off option strict)
    fontStyle = fontStyle.Parse(enumType:=styleType, _
      value:=g_FontStyle)

    'create a new font based on global values
    font = New Font(family:=fontFamily, _
        emSize:=CSng(g_FontSize), _
        style:=fontStyle, _
        unit:=System.Drawing.GraphicsUnit.Point)

    'reset the font on the control
    Me.richTextBox.Font = font

End Sub
```

The form load event initializes the `RichTextBox`.

```
Private Sub Form1_Load(ByVal sender As System.Object, _
    ByVal e As System.EventArgs) Handles MyBase.Load

  'purpose:   init. the application, load any controls

  'set the text property of the rich text box
  richTextBox().Text = ""

  'set the font properties to their defaults
  resetRichTextBox()
  g_FontPad = Me

End Sub
```

When users click the `Font` item on the `Format` menu, the following code executes to show the Font Selection dialog box.

```
Private Sub menuItemFont_Click(ByVal sender As System.Object, _
    ByVal e As System.EventArgs) Handles menuItemFont.Click

  'purpose:   show the font dialog when the user clicks
  '              the font menu item

  'local scope
  Dim dialogFont As FontSettings

  'create new suface form
  dialogFont = New FontSettings()

  'set the start position of the modal dialog to the center
  '  positions of its parent
  dialogFont.StartPosition = FormStartPosition.CenterParent

  'show the form as modal dialog
  dialogFont.ShowDialog(Me)

End Sub
```

When users click the `Exit` item on the `File` menu, the application ends.

```
Private Sub menuItemExit_Click(ByVal sender As System.Object, _
    ByVal e As System.EventArgs) Handles menuItemExit.Click

  'purpose:   end the application

  'close the form
  Me.Close()

End Sub
```

```
#End Region

End Class
```

FontPad Font Settings Dialog Box

The Font Settings dialog box is also similar in feel to that of Notepad's. For example, the settings apply to the application as a whole (this is a text editor and not a word processor). Users can browse a list of font families, styles, and sizes (see Figure 6.2). As a user selection changes, an example of the most recent selection is displayed inside the sample group box. This gives users a visual cue before selecting a new font setting.

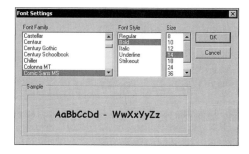

FIGURE 6.2

FontPad: Font Settings form (formFontSettings.vb).

Code Walkthrough

Again, .NET makes the code rather simple. Listing 6.3 represents the code behind the form.

The listing starts with the form and control setup code.

LISTING 6.3 FontPad Font Settings Form

```
Option Strict Off

Public Class FontSettings
  Inherits System.Windows.Forms.Form

#Region " Windows Form Designer generated code "

  Public Sub New()
    MyBase.New()

      'This call is required by the Windows Form Designer.
      InitializeComponent()
```

LISTING 6.3   Continued

```
    'Add any initialization after the InitializeComponent() call

End Sub

'Form overrides dispose to clean up the component list.
Protected Overloads Overrides Sub Dispose(ByVal disposing As Boolean)
  If disposing Then
    If Not (components Is Nothing) Then
      components.Dispose()
    End If
  End If
  MyBase.Dispose(disposing)
End Sub

Private WithEvents label4 As System.Windows.Forms.Label
Private WithEvents label2 As System.Windows.Forms.Label
Private WithEvents label3 As System.Windows.Forms.Label
Private WithEvents groupBox1 As System.Windows.Forms.GroupBox
Private WithEvents labelSample As System.Windows.Forms.Label
Private WithEvents listBoxSizes As System.Windows.Forms.ListBox
Private WithEvents buttonOk As System.Windows.Forms.Button
Private WithEvents buttonCancel As System.Windows.Forms.Button
Private WithEvents listBoxFamilies As System.Windows.Forms.ListBox
Private WithEvents listBoxStyles As System.Windows.Forms.ListBox

'Required by the Windows Form Designer
Private components As System.ComponentModel.Container

'NOTE: The following procedure is required by the Windows Form Designer
'It can be modified using the Windows Form Designer.
'Do not modify it using the code editor.
<System.Diagnostics.DebuggerStepThrough()> _
Private Sub InitializeComponent()
  Me.labelSample = New System.Windows.Forms.Label()
  Me.listBoxSizes = New System.Windows.Forms.ListBox()
  Me.buttonOk = New System.Windows.Forms.Button()
  Me.buttonCancel = New System.Windows.Forms.Button()
  Me.listBoxFamilies = New System.Windows.Forms.ListBox()
  Me.listBoxStyles = New System.Windows.Forms.ListBox()
  Me.label2 = New System.Windows.Forms.Label()
  Me.label4 = New System.Windows.Forms.Label()
  Me.groupBox1 = New System.Windows.Forms.GroupBox()
  Me.label3 = New System.Windows.Forms.Label()
  Me.labelSample.BorderStyle = System.Windows.Forms.BorderStyle.Fixed3D
  Me.labelSample.Location = New System.Drawing.Point(12, 24)
```

LISTING 6.3 Continued

```
Me.labelSample.Size = New System.Drawing.Size(344, 80)
Me.labelSample.TabIndex = 0
Me.labelSample.Text = "AaBbCcDd - WwXxYyZz"
Me.labelSample.TextAlign = System.Drawing.ContentAlignment.MiddleCenter
Me.listBoxSizes.Location = New System.Drawing.Point(320, 28)
Me.listBoxSizes.Size = New System.Drawing.Size(56, 95)
Me.listBoxSizes.TabIndex = 2
Me.buttonOk.Location = New System.Drawing.Point(384, 28)
Me.buttonOk.TabIndex = 3
Me.buttonOk.Text = "OK"
Me.buttonCancel.DialogResult = System.Windows.Forms.DialogResult.Cancel
Me.buttonCancel.Location = New System.Drawing.Point(384, 60)
Me.buttonCancel.TabIndex = 4
Me.buttonCancel.Text = "Cancel"
Me.listBoxFamilies.Location = New System.Drawing.Point(12, 28)
Me.listBoxFamilies.Size = New System.Drawing.Size(196, 95)
Me.listBoxFamilies.TabIndex = 0
Me.listBoxStyles.Location = New System.Drawing.Point(216, 28)
Me.listBoxStyles.Size = New System.Drawing.Size(96, 95)
Me.listBoxStyles.TabIndex = 1
Me.label2.Location = New System.Drawing.Point(216, 12)
Me.label2.Size = New System.Drawing.Size(120, 20)
Me.label2.TabIndex = 7
Me.label2.Text = "Font Style"
Me.label4.Location = New System.Drawing.Point(320, 12)
Me.label4.Size = New System.Drawing.Size(52, 20)
Me.label4.TabIndex = 9
Me.label4.Text = "Size"
Me.groupBox1.Controls.AddRange(New System.Windows.Forms.Control() _
  {Me.labelSample})
Me.groupBox1.Location = New System.Drawing.Point(12, 136)
Me.groupBox1.Size = New System.Drawing.Size(364, 112)
Me.groupBox1.TabIndex = 5
Me.groupBox1.TabStop = False
Me.groupBox1.Text = "Sample"
Me.label3.Location = New System.Drawing.Point(12, 12)
Me.label3.Size = New System.Drawing.Size(120, 20)
Me.label3.TabIndex = 8
Me.label3.Text = "Font Family"
Me.AcceptButton = Me.buttonOk
Me.AutoScaleBaseSize = New System.Drawing.Size(5, 13)
Me.FormBorderStyle = System.Windows.Forms.FormBorderStyle.FixedDialog
Me.CancelButton = Me.buttonCancel
Me.ClientSize = New System.Drawing.Size(473, 262)
```

LISTING 6.3 Continued

```
    Me.Controls.AddRange(New System.Windows.Forms.Control() _
        {Me.listBoxSizes, Me.listBoxStyles, Me.listBoxFamilies, Me.label4, _
        Me.label3, Me.label2, Me.groupBox1, Me.buttonCancel, Me.buttonOk})
    Me.MaximizeBox = False
    Me.MinimizeBox = False
    Me.Text = "Font Settings"

End Sub
```

The form's load event initializes all the controls on the form. It uses the
`InstalledFontsCollection` class to load the font-family list box (`listBoxFamilies`). The
font styles are loaded from the `FontStyle` enumeration member names using a method from
the `Reflection` classes. The size list box values are hard-coded from an array on the form
load.

Last, we set the selected items for each list box to be that of the application's default values.
Notepad actually stores these user-configurable values between each use. We will leave this
code up to you—perhaps you could create an XML file for these settings. FontPad's default
settings are stored in global variables.

```
Private Sub formFontSettings_Load(ByVal sender As System.Object, _
        ByVal e As System.EventArgs) Handles MyBase.Load

    'purpose:   init. the controls on the form

    'declare variables of local scope
    Dim myFonts As System.Drawing.Text.InstalledFontCollection
    Dim i As Integer
    Dim myType As System.Type
    Dim myStyle As FontStyle
    Dim myArray() As String

    'return the collection of installed fonts
    myFonts = New System.Drawing.Text.InstalledFontCollection()

    'loop through the font families and add to the list box
    For i = 1 To UBound(myFonts.Families)
      listBoxFamilies().Items.Add(myFonts.Families(i).Name)
    Next

    'get a type object based on the font style enumeration
    myType = myStyle.GetType()

    'fill an array with the font style member names
    myArray = myStyle.GetNames(myType)
```

Font, Text, and Printing Operations

CHAPTER 6

175

6

FONT, TEXT, AND
PRINTING
OPERATIONS

```
'loop through the array
For i = 0 To UBound(myArray)

    'fill the list box with the font styles
    listBoxStyles().Items.Add(myArray(i))

Next

'add basic font sizes
listBoxSizes().Items.Add("8")
listBoxSizes().Items.Add("10")
listBoxSizes().Items.Add("12")
listBoxSizes().Items.Add("14")
listBoxSizes().Items.Add("18")
listBoxSizes().Items.Add("24")
listBoxSizes().Items.Add("36")
listBoxSizes().Items.Add("48")
listBoxSizes().Items.Add("72")

'select the current settings in the lists
listBoxStyles().SelectedItem = g_FontStyle
listBoxFamilies().SelectedItem = g_FontFamily
listBoxSizes().SelectedItem = g_FontSize

End Sub
```

The next procedure, `SetSampleText`, is responsible for keeping the label control on the font settings form in synch with user selections. Each list box's index change event calls this subroutine. The code itself creates a `Font` instance from the values selected in the three list boxes and applies this object to the sample label's `Font` property.

```
Private Sub setSampleText()

    'purpose:   reset the sample label as a visual cue to users

    'local scope
    Dim font As Font
    Dim fontStyle As FontStyle
    Dim fontFamily As FontFamily
    Dim styleType As System.Type
    Dim fontFamilyName As String
    Dim fontSize As String
    Dim fontStyleName As String

    'get values from family list box
    If listBoxFamilies().SelectedIndex = -1 Then
```

```
    'nothing is selected: set to default
    fontFamilyName = g_FontFamily

Else

    'return selected item
    fontFamilyName = listBoxFamilies().SelectedItem.ToString

End If

'get values from size list box
If listBoxSizes().SelectedIndex = -1 Then

    'nothing is selected: set to default
    fontSize = g_FontSize

Else

    'return selected item
    fontSize = listBoxSizes().SelectedItem.ToString

End If

'get values from the style list box
If listBoxStyles().SelectedIndex = -1 Then

    'nothing is selected: set to default
    fontStyleName = g_FontStyle

Else

    'return selected item
    fontStyleName = listBoxStyles().SelectedItem.ToString

End If

'set a font style type
styleType = fontStyle.GetType

'create a font family object
fontFamily = New FontFamily(fontFamilyName)

'get a font style object (note: must turn off option strict)
fontStyle = fontStyle.Parse(enumType:=styleType, value:=fontStyleName)

'create a new font based on global values
font = New Font(family:=fontFamily, _
```

```
            emSize:=CSng(fontSize), _
            style:=fontStyle, _
            unit:=System.Drawing.GraphicsUnit.Point)

    'reset the font on the label control
    labelSample().Font = font

End Sub
```

When a user clicks the OK button, the global font values are updated and FontPad's
ResetRichTextBox procedure is called, thus applying the new settings.

```
Private Sub buttonOk_Click(ByVal sender As System.Object, _
    ByVal e As System.EventArgs) Handles buttonOk.Click

    'purpose:   respond to the user's request to apply the form's changes

    'reset the aplication's font settings from the list boxes
    g_FontFamily = listBoxFamilies().SelectedItem.ToString()
    g_FontSize = listBoxSizes().SelectedItem.ToString()
    g_FontStyle = listBoxStyles().SelectedItem.ToString()

    'apply the settings to the rich text box
    Call g_FontPad.resetRichTextBox()

    'close the dialog
    Me.Close()

End Sub
```

When a user clicks the Cancel button, the form simply closes without applying any changes.

```
Private Sub buttonCancel_Click(ByVal sender As System.Object, _
    ByVal e As System.EventArgs) Handles buttonCancel.Click

    'purpose:   respond to the user's request to cancel the form

    'close the font settings dialog
    Me.Close()

End Sub
```

The following are the change events for the various list boxes. Each simply makes a call to
SetSampleText to update the label control used as a visual cue.

```
Private Sub listBoxFamilies_SelectedIndexChanged( _
    ByVal sender As System.Object, _
    ByVal e As System.EventArgs) Handles listBoxFamilies.SelectedIndexChanged

    'purpose:   synch. the sample label with the selected item
```

```
    'call the sample update procedure
    Call setSampleText()

  End Sub

  Private Sub listBoxStyles_SelectedIndexChanged( _
      ByVal sender As System.Object, _
      ByVal e As System.EventArgs) Handles listBoxStyles.SelectedIndexChanged

    'purpose:    synch. the sample label with the selected item

    'call the sample update procedure
    Call setSampleText()

  End Sub

  Private Sub listBoxSizes_SelectedIndexChanged( _
      ByVal sender As System.Object, _
      ByVal e As System.EventArgs) Handles listBoxSizes.SelectedIndexChanged

    'purpose:    synch. the sample label with the selected item

    'call the sample update procedure
    Call setSampleText()

  End Sub

#End Region

End Class
```

FontPad Module

We use a standard module in the FontPad application to store global variables. Listing 6.4 represents our three font settings and a reference to the main FontPad form.

LISTING 6.4   FontPad Module

```
Module modFontPad

    'declare variables that have global scope & set the defaults
    Public g_FontFamily As String = "Courier New"
    Public g_FontStyle As String = "Regular"
    Public g_FontSize As String = "10"

    'used to maintain a reference to the main form
  Public g_FontPad As FormMain

End Module
```

Font, Text, and Printing Operations

CHAPTER 6

179

6

FONT, TEXT, AND
PRINTING
OPERATIONS

Printing

Previous to .NET, printing with Visual Basic involved either using the common print dialog control and/or the Win32 API. The former did not always provide enough flexibility and the later sapped the productivity level to which VB developers have become accustomed. System.Drawing.Printing to the rescue! This namespace provides us with a ton of flexibility while encapsulating the low-level stuff that can often bog down programmers.

Sending Output to the Printer

Printing in Windows involves a printer device context. The good news is that this context can be used the same way as any other device context. All the drawing functions presented in the following chapter, for instance, work the same way for printers as they do for display devices. This is one of the reasons you find the Printing namespace tucked under Drawing. This device independence is one of the powerful features that Windows provides. It is possible to render output to either the screen or the printer just by switching device contexts.

Typically, programmers execute the following basic steps when writing printing functionality using the .NET Class Library:

1. Create a new instance of the PrintDocument class from the System.Drawing.Printing namespace. This is the principal object used to control our printing operation.

   ```
   Dim printDocument As New System.Drawing.Printing.PrintDocument
   ```

2. Set properties of the PrintDocument class to describe how and where to print. Of course, in an actual application, we would not hard-code the printer's name but would query the system for the default printer instead.

   ```
   'tell the print document object the name of the printer
   printDocument.PrinterSettings.PrinterName = _
       "Epson Stylus COLOR 640 ESC/P 2"

   'set the page orientation to landscape
   printDocument.PrinterSettings.DefaultPageSettings.Landscape = False
   ```

3. Set an event handler to intercept calls from a delegate when a page is printed. We do this by telling PrintDocument that we want to intercept its PrintPage event. This ensures that the procedure PrintPage_handler will receive the PrintDocument's PrintPage event. This event gets fired for every page that needs to be printed.

   ```
   AddHandler printDocument.PrintPage, AddressOf Me.printPage_handler
   ```

4. Call the Print method to print the document and raise the print event.

   ```
   printDocument.Print()
   ```

5. Define an event handler routine to process the printing. Note: The handler's
`PrintPageEventArgs` passes the appropriate `Graphics` object used to send output to the
printer.

```
Private Sub printPage_handler(ByVal sender As Object, _
    ByVal ev As System.Drawing.Printing.PrintPageEventArgs)

    'draw the string to the printer device
    ev.Graphics.DrawString(s:="Hello World!", _
    font:= New Font("Arial", 10), brush:=Brushes.Black, _
    x:= ev.MarginBounds.Left, y:=ev.MarginBounds.Top, _
    format:=New StringFormat())

End Sub
```

Printer Configuration

The `Printing` namespace provides a number of enumerations that enable us to manage various
printer configuration settings. This section provides an overview of what is available. It is
arranged into a number of tables that describe the enumerations and their members.

Table 6.7 lists the `Duplex` enumeration members. This enables you to read and write the
printer's duplex setting. *Duplex*, in printing, describes how printers print on both sides of the
paper. This enumeration provides values for the `PrinterSettings` class's `Duplex` property. A
`PrinterSettings` instance is used to control how a printer is configured to send output.

TABLE 6.7   Duplex Enumeration Members

Member	Description
Default	Select the printer's default duplex setting.
Horizontal	Select double-sided, horizontal (landscape) printing.
Simplex	Select single-sided printing (do not use duplex functionality).
Vertical	Select double-sided, vertical (portrait) printing.

`PaperKind` refers to the physical type of paper loaded into the printer. The enumeration is used
by the `PaperSize` class for its `Kind` property. `PaperSize` itself is used by the `PrinterSettings`
class when specifying the `PaperSizes` property. The `PaperSizes` property is a collection of
`PaperSize` objects that indicate the various sizes of paper the given printer supports. Table 6.8
lists some of the key `PaperKind` members most commonly used in the United States.

TABLE 6.8 PaperKind Enumeration

Member	Description
Executive	Standard executive paper (7.5 in. by 10.5 in.)
Folio	Standard folio paper (8.5 in. by 13 in.)
Ledger	Standard ledger paper (17 in. by 11 in.)
Legal	Standard legal paper (8.5 in. by 14 in.)
Letter	Standard letter paper (8.5 in. by 11 in.)
Tabloid	Standard tabloid paper (11 in. by 17 in.)

Table 6.9 documents the PaperSourceKind enumeration members. Paper sources can be thought of as paper trays and the like on a physical printer. The enumeration is used by the PaperSource class for its Kind property. This property is used to both return and to set the source of the paper used when printing. PaperSource itself is used by the PrinterSettings class when specifying the PaperSources property. The PaperSources property is a collection of PaperSource objects that indicates the various paper sources a given printer supports. The most common setting is AutomaticFeed, which tells most printers that they should handle the source from where the paper comes.

TABLE 6.9 PaperSourceKind Enumeration Members

Member	Description
AutomaticFeed	Indicates that the source of the paper is automatically fed paper.
Cassette	Indicates that the source of the paper is a paper cassette.
Custom	Indicates that the source of the paper is a printer-specific paper source.
Envelope	Indicates that the source of the paper is an envelope.
FormSource	Indicates that the source of the paper is the printer's default input bin.
LargeCapacity	Indicates that the source of the paper is the printer's large-capacity bin.
LargeFormat	Indicates that the source of the paper is large-format paper.
Lower	Indicates that the source of the paper is the lower bin of a printer. Note: If the printer has only one bin, it will be used.
Manual	Indicates that the source of the paper is manually fed paper.
ManualFeed	Indicates that the source of the paper is manually fed envelopes.
Middle	Indicates that the source of the paper is the middle bin of a printer.
SmallFormat	Indicates that the source of the paper is small-format paper.
TractorFeed	Indicates that the source of the paper is a tractor feed.
Upper	Indicates that the source of the paper is the upper bin of a printer. Note: If the printer has only one bin, it will be used.

Table 6.10 lists the various printer resolution settings that are available to your applications. The PrinterResolutionKind enumeration members enable you to tell the printer to output documents based on some standard resolutions. The enumeration is used by the PrinterResoultion class for its Kind property. PrinterResoultion itself is used by the PrinterSettings class when specifying the PrinterResolutions property. The PrinterResolutions property is a collection of PrinterResolution objects that indicate the various resolutions supported by a given printer. These properties are handy when users want a quick version, or draft, of their documents for proofing, or a slower, but high-quality version for release.

TABLE 6.10   System.Printing *and* PrinterResolutionKind Enumeration Members

Member	Description
Custom	Specifies a custom printer resolution setting. If this is set to custom, use the *x* and *y* properties of the PrinterResolution class to determine the printer resolution in the horizontal and vertical directions, respectively.
Draft	Specifies the draft printer resolution setting.
High	Specifies the high printer resolution setting.
Low	Specifies the low printer resolution setting.
Medium	Specifies the medium printer resolution setting.

Table 6.11 lists the PrintRange enumeration members. The enumeration is used to represent the portions of the document that should be output to the printer. This enumeration is used by the PrinterSettings class to indicate the range that should be printed.

TABLE 6.11   System.Printing *and* PrintRange Enumeration Members

Member	Description
AllPages	Indicates that all pages in the document should be printed.
Selection	Indicates that only the selected pages in the document should be printed.
SomePages	Indicates that only some pages (those from *x* to *y*) in the document should be printed. If using this value, reference the PrinterSettings class, fromPage and toPage properties.

Previewing Documents Prior to Printing

Before sending documents to the printer, users often need to see how their output is going to look. This saves paper, ink, and time. For instance, Microsoft Word provides the print previewing functionality. .NET exposes two classes that enable developers to simulate this functionality. The PreviewPrintController class is a print controller that displays documents

Font, Text, and Printing Operations

CHAPTER 6

183

6

FONT, TEXT, AND
PRINTING
OPERATIONS

to the screen as a series of images. This class makes extensive use of the `PreviewPageInfo` class. The `PreviewPageInfo` class represents the print preview information of one specific page. The following is a step-by-step walkthrough of adding print preview capabilities to your application:

1. First, you declare a number of variables to represent the classes you will need.

```
Dim printDocument As System.Drawing.Printing.PrintDocument
Dim previewController As System.Drawing.Printing.PreviewPrintController
Dim pageInfoArray() As System.Drawing.Printing.PreviewPageInfo
Dim i As Integer
```

2. Next, create an instance of a `PrintDocument` class:

```
printDocument = New System.Drawing.Printing.PrintDocument()
```

3. Then, create an instance of the `PreviewPrintController` class.

```
previewController = New System.Drawing.Printing.PreviewPrintController()
```

4. Set the `PrintDocument` object's `PrintController` property to your `PreviewPrintController` object. This ensures that your output is sent to a set of images rather than to the printer.

```
printDocument.PrintController = previewController
```

5. Next, indicate an event handler for each page that is output. Note: The event handler can be identical to the one defined in the basic printing walkthrough. Perhaps one exception is that you might want to add the line `ev.Graphics.ScaleTransform(sx:=0.25,` `sy:=0.25)` to the `printPage_handler` routine. This code scales the output of the `Graphics` object by 25%, which makes viewing print images a little easier.

```
AddHandler printDocument.PrintPage, AddressOf Me.printPage_handler
```

6. Now call the Print method of the `PrintDocument` instance. This raises a call to the event handler and forces the printed content into the preview print controller.

```
printDocument.Print()
```

7. All that is left is to view the preview images. After the document is finished printing, the `PreviewPrintController` instance that you set as the target of the print output is filled with a collection of `PreviewPageInfo` objects. There is one item in the collection per printed page. Return the images by calling the `GetPreviewPageInfo` method of the `PreviewPrintController` object. You can then loop through the array and output each image into a picture box defined on a form.

```
'return an array of PreviewPageInfo objects from the print controller
pageInfoArray = previewController.GetPreviewPageInfo()

'loop through the array and display each image
For i = 0 To UBound(pageInfoArray)
    Me.pictureBoxPreview.Image = pageInfoArray(i).Image
Next
```

Learning by Example: Adding Printing Capabilities to FontPad

In this example, we extend the FontPad application that we created in the previous section to include printing functionality. We do so by adding a Page Setup form that allows users to indicate things such as page size and orientation. We then create a simple Print Dialog form that enables users to indicate which printer they want to use and what pages they want printed.

Key Concepts Covered

The following represents the key class and concepts demonstrated with this sample application:

- Setting and enforcing margins on a printed page
- Using the `PrintDocument` class to output text to the printer
- Using the `PaperSizes` and `PaperSources` properties of the `PrinterSettings` class to return the sizes and sources that a given printer supports
- Printing a stream of text using the `System.IO.StringReader` class

Main Form Changes

The main form is identical to Figure 6.1 except that we now add two new menu items: Page Setup and Print.

Code Walkthrough

The additional code behind each new menu item's click event is in Listing 6.5.

LISTING 6.5   FontPad Main Form (moduleFontSample.vb) Changes

When the user clicks Print, Page Setup, we display the Page Setup dialog box to him.

```
Private Sub menuItemPageSetup_Click(ByVal sender As System.Object, _
  ByVal e As System.EventArgs) Handles menuItemPageSetup.Click

  'purpose: display the page setup dialog

  'local scope
  Dim dialogPageSetup As PageSetup

  'create new page setup form
  dialogPageSetup = New PageSetup()

  'set the start position of the modal dialog to the center
  '  positions of its parent
```

Font, Text, and Printing Operations

CHAPTER 6

185

6

FONT, TEXT, AND
PRINTING
OPERATIONS

LISTING 6.5 Continued

```
dialogPageSetup.StartPosition = FormStartPosition.CenterParent

'show the form as modal dialog
dialogPageSetup.ShowDialog(Me)

End Sub
```

When the user fires the `menuItemPrint_Click` event, we get the text from the `RichTextBox` control (`printString = Me.richTextBox.Text`). This gives us a text string to load into the `StreamReader` class. The StreamReader will be used when we actually send output to the printer. Of course, we then show the dialog box to the user.

```
Private Sub menuItemPrint_Click(ByVal sender As System.Object, _
    ByVal e As System.EventArgs) Handles menuItemPrint.Click

    'purpose: display the print dialog

    'local scope
    Dim dialogPrint As Print

    'set the contents of what to print
    printString = Me.richTextBox.Text

    'create new print form
    dialogPrint = New Print()

    'set the start position of the modal dialog to the center
    '  positions of its parent
    dialogPrint.StartPosition = FormStartPosition.CenterParent

    'show the form as modal dialog
    dialogPrint.ShowDialog(Me)

End Sub
```

Page Setup

The Page Setup dialog box enables users to select the paper size, the printer's paper source, the page orientation, and the page margins. Figure 6.3 shows the Page Setup dialog box. Note its similarities to Notepad's Page Setup dialog box.

FIGURE 6.3

FontPad: Page Setup form (formPageSetup.vb).

Code Walkthrough

The code behind the Page Setup form can be read in Listing 6.6.

LISTING 6.6   Page Setup Form

The code starts by setting up and defining the form and the controls it contains.

```
Public Class PageSetup
  Inherits System.Windows.Forms.Form

#Region " Windows Form Designer generated code "

  Public Sub New()
    MyBase.New()

    'This call is required by the Windows Form Designer.
    InitializeComponent()

    'Add any initialization after the InitializeComponent() call

  End Sub


  'Form overrides dispose to clean up the component list.
  Protected Overloads Overrides Sub Dispose(ByVal disposing As Boolean)
    If disposing Then
      If Not (components Is Nothing) Then
        components.Dispose()
      End If
    End If
    MyBase.Dispose(disposing)
  End Sub
```

Font, Text, and Printing Operations

CHAPTER 6

187

6

FONT, TEXT, AND
PRINTING
OPERATIONS

LISTING 6.6 Continued

```vbnet
Private WithEvents groupBox2 As System.Windows.Forms.GroupBox
Private WithEvents groupBox3 As System.Windows.Forms.GroupBox
Private WithEvents groupBox1 As System.Windows.Forms.GroupBox
Private WithEvents textBoxBottom As System.Windows.Forms.TextBox
Private WithEvents comboBoxSize As System.Windows.Forms.ComboBox
Private WithEvents buttonCancel As System.Windows.Forms.Button
Private WithEvents label4 As System.Windows.Forms.Label
Private WithEvents label5 As System.Windows.Forms.Label
Private WithEvents label6 As System.Windows.Forms.Label
Private WithEvents label7 As System.Windows.Forms.Label
Private WithEvents textBoxRight As System.Windows.Forms.TextBox
Private WithEvents label1 As System.Windows.Forms.Label
Private WithEvents label2 As System.Windows.Forms.Label
Private WithEvents label3 As System.Windows.Forms.Label
Private WithEvents textBoxTop As System.Windows.Forms.TextBox
Private WithEvents comboBoxSource As System.Windows.Forms.ComboBox
Private WithEvents buttonOk As System.Windows.Forms.Button
Private WithEvents textBoxLeft As System.Windows.Forms.TextBox
Private WithEvents radioButton1 As System.Windows.Forms.RadioButton
Private WithEvents radioButton2 As System.Windows.Forms.RadioButton
Private WithEvents radioButtonLandscape As System.Windows.Forms.RadioButton
Private WithEvents radioButtonPortrait As System.Windows.Forms.RadioButton

'Required by the Windows Form Designer
Private components As System.ComponentModel.Container

'NOTE: The following procedure is required by the Windows Form Designer
'It can be modified using the Windows Form Designer.
'Do not modify it using the code editor.
<System.Diagnostics.DebuggerStepThrough()> Private Sub InitializeComponent()
  Me.groupBox1 = New System.Windows.Forms.GroupBox()
  Me.comboBoxSource = New System.Windows.Forms.ComboBox()
  Me.comboBoxSize = New System.Windows.Forms.ComboBox()
  Me.label3 = New System.Windows.Forms.Label()
  Me.label2 = New System.Windows.Forms.Label()
  Me.label1 = New System.Windows.Forms.Label()
  Me.groupBox2 = New System.Windows.Forms.GroupBox()
  Me.radioButtonLandscape = New System.Windows.Forms.RadioButton()
  Me.radioButtonPortrait = New System.Windows.Forms.RadioButton()
  Me.groupBox3 = New System.Windows.Forms.GroupBox()
  Me.textBoxBottom = New System.Windows.Forms.TextBox()
  Me.textBoxRight = New System.Windows.Forms.TextBox()
  Me.textBoxTop = New System.Windows.Forms.TextBox()
  Me.textBoxLeft = New System.Windows.Forms.TextBox()
  Me.label7 = New System.Windows.Forms.Label()
```

LISTING 6.6   Continued

```
Me.label6 = New System.Windows.Forms.Label()
Me.label5 = New System.Windows.Forms.Label()
Me.label4 = New System.Windows.Forms.Label()
Me.buttonCancel = New System.Windows.Forms.Button()
Me.buttonOk = New System.Windows.Forms.Button()
Me.groupBox1.SuspendLayout()
Me.groupBox2.SuspendLayout()
Me.groupBox3.SuspendLayout()
Me.SuspendLayout()
'
'groupBox1
'
Me.groupBox1.Controls.AddRange(New System.Windows.Forms.Control() _
  {Me.comboBoxSource, Me.comboBoxSize, Me.label3, Me.label2, Me.label1})
Me.groupBox1.Location = New System.Drawing.Point(12, 12)
Me.groupBox1.Name = "groupBox1"
Me.groupBox1.Size = New System.Drawing.Size(344, 84)
Me.groupBox1.TabIndex = 0
Me.groupBox1.TabStop = False
Me.groupBox1.Text = "Paper"
'
'comboBoxSource
'
Me.comboBoxSource.DropDownWidth = 276
Me.comboBoxSource.Location = New System.Drawing.Point(60, 52)
Me.comboBoxSource.Name = "comboBoxSource"
Me.comboBoxSource.Size = New System.Drawing.Size(276, 21)
Me.comboBoxSource.TabIndex = 1
'
'comboBoxSize
'
Me.comboBoxSize.DropDownWidth = 276
Me.comboBoxSize.Location = New System.Drawing.Point(60, 20)
Me.comboBoxSize.Name = "comboBoxSize"
Me.comboBoxSize.Size = New System.Drawing.Size(276, 21)
Me.comboBoxSize.TabIndex = 0
'
'label3
'
Me.label3.Location = New System.Drawing.Point(12, 56)
Me.label3.Name = "label3"
Me.label3.TabIndex = 2
Me.label3.Text = "Source"
'
'label2
'
```

Font, Text, and Printing Operations

CHAPTER 6

189

6

FONT, TEXT, AND
PRINTING
OPERATIONS

LISTING 6.6 Continued

```vb
Me.label2.Location = New System.Drawing.Point(4, 76)
Me.label2.Name = "label2"
Me.label2.Size = New System.Drawing.Size(4, 0)
Me.label2.TabIndex = 1
Me.label2.Text = "label2"
'
'label1
'
Me.label1.Location = New System.Drawing.Point(12, 24)
Me.label1.Name = "label1"
Me.label1.TabIndex = 0
Me.label1.Text = "Size"
'
'groupBox2
'
Me.groupBox2.Controls.AddRange(New System.Windows.Forms.Control() _
   {Me.radioButtonLandscape, Me.radioButtonPortrait})
Me.groupBox2.Location = New System.Drawing.Point(12, 108)
Me.groupBox2.Name = "groupBox2"
Me.groupBox2.Size = New System.Drawing.Size(108, 80)
Me.groupBox2.TabIndex = 1
Me.groupBox2.TabStop = False
Me.groupBox2.Text = "Orientation"
'
'radioButtonLandscape
'
Me.radioButtonLandscape.Location = New System.Drawing.Point(12, 48)
Me.radioButtonLandscape.Name = "radioButtonLandscape"
Me.radioButtonLandscape.Size = New System.Drawing.Size(80, 24)
Me.radioButtonLandscape.TabIndex = 1
Me.radioButtonLandscape.Text = "Landscape"
'
'radioButtonPortrait
'
Me.radioButtonPortrait.Location = New System.Drawing.Point(12, 24)
Me.radioButtonPortrait.Name = "radioButtonPortrait"
Me.radioButtonPortrait.Size = New System.Drawing.Size(60, 24)
Me.radioButtonPortrait.TabIndex = 0
Me.radioButtonPortrait.Text = "Portrait"
'
'groupBox3
'
Me.groupBox3.Controls.AddRange(New System.Windows.Forms.Control() _
   {Me.textBoxBottom, Me.textBoxRight, Me.textBoxTop, Me.textBoxLeft, _
   Me.label7, Me.label6, Me.label5, Me.label4})
```

LISTING 6.6   Continued

```
Me.groupBox3.Location = New System.Drawing.Point(128, 108)
Me.groupBox3.Name = "groupBox3"
Me.groupBox3.Size = New System.Drawing.Size(228, 80)
Me.groupBox3.TabIndex = 2
Me.groupBox3.TabStop = False
Me.groupBox3.Text = "Margins (inches)"
'
'textBoxBottom
'
Me.textBoxBottom.Location = New System.Drawing.Point(156, 48)
Me.textBoxBottom.Name = "textBoxBottom"
Me.textBoxBottom.Size = New System.Drawing.Size(40, 20)
Me.textBoxBottom.TabIndex = 3
Me.textBoxBottom.Text = ""
'
'textBoxRight
'
Me.textBoxRight.Location = New System.Drawing.Point(156, 20)
Me.textBoxRight.Name = "textBoxRight"
Me.textBoxRight.Size = New System.Drawing.Size(40, 20)
Me.textBoxRight.TabIndex = 1
Me.textBoxRight.Text = ""
'
'textBoxTop
'
Me.textBoxTop.Location = New System.Drawing.Point(52, 48)
Me.textBoxTop.Name = "textBoxTop"
Me.textBoxTop.Size = New System.Drawing.Size(40, 20)
Me.textBoxTop.TabIndex = 2
Me.textBoxTop.Text = ""
'
'textBoxLeft
'
Me.textBoxLeft.Location = New System.Drawing.Point(52, 20)
Me.textBoxLeft.Name = "textBoxLeft"
Me.textBoxLeft.Size = New System.Drawing.Size(40, 20)
Me.textBoxLeft.TabIndex = 0
Me.textBoxLeft.Text = ""
'
'label7
'
Me.label7.Location = New System.Drawing.Point(112, 52)
Me.label7.Name = "label7"
Me.label7.TabIndex = 3
Me.label7.Text = "Bottom"
'
```

LISTING 6.6 Continued

```
'label6
'
Me.label6.Location = New System.Drawing.Point(112, 24)
Me.label6.Name = "label6"
Me.label6.TabIndex = 2
Me.label6.Text = "Right"
'
'label5
'
Me.label5.Location = New System.Drawing.Point(12, 52)
Me.label5.Name = "label5"
Me.label5.TabIndex = 1
Me.label5.Text = "Top"
'
'label4
'
Me.label4.Location = New System.Drawing.Point(12, 24)
Me.label4.Name = "label4"
Me.label4.TabIndex = 0
Me.label4.Text = "Left"
'
'buttonCancel
'
Me.buttonCancel.DialogResult = System.Windows.Forms.DialogResult.Cancel
Me.buttonCancel.Location = New System.Drawing.Point(280, 200)
Me.buttonCancel.Name = "buttonCancel"
Me.buttonCancel.TabIndex = 4
Me.buttonCancel.Text = "Cancel"
'
'buttonOk
'
Me.buttonOk.Location = New System.Drawing.Point(196, 200)
Me.buttonOk.Name = "buttonOk"
Me.buttonOk.TabIndex = 3
Me.buttonOk.Text = "OK"
'
'PageSetup
'
Me.AcceptButton = Me.buttonOk
Me.AutoScaleBaseSize = New System.Drawing.Size(5, 13)
Me.CancelButton = Me.buttonCancel
Me.ClientSize = New System.Drawing.Size(367, 236)
Me.Controls.AddRange(New System.Windows.Forms.Control() _
  {Me.buttonOk, Me.buttonCancel, Me.groupBox3, Me.groupBox2, Me.groupBox1})
Me.FormBorderStyle = System.Windows.Forms.FormBorderStyle.FixedDialog
```

LISTING 6.6 Continued

```
    Me.MaximizeBox = False
    Me.MinimizeBox = False
    Me.Name = "PageSetup"
    Me.Text = "FontPad: Page Setup"
    Me.groupBox1.ResumeLayout(False)
    Me.groupBox2.ResumeLayout(False)
    Me.groupBox3.ResumeLayout(False)
    Me.ResumeLayout(False)


 End Sub


#End Region
```

When users click the Cancel button, the form simply closes and no setup changes are made.

```
 Private Sub buttonCancel_Click(ByVal sender As System.Object, _
    ByVal e As System.EventArgs) Handles buttonCancel.Click

    'purpose: cancel the form without applying the changes

    'close the page setup dialog
    Me.Close()

 End Sub
```

Inside the OK button's click event, we simply store the user-selected form values to our global variables. This makes sure that these user-defined settings are available to us inside our Print dialog box.

```
 Private Sub buttonOk_Click(ByVal sender As System.Object, _
    ByVal e As System.EventArgs) Handles buttonOk.Click

    'purpose: reset the page setup values for the application

    'local scope
    Dim isValid As Boolean

    'validate the text box fields
    isValid = True
    If Not IsNumeric(textBoxBottom().Text) Then isValid = False
    If Not IsNumeric(textBoxTop().Text) Then isValid = False
    If Not IsNumeric(textBoxLeft().Text) Then isValid = False
    If Not IsNumeric(textBoxRight().Text) Then isValid = False

    'check if passed validation
```

```
   If isValid Then

      'set the global values

      'set paper size and paper source
      If comboBoxSize().SelectedIndex <> -1 Then
        paperSize = comboBoxSize().SelectedItem.ToString
      End If
      If comboBoxSource().SelectedIndex <> -1 Then
        paperSource = comboBoxSource().SelectedItem.ToString
      End If

      'set the page orientation value
      If radioButtonPortrait().Checked = True Then
        pageOrientation = "PORTRAIT"
      Else
        pageOrientation = "LANDSCAPE"
      End If

      'set margin values
      marginLeft = CSng(textBoxLeft().Text)
      marginTop = CSng(textBoxTop().Text)
      marginRight = CSng(textBoxRight().Text)
      marginBottom = CSng(textBoxBottom().Text)

      'close the form
      Me.Close()

   Else

      'of course we can do better than this ...
      Beep()

   End If

End Sub
```

Inside the form's load event, we select the user's current default settings. These variables are declared in a global module. Among the settings is the user's default printer. Inside this event, we create a PrintDocument instance and set it to this printer. We then enumerate the PaperSizes and PaperSources collections, adding their values to the associated combo boxes. This ensures that the paper size and source is relevant to the current printer and allows users to select appropriate values.

```
Private Sub PageSetup_Load(ByVal sender As System.Object, _
   ByVal e As System.EventArgs) Handles MyBase.Load
```

```
'purpose:   load the form and init. the control values

'local scope
Dim printDocument As System.Drawing.Printing.PrintDocument
Dim i As Integer
Dim paperSizes As _
    System.Drawing.Printing.PrinterSettings.PaperSizeCollection
Dim paperSources As _
    System.Drawing.Printing.PrinterSettings.PaperSourceCollection

'create a new print document
printDocument = New System.Drawing.Printing.PrintDocument()

'set margin values
textBoxBottom().Text = CStr(marginBottom)
textBoxTop().Text = CStr(marginTop)
textBoxLeft().Text = CStr(marginLeft)
textBoxRight().Text = CStr(marginRight)

'set the page orientation values
Select Case pageOrientation

  Case "PORTRAIT"
    radioButtonPortrait().Checked = True

  Case Else
    radioButtonLandscape().Checked = True

End Select

'tell the print document object the name of the selected printer
printDocument.PrinterSettings.PrinterName = printerDefault

'set paper sizes
paperSizes = printDocument.PrinterSettings.PaperSizes
For i = 0 To paperSizes.Count - 1

  'add the paper sizes to the combo box
  comboBoxSize().Items.Add(paperSizes.Item(i).PaperName)

Next

'set the paper sources
paperSources = printDocument.PrinterSettings.PaperSources
For i = 0 To paperSources.Count - 1
```

Font, Text, and Printing Operations

CHAPTER 6

195

6

FONT, TEXT, AND
PRINTING
OPERATIONS

```
        'add the paper sizes to the combo box
        comboBoxSource().Items.Add(paperSources.Item(i).SourceName)

    Next

    'select the user settings
    comboBoxSize().SelectedItem = paperSize
    comboBoxSource().SelectedItem = paperSource

    'close objects
    printDocument.Dispose()

    End Sub

End Class
```

Print Dialog Box

The Print dialog box for FontPad enables users to select an installed printer, set the print range, the number of copies, and whether to collate the output. Figure 6.4 shows the Print dialog box.

FIGURE 6.4
FontPad: Print form (formPrint.vb).

Code Walkthrough

The code behind the print form is similar to our print example earlier in the chapter. Listing 6.7 provides the code for you to reference.

LISTING 6.7   Print Form (formPrint.vb)

The code starts by setting up the form and its associated controls. Note that we declare an instance of the `PrintDocument` class and the `StringReader` class at the form level. This enables us to use these objects from within all the procedures in the form module.

LISTING 6.7   Continued

The StringReader class is part of the System.IO namespace, and is discussed in Chapter 7, "Stream and File Operations." It provides us with a version of a stream object that is based on a string. We populate this with our RichTextBox contents (printString) and output it line-by-line to the printer.

```
Public Class Print
  Inherits System.Windows.Forms.Form

#Region " Windows Form Designer generated code "

  Public Sub New()
    MyBase.New()

    'This call is required by the Windows Form Designer.
    InitializeComponent()

    'Add any initialization after the InitializeComponent() call

  End Sub

  'Form overrides dispose to clean up the component list.
  Protected Overloads Overrides Sub Dispose(ByVal disposing As Boolean)
    If disposing Then
      If Not (components Is Nothing) Then
        components.Dispose()
      End If
    End If
    MyBase.Dispose(disposing)
  End Sub

  Private WithEvents textBoxFrom As System.Windows.Forms.TextBox
  Private WithEvents label8 As System.Windows.Forms.Label
  Private WithEvents buttonCancel As System.Windows.Forms.Button
  Private WithEvents label1 As System.Windows.Forms.Label
  Private WithEvents label2 As System.Windows.Forms.Label
  Private WithEvents radioButtonAll As System.Windows.Forms.RadioButton
  Private WithEvents label11 As System.Windows.Forms.Label
  Private WithEvents buttonOk As System.Windows.Forms.Button
  Private WithEvents groupBox1 As System.Windows.Forms.GroupBox
  Private WithEvents groupBox2 As System.Windows.Forms.GroupBox
  Private WithEvents groupBox3 As System.Windows.Forms.GroupBox
  Private WithEvents comboBoxPrinterName As System.Windows.Forms.ComboBox
  Private WithEvents radioButtonSelection As System.Windows.Forms.RadioButton
  Private WithEvents textBoxTo As System.Windows.Forms.TextBox
  Private WithEvents radioButtonPages As System.Windows.Forms.RadioButton
```

LISTING 6.7 Continued

```
Private WithEvents numericUpDownCopies As System.Windows.Forms.NumericUpDown
Private WithEvents labelStatus As System.Windows.Forms.Label
Private WithEvents labelTo As System.Windows.Forms.Label
Private WithEvents labelFrom As System.Windows.Forms.Label
Private WithEvents checkBoxCollate As System.Windows.Forms.CheckBox
Private WithEvents labelColor As System.Windows.Forms.Label

'Required by the Windows Form Designer
Private components As System.ComponentModel.Container

'NOTE: The following procedure is required by the Windows Form Designer
'It can be modified using the Windows Form Designer.
'Do not modify it using the code editor.
<System.Diagnostics.DebuggerStepThrough()> Private Sub InitializeComponent()
  Me.labelFrom = New System.Windows.Forms.Label()
  Me.radioButtonPages = New System.Windows.Forms.RadioButton()
  Me.radioButtonAll = New System.Windows.Forms.RadioButton()
  Me.label11 = New System.Windows.Forms.Label()
  Me.textBoxTo = New System.Windows.Forms.TextBox()
  Me.labelColor = New System.Windows.Forms.Label()
  Me.buttonCancel = New System.Windows.Forms.Button()
  Me.buttonOk = New System.Windows.Forms.Button()
  Me.checkBoxCollate = New System.Windows.Forms.CheckBox()
  Me.groupBox1 = New System.Windows.Forms.GroupBox()
  Me.comboBoxPrinterName = New System.Windows.Forms.ComboBox()
  Me.label2 = New System.Windows.Forms.Label()
  Me.label1 = New System.Windows.Forms.Label()
  Me.groupBox2 = New System.Windows.Forms.GroupBox()
  Me.textBoxFrom = New System.Windows.Forms.TextBox()
  Me.labelTo = New System.Windows.Forms.Label()
  Me.label8 = New System.Windows.Forms.Label()
  Me.groupBox3 = New System.Windows.Forms.GroupBox()
  Me.numericUpDownCopies = New System.Windows.Forms.NumericUpDown()
  Me.groupBox1.SuspendLayout()
  Me.groupBox2.SuspendLayout()
  Me.groupBox3.SuspendLayout()
  CType(Me.numericUpDownCopies, _
    System.ComponentModel.ISupportInitialize).BeginInit()
  Me.SuspendLayout()
  '
  'labelFrom
  '
  Me.labelFrom.Location = New System.Drawing.Point(76, 64)
  Me.labelFrom.Name = "labelFrom"
  Me.labelFrom.Size = New System.Drawing.Size(40, 23)
```

LISTING 6.7 Continued

```
Me.labelFrom.TabIndex = 5
Me.labelFrom.Text = "from"
'
'radioButtonPages
'
Me.radioButtonPages.Location = New System.Drawing.Point(12, 56)
Me.radioButtonPages.Name = "radioButtonPages"
Me.radioButtonPages.TabIndex = 1
Me.radioButtonPages.Text = "Pages"
'
'radioButtonAll
'
Me.radioButtonAll.Checked = True
Me.radioButtonAll.Location = New System.Drawing.Point(12, 24)
Me.radioButtonAll.Name = "radioButtonAll"
Me.radioButtonAll.TabIndex = 0
Me.radioButtonAll.TabStop = True
Me.radioButtonAll.Text = "All"
'
'label11
'
Me.label11.Location = New System.Drawing.Point(12, 24)
Me.label11.Name = "label11"
Me.label11.TabIndex = 0
Me.label11.Text = "Number of copies"
'
'textBoxTo
'
Me.textBoxTo.Location = New System.Drawing.Point(172, 60)
Me.textBoxTo.Name = "textBoxTo"
Me.textBoxTo.Size = New System.Drawing.Size(40, 20)
Me.textBoxTo.TabIndex = 6
Me.textBoxTo.Text = ""
'
'labelColor
'
Me.labelColor.Location = New System.Drawing.Point(112, 48)
Me.labelColor.Name = "labelColor"
Me.labelColor.Size = New System.Drawing.Size(244, 23)
Me.labelColor.TabIndex = 4
'
'buttonCancel
'
Me.buttonCancel.DialogResult = System.Windows.Forms.DialogResult.Cancel
Me.buttonCancel.Location = New System.Drawing.Point(296, 220)
```

Font, Text, and Printing Operations

CHAPTER 6

199

6

FONT, TEXT, AND
PRINTING
OPERATIONS

LISTING 6.7 Continued

```
Me.buttonCancel.Name = "buttonCancel"
Me.buttonCancel.TabIndex = 0
Me.buttonCancel.Text = "Cancel"
'
'buttonOk
'
Me.buttonOk.Location = New System.Drawing.Point(212, 220)
Me.buttonOk.Name = "buttonOk"
Me.buttonOk.TabIndex = 1
Me.buttonOk.Text = "OK"
'
'checkBoxCollate
'
Me.checkBoxCollate.Checked = True
Me.checkBoxCollate.CheckState = System.Windows.Forms.CheckState.Checked
Me.checkBoxCollate.Location = New System.Drawing.Point(12, 80)
Me.checkBoxCollate.Name = "checkBoxCollate"
Me.checkBoxCollate.TabIndex = 2
Me.checkBoxCollate.Text = "Collate"
'
'groupBox1
'
Me.groupBox1.Controls.AddRange(New System.Windows.Forms.Control() _
  {Me.comboBoxPrinterName, Me.labelColor, Me.label2, Me.label1})
Me.groupBox1.Location = New System.Drawing.Point(8, 8)
Me.groupBox1.Name = "groupBox1"
Me.groupBox1.Size = New System.Drawing.Size(364, 76)
Me.groupBox1.TabIndex = 2
Me.groupBox1.TabStop = False
Me.groupBox1.Text = "Printer"
'
'comboBoxPrinterName
'
Me.comboBoxPrinterName.DropDownWidth = 304
Me.comboBoxPrinterName.Location = New System.Drawing.Point(52, 20)
Me.comboBoxPrinterName.Name = "comboBoxPrinterName"
Me.comboBoxPrinterName.Size = New System.Drawing.Size(304, 21)
Me.comboBoxPrinterName.TabIndex = 7
'
'label2
'
Me.label2.Location = New System.Drawing.Point(12, 48)
Me.label2.Name = "label2"
Me.label2.TabIndex = 1
Me.label2.Text = "Supports Color:"
'
```

LISTING 6.7   Continued

```
'label1
'
Me.label1.Location = New System.Drawing.Point(12, 24)
Me.label1.Name = "label1"
Me.label1.TabIndex = 0
Me.label1.Text = "Name"
'
'groupBox2
'
Me.groupBox2.Controls.AddRange(New System.Windows.Forms.Control() _
  {Me.textBoxFrom, Me.labelFrom, Me.textBoxTo, Me.labelTo, _
  Me.label8, Me.radioButtonPages, Me.radioButtonAll})
Me.groupBox2.Location = New System.Drawing.Point(8, 92)
Me.groupBox2.Name = "groupBox2"
Me.groupBox2.Size = New System.Drawing.Size(220, 120)
Me.groupBox2.TabIndex = 3
Me.groupBox2.TabStop = False
Me.groupBox2.Text = "Print Range"
'
'textBoxFrom
'
Me.textBoxFrom.Location = New System.Drawing.Point(108, 60)
Me.textBoxFrom.Name = "textBoxFrom"
Me.textBoxFrom.Size = New System.Drawing.Size(40, 20)
Me.textBoxFrom.TabIndex = 7
Me.textBoxFrom.Text = ""
'
'labelTo
'
Me.labelTo.Location = New System.Drawing.Point(152, 64)
Me.labelTo.Name = "labelTo"
Me.labelTo.Size = New System.Drawing.Size(20, 23)
Me.labelTo.TabIndex = 4
Me.labelTo.Text = "to"
'
'label8
'
Me.label8.Location = New System.Drawing.Point(116, 60)
Me.label8.Name = "label8"
Me.label8.Size = New System.Drawing.Size(4, 0)
Me.label8.TabIndex = 3
Me.label8.Text = "label8"
'
'groupBox3
'
```

LISTING 6.7   Continued

```vbnet
    Me.groupBox3.Controls.AddRange(New System.Windows.Forms.Control() _
        {Me.checkBoxCollate, Me.numericUpDownCopies, Me.label11})
    Me.groupBox3.Location = New System.Drawing.Point(236, 92)
    Me.groupBox3.Name = "groupBox3"
    Me.groupBox3.Size = New System.Drawing.Size(136, 120)
    Me.groupBox3.TabIndex = 4
    Me.groupBox3.TabStop = False
    Me.groupBox3.Text = "Copies"
    '
    'numericUpDownCopies
    '
    Me.numericUpDownCopies.Location = New System.Drawing.Point(12, 48)
    Me.numericUpDownCopies.Maximum = New Decimal(New Integer() {99, 0, 0, 0})
    Me.numericUpDownCopies.Minimum = New Decimal(New Integer() {1, 0, 0, 0})
    Me.numericUpDownCopies.Name = "numericUpDownCopies"
    Me.numericUpDownCopies.Size = New System.Drawing.Size(44, 20)
    Me.numericUpDownCopies.TabIndex = 1
    Me.numericUpDownCopies.Value = New Decimal(New Integer() {1, 0, 0, 0})
    '
    'Print
    '
    Me.AcceptButton = Me.buttonOk
    Me.AutoScaleBaseSize = New System.Drawing.Size(5, 13)
    Me.CancelButton = Me.buttonCancel
    Me.ClientSize = New System.Drawing.Size(389, 258)
    Me.Controls.AddRange(New System.Windows.Forms.Control() _
        {Me.groupBox3, Me.groupBox2, Me.groupBox1, Me.buttonOk, Me.buttonCancel})
    Me.FormBorderStyle = System.Windows.Forms.FormBorderStyle.FixedDialog
    Me.MaximizeBox = False
    Me.MinimizeBox = False
    Me.Name = "Print"
    Me.Text = "FontPad: Print"
    Me.groupBox1.ResumeLayout(False)
    Me.groupBox2.ResumeLayout(False)
    Me.groupBox3.ResumeLayout(False)
    CType(Me.numericUpDownCopies, _
        System.ComponentModel.ISupportInitialize).EndInit()
    Me.ResumeLayout(False)

End Sub

#End Region

    'form-level scope
    Private printDocument As New System.Drawing.Printing.printDocument()
    Private printStream As System.IO.StringReader
```

Inside the load event of the print form, we load a combo box with all the installed printers on the system. This is done with the `PrintDocument.InstalledPrinters` collection. We then set the selected printer in the combo box to the user's default settings as stored in our application-wide variable `printerDefault`.

```
Private Sub Print_Load(ByVal sender As System.Object, _
   ByVal e As System.EventArgs) Handles MyBase.Load

   'purpose:   load the form, init. the controls

   'local scope
   Dim i As Integer

   'use the printDocument object to return all installed printers
   '  loop through the list
   For i = 0 To printDocument.PrinterSettings.InstalledPrinters.Count - 1

     'set the printer combo box to all installed printers
     comboBoxPrinterName().Items.Add( _
        printDocument.PrinterSettings.InstalledPrinters.Item(i).ToString())

   Next

   'select the default printer in the list
   comboBoxPrinterName().SelectedItem = printerDefault

End Sub
```

When users click the Cancel button, we simply unload the form and do not send output to the printer.

```
Private Sub buttonCancel_Click(ByVal sender As System.Object, _
   ByVal e As System.EventArgs) Handles buttonCancel.Click

   'purpose:   cancel the dialog without applying changes

   'close the form
   Me.Close()

End Sub
```

When a user clicks the form's OK button, we start the printing process. First, we do some simple form-field validation. Then we call the `printText` procedure, passing the form's values as parameters. This gives us a slightly more generic print method that could be used elsewhere.

```
Private Sub buttonOk_Click(ByVal sender As System.Object, _
   ByVal e As System.EventArgs) Handles buttonOk.Click

   'purpose:   print the document based on settings
```

```
'local scope
Dim isValid As Boolean
Dim fromPage As Integer
Dim toPage As Integer

'validate text boxes
isValid = True

'validate the from text box
If textBoxFrom().Enabled = True Then

  If Not IsNumeric(textBoxFrom().Text) Then
    isValid = False
  Else
    'set the from page value
    fromPage = CInt(textBoxFrom().Text)
  End If

End If

'validate the to text box
If textBoxTo().Enabled = True Then

  If Not IsNumeric(textBoxTo().Text) Then
    isValid = False
  Else
    'set the to page value
    toPage = CInt(textBoxTo().Text)
  End If

End If

'check for valid range
If fromPage > toPage Then isValid = False

'check if valid input
If isValid Then

  'print the document
  Call printText(fromPage:=fromPage, _
      toPage:=toPage, _
      copiesToPrint:=numericUpDownCopies().Value, _
      isCollate:=checkBoxCollate().Checked)

  'close the form
```

```
   Me.Close()

  Else

    Beep()

  End If

End Sub
```

Inside the `PrintText` procedure, we control the printing process and set printer settings. We first create a new instance of the `StringReader` class and set its string constructor value to our `printString` value. Then we tell the `PrintDocument` object that we will handle its `PrintPage` event with our own procedure, `printPage_handler`.

The page ranges to print are then set.

Next, we create an instance of the `Margins` class based on the user's defined margin settings. Note that margin values are indicated in hundredths of an inch.

Then we set the orientation, paper size, paper source, number of copies, and collate properties of the `PrintDocument.PrinterSettings` object.

Finally, we call the `Print` method of the `PrintDocument` class. This will fire the `PrintPage` event (which we intercept) for every page that it needs to print.

```
Private Sub printText(ByVal fromPage As Integer, _
   ByVal toPage As Integer, _
   ByVal copiesToPrint As Integer, _
   ByVal isCollate As Boolean)

   'purpose:   print the contents of the rich text box to the selected printer

   'local scope
   Dim margins As System.Drawing.Printing.Margins
   Dim count As Integer

   'create a new instance of the string reader class
   '    contruct it based on the contents to print from the rich text box
   '    this value (printString) is set just before the print
   '      dialog is displayed
   printStream = New System.IO.StringReader(s:=printString)

   'intercept the print page event with our own handler
   AddHandler printDocument.PrintPage, _
       AddressOf Me.printPage_handler

   'set the range of pages to print
```

Font, Text, and Printing Operations

CHAPTER 6

205

6

FONT, TEXT, AND
PRINTING
OPERATIONS

```vb
If fromPage > 0 And toPage > 0 Then
   printDocument.PrinterSettings.FromPage = fromPage
   printDocument.PrinterSettings.ToPage = toPage
End If


'set the page margin values based on user settings (hundredth of an inch)
margins = New System.Drawing.Printing.Margins(Left:=(marginLeft * 100), _
    Right:=(marginRight * 100), Top:=(marginTop * 100), _
    Bottom:=(marginBottom * 100))
printDocument.DefaultPageSettings.Margins = margins

'set page orientation values based on user settings
If pageOrientation = "PORTRAIT" Then
   printDocument.DefaultPageSettings.Landscape = False
Else
   printDocument.DefaultPageSettings.Landscape = True
End If


'set the paper size to print from by looping through the paper
'    sizes collection, matching the paper size name that the
'      user has selected,
'    and setting the paperSize property of defaultPageSettings =
'    to the correct paperSize
For count = 0 To printDocument.PrinterSettings.PaperSizes.Count - 1
   If printDocument.PrinterSettings.PaperSizes.Item(count).PaperName = _
      paperSize Then

      printDocument.DefaultPageSettings.PaperSize = _
         printDocument.PrinterSettings.PaperSizes.Item(count)


      Exit For


   End If
Next

'set the paper source to print from by looping through
'    the paper sources collection,
'    matching the paper source name that the user has selected,
'    and setting the paperSource property of pageSettings =
'    to the correct paperSource
For count = 0 To printDocument.PrinterSettings.PaperSources.Count - 1
   If printDocument.PrinterSettings.PaperSources.Item(count).SourceName = _
      paperSource Then

      printDocument.DefaultPageSettings.PaperSource = _
         printDocument.PrinterSettings.PaperSources.Item(count)

      Exit For
```

```
      End If
    Next

    'set the number of copies to print
    printDocument.PrinterSettings.Copies = copiesToPrint

    'set the collate property
    printDocument.PrinterSettings.Collate = isCollate

    'print the document
    printDocument.Print()

    'close the connection to the text document
    printStream.Close()

End Sub
```

Within our custom print page event handler (printPage_handler), we first set the print font to that of the user's defined font setting for the application. Next, we start drawing lines to the printer, one at a time. We calculate the number of lines per page and begin looping through our count (linesPerPage). We use the StringReader instance (printStream) to read each line and the Graphics class DrawString method to output the string to the printer.

```
Private Sub printPage_handler(ByVal sender As Object, _
    ByVal ev As System.Drawing.Printing.PrintPageEventArgs)

    'purpose:    intercept and handle the printPage event
    '            of the PrintDocument object
    '            prints 1 page at a time

    'local scope
    Dim linesPerPage As Single = 0
    Dim yPos As Single = 0
    Dim count As Integer = 0
    Dim leftMargin As Single = ev.MarginBounds.Left
    Dim topMargin As Single = ev.MarginBounds.Top
    Dim line As String = ""
    Dim printFont As Font
    Dim fontStyle As FontStyle
    Dim fontFamily As FontFamily
    Dim styleType As System.Type

    'set a font style type
    styleType = fontStyle.GetType
```

Font, Text, and Printing Operations

CHAPTER 6

207

6

FONT, TEXT, AND
PRINTING
OPERATIONS

```
'create a font family object
fontFamily = New FontFamily(fontFamilySetting)

'get a font style object (note: must turn off option strict)
fontStyle = fontStyle.Parse(enumType:=styleType, value:=fontStyleSetting)

'create a new font object for the printer based on user selected font
'  set it to the user's selected font setting
printFont = New Font(family:=fontFamily, _
    emSize:=CSng(fontSizeSetting), _
    style:=fontStyle, _
    unit:=System.Drawing.GraphicsUnit.Point)

'calculate the number of lines per page
linesPerPage = ev.MarginBounds.Height / _
    printFont.GetHeight(ev.Graphics)

'iterate through the file, printing each line
count = 0
Do While count < linesPerPage

  'increment count variable
  count = count + 1

  'read a line of text from the file
  line = printStream.ReadLine

  'set y coordinate of the printing position
  yPos = topMargin + (count * printFont.GetHeight(ev.Graphics))

  'draw the string to the printer device
  ev.Graphics.DrawString(s:=line, Font:=printFont, _
      brush:=Brushes.Black, _
      x:=leftMargin, y:=yPos, _
      Format:=New StringFormat())

  'check for more pages to print
  'NOTE: need to figure out how to tell if at the end of the document
  If line <> "" Then
    ev.HasMorePages = True
  Else
    ev.HasMorePages = False
  End If

Loop

End Sub
```

The following are simply click events used to control our form operations:

```
Private Sub toggleRange(ByVal toggleValue As Boolean)

    'purpose:   enable from and to controls when user selects a range

    labelFrom().Enabled = toggleValue
    labelTo().Enabled = toggleValue
    textBoxFrom().Enabled = toggleValue
    textBoxTo().Enabled = toggleValue

End Sub

Private Sub radioButtonPages_CheckedChanged(ByVal sender As System.Object, _
    ByVal e As System.EventArgs) Handles radioButtonPages.CheckedChanged

    'purpose: enable related controls

    Call toggleRange(True)

End Sub

Private Sub radioButtonAll_CheckedChanged(ByVal sender As System.Object, _
    ByVal e As System.EventArgs) Handles radioButtonAll.CheckedChanged

    'purpose: disable related controls

    Call toggleRange(False)

End Sub

Private Sub comboBoxPrinterName_SelectedIndexChanged( _
    ByVal sender As System.Object, _
    ByVal e As System.EventArgs) Handles _
        comboBoxPrinterName.SelectedIndexChanged

    'tell the print document object the name of the selected printer
    printDocument.PrinterSettings.PrinterName = _
        comboBoxPrinterName().SelectedItem.ToString

    'set the information label to the printer settings
    labelColor().Text = CStr(printDocument.PrinterSettings.SupportsColor)

End Sub

End Class
```

FontPad Print Example Module Changes

The only changes that were made to FontPad's module code were additions to the global scope declarations. We added the page setup and the printer settings values. Listing 6.8 lists this code for your reference.

LISTING 6.8 FontPad Module (moduleFonts.vb)

```
Module modFontPad

    'purpose: declare variables that have global scope & set the defaults

    'font settings
    Public g_FontFamily As String = "Courier New"
    Public g_FontStyle As String = "Regular"
    Public g_FontSize As String = "10"

    'group of values used for the font settings dialog
    Public fontFamilySetting As String = "Courier New"
    Public fontStyleSetting As String = "Regular"
    Public fontSizeSetting As String = "10"

    'group of values used for the page setup dialog
    Public paperSize As String = "Letter"
    Public paperSource As String = "Automatically Select"
    Public pageOrientation As String = "PORTRAIT"
    Public marginLeft As Single = 0.75
    Public marginTop As Single = 0.75
    Public marginRight As Single = 1
    Public marginBottom As Single = 1

    'values for the print dialog
    Public printerDefault As String = "Epson Stylus COLOR 640 ESC/P 2"
    Public printString As String = ""

    'used to maintain a reference to the main form
    Public formFontPad As FormMain
```

Suggestions for Further Exploration

⟳ Extend the FontPad printing capabilities to include a Print Preview feature. Use the `PreviewPrintController` and `PreviewPageInfo` classes on the Page Setup dialog box to allow users to click through a visual representation of their printed document.

⟳ Print shapes and bitmaps to the printer using the various `Graphics` class methods as referenced in Chapter 9, "Drawing Functions."

Printing and Font-Related Controls and Dialog Boxes

The .NET namespaces (and VB .NET) would be lacking if they did not provide programmers with a solid set of controls and common dialog boxes. Although this material is beyond the scope of this book (as are the rest of the form controls), it is important that you be aware of their existence. All the classes defined by these controls and dialog boxes make use of the namespaces we've been discussing in this chapter.

Table 6.12 lists the various controls and dialog classes that are available for embedding into an application. The use of these controls is straightforward enough. Of course, now that you know how to use the classes from which these dialogs are derived, you'll be able to roll your own custom versions of these dialogs.

TABLE 6.12 `System.Windows.Forms` Printing-Related Controls

Member	Description
PrintDialog	The `PrintDialog` class enables programmers to easily create a form that gives users access to printer and print property selections.
PrintPreviewControl	The `PrintPreviewControl` class encapsulates the print previewing process without any dialog boxes.
PrintPreviewDialog	The `PrintPreviewDialog` class allows programmers to easily display print preview information to users of their application. The `PrintPreviewDialog` uses a `PrintPreviewControl`.
PageSetupDialog	The `PageSetupDialog` class enables you to create a dialog box that can be manipulated by users to modify page settings, margins, and paper orientation.
FontDialog	The `FontDialog` class gives you a form to display to users representing a list of fonts that are currently installed on a system. Users can select a font, size, and style.
FileDialog	The `FileDialog` class enables programmers to easily create a form that will allow users to navigate their machine and network in search of a file.

Summary

The items we've covered in this chapter represent the foundation for manipulating fonts and sending output to the printer with the .NET Class Library. From here you should be able to easily strengthen this foundation through your own explorations as you extend your knowledge into your own application development.

The following are key points to writing code for font, text, and printing functionality with the .NET Class Library:

- A font describes the way text appears on a device. Fonts can vary in size, weight, and style.
- The Font class encapsulates an individual font inside of .NET.
- The InstalledFontCollection class enables you to return all fonts installed on a given system.
- The PrivateFontsCollection class enables you to work with custom fonts without actually installing them on a system.
- The PrintDocument class is used to control output to a printer.
- To set and retrieve specific settings on a given printer, use the PrinterSettings class.
- The PreviewPrintController class provides a print controller that outputs printed pages as images that can be viewed prior to submission to the printer.

Stream and File Operations

IN THIS CHAPTER

One of the most important issues any programmer faces is how to go about storing and retrieving information on disk. This issue can be surprisingly complex. The .NET Base Class Library provides a number of classes that simplify the issue somewhat. The library is a substantial improvement over the file-related operations Visual Basic programmers had available to them previously.

This chapter focuses on the .NET namespaces related to directories, files, and synchronous and asynchronous reading from and writing to data streams. First, an overview is presented that details the key classes within the namespace. Then we get into files, streams, and data types. And finally, we write a file-monitoring application that demonstrates the use of these classes.

After reading this chapter, you should be able to do the following:

- Manage directories and files including creating, deleting, and accessing their property information
- Monitor the file system and respond to basic system events
- Read and write files as streams of data both synchronously and asynchronously
- Access file data at the binary level
- Understand some of the basic design considerations for choosing a file I/O strategy

Key Classes Related to File I/O

Every application, image, database, message, and document is stored as some form of a file. Directories and files are the warehouses and boxes of our applications. All our applications spend time interacting with the file system at some level. And most of our applications require us to read, write, or manipulate files and directories.

The .NET System.IO namespace provides us with a rich set of tools to write effective file I/O code in a productive manner. This namespace encapsulates functionality related to both synchronous and asynchronous reading and writing to files and streams. Table 7.1 presents the key classes contained in the namespaces. These classes represent those primarily used by developers when implementing features based on directories, files, and streams.

TABLE 7.1 Key Classes of the System.IO Namespace

Class	Description
	Managing Directories
Directory	The Directory class allows you to create, move, and enumerate directories and subdirectories. All of its methods are static and require a security check for each call. Consider the DirectoryInfo class if you plan to reuse the object and do not want the overhead of the security checks.

TABLE 7.1 Continued

Class	Description
Managing Directories	
DirectoryInfo	The DirectoryInfo class is similar to the Directory class but contains only instance methods. All objects created using this class reference a specific directory. As a result, a security check is performed only when the instance is created.
Path	The Path class allows you to process directory strings in a cross-platform manner.
Manipulating Files	
File	The File class allows you to write code to create, copy, delete, move, and open files. All its methods are static and thus perform a security check on every call. If you plan to reuse the File instance on a single file, use the instance class, FileInfo.
FileInfo	The FileInfo class is similar to the File, but like DirectoryInfo, provides instance methods.
Reading and Writing to Files and Streams	
FileStream	The FileStream class allows you to create a stream instance based on a file.
StreamReader	The StreamReader class implements a TextReader object that reads characters from a byte stream in a particular encoding.
StreamWriter	The StreamWriter class implements a TextWriter object for writing characters to a stream in a particular encoding.
StringReader	The StringReader class implements a TextReader object that reads from a string.
StringWriter	The StringWriter class implements a TextWriter object that writes information to a string. The information is stored in an underlying StringBuilder class (from the System.Text namespace).
BinaryReader	The BinaryReader class allows you to access file data at the binary level.
BinaryWriter	The BinaryWriter class allows you to write binary data out to files.
Monitoring File System Activity	
FileSystemWatcher	The FileSystemWatcher class allows you to listen to the file system change notifications and intercept events when a directory or file changes.

7

STREAM AND FILE
OPERATIONS

Directory and File Operations

In past versions of Visual Basic, we were relegated to the `FileSystemObject` (or a similar third-party control) or the Win32 API to implement most file operations. The `System.IO` namespace provides a robust set of objects for our tool belt. These objects can be leveraged to solve a host of problems and ease and simplify interaction with the file system.

As programmers, it is important for us to understand the key aspects of the Windows file system. A *file*, in Windows, is an ordered and named collection of a sequence of bytes having persistent storage. When you think of files, you think of a filename, file size, attributes, and directory path. *Directories* in Windows are simply another type of file that contains other files and subdirectories. This section illustrates how to interact with the Windows file system using the `System.IO` namespace.

Access and Attributes

To access directories and files using the .NET Class Library you work with two primary classes: `DirectoryInfo` and `FileInfo`. These classes are designed to provide most of the file system functionality and information that your applications need.

The `DirectoryInfo` and `Directory` classes are used to create, move, and enumerate through directories and subdirectories. The `Directory` class contains the associated static methods, while `DirectoryInfo` contains the instance methods. An instance of the `DirectoryInfo` class represents one physical directory. With it, you can call the `GetDirectories` method to return a list of the directory's subdirectories. You can also return a list of files in the directory with the `GetFiles` method. Of course, there are a number of other important properties and methods inside the `DirectoryInfo` class.

The `FileInfo` and `File` classes are used to create, copy, delete, move, and open files. The `File` class contains the associated static methods, where `FileInfo` contains the instance methods. Using an instance of the `FileInfo` class, you can return specific attributes of a given file. For example, you can read the file's name, size, and parent directory. The actual content of a file is accessed via the `FileStream` object. The `FileStream` class allows for both synchronous and asynchronous read and writes to a file.

To best illustrate the use of these classes, we will create a simple directory and file listing application. The application will read a list of directories, and for each directory, display a list of files contained by it. Additionally, for both the selected file and the selected directory, we will list a number of key attributes. Figure 7.1 illustrates the form that we will use to display the application's information. Of course, I use the term application loosely. This is just some sample code with an attached form.

FIGURE 7.1

Access and attributes form.

The code for the example is provided in Listing 7.1. It involves code to create the form, a form load event, and a pair of index change events for the two list boxes.

The code starts with a few global variable declarations to store a path, directory, and filename. This is followed by the basic form creation code.

LISTING 7.1 Access and Attributes

```
Public Class Form2
    Inherits System.Windows.Forms.Form

    'form-level scope declarations
    Dim myPath As String = "c:\"
    Dim myDirName As String
    Dim myFileName As String

#Region " Windows Form Designer generated code "

    Public Sub New()
        MyBase.New()

        'This call is required by the Windows Form Designer.
        InitializeComponent()

        'Add any initialization after the InitializeComponent() call
    End Sub

    'Form overrides dispose to clean up the component list.
```

LISTING 7.1 Continued

```
Public Overloads Overrides Sub Dispose()
    MyBase.Dispose()
    If Not (components Is Nothing) Then
        components.Dispose()
    End If
End Sub

Private WithEvents label1 As System.Windows.Forms.Label
Private WithEvents label2 As System.Windows.Forms.Label
Private WithEvents labelDirectoryInfo As System.Windows.Forms.Label
Private WithEvents listBoxFiles As System.Windows.Forms.ListBox
Private WithEvents labelFileInfo As System.Windows.Forms.Label
Private WithEvents listBoxDirectories As System.Windows.Forms.ListBox
Private WithEvents buttonClose As System.Windows.Forms.Button

'Required by the Windows Form Designer
Private components As System.ComponentModel.Container

'NOTE: The following procedure is required by the Windows Form Designer
'It can be modified using the Windows Form Designer.
'Do not modify it using the code editor.
<System.Diagnostics.DebuggerStepThrough()> Private Sub _
    InitializeComponent()
    Me.labelFileInfo = New System.Windows.Forms.Label()
    Me.listBoxFiles = New System.Windows.Forms.ListBox()
    Me.labelDirectoryInfo = New System.Windows.Forms.Label()
    Me.listBoxDirectories = New System.Windows.Forms.ListBox()
    Me.buttonClose = New System.Windows.Forms.Button()
    Me.label1 = New System.Windows.Forms.Label()
    Me.label2 = New System.Windows.Forms.Label()
    Me.labelFileInfo.BorderStyle = System.Windows.Forms.BorderStyle.Fixed3D
    Me.labelFileInfo.Location = New System.Drawing.Point(248, 216)
    Me.labelFileInfo.Size = New System.Drawing.Size(200, 160)
    Me.labelFileInfo.TabIndex = 4
    Me.labelFileInfo.Text = "label3"
    Me.listBoxFiles.Location = New System.Drawing.Point(8, 216)
    Me.listBoxFiles.Size = New System.Drawing.Size(232, 160)
    Me.listBoxFiles.TabIndex = 1
    Me.labelDirectoryInfo.BorderStyle = _
        System.Windows.Forms.BorderStyle.Fixed3D
    Me.labelDirectoryInfo.Location = New System.Drawing.Point(248, 24)
    Me.labelDirectoryInfo.Size = New System.Drawing.Size(200, 160)
    Me.labelDirectoryInfo.TabIndex = 4
    Me.labelDirectoryInfo.Text = "label3"
    Me.listBoxDirectories.Location = New System.Drawing.Point(8, 24)
```

LISTING 7.1   Continued

```
    Me.listBoxDirectories.Size = New System.Drawing.Size(232, 160)
    Me.listBoxDirectories.TabIndex = 0
    Me.buttonClose.Location = New System.Drawing.Point(376, 384)
    Me.buttonClose.TabIndex = 5
    Me.buttonClose.Text = "Close"
    Me.label1.Location = New System.Drawing.Point(8, 8)
    Me.label1.TabIndex = 2
    Me.label1.Text = "Directories"
    Me.label2.Location = New System.Drawing.Point(8, 200)
    Me.label2.TabIndex = 3
    Me.label2.Text = "Files"
    Me.AcceptButton = Me.buttonClose
    Me.AutoScaleBaseSize = New System.Drawing.Size(5, 13)
    Me.FormBorderStyle = System.Windows.Forms.FormBorderStyle.FixedDialog
    Me.ClientSize = New System.Drawing.Size(453, 410)
    Me.Controls.AddRange(New System.Windows.Forms.Control() _
        {Me.buttonClose, Me.labelFileInfo, Me.listBoxFiles, _
        Me.listBoxDirectories, Me.labelDirectoryInfo, Me.label2, _
        Me.label1})
    Me.Text = "Directory And Files"

End Sub
```

Inside the form's load event we return a list of directories. To do so, first we instantiate a DirectoryInfo class with the line

```
Dim myDirectory As New System.IO.DirectoryInfo(path:=myPath).
```

where myPath is a valid path (c:\). Next, we call the GetDirectories method of the DirectoryInfo class. This returns an array of DirectoryInfo objects that represent the path's subdirectories. Finally, we select an item in the directory list box. This fires the index-changed event of the directory list box.

```
Private Sub Form1_Load(ByVal sender As System.Object, _
        ByVal e As System.EventArgs) Handles MyBase.Load

    'purpose:   load the form, set the control values

    'local scope
    Dim myDirectories() As System.IO.DirectoryInfo
    Dim i As Integer

    'create a new directory object pointed at c:
    Dim myDirectory As New System.IO.DirectoryInfo(path:=myPath)
```

```
          'return the sub directories of c: from the global directory object
          myDirectories = myDirectory.GetDirectories()

          'loop through the directories and add them to the list box
          For i = 0 To UBound(myDirectories) - 1

              'add the directory name to the list
              listBoxDirectories().Items.Add(myDirectories(i).Name)

          Next

          'select the first directory in the list
          '   note: this will trigger the events that fill the label control
          '         and the files list box and its label control
          listBoxDirectories().SelectedIndex = 0

      End Sub
```

Once a user selects a directory, we must return to her a list of files. In our example, we do this inside the `listBoxDirectories` index change event (`listBoxDirectories_SelectedIndexChanged`). We first create a new `DirectoryInfo` object based on our starting path value and the user's selected directory:

```
myDirectory = New System.IO.DirectoryInfo(path:=(myPath & myDirName))
```

Next we return an array of `FileInfo` objects using the method `GetFiles` of the `DirectoryInfo` class. Finally, we loop through the array and add the filenames to the list box and select the first file in the list.

```
      Private Sub listBoxDirectories_SelectedIndexChanged(ByVal sender As _
          System.Object, ByVal e As System.EventArgs) Handles _
          listBoxDirectories.SelectedIndexChanged

          'purpose: synchronize the files list box with the selected directory
          '         and display the selected directory's information

          'local scope
          Dim myDirectory As System.IO.DirectoryInfo
          Dim dirInfo As String
          Dim myFiles() As System.IO.FileInfo
          Dim i As Integer

          'clear the listbox of its current contents
          listBoxFiles().Items.Clear()

          'get a directory info object based on the user's selection
          myDirName = listBoxDirectories().SelectedItem.ToString & "\"
```

```
    myDirectory = New System.IO.DirectoryInfo( _
        path:=(myPath & myDirName))

    'set the dir info
    dirInfo = dirInfo & "Path: " & myDirectory.FullName & vbCrLf
    dirInfo = dirInfo & "Attributes: " & myDirectory.Attributes.ToString _
        & vbCrLf
    labelDirectoryInfo().Text = dirInfo

    'get the files in the directory
    myFiles = myDirectory.GetFiles()

    'check for files
    If UBound(myFiles) >= 0 Then

        'loop through the files array and add to the listbox
        For i = 0 To UBound(myFiles) - 1
            listBoxFiles().Items.Add(myFiles(i).Name)
        Next

        'select the file in the list, this will trigger the event to change
        '   the file info label control
        listBoxFiles().SelectedIndex = 0

    End If

End Sub
```

As a filename is selected (`listBoxFiles_SelectedIndexChanged` event) we update the contents of the file information label. To do this we create an instance of the `FileInfo` class based on the file's path and name. We then read some of the file's properties and display them to a label control.

```
Private Sub listBoxFiles_SelectedIndexChanged(ByVal sender As _
    System.Object, ByVal e As System.EventArgs) Handles _
    listBoxFiles.SelectedIndexChanged

    'purpose:   change the contents of the file properties label

    'local scope
    Dim myFile As System.IO.FileInfo
    Dim fileInfo As String

    'set the file name
    myFileName = listBoxFiles().SelectedItem.ToString

    'create a new file object
```

```
        myFile = New System.IO.FileInfo(fileName:=myPath & myDirName & _
            myFileName)

        'set the file info to display
        fileInfo = fileInfo & "Directory: " & myFile.DirectoryName & vbCrLf
        fileInfo = fileInfo & "Created Time: " & myFile.CreationTime & vbCrLf
        fileInfo = fileInfo & "Size: " & myFile.Length & vbCrLf
        fileInfo = fileInfo & "Last Accessed: " & myFile.LastAccessTime & _
            vbCrLf
        fileInfo = fileInfo & "Attributes: " & myFile.Attributes.ToString & _
            vbCrLf

        'set the label to the file's info
        labelFileInfo().Text = fileInfo

    End Sub

    Private Sub buttonClose_Click(ByVal sender As System.Object, _
        ByVal e As System.EventArgs) Handles buttonClose.Click

        'purpose:   end the application

        'close the form
        Me.Close()

    End Sub

#End Region

End Class
```

In the prior example we used the FileInfo class to display file attributes to the user. This class has a number of properties that are useful when working with files. Some of these that are of keen interest are listed in Table 7.2.

TABLE 7.2   Properties of the FileInfo Class

Property	Data Type	Description
Attributes	FileSystemInfo.Attributes	The Attributes property is used to get or set the file's attributes. The value of the property is based on a combination of the file-attribute flags found in FileSystemInfo.Attributes. Values include: archive, compressed, directory, hidden, offline, read-only, system, and temporary.

TABLE 7.2 Continued

Property	Data Type	Description
CreationTime	Datetime	The CreationTime property returns or sets the time that a file was created.
Directory	Directory class	The Directory property returns an instance of the file's parent directory as the Directory class.
DirectoryName	String	The DirectoryName property returns the full path to the file.
Exists	Boolean	The Exists property returns true if a file physically exists and false if it does not.
Extension	String	The Extension property returns the file's extension (.txt for text files).
FullName	String	The FullName property returns the complete path to the file and its name.
LastAcccessTime	DateTime	The LastAccessTime property returns or sets the time that the file was last accessed.
LastWriteTime	DateTime	The LastWriteTime property returns or sets the time the file was last written to.
Length	Long	The Length property returns the size of the file in bytes.
Name	String	The Name property returns the name of the file.

Creation, Deletion, and Manipulation

So far we've looked at how we access directories and files and return their attributes. Now we will explore the basic tasks of creating, deleting, and moving files and directories. The .NET Framework's System.IO offers us all the necessary methods to perform these tasks.

Directories

For manipulating directories we primarily use five basic methods: Create, CreateSubdirectory, Delete, MoveTo, and Refresh. These methods are called from the DirectoryInfo class:

- The Create method creates the directory to which the DirectoryInfo object refers. The CreateSubdirectory method accepts the subdirectory's path as a parameter. It then creates the subdirectory and returns it as a DirectoryInfo instance.

- The Delete method has two overloaded parameter sets. The first takes no parameters and simply deletes the directory and its contents to which the DirectoryInfo instance refers. The second takes a Boolean value that indicates whether the delete call should also be recursive; that is, whether it should delete all its subdirectories and their contents.

- The MoveTo method takes a string as a parameter (destDirName) that represents the destination path. The destination path, as you may have guessed, defines the directory and its path to which the current directory (defined by the DirctoryInfo instance) should be moved.

- The Refresh method refreshes the DirectoryInfo object instance. The method reloads the directory information. This is useful for long-running objects to maintain the most up-to-date information on the directory attributes.

Listing 7.2 is a procedure that demonstrates these methods. The procedure can be copied into a console application and executed.

LISTING 7.2   Directories Create, Move, and Delete

```
Module Module1

    Sub Main()

        'purpose:    demonstrate code that does the following:
        '            1. creates a directory
        '            2. creates a sub directory
        '            3. moves the sub directory under the first directory
        '            4. deletes the sub directory

        'local scope
        Dim myDirectoryParent As System.IO.DirectoryInfo
        Dim myDirectory2 As System.IO.DirectoryInfo

        'create a new instance of the directory info object
        myDirectoryParent = New System.IO.DirectoryInfo(path:="c:\")

        'create a sub directory under the parent directory
        myDirectoryParent.CreateSubdirectory(path:="new directory 1")

        'create another sub directory under the parent directory
        myDirectoryParent.CreateSubdirectory(path:="new directory 2")
```

LISTING 7.2 Continued

```
        'create a directory object based on the 2nd directory
        myDirectory2 = New System.IO.DirectoryInfo( _
            path:="c:\new directory 2")

        'move the second directory under the first
        'note: you must supply its new name (can be the same)
        myDirectory2.MoveTo( _
            destDirName:="c:\new directory 1\new directory 2")

        'delete the second directory and its contents
        'note: you could set the recursive property to true
        '      to delete its sub directories as well
        myDirectory2.Delete()

    End Sub

End Module
```

Files

For working with files we use a similar set of methods found in the FileInfo class. The Create, Delete, MoveTo, and Refresh methods are all present. However, programming with files requires a few additional methods: AppendText, CopyTo, CreateText, Open, OpenRead, and OpenWrite (all of which will be defined later in this chapter).

The Create, MoveTo, and Delete methods are very similar to the DirectoryInfo class. The CopyTo method copies a version of the file to which the FileInfo instance refers. The method is overloaded with two parameter sets. The first copies an instance of the given file to the new directory specified in the parameter destFileName. This method raises an exception if a file with the same name already exists in the destination directory. Upon success, the method returns an instance of the FileInfo class based on the copied file. The second overloaded method takes both the destFileName and the parameter overwrite as a Boolean. Set this parameter to True if you want the Copy method to overwrite any existing file with the same name and False if you do not. Sample code that illustrates these methods is provided for you in Listing 7.3.

Note the return type of the Create method. On file create, we are returned an instance of the FileStream object. This object is a *stream object* based on the new file. The stream object provides us the ability to read and write to the file. Streams, as well as reading and writing to files, are discussed later in this chapter.

LISTING 7.3   Files Create, Move, CopyTo, and Delete

```vb
Imports System.IO

Module Module1

    Sub Main()

        'purpose:    demonstrate code that does the following:
        '                1. creates a file
        '                3. moves the file to a different directory
        '                4. copies the file to another directory
        '                5. deletes the file

        'local scope
        Dim myFileStream As FileStream
        Dim myFile As FileInfo
        Dim myCopiedFile As FileInfo

        'check if file exists, if so delete it
        If File.Exists(path:="c:\newFile.txt") Then
            File.Delete(path:="c:\newFile.txt")
        End If

        'create a new file using, set = to file stream object
        myFileStream = File.Create(path:="c:\newFile.txt")

        'close the file stream object
        myFileStream.Close()

        'get the newly created file
        myFile = New FileInfo(fileName:="c:\newFile.txt")

        'check if move to file exists, if so delete it
        If File.Exists(path:="c:\moveFile.txt") Then
            File.Delete(path:="c:\moveFile.txt")
        End If

        'move the file
        myFile.MoveTo(destFileName:="c:\moveFile.txt")

        'check to see if directory exists, else create it
        If Not System.IO.Directory.Exists(path:="C:\new directory 1") Then
            System.IO.Directory.CreateDirectory( _
                path:="C:\new directory 1")
        End If

        'copy the file back to the directory
```

LISTING 7.3 Continued

```
        'overwrite an existing file if need be
        myCopiedFile = myFile.CopyTo( _
            destFileName:="C:\new directory 1\copyFile.txt", _
            overwrite:=True)

        'wait for the user to stop the console application
        'this allows you to view the directories and the results
        Console.WriteLine("Enter 's' to stop the application.")

        'loop until user presses s key
        Do While Console.ReadLine <> "s" : Loop

        'delete the files
        myFile.Delete()
        myCopiedFile.Delete()

    End Sub

End Module
```

The level of access users are granted to a file is controlled by the FileAccess enumeration. The parameter is specified in many of the constructors of the File, FileInfo, and FileStream classes. Table 7.3 lists the members of the enumeration and a brief description of each.

TABLE 7.3 FileAccess Enumeration Members

Member	Description
Read	The Read member indicates that data can be read from a file.
ReadWrite	The ReadWrite member defines both read and write access to a given file.
Write	The Write member provides write access to a file.

The various attribute values for files and directories are controlled using the FileAttributes enumeration. It should be noted that not all members are applicable to both files and directories. Table 7.4 lists the members of the FileAttributes enumeration.

TABLE 7.4 FileAttributes Enumeration Members

Member	Description
Archive	The Archive member indicates a file's archive status. The archive status is often used to mark files for backup or removal.
Compressed	The Compressed member indicates that a file is compressed.

TABLE 7.4 Continued

Member	Description
Directory	The Directory file attribute indicates that a file is actually a directory.
Encrypted	The Encrypted member indicates that a file is encrypted.
Hidden	The Hidden value indicates that the file is hidden, and thus not included in an ordinary directory listing.
Normal	The Normal value indicates the file has no other attributes set.
NotContentIndexed	The NotContentIndexed value indicates that the file will not be indexed by Windows' indexing service.
Offline	The Offline value indicates that the file's data is not readily accessible (offline).
ReadOnly	The ReadOnly member indicates that the file cannot be modified; it is for reading only.
ReparsePoint	The ReparsePoint member indicates that the file contains a block of user-defined data (reparse point).
SparsePoint	The SparsePoint member indicates that the file is a sparse file. Sparse files are large files whose data are mostly zero values.
System	The System member marks a file as being part of the operating system or used exclusively by the operating system.
Temporary	The Temporary value indicates that a file is temporary. Temporary files should be created and deleted by applications as they are needed and no longer needed.

To control whether a file is created, overwritten, opened, or some combination thereof, you use the FileMode enumeration. It is used in many of the constructors of the FileStream, File, FileInfo, and IsolatedStorageFileStream classes. Table 7.5 lists the members of the FileMode enumeration.

TABLE 7.5 FileMode Enumeration Members

Member	Description
Append	The Append parameter specifies that a file be opened or created, and its end searched (seek) out. FileMode.Append can only be used in conjunction with FileAccess.Write. Any attempt to read fails and throws an ArgumentException.

TABLE 7.5 Continued

Member	Description
Create	The Create parameter specifies that Windows create a new file. If the file already exists, it will be overwritten. This requires FileIOPermissionAccess.Write and FileIOPermissionAccess.Append FileIOPermission.
CreateNew	The CreateNew parameter indicates that Windows should create a new file. This requires FileIOPermissionAccess.Read and FileIOPermissionAccess.Append FileIOPermission. If the file already exists, an IOException is thrown.
Open	The Open member indicates that Windows should open an existing file. This requires FileIOPermissionAccess.Read FileIOPermission.
OpenOrCreate	The OpenOrCreate member indicates that Windows should open a file if it exists; otherwise, a new file should be created. If the file is opened with FileAccess.Read, FileIOPermissionAccess.Read FileIOPermission is required. If file access is FileAccess.ReadWrite and the file exists, FileIOPermissionAccess.Write FileIOPermission is required. If file access is FileAccess.ReadWrite and the file does not exist, FileIOPermissionAccess.Append FileIOPermission is required in addition to Read and Write.
Truncate	The truncate member indicates that Windows should open an existing file and truncate its size to zero bytes. This requires FileIOPermissionAccess.Write FileIOPermission.

Use the FileShare enumeration to control whether two processes can access a given file simultaneously. For example, if a user opens a file marked FileShare.Read, other users can open the file for reading but cannot save or write to it. The FileShare enumeration is used in some of the constructors for the FileStream, File, FileInfo, and IsolatedStorageFileStream classes. Table 7.6 lists the FileShare enumeration members.

TABLE 7.6 FileShare Enumeration Members

Member	Description
None	The None value indicates that the file should not be shared in any way. All requests to open the file will fail until the file is closed.
Read	The Read member allows users to open a given file for reading only. Attempts to save the file (or write to it) but read-only processes will fail.
ReadWrite	The ReadWrite parameter indicates that a file can be opened for both reading and writing by multiple processes. Obviously this can cause problems because the last user to save has his changes applied.

TABLE 7.6 Continued

Member	Description
Write	The Write parameter indicates that a file can be open for writing but not necessarily reading. This can be combined with Read to mimic the ReadWrite parameter.

Monitoring the File System

It seems there is always a need to monitor a directory for file drops or respond to file system events. For example, suppose your team needs to be notified whenever a documentation artifact for the project you're working on is created or modified. Wouldn't it be nice if you could write a simple monitoring service that responds to these events and notifies the team?

One of the most interesting objects in the namespace is the FileSystemWatcher class. This class can be easily configured to monitor events within directories. Before the file watcher class, Visual Basic programmers often had to implement a message queue application, monitor SMTP, or write a service which, at different intervals, queried a directory to check for changes. .NET provides the FileSystemWatcher as an easy-to-use class to solve these common programming dilemmas.

Identifying What to Monitor

The FileSystemWatcher can be used to monitor changes made to files and subdirectories of a specified parent directory. The component can be configured to work with the local file system, a directory on the local network, or a remote machine.

The FileSystemWatcher class allows you to

- Watch files from either a Windows 2000 or an NT 4 install.
- Watch all files, including those marked hidden.

The FileSystemWatcher does *not* allow you to

- Watch a *remote* NT 4 computer from another NT 4 computer.
- Work with CDs or DVDs because files on these devices are fixed and cannot change.

There are a number of properties of the FileSystemWatcher class that allow us to target the objects we wish to watch. The properties developers will use most often are Filter and Path. Path simply indicates the directory path to watch. Filter indicates the type of files to watch. The format for Filter uses Windows' standard wildcard notation to set its value. If you do not set the filter property, its default is *.* (star dot star), which indicates that you are monitoring all files in the directory. If you are trying to monitor only Microsoft Excel files, then you'd set the Filter property to *.xls. Table 7.7 lists additional properties and describes when you would implement their use.

TABLE 7.7 Configuration Properties of the `FileSystemWatcher` Class

Property	Scenario Description
Path	The `Path` property lets you indicate what directory to watch. You can indicate a path using standard directory path notation (c:\myDirectory) or in UNC format (\\serverName\directory\name).
Filter	Set the `Filter` property to watch for changes made to a file or directory that are of a specific type.
Target	Use the `Target` property to watch for changes on only a file, only a directory, or both a file and a directory. By default, the `Target` property is set to watch for changes to both directory and file-level items.
IncludeSubDirectories	Set the `IncludeSubDirectories` property to `True` to monitor changes made to subdirectories that the root directory contains. The watcher will watch for the same changes in all directories.
ChangedFilter	Use the `ChangedFilter` property to watch for specific changes to a file or directory when handling the `Changed` event. Changes can apply to `Attributes`, `LastAccess`, `LastWrite`, `Security`, or `Size`.

Once you've decided what objects you are monitoring you'll need to indicate the events or actions to which you are listening. The changes that the `FileSystemWatcher` can monitor include changes in the directory's or file's properties, size, last write time, last access time, and security settings.

You use the `NotifyFilters` enumeration of the `FileSystemWatcher` class to specify changes for which to watch on files and directories. The members of this enumeration can be combined using `BitOr` (bitwise or comparisons) to watch for multiple kinds of changes. An event is raised when any change you are watching for is made. Table 7.8 lists the members of the `NotifyFilters` enumeration and provides a brief description of each.

TABLE 7.8 NotifyFilters Enumeration Members

Member	Description
Attributes	The Attributes member allows you to watch for changes made to the attributes of a file or directory.
CreationTime	The CreationTime member allows you to watch for changes made to the time the file or directory was created.
DirectoryName	The DirectoryName member allows you to watch for changes made to the name of the file or directory.
FileName	The FileName member allows you to watch for changes made to the name of a file.
LastAccess	The LastAccess member allows you to watch for changes made to the date the file or directory was last opened.
LastWrite	The LastWrite member allows you to watch for changes made to the date the file or directory had data written to it.
Security	The Security member allows you to watch for changes made to the security settings of the file or directory.
Size	The Size member allows you to watch for changes made to the size of the file or directory.

Responding to File System Events

At this point, we've indicated what we are watching and what events interest us; now we must hook up those events to our application. The FileSystemWatcher raises an event when files or directories are created, deleted, renamed, or otherwise changed. The events are raised and stored in a buffer before being passed to our instance of the FileSystemWatcher.

> **NOTE**
>
> You might notice that some common tasks such as file copy or move do not correspond directly to an event raised by the component. However, upon closer examination, you will notice that when a file is copied, the system raises a created event to the directory to which the file was copied. Similarly, when a file is moved, the system raises both a deleted event in the file's original directory and a created event in the file's new directory. These events serve in place of actual copy and move to events.

This buffer becomes very important in high-volume monitoring applications. It has the potential to receive a lot of events. Let's examine this further. Every change to a file in a directory raises a separate event. This sounds simple enough, but we have to be careful. For example, if we are monitoring a directory that contains 25 files and we reset the security settings on the directory, we will get 25 separate change events. Now if we write an application that renames those files and resets their security we'll get 50 events: one for each file for both change and rename.

All these events are stored in the `FileSystemWatcher`'s internal buffer, which has a maximum size limit and can overflow. If this buffer overflows, the `FileSystemWatcher` will raise the `InternalBufferOverflow` event. Fortunately, the component allows us to increase this buffer size.

The default buffer size is set to 8KB. Microsoft indicates that this can track changes on approximately 160 files in a directory. You can reset the buffer size to better match your needs using the `InternalBufferSize` property. For best performance, this property should be set in increments of 4K (4096, 8192, 12288, and so on) because this corresponds to the operating system's (Windows 2000) default page size.

Increasing this internal buffer comes at a cost. The buffer uses non-paged memory that cannot be swapped to disk. Therefore, we need to keep the buffer size as small as possible. Strategies to limit the buffer's size include the `NotifyFilter` and `IncludeSubDirectories` properties to filter out those change notifications in which we have no interest. It should be noted that the `Filter` property actually has no effect on the buffer size since the filter is applied after the notifications are written to the buffer.

To actually connect to the `FileSystemWatcher`'s events we add handlers in our code as we would with any other event. For example, to hook into the `Changed` event, we add code similar to the following:

```
AddHandler myWatcher.Changed, AddressOf watcher_OnChange
```

This tells your application to intercept the `Changed` event and process through a custom event called `watcher_onChange`. The custom event need only have the correct function signature. Table 7.9 lists the events to which you can subscribe and their associated function signatures.

TABLE 7.9 `FileSystemWatcher` Events

Event	VB Handler and Function Signature
Changed	`AddHandler myWatcher.Changed, AddressOf watcher_OnChange Sub watcher_OnChange(ByVal source As Object, _ByVal e As IO.FileSystemEventArgs)`
Created	`AddHandler myWatcher.Created, AddressOf watcher_OnCreate Sub watcher_OnCreate(ByVal source As Object, _ByVal e As IO.FileSystemEventArgs)`

TABLE 7.9   Continued

Event	VB Handler and Function Signature
Deleted	AddHandler myWatcher.Deleted, AddressOf watcher_OnDelete Sub watcher_OnChange(ByVal source As Object, _ByVal e As IO.FileSystemEventArgs)
Error	AddHandler myWatcher.Error, AddressOf watcher_OnError Sub watcher_OnError(ByVal source As Object, _ByVal e As IO.ErrorEventHandler)
Renamed	AddHandler myWatcher.Renamed, AddressOf watcher_OnRename Sub watcher_OnRename(ByVal source As Object, _ByVal e As IO. RenamedEventHandler)

Once inside the event, we have access to a number of properties related to the event and event type. These properties come from the event arguments that are passed to us when the event is raised. They include things like the change type and the path and name to the file or directory.

The WatcherChangeTypes enumeration is used by events of the FileSystemWatcher class. The enumeration's members indicate to the event the type of change that occurred to a file or directory. Table 7.10 lists the members of the WatcherChangeTypes enumeration.

TABLE 7.10   WatcherChangeTypes Enumeration Members

Member	Description
All	The All member indicates that any of the creation, deletion, change, or renaming of a file or folder actions occurred.
Changed	The Changed member indicates that a change action occurred to a file or event. Changes can include: size, attributes, security, last write, and last access time.
Created	The Created member indicates that a file or folder was created.
Deleted	The Deleted member indicates that a file or folder was deleted.
Renamed	The Renamed member indicates that a file or folder was renamed.

Listing 7.4 provides a sample FileSystemWatcher application that serves to further illustrate these concepts. The code can be executed inside a console application (and downloaded from www.samspublishing.com). The application monitors a directory for changes to text files. When a change occurs, the user is notified with a simple call to Console.WriteLine from within the intercepted change event.

LISTING 7.4 FileSystemWatcher Directory Monitor

```vb
Imports System.IO

Module Module1

    Sub Main()

        'Call directory()
        Call watchDirectory(watchPath:="c:\watch")

    End Sub

    Sub watchDirectory(ByVal watchPath As String)

        'purpose:   watch a directory for changes to files

        'local scope
        Dim myWatcher As FileSystemWatcher
        Dim stopValue As String

        'check if directory exits, no = create
        If Not Directory.Exists(path:=watchPath) Then
            Directory.CreateDirectory(path:=watchPath)
        End If

        'instantiate a new system watcher object
        myWatcher = New FileSystemWatcher()

        'set the path of directory to watch
        myWatcher.Path = watchPath

        'tell the watcher object to watch only for text files
        myWatcher.Filter = "*.txt"

        'tell the watcher the type of changes to watch for
        myWatcher.NotifyFilter = IO.NotifyFilters.DirectoryName _
            Or IO.NotifyFilters.LastAccess _
            Or IO.NotifyFilters.LastWrite _
            Or IO.NotifyFilters.FileName

        'intercept the watcher events
        AddHandler myWatcher.Changed, AddressOf watcher_OnChange
        AddHandler myWatcher.Deleted, AddressOf watcher_OnChange
        AddHandler myWatcher.Created, AddressOf watcher_OnChange
        AddHandler myWatcher.Renamed, AddressOf watcher_OnRename
```

LISTING 7.4 Continued

```vb
        'tell the watcher to start watching
        myWatcher.EnableRaisingEvents = True

        'tell the user that watching is on
        Console.WriteLine("Watching " & watchPath & "...")

        'wait for the user to stop the console application
        Console.WriteLine("Press 's' to stop the application.")

        'loop until user presses s key
        Do While Console.ReadLine <> "s" : Loop

    End Sub

    Sub watcher_OnChange(ByVal source As Object, _
        ByVal e As IO.FileSystemEventArgs)

        'purpose:    respond to the changed notify event
        '            (created, changed, deleted)

        'indicate that a file is changed, created, or deleted
        Console.WriteLine("File: " & e.FullPath & " " & e.ChangeType)

    End Sub

    Sub watcher_OnRename(ByVal source As Object, _
        ByVal e As IO.RenamedEventArgs)

        'purpose:    respond to the renamed watcher notify event

        'tell the user the file that was renamed
        Console.WriteLine("File: {0} renamed to {1}", e.OldFullPath, _
            e.FullPath)

    End Sub

End Module
```

 ## Suggestions for Further Exploration

⊃ To read similar information about working with file I/O in .NET, read the MSDN chapter found at: Visual Studio .NET/.NET Framework/Programming with the .NET Framework/Working with I/O.

⊃ For additional information on .NET security issues (for user, file, directory, and code access), start with the System.Security namespace. Of course, you will also want to read Appendix D, ".NET Framework Base Data Types," which deals specifically with security in .NET.

⊃ You will want to check out the FileDialog class found in System.Windows.Forms. This class allows you to easily display a window's dialog that allows users to select a file. The class is the replacement of the old common dialog control.

Reading and Writing to Files and Streams

As programmers, we often have to write directly to a file or data stream. If you've communicated with disparate systems, you are undoubtedly familiar with writing out CSV or XML files as a means of exchanging data. The .NET Framework gives us a group of classes and methods inside the System.IO namespace that allows us to access data streams and files both synchronously and asynchronously.

This section will define the AppendText, CreateText, Open, OpenRead, and OpenWrite methods of the FileInfo class.

File and data streams are essentially the same thing. They both are a type of stream. Their differences lie in their *backing store*. Backing store refers to a storage medium, such as a disk, tape, memory, network, and so on. Every backing store implements its own stream type as a version of the Stream class. This allows each stream type to read and write bytes to and from its own backing store. These streams that connect directly to backing stores are called base streams in .NET. An example of a base stream is the FileStream class. This class gives us access to files stored on disk inside of directories.

Reading and Writing Files

To read data to and from files using the System.IO namespace, we primarily use two classes: FileInfo and FileStream. The FileInfo class exposes a number of methods that allow us access to stream-related functions based on a file. These methods simply use the FileStream and related classes to expose this functionality. However, they are useful as you often already have an instance of FileInfo that is specific to a given file. You can then call these methods to return and write to the contents of this file. Table 7.11 lists these methods and their associated return types.

TABLE 7.11 `FileInfo` Streaming Methods

Member	Description
AppendText	The `AppendText` method creates an instance of the `StreamWriter` class that allows us to append text to a file. The `StreamWriter` class implements a `TextWriter` instance to output the characters in a specific encoding.
CreateText	The `CreateText` method creates an instance of the `StreamWriter` class that creates a new text file to which to write.
Open	The `Open` method opens a file and returns it to us as a `FileStream` object. The method has three constructors that allow us to specify the open mode (open, create, append, and so on), the file access (read, write, read and write), and how we want the file to be shared by other `FileStream` objects.
OpenText	The `OpenText` method creates a `StreamReader` object based on the associated text file.
OpenRead	The `OpenRead` method creates a `FileStream` object that is read only.
OpenWrite	The `OpenWrite` method creates a `FileStream` object that is both read and write.

You can see that the `FileInfo` class makes extensive use of the `FileStream`, `StreamWriter`, and `StreamReader` classes. These classes expose the necessary functionality to read and write to files in .NET. As you might have guessed, these objects are designed to work with persisted text files. They are based on the `TextWriter` and `TextReader` classes.

The `FileStream` class can be created explicitly. You've already seen that `FileInfo` uses this class to expose reading and writing to files. Table 7.12 lists the version of the `FileStream` constructors that can be used to create a `FileStream` object.

TABLE 7.12 `FileStream` Constructors

New FileStream (ByVal handle as IntPtr, ByVal access as FileAccess)

    `handle`: A valid handle to a file.

    `access`: A member of the `FileAccess` enumeration (Read, ReadWrite, Write).

    Note: Use this constructor when you have a valid file pointer and need to specify the read/write permissions.

New FileStream (ByVal path as String, ByVal mode as FileMode)

    `path`: A valid path to the file that the `FileStream` object will represent.

    `mode`: A member of the `FileMode` enumeration (Append, Create, CreateNew, Open, OpenOrCreate, Truncate) that specifies how the file should be opened.

    Note: Use this constructor when you know the file's path and wish to specify how the file is opened.

TABLE 7.12 Continued

New FileStream (ByVal handle as IntPtr, ByVal access as FileAccess, _ByVal ownsHandle as Boolean)

handle: A valid handle to a file.

access: A member of the FileAccess enumeration (Read, ReadWrite, Write).

ownsHandle: Indicates if the file's handle will be owned by the given instance of the FileStreamObject.

Note: Use this constructor when you have a valid file pointer, need to specify the read/write permissions, and wish to own (or pass off) the file's handle. If the FileStream object owns the file's handle, a call to the Close method will also close the file's handle and thus decrement its handle count by one.

New FileStream (ByVal path as String, ByVal mode as FileMode, _ByVal access as FileAccess)

path: A valid path to the file that the FileStream object will represent.

mode: A member of the FileMode enumeration (Append, Create, CreateNew, Open, OpenOrCreate, Truncate) that specifies how the file should be opened.

access: A member of the FileAccess enumeration (Read, ReadWrite, Write).

Note: Use this constructor when you know the file's path, wish to specify how the file is opened, and need to specify the read/write permissions on the file.

New FileStream (ByVal handle as IntPtr, ByVal access as FileAccess, _ByVal ownsHandle as Boolean, ByVal bufferSize as Integer)

handle: A valid handle to a file.

access: A member of the FileAccess enumeration (Read, ReadWrite, Write).

ownsHandle: Indicates if the file's handle will be owned by the given instance of the FileStreamObject.

bufferSize: Indicates the size of the buffer in bytes.

Note: Use this constructor when you have a valid file pointer, need to specify the read/write permissions, with to own the file's handle, and need to set the stream's buffer size.

New FileStream (ByVal path as String, ByVal mode as FileMode, _ByVal access as FileAccess, ByVal share as FileShare)

path: A valid path to the file that the FileStream object will represent.

mode: A member of the FileMode enumeration (Append, Create, CreateNew, Open, OpenOrCreate, Truncate) that specifies how the file should be opened.

access: A member of the FileAccess enumeration (Read, ReadWrite, Write).

share: A member of the FileShare enumeration that indicates how the file will be shared.

TABLE 7.12 Continued

FileShare controls how other FileStream objects can access the same file. Values include: Inheritable, None, Read, ReadWrite, and Write.

Note: Use this constructor when you know the file's path, wish to specify how the file is opened, and need to specify the read/write permissions on the file.

New FileStream (ByVal handle as IntPtr, ByVal access as FileAccess, _ByVal ownsHandle as Boolean, ByVal bufferSize as Integer, _ByVal isAsync as Boolean)

handle: A valid handle to a file.

access: A member of the FileAccess enumeration (Read, ReadWrite, Write).

ownsHandle: Indicates if the file's handle will be owned by the given instance of the FileStreamObject.

bufferSize: Indicates the size of the buffer in bytes.

isAsync: Indicates if the file should be opened asynchronously.

Note: Use this constructor when you have a valid file pointer, need to specify the read/write permissions, wish to own (or pass off) the file's handle, need to set the buffer size, and wish to indicate the file should be opened asynchronously.

New FileStream (ByVal path as String, ByVal mode as FileMode, _ByVal access as FileAccess, ByVal share as FileShare, _ByVal bufferSize as Integer)

path: A valid path to the file that the FileStream object will represent.

mode: A member of the FileMode enumeration (Append, Create, CreateNew, Open, OpenOrCreate, Truncate) that specifies how the file should be opened.

access: A member of the FileAccess enumeration (Read, ReadWrite, Write).

share: A member of the FileShare enumeration that indicates how the file will be shared. FileShare controls how other FileStream objects can access the same file. Values include: Inheritable, None, Read, ReadWrite, and Write.

bufferSize: Indicates the size of the buffer in bytes.

Note: Use this constructor when you know the file's path, wish to specify how the file is opened, need to specify the read/write permissions on the file, and need to set the stream's buffer size.

New FileStream (ByVal path as String, ByVal mode as FileMode, _ByVal access as FileAccess, ByVal share as FileShare, _ByVal bufferSize as Integer, ByVal useAsynch as Boolean)

path: A valid path to the file that the FileStream object will represent.

mode: A member of the FileMode enumeration (Append, Create, CreateNew, Open, OpenOrCreate, Truncate) that specifies how the file should be opened.

access: A member of the FileAccess enumeration (Read, ReadWrite, Write).

share: A member of the FileShare enumeration that indicates how the file will be shared.

TABLE 7.12   Continued

FileShare controls how other `FileStream` objects can access the same file. Values include: `Inheritable`, `None`, `Read`, `ReadWrite`, and `Write`.

`bufferSize`: Indicates the size of the buffer in bytes.

`useAsync`: Indicates if the file should be opened asynchronously.

Note: Use this constructor when you know the file's path, wish to specify how the file is opened, need to specify the read/write permissions on the file, need to set the stream's buffer size, and need to indicate if the file is being opened for asynchronous read/write.

Listing 7.5 provides an example of the `FileStream`, `StreamWriter`, and `StreamReader` classes. This example is a simple, console-based application. It creates a new `FileStream` object based on a physical file. It then creates a `StreamWriter` instance based on the `FileStream` class. It calls the `WritLine` method of `StreamWriter` to output a line of text to the file. After it closes the `StreamWriter` instance, it creates a `StreamReader` instance based on a `FileStream` object. Finally, it loops through the lines in the file and outputs them to the console for your viewing.

LISTING 7.5   `FileStream`, `StreamWriter`, and `StreamReader`

```
Imports System.IO

Module Module1

    Sub Main()

        'purpose:   open a file and append infromation to its end

        'local scope
        Dim fileStream As FileStream
        Dim streamWriter As StreamWriter
        Dim streamReader As StreamReader

        'create a new instance of the file stream object
        'note: if the file does not exist, the constructor create it
        fileStream = New fileStream(path:="c:\test.txt", _
            mode:=FileMode.OpenOrCreate, access:=FileAccess.Write)

        'create an instance of a character writer
        streamWriter = New StreamWriter(stream:=fileStream)

        'set the file pointer to the end of the file
        streamWriter.BaseStream.Seek(offset:=0, origin:=SeekOrigin.End)

        'write a line of text to the end of the file
        streamWriter.WriteLine(value:="This is a test")
```

LISTING 7.5   Continued

```
            'apply the update to the file
            streamWriter.Flush()

            'close the stream writer
            streamWriter.Close()

            'close the file stream object
            fileStream.Close()

            'create a new instance of file stream to read the file back
            fileStream = New fileStream(path:="c:\test.txt", _
                mode:=FileMode.OpenOrCreate, access:=FileAccess.Read)

            'create a stream reader instance
            streamReader = New StreamReader(stream:=fileStream)

            'set the file pointer to the start of the file
            streamReader.BaseStream.Seek(offset:=0, _
                origin:=SeekOrigin.Begin)

            'loop through the file and write to console until the
            ' end of file reached
            Do While streamReader.Peek > -1
                Console.WriteLine(value:=streamReader.ReadLine())
            Loop

            'close the stream reader
            streamReader.Close()

            'wait for the user to stop the console application
            Console.WriteLine("Press 's' to stop the application.")

            'loop until users presses s key
            Do While Console.ReadLine <> "s" : Loop

    End Sub

End Module
```

Asynchronous Reading and Writing

As stated earlier, streaming with the .NET Framework classes can be done both synchronously and asynchronously. Synchronous reading and writing blocks methods from continuing until the operation is complete. For instance, suppose your application takes orders in the form of text files written to a queue. When a file is placed in the queue (or directory), your application reads the contents of the file and processes the order(s) accordingly. Each file can represent one order, or can contain a batch of orders. If your application is set up to handle each order from start to finish as it comes in (synchronously), then a long order will block your application from continuing to process orders while simply reading the file.

For a more efficient use of your resources, you will want to read orders asynchronously. That is, as an order comes in, you will tell a version of the `Stream` object to start reading the file and to let you know when it is done. This way, once you fire the `BeginRead` method, you can continue executing other program logic including responding to and processing additional orders.

With asynchronous file I/O, the main thread of your application continues to execute code while the I/O process finishes. In fact, multiple asynchronous IO requests can process simultaneously. Generally, an asynchronous design offers your application better performance. The tradeoff to this performance is that a greater coding effort is required.

The `FileStream` class provides us the `BeginRead` method for asynchronous file input and the `BeginWrite` method for asynchronous file output. As a parameter to each, we pass the name of the method we wish to have called when the operation is complete (`userCallback as AsynchCallback`). In VB .NET, the syntax looks like this:

```
New AsyncCallback(AddressOf myCallbackMethod)
```

Where `myCallbackMethod` is the name of the method you wish to have intercept and process the completed operation notification. From within this callback method, you should call `EndRead` or `EndWrite` as the case dictates. These methods end their respective operations. `EndRead` returns the number of bytes that were read during the operation. Both methods take a reference to the pending asynchronous I/O operation (`AsynchResult as IAsynchResult`). This object comes to us as a parameter to our custom callback method. The code in Listing 7.6 further illustrates these concepts.

The application's `Sub Main` simply controls the calls to the read operation. You can see in Listing 7.6 that we execute three separate read requests on three different files. The remaining bits of functionality are nicely encapsulated and thus, should be easy to reuse.

LISTING 7.6 Asynchronous File Reading

```
Imports System.IO

Module Module1

    Sub Main()
```

LISTING 7.6 Continued

```
'purpose: provide example code of asynch. file I/O

'steps:    1. start asynch. read and processing of 3 files of
'             varying lengths
'          2. wait for callback and display to screen

'local scope
Dim myFiles(3) As String
Dim i As Int16

myFiles(0) = "c:\file1.txt"
myFiles(1) = "c:\file2.txt"
myFiles(2) = "c:\file3.txt"

'call each asynch. read
For i = 0 To 2
    Console.WriteLine("Starting file read: " & myFiles(i))
    Call asynchRead(filePath:=myFiles(i))
Next

'NOTE: now that file reads have started, our application can
'      continue processing other information and await a callback
'      from the read operation indicating read is complete

'wait for the user to stop the console application
Console.WriteLine("******** Enter 's' to stop the application.")

'loop until user presses s key
Do While Console.ReadLine <> "s" : Loop

End Sub
```

The procedure asynchRead sets up the asynchronous file input. The class StateObject is a simple state object that allows us to maintain file input information, in the form of properties, across read requests.

Notice that when calling BeginRead, in addition to indicating a callback method, we must specify both a byte array (array() as Byte) and the total number of bytes (numBytes as Integer) we wish to have read. To store the bytes, we dimension an array of type byte inside our state object. We pass byteArraySize in the object's constructor. We get its size by reading the file size from the FileInfo object's Length property. This allows us to create an array of the exact size we need. Similarly, when we set the number of bytes to read, we use

FileInfo.Length again to indicate we want to read the entire file.

```
Private Sub asynchRead(ByVal filePath As String)

    'purpose: execute an asynch. read against a given file
    '         throw an exception if the file is not found

    'local scope
    Dim fileStream As FileStream
    Dim state As StateObject
    Dim fileInfo As FileInfo

    'check to see if the file exists
    If Not File.Exists(path:=filePath) Then

        'file does not exist = throw an exception
        Throw New Exception(message:="File not found.")

    End If

    'file exists = create an open instance of the file
    fileStream = New FileStream(path:=filePath, mode:=FileMode.Open)

    'determine size of the file to set the number of bytes
    fileInfo = New FileInfo(fileName:=filePath)
    Console.WriteLine("File length: " & fileInfo.Length)

    'create a state object
    state = New StateObject(filePath:=filePath, _
        byteArraySize:=fileInfo.Length)

    'set fileStream prop (useful for callback)
    state.FileStream = fileStream

    'begin the file read
    fileStream.BeginRead(array:=state.ByteArray, offset:=0, _
        numBytes:=fileInfo.Length, _
        userCallback:=New AsyncCallback(AddressOf fileRead), _
        stateObject:=state)

End Sub
```

The fileRead method is the application's callback implementation. This method receives notification when a BeginRead has completed for a given file.

```
Private Sub fileRead(ByVal asyncResult As IAsyncResult)

    'purpose: provide a callback method for asynch reads
```

```vb
            'local scope
            Dim state As StateObject
            Dim bytesRead As Integer

            'set the state object = to the one returned by the asynch results
            state = asyncResult.AsyncState

            'write out the path of the object read
            Console.WriteLine(state.FilePath)

            'indicate that the file was read asynch.
            If asyncResult.CompletedSynchronously Then
                Console.WriteLine("File was read synchronously.")
            Else
                Console.WriteLine("File was read asynchronously.")
            End If

            'determine the number of bytes read by calling EndRead
            bytesRead = state.FileStream.EndRead(asyncResult)

            'write out bytes read
            Console.WriteLine("Bytes read: " & bytesRead)

            'close the file stream
            state.FileStream.Close()

    End Sub

End Module

Public Class StateObject

    'purpose: maintain state information across asynch calls

    'class-level scope
    Private localFilePath As String
    Private localByteArray() As Byte

    'public properties
    Public FileStream As FileStream

    Public Property ByteArray() As Byte()

        'purpose: get and set ByteArray property
```

```
        Get
            Return localByteArray
        End Get

        Set(ByVal Value() As Byte)
            localByteArray = Value
        End Set

    End Property

    Public Property FilePath() As String

        'purpose: get and set FilePath prop.

        Get
            Return localFilePath
        End Get

        Set(ByVal Value As String)
            localFilePath = Value
        End Set

    End Property

    Sub New(ByVal filePath As String, ByVal byteArraySize As Integer)

        'purpose: constructor, allows setting of file path info.
        '         and byte array size info.

        'set local file path info
        localFilePath = filePath

        'dimension the size of the byte array
        ReDim localByteArray(byteArraySize)

    End Sub

End Class
```

Figure 7.2 represents the output of the code listing. Notice that in this case, each file was read in the same order the request was made. However, there is no guarantee of processing order due to the asynchronous nature of the request and additional factors like file size and processor availability. Also notice that after the first (and subsequent) read requests were made, our code did not stop executing. Rather, it made additional requests, and ultimately, waited on user input to stop the application. Finally, as each read completed, the notification was sent to our readFile method and the results of the operation were written to the console.

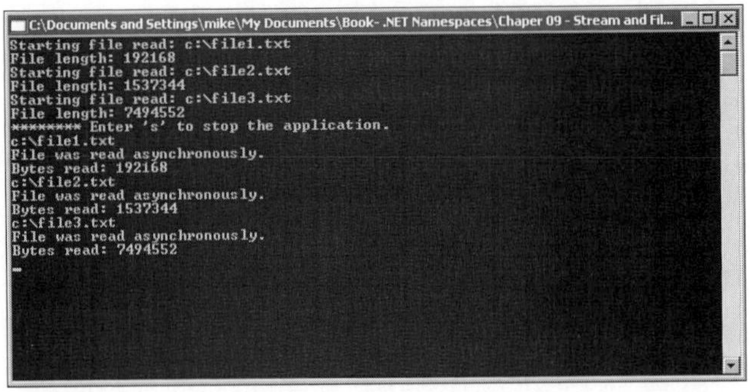

FIGURE 7.2
Output of asynchronous example.

Binary Reading and Writing

Thus far, we've dealt primarily with text files. While it is true that text files make up the majority of business programming I/O tasks, you will often need to read and write files of a proprietary type. To do so, you will access them at the binary level. Suppose that you need to accept an Excel file streaming across the wire, chances are you will want to persist it to disk using a binary reader and writer. Or suppose you want to read image files and store them in your database. Again, a binary reader will make this operation go smoothly.

We have a number of options open to us for file I/O at the binary level. The principal ones include using the `BinaryReader`, `BinaryWriter`, and `FileStream` classes. The best thing is that, for the most part, you already know how to use these objects. `BinaryReader` and `BinaryWriter` are similar to `StreamReader` and `StreamWriter`, respectively. Like these classes, `BinaryReader` and `BinaryWriter` take an instance of a valid `Stream` object as a parameter of their constructor. The `Stream` object represents the backing store that is being read from or written to.

The `BinaryReader` class provides a number of read methods that allow us to access primitive data types from our file streams. Each read method returns the given data from the stream and advances the current position in the stream ahead of the returned data. The reader you're likely to use most often is `ReadByte`. This returns one byte of data from the stream and advances the current stream position to the next byte. When the end of the stream is reached, the exception, `EndOfStreamException`, is thrown by the method. Other read methods include `ReadBytes`, `ReadString`, `ReadDecimal`, and `ReadBoolean` to name a few.

Similarly, `BinaryWriter` provides a number of write methods for writing primitive data to a stream. Unlike `BinaryReader`, `BinaryWriter` exposes only one method, `WriteByte`, for executing binary writes. However, this method has a number of overloads that allow us to specify whether we are writing byte data or string, decimal, and so on. Calls to WriteByte write out the given data to the stream and advance its current position by the length of the data. Again, WriteByte(value as Byte) will be the most commonly used method.

The FileStream class also exposes the basic binary methods, ReadByte and WriteByte. ReadByte and WriteByte behave in the exact same manner as BinaryReader.ReadByte and BinaryWriter.WriteByte(value as Byte). It is often easier to simply use FileStream for all your basic needs; this is why it exists. Should you need additional functionality, then you will want to implement one or more of the binary classes.

Listing 7.7 provides an example of the BinaryReader and BinaryWriter classes. In the example, we use BinaryReader to read the contents of a bitmap file, one byte at a time. At the same time, we write each byte out to another file using BinaryWriter. The result is two identical files. Notice that to create both the reader and the writer we must first create a valid FileStream (or similar Stream derivation) for the instances to use as their backing.

LISTING 7.7 Binary Reading and Writing

```vb
Imports System.IO

Module Module1

    Sub Main()

        'purpose: read a binary file and write contents to diff. file

        'local scope
        Dim fsRead As FileStream
        Dim fsWrite As FileStream
        Dim bRead As BinaryReader
        Dim b As Byte
        Dim bWrite As BinaryWriter

        'check if read file exists
        If Not File.Exists(path:="c:\test.bmp") Then

            Console.WriteLine("File, test.bmp, not found")

            'waite for user input
            Console.WriteLine("Enter 's' to stop the application.")
            Do While Console.ReadLine <> "s" : Loop

            End
```

LISTING 7.7 Continued

```
    End If

    'create a fileStream instance to pass to BinaryReader object
    fsRead = New FileStream(path:="c:\test.bmp", mode:=FileMode.Open)

    'check if write file exists
    If File.Exists(path:="c:\test2.bmp") Then

        'delete file
        File.Delete(path:="c:\test2.bmp")

    End If

    'create a fileStream instance to pass to BinaryWriter object
    fsWrite = New FileStream(path:="c:\test2.bmp", _
        mode:=FileMode.CreateNew, access:=FileAccess.Write)

    'create binary writer instance
    bWrite = New BinaryWriter(output:=fsWrite)

    'create instance of binary reader
    bRead = New BinaryReader(Input:=fsRead)

    'set the file pointer to the start of the file
    bRead.BaseStream.Seek(offset:=0, _
        origin:=SeekOrigin.Begin)

    'loop until can no longer read bytes from file
    Do While True

        Try

            'read next byte and advance reader
            b = bRead.ReadByte

        Catch
            Exit Do
        End Try

        'write byte out
        bWrite.Write(value:=b)
```

LISTING 7.7 Continued

```
    Loop

    'close the reader
    bRead.Close()

    'close the writer
    bWrite.Close()

    'close the file streams
    fsRead.Close()
    fsWrite.Close()

    'wait for the user to stop the console application
    Console.WriteLine("Operation complete.")
    Console.WriteLine("Enter 's' to stop the application.")

    'loop until user presses s key
    Do While Console.ReadLine <> "s" : Loop

  End Sub

End Module
```

 ## Suggestions for Further Exploration

➲ To create a stream whose backing is memory (and not disk), check out the MemoryStream class. This class is useful in that it can reduce your need for direct file I/O inside your application and provide you with a temporary buffer.

➲ Depending on your application, you can sometimes garner additional performance by implementing the BufferedStream class. Note that FileStream has internal buffering of its own and is often sufficient. Programming with BufferedStream is similar to the other stream classes we've discussed.

➲ To store data using isolated stores, check out the namespace System.IO.IsolatedStorage. Isolated stores are secure data compartments that are only accessible by the given user or code assembly. Data can also be isolated at the domain level and user data can travel with them using roaming profiles. For more information, check out the MSDN chapter at: Visual Studio .NET/.NET Framework/Programming with the .NET Framework/Working with I/O/Performing Isolated Storage Tasks.

Learning By Example: Adding Open and Save to FontPad

Recall FontPad from Chapter 6, "Font, Text, and Printing." This was our basic text editor to which we then added printing capabilities. We will round out this application by adding basic file I/O. After all, what's a text editor worth if it can't open and save files? By the time we're done, we should have completely replaced (or duplicated, anyway) the functionality of Notepad.

This example extends FontPad with an open and save dialog. Therefore, only the open and save dialogs are discussed here. To run the application, you should download the full source at www.samspublishing.com. After walking through the application, you should be able to extend the example as a test harness in which you can experiment with your own code.

Key Concepts Covered

The following represents the key class and concepts demonstrated with this sample application:

- Accessing directory properties and enumerating directories with the `DirectoryInfo` class.
- Accessing file properties and enumerating files in a directory with the `FileInfo` class.
- Reading a file with the `FileStream` and `StreamReader` classes.
- Persisting a file to disk with the `FileStream` and `StreamWriter` classes.

Open Dialog

To open files, we must present users with a method to browse the file system. .NET provides us with a `FileDialog` class specifically designed for this purpose. This class is similar to the common dialogs with which we're familiar from the VB of old. The .NET team built the dialog using the namespace we've presented in this chapter.

In our example application we will create our own dialog using the namespace rather than `FileDialog`. This makes sense because our objective is to teach the namespace. However, we suggest you further explore this class if you need fast and easy access to the file system. Figure 7.3 is a screen capture of our open dialog.

Obviously, this form will not win any usability or user interface design awards; it was built to illustrate code. There are two list boxes on the form. One maintains a current list of subdirectories of the given path. The other displays files of type text within the selected directory. Users navigate down through subdirectories by double-clicking a directory. To navigate back, they click the Up button. As directories and files are selected, we write related information to a couple of label controls.

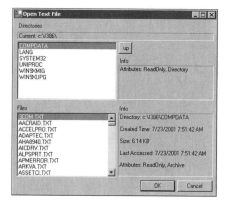

FIGURE 7.3

FontPad: Open form screen shot.

Code Walkthrough

The code used by the open dialog should be very familiar to you by now. The code can be found in Listing 7.8.

The code starts with some form-level declarations for directory name and filename. This is followed by the basic code to build the form.

LISTING 7.8 FontPad: Open Form (formOpen.vb)

```
Public Class formOpen

    Inherits System.Windows.Forms.Form

    'form-level scope declarations
    Dim myDirName As String
    Dim myFileName As String

#Region " Windows Form Designer generated code "

    Public Sub New()
        MyBase.New()

        'This call is required by the Windows Form Designer.
        InitializeComponent()

        'Add any initialization after the InitializeComponent() call

    End Sub
```

LISTING 7.8 Continued

```vb
'Form overrides dispose to clean up the component list.
Public Overloads Overrides Sub Dispose()
    MyBase.Dispose()
    If Not (components Is Nothing) Then
        components.Dispose()
    End If
End Sub

Private WithEvents buttonOk As System.Windows.Forms.Button
Private WithEvents buttonCancel As System.Windows.Forms.Button
Private WithEvents listBox1 As System.Windows.Forms.ListBox
Private WithEvents labelCurrentDir As System.Windows.Forms.Label
Private WithEvents buttonUp As System.Windows.Forms.Button
Private WithEvents labelDirInfo As System.Windows.Forms.Label
Private WithEvents label2 As System.Windows.Forms.Label
Private WithEvents label1 As System.Windows.Forms.Label
Private WithEvents labelFileInfo As System.Windows.Forms.Label
Private WithEvents listBoxFiles As System.Windows.Forms.ListBox
Private WithEvents listBoxDirectories As System.Windows.Forms.ListBox
Private WithEvents label5 As System.Windows.Forms.Label
Private WithEvents label3 As System.Windows.Forms.Label


'Required by the Windows Form Designer
Private components As System.ComponentModel.Container

'NOTE: The following procedure is required by the Windows Form Designer
'It can be modified using the Windows Form Designer.
'Do not modify it using the code editor.
<System.Diagnostics.DebuggerStepThrough()> Private Sub _
    InitializeComponent()
    Me.labelDirInfo = New System.Windows.Forms.Label()
    Me.listBoxFiles = New System.Windows.Forms.ListBox()
    Me.labelCurrentDir = New System.Windows.Forms.Label()
    Me.buttonCancel = New System.Windows.Forms.Button()
    Me.buttonUp = New System.Windows.Forms.Button()
    Me.listBoxDirectories = New System.Windows.Forms.ListBox()
    Me.listBox1 = New System.Windows.Forms.ListBox()
    Me.label5 = New System.Windows.Forms.Label()
    Me.labelFileInfo = New System.Windows.Forms.Label()
    Me.buttonOk = New System.Windows.Forms.Button()
    Me.label1 = New System.Windows.Forms.Label()
    Me.label2 = New System.Windows.Forms.Label()
    Me.label3 = New System.Windows.Forms.Label()
    Me.labelDirInfo.BorderStyle = System.Windows.Forms.BorderStyle.Fixed3D
    Me.labelDirInfo.Location = New System.Drawing.Point(224, 96)
```

LISTING 7.8   Continued

```
Me.labelDirInfo.Size = New System.Drawing.Size(204, 72)
Me.labelDirInfo.TabIndex = 7
Me.listBoxFiles.Location = New System.Drawing.Point(8, 196)
Me.listBoxFiles.Size = New System.Drawing.Size(212, 134)
Me.listBoxFiles.TabIndex = 9
Me.labelCurrentDir.BorderStyle = _
    System.Windows.Forms.BorderStyle.Fixed3D
Me.labelCurrentDir.Location = New System.Drawing.Point(8, 28)
Me.labelCurrentDir.Size = New System.Drawing.Size(420, 16)
Me.labelCurrentDir.TabIndex = 6
Me.labelCurrentDir.Text = "Current: "
Me.buttonCancel.DialogResult = System.Windows.Forms.DialogResult.Cancel
Me.buttonCancel.Location = New System.Drawing.Point(352, 336)
Me.buttonCancel.TabIndex = 0
Me.buttonCancel.Text = "Cancel"
Me.buttonUp.Location = New System.Drawing.Point(224, 48)
Me.buttonUp.Size = New System.Drawing.Size(28, 24)
Me.buttonUp.TabIndex = 5
Me.buttonUp.Text = "up"
Me.listBoxDirectories.Location = New System.Drawing.Point(8, 48)
Me.listBoxDirectories.Size = New System.Drawing.Size(212, 121)
Me.listBoxDirectories.TabIndex = 4
Me.listBox1.Location = New System.Drawing.Point(20, 60)
Me.listBox1.Size = New System.Drawing.Size(0, 4)
Me.listBox1.TabIndex = 3
Me.label5.Location = New System.Drawing.Point(224, 180)
Me.label5.Size = New System.Drawing.Size(92, 16)
Me.label5.TabIndex = 2
Me.label5.Text = "Info"
Me.labelFileInfo.BorderStyle = System.Windows.Forms.BorderStyle.Fixed3D
Me.labelFileInfo.Location = New System.Drawing.Point(224, 196)
Me.labelFileInfo.Size = New System.Drawing.Size(204, 132)
Me.labelFileInfo.TabIndex = 7
Me.buttonOk.Location = New System.Drawing.Point(272, 336)
Me.buttonOk.TabIndex = 1
Me.buttonOk.Text = "OK"
Me.label1.Location = New System.Drawing.Point(8, 8)
Me.label1.Size = New System.Drawing.Size(100, 16)
Me.label1.TabIndex = 8
Me.label1.Text = "Directories"
Me.label2.Location = New System.Drawing.Point(224, 80)
Me.label2.Size = New System.Drawing.Size(92, 16)
Me.label2.TabIndex = 2
Me.label2.Text = "Info"
Me.label3.Location = New System.Drawing.Point(6, 180)
```

7

LISTING 7.8 Continued

```
        Me.label3.Size = New System.Drawing.Size(100, 16)
        Me.label3.TabIndex = 8
        Me.label3.Text = "Files"
        Me.AcceptButton = Me.buttonOk
        Me.AutoScaleBaseSize = New System.Drawing.Size(5, 13)
        Me.FormBorderStyle = System.Windows.Forms.FormBorderStyle.FixedDialog
        Me.CancelButton = Me.buttonCancel
        Me.ClientSize = New System.Drawing.Size(433, 366)
        Me.Controls.AddRange(New System.Windows.Forms.Control() {Me.label5, _
            Me.labelFileInfo, Me.label3, Me.listBoxFiles, Me.label1, _
            Me.labelCurrentDir, Me.buttonUp, Me.listBoxDirectories, _
            Me.labelDirInfo, Me.label2, Me.listBox1, Me.buttonOk, _
            Me.buttonCancel})
        Me.Text = "Open Text File"

End Sub
```

On the form load event we simply make a call to the sub procedure that loads the directory list box.

```
    Private Sub formOpen_Load(ByVal sender As System.Object, _
        ByVal e As System.EventArgs) Handles MyBase.Load

        'purpose:    load the form, init the controls

        'local scope

        'load the directory list box
        Call loadDirListBox()

    End Sub
```

The procedure `loadDirListBox` refreshes the contents of the directory list box when the form loads and as users double-click a subdirectory or press the Up button.

```
    Private Sub loadDirListBox()

        'purpose:    load the list box control based on the current path

        'local scope
        Dim myDirectory As System.IO.DirectoryInfo
        Dim myDirectories() As System.IO.DirectoryInfo
        Dim i As Integer
```

LISTING 7.8 Continued

```
    'clear the directory list box
    listBoxDirectories().Items().Clear()

    'create a new directory object
    myDirectory = New System.IO.DirectoryInfo(path:=myPath)

    'return the sub directories from the global directory object
    myDirectories = myDirectory.GetDirectories()

    'loop through the directories and add them to the list box
    For i = 0 To UBound(myDirectories) - 1

        'add the directory name to the list
        listBoxDirectories().Items.Add(myDirectories(i).Name)

    Next

    'set the current label to indicate the current path
    labelCurrentDir().Text = "Current: " & myPath

    'select the first directory in the list
    '  note: this will trigger the events that fill the label control
    '        and the files list box and its label control
    If listBoxDirectories().Items.Count > 0 Then
        listBoxDirectories().SelectedIndex = 0
    End If

End Sub
```

Once the user has selected a file to open and has clicked the OK button, the button's click
event calls a custom procedure we call readFile.

```
Private Sub buttonOk_Click(ByVal sender As System.Object, _
    ByVal e As System.EventArgs) Handles buttonOk.Click

    'purpose:   respond to the OK button event
    '           validate the form
    '           open the user's selected file

    'determine if the user does indeed have a text file selected
    If Not (listBoxFiles().SelectedIndex > -1) Then

        'tell the user to select a text file to continue
        MsgBox(prompt:="Please select a text file.", _
            buttons:=MsgBoxStyle.Information, title:="FontPad Open")
```

LISTING 7.8 Continued

```
      Else

          'open the text file as a stream and read it into our editor
          'note: this new file will replace the current file without saving
          Call readFile()

          'close the form
          Me.Close()

      End If

   End Sub
```

The readFile procedure creates a StreamReader object, sets its read position to the start of the file, and reads the file line-by-line. Finally, our rich text box control is updated with the contents of the opened file.

```
Private Sub readFile()

      'purpose:   read a file as a stream object
      '             and put its content in the rich text box

      'local scope
      Dim fileStream As IO.FileStream
      Dim streamReader As IO.StreamReader

      'handle any errors the occur when loading the file stream
      Try
          'create a new instance of the file stream object
          '   based on the current path and selected file
          fileStream = New IO.FileStream(path:=myPath & myDirName & _
              myFileName, mode:=IO.FileMode.Open, access:=IO.FileAccess.Read)

          'create a stream reader instance
          streamReader = New IO.StreamReader(stream:=fileStream)

          'set the file pointer to the start of the file
          streamReader.BaseStream.Seek(offset:=0, _
          origin:=IO.SeekOrigin.Begin)

          'set the textContents to nothing
          'note the rich text box will be updated on form close
          textContents = ""
```

LISTING 7.8   Continued

```
        'loop through the file and write to internal string variable
        '    until end of file reached
        Do While streamReader.Peek > -1
            textContents = textContents & streamReader.ReadLine() & vbCrLf
        Loop

        'close the stream reader
        streamReader.Close()

    Catch

        'indicate to the user that the file cannot be opened
        MsgBox(prompt:="Sorry, unable to open the selected file", _
            buttons:=MsgBoxStyle.Exclamation, title:="FontPad Open")

    End Try

End Sub
```

Inside the `listBoxDirectories` double-click event we simply reset the path (`myPath`) and call load directories sub (`loadDirListBox`).

```
Private Sub listBoxDirectories_DoubleClick(ByVal sender As System.Object, _
        ByVal e As System.EventArgs) Handles listBoxDirectories.DoubleClick

        'purpose:   manange the double-click event
        '           which allows users to navigate down directories

        'local scope

        'set the new global path
        myPath = myPath & myDirName

        'update the list directory list box
        Call loadDirListBox()

End Sub
```

When users select a directory from the list box, the directory list box's index change event gets fired. This event loads the file's list box based on the user-selected subdirectory. Inside this event, we trap for file security access issues. For instance, if you call the `GetFiles` method of the `Directory` object and the user is not granted access to the directory's files, we must raise this issue to our user.

LISTING 7.8   Continued

```
Private Sub listBoxDirectories_SelectedIndexChanged( _
        ByVal sender As System.Object, ByVal e As System.EventArgs) _
        Handles listBoxDirectories.SelectedIndexChanged

        'purpose:    update the directory info label and the file's list box
        '            when users select a directory

        'local scope
        Dim myDirectory As System.IO.DirectoryInfo
        Dim dirInfo As String
        Dim myFiles() As System.IO.FileInfo
        Dim i As Integer

        'clear the listbox of its current contents
        listBoxFiles().Items.Clear()

        'clear the list box label
        labelFileInfo().Text = ""

        'get a directory info object based on the user's selection
        myDirName = listBoxDirectories().SelectedItem.ToString & "\"
        myDirectory = New System.IO.DirectoryInfo( _
            path:=(myPath & myDirName))

        'set the dir info
        dirInfo = dirInfo & "Attributes: " & myDirectory.Attributes.ToString
        labelDirInfo().Text = dirInfo

        'get the files in the directory that are of type text
        'NOTE: we handle security access exceptions
        Try
            myFiles = myDirectory.GetFiles(searchPattern:="*.txt")

            'check for files
            If UBound(myFiles) >= 0 Then

                'loop through the files array and add to the listbox
                For i = 0 To UBound(myFiles) - 1
                    listBoxFiles().Items.Add(myFiles(i).Name)
                Next

                'select the file in the list, this will trigger the event to _
                    change
```

LISTING 7.8 Continued

```
            '   the file info label control
            If listBoxFiles().Items.Count > 0 Then
                listBoxFiles().SelectedIndex = 0
            End If

        End If

    Catch
        MsgBox(prompt:= _
            "Sorry, but you do not have access to browse this folder's _
            files.", buttons:=MsgBoxStyle.Exclamation, title:="FontPad _
            Exception")
    End Try

End Sub
```

When a user selects a file, the `SelectedIndexChanged` event is fired. This event allows us to set the selected filename (`myFileName`) and update the file properties to the user.

```
Private Sub listBoxFiles_SelectedIndexChanged(ByVal sender As System.Object, _
    ByVal e As System.EventArgs) Handles listBoxFiles.SelectedIndexChanged

    'purpose:   change the contents of the file properties label

    'local scope
    Dim myFile As System.IO.FileInfo
    Dim fileInfo As String

    'set the file name
    myFileName = listBoxFiles().SelectedItem.ToString

    'create a new file object
    myFile = New System.IO.FileInfo(fileName:=myPath & myDirName & _
        myFileName)

    'set the file info to display
    fileInfo = fileInfo & "Directory: " & _
        myFile.DirectoryName & vbCrLf & vbCrLf
    fileInfo = fileInfo & "Created Time: " & _
        CStr(myFile.CreationTime) & vbCrLf & vbCrLf
    fileInfo = fileInfo & "Size: " & _
        CStr(myFile.Length / 100) & " KB" & vbCrLf & vbCrLf
    fileInfo = fileInfo & "Last Accessed: " & _
        CStr(myFile.LastAccessTime) & vbCrLf & vbCrLf
    fileInfo = fileInfo & "Attributes: " & myFile.Attributes.ToString
```

Listing 7.8 Continued

```
        'set the label to the file's info
        labelFileInfo().Text = fileInfo

    End Sub
```

The Up button's click event simply navigates the user back up one folder.

```
    Private Sub buttonUp_Click(ByVal sender As System.Object, _
        ByVal e As System.EventArgs) Handles buttonUp.Click

        'purpose:   move back one directory

        'local scope
        Dim intPos As Integer

        'find the \ at the end of the path
        intPos = InStrRev(stringCheck:=Mid(myPath, 1, Len(myPath) - 1), _
            stringMatch:="\")

        If intPos = 0 Then
            'no more path info
            Beep()
        Else
            'trim the path back
            myPath = Mid(myPath, 1, intPos)
            Call loadDirListBox()
        End If

    End Sub

#End Region

End Class
```

Save Dialog

Our application needs a way to persist its data to the file system. We create a Save dialog and associated code to do just that. Figure 7.4 is a screen capture of the Save dialog in action. Again, this dialog is sure to offend UI designers but it serves to illustrate the use of the classes.

The directory list box and associated Up button were stolen from the Open form. This simple paradigm provides users with access to the file system. A text box is provided for users to type the name to which they want to save the file.

FIGURE 7.4
FontPad: Save form.

The directory browsing provided by the form's code is nearly the same as the Open example (we might have considered creating a common dialog to be used by both features).

Code Walkthrough

Listing 7.9 presents the code behind the Open form.

Listing 7.9 starts with a form-level declare for storing the directory name. This is followed by the basic form code. After that, much of the code is similar to the code in the open dialog with the exception of the saveFile function.

LISTING 7.9   FontPad: Save Form (formSave.vb)

```
Public Class formSave
    Inherits System.Windows.Forms.Form

    'form-level scope declarations
    Dim myDirName As String

    'note:  issues
    '1. cannot save to the root directory
    '2. the return character not coming out right
    '3. files saved cannot be seen by the open
    '4. delete the file if exists??

#Region " Windows Form Designer generated code "
```

LISTING 7.9   Continued

```vb
Public Sub New()
    MyBase.New()

    'This call is required by the Windows Form Designer.
    InitializeComponent()

    'Add any initialization after the InitializeComponent() call

End Sub

'Form overrides dispose to clean up the component list.
Public Overloads Overrides Sub Dispose()
    MyBase.Dispose()
    If Not (components Is Nothing) Then
        components.Dispose()
    End If
End Sub
Private WithEvents label1 As System.Windows.Forms.Label
Private WithEvents buttonOk As System.Windows.Forms.Button
Private WithEvents buttonCancel As System.Windows.Forms.Button
Private WithEvents buttonUp As System.Windows.Forms.Button
Private WithEvents label2 As System.Windows.Forms.Label
Private WithEvents textBoxFileName As System.Windows.Forms.TextBox
Private WithEvents listBoxDirectories As System.Windows.Forms.ListBox
Private WithEvents labelSaveTo As System.Windows.Forms.Label

'Required by the Windows Form Designer
Private components As System.ComponentModel.Container

'NOTE: The following procedure is required by the Windows Form Designer
'It can be modified using the Windows Form Designer.
'Do not modify it using the code editor.
<System.Diagnostics.DebuggerStepThrough()> Private Sub _
    InitializeComponent()
    Me.label1 = New System.Windows.Forms.Label()
    Me.buttonOk = New System.Windows.Forms.Button()
    Me.label2 = New System.Windows.Forms.Label()
    Me.buttonCancel = New System.Windows.Forms.Button()
    Me.listBoxDirectories = New System.Windows.Forms.ListBox()
    Me.labelSaveTo = New System.Windows.Forms.Label()
    Me.textBoxFileName = New System.Windows.Forms.TextBox()
    Me.buttonUp = New System.Windows.Forms.Button()
    Me.SuspendLayout()
    '
    'label1
    '
```

LISTING 7.9 Continued

```vb
    Me.label1.Location = New System.Drawing.Point(8, 8)
    Me.label1.Name = "label1"1
    Me.label1.Size = New System.Drawing.Size(124, 23)
    Me.label1.TabIndex = 2
    Me.label1.Text = "Save to directory:"
    '
    'buttonOk
    '
    Me.buttonOk.Location = New System.Drawing.Point(136, 220)
    Me.buttonOk.Name = "buttonOk"
    Me.buttonOk.TabIndex = 1
    Me.buttonOk.Text = "OK"
    '
    'label2
    '
    Me.label2.Location = New System.Drawing.Point(4, 172)
    Me.label2.Name = "label2"
    Me.label2.TabIndex = 2
    Me.label2.Text = "File name:"
    '
    'buttonCancel
    '
    Me.buttonCancel.DialogResult = System.Windows.Forms.DialogResult.Cancel
    Me.buttonCancel.Location = New System.Drawing.Point(216, 220)
    Me.buttonCancel.Name = "buttonCancel"
    Me.buttonCancel.TabIndex = 0
    Me.buttonCancel.Text = "Cancel"
    '
    'listBoxDirectories
    '
    Me.listBoxDirectories.Location = New System.Drawing.Point(8, 72)
    Me.listBoxDirectories.Name = "listBoxDirectories"
    Me.listBoxDirectories.Size = New System.Drawing.Size(244, 95)
    Me.listBoxDirectories.TabIndex = 3
    '
    'labelSaveTo
    '
    Me.labelSaveTo.BorderStyle = System.Windows.Forms.BorderStyle.Fixed3D
    Me.labelSaveTo.Location = New System.Drawing.Point(8, 28)
    Me.labelSaveTo.Name = "labelSaveTo"
    Me.labelSaveTo.Size = New System.Drawing.Size(280, 36)
    Me.labelSaveTo.TabIndex = 6
    '
    'textBoxFileName
    '
```

LISTING 7.9   Continued

```
        Me.textBoxFileName.Location = New System.Drawing.Point(8, 192)
        Me.textBoxFileName.Name = "textBoxFileName"
        Me.textBoxFileName.Size = New System.Drawing.Size(280, 20)
        Me.textBoxFileName.TabIndex = 5
        Me.textBoxFileName.Text = ""
        '
        'buttonUp
        '
        Me.buttonUp.Location = New System.Drawing.Point(256, 72)
        Me.buttonUp.Name = "buttonUp"
        Me.buttonUp.Size = New System.Drawing.Size(32, 23)
        Me.buttonUp.TabIndex = 4
        Me.buttonUp.Text = "up"
        '
        'formSave
        '
        Me.AcceptButton = Me.buttonOk
        Me.AutoScaleBaseSize = New System.Drawing.Size(5, 13)
        Me.CancelButton = Me.buttonCancel
        Me.ClientSize = New System.Drawing.Size(298, 250)
        Me.Controls.AddRange(New System.Windows.Forms.Control() _
            {Me.labelSaveTo, Me.textBoxFileName, Me.label2, Me.buttonUp, _
            Me.listBoxDirectories, Me.label1, Me.buttonOk, Me.buttonCancel})
        Me.FormBorderStyle = System.Windows.Forms.FormBorderStyle.FixedDialog
        Me.Name = "formSave"
        Me.Text = "Save Text File"
        Me.ResumeLayout(False)

    End Sub

    Private Sub formSave_Load(ByVal sender As System.Object, _
        ByVal e As System.EventArgs) Handles MyBase.Load

        'purpose:   load the form

        'local scope

        'load the directory list box
        Call loadDirListBox()

    End Sub

    Private Sub loadDirListBox()

        'purpose:   load the list box control based on the current path
        '           note: this procedure is the same as the one in formOpen
```

LISTING 7.9 Continued

```
        'local scope
        Dim myDirectory As System.IO.DirectoryInfo
        Dim myDirectories() As System.IO.DirectoryInfo
        Dim i As Integer

        'clear the directory list box
        listBoxDirectories().Items().Clear()

        'create a new directory object
        myDirectory = New System.IO.DirectoryInfo(path:=myPath)

        'return the sub directories from the global directory object
        myDirectories = myDirectory.GetDirectories()

        'loop through the directories and add them to the list box
        For i = 0 To UBound(myDirectories) - 1

            'add the directory name to the list
            listBoxDirectories().Items.Add(myDirectories(i).Name)

        Next

        'select the first directory in the list
        '  note: this will trigger the events that fill the label control
        '        and the files list box and its label control
        If listBoxDirectories().Items.Count > 0 Then
            listBoxDirectories().SelectedIndex = 0
        End If

    End Sub
    Private Sub listBoxDirectories_SelectedIndexChanged( _
        ByVal sender As System.Object, ByVal e As System.EventArgs) _
        Handles listBoxDirectories.SelectedIndexChanged

        'purpose:   update the directory name when users select a directory

        'local scope

        'set the directory's name
        myDirName = listBoxDirectories().SelectedItem.ToString & "\"

        'reset the save to directory
        labelSaveTo().Text = myPath & myDirName

    End Sub
```

LISTING 7.9   Continued

```
Private Sub buttonUp_Click(ByVal sender As System.Object, _
    ByVal e As System.EventArgs) Handles buttonUp.Click

    'purpose:   move back one directory
    '           note: this proc. is the same as formOpen

    'local scope
    Dim intPos As Integer

    'find the \ at the end of the path
    intPos = InStrRev(stringCheck:=Mid(myPath, 1, Len(myPath) - 1), _
        stringMatch:="\")

    If intPos = 0 Then
        'no more path info
        Beep()
    Else
        'trim the path back
        myPath = Mid(myPath, 1, intPos)
        Call loadDirListBox()
    End If

End Sub

Private Sub listBoxDirectories_DoubleClick(ByVal sender As System.Object, _
    ByVal e As System.EventArgs) Handles listBoxDirectories.DoubleClick

    'purpose:   manange the double-click event
    '           which allows users to navigate down directories
    '           note: same as formOpen's

    'local scope

    'set the new global path
    myPath = myPath & myDirName

    'reset the selected directory to nothing
    myDirName = ""

    'update the list directory list box
    Call loadDirListBox()

End Sub

Private Sub buttonOk_Click(ByVal sender As System.Object, _
    ByVal e As System.EventArgs) Handles buttonOk.Click
```

LISTING 7.9 Continued

```
    'purpose:   user has indicated they would like to apply their
    'selections

    'local scope
    Dim fileName As String

    'get the file name
    fileName = Trim(textBoxFileName().Text)

    'validate filename
    If fileName = "" Then

        'raise a message to the user
        MsgBox(prompt:="Please enter a file name.", _
            buttons:=MsgBoxStyle.Exclamation, title:="FontPad Save")

        'position cursor
        textBoxFileName().Focus()

    Else

        'check the file name's extension
        If Not fileName.EndsWith(".txt") Then
            fileName = fileName.Insert(fileName.Length, ".txt")
        End If

        'call save file method
        Call saveFile(fileName:=fileName)

        'close the form
        Me.Close()

    End If

End Sub
```

The primary piece of functionality (save) can be found in the saveFile procedure. First, we use methods of the File class to determine if the file already exists. If a file does exist, we handle the situation by first deleting it and then saving it as new. This is a shortcut and not the best solution. A more robust design would tell the user the file already exists and prompt him to overwrite. Next, we create the FileStream object to write out the file. We open a StreamWriter instance and set it to start writing at the beginning of our file. After this, we call the Write method and pass it our contents as a string value. Finally we Flush and Close the StreamWriter instance. Our new file is now saved to disk.

```
Private Sub saveFile(ByVal fileName As String)

        'purpose:   save the contents of the rtb to a file

        'local scope
        Dim fileStream As IO.FileStream
        Dim streamWriter As IO.StreamWriter
        Dim filePath As String

        'set the full path of the file
        filePath = myPath & myDirName & fileName

        'check if the file already exists in the directory
        If IO.File.Exists(path:=filePath) Then

            'the file already exists, we cheat and delete it
            IO.File.Delete(path:=filePath)

        End If

        'create a new instance of the file stream object
        'note: if the file does not exist, the constructor will create it
        fileStream = New IO.FileStream(path:=filePath, _
            mode:=IO.FileMode.OpenOrCreate, access:=IO.FileAccess.Write)

        'create an instance of a character writer
        streamWriter = New IO.StreamWriter(stream:=fileStream)

        'set the file pointer to the end of the file
        streamWriter.BaseStream.Seek(offset:=0, origin:=IO.SeekOrigin.Begin)

        'write a line of text to the end of the file
        streamWriter.Write(value:=textContents)

        'apply the update to the file
        streamWriter.Flush()

        'close the stream writer
        streamWriter.Close()

        'close the file stream object
        fileStream.Close()

    End Sub

#End Region

End Class
```

Summary

The ability to handle common file I/O tasks is essential to all developers. The .NET Framework namespace, System.IO, exposes this functionality. By now, you should have a solid foothold in this namespace that will support you in your further explorations.

The following is a summary of some of the key points regarding common file I/O programming tasks:

- DirectoryInfo and FileInfo classes contain specific instance methods related to a given directory or file. Whereas, the Directory and File classes pertain to static methods and are thus used in more generic cases.

- Use the following four basic methods of the Directory class for manipulating directories: Create, CreateSubdirectory, Delete, MoveTo, and Refresh.

- Use the GetFiles method of Directory to access the files in a specific directory.

- Use the following methods of FileInfo to manipulate files: Create, Delete, MoveTo, Refresh, CopyTo, Open, OpenRead, and OpenWrite.

- The class, FileSystemWatcher, allows us to monitor the file system for new files, files being renamed, moved, and so on.

- Use the FileStream object for all basic file reading and writing including asynchronous and binary.

- To read files asynchronously, we call FileStream.BeginRead and pass the name of a procedure to receive callback notification when the operation is complete.

- StreamWriter, StreamReader, BinaryWriter, and BinaryReader all provide additional, more advanced file streaming functionality.

- ReadByte and WriteByte are the primary methods used for reading and writing binary data.

Networking Functions

IN THIS CHAPTER

This chapter begins our in-depth discussion of namespaces by examining the functionality exposed by the System.Net and System.Net.Sockets namespaces. This chapter will show you how to accomplish common network-based programming tasks using the components exposed in these two namespaces. We'll begin by examining how the network classes in these namespaces provide comprehensive coverage of both high and low-level network programming tasks. Then, by working our way from the low-level classes dealing with protocol-independent sockets to the high-level classes that operate over HTTP, we will paint a picture of the exact functionality offered by these base classes. We will also look at how they can serve as a great foundation for building network-enabled .NET applications.

After reading this chapter, you should be able to:

- Discuss the layered approach to network functionality offered by the classes of the System.Net and System.Net.Sockets namespaces
- Create and use sockets for bidirectional communication
- Send and receive TCP or UDP packets across a network
- Issue and respond to HTTP requests
- Download and upload Web-based resources
- Use credentials to access privileged resources
- Configure your code to work with proxy servers
- Build asynchronous design patterns into your networking code

Key Classes Related to Network Programming

At its simplest, network programming is about physically moving bits from point A to point B across a wire and responding to data that is being moved from point A to point B across a network. Conceptually, this is a simple task. Physically, it can get very complicated. The .NET Framework Class Library gives us a very useful foundation of code constructs that can either shelter us from, or expose us to, low-level networking concepts.

Programmers familiar with Windows sockets programming will feel right at home (and even a little spoiled) when dealing with the classes in System.Net.Sockets. At the same time, developers new to network programming will find the network classes approachable and easy to use despite their amazing range of functionality.

Table 8.1 shows the classes that we will be talking about in this chapter.

TABLE 8.1 Classes Discussed in This Chapter

Class	Description
Socket Classes	
Socket	The Socket class represents a network socket. On the Microsoft Windows platform, this class abstracts the WinSock API.
SocketException	The SocketException class is used to signal socket-specific errors that occur.
TCP/UDP Classes	
TcpClient	The TCPClient class allows you to create TCP connections to a remote server. This class is a further abstraction, or later, on top of the socket level of functionality.
TcpListener	The TCPListener class allows applications to listen for, and react to, TCP connections from other network clients.
UdpClient	Similar to the TCPClient class, this class deals specifically with the UDP protocol.
HTTP Request/Response Classes	
HttpWebRequest	This is an implementation of the WebRequest class, specifically designed to work with the HTTP protocol.
HttpWebResponse	This is an implementation of the WebResponse class, specifically designed to work with the HTTP protocol.
Generic Request/Response Classes	
FileWebRequest	The FileWebRequest class allows you to issue requests for files to remote servers. In other words, this class encapsulates "file://" requests.
FileWebResponse	The FileWebResponse class provides access to a file response stream sent from a remote server.
WebRequest	The WebRequest class abstracts Web-based server requests. This class is protocol agnostic.
WebResponse	The WebResponse class is used to work with Web-based server responses. This class is protocol agnostic.
WebClient	The WebClient class represents the highest level of abstraction in the .NET networking stack. It allows for simple sending and receiving of data from a resource. This class is protocol agnostic.
WebException	The WebException class signals errors encountered with any of the pluggable network protocols supported by .NET.

8

NETWORKING
FUNCTIONS

TABLE 8.1   Continued

Class	Description
Authentication Classes	
AuthenticationManager	This class handles the varied network authentication modules that an application may use.
CredentialCache	The CredentialCache class provides for centralized storage and retrieval of networking credentials.
NetworkCredential	The NetworkCredential class stores a particular instance of application or user network credentials.
Utility Classes	
NetworkStream	The Point class implements network-based stream operations.
DNS	The DNS class allows server names to be resolved into IP addresses.
IPAddress	The IPAddress class is used to encapsulate an IP address.
IPEndpoint	The IPEndpoint class represents one end point on a specific network connection. An end point is typically identified by an IP address and a port number.
IPHostEntry	The IPHostEntry class is used in conjunction with the DNS class. It stores a specific DNS host entry.
WebProxy	The WebProxy class provides proxy services that can be used by the WebRequest class and its descendants.

Mapping the Network Classes in .NET

The .NET namespaces System.Net and System.Net.Sockets expose a continuum of network functionality for developers to use. In other words, if we want or need to interact with a network at a very low level, we can. The "bottom" level of functionality exposed by .NET allows us to deal directly with something called a socket (more on this in a little bit). Likewise, we can also deal with some very high-level constructs that enable us to do things like open a connection to a URL and retrieve its response using only one line of code.

Figure 8.1 shows how the .NET networking classes range across a spectrum of control versus simplicity to provide developers with the appropriate level of functionality for their specific programming task.

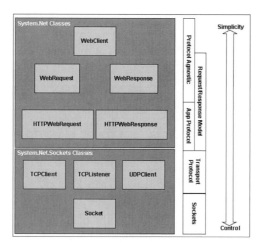

FIGURE 8.1

The network class layers in .NET.

Working from the most complex, highest level of control to the least complex, least amount of control, the base classes can be grouped in the following way:

- The socket level of functionality allows direct interaction with *datagrams* and *streams*. Representative classes include the Socket class.

- The transport level of functionality allows us access to TCP- and UDP-based features. The core classes here are the TCPClient, UDPClient, and TCPListener.

- The application level of functionality deals principally with HTTP-based Web communications. The HTTPWebRequest and HTTPWebResponse classes represent this level of control.

- The "Protocol Agnostic" level of functionality allows easy connection and communication to a URI without worrying about protocol specifics. A URL (for example, www.microsoft.com) is a common form of a URI. The WebRequest, WebResponse, and WebClient classes represent this level of functionality.

Each successive layer of the networking classes builds on the layer below it, abstracting functionality and complexity for us until we reach the pinnacle of ease: the WebClient class which can, with one line of code, open a connection to a URI (Uniform Resource Identifier) and retrieve a result.

8

NETWORKING
FUNCTIONS

> **NOTE**
>
> URI stands for *Uniform Resource Identifier*; it is a string that uniquely identifies a resource. URLs, or Uniform Resource Locators, are one form of a URI that describe Web addresses.

The .NET networking classes offer a few distinct advantages to the old Windows DNA/Win32 API style of networking code. For one, the classes are specifically designed to function in high-load environments. That means that you won't have to worry about their performance, whether you are deploying them on the server side, where scalability and speed are critical, or on the client side, where functionality tends to be more important than scalability or speed. In addition, they provide a way to implement a simple architecture that can achieve complex results by exposing a logical, hierarchical component object model for use.

Now that we've examined the general concepts of networking and seen how the `System.Net` and `System.Net.Sockets` classes are arranged to provide programmatic access to these networking tasks, we can start looking at the tangible code structures that we'll deal with when writing our network-level software. We will start at the bottom with the `Socket` class.

Sockets

A socket can be thought of as a two-way pipe; it connects two end points and allows data to flow across the pipe from one end point to the other. As a technology, it was first implemented as a method for exposing the TCP/IP suite to calling applications. Today, most socket APIs are generic enough to be used for almost any interprocess communication request. From an application developer's point of view, a socket is something that can be "plugged into" to allow data to be sent from one endpoint to another.

Sockets are a core technology for programming applications that communicate across IP networks—if you program against the Winsock API or use the Winsock Control (an OCX) in Visual Basic 6, you are already familiar with sockets and what they can do. The `System.Net.Sockets` namespace provides straightforward access to this general purpose networking API. Working with the `Socket` class in .NET very closely resembles working with the socket calls in the Win32 API. When run on the Microsoft Windows platform, the `Socket` class is merely an abstraction of the Winsock libraries; in many cases it just passes its calls into the Winsock API for execution.

> **Note**
>
> Keep in mind that the .NET Framework is meant to port to platforms other than Windows. Should that happen, the Socket class would, of course, have to talk to something other than the WinSock API, which doesn't exist outside of Windows.

The other `System.Net` and `System.Net.Sockets` classes often build directly on top of the `Socket` class for their functionality.

Creating Sockets

A common analogy used to describe the process of socket communication is the concept of a telephone call: Before you start talking, you first have to dial a number. In our world of network classes, this means establishing a connection; and that means first creating an instance of the `Socket` class.

When dealing with sockets-based communication, we are primarily concerned with the two following classes:

- `Socket` class (from the `System.Net.Sockets` namespace)—This represents an instance of a sockets interface. Remember that this is a bidirectional pipeline that is used to send and receive data across a network.
- `IPEndPoint` class (from the `System.Net` namespace)—This class encapsulates an IP address (and thus, one end of our "pipe").

Instancing a socket object from the `Socket` class is straightforward. Its constructor takes three arguments: the address family that the socket will use, the type of socket to create, and the type of protocol that the socket will use once created. Let's examine each one of these in order.

The address family identifies which type of addressing schema or scope the socket will use .NET provides us with an enumeration constant that we can use to identify our desired address family. Appropriately, it is named `AddressFamily`. Table 8.2 shows the different values supported by this enumeration.

For our purposes here, we will use the InterNetwork address family (for Internet protocol addressing).

TABLE 8.2 AddressFamily Enumeration

Name	Description
AppleTalk	AppleTalk Addressing
Atm	Asynchronous Transfer Mode addressing
Banyan	Banyan networking addressing
Ccitt	CCITT (X.400/X.500 addressing)
Chaos	MIT CHAOS addressing
Cluster	Microsoft cluster addressing
DataKit	DataKit protocol addressing
DataLink	DataLink interface addressing
DecNet	DECNet addressing
ECMA	European Computer Manufacturers Association addressing
FireFox	FireFox addressing
HyperChannel	NSC Hyperchannel addressing
Ieee12844	IEEE 1284.4 workgroup addressing
ImpLink	ARPANET IMP addressing
InterNetwork	IP v4 addressing
InterNetworkv6	IP v6 addressing
Ipx	Internetwork Packet Exchange addressing
Irda	Infrared Data Association addressing
Iso	ISO protocol addressing
Lat	Local Address Table addressing
Max	MAX addressing
NetBios	Network Basic Input/Output System addressing
NetworkDesigners	NetworkDesigners OSI protocols addressing
NS	Xerox NS addressing
Osi	OSI protocol addressing
Pup	PUP protocol addressing
Sna	IBM SNA addressing
Unix	Unix local to host addressing
Unknown	<unknown address family>
Unspecified	<unspecified address family>
VoiceView	VoiceView addressing

We would express the enumeration value like this:

```
AddressFamily.InterNetwork
```

The next parameter into our socket constructor is the socket type. There are two types available to us: *stream* or *datagram*.

> **NOTE**
>
> In general, stream-based communication protocols are more reliable because they have the capability to resend packets that have been received with an error. Datagram-based communication tends to be faster because it doesn't have any of the error control functionality as overhead, but of course you pay the price in reliability. TCP packets are stream oriented, and UDP packets are datagram oriented.

Since we are specifically talking about TCP transmissions here, we will select stream. Just as with the previous example, the `System.Net.Sockets` namespace contains an enumeration, `SocketType` (see Table 8.3), that we can use to easily specify our stream socket type like this:

```
SocketType.SockStream
```

TABLE 8.3 SocketType Enumeration

Name	Description
Dgram	Datagram socket
Raw	Raw socket
Rdm	Reliably-Delivered Messages socket
SeqPacket	Sequential packet socket
Stream	Stream socket
Unknown	Unknown socket

The last parameter required by our socket constructor is the protocol type. Once again, an enumeration comes to the rescue. The `ProtocolType` enumeration (see Table 8.4) allows us to easily specify protocols such as TCP, UDP, or SPX among others:

```
ProtocolType.Tcp
```

TABLE 8.4 ProtocolType Enumeration

Name	Description
Ggp	Gateway to Gateway Protocol
Icmp	Internet Control Message Protocol
Idp	Internet Datagram Protocol
Igmp	Internet Group Management Protocol
IP	Internet Protocol
Ipx	Internetwork Packet Exchange
ND	Net Disk Protocol
Pup	PUP Protocol
Raw	RAW UP Protocol
Spx	Sequence Packet Exchange Protocol
SpxII	Sequence Packet Exchange II Protocol
Tcp	Transmission Control Protocol
Udp	User Datagram Protocol
Unknown	Unknown Protocol
Unspecified	Unspecified Protocol

Putting all of this together, we arrive at the following statement that creates an instance of the Socket class with the appropriate properties set through its constructor:

```
Dim ourSocket As Socket = New Socket(AddressFamily.InterNetwork, _
    SocketType.Stream, ProtocolType.Tcp)
```

Sending Data

Now that the socket has been created, we need to connect it to its end points. Since we are talking in terms of TCP/IP in this example, our end points will be IP addresses. The IPEndPoint class embodies the concept of an IP-based end point, and is available in the System.Net library. Also in the System.Net namespace is the IPAddress class. We will use an IPAddress instance to create our IPEndPoint instance. The first order of business is to create an IPAddress object from a valid IP address. One convenient way of doing this is by using the IPAddress.Parse method. We can supply this method with an IP address in dotted quad form and have an IPAddress object returned to us:

```
Dim localAddress As IPAddress = IPAddress.Parse("10.0.0.1")
```

Now, to create an `IPEndPoint` instance, we pass our `IPAddress` into the constructor, along with a port number, like this:

```
Dim localEndPoint As IPEndPoint = New IPEndPoint(localAddress, 8080)
```

We have now specified our local address (that is, the "near" side of the connection). Now we need to set up the remote address (the far side of the connection). Here we will assume that we don't know the actual IP address of the machine to which we want to connect—we just know its host name. To resolve a host name into an IP address, we turn to the `DNS` class, also located in the `System.Net` library. The `DNS` class has a `Resolve` method that will accept a host/server name:

```
Dim targetAddress As IPAddress
targetAddress = DNS.Resolve("www.microsoft.com").AddressList(0)
Dim endPoint As IPEndPoint = New IPEndPoint(targetAddress, 8080)
```

The `Resolve` method returns an `IPHostEntry` object. This isn't quite what we are looking for; we just want an `IPAddress` object. But the `IPHostEntry` object exposes an `AddressList` property that will return what we are looking for. In the code example, you can see that we are going after the first IP address associated with that particular `IPHostEntry` by typing this: `.AddressList(0)`.

Now, all that is left to do is connect our socket to the two end points. The `Socket.Bind` method will connect us with our local end point:

```
'connect the socket to the local end-point
ourSocket.Bind(localEndPoint)
```

And the `Socket.Connect` method will connect us with the remote end point:

```
'connect the socket using our endpoint object
ourSocket.Connect(endPoint)
```

Once the socket is fully connected, we can move data across the pipe. What would it take to send a plain text message across the socket to our end point? Not much. `Socket.Send` accepts a byte array for transmission across the socket. If we wanted to send a test message like "socket programming is easy!" we first have to massage it into the required byte array form. Again, the .NET namespaces provide us with the answer in the form of another ready to use class. The `Encoding` class from the `System.Text` library and its `GetBytes` method provide a quick way to get what we want—an array of bytes.

```
Dim encoder As Encoding
Dim ourMsg As Byte() = encoder.GetBytes("socket programming is easy!")
```

To send, the string requires a `Send` method call from our `Socket` class:

```
ourSocket.Send(ourMsg)
```

Receiving Data

If your application is one that sits on the other end of the pipe and is a data recipient, or if you are expecting a reply back from data that you have sent out across the socket, you will employ the Receive method of the Socket class.

The Receive method acts in much the same way as the Send method in that it deals with byte arrays instead of serialized strings. To get the byte array into a more usable form, we can again use the Encoding class. This time we will call the GetString method, passing it the byte array.

Examine the code in Listing 8.1. First, we create an empty buffer to hold the data coming in via the Receive method. The buffer is a byte array, pre-declared at a set size (we could have used a variable array here as well). The Receive function expects an array to store the data, and also needs to know the total length of the array and in what position in the array it should start filling the data. Besides filling the provided buffer with the incoming data, the receive method also returns the number of bytes received as its return parameter—and starts filling from the beginning of the array.

After receiving all of the data, we want to shut the socket down. This is supported through the Socket.Shutdown method. This method takes an instance of the SocketShutdown enumeration (see Table 8.5). We can tell the socket that we want to shut down its ability to send data, receive data, or both send and receive data.

TABLE 8.5 SocketShutdown Enumeration

Name	Description
Both	Shut down the socket from sending and receiving data
Receive	Shut down the socket for receiving data
Send	Shut down the socket for sending data

LISTING 8.1 Receiving Data on a Socket

```
Imports System.Net
Imports System.Net.Sockets
Imports System.Text

Module Module1

    Sub ReceiveOverSocket()
        'buffer for the incoming data (capped at 256)
        Dim buffArray(256) As Byte

        'holds number of bytes returned from the receive method
        Dim numBytes As System.Int32
```

LISTING 8.1 Continued

```vb
        'holds the resulting string from the received bytes
        Dim dataString As String

        Dim dataEncoder As Encoding

        'Create the socket object:
        'TCP/IP, stream based with Internet addressing
        Dim ourSocket As Socket = New Socket(AddressFamily.InterNetwork, _
                SocketType.Stream, ProtocolType.Tcp)

        'Create the local end-point
        '(change this to the IP of the machine you will run this code from
        Dim localAddress As IPAddress = IPAddress.Parse("10.0.0.1")
        Dim localEndPoint As IPEndPoint = New IPEndPoint(localAddress, _
        8080)

        'Create the remote end-point
        Dim targetAddress As IPAddress

        'Here, we resolve a host name to an IP address
        'Resolve returns an IPHostEntry; AddressList is an array of
        'IPAddress(objects)
        'A host may have more than one IP attached to it; we just want the
        'first one returned in the AddressList property (zero based)
        targetAddress = Dns.Resolve("www.microsoft.com").AddressList(0)
        Dim endPoint As IPEndPoint = New IPEndPoint(targetAddress, 8080)

        'connect the socket to the local end-point
        ourSocket.Bind(localEndPoint)

        'connect the socket to the remote end-point
        ourSocket.Connect(endPoint)

        'Using our netSocket created earlier, we call the receive method...
        numBytes = ourSocket.Receive(buffArray, buffArray.Length, 0)

        'To serialize, just pass the byte array through the GetString
        'method.
        dataString = dataEncoder.GetString(buffArray, 0, numBytes)

        Console.WriteLine("Data received: {0}", dataString)
        Console.WriteLine("Shutting the socket down...")

        ourSocket.Shutdown(SocketShutdown.Both)

    End Sub

End Module
```

8

NETWORKING FUNCTIONS

Handling Socket Exceptions

If you are using a structured exception handling approach to trapping errors in your code, you should know that socket classes will throw `SocketException` instances when problems are encountered with the network. (We talked about exception handlers in Chapter 4, "Introduction to the .NET Framework Class Library," and also in Chapter 20, "Profiling, Debugging, and Exception Handling.")

The `SocketException` class derives from the `Exception` class. It overrides the `Exception.ErrorCode` property to return an integer that maps to the error codes defined in the Winsock 2.0 API. For instance, a return value of 10061 maps to the Winsock 2 error of "WSAECONNREFUSED," and indicates that the target of the socket connection refused the connection. Essentially, the `ErrorCode` property is returning the last known operating system WinSock error. Table 8.6 shows some of the more common errors returned from the WinSock API (version 2). For an exhaustive list, please consult the actual WinSock 2.0 API documentation.

> **NOTE**
>
> If you have written any socket-oriented applications in Visual Basic before, you may already have a routine ripe for porting to .NET that will map these error numbers to their more meaningful error descriptions.

TABLE 8.6 Common `SocketException` Error Codes and Descriptions

Error Code	WinSock Constant	Description
10013	WSAEACCESS	A socket has attempted an action that was denied to it by the associated permission levels.
10048	WSAEADDRINUSE	Address is already in use. This is usually raised when a socket has attempted to bind to an address already bound to another socket instance.
10049	WSAEADDRNOTAVAIL	The address cannot be assigned. This is usually raised when the socket has attempted to bind to an address that is not available on the local machine.
10056	WSAEISCONN	An attempt was made to connect a socket that has already been connected.
100057	WSAENOTCONN	An attempt was made to send or receive data over a socket that is not connected.

TABLE 8.6 Continued

Error Code	WinSock Constant	Description
10060	WSAETIMEDOUT	The connection attempt has timed out.
10061	WSAECONNREFUSED	The target machine has refused the request for a connection.

So, we can add a catch block to a generic exception handler to deal specifically with socket exceptions:

```
Sub Main()
        'The exception handler is initiated with the 'try' block
        Try
            'this is where we would put some code that deals with
            'sockets

        Catch sockError As SocketException
            'Handle a specific socket error here. You can
            'cross-reference the ErrorCode returned against the
            'Winsock 2.0 API error codes.
            MsgBox("Socket error number:" & sockError.ErrorCode)

        Catch appError As Exception
            'handle the error; here, we just alert the user
            'through a message box. To get more detailed
            'debugging level info, we could use the
            'Exception.StackTrace property...
            MsgBox("Error:" & appError.Message)

        Finally

            Beep()

        End Try
    End Sub
```

NOTE

Any class that inherits from the Socket class will throw SocketException instances. This includes the DNS class as well as the TCPClient, TCPListener, and UDPClient classes.

Suggestions for Further Exploration

⊃ If you are curious about how to restrict or permit socket communications, investigate the SocketPermission class. It is located in the System.Net namespace and will restrict or allow an application to accept connections or contact servers based on a host, port number, and transport protocol.

⊃ To implement multicasting into your socket applications, check out the MulticastOption class. It can be used in conjunction with the SetSocketOption property on the Socket class to indicate a list of IP address values for IP multicast packets.

⊃ The LingerOption class, in the System.Net.Sockets namespace, will enable you to specify the amount of time a socket will remain open after closing the socket *if* there is any remaining data to be sent. Experiment with using this class to avoid premature shutdown and subsequent loss of pending data.

⊃ The Socket class provides a way to interactively check its current status. Please consult the Framework documentation on the Socket.Poll method.

A More Simplified Approach to Socket Programming

Moving up to the next layer of functionality offered by the .NET classes, we arrive at the TCPClient, UDPClient, and TCPListener classes. These classes offer a more simplified approach to socket programming, while retaining quite a bit of power. The two client classes are very similar with some fundamental differences between them that are worth pointing out:

- The TCPClient class deals with TCP connections; thus, it is stream oriented.
- The UDPClient class deals with UDP connections and is datagram oriented.
- Send and receive operations with the TCPClient class are done through Stream class instances.
- Send and receive operations with the UDPClient class can be accomplished by calling the Send and Receive methods and passing an array holding the actual datagram data.

We will focus on the TCPClient class as opposed to the UDPClient class. Understanding one should enable you to easily deal with the other.

The TCPClient class has an overloaded constructor that can accept either an IPEndPoint instance or a host/port name combination. This allows you to quickly establish a socket to a remote end point with only one line of code. There is no need to involve the IPEndPoint class, and no need to involve the DNS class to resolve host names because the TCPClient constructor is robust enough to handle these dynamics. Here is an example:

```
Dim tcp As TCPClient = New TCPClient("www.samspublishing.com",80)
```

The previous instantiation code handles the details of actually obtaining a connection to the URI that we want. Writing data to the resulting socket is also simple. The GetStream method defined by the TCPClient class returns an interesting structure that deserves more investigation—a NetworkStream.

Network Streams

With .NET, Microsoft has generalized the many different applications and uses of data streams into one super-class called Stream. This powerful class, which is represented in the System.IO namespace, can be used to represent and interact with any type of stream that you can think of including file streams, network streams, XML data streams, and data streams from databases, among others. As you gain more exposure to the .NET base classes, you will realize that streams are a consistent concept that runs through the entire fabric of .NET. In fact, the System.Net.Sockets library contains a class called NetworkStream that is a direct subclass of the Stream class.

> **NOTE**
>
> Although the NetworkStream class is derived from the parent Stream class, there are a few methods and properties that are not supported. The Seek and Position methods that are defined in the Stream class will throw an exception if you try to use them. And NetworkStream objects are not seekable (you can test for this by examining the CanSeek property—it will always return false).

8

NETWORKING
FUNCTIONS

The Write method available off of the NetworkStream class can be used to send data across the stream to the target end point. Similar to the example we looked at with the Socket send method, the NetworkStream Write method accepts a byte array containing the actual data to be sent across the stream. It also accepts an offset into the byte array (the point at which you want to start sending data) and an integer representing the total number of bytes to send:

```
Dim netStream As NetworkStream = Tcp.GetStream()
netStream.Write(bytArray, 0, bytArray.Length)
```

If we were to rewrite our previous socket code using the TCPClient class, it would look something like this:

```
'create our TCPClient class
Dim tcp As TCPClient = New TCPClient("www.microsoft.com",8080)

'get NetworkStream object for write operation
Dim netStream As NetworkStream = Tcp.GetStream()
```

```
'encode our message in a byte array
Dim encoder As ASCIIEncoding
Dim buffArray() As Byte = encoder.GetBytes("TCPClient programming is even _
    easier!")

'write the message into the stream
netStream.Write(buffArray, 0, buffArray.Length)
```

The third class we need to discuss at this level of networking code is the TCPListener class. But before moving on, let's take a minute to recap network operations using the Socket class and the TCPClient class by looking at their key differentiators.

Socket

- Allows programming and interoperability across a wide range of protocols (including custom protocols).
- Represents the lowest level of control over network communications in the Framework Class Library.

TCPClient

- Streamlined and simplified specifically for Internet-based TCP communication.
- Leverages the NetworkStream class for reads and writes.
- Knows only about TCP packet construction.
- Actually built on top of the Socket class; represents a higher level of abstraction.

Listening for Connections

Objects created from the TCPListener class have the ability to wait and listen for TCP connection requests from other TCP clients. Once a connection request is "heard," you can decide how to react; you may want to send data immediately, wait for incoming data to arrive, and so on.

> **NOTE**
>
> There is no equivalent to the TCPListener class for UDP packets; in other words, the UDPListener class does not exist.

The TCPListener class has an overloaded constructor. You can create an instance by providing one of the following: a port to listen to, an IPEndPoint, or an IP address and port. Once instantiated, use the Start method and Accept methods to access any incoming connection through its socket. The Start method initiates the listener, while the Accept method actually allows a connection to be made, returning either a `Socket` instance or a `TCPClient` instance that you can then use to talk across the connection. The code in Listing 8.2 shows the specifics of listening and reacting to TCP connections. The following example creates a listener object that waits for a TCP connection on port 8080.

LISTING 8.2   Listening for TCP Connections

```
Imports System.Net.Sockets
Imports System.Text

Module Module1

    'This simple subroutine waits for a connection to come across port
    '8080. It then responds back to the client that made the connection
    'with the message "connection accepted".
    Sub Main()
        Dim listener As TcpListener = New TcpListener(8080)

        'This starts the actual listening process...
        listener.Start()

        Console.WriteLine("Waiting for TCP connection...")

        'If a connection is requested, the next line of code will
        'return a TCPClient object. If you wanted a socket object
        'instead of a TCPClient object, you could do the following
        'instead:
        'Dim objSocket As Socket = objListener.AcceptSocket()
        'Code will block here until a connection is attempted
        Dim tcp As TcpClient = listener.AcceptTcpClient()

        'Our tcp object now holds the reference to the client

        'get NetworkStream object for write operation
        Dim netStream As NetworkStream = tcp.GetStream()
        Dim encoder As ASCIIEncoding
        Dim bytArray() As Byte = encoder.GetBytes("connection accepted")

        'write the message into the stream
        netStream.Write(bytArray, 0, bytArray.Length)

        'Stop the listener
        listener.Stop()

    End Sub

End Module
```

Implementing a Request/Response Model

Continuing on our journey up through the layers of the .NET networking libraries we arrive at those classes that implement a standard request/response model: the WebRequest and WebResponse classes. These classes are layered above the socket and stream level of interaction and deal with request/response traffic across the Internet. Here, we are afforded the ability to either deal at a protocol-specific level with items, or deal in a protocol-agnostic fashion. This will depend largely on the programming task that you are working on but the important thing to note is that you, as a .NET programmer, have a choice.

Creating Requests

The WebRequest and WebResponse classes form the underpinnings for the request/response model in .NET. They represent a protocol-agnostic view; the classes themselves contain a class factory that will manufacture the appropriate protocol-specific class depending on what Uniform Resource Identifier (URI) you are trying to connect to. These so-called *descendant classes* are protocol-specific implementations of the more generic WebRequest/WebResponse classes. A request to an HTTP URI, for instance, would generate a HTTPWebRequest class, a request to a file-based URI would generate an FileWebRequest class, and so on. For example, the following code attempts a connection to a URL through the WebRequest class:

```
Dim rqst = WebRequest.Create("http://www.samspublishing.com")
```

Retrieving Responses

We can then use the GetResponse method off of the WebResponse class to retrieve the response generated by our target URI:

```
Dim resp = rqst.GetResponse()
```

It is important to note a subtle difference in dealing with these classes: You do not directly create instances of these classes. Rather, you must rely on the Create method to generate new instances of the WebRequest class and the GetResponse method to generate new instances of the WebResponse class.

After retrieving the response, we can deal with the stream it represents by using the GetResponseStream method:

```
Dim netStream As New NetworkStream = resp.GetResponseStream()
```

From this point, our interaction can follow the same design patterns that we previously saw when discussing streams created from the TCPClient class.

> **NOTE**
>
> If there is no compelling reason to deal with protocol-specific properties, it is better to construct your request/response designs by using the WebRequest and WebResponse classes. In this way, if new protocols are added to .NET, your code will automatically function appropriately with those protocols with no coding changes necessary.

Working with HTTP-Specific Requests and Responses

If you have the need to deal with, say, HTTP-specific header properties, you can access them by simply casting your WebRequest or WebResponse objects into an HTTPWebRequest or HTTPWebResponse object through the CType command. This process is illustrated through the following code (continued from the previous example):

```
Dim http As HttpWebResponse = CType(resp, HttpWebResponse)
```

The resulting HTTPWebResponse object offers a slightly different pattern of properties and methods than the parent WebResponse class. We now have access to new properties and methods that were not previously available. In addition, the methods and properties defined by the WebResponse class have been overridden to return or process HTTP information. The ProtocolVersion property, for instance, does not exist on the WebResponse base class but is implemented on the HTTPWebResponse class to return the actual version of the HTTP protocol with which the response was formatted. This is a good example of a subclass providing a new member to the base class. An example of a property being overridden is found in the Headers property: This method now returns HTTP-specific name/value pairs. For more information on actual properties and methods supported, see the reference located at the end of this chapter.

You can examine the StatusCode property on the HttpWebResponse class to get access to the HTTP status codes returned as part of a response. It returns an enumeration that evaluates to the HttpStatusCode enumeration, shown in Table 8.7.

TABLE 8.7 HttpStatusCode Enumeration

Name	Equivalent HTTP Status Code	Description
Accepted	202	The request was accepted.
Ambiguous	300	The server couldn't decide what to return (equivalent to MultipleChoices).
BadGateway	502	An intermediate proxy server received a bad response.

TABLE 8.7   Continued

Name	Equivalent HTTP Status Code	Description
BadRequest	400	The server did not understand the request.
Conflict	409	There was a conflict on the server with the current state of a resource.
Continue	100	The request can be continued.
Created	201	The request was fulfilled, resulting in the creation of a new resource.
ExpectationFailed	417	An expectation specified in the Expect header could not be met by the server.
Forbidden	403	The server understood the request but has refused to respond.
Found	302	The server has indicated a redirect to the desired resource (equivalent to Redirect).
GatewayTimeout	504	The request timed out waiting for a gateway to respond.
Gone	410	The resource that was requested no longer resides on the server.
HttpVersionNotSupported	505	The server does not support the HTTP version specified in the request.
InternalServerError	500	The server encountered an unexpected error that is preventing it from responding to the request.
LengthRequired	411	The server is refusing to answer the request because it was sent without a Content-length header.
MethodNotAllowed	405	The server does not allow the method used for the request.
Moved	301	The requested resource now lives at a different URI (the server will return the URI in its response in the Location header) if the initial request was a POST, the redirect will instead use a GET.

TABLE 8.7 Continued

Name	Equivalent HTTP Status Code	Description
MovedPermanently	301	See above.
MultipleChoices	300	The server couldn't decide what to return (synonym for Ambiguous).
NoContent	204	The server has intentionally returned a blank response to the request.
NonAuthoritativeInformation	203	The server returned meta information that was from a cache of the original information and may therefore be incorrect.
NotAcceptable	406	The server was unable to find a response that was acceptable to the client (the client has issued a list of acceptable responses in the Accept header).
NotFound	404	The resource that was requested could not be found on the server.
NotImplemented	501	The server does not have the functionality required to fulfill the request.
NotModified	304	The requested resource has not been changed from the client's cached copy.
OK	200	The request was successful, the requested data is in the response.
PartialContent	206	In response to a GET command that included a byte range, the server answered with a partial response.
PaymentRequired	402	Not currently defined in the HTTP protocol.
PreconditionFailed	412	The server can not meet one or more of the conditional request headers specified.

8

NETWORKING
FUNCTIONS

TABLE 8.7   Continued

Name	Equivalent HTTP Status Code	Description
ProxyAuthenticationRequired	407	The requested proxy requires authentication—the response will indicate how to perform the authentication in the Proxy-authenticate header.
Redirect	302	The server has indicated a redirect to the desired resource (equivalent to Found).
RedirectKeepVerb	307	The requested resource is available at the URI identified in the Location header. If the initial request was a POST, the redirect will also use a POST (equivalent to TemporaryRedirect).
RedirectMethod	303	The server is automatically redirecting the request to the URI identified in the Location header—the redirected request will be made with a GET (synonym for SeeOther).
RequestedRangeNotSatisfiable	416	The server could not return the range of data indicated because the beginning occurred before the beginning of the data range, or the end occurred after the end of the data range.
RequestEntityTooLarge	413	The server cannot process the request—it is too large.
RequestTimeout	408	The server timed out while waiting for the request.
RequestUriTooLong	414	The server has refused the request because the URI is longer than it will permit.
ResetContent	205	The client should reset the current resource.

TABLE 8.7   Continued

Name	Equivalent HTTP Status Code	Description
SeeOther	303	The server is automatically redirecting the request to the URI identified in the Location header— the redirected request will be made with a GET (equivalent to RedirectMethod).
ServiceUnavailable	503	The server is currently unavailable.
SwitchingProtocols	101	Either the version of the protocol or the actual protocol is being changed.
TemporaryRedirect	307	The requested resource is available at the URI identified in the Location header. If the initial request was a POST, the redirect will also use a POST (equivalent to RedirectKeepVerb).
Unauthorized	401	The requested resource requires proper authentication, which was not supplied.
UnsupportedMediaType	415	The server has refused the request because the request itself is an unsupported type.
Unused	306	Not currently defined in HTTP 1.1.
UseProxy	305	The requested resource needs to be accessed through the proxy identified in the Location header.

8

NETWORKING
FUNCTIONS

Handling Web Exceptions

The WebRequest and WebResponse classes, and their descendants, will throw WebException instances when errors are encountered. By examining the WebException.Status property, you can find what type of error was encountered. This property returns a member of the WebExceptionStatus enumeration, which is detailed in Table 8.8.

TABLE 8.8   Members of the `WebExceptionStatus` Enumeration

Name	Description
ConnectFailure	The connection attempt to the target address has failed.
ConnectionClosed	The connection was closed.
KeepAliveFailure	A request has specified a keep-alive in its header, and the request connection was closed.
NameResolutionFailure	The host name could not be resolved.
Pending	An async request is still pending.
ProtocolError	A response was received from the target address indicating that a protocol-level error was encountered.
ProxyNameResolutionFailure	The proxy host name could not be resolved.
ReceiveFailure	A complete response was not received from the target address.
RequestCanceled	The request was canceled.
SecureChannelFailure	An error was encountered while trying to establish a secure channel link.
SendFailure	The request could not be sent to the target address.
ServerProtocolViolation	The response received was not a valid HTTP response.
Success	No error was encountered.
Timeout	The request has timed out.
TrustFailure	The server certificate could not be authenticated.

Listing 8.3 pulls together all the request/response objects we have talked about for creating requests, receiving responses, and dealing with exceptions. This console application attempts to open a Web page (by issuing a request), and then displays the results to the console window (by writing out the response). Any errors encountered along the way are also written out to the console window.

LISTING 8.3   Creating Requests and Processing Responses

```
Imports System.Net
Imports System.Net.Sockets

Module Module1

    Sub Main()

        Try
```

LISTING 8.3 Continued

```vb
    'Buffer byte array to hold the stream data
    Dim buffArray(1024) As Byte

    'Var for the stream looping
    Dim currIndex As System.Int32

    'Var to hold the number of bytes read
    Dim numBytes As System.Int32

    'Create the request for a web page
    Dim rqst = WebRequest.Create("http://www.brilliantstorm.com")

    'Get the response to our request
    Dim resp = rqst.GetResponse()

    'Create a stream object and assign it to the response stream
    Dim netStream As NetworkStream = resp.GetResponseStream()

    'Read from the stream and write any data to the console.
    numBytes = netStream.Read(buffArray, 0, buffArray.Length)
    While numBytes > 0
        For currIndex = 0 To numBytes - 1
            Console.Write("{0}", buffArray(currIndex))
        Next currIndex

        Console.WriteLine()
        numBytes = netStream.Read(buffArray, 0, buffArray.Length)
    End While

    'Close the request and response objects
    rqst.Close()
    resp.Close()


Catch webErr As WebException
    'Setup containers for the WebExceptionStatus enum and its
    'underlying text
    Dim webStatusEnum As WebExceptionStatus
    Dim webStatusDesc As String

    'Setup containers for the HttpStatusCode enum and its
    'underlying text
    Dim httpStatusEnum As HttpStatusCode
    Dim httpStatusDesc As String
```

LISTING 8.3   Continued

```
            'If we get a protocol error back, we will need an HTTPWebResponse
            'object to get at the underlying http status code
            Dim httpResp As HttpWebResponse

            'Get the desc. of the web exception
            webStatusDesc = webStatusEnum.GetName(webStatusEnum.GetType, _
                webErr.Status)

            'Write out the WebException text to the console
            Console.WriteLine("A web error was encountered: {0}", _
                webStatusDesc)

            'If we encountered a protocol error
            '(WebExceptionStatus.ProtocolError), cast the web response to an
            'http web response and then examine the http status code info
            If webErr.Status = WebExceptionStatus.ProtocolError Then
                httpResp = CType(webErr.Response, HttpWebResponse)
                httpStatusEnum = httpResp.StatusCode
                httpStatusDesc = httpStatusEnum.GetName
➥(httpStatusEnum.GetType, httpResp.StatusCode)

                'write out the http status code to the console
                Console.Write("HTTP Status Code: {0}", httpStatusDesc)

            End If
        Catch appErr As Exception
            ' non-web error raised...
            Console.WriteLine("An app error was encountered: {0}", _
                appErr.ToString)

        Finally
            Console.WriteLine("...")
            Console.WriteLine("Finished.")
            Console.WriteLine("Hit <ENTER> to exit.")
            Console.ReadLine()
        End Try
    End Sub

End Module
```

Using the `WebClient` Class

The `WebClient` class represents the most abstract level of functionality provided by the .NET network classes: It is the easiest and quickest way to establish network communications. The `WebClient` class allows:

- Resolution of a URI using one line of code
- Uploading and downloading of files, buffers, streams, and name/value pairs
- HTTP, HTTPS, and FILE protocols transmissions

This section discusses the particular ease of use offered by this class.

Uploads and Downloads

One of the things that the `WebClient` class allows you to do very simply is the uploading or downloading of resources to or from a server. There are two sets of methods that we are concerned with: the `DownloadData` and `DownloadFile` methods, and the `UploadData` and `UploadFile` methods. Their syntax is brief and concise.

To upload data to a server, all we need to know is the URI and a byte array with the data that we want to send. The following code shows how easy this is:

```
Dim web As New WebClient()
web.UploadData(myURL, byteArray())
```

Uploading an actual file is just a slight variation on this syntax. Instead of a byte array of data, we pass in a fully qualified filename:

```
web.UploadFile(myURL, myFile)
```

> **NOTE**
>
> Both the `UploadData` and `UploadFile` methods perform their work through HTTP `POST` commands.

The `DownloadData` and `DownloadFile` methods are mirrors of their upload counterparts that we just discussed. The `DownloadData` method takes an address parameter and returns a byte array of the data that was downloaded. The `DownloadFile` method takes an address and a fully qualified filename (and doesn't return anything).

```
buffArray() = web.DownloadData(myURL)
web.DownloadFile(myURL, localFilename)
```

Working with Streams

Of course, the WebClient class would not be complete without support for streams. Using the OpenRead and OpenWrite methods, you can obtain stream references that you can read and write into.

```
Dim myStream As Stream
Dim web As New WebClient()

'obtain a stream reference for reading data…
myStream = web.OpenRead(myURL)

'or writing data.
myStream = web.OpenWrite(myURL)
```

 ## Suggestions for Further Exploration

- ⊃ Investigate the WebPermission class to see how to control rights and permissions for a specific Internet resource.

- ⊃ The WebClient.UploadValues method provides a way to send name/value pairs to a server and retrieve the response. Examine the Framework documentation for this method and for the NameValueCollection class (in the System.Collections.Specialized namespace) to see how to use them in your networking code.

An Asynchronous Request/Response Pattern

Until now, all of our focus has been on using the networking classes in a synchronous fashion. However, the Internet itself is asynchronous in nature, and there are many programming tasks that are not well served by synchronous software design. In this section, we'll look at a design pattern for implementing an asynchronous request/response model using the WebRequest and WebResponse classes.

Overview

First, let's talk through a scenario: You want to issue a request for a Web page from a server. After the request has been made, your application should continue without waiting for the response. Once the response comes back, your application should be signaled somehow, so that it can now deal with the data it has received. This sets the stage for our asynchronous request/response design pattern.

With this scenario in mind, let's walk through each step and see how we can use the intrinsic capabilities of the .NET Framework and the networking classes to handle each piece of this pattern.

Issuing an Asynchronous Request

Recall that, with the `WebRequest` class, a request is issued for a resource by calling the `GetResponse` method. This is done in a synchronous fashion; the application will block on that line of code until the response has been received. To issue an asynchronous request, we use the `BeginGetResponse` method. This is what kicks the whole process off. The `BeginGetResponse` method, unlike the `GetResponse` method, takes some parameters that equip it to work asynchronously. These parameters are an `AsyncCallBack` instance, and a generic "container" object instance for holding state.

The callback that we pass into the `BeginGetResponse` method essentially tells the class: "When a response has been received, fire off the code pointed to by the callback." So, if we had a subroutine called "ReceiveResponse", we can specify its callback into the `BeginGetResponse` method like this:

```
New AsyncCallback(AddressOf ReceiveResponse)
```

This will create an `AsyncCallBack` instance with the address of the subroutine that needs to react to the callback.

The state object, used in the `BeginGetResponse` method call, is a little tricky to understand until we get farther into the async process. For now, just accept the fact that it is used to persist data between asynchronous method calls. One of the things that we are interested in persisting is the actual `WebRequest` object used to make the `BeginGetResponse` call. Other than its slightly confusing reason for existence at this point, there is really no mystery to this state object. It is simply an instance of a class that you create to hold state through properties. In this example, we could define the class like this:

```
Public Class State
    Public httpRqst As HttpWebRequest

    Public Sub New()
        rqst = Nothing
    End Sub
End Class
```

Note that we have explicitly defined the request property as an `HttpWebRequest` instance since we know we are going after a Web page. To actually issue our async request, two things need to be done. First, the request object itself must be instantiated and then assigned into an instance of the `State` class that we created:

```
Dim rqst As HttpWebRequest = WebRequest.Create(someURL)
Dim aState As State = New State()

aState.httpRqst = rqst
```

Next, we will finally call `BeginGetResponse`:

```
rqst.BeginGetResponse(New AsyncCallback(AddressOf ReceiveResponse), _
aState)
```

This brings us to the next step in the pattern.

Receiving the Response Asynchronously

After making the resource request, the application will continue on its execution path until it is signaled that the data in response to the request has finally arrived. Our subroutine that handles the callback—in this case called `ReceiveResponse`—will have an `IAsyncResult` object passed to it. The `IASyncResult` interface exposes a property, `AsyncState`, which will return to us the state object that we had originally passed in to the `BeginGetResponse` method:

```
Public Sub ReceiveResponse(rslt As IAsyncResult)

End Sub
```

This `IAsyncResult` interface is the key here: We will use it to get to the response object. Remember that the `WebResponse` object is what is created in response to the `GetResponse` method. The same holds true for our `BeginGetResponse` call—we will need to get a handle to the resulting `WebResponse` object in order to examine the response data. The `EndGetResponse` method will return us the response object that we are looking for. First, the request object will need to be pulled back out of the state object's property, and then the `EndGetResponse` method will be called:

```
Public Sub ReceiveResponse(rslt As IAsyncResult)
    Dim retState As State = CType(rslt.AsyncState, State)
    Dim httpRqst As HttpWebRequest = retState.httpRqst

    Dim httpResp As HttpWebResponse = _req.EndGetResponse(ar), _
    HttpWebResponse)

    Dim resp As WebResponse = rqst.EndGetResponse(ar)
    .
    .
    .
End Sub
```

Reading the Response Asynchronously

Just like the `WebRequest` class, the `Stream` class also has explicit support for asynchronous operations. The `Stream.BeginRead` method is simply the asynchronous equivalent to the `Stream.Read` method. Just as with the `WebRequest` class, this method requires an `AsyncCallBack` instance and a state object instance.

> **NOTE**
>
> Just because you have implemented an async pattern with the `WebRequest` and `WebResponse` classes doesn't mean that you have to do so with the `Stream` class as well. After receiving the response instance, you could simply interact with its stream synchronously. Microsoft, however, strenuously advises against "mixing" synchronous access with asynchronous in a tightly bound process like this for performance reasons.

It is often easiest to just reuse the state object you have already created; add a few new properties to the class to hold the read buffer for the stream, and perhaps the concatenated results of the multiple stream reads, and you are all set.

```
Dim respStream As Stream = resp.GetResponseStream()

retState.respStream = respStream

respStream.BeginRead(respStream.BufferRead, 0, 1024, New _
AsyncCallback(AddressOf ReadStream)
```

A new subroutine will be needed to process the results of the stream read where we again will use the passed in `IAsyncResult` object to get at the state object, and thus the stored stream. At this point, you should recognize the stream read pattern from our previous sections.

```
Public Sub ReadStream(rslt As IAsyncResult)
    Dim retState As RequestState = rslt.AsyncState

    Dim respStream As Stream = retState.respStream

    Dim dataBytes As Integer = respStream.EndRead(rslt)
    If dataBytes > 0 Then
        ' Data still left in the stream... parse it out
        ' Then issue another BeginRead...
    Else
        'all done
    End If

    'close the stream
    responseStream.Close()
    .
    .
    .
End Sub
```

Figure 8.2 shows the entire pattern laid out from a process flow perspective. You can see that Step 1 is indeed a call to `BeginGetResponse`.

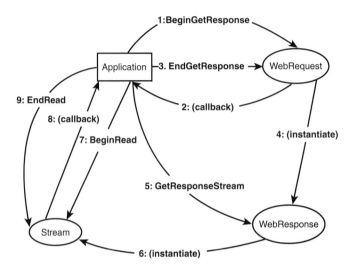

FIGURE 8.2

A basic async flow for the `WebRequest`/`WebResponse` *classes.*

To summarize the steps once more:

1. Call the `BeginGetResponse` method.

   The calling application first makes a call to the `BeginGetResponse` method off an instantiated `WebRequest` object.

2. The `WebRequest` object places the callback.

   Once the `WebRequest` object has received a response from the server, it will call back to the routine that we passed it in Step 1. During this callback, it will pass an instance of an `IAsyncResult`—more on this in the next step.

3. Call the `EndGetResponse` method.

   The callback routine will now want to place a call to the `EndGetResponse` method. This will take the `IAsyncResult` object that was passed over from the `WebRequest` object. The `EndGetResponse` method is the async equivalent of the `GetResponse` method, and effectively completes the circle by returning a `WebResponse` object (which, if you recall, is what we can use to get access to the actual data sent in response to our request).

4. The `WebRequest` creates a `WebResponse` object.

   The `WebRequest` object will return a `WebResponse` object to us after we call the `EndGetResponse` method. We'll use this response to get access to that actual raw data sent from the server.

5. Call the GetResponseStream method.

From this point our pattern looks like the previous code, which we looked at for dealing with WebResponse objects. We will first get a Stream object representation of the response.

6. The WebResponse creates the Stream object.

From the GetResponseStream, we will get a Stream object that we will use as our final interaction point with the response. Again, this is identical to the previous code, which we examined in our section on the WebRequest/WebResponse classes.

7–9. Interactively read the stream with BeginRead.

The async design pattern continues here with the reading of the response stream. This follows the same pattern as our request/response pattern.

The sample application "ISBNCrawler," located at the end of this chapter, demonstrates asynchronous request/response code.

Authentication and Proxies

In all our previous discussions on the network classes, we dealt with accessing URIs and establishing connections in a very simplistic fashion; we have assumed an open and free landscape of network resources and servers that blindly accept our requests for connections, file downloads, resource uploads, and protocol queries. This has been useful to conduct our quick tour of these networking classes, but the real world acts a bit differently: Conscientious server administrators and software architects tend to require proper credentials from a client before handing over the rights to access files or traverse Web directories. In this section, we will talk about the System.Net structures that allow programmers to provide credentials when querying resources. We will also talk a bit about using proxies in our programming efforts.

Authentication Methods

Before we look at the actual helper classes for dealing with credentials and authentication, we'll take a high-level look at the different types of authentication supported by the .NET classes. For Internet communication, there are primarily five different types of authentication supported: *Basic*, *Digest*, *NTLM*, *Kerberos*, and *Negotiate*.

You may already be familiar with these concepts if you have been responsible for structuring security on IIS Web servers before—particularly, with IIS 8.0 and above. For a more in-depth treatment of security in general, you may want to look at Chapter 14, "Browser/Server Communications," where we cover security functions. Because we will be referencing some of these in our code examples in this section, here is some basic information on these different authentication methods:

- Basic Authentication: This is a clear-text method in which the username and password are encoded (not encrypted) and then sent to the server.

- Digest Authentication: This is an encrypted method of authentication: The server will issue a *nonce*—a random data string—that the client then uses to encrypt its credential information. This information is sent back to the server where it is compared to the expected values. If the two match, authentication is accomplished.

- Kerberos Authentication: This method of authentication relies on users being authenticated by a Kerberos Authentication Server. Once authenticated, the user uses this encrypted "ticket" as a pass to access specific services.

- NTLM: Probably more commonly known as Windows NT Challenge/Response, this also is an encrypted method of sending user credentials. In this case, the encryption is based on a hash algorithm and it is also uuencoded. NTLM stands for NT LAN Manager.

Now let's look at the specific classes that will help us to actually use credentials when querying network resources.

Encapsulating Credentials

The `NetworkCredential` class is used to encapsulate *credentials* for use when requesting a resource. Credentials are simply pieces of identifying data that can be associated with a level of authorization in a given system. When we log into a Windows 2000 Server, we supply a login name (or username) and password as credentials.

> **NOTE**
>
> Other authentication schemes may make use of other forms of credentials, but the login name and password pair is arguably the most common form that you will bump into in your programming efforts, and certainly the prevailing form of credentials on the Web.

As we saw in the previous paragraphs, these credentials are commonly encoded or encrypted using standardized methods.

The `NetworkCredential` class is fairly light in terms of properties and methods. It allows you to supply password and username pairs through the `Password` and `UserName` properties—you can also specify these items through the class constructor. The class also supports specification of a domain through the `Domain` property. In terms of methods, its one unique method is the `GetCredential` method that accepts a URI and an authentication type and returns a `NetworkCredential` instance.

Probably the most common and easiest use of this class will be through simple instantiation and the use of its constructor. The following code creates a `NetworkCredential` instance with the username "John Doe", password "fortknox":

```
Dim creds As NetworkCredential = new NetworkCredential( "John Doe", _
    "fortknox")
```

The `NetworkCredential` class is to be used in conjunction with some of the other classes that we have talked about in the previous sections of this chapter. Let's take a look at how we can use an instance of the `NetworkCredential` class in conjunction with the `WebClient` class and the `WebRequest` class. In general, most of the network classes support the specification of credentials through a `Credentials` property. This property can be assigned an instance of a `NetworkCredential` object. The specified data is then presented for authentication (if needed) to the resource controller (server). In essence, this is meant to provide evidence of your code's capability to perform the particular function or access the particular resource that you are targeting. Thus, to specify credentials for use with a `WebClient` instance, we can say:

```
Dim web as WebClient
web.Credentials = New NetworkCredential("John Doe", "fortknox")
```

With the `WebRequest` class, our signature is identical:

```
Dim rqst as WebRequest
rqst.Credentials = New NetworkCredential("John Doe", "fortknox")
```

Table 8.9 shows the classes in the `System.Net` and `System.Net.Sockets` namespaces that support the use of the `Credentials` property.

TABLE 8.9 Networking Classes That Support the `Credentials` Property

FileWebRequest

HTTPWebRequest

WebClient

WebProxy

WebRequest

Using the `NetworkCredential` class in the ways we have shown is best if you are dealing only with a small number of URIs that you need to access, or if you will be providing the same set of credentials for each of the URIs you need to access. If you are dealing with a multitude of URIs, each with their own credentials that have to be passed, the preferred solution is to use the `System.Net` structure for caching credentials: the `CredentialCache` class.

Optimizing Credentials Through the Cache

The CredentialCache class is actually a collection class: It can maintain multiple credential entries, each associated with a specific URI and authentication method. Your code can then extract the appropriate credentials by using the GetCredential method, passing in the URI and authentication method. The class will then return the first matching set of credentials through an instance of a NetworkCredential class. If no matching credentials are found, it returns a null object (Nothing). The following code illustrates the use of a credential cache with a WebClient object:

```
Imports System.Net

Module Module1

    Sub Main()
        'the WebClient we will use with the cred cache
        Dim myClient As WebClient

        'private instance of a credential cache
        Dim myCache As New CredentialCache()

        'the first parameter to the credential cache's
        'add method is a URI object; here we create two
        Dim uri1 = New Uri("www.microsoft.com")
        Dim uri2 = New Uri("www.samspublishing.com")

        'The second parameter required is a NetworkCredential
        'instance (login ID and passworD)
        Dim myLogin = New NetworkCredential("John Doe", "fortknox")

        'Now, we add the two different sets of credentials to the
        'cache
        creds.Add(uri1, "Basic", myLogin)
        creds.Add(uri2, "NTLM", myLogin)

        'By setting the credentials prop equal to one of the stored
        'credentials in the cache, we are able to carry along our
        'login information with the WebClient object
        myClient.Credentials = creds.GetCredential(uri1, "Basic")
    End Sub

End Module
```

Caching your credentials centralizes maintenance of logins in your code, and helps to make for a much more robust solution.

Dealing with Proxies

Besides credentials, when working with Internet-based connections, you may need to worry about specifying proxy server information. The WebRequest class and its descendant classes allow you to specify a proxy server through the Proxy property; you must set this property equal to an instance of a WebProxy class. The following code shows how this can be done.

```
'First create a WebProxy instance
Dim myProxy As WebProxy = New WebProxy("http://ourproxy:8080")

'rqst is a WebRequest instance; set its Proxy prop to route
'requests appropriately...
rqst.Proxy = myProxy

'now, use the request object like you normally would.
```

> **NOTE**
>
> The WebProxy constructor has many different, overloaded forms. We could, for instance, have supplied a URI instance instead of a string to specify our URL. Check with the .NET Framework SDK documentation to see which constructor works best for your particular situation.

If you do not specify a proxy when using the request classes, the system will use the global proxy server setting. By default, this will be set to whatever your local Internet Explorer settings are set. You can also change this global setting by using the GlobalProxySelection class. Let's look at some code that sets a global proxy server; the proxy settings we implement will hold for all created instances of WebRequest/HTTPWebRequest objects, unless we choose to explicitly override them by using the Proxy property that we just discussed.

This code will have the same effect as our previous code example: All requests made through the request object that we have created will be routed through http://ourproxy:8080.

```
Dim myProxy As WebProxy = New WebProxy("http://ourprxy:8080")

GlobalProxySelection.Select = myProxy
```

 ## Suggestions for Further Exploration

⊃ The ServicePointManager class holds a cache or collection of ServicePoint objects in much the same way that the CredentialsCache holds instances of NetworkCredential objects. A ServicePoint is an object that holds connection information for a particular URI; the ServicePointManager class can return a ServicePoint based on the URI you are trying to connect. Refer to the .NET Framework SDK documentation for more information on how this class can help you to centralize connection management and speed up URI requests.

⊃ General information on security in the .NET Framework can be found in Appendix C, ".NET Security Models."

Learning by Example: A Socket Transmitter Application

The "SocketTransmitter" application ties together some of the primary concepts that we have talked about in relationship to communicating using the Socket class. The application has a single form that allows you to play around with Socket messaging by entering different commands that can be sent to the server address of your choice. The application will then show you the reply you get back from the server.

Key Concepts Covered

This application showcases the following:

- Creating a socket object
- Binding and connecting a socket instance to its respective end points
- Using the DNS class to resolve host names to an IPAddress instance
- Using the IPAddress.Parse method to derive an IPAddress instance from a string representation of an IP address in dotted quad form
- Sending data across a socket with the Socket.Send method
- Receiving data across a socket using the Socket.Receive method
- Catching and responding to SocketException errors

Figure 8.3 shows the Socket Transmitter form.

To take the application for a spin, you must first have a connection established to the Internet. Try the following:

1. Type either a host name or IP address for the local end point (near side of the connection). If you type a host name instead of a valid IP address, make sure you have the "Resolve Local Host" checkbox checked. Click the "Bind" button. If successful, you should see the status bar indicate that the socket has been bound.

2. Now type in a host name or IP address for the remote end point (the far side of the connection). Again, make sure you have the "Resolve Remote Host" checkbox checked if you didn't type in an actual IP address. Click on the "Connect" button. If successful, the status bar should report that the socket has been connected.

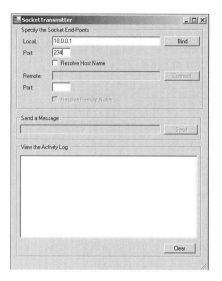

FIGURE 8.3

The SocketTransmitter application.

3. Type in a message/command to send to the remote end point. Confused about what to enter for a command? Try researching the different protocol standards to see what common sets of commands they have defined. To get you started, you could try the following:

- Connect to a server that you know is a newsgroup server. Then issue NNTP-specific commands such as "authinfo user xxxx pass yyyy" where xxxx is your login id and yyyy is your password. Once logged in, try selecting a specific newsgroup by sending "GROUP xxxx" where xxxx is the newsgroup name. From there, you can read different articles by using the article command ("ARTICLE xxxx", where xxxx is the article number).

- Connect to an HTTP server and then request a Web page by using the GET command. "GET / HTTP/1.1\r\nHost: " + server + "\r\nConnection: Close\r\n".

- You can get more ideas of command by examining the actual Request for Comments or Standards available at www.w3.org.

4. The messages sent out, the responses received, and any errors encountered should all show up in the Activity Log.

8

NETWORKING
FUNCTIONS

Code Walkthrough

Listing 8.4 walks you through the code of a sample application—the Socket Transmitter.

LISTING 8.4   Sample Application: Socket Transmitter

We first reference the three namespaces that will provide us with the objects we need. Note that at the class scope, we have created a global socket instance called 'sock'.

```
Imports System.Text
Imports System.Net
Imports System.Net.Sockets

Public Class SocketTransmitter
    Inherits System.Windows.Forms.Form

    Dim netSocket As Socket

#Region " Windows Form Designer generated code "

    Public Sub New()
        MyBase.New()

        'This call is required by the Windows Form Designer.
        InitializeComponent()
```

For the most part, the Windows Forms designer generates this code. We have added code to initialize the visual state of the form and to actually instantiate a socket instance through a call to a private subroutine called `CreateSocket`.

```
        'Add any initialization after the InitializeComponent() call
        SetFormState("INITIAL")
        CreateSocket()
    End Sub

    'Form overrides dispose to clean up the component list.
    Protected Overloads Overrides Sub Dispose(ByVal disposing As Boolean)
        If disposing Then
            If Not (components Is Nothing) Then
                components.Dispose()
            End If
        End If
        MyBase.Dispose(disposing)
    End Sub
    Friend WithEvents GroupBox1 As System.Windows.Forms.GroupBox
    Friend WithEvents Label1 As System.Windows.Forms.Label
    Friend WithEvents textBoxLocal As System.Windows.Forms.TextBox
    Friend WithEvents Label2 As System.Windows.Forms.Label
```

LISTING 8.4   Continued

```
Friend WithEvents buttonBind As System.Windows.Forms.Button
Friend WithEvents buttonConnect As System.Windows.Forms.Button
Friend WithEvents checkResolveLocal As System.Windows.Forms.CheckBox
Friend WithEvents checkResolveRemote As System.Windows.Forms.CheckBox
Friend WithEvents GroupBox2 As System.Windows.Forms.GroupBox
Friend WithEvents GroupBox3 As System.Windows.Forms.GroupBox
Friend WithEvents textBoxSend As System.Windows.Forms.TextBox
Friend WithEvents buttonSend As System.Windows.Forms.Button
Friend WithEvents StatusBar As System.Windows.Forms.StatusBar
Friend WithEvents buttonClear As System.Windows.Forms.Button
Friend WithEvents textBoxRemote As System.Windows.Forms.TextBox
Friend WithEvents listBoxActivity As System.Windows.Forms.ListBox
Friend WithEvents Label3 As System.Windows.Forms.Label
Friend WithEvents textBoxLocalPort As System.Windows.Forms.TextBox
Friend WithEvents textBoxRemotePort As System.Windows.Forms.TextBox
Friend WithEvents Label4 As System.Windows.Forms.Label


'Required by the Windows Form Designer
Private components As System.ComponentModel.Container

'NOTE: The following procedure is required by the Windows Form Designer
'It can be modified using the Windows Form Designer.
'Do not modify it using the code editor.
<System.Diagnostics.DebuggerStepThrough()> Private Sub _
    InitializeComponent()
    Me.Label4 = New System.Windows.Forms.Label()
    Me.buttonBind = New System.Windows.Forms.Button()
    Me.Label1 = New System.Windows.Forms.Label()
    Me.Label2 = New System.Windows.Forms.Label()
    Me.Label3 = New System.Windows.Forms.Label()
    Me.textBoxLocalPort = New System.Windows.Forms.TextBox()
    Me.checkResolveRemote = New System.Windows.Forms.CheckBox()
    Me.GroupBox2 = New System.Windows.Forms.GroupBox()
    Me.buttonSend = New System.Windows.Forms.Button()
    Me.textBoxSend = New System.Windows.Forms.TextBox()
    Me.GroupBox3 = New System.Windows.Forms.GroupBox()
    Me.listBoxActivity = New System.Windows.Forms.ListBox()
    Me.buttonClear = New System.Windows.Forms.Button()
    Me.checkResolveLocal = New System.Windows.Forms.CheckBox()
    Me.buttonConnect = New System.Windows.Forms.Button()
    Me.textBoxLocal = New System.Windows.Forms.TextBox()
    Me.textBoxRemote = New System.Windows.Forms.TextBox()
    Me.StatusBar = New System.Windows.Forms.StatusBar()
    Me.GroupBox1 = New System.Windows.Forms.GroupBox()
    Me.textBoxRemotePort = New System.Windows.Forms.TextBox()
    Me.GroupBox2.SuspendLayout()
```

LISTING 8.4   Continued

```
Me.GroupBox3.SuspendLayout()
Me.GroupBox1.SuspendLayout()
Me.SuspendLayout()
'
'Label4
'
Me.Label4.Location = New System.Drawing.Point(12, 120)
Me.Label4.Name = "Label4"
Me.Label4.Size = New System.Drawing.Size(60, 12)
Me.Label4.TabIndex = 0
Me.Label4.Text = "Port:"
'
'buttonBind
'
Me.buttonBind.Location = New System.Drawing.Point(316, 20)
Me.buttonBind.Name = "buttonBind"
Me.buttonBind.Size = New System.Drawing.Size(76, 20)
Me.buttonBind.TabIndex = 2
Me.buttonBind.Text = "Bind"
'
'Label1
'
Me.Label1.Location = New System.Drawing.Point(12, 24)
Me.Label1.Name = "Label1"
Me.Label1.Size = New System.Drawing.Size(60, 12)
Me.Label1.TabIndex = 0
Me.Label1.Text = "Local:"
'
'Label2
'
Me.Label2.Location = New System.Drawing.Point(12, 96)
Me.Label2.Name = "Label2"
Me.Label2.Size = New System.Drawing.Size(60, 12)
Me.Label2.TabIndex = 0
Me.Label2.Text = "Remote:"
'
'Label3
'
Me.Label3.Location = New System.Drawing.Point(12, 48)
Me.Label3.Name = "Label3"
Me.Label3.Size = New System.Drawing.Size(60, 12)
Me.Label3.TabIndex = 0
Me.Label3.Text = "Port:"
'
'textBoxLocalPort
'
```

LISTING 8.4 Continued

```
    Me.textBoxLocalPort.Location = New System.Drawing.Point(76, 44)
    Me.textBoxLocalPort.MaxLength = 5
    Me.textBoxLocalPort.Name = "textBoxLocalPort"
    Me.textBoxLocalPort.Size = New System.Drawing.Size(40, 20)
    Me.textBoxLocalPort.TabIndex = 1
    Me.textBoxLocalPort.Text = ""
    '
    'checkResolveRemote
    '
    Me.checkResolveRemote.Location = New System.Drawing.Point(76, 144)
    Me.checkResolveRemote.Name = "checkResolveRemote"
    Me.checkResolveRemote.Size = New System.Drawing.Size(156, 16)
    Me.checkResolveRemote.TabIndex = 3
    Me.checkResolveRemote.Text = "Resolve Remote Name"
    '
    'GroupBox2
    '
    Me.GroupBox2.Controls.AddRange(New System.Windows.Forms.Control() _
        {Me.buttonSend, Me.textBoxSend})
    Me.GroupBox2.Location = New System.Drawing.Point(8, 188)
    Me.GroupBox2.Name = "GroupBox2"
    Me.GroupBox2.Size = New System.Drawing.Size(396, 52)
    Me.GroupBox2.TabIndex = 1
    Me.GroupBox2.TabStop = False
    Me.GroupBox2.Text = "Send a Message"
    '
    'buttonSend
    '
    Me.buttonSend.Location = New System.Drawing.Point(316, 20)
    Me.buttonSend.Name = "buttonSend"
    Me.buttonSend.Size = New System.Drawing.Size(72, 20)
    Me.buttonSend.TabIndex = 1
    Me.buttonSend.Text = "Send"
    '
    'textBoxSend
    '
    Me.textBoxSend.Location = New System.Drawing.Point(8, 20)
    Me.textBoxSend.Name = "textBoxSend"
    Me.textBoxSend.Size = New System.Drawing.Size(300, 20)
    Me.textBoxSend.TabIndex = 0
    Me.textBoxSend.Text = ""
    '
    'GroupBox3
    '
    Me.GroupBox3.Controls.AddRange(New System.Windows.Forms.Control() _
        {Me.listBoxActivity, Me.buttonClear})
```

LISTING 8.4   Continued

```
        Me.GroupBox3.Location = New System.Drawing.Point(8, 248)
        Me.GroupBox3.Name = "GroupBox3"
        Me.GroupBox3.Size = New System.Drawing.Size(396, 236)
        Me.GroupBox3.TabIndex = 2
        Me.GroupBox3.TabStop = False
        Me.GroupBox3.Text = "View the Activity Log"
        '
        'listBoxActivity
        '
        Me.listBoxActivity.HorizontalScrollbar = True
        Me.listBoxActivity.Location = New System.Drawing.Point(8, 24)
        Me.listBoxActivity.Name = "listBoxActivity"
        Me.listBoxActivity.Size = New System.Drawing.Size(380, 173)
        Me.listBoxActivity.TabIndex = 2
        '
        'buttonClear
        '
        Me.buttonClear.Location = New System.Drawing.Point(316, 208)
        Me.buttonClear.Name = "buttonClear"
        Me.buttonClear.Size = New System.Drawing.Size(68, 20)
        Me.buttonClear.TabIndex = 1
        Me.buttonClear.Text = "Clear"
        '
        'checkResolveLocal
        '
        Me.checkResolveLocal.Location = New System.Drawing.Point(76, 68)
        Me.checkResolveLocal.Name = "checkResolveLocal"
        Me.checkResolveLocal.Size = New System.Drawing.Size(156, 16)
        Me.checkResolveLocal.TabIndex = 3
        Me.checkResolveLocal.Text = "Resolve Host Name"
        '
        'buttonConnect
        '
        Me.buttonConnect.Enabled = False
        Me.buttonConnect.Location = New System.Drawing.Point(316, 92)
        Me.buttonConnect.Name = "buttonConnect"
        Me.buttonConnect.Size = New System.Drawing.Size(76, 20)
        Me.buttonConnect.TabIndex = 2
        Me.buttonConnect.Text = "Connect"
        '
        'textBoxLocal
        '
        Me.textBoxLocal.Location = New System.Drawing.Point(76, 20)
        Me.textBoxLocal.MaxLength = 1024
        Me.textBoxLocal.Name = "textBoxLocal"
        Me.textBoxLocal.Size = New System.Drawing.Size(232, 20)
```

LISTING 8.4 Continued

```
Me.textBoxLocal.TabIndex = 1
Me.textBoxLocal.Text = ""
'
'textBoxRemote
'
Me.textBoxRemote.Location = New System.Drawing.Point(76, 92)
Me.textBoxRemote.MaxLength = 1024
Me.textBoxRemote.Name = "textBoxRemote"
Me.textBoxRemote.Size = New System.Drawing.Size(232, 20)
Me.textBoxRemote.TabIndex = 1
Me.textBoxRemote.Text = ""
'
'StatusBar
'
Me.StatusBar.Location = New System.Drawing.Point(0, 489)
Me.StatusBar.Name = "StatusBar"
Me.StatusBar.Size = New System.Drawing.Size(416, 20)
Me.StatusBar.TabIndex = 3
'
'GroupBox1
'
Me.GroupBox1.Controls.AddRange(New System.Windows.Forms.Control() _
    {Me.Label4, Me.textBoxRemotePort, Me.textBoxLocalPort, Me.Label3, _
    Me.checkResolveRemote, Me.checkResolveLocal, Me.buttonConnect, _
    Me.buttonBind, Me.Label2, Me.textBoxRemote, Me.textBoxLocal, _
    Me.Label1})
Me.GroupBox1.Location = New System.Drawing.Point(8, 4)
Me.GroupBox1.Name = "GroupBox1"
Me.GroupBox1.Size = New System.Drawing.Size(400, 172)
Me.GroupBox1.TabIndex = 0
Me.GroupBox1.TabStop = False
Me.GroupBox1.Text = "Specify the Socket End-Points"
'
'textBoxRemotePort
'
Me.textBoxRemotePort.Location = New System.Drawing.Point(76, 116)
Me.textBoxRemotePort.MaxLength = 5
Me.textBoxRemotePort.Name = "textBoxRemotePort"
Me.textBoxRemotePort.Size = New System.Drawing.Size(40, 20)
Me.textBoxRemotePort.TabIndex = 1
Me.textBoxRemotePort.Text = ""
'
'SocketTransmitter
'
Me.AutoScaleBaseSize = New System.Drawing.Size(5, 13)
Me.ClientSize = New System.Drawing.Size(416, 509)
```

LISTING 8.4 Continued

```
        Me.Controls.AddRange(New System.Windows.Forms.Control() _
            {Me.StatusBar, Me.GroupBox3, Me.GroupBox2, Me.GroupBox1})
        Me.Name = "SocketTransmitter"
        Me.Text = "SocketTransmitter"
        Me.GroupBox2.ResumeLayout(False)
        Me.GroupBox3.ResumeLayout(False)
        Me.GroupBox1.ResumeLayout(False)
        Me.ResumeLayout(False)


    End Sub


#End Region


    Private Sub SocketTransmitter_Load(ByVal sender As System.Object, ByVal e
As System.EventArgs) Handles MyBase.Load


    End Sub
```

This routine creates a new socket instance. We use a structured exception handler to catch any errors at this point and display them to the user.

```
    Private Sub CreateSocket()
        'This creates our socket object; we have hard-coded the address family,
        'socket type, and protocol type. Feel free to lay around with these
        'settings...

        Try
            netSocket = New Socket(AddressFamily.InterNetwork, _
                SocketType.Stream, ProtocolType.Unspecified)

        Catch appErr As Exception
            'If we are unable to create the socket, raise the error to the
            'screen and then close the form
            WriteStatus("Error: unable to create socket")
            MsgBox("Unable to create a socket, closing the application..." & _
                vbCrLf & vbCrLf & "Error:" & appErr.Message & vbCrLf & "Stack _
                Trace: " & appErr.StackTrace)
            Me.Close()
        End Try

    End Sub
```

Clicking on the Bind button will call this routine. This assumes that CreateSocket has previously been called, and that we now have a valid socket object (netSocket) to work with. If the local end point address requires DNS resolution, we indicate this through the useDNS Boolean parameter. The local parameter identifies the local address for the bind, and the port parameter identifies the local port for the bind.

LISTING 8.4   Continued

```
Private Sub BindSocket(ByVal useDNS As Boolean, ByVal local As String, _
    ByVal port As System.Int32)
    Try

        'This will hold our local IPAddress for the bind
        Dim localAddress As IPAddress

        If useDNS Then
            'User has supplied a server name; we first need to resolve it
            'using the DNS class
            localAddress = Dns.Resolve("local").AddressList(0)
        Else
            'User has supplied an IP address in dotted quad format; just
            'use the IPAddress.Parse method to get at the actual
            'IPAddress instance
            localAddress = IPAddress.Parse(local)
        End If

        Dim localEP As IPEndPoint = New IPEndPoint(localAddress, port)

        netSocket.Bind(localEP)

    Catch sockErr As SocketException
        'A socket exception was encountered.

        'Retrieve and then write out the actual winsock error
        'description
        Dim convert As WinSockError = New WinSockError()
        Dim errDesc As String = convert.GetDescription(sockErr.ErrorCode)

        WriteStatus("Error binding the socket.")
        WriteActivity("Error: " & errDesc, "APP")

        'Re-set the form to its initial state
        SetFormState("INITIAL")

    Catch appErr As Exception
        'This is our catch-all for any other types of errors.
        WriteStatus("Error binding the socket.")
        WriteActivity("Error: " & appErr.Message, "APP")

        'Re-set the form to its initial state
        SetFormState("INITIAL")

    End Try

End Sub
```

Listing 8.4   Continued

The next step, after binding the socket to its local end point, is to connect it to its remote end point. This routine functions nearly identically to the BindSocket routine.

```
Private Sub ConnectSocket(ByVal useDNS As Boolean, _
    ByVal server As String, ByVal port As Integer)
    Try
        Dim serverAddress As IPAddress

        If useDNS Then
            'User has supplied a server name; we first need to resolve it
            'using the DNS class
            serverAddress = Dns.Resolve(server).AddressList(0)
        Else
            'User has supplied an IP address in dotted quad format; just
            'use the IPAddress.Parse method to get at the actual
            serverAddress = IPAddress.Parse(server)

        End If

        'Now that we had an IPAddress instance, we can use this
        'to establish our IPEndPoint object
        Dim serverEP As IPEndPoint = New IPEndPoint(serverAddress, port)

        'establish the connection
        netSocket.Connect(serverEP)

        'Set the form state to "connected"
        SetFormState("CONNECTED")

        'Write out the success message
        WriteStatus("Connected to " & server & ".")
        WriteActivity("Socket connect to " & server & ".", "APP")

    Catch sockErr As SocketException
        'A socket exception was encountered.

        'Retrieve and then write out the actual winsock error
        'description
        Dim convert As WinSockError = New WinSockError()
        Dim errDesc As String = convert.GetDescription(sockErr.ErrorCode)

        WriteStatus("Error binding the socket.")
        WriteActivity("Error: " & errDesc, "APP")

        'Re-set the form to its initial state
        SetFormState("INITIAL")
```

LISTING 8.4 Continued

```
    Catch appErr As Exception
        'This is our catch-all for any other types of errors.
        WriteStatus("Error binding the socket.")
        WriteActivity("Error: " & appErr.Message, "APP")

        'Re-set the form to bound state
        SetFormState("BOUND")

    End Try

End Sub
```

This is where all of the action is. The SendToSocket routine takes the text "command" or message typed in and sends it across the socket to the machine sitting at the remote end point. After sending the message, the ReceiveFromSocket routine is called.

```
Private Sub SendToSocket(ByVal msg As String)
    'This routine sends data across the socket and then
    'receives the reply.

    'Translate the string into a byte array
    Dim encoder As Encoding

    Dim sendMsg As Byte() = encoder.GetBytes(msg)

    Try
        Dim bytesSent As System.Int32

        'Send the message to the server
        bytesSent = netSocket.Send(sendMsg)

        ReceiveFromSocket()

        WriteActivity(msg & "(" & bytesSent & " bytes)", "MSG")

    Catch sockErr As SocketException
        'A socket exception was encountered.

        'Retrieve and then write out the actual winsock error
        'description
        Dim convert As WinSockError = New WinSockError()
        Dim errDesc As String = convert.GetDescription(sockErr.ErrorCode)

        WriteStatus("Error sending across the socket.")
        WriteActivity("Error: " & errDesc, "APP")
```

LISTING 8.4   Continued

```
                'Re-set the form to its connected state
                SetFormState("CONNECTED")

        Catch appErr As Exception
                'This is our catch-all for any other types of errors.
                WriteStatus("Error sending across the socket.")
                WriteActivity("Error: " & appErr.Message, "APP")

                'Re-set the form to bound state
                SetFormState("CONNECTED")

        End Try

    End Sub
```

The `ReceiveFromSocket` subroutine collects data coming back across the socket in response to the message sent. It will loop through the bytes received until there are no more left; it then writes the response out to the activity log on the main form.

```
    Private Sub ReceiveFromSocket()
        Try
                Dim bytesRcvd As System.Int32
                Dim rcvBuffer As Byte()
                Dim reply As String

                'For translations between strings and byte arrays
                Dim encoder As Encoding

                'Receive the reply message across the socket
                bytesRcvd = netSocket.Receive(rcvBuffer, 1024, SocketFlags.None)

                'We need to loop until there is no more data coming across
                While bytesRcvd > 0
                        WriteStatus("Receiving across the socket (" & bytesRcvd & " _
                            bytes)")
                        bytesRcvd = netSocket.Receive(rcvBuffer, rcvBuffer.Length, _
                            SocketFlags.None)
                        reply = reply & encoder.GetString(rcvBuffer, 0, bytesRcvd)
                End While

                'concatenated response from the server is now stored in the
                ' "reply" variable
                WriteActivity(reply, "RESP")

        Catch sockErr As SocketException
                'A socket exception was encountered.
```

LISTING 8.4   Continued

```
              'Retrieve and then write out the actual winsock error
              'description
              Dim convert As WinSockError = New WinSockError()
              Dim errDesc As String = convert.GetDescription(sockErr.ErrorCode)

              WriteStatus("Error sending across the socket.")
              WriteActivity("Error: " & errDesc, "APP")

              'Re-set the form to its connected state
              SetFormState("CONNECTED")

         Catch appErr As Exception
              'This is our catch-all for any other types of errors.
              WriteStatus("Error sending across the socket.")
              WriteActivity("Error: " & appErr.Message, "APP")

              'Re-set the form to bound state
              SetFormState("CONNECTED")

         End Try

    End Sub
```

This is just a utility routine; it is responsible for doing some basic formatting on the "messages" we write to the screen by way of the activity log.

```
    Private Sub WriteActivity(ByVal msg As String, ByVal msgType As String)
        Dim prefix As String

        Select Case msgType
            Case "APP"
                prefix = "--->"
            Case "MSG"
                prefix = "Msg Sent:"
            Case "RESP"
                prefix = "Response:"
            Case Else
                prefix = ""
        End Select

        listBoxActivity.Items.Add(prefix & msg)

    End Sub

    Private Sub WriteStatus(ByVal msg As String)
        'this routine just writes status messages
        'to the statusbar control on the form
```

LISTING 8.4   Continued

```
       StatusBar().Text = msg
End Sub

Private Sub SetFormState(ByVal state As String)

    Select Case state
        Case "INITIAL"
            textBoxLocal.Enabled = True
            buttonBind.Enabled = True
            checkResolveLocal.Enabled = True
            textBoxRemote.Enabled = False
            checkResolveRemote.Enabled = False
            textBoxSend.Enabled = False
            buttonSend.Enabled = False

        Case "BOUND"
            textBoxLocal.Enabled = False
            buttonBind.Enabled = False
            checkResolveLocal.Enabled = False
            textBoxRemote.Enabled = False
            checkResolveRemote.Enabled = False
            textBoxSend.Enabled = False
            buttonSend.Enabled = False

        Case "CONNECTED"
            textBoxLocal.Enabled = False
            buttonBind.Enabled = False
            checkResolveLocal.Enabled = False
            textBoxRemote.Enabled = False
            checkResolveRemote.Enabled = False
            textBoxSend.Enabled = True
            buttonSend.Enabled = True
    End Select
End Sub

Private Sub buttonBind_Click(ByVal sender As System.Object, _
ByVal e As System.EventArgs) Handles buttonBind.Click
    BindSocket(checkResolveLocal.Checked, Trim(textBoxLocal.Text), _
    Trim(textBoxLocalPort.Text))
End Sub

Private Sub buttonConnect_Click(ByVal sender As System.Object, ByVal e As _
    System.EventArgs) Handles buttonConnect.Click
    ConnectSocket(checkResolveRemote.Checked, Trim(textBoxRemote.Text), _
        Trim(textBoxRemotePort.Text))
End Sub
```

LISTING 8.4   Continued

```
    Private Sub buttonSend_Click(ByVal sender As System.Object, ByVal e As _
        System.EventArgs) Handles buttonSend.Click
        SendToSocket(Trim(textBoxSend.Text))
    End Sub
End Class
```

This is a helper class that we use to provide more descriptive error descriptions whenever the application encounters an actual WinSock exception.

```
Public Class WinSockError
    Public Function GetDescription(ByVal errNum As System.Int32) As String

        'Return a winsock specific error message based on the passed
        'in errNum integer
        Select Case errNum
            Case 10013
                GetDescription = "Permission denied"
            Case 10048
                GetDescription = "Address already in use"
            Case 10049
                GetDescription = "Cannot assign request address"
            Case 10047
                GetDescription = "Address family not supported by protocol _
                    family"
            Case 10037
                GetDescription = "Operation already in progress"
            Case 10053
                GetDescription = "Software caused connection abort"
            Case 10061
                GetDescription = "Connection refused"
            Case 10054
                GetDescription = "Connection reset by peer"
            Case 10039
                GetDescription = "Destination address required"
            Case 10014
                GetDescription = "Bad address"
            Case 10064
                GetDescription = "Host is down"
            Case 10065
                GetDescription = "No route to host"
            Case 10036
                GetDescription = "Operation now in progress"
            Case 10004
                GetDescription = "Interrupted function call"
            Case 10022
                GetDescription = "Invalid argument"
```

LISTING 8.4 Continued

```
Case 10056
    GetDescription = "Socket is already connected"
Case 10024
    GetDescription = "Too many open files"
Case 10040
    GetDescription = "Message too long"
Case 10050
    GetDescription = "Network is down"
Case 10052
    GetDescription = "Network dropped connection on reset"
Case 10051
    GetDescription = "Network is unreachable"
Case 10055
    GetDescription = "No buffer space available"
Case 10042
    GetDescription = "Bad protocol option"
Case 10057
    GetDescription = "Socket is not connected"
Case 10038
    GetDescription = "Socket operation on non-socket"
Case 10045
    GetDescription = "Operation not supported"
Case 10046
    GetDescription = "Protocol family not supported"
Case 10067
    GetDescription = "Too many processes"
Case 10043
    GetDescription = "Protocol not supported"
Case 10041
    GetDescription = "Protocol wrong type for socket"
Case 10058
    GetDescription = "Cannot send after socket shutdown"
Case 10044
    GetDescription = "Socket type not supported"
Case 10060
    GetDescription = "Connection timed out"
Case 10109
    GetDescription = "Class type not found"
Case 10035
    GetDescription = "Resource temporarily unavailable"
Case 11001
    GetDescription = "Host not found"
Case 10091
    GetDescription = "Network subsystem is unavailable"
Case 11002
    GetDescription = "Non-authoritative host not found"
```

LISTING 8.4   Continued

```
         Case 10101
            GetDescription = "Graceful shutdown in progress"
         Case Else
            GetDescription = "unknown"
      End Select

   End Function
End Class
```

Learning by Example: ISBNCrawler Application

With this sample application, we'll spend some time looking at a good design pattern revolving around the use of the WebClient class and the WebRequest/WebResponse classes to access and interact with Web-based resources. At the same time, we'll introduce a key advanced concept—asynchronous processing.

This application will crawl a few different Web sites looking for pricing information on a specific book (referenced by its ISBN number). Each request, and corresponding response, is performed asynchronously. You will see responses coming in by examining the "activity log" on the form and by watching the actual price column—it will transition from "waiting" to an actual dollar amount (that is, if the program was successful in parsing a price out of the HTML response). Here are a few notes on the application:

- The application will prompt you for an ISBN number (some very basic bounds and pattern checking will be done to see if you actually typed in a valid ISBN from a format perspective).

- The application will then go out and query a list of Web site resources that function as ISBN-based interfaces into a bookseller's Web site.

- The resulting HTML response is parsed in an attempt to find the price of the book. The application stores a specific string pattern by each site entry; it will look for this pattern when attempting to discern the actual pricing information. Note that HTML parsing is a pretty poor way to derive data from a Web page; it would be far better if the data was delineated in an XML format!

Key Concepts Covered

Specifically, we will show how to:

- Use the WebRequest class and WebResponse class to retrieve a specific HTML document from a list of sites.

- Asynchronously download data from the sites.

- Parse the data and present it to the user on the screen as it becomes available.

Code Walkthrough—A Basic Async Design Pattern

Asynchronous request/response patterns are common when accessing Web-based resources. For instance, code that blocks while waiting for a reply back from a Web server may not be a good thing.

The ISBNCrawler application follows a standard design pattern in .NET for writing code that uses asynchronous callbacks. This is the same pattern we discussed earlier in this chapter (see Figure 8.4).

FIGURE 8.4
ISBNCrawler: The main dialog.

This dialog is pretty self-explanatory. Simply select which of the "big three" you want to query for a particular book, enter the ISBN number in the text box, and press the Go button. You should see a message that the server is being queried. After being queried, the hourglass should go away, control should be returned back to the application, and the form will indicate that it is waiting for a response.

Once the response is received, the raw HTML will be displayed in the Returned HTML text box. If the application was successful at parsing a price out of the HTML, it will show up to the right of the Go button.

Code Walkthrough

Listing 8.5 walks you through the code of a sample application—the ISBNCrawler.

LISTING 8.5 Sample Application: ISBN Crawler

```
Imports System.Net
Imports System.IO
Imports System.Text
```

LISTING 8.5   Continued

```
Public Class Form1
    Inherits System.Windows.Forms.Form
```

We hold the actual URL of the site to be queried in the form-local variable `targetSite`. We also hold our State object at this scope as well.

```
'Currently targeted site
Dim targetSite As String
Dim aState As State = New State()
```

These are the constants being used for the ISBN query facility for each site.

```
Const AMAZON_QRY As String = "/exec/obidos/ASIN/"
Const BARNES_QRY As String = "/isbninquiry.asp?isbn="
Const BORDERS_QRY As String = "/fcgi-bin/db2www/search/search.d2w/
➥Details?mediaType=Book&searchType=ISBNUPC&code="
```

Windows Form Designer Code: nothing special here, although we do "initialize" the targetSite variable with the URL for Amazon.com.

```
#Region " Windows Form Designer generated code "

    Public Sub New()
        MyBase.New()

        'This call is required by the Windows Form Designer.
        InitializeComponent()

        'Add any initialization after the InitializeComponent() call
        targetSite = "http://www.amazon.com" & AMAZON_QRY
    End Sub

    'Form overrides dispose to clean up the component list.
    Public Overloads Sub Dispose()
        MyBase.Dispose()
        If Not (components Is Nothing) Then
            components.Dispose()
        End If
    End Sub

    Private WithEvents groupBox1 As System.Windows.Forms.GroupBox
    Private WithEvents textBox1 As System.Windows.Forms.TextBox
    Private WithEvents button1 As System.Windows.Forms.Button
    Private WithEvents label1 As System.Windows.Forms.Label
    Private WithEvents label2 As System.Windows.Forms.Label
    Private WithEvents listBox2 As System.Windows.Forms.ListBox
    Private WithEvents listBox1 As System.Windows.Forms.ListBox
    Private WithEvents listView1 As System.Windows.Forms.ListView
    Private WithEvents button3 As System.Windows.Forms.Button
```

LISTING 8.5   Continued

```
Private WithEvents textBoxISBN As System.Windows.Forms.TextBox
Private WithEvents buttonGo As System.Windows.Forms.Button
Friend WithEvents GroupBox2 As System.Windows.Forms.GroupBox
Friend WithEvents RadioButton1 As System.Windows.Forms.RadioButton
Friend WithEvents RadioButton2 As System.Windows.Forms.RadioButton
Friend WithEvents RadioButton3 As System.Windows.Forms.RadioButton
Friend WithEvents ReportedPrice As System.Windows.Forms.Label

'Required by the Windows Form Designer
Private components As System.ComponentModel.Container

'NOTE: The following procedure is required by the Windows Form Designer
'It can be modified using the Windows Form Designer.
'Do not modify it using the code editor.
<System.Diagnostics.DebuggerStepThrough()> Private Sub _
    InitializeComponent()
    Me.buttonGo = New System.Windows.Forms.Button()
    Me.label1 = New System.Windows.Forms.Label()
    Me.button3 = New System.Windows.Forms.Button()
    Me.groupBox1 = New System.Windows.Forms.GroupBox()
    Me.textBoxHTML = New System.Windows.Forms.TextBox()
    Me.GroupBox2 = New System.Windows.Forms.GroupBox()
    Me.RadioButton3 = New System.Windows.Forms.RadioButton()
    Me.RadioButton2 = New System.Windows.Forms.RadioButton()
    Me.RadioButton1 = New System.Windows.Forms.RadioButton()
    Me.listBox2 = New System.Windows.Forms.ListBox()
    Me.textBoxISBN = New System.Windows.Forms.TextBox()
    Me.ReportedPrice = New System.Windows.Forms.Label()
    Me.groupBox1.SuspendLayout()
    Me.GroupBox2.SuspendLayout()
    Me.SuspendLayout()
    '
    'buttonGo
    '
    Me.buttonGo.Location = New System.Drawing.Point(272, 60)
    Me.buttonGo.Name = "buttonGo"
    Me.buttonGo.Size = New System.Drawing.Size(75, 20)
    Me.buttonGo.TabIndex = 2
    Me.buttonGo.Text = "Go!"
    '
    'label1
    '
    Me.label1.Location = New System.Drawing.Point(236, 24)
    Me.label1.Name = "label1"
    Me.label1.Size = New System.Drawing.Size(36, 16)
    Me.label1.TabIndex = 1
    Me.label1.Text = "ISBN:"
```

LISTING 8.5 Continued

```vb
'
'button3
'
Me.button3.Location = New System.Drawing.Point(364, 208)
Me.button3.Name = "button3"
Me.button3.Size = New System.Drawing.Size(75, 20)
Me.button3.TabIndex = 0
Me.button3.Text = "Clear"
'
'groupBox1
'
Me.groupBox1.Controls.AddRange(New System.Windows.Forms.Control() _
    {Me.textBoxHTML, Me.button3})
Me.groupBox1.Location = New System.Drawing.Point(16, 132)
Me.groupBox1.Name = "groupBox1"
Me.groupBox1.Size = New System.Drawing.Size(448, 236)
Me.groupBox1.TabIndex = 3
Me.groupBox1.TabStop = False
Me.groupBox1.Text = "Returned HTML"
'
'textBoxHTML
'
Me.textBoxHTML.Location = New System.Drawing.Point(12, 24)
Me.textBoxHTML.Multiline = True
Me.textBoxHTML.Name = "textBoxHTML"
Me.textBoxHTML.Size = New System.Drawing.Size(424, 180)
Me.textBoxHTML.TabIndex = 4
Me.textBoxHTML.Text = ""
'
'GroupBox2
'
Me.GroupBox2.Controls.AddRange(New System.Windows.Forms.Control() _
    {Me.RadioButton3, Me.RadioButton2, Me.RadioButton1})
Me.GroupBox2.Location = New System.Drawing.Point(16, 12)
Me.GroupBox2.Name = "GroupBox2"
Me.GroupBox2.Size = New System.Drawing.Size(208, 112)
Me.GroupBox2.TabIndex = 1
Me.GroupBox2.TabStop = False
Me.GroupBox2.Text = "Target Site"
'
'RadioButton3
'
Me.RadioButton3.Location = New System.Drawing.Point(20, 80)
Me.RadioButton3.Name = "RadioButton3"
Me.RadioButton3.Size = New System.Drawing.Size(172, 16)
Me.RadioButton3.TabIndex = 2
Me.RadioButton3.Text = "Borders.com"
'
```

LISTING 8.5 Continued

```
'RadioButton2
'
Me.RadioButton2.Location = New System.Drawing.Point(20, 56)
Me.RadioButton2.Name = "RadioButton2"
Me.RadioButton2.Size = New System.Drawing.Size(172, 16)
Me.RadioButton2.TabIndex = 1
Me.RadioButton2.Text = "BarnesAndNoble.com"
'
'RadioButton1
'
Me.RadioButton1.Checked = True
Me.RadioButton1.Location = New System.Drawing.Point(20, 32)
Me.RadioButton1.Name = "RadioButton1"
Me.RadioButton1.Size = New System.Drawing.Size(172, 16)
Me.RadioButton1.TabIndex = 0
Me.RadioButton1.TabStop = True
Me.RadioButton1.Text = "Amazon.com"
'
'listBox2
'
Me.listBox2.Location = New System.Drawing.Point(244, 72)
Me.listBox2.Name = "listBox2"
Me.listBox2.Size = New System.Drawing.Size(120, 95)
Me.listBox2.TabIndex = 1
'
'textBoxISBN
'
Me.textBoxISBN.Location = New System.Drawing.Point(272, 20)
Me.textBoxISBN.Name = "textBoxISBN"
Me.textBoxISBN.Size = New System.Drawing.Size(172, 20)
Me.textBoxISBN.TabIndex = 0
Me.textBoxISBN.Text = ""
'
'ReportedPrice
'
Me.ReportedPrice.Font = New System.Drawing.Font("Microsoft Sans _
    Serif", 9!, _
System.Drawing.FontStyle.Bold, System.Drawing.GraphicsUnit.Point, _
    CType(0, Byte))
Me.ReportedPrice.ForeColor = System.Drawing.Color.Blue
Me.ReportedPrice.Location = New System.Drawing.Point(352, 60)
Me.ReportedPrice.Name = "ReportedPrice"
Me.ReportedPrice.Size = New System.Drawing.Size(124, 20)
Me.ReportedPrice.TabIndex = 5
Me.ReportedPrice.Text = "Price: <not found>"
'
'Form1
```

LISTING 8.5 Continued

```
        '
        Me.AutoScaleBaseSize = New System.Drawing.Size(5, 13)
        Me.ClientSize = New System.Drawing.Size(496, 373)
        Me.Controls.AddRange(New System.Windows.Forms.Control() _
            {Me.ReportedPrice, _
        Me.GroupBox2, Me.buttonGo, Me.groupBox1, Me.label1, Me.textBoxISBN})
        Me.Name = "Form1"
        Me.Text = "ISBNCrawler"
        Me.groupBox1.ResumeLayout(False)
        Me.GroupBox2.ResumeLayout(False)
        Me.ResumeLayout(False)

    End Sub

    Private Sub MainForm_Load(ByVal sender As System.Object, _
        ByVal e As System.EventArgs) Handles MyBase.Load
    End Sub

#End Region
```

When you press the Go button, we first check to see if a valid ISBN number was entered (this is a rudimentary check at best). If everything checks out, we change the cursor, display a message through the form title bar, and then call `IssueAsyncRequest`.

```
    Private Sub buttonGo_Click(ByVal sender As System.Object, ByVal e As _
        System.EventArgs) Handles buttonGo.Click

        'We will first pass the ISBN number through a short validation
        'routine; if everything looks good, we can go ahead and issue our async
        'requests.
        If ValidISBN(Trim(textBoxISBN().Text)) Then

            buttonGo.Enabled = False
            Me.Cursor = System.Windows.Forms.Cursors.WaitCursor
            Me.textBoxHTML.Text = ""
            Me.Text = "ISBNCrawler - Issuing request"
            targetSite = targetSite & Trim(textBoxISBN.Text)
            IssueAsyncRequest()
            Me.Text = "ISBNCrawler - Waiting for response..."
            Me.Cursor = System.Windows.Forms.Cursors.Default
            buttonGo.Enabled = True

        Else

            MsgBox("You have entered an incorrectly formatted ISBN number. _
                The ISBN you enter should be numeric, and should have 10 _
                digits without any dashes or spaces." & vbCrLf & vbCrLf & _
                "Please try again.")
```

LISTING 8.5   Continued

```
        End If
    End Sub
```

IssueAsyncRequest launches a request object, thereby starting off the async design pattern. The WebRequest object is created with the URL specified in targetSite, and then the BeginGetResponse method is called.

```
    Private Sub IssueAsyncRequest()
        Try
            Dim req As WebRequest    'encapsulates our request
            Dim indx As Integer      'used to loop through the site array

            'Create the request object
            req = WebRequest.Create(targetSite)

            'Assign the request object into the state object
            aState.HttpRequest = req

            'This kicks off the whole async request
            req.BeginGetResponse(New AsyncCallback(AddressOf _
                ReceiveResponse), aState)

        Catch webErr As WebException    'catch a WebRequest error
            Dim status As WebExceptionStatus = webErr.Status

            ResetFormCursor()

            MsgBox("An error occurred while creating the WebRequest->" & _
            webErr.Message & ";" & webErr.StackTrace)

        Catch appErr As Exception

            ResetFormCursor()

            MsgBox("An application error occured->" & appErr.Message & ";" & _
            appErr.StackTrace)

        End Try

    End Sub
```

This is the subroutine, which should receive the callback once a response is received. After retrieving the response stream, an asynchronous read is started on the stream by calling BeginRead.

LISTING 8.5 Continued

```vb
Private Sub ReceiveResponse(ByVal rslt As IAsyncResult)
    Dim priceGuess As String 'hold the price string that we have _
        attempted to parse

    'Start our block of structured exception handling
    Try
        'Indicate that a response has been received
        Me.Cursor = System.Windows.Forms.Cursors.WaitCursor
        Me.Text = "ISBNCrawler - Response received."

        'Get the state object from the async result
        Dim retState As State = CType(rslt.AsyncState, State)

        'Now, pull the HttpWebRequest object out of the state object
        Dim httpRequest As HttpWebRequest = retState.HttpRequest

        'Call EndGetResponse, which will produce the HttpWebResponse object
        'that came from the request issued above
        Dim httpResp As HttpWebResponse = httpRequest.EndGetResponse(rslt)

        'Grab the stream from the response object
        Dim respStream As Stream = httpResp.GetResponseStream()

        ' Store the reponse stream in State to read
        ' the stream asynchronously.
        retState.RespStream = respStream

        'Start the async stream reads;
        'here, we use the StreamBuffer prop and set the callback to the
        'ReadStream routine
        respStream.BeginRead(retState.StreamBuffer, 0, 1024, New _
        AsyncCallback(AddressOf ReadStream), retState)

    Catch webErr As WebException   ' Catch the error.

        Dim status As WebExceptionStatus = webErr.Status()

        ResetFormCursor()

        MsgBox("An error was encountered retrieving the server _
            response->" & webErr.Message & ";" & webErr.StackTrace)
```

LISTING 8.5 Continued

```
                'Try to present some useful information if a protocol error
                'has occurred.
                If status = WebExceptionStatus.ProtocolError Then
                    MsgBox("PROTOCOL ERROR: " & status.ToString)
                End If

                MessageBox.Show(Err().ToString) ' Show friendly error message.


        Catch appErr As Exception     ' Catch the error.

            ResetFormCursor()

            'Any other error type should fall into here...
            MsgBox("An application error occurred->" & appErr.Message & ";" & _
            appErr.StackTrace)

        End Try

    End Sub
```

The ReadStream subroutine received the call back from the async stream read. If more bytes remain to be read, it will call itself again until the data is exhausted. Once all of the data has been read in, its entirety is written out to the HTML results box, and the parsed price (if one was found) is displayed to the screen as well.

```
Private Sub ReadStream(ByVal rslt As IAsyncResult)
    Try
        'Get the state object from the async result
        Dim retState As State = CType(rslt.AsyncState, State)

        ' Retrieve the stream from the state object
        Dim respStream As Stream = retState.RespStream

        Dim bytesRead As Integer = respStream.EndRead(rslt)

        'If the stream still contains data...
        If bytesRead > 0 Then

            'Use the encoder to x-late the byte array into a string
            Dim streamStr As String = _
                Encoding.ASCII.GetString(retState.StreamBuffer)

            'Concat the string into the stringbuilder in the state object
            retState.RqstData.Append(streamStr)
```

LISTING 8.5   Continued

```
                'Call for another read
                respStream.BeginRead(retState.StreamBuffer, 0, 1024, New _
                AsyncCallback(AddressOf ReadStream), retState)

        Else
                'No more data in the stream; parse the price out and
                'write the HTML to the form
                Dim price As String = ParsePrice(retState.RqstData.ToString)
                Me.textBoxHTML.Text = retState.RqstData.ToString

                ' Close down the response stream.
                respStream.Close()

                Me.Cursor = System.Windows.Forms.Cursors.Default

        End If

    Catch streamErr As IOException

        ResetFormCursor()

        MsgBox("An IO error occurred with the stream object->" & _
        streamErr.Message & ";" & streamErr.StackTrace)


    Catch appErr As Exception

        ResetFormCursor()

        'Any other error type should fall into here...
        MsgBox("An application error occurred->" & appErr.Message & ";" & _
        appErr.StackTrace)

    End Try

End Sub
```

`ParsePrice` attempts to pull the actual book price out of a string by looking for the pattern "Our Price:". Again, this is not the best way to do things, but it suffices for the scope of this demonstration.

```
Private Function ParsePrice(ByVal resp As String) As String
        'This routine just performs some rudimentary guessing in terms of the
        'price returned to us in the response object
        Dim currPos As Integer
        Dim priceGuess As String
```

LISTING 8.5   Continued

```
    Const PATTERN_MATCH As String = "Our Price: "

    currPos = InStr(resp, PATTERN_MATCH)

    priceGuess = Mid(resp, currPos + PATTERN_MATCH.Length, 7)

End Function
```

Another utility routine performs a rudimentary validation on an ISBN number.

```
Private Function ValidISBN(ByVal isbn As String) As Boolean
    'assume isbn is accurate...
    ValidISBN = True

    'now look for evidence that it is not (these are not exhaustive _
        obviously...)
    If isbn.Length > 10 Or isbn.Length < 10 Then
        ValidISBN = False
    ElseIf Not IsNumeric(isbn) Then
        ValidISBN = False
    End If

End Function


Private Sub WriteResult(ByVal price As String)
    ReportedPrice.Text = "Price: " & price
End Sub


Private Sub RadioButton1_CheckedChanged(ByVal sender As System.Object, _
    ByVal e As System.EventArgs) Handles RadioButton1.CheckedChanged
    If RadioButton1.Checked Then
        Me.targetSite = "http://www." & RadioButton1.Text & AMAZON_QRY
    End If
End Sub

Private Sub RadioButton2_CheckedChanged(ByVal sender As System.Object, _
    ByVal e As System.EventArgs) Handles RadioButton2.CheckedChanged
    If RadioButton2.Checked Then
        Me.targetSite = "http://www." & RadioButton2.Text & BARNES_QRY
    End If
End Sub

Private Sub RadioButton3_CheckedChanged(ByVal sender As System.Object, _
    ByVal e As System.EventArgs) Handles RadioButton3.CheckedChanged
    If RadioButton3.Checked Then
```

LISTING 8.5   Continued

```
            Me.targetSite = "http://search." & RadioButton3.Text & BORDERS_QRY
        End If

    End Sub

    Private Sub ResetFormCursor()
        Me.Cursor = System.Windows.Forms.Cursors.Default
    End Sub

    Private Sub button3_Click(ByVal sender As System.Object, ByVal e As _
        System.EventArgs) Handles button3.Click
        textBoxHTML.Text = ""
    End Sub

    Friend WithEvents textBoxHTML As System.Windows.Forms.TextBox
End Class
```

This class is our state class, responsible for holding onto our stream items and request/response items between async calls.

```
Imports System
Imports System.Net
Imports System.Text
Imports System.IO

Public Class State

    'Object to hold the WebRequest instance
    Public HttpRequest As HttpWebRequest

    'Object to hold the stream from the response object
    Public RespStream As Stream

    'Buffer for holding our reads into the stream
    Public StreamBuffer(1024) As Byte

    'Because our stream reads will be done async, we need to
    'build up the entire response stream content through
    'concatenation - this will hold the concatenated response
    'data:
    Public RqstData As New StringBuilder("")

    Public Sub New()

    End Sub
End Class
```

Summary

The networking classes exposed in the class library represent a very powerful tool for the Visual Basic .NET developer. The ease with which developers can perform complex operations, coupled with the capability to write low-level network functions, represents a large step forward from Visual Basic's previous abilities in this arena.

In this chapter, we examined:

- Socket programming using the `System.Net.Sockets` namespace
- Sending and receiving TCP/IP network traffic using the `TCPListener` and `TCPClient` classes
- Using HTTP-specific, as well as protocol-agnostic, classes to issue requests to Web servers and react to their responses
- How to employ a typical .NET design pattern with the networking classes to allow applications to issue and receive data in an asynchronous fashion
- Creating variables that are specific and local to individual threads

Drawing Functions

IN THIS CHAPTER

Nothing in Windows gets to the user's screen without the aid of a drawing function. This includes images, colors, and even text. The OS must render all things visually by drawing pixels to an output device (monitor, printer, and so on). Of course, Windows does a good job of hiding drawing functions from the average developer. When did you last need to call an API function to display text to the screen or change the background color of a button? Our controls, compiler, and operating system serve to limit our need to make direct calls into the drawing library. However, there is always the case where your application requirements are beyond the scope of what can be done with controls and so on. Perhaps you must create custom pie charts for your users on-the-fly. Or maybe you need to allow your users to view a group of fonts or send output to the printer. Chances are that you will eventually need to write your own custom visual display code. This is where the .NET drawing library comes into play. It provides you with a host of classes that make adding drawing capabilities to your application easy and fun.

This chapter illustrates common programming tasks using the namespaces related to drawing in the .NET Framework Class Library. The chapter starts by illustrating the key classes used to execute drawing functions with the namespace. Then follows a detailed discussion of these key classes and related code examples. Lastly, we will create a simple drawing application that serves to demonstrate how these classes can be used in the context of a larger application and serves as an experimental ground.

After reading this chapter, you should be able to do the following:

- Understand how Windows manages coordinates
- Draw basic shapes including lines, curves, rectangles, and polygons
- Fill shapes and lines with various colors, patterns, and gradients
- Work with groups of shapes
- Work with bitmaps and icons in your application
- Rotate, stretch, and skew graphics

Key Classes Related to Drawing

The process of drawing with the .NET Framework Class Library involves a whole host of classes. These classes can be found inside of the System.Drawing namespace and its associated third-level namespaces. At a glance, the drawing namespace in .NET is made up of the following:

- System.Drawing: Provides basic graphics functionality. This chapter focuses on this namespace.
- System.Drawing.Design: Focuses on providing functionality for extending the design time environment. This namespace is beyond the scope of this book.

- `System.Drawing.Drawing2D`: Provides two-dimensional and vector graphics classes and methods. This namespace is covered within this chapter.

- `System.Drawing.Imaging`: Exposes advanced imaging functionality. This namespace is beyond the scope of this book.

- `System.Drawing.Printing`: Gives you classes to manage output to a print device. Chapter 6, "Font, Text, and Printing Operations," covers this namespace.

- `System.Drawing.Text`: Wraps fonts and type management. Chapter 6 covers this namespace.

This chapter is focused on the `System.Drawing` and `System.Drawing.Drawing2D` namespaces. These two namespaces contain classes that are fundamental to the execution of common programming tasks with .NET. The namespaces `Printing` and `Text` are covered elsewhere in the book, and `Design` and `Imaging` are simply beyond the scope of this book as they encapsulate more specialized features. There are certainly great classes within these namespaces, and we encourage you to use this chapter as a leaping-off point to your own exploring. Table 9.1 lists the key classes we will be discussing.

TABLE 9.1   Key Classes of `System.Drawing` and `System.Drawing.Drawing2D`

Class	Description
Functional Drawing Classes	
Graphics	The `Graphics` class is the premier class within the namespace for executing drawing and filling shapes.
GraphicsState	The `GraphicsState` class is used to save the state of the `Graphics` object between calls to transformations and the like. This class is used with the `BeginContainer` and `EndContainer` methods of the `Graphics` class.
Drawing Basics	
Pen	The `Pen` class is used to draw the outlines of objects (lines, rectangles, ellipses, and so on). It defines the line weight and color similar to an actual pen.
Rectangle	The `Rectangle` structure stores information about a rectangle (location, width, and height). This structure is used to draw rectangles, ellipses, pies, and so on.
CustomLineCap	The `CustomLineCap` class is used to create a custom, user-defined end cap for a line.

TABLE 9.1 Continued

Class	Description
	Working with Images
Bitmap	The Bitmap class encapsulates an image of type bitmap.
Icon	The Icon class encapsulates a small bitmap image used to represent an object.
Image	The Image class is the abstract base class used for both the Bitmap and the Icon classes.
	Graphic Fills
Brush	The abstract Brush class is the base class for the various brush classes throughout the drawing namespace. Brushes are used to fill shapes with colors, textures, and patterns.
SolidBrush	The SolidBrush class is a brush made of one solid color.
TextureBrush	The TextureBrush class is a brush made up of an image. It allows you to fill shapes with various versions of an image.
HatchBrush	The HatchBrush class is used to create a brush based on a predefined pattern, a foreground color, and a background color.
LinearGradientBrush	The LinearGradientBrush is used to create brushes that blend two colors across an object.
PathGradientBrush	The PathGradientBrush can create a brush object that can be used to fill paths.
	Graphic Storage
Region	The Region class is used to describe the inside of a graphics shape made of rectangles and paths.
RegionData	The RegionData class is used to store the data that makes up a region.
GraphicsPath	The GraphicsPath class groups connected lines and curves for manipulation as a whole.
PathData	The PathData class is used to store data that makes up a GraphicsPath.
	Utility Classes
Point	The Point structure allows you to group x and y coordinates as a single object or point on a 2D plane.
Size	Similar to the Point structure, the Size structure groups width and height.
Matrix	The Matrix class is the mathematical foundation used to transform graphics.

Drawing with the .NET Namespaces

Windows has a very rich user interface. Users interact with it through a visual display; they click menus, buttons, and toolbars; they read text and respond to dialog boxes. All of these are things that must be drawn to the screen. A button is simply a bitmap image—a set of pixels. As such, it must be drawn, and someone must write the code to draw it.

GDI+

All drawing with .NET-managed code happens through the *Graphics Device Interface plus* (GDI+) layer. GDI+ is the new API Windows uses to provide the .NET Framework with graphics, imaging, printing, and typography capabilities. Prior to .NET, VB programmers mostly had to rely on Win32 API calls into GDI to execute drawing functions. In .NET, GDI+ is wrapped by the drawing namespace. This provides easy, object-oriented access to drawing functions from all .NET languages.

GDI+ shields your application from having to deal with the details and particulars of device drivers. It allows you to send output to the screen or printer without concern for calling into the driver that manages a given device. For example, your application need not write new code to support an Epson printer versus an HP; think if you had to write new code for every graphics card your application had to support. Instead, GDI+ makes the calls to the specific device driver for us, thus insulating our application from the hardware and allowing us to easily create device-independent software.

Practical Applications

GDI+ provides objects like pens and brushes—objects used by programmers to illustrate ideas and to create tools for their users to do the same. If you are creating applications with illustrating capabilities, you see the obvious need for drawing functions. For instance, if your application allows users to select a color, you'll most likely use the Color structure or the ColorPalette class.

Beyond illustration applications, however, you might be surprised by how often drawing functions are required. For instance, word processing applications use lines and curves to render borders for tables, pages, and around text. A search word game might use the DrawLine function to cross out words as users find them. Spreadsheet applications and the like could use the DrawPie method to create pie charts based on user data. CAD (computer-aided design) applications outline objects and calculate distance between points with lines and curves. Even Web applications might create graphics on the server based on user-submitted data. These images could be stored to the file system and displayed out to the user's browser. You can see that, before long, you will more than likely need to execute drawing functions with the .NET Framework Class Library. So, let's get started learning to draw using the .NET namespaces.

Suggestions for Further Exploration

➲ If you're familiar with using GDI and want a quick primer on what's new, check out "What's New in GDI+" inside of the MSDN library, "Programming with the .NET Framework."

➲ For more information on the Win32 GDI functions, see MSDN: Library/Graphics and Multimedia/Windows GDI.

➲ For specific Win32 API calls for the Visual Basic programmer, see Dan Appleman's *Visual Basic Programmer's Guide to the Win32 API.*

Drawing Basics

Most computer-based drawing is done on a two-dimensional plane using a basic set of objects. These objects are like building blocks. In the hands of a competent craftsman, they can be manipulated to create interesting effects and complex shapes. But before we can build the skyscraper, we must first set the basic foundation.

Understanding Windows Coordinate Systems

The default coordinate system in Windows has the origin (0, 0) in the upper-left corner of the drawing surface. The x-axis extends to the right, while the y-axis extends downward. The pixel is the unit of measurement in the default coordinate system. To draw to a surface, you specify what pixels you want your monitor to "turn on" to create the graphic. For instance, a line can be defined by joining the pixels between a start and an end coordinate. Figure 9.1 illustrates these concepts.

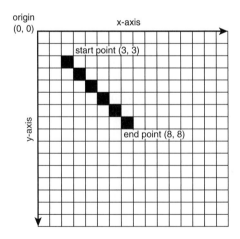

FIGURE 9.1

Windows default coordinate system.

The `Graphics` Class

The `Graphics` class is used to render the majority of all two-dimensional drawing in .NET. It is far and away the class you will most often use to execute basic drawing tasks. The class provides methods for drawing all the basic 2D shapes, including: lines, rectangles, ellipses, polygons, arcs, cardinal splines, and Bèzier splines. For the most part, if you need to draw a shape, there will be an associated method of the `Graphics` class. For example, the `DrawLine` method is used to draw a line and the `DrawRectangle` method is used for a rectangle. In fact, you can often draw several graphic elements with a single method call. To do so, you simply use the plural version of a given drawing method, such as `DrawLines` or `DrawRectangles`. All of these methods (and the `Graphics` class itself) are covered in-depth throughout the rest of this chapter.

Pens

The companion to the `Graphics` class is the `Pen` class. In fact, in order to draw nearly anything, you'll need at least a `Graphics` and a `Pen` instance. The `Pen` class is used to define how the outlines of shapes are rendered to the surface. Similar to a real pen, the `Pen` class defines a width color that will be used to do the drawing. Additionally, you can create a `Pen` based on a `Brush` instance. This allows you to draw with more stylized lines. Table 9.2 demonstrates the various constructors that are available to you when creating new `Pen` instances.

TABLE 9.2 Pen Constructors

Constructor	Description
New Pen(Color, Single)	Creates a `Pen` object based on a color (`Color` structure) and a width (Single) in pixels.
New Pen(Color)	Creates a `Pen` object based on a color defined by the `Color` structure. Sets the pen's width to the default of 1 pixel.
New Pen(Brush, Single)	Creates a `Pen` object using a valid class derived from the `Brush` base class. The pen's width (Single) is defined in pixels.
New Pen(Brush)	Creates a `Pen` object based on a valid `Brush` object. Sets the pen's width to the default of 1.0 pixels.

The `Color` parameter, used in the `Pen` constructor, is defined by an instance of the `Color` structure. The `Color` structure represents an ARGB (Alpha, Red, Green, and Blue) color. Most colors come predefined as properties of the `Color` structure for easy use. For example, `Color.Red` indicates the ARGB equivalent of red. There are a wide variety of predefined colors, everything from `LawnGreen` to `Tomato` to `Transparent`. Additionally, you can call methods of the `Color` structure to create custom colors or return the brightness, saturation, and hue of a given color.

Lines

So far, we've talked about pens and drawing methods but have yet to render anything to the screen. Now we'll use a Pen object to draw a line onto a form. This may not seem exciting, but it provides a foundation.

A line is a set of pixels linked by a start and end point. Line attributes are defined by the Pen object with which they are drawn. Of course, as pens can vary in width and color, so to can lines. To draw a line, we use the DrawLine method of the Graphics class. This method is overloaded; it defines a number of ways you can pass it parameters. For instance, you can pass it a Pen object and two Point structures between which GDI+ will draw the line. A Point structure stores the x and y coordinates of a point on a 2D plane.

The following code uses the DrawLine method and a Pen instance to draw a blue line onto a form. You can test this code, create a new form-based application, add a button to it, and add the code in the listing to the button's click event.

```
'local scope
Dim myGraphics As Graphics
Dim myPen As Pen

'return the current form as a drawing surface
myGraphics = Graphics.FromHwnd(hwnd:=ActiveForm().Handle)

'instantiate a new pen object using the color structure
myPen = New Pen(color:=Color.Blue, Width:=4)

'draw the line on the form using the pen object
myGraphics.DrawLine(pen:=myPen, x1:=1, y1:=1, x2:=25, y2:=50)
```

Note that before we could draw anything to the screen, we needed to return a valid drawing surface. To do so, we created an instance of the Graphics class. This provides us an object on which to draw. The constructor accepts a Windows handle as its parameter. We pass it the active Windows handle. This sets up the Graphics object to use the active form as its target for drawing our line.

Next, a Pen instance is created. We pass its constructor a valid color and width. Finally, the DrawLine method of the Graphics object is called to render the line onto the form. The version of the DrawLine method we used requires a Pen instance and a set of start and end coordinates. These coordinates are simply passed in order as two points defined as (x1, y1) and (x2, y2). The method connects the two coordinate points with a blue line based on our Pen object.

Dashes and Caps

What if you want to add an arrow to the end of your line? Or maybe, you need a dotted line to get your point across. In addition to defining color and width, the Pen class is used to create dashed lines and to attach start and end line caps. Line caps can be as simple as an arrowhead or as complex as a custom-defined cap. Table 9.3 lists properties of the Pen class that are specific to dashes and caps.

TABLE 9.3 Pen Class Dash and Cap Properties

Property	Description
CustomStartCap	The CustomStartCap property is used to set or get a custom-defined line cap. The CustomStartCap property defines the cap at a line's start. The property is of type CustomLineCap.
CustomEndCap	The CustomEndCap property is used to set or get a custom-defined line cap. The CustomEndCap property defines the cap at a line's end. The property is of type CustomLineCap.
DashCap	The DashCap property is used to set or get the style used for the start or end caps of dashed lines.
DashOffset	The DashOffset property is used to set or get the distance between the start of a line and the start of the dash pattern.
DashPattern	The DashPattern property sets or gets an array of integers that indicates the distances between dashes in dash-patterned lines.
DashStyle	The DashStyle property sets or gets the style used for dashing a line. The property is of the type DashStyle enumeration. DashStyle enumeration members include the following: Dash, DashDot, DashDotDot, Dot, Solid.
EndCap	The EndCap property sets or gets the LineCap object used to define the end of the line. EndCap is of the type LineCap. The LineCap enumeration includes the following members: AnchorMask, ArrowAnchor, Custom, DiamondAnchor, Flat, NoAnchor, Round, RoundAnchor, Square, SquareAnchor, and Triangle.
StartCap	The StartCap property sets or gets the LineCap object used to define the start of the line. StartCap is of the type LineCap. The LineCap enumeration includes the following members: AnchorMask, ArrowAnchor, Custom, DiamondAnchor, Flat, NoAnchor, Round, RoundAnchor, Square, SquareAnchor, and Triangle.

9

DRAWING FUNCTIONS

The following code demonstrates setting the styles and cap properties of a Pen object. The code first creates a Pen object of the color blue. It then sets the EndCap property to an arrow using the LineCap enumeration. Last, it indicates the line's DashStyle to be a dash followed by a dot (DashDot).

```
'dimension a local variable of type Pen
Dim myPen As Pen

'instantiate a Pen using the color structure and width constructor
myPen = New Pen(color:=Color.Blue, Width:=5)

'set the Pen's end cap to be of type arrow
myPen.EndCap = Drawing.Drawing2D.LineCap.ArrowAnchor

'set the Pen's dash style to be a dash followed by a dot
myPen.DashStyle = Drawing.Drawing2D.DashStyle.DashDot
```

Joins

Suppose we have multiple lines that are joined to indicate a shape or routing direction through a diagram. The point at which two lines are joined can be rendered with three distinct styles. The Pen class defines how lines are joined. To do so, it provides the LineJoin property. This property is of the type LineJoin enumeration whose members include those listed in Table 9.4.

TABLE 9.4 LineJoin Enumeration Members

Member	Example	Description
Bevel		The Bevel member indicates a beveled join between the lines.
Miter		The Miter member specifies an angled join.
Round		The Round member creates a smooth and rounded join.

To join lines, you must add each line to a Path object (discussed later in the chapter). The path is drawn to the surface using one Pen instance. Intersecting lines are then joined based on the LineJoin property of the given Pen instance. The following snippet illustrates this with code.

```
'local scope
Dim myPath As New System.Drawing.Drawing2D.GraphicsPath()
Dim myGraphics As Graphics
Dim myPen As New Pen(color:=Color.Blue, Width:=8)

'return the current form as a drawing surface
myGraphics = Graphics.FromHwnd(hwnd:=ActiveForm().Handle)

'add 2 intersecting lines to a path
myPath.AddLine(10, 10, 50, 10)
myPath.AddLine(50, 10, 50, 50)
```

```
'set the line join property
myPen.LineJoin = Drawing.Drawing2D.LineJoin.Miter

'draw the line to the form
myGraphics.DrawPath(pen:=myPen, path:=myPath)
```

Curves

A curve is an array of points defining the perimeter of a conic section. Curves can be used for such things as connecting points on a graph or drawing a handlebar mustache.

There are two types of curves in the .NET library: cardinal splines and Bèzier splines. There are also a number of methods of the Graphics class that can be used to draw curves. Table 9.5 lists these methods. For our discussion, we will focus on the DrawCurve and DrawBezierCurve methods.

TABLE 9.5 Graphics Class Curve Drawing Methods

Method	Description
DrawCurve	The DrawCurve method connects an array of points using a curved line.
DrawClosedCurve	The DrawClosedCurve method draws a closed curve using an array of points. A closed curve ensures that the shape is closed. For instance, if you drew a curve between three points, the method would close the curve by connecting the third point with the first.
DrawBezier	The DrawBezier method is used to draw a Bèzier curve.
DrawArc	The DrawArc method draws an arc from a specified ellipse.

Cardinal Splines

A *cardinal spline* is an array of points through which a line smoothly passes. The curve or bend of the line is defined by a tension parameter. The curve's tension indicates how tightly the curve bends, the lower the tension on a given curve, the flatter (straighter) the line. A curve with a tension of zero (0), for instance, is equivalent to drawing a straight line between points.

To create a cardinal spline, you use the DrawCurve method. This method allows us to control the curve's tension and define the number of points in a given curve. The method is overloaded, and as such, provides a number of ways to display a curve. In the following example, we create a blue curve that passes through three points. Notice that we did not specify the tension. When left blank, the method uses the default tension of 0.5.

```
'declare local variables
Dim myGraphics As Graphics
Dim myPen As Pen
Dim myPoints(2) As Point

'create a 3-item array of point structures
myPoints(0) = New Point(100, 75)
myPoints(1) = New Point(125, 50)
myPoints(2) = New Point(150, 75)

'return the current form as a drawing surface
myGraphics = Graphics.FromHwnd(hwnd:=ActiveForm().Handle)

'instantiate a new pen object using the color structure
myPen = New Pen(color:=Color.Blue, Width:=2)

'draw curve between the 3 points defined in the array
myGraphics.DrawCurve(pen:=myPen, points:=myPoints)
```

Figure 9.2 helps illustrate the concept of curve tension. The innermost line is drawn with a tension setting of zero. Each successive line increases the tension by .5 until we reach 2.0.

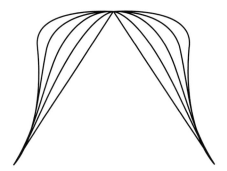

FIGURE 9.2
Curve tension.

Bèzier Splines

Bèzier splines can be used to create a wide variety of shapes. Fonts, for instance, often use Bèzier splines for outlining characters. Four points define a Bèzier spline: a start and end point and two control points. The curve is drawn between the start and end point. The control points influence how the curve flows between the points. As the curve moves from point to point, it is "pulled" toward the nearest control point.

Consider the following code:

```
'declare local variables
Dim myGraphics As Graphics
Dim myPen As Pen
Dim myPoints(3) As Point

'create a 4-item array of point structures
myPoints(0) = New Point(100, 75)
myPoints(1) = New Point(125, 50)
myPoints(2) = New Point(150, 75)
myPoints(3) = New Point(175, 50)

'return the current form as a drawing surface
myGraphics = Graphics.FromHwnd(ActiveForm().Handle)

'instantiate a new pen object using the color structure
myPen = New Pen(Color.Blue, 2)

'draw bezier using the points defined in the array
myGraphics.DrawBezier(pen:=myPen, pt1:=myPoints(0), pt2:=myPoints(1), _
    pt3:=myPoints(2), pt4:=myPoints(3))
```

In the preceding example, we created a Bézier curve using the `DrawBezier` method. First, we defined a set of four points. The first point (100, 75) is the starting point. The next two points, (125, 50) and (150, 75) act as the control points. The curve ends at the point (175, 50).

 ## Suggestions for Further Exploration

⊃ For a complete listing of colors available through the Color structure, check out MSDN: Visual Studio .NET/.NET Framework Class Library/System.Drawing/Color Structure/Properties.

⊃ Use the curve code examples presented in this section to experiment with the `DrawArc` and `DrawClosedCurve` methods.

⊃ Use `DrawBeziers` method to create a series of Bèzier curves.

Drawing Basic Shapes

We continue our exploration of the namespace by drawing some basic shapes. Again, the variety and features contained in the namespace are astounding; we'll try to take a path that focuses on the shapes and illustration details you're most likely to employ in building your application.

Rectangles

The Rectangle structure is the backbone of the shapes presented in this section. Classes like Ellipse and Pie use it to bind their shape. The structure stores the size and location of a rectangular region.

We have two constructors available to create an instance of the Rectangle structure. One creates the rectangle based on the upper-left x and y coordinate, the width of the rectangle, and its height. To the other constructor, you pass both location as an instance of the Point structure, and Size as an instance of the Size structure.

Listing 9.1 illustrates both rectangle constructors. The code is simply fired by a button's click event. The rectangles are output to the active form.

LISTING 9.1   DrawRectangle

```
Private Sub Button1_Click(ByVal sender As System.Object, _
    ByVal e As System.EventArgs) Handles Button1.Click

    'dimension variables of local scope
    Dim myGraphics As Graphics
    Dim myRectangle As Rectangle
    Dim myPen As New Pen(Color.Blue)

    'return the current form as a drawing surface
    myGraphics = Graphics.FromHwnd(ActiveForm().Handle)

    'create a rectangle based on x,y coordinates, width, & height
    myRectangle = New Rectangle(x:=5, y:=5, Width:=10, Height:=40)

    'draw rectangle from pen and rectangle objects
    myGraphics.DrawRectangle(pen:=myPen, rect:=myRectangle)

    'create a rectangle based on Point and Size objects
    myRectangle = New Rectangle(Location:=New Point(10, 10), _
        Size:=New Size(Width:=20, Height:=60))

    'draw another rectangle from Pen and new Rectangle object
    myGraphics.DrawRectangle(pen:=myPen, rect:=myRectangle)

    'draw a rectangle from a Pen object, a rectangle's x & y,
    '  width, & height
    myGraphics.DrawRectangle(pen:=myPen, x:=20, y:=20, _
        Width:=30, Height:=80)

End Sub
```

The DrawRectangle method of the Graphics object allows us to draw the outline of a rectangle to the drawing surface. The method is overloaded with three different sets of parameters. The first set allows you to create a rectangle based on a Pen and Rectangle instance. The other two sets create a rectangle directly from a Pen instance and the rectangle's x and y coordinates (width and height). The difference between these two is the data types used to define the coordinates and size. One uses the Int32 data type, and the other uses a Single.

Ellipses

An ellipse is simply a circle or oval bound inside a Rectangle structure. To draw an ellipse, you can use the DrawEllipse method of the Graphics class. This method requires a Pen object and some semblance of a rectangle definition (structure instance, coordinates, and so on). The following code illustrates drawing an ellipse inside of a defined Rectangle instance.

```
'dimension variables of local scope
Dim myGraphics As Graphics

'return the current form as a drawing surface
myGraphics = Graphics.FromHwnd(ActiveForm().Handle)

'draw an ellipse inside a bounding rectangle with a Pen instance
myGraphics.DrawEllipse(pen:=New Pen(color.Blue), _
    rect:=New Rectangle(x:=5, y:=5, width:=70, height:=25))
```

Polygons

A polygon is a closed plane, or object, represented by at least three lines (segments). To draw polygons with the namespace, we simply play connect-the-dots. We first create the dots using the Point structure. These dots are actually a series of coordinates through which we will draw lines. Figure 9.3 shows a set of six points using the basic Windows coordinate system.

To connect the dots, we use the DrawPolygon method of the Graphics class. We indicate the order in which to connect the points of the polygons by their order in our Point array. You can see from code Listing 9.2 that the points can be connected in a variety of ways to produce varied results.

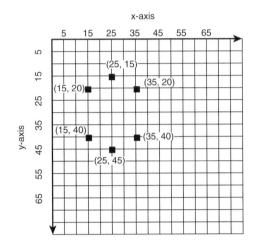

FIGURE 9.3

Polygon coordinates.

LISTING 9.2   DrawPolygon

```
Private Sub Button1_Click(ByVal sender As System.Object, _
    ByVal e As System.EventArgs) Handles Button1.Click

    'declare variables of local scope
    Dim myGraphics As Graphics
    Dim myPoints() As Point

    'return the current form as a drawing surface
    myGraphics = Graphics.FromHwnd(hwnd:=ActiveForm().Handle)

    'create a 7-item array of point structures in order of connection
    ReDim myPoints(6)
    myPoints(0) = New Point(15, 20)
    myPoints(1) = New Point(25, 15)
    myPoints(2) = New Point(35, 20)
    myPoints(3) = New Point(35, 40)
    myPoints(4) = New Point(25, 45)
    myPoints(5) = New Point(15, 40)
    myPoints(6) = New Point(15, 20)

    'draw the polygon (connect the dots between the points in the array)
    myGraphics.DrawPolygon(pen:=New Pen(Color.Blue, Width:=2), _
      points:=myPoints)

    'create a new 7-item array (y + 50 for offset)
```

LISTING 9.2 Continued

```
    ReDim myPoints(6)
    myPoints(0) = New Point(15, 70)
    myPoints(1) = New Point(25, 65)
    myPoints(2) = New Point(35, 70)
    myPoints(3) = New Point(15, 90)
    myPoints(4) = New Point(25, 95)
    myPoints(5) = New Point(35, 90)
    myPoints(6) = New Point(15, 70)

    'draw the polygon (connect the dots between the points in the array)
    myGraphics.DrawPolygon(pen:=New Pen(Color.Blue, Width:=2), _
        points:=myPoints)

End Sub
```

Notice that the last member of the array in Listing 9.2 always points back to the starting point. This closes the polygon. If you omit this last element in the array, the method assumes it and will close the polygon for you.

Pies

A pie is simply a wedge of a circle, similar to a section in a pie chart or a piece of pie. GDI+ defines a pie section by an `Ellipse` object (which is contained by a `Rectangle`), and the two radial lines that intersect with the endpoints of the arc defined by the `Ellipse`. Figure 9.4 illustrates this point.

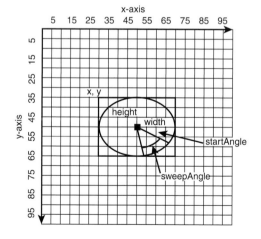

FIGURE 9.4
`DrawPie` *method.*

From Figure 9.4, you can see that the x and y coordinates actually define the upper-left corner (or starting point) of the bounding rectangle. The pie piece is drawn from the center of this rectangle. The width and height of the rectangle define the size of the ellipse, which in turn defines the size of our wedge.

To create a pie wedge we use, you guessed it, the Graphics class. The DrawPie method has two key parameters (in addition to the Rectangle that defines the Ellipse and the Pen object that is used to draw the pie), startAngle and sweepAngle. The startAngle parameter is an angle that is defined clockwise from the x-axis to the first side of the pie. The parameter, sweepAngle, is defined clockwise from the first side of the pie to the second side of the pie section. This is easier to grasp by looking at both the code in Listing 9.3.

LISTING 9.3 DrawPie

```
Private Sub Button1_Click(ByVal sender As System.Object, _
    ByVal e As System.EventArgs) Handles Button1.Click

    'dimension variables of local scope
    Dim myGraphics As Graphics
    Dim myRectangle As Rectangle
    Dim myPen As New Pen(color:=Color.Blue, Width:=1)

    'return the current form as a drawing surface
    myGraphics = Graphics.FromHwnd(ActiveForm().Handle)

    'create a rectangle based on x,y coor. width & height
    myRectangle = New Rectangle(x:=5, y:=5, Width:=50, Height:=50)

    'draw the upper-right pie section
    myGraphics.DrawPie(pen:=myPen, rect:=myRectangle, _
     startAngle:=0, sweepAngle:=-90)

    'draw the upper-left pie section
    myGraphics.DrawPie(pen:=myPen, rect:=myRectangle, _
     startAngle:=-90, sweepAngle:=-90)

    'draw the bottom-left pie section
    myGraphics.DrawPie(pen:=myPen, rect:=myRectangle, _
     startAngle:=-180, sweepAngle:=-90)

    'draw the bottom-right pie section
    myGraphics.FillPie(New SolidBrush(Color.Chartreuse), _
     rect:=New Rectangle(x:=8, y:=8, Width:=50, Height:=50), _
     startAngle:=-270, sweepAngle:=-90)

End Sub
```

From Listing 9.3, you can see that when the first section of the pie is created, we set the start angle to 0 and the sweep angle to 90° counterclockwise (negative). The next piece starts where the last one left off and again creates a section of equal value (90°). Note how the last piece was created with the FillPie method with an offset to add extra highlighting to the piece.

 Suggestions for Further Exploration

- ⊃ Experiment with the following methods of the Rectangle structure: inflate, intersects, and contains.
- ⊃ Check out the Graphics class methods: DrawRectangles, DrawLines, FillRectangle, and FillPolygon.

Filling Shapes

So far, we've dealt with the outline of a shape. Now we will focus on the interior, or fill area, of a shape. GDI+ gives us the concept of a brush to indicate how a shape is filled. Brushes are useful when blending colors for a desired effect like a fade or indicating a shape's texture like sand, stone, or brick. Brushes can be a single solid color, a blend of colors, a texture, a bitmap, or a hatched pattern.

To create brush objects in our code, we use a derivative of the Brush class. Brush is an abstract base class. Classes that derive from Brush are as follows: SolidBrush, TextureBrush, RectangleGradientBrush, LinearGradientBrush, and HatchBrush. This section discusses the various Brush derivatives.

SolidBrush

The SolidBrush class could not be more basic. It works just as it sounds; it provides a single-colored brush with which to fill shapes. It has one constructor and one property, Color. Of course, this property is of the type Color structure. The following is an example of how to create a SolidBrush object:

```
Dim myBrush as New SolidBrush(color:=Color.Red)
```

TextureBrush

To create custom fill effects, you use the TextureBrush class. Custom fills are useful when you want to apply your own design to the interior of a shape. For example, suppose you've created a bar graph and you want to fill each bar with the logo of a different company. The TextureBrush class would allow you to use a bitmap of each company's logo to fill each rectangle or bar in the graph. Using the TextureBrush class and bitmap images, you can create endless fill patterns.

The following code creates a TextureBrush instance based on a simple bitmap made up of three 45° lines. The bitmap is defined inside of an ImageList control (imageList1). When we create the object instance, we set the WrapMode parameter to the TileFlipXY enumeration member. This reverses the image both vertically and horizontally before it is applied to the graphic surface.

```
'dimension a local variable of type TextureBrush Class
Dim myBrush As TextureBrush

'create a new instance of TextureBrush
myBrush = New TextureBrush(imageList1().Images.Item(0), _
        Drawing.Drawing2D.WrapMode.TileFlipXY)
```

Table 9.6 demonstrates how you can use the WrapMode property to tile an image inside the TextureBrush object to create a desired effect.

TABLE 9.6   TextureBrush WrapMode Enumeration

Effect	Description
//	This is the original 16 × 16 bitmap that is used to create the various effects.
////	A 32 × 32 filled area using the WrapMode.Tile property. The 16 × 16 bitmap is repeated four times in a tiled fashion.
⟨◇⟩	A 32 × 32 filled area using the WrapMode.TileFlipX property. The 16 × 16 bitmap is reversed horizontally and then repeated four times (tiled).
⟪⟪⟪	A 32 × 32 filled area using the WrapMode.TileFlipY property. The 16 × 16 bitmap is reversed vertically and then repeated four times (tiled).
⟪⟪⟪	A 32 × 32 filled area using the WrapMode.TileFlipXY property. The 16 × 16 bitmap is reversed vertically and horizontally before being tiled.

LinearGradientBrush

In Windows 9x and above, you've undoubtedly seen how you can blend two colors across the title bar of a window from within the "Display Settings" control panel. Well, the LinearGradientBrush class allows us to do just that; we can blend two colors across a given shape.

To do so, we first create an instance of the class based on two colors and a blend style. Blend styles are defined by the LinearGradientMode enumeration. We then use a fill method of the Graphics object to paint our shape with the blended style. Listing 9.4 illustrates this by creating a Rectangle object and then using the blended LinearGradientBrush to fill its interior by calling FillRectangle.

LISTING 9.4 LinearGradientBrush

```
Private Sub Button1_Click(ByVal sender As System.Object, _
    ByVal e As System.EventArgs) Handles Button1.Click

    'local scope
    Dim myGraphics As Graphics
    Dim myBrush As System.Drawing.Drawing2D.LinearGradientBrush
    Dim myRectangle As Rectangle

    'return the current form as a drawing surface
    myGraphics = Graphics.FromHwnd(hwnd:=ActiveForm().Handle)

    'create a rectangle object
    myRectangle = New Rectangle(x:=5, y:=5, Width:=40, Height:=50)

    'draw the rectangle to the surface
    myGraphics.DrawRectangle(pen:=New Pen(Color.Black), rect:=myRectangle)

    'create the gradient brush
    myBrush = New System.Drawing.Drawing2D.LinearGradientBrush( _
        rect:=myRectangle, _
        color1:=Color.White, _
        color2:=Color.DarkSlateBlue, _
        LinearGradientMode:= _
        System.Drawing.Drawing2D.LinearGradientMode.Vertical)

    'fill the rectangle using the gradient brush
    myGraphics.FillRectangle(brush:=myBrush, rect:=myRectangle)

End Sub
```

Notice that when we created the brush, we set the LinearGradientMode parameter to indicate a blend from the top of the shape to its bottom (Vertical). You can get the four effects defined in Table 9.7 by using this enumeration.

TABLE 9.7 LinearGradientMode Enumeration

Member	Effect	Description
Vertical		The Vertical member indicates a fill pattern from the top of the object to the bottom.
Horizontal		The Horizontal member indicates a fill pattern from the left of an object to its right.

TABLE 9.7 Continued

Member	Effect	Description
ForwardDiagonal		The ForwardDiagonal member indicates a fill pattern from the upper-left corner of an object to the lower-right corner.
BackwardDiagonal		The BackwardDiagonal member indicates a fill pattern from the upper-right corner of an object to the lower-left corner.

HatchBrush

Remember the first paint programs? Remember showing your friends a wall built out of red brick that you drew with a rectangle and filled with the brick pattern? Well, the HatchBrush class allows us to create numerous predefined fill patterns, including brick.

We create a HatchBrush by passing in a hatch style, using the HatchStyle enumeration, and a foreground and background color to be used by the hatch style. Listing 9.5 fills an ellipse using a checkerboard HatchBrush instance.

LISTING 9.5 HatchBrush

```
Private Sub Button1_Click(ByVal sender As System.Object, _
    ByVal e As System.EventArgs) Handles Button1.Click

    'local scope
    Dim myGraphics As Graphics
    Dim myBrush As System.Drawing.Drawing2D.HatchBrush
    Dim myRectangle As Rectangle

    'return the current form as a drawing surface
    myGraphics = Graphics.FromHwnd(hwnd:=ActiveForm().Handle)

    'create a rectangle object to bind the ellipse
    myRectangle = New Rectangle(x:=5, y:=5, Width:=70, Height:=60)

    'draw the ellipse to the surface
    myGraphics.DrawEllipse(pen:=New Pen(Color.Black), rect:=myRectangle)

    'create the hatch brush
    myBrush = New System.Drawing.Drawing2D.HatchBrush( _
        hatchstyle:=Drawing.Drawing2D.HatchStyle.LargeCheckerBoard, _
        ForeColor:=Color.Black, _
        BackColor:=Color.White)
```

LISTING 9.5 Continued

```
    'fill the ellipse using the hatch brush
    myGraphics.FillEllipse(brush:=myBrush, rect:=myRectangle)

End Sub
```

Table 9.8 provides a visual representation of the various patterns possible using the
HatchBrush class. Hopefully, this will serve as a handy reference when you need to pick
the perfect pattern. A description of each member is not necessary; the associated graphic
tells the whole story. Remember, the table uses black and white, but you can use any color
for the foreColor and backColor parameters for nearly unlimited effects.

TABLE 9.8 HatchStyle Enumeration

Member	Effect	Member	Effect
Horizontal		Vertical	
LightHorizontal		LightVertical	
DarkHorizontal		DarkVertical	
DashedHorizontal		DashedVertical	
NarrowHorizontal		NarrowVertical	
DiagonalBrick		Cross	
HorizontalBrick		DiagonalCross	
SmallGrid		SolidDiamond	
LargeGrid		DottedDiamond	
DottedGrid		OutlinedDiamond	
SmallCheckerBoard		SmallConfetti	
LargeCheckerBoard		LargeConfetti	

9

DRAWING
FUNCTIONS

TABLE 9.8   Continued

Member	Effect	Member	Effect
Percent05		Percent10	
Percent20		Percent25	
Percent30		Percent40	
Percent50		Percent60	
Percent70		Percent75	
Percent80		Percent90	
Plaid		Sphere	
Trellis		Shingle	
Wave		Weave	
BackwardDiagonal		ForwardDiagonal	
DarkDownwardDiagonal		LightDownwardDiagonal	
DarkUpwardDiagonal		LightUpwardDiagonal	
DashedDownwardDiagonal		DashedUpwardDiagonal	
WideDownwardDiagonal		WideUpwardDiagonal	
Divot			

Collections of Shapes

It is often useful to collect various "building block" shapes into a single unit. Rather than managing each rectangle in a bar graph, for instance, it is often easier to group these objects into a single, manageable unit. If the objects need to be moved or redrawn, you can simply make one method call. Similarly, if you are transforming the objects, maybe rotating them all 45°, it is much easier to transform a group than transform each item independently. The System.Drawing.Drawing2D namespace provides us the Path class for grouping shapes.

Additionally, once you've defined your various object groups, it is often necessary to indicate how those groups interact with one another. If you've ever used a drawing application, you are undoubtedly familiar with the concepts of bring-to-front and send-to-back. These are features that allow an artist to indicate how shapes (or groups of shapes) relate to one another in layers. The System.Drawing namespace gives us the Region class for indicating object interaction and layers.

Paths

Paths enable more advanced drawing techniques in .NET. A path is made of one or more geometric shapes (rectangle, line, curve, and so on). By grouping shapes together in a path, we are able to manage and manipulate the group as one object. We add shapes to a path for storage in what is called the *world coordinate space*. This coordinate system is essentially virtual. It is the place where the shapes logically exist in memory relative to one another. The graphic can then be manipulated as a whole. It can be drawn to the screen over and over. In addition, it can be transformed (rotated, sheared, reflected, scaled) when moving from this logical world space to the physical device space (form). For example, you might have a 10×20 rectangle stored inside a path. When you place it on the form, you can rotate it 20° and sheer the rectangle. The key is that the rectangle still exists as a 10×20 rectangle (not rotated, not sheared) in the world space.

To create a path, we use the GraphicsPath class. This class provides methods like AddLine, AddRectangle, AddArc, and so on; each adds their shape to the path. Paths can contain multiple *figures* or groups of shapes that represent one object. When adding a shape to a path, it is best to indicate to which figure the shape belongs. We do this by calling the StartFigure method. Each subsequent call to an add function adds the shape to the figure. If we call StartFigure again, a new figure is started and all following shapes are added to the new figure. We call the CloseFigure method prior to starting a new figure if we wish the figure to be closed off, or connected from start point to end point.

Listing 9.6 creates a GraphicsPath instance. We add a few shapes to the GraphicsPath class and then display the path to the form.

LISTING 9.6   GraphicsPath

```
Private Sub Button1_Click(ByVal sender As System.Object, _
    ByVal e As System.EventArgs) Handles Button1.Click

    'dimension variables of local scope
    Dim myGraphics As Graphics
    Dim myPen As New Pen(color:=Color.Blue, Width:=2)
    Dim myPath As System.Drawing.Drawing2D.GraphicsPath
    Dim myPoints(2) As Point

    'create a new GraphicsPath instance with default values
    myPath = New System.Drawing.Drawing2D.GraphicsPath()

    'start the figure
    myPath.StartFigure()

    'add an ellipse for the head
    myPath.AddEllipse(x:=0, y:=0, Width:=50, Height:=70)

    'add 2 ellipses to the eyes
    myPath.AddEllipse(x:=10, y:=10, Width:=10, Height:=8)
    myPath.AddEllipse(x:=30, y:=10, Width:=10, Height:=8)

    'add bezier for the nose
    myPath.AddBezier( _
        pt1:=New Point(x:=25, y:=30), _
        pt2:=New Point(x:=15, y:=30), _
        pt3:=New Point(x:=20, y:=40), _
        pt4:=New Point(x:=25, y:=40))

    'add a points to make a curve for the mouth
    myPath.StartFigure()
    myPoints(0) = New Point(x:=10, y:=50)
    myPoints(1) = New Point(x:=25, y:=60)
    myPoints(2) = New Point(x:=40, y:=50)
    myPath.AddCurve(points:=myPoints)

    'return the current form as a drawing surface
    myGraphics = Graphics.FromHwnd(hwnd:=ActiveForm().Handle)

    'output the Path to the drawing surface of the form
    myGraphics.DrawPath(pen:=myPen, path:=myPath)

End Sub
```

If you use paths a lot, you will want to check out the `Flatten` method of the `GraphicsPath` class. This method allows you to change how items are stored within the object instance. By default, state is maintained for each item added to the path. This means that if a curve and an ellipse, for instance, are stored in a `GraphicsPath`, then data for the curve's points and control points as well as data that defines the ellipse is stored in the object. By flattening the path, you allow the object to manage the shape as a series of line segments, thus reducing overhead. In a completely flattened path, all points are stored as points to be connected by line segments.

Regions and Clipping

A region is a section of the screen defined by a given path or rectangle. Regions allow you to define clip areas and do hit-testing based on a graphics area. *Clipping* involves one shape defining the border, or area, of another shape. Additional items drawn within a defined region are constrained by the region; that is, a line with a width of 50 drawn within a rectangular region whose width is 20 will be cropped to 20 for display. *Hit-testing* simply allows your application to know when the user has placed the mouse over a given region or if another shape is contained within the area defined by the region. For example, if you define a region based on a rectangle, you can trap when a user clicks on the rectangle or when his or her mouse travels over the rectangle.

You use the `Region` class to create regions with the namespace. An instance of the `Region` class can be created with either a valid `Rectangle` instance or a `Path` object. To hit-test, you use the `IsVisible` method of the `Region` class. Once a region has been defined, you can pass a point or a rectangle and a valid graphics surface as parameters to the `IsVisible` method. This method simply returns `True` if the given point or rectangle is contained within the `Region`; otherwise, it returns `False`. The following is an example of this method call; it displays the return of the `IsVisible` method to a message box.

```
MsgBox(prompt:=myRegion.IsVisible(x:=75, y:=75, g:=myGraphics))
```

You still draw with the `Graphics` class, but the `Region` class allows you to set parameters for drawing. For example, you set the region parameter of the `SetClip` method of the `Graphics` object to your instance of `Region`. This tells the graphics object that your `Region` further defines the graphics area on the given drawing surface.

Listing 9.7 presents a clipping example. We first draw a rectangle and add it to a `Path` object. We then define a `Region` instance based on the `Path` object. After that, we call the `SetClip` method of our `Graphics` container and pass in the `Region` object. Finally, we draw a number of strings to the graphic surface; notice how our defined region clips them.

LISTING 9.7   Clipping with the `Region` Class

```
Private Sub Button1_Click(ByVal sender As System.Object, _
    ByVal e As System.EventArgs) Handles Button1.Click

    'local scope
    Dim myGraphics As Graphics
    Dim myPen As New Pen(color:=Color.Blue, Width:=2)
    Dim myPath As New System.Drawing.Drawing2D.GraphicsPath()
    Dim myPoints(2) As Point
    Dim myRegion As Region
    Dim i As Short

    'define a triangle
    myPath.StartFigure()
    myPoints(0) = New Point(x:=100, y:=20)
    myPoints(1) = New Point(x:=50, y:=100)
    mvPoints(2) = New Point(x:=150. v:=100)

    'add triangle to the path
    myPath.AddPolygon(points:=myPoints)

    'create a region based on the path
    myRegion = New Region(path:=myPath)

    'return the current form as a drawing surface
    myGraphics = Graphics.FromHwnd(hwnd:=ActiveForm().Handle)

    'draw the region's outline to the screen
    myGraphics.DrawPath(pen:=myPen, path:=myPath)

    'set the clipping region
    myGraphics.SetClip(Region:=myRegion, _
        combineMode:=Drawing.Drawing2D.CombineMode.Replace)

    'draw the string multiple times
    For i = 20 To 100 Step 20

        'draw clipped text
        myGraphics.DrawString(s:="Clipping Region", _
        Font:=New Font(familyName:="Arial", emSize:=18, _
        style:=FontStyle.Regular, _
        unit:=GraphicsUnit.Pixel), _
        brush:=New SolidBrush(color:=Color.Red), _
        x:=50, v:=i)

    Next

End Sub
```

Did you notice that when we called `SetClip` we also set something called the `combineMode`? This indicates how the two regions or shapes should be combined. In our case, we had a triangular `Region` object and a few strings that we drew. We set the `combineMode` enumeration to `Replace` to indicate that the string information should replace the region inside the triangle. Of course, there are a number of additional members to this enumeration. Table 9.9 lists them. Also, note that each enumeration member has a corresponding method on the `Region` class (`Region.Replace` for example).

TABLE 9.9   Region Combine Modes

Enumeration Member	Example Output	Description
		This is an example of the two objects that we are combining. The rectangle represents the clipping region.
Complement		The `Complement` member indicates that only the portion of the second region that does not intersect with the first should be updated.
Exclude		The `Exclude` member indicates that the intersecting portion of the second region should be excluded from the first region. The result is only points that belong to the first region specifically.
Intersect		The `Intersect` member indicates that only points common to both regions should be valid.
Replace		The `Replace` member indicates that the second region replaces the internal region defined by the first. That is, the first region now contains, or defines the area for, the second region.
Union		The `Union` member indicates that both regions should be joined. The result is an area that is defined by all points in both regions.
Xor		The `Xor` member is the opposite of the `Intersect` member. It contains all points that are *not* common to either region.

The following code was used to create the example graphics in the previous table. Note that we created two regions and combined them using the `Region.[Method]` syntax.

```
'local scope
Dim myGraphics As Graphics
Dim myPath As New System.Drawing.Drawing2D.GraphicsPath()
Dim myPath2 As New System.Drawing.Drawing2D.GraphicsPath()
Dim myRegion As Region
Dim myRegion2 As Region

'return the current form as a drawing surface
myGraphics = Graphics.FromHwnd(hwnd:=ActiveForm().Handle)

'create the first path and region
myPath.StartFigure()
myPath.AddRectangle(rect:=New Rectangle(x:=50, y:=50, Width:=50, _
    Height:=20))
myRegion = New Region(path:=myPath)

'create the first path and region
myPath2.StartFigure()
Dim myRec As New Rectangle(x:=35, y:=45, Width:=50, Height:=30)
myPath2.AddEllipse(rect:=myRec)
myRegion2 = New Region(path:=myPath2)

'add the paths together
myRegion.Complement(Region:=myRegion2)

'fill the region
myGraphics.FillRegion(brush:=New SolidBrush(Color.Black), _
    Region:=myRegion)
```

Suggestions for Further Exploration

⊃ Write code using the following methods of the GraphicsPath class: Warp and Widen.

⊃ Use the interior of text to outline a clipping region. Create a Path based on a string and use the path to create the Region.

Working with Images

In this section, you will see how to use two of the most common graphic types a programmer interacts with: bitmaps and icons. As stated earlier in the chapter, all user-interface objects in Windows are some form of a bitmap; a bitmap is simply a collection of pixels set to various colors.

Images

The namespace library gives us three classes for working with images: `Image`, `Bitmap` and `Icon`. `Image` is simply the base class from which the others inherit. `Bitmap` allows us to convert a graphics file into the native GDI+ format (bitmap). This class can be used to define images as fill patterns, transform images for display, define the look of a button—its uses are many. Although the bitmap format is used to manipulate images at the pixel level, GDI+ can actually work with the following image types:

- Bitmaps (BMP)
- Graphics Interchange Format (GIF)
- Joint Photographic Experts Group (JPEG)
- Exchangeable Image File (EXIF)
- Portable Network Graphics (PNG)
- Tag Image File Format (TIFF)

Creating an instance of `Bitmap` requires a filename, stream, or another valid `Image` instance. For example, the following line of code will instantiate a `Bitmap` object based on a JPEG file:

```
Dim myBitmap As New System.Drawing.Bitmap(fileName:="Sample.jpg")
```

Once instantiated, we can do a number of things with the image. For instance, we can change its resolution with the `SetResolution` method or make part of the image transparent with `MakeTransparent`. Of course, we will also want to draw our image to the form. We use the `DrawImage` method of the `Graphics` class to output the image to the screen. The `DrawImage` method has over 30 overloaded parameter sets. In its simplest form, we pass the method an instance of `Bitmap` and the upper-left coordinate of where we want the method to begin drawing. For example:

```
myGraphics.DrawImage(image:=myBitmap, point:=New Point(x:=5, y:=5))
```

Scaling and Cropping

It is often helpful to be able to scale or crop an image to a different size. Suppose you need a 100×100 image to fit in a 20×20 space, or you want to give your users the ability to zoom in on a portion of an image. You use a variation of the `DrawImage` method to scale images. This overloaded method takes a `Rectangle` instance as the destination for drawing your image. However, if the rectangle is smaller or larger than your image, the method will automatically scale the image to match the bounds of the rectangle.

Another version of the `DrawImage` method takes both a source rectangle and a destination rectangle. The source rectangle defines the portion of the original image to be drawn into the destination rectangle. This, effectively, is cropping. The source rectangle defines how the image gets cropped when applied to the destination. Of course, you can crop to the original size or scale the cropped portion to a new size. Listing 9.8 provides a detailed code example of both scaling and cropping an image.

LISTING 9.8   Scale and Crop

```
Protected Overrides Sub OnClick(ByVal e As System.EventArgs)

    'local scope
    Dim myBitmap As System.Drawing.Bitmap
    Dim myGraphics As Graphics
    Dim mySource As Rectangle
    Dim myDestination As Rectangle

    'create an instance of bitmap based on a file
    myBitmap = New System.Drawing.Bitmap(fileName:="dotnet.gif")

    'return the current form as a drawing surface
    myGraphics = Graphics.FromHwnd(ActiveForm().Handle)

    'define a rectangle as the size of the original image (source)
    mySource = New Rectangle(x:=0, y:=0, Width:=81, Height:=45)

    'draw the original bitmap to the source rectangle
    myGraphics.DrawImage(image:=myBitmap, rect:=mySource)

    'create a destination rectangle
    myDestination = New Rectangle(x:=90, y:=0, Width:=162, Height:=90)

    'output the image to the dest. rectangle (scale)
    myGraphics.DrawImage(image:=myBitmap, rect:=myDestination)

    'output a cropped portion of the source
    myGraphics.DrawImage(image:=myBitmap, _
        destRect:=New Rectangle(x:=0, y:=100, Width:=30, Height:=30), _
        srcRect:=New Rectangle(x:=0, y:=35, Width:=14, Height:=14), _
        srcUnit:=GraphicsUnit.Pixel)

End Sub
```

Notice that we actually drew the image to the form three times. The first time, we drew the image into a rectangle (`mySource`) based on its original size. The second time, we scaled the image to two times its original size (`myDestination`) by creating a larger rectangle and outputting the image accordingly. Finally, we cropped a portion of the original output and put it in a new, larger rectangle. Figure 9.5 shows the code's output to the form.

FIGURE 9.5
Scale and crop output.

Icons

An icon in Windows is a small bitmap image that represents an object. You cannot go far in without seeing and working with icons. For example, the File Explorer uses icons to represent folders and files; your desktop contains icons for My Computer, Recycle Bin, and My Network Places.

We use the `Icon` class to work with icons in .NET. We can instantiate an `Icon` instance in much the same way we created `Bitmap` objects. The following code creates an icon based on a file name:

```
Dim myIcon as New Icon(fileName:="myIcon.ico")
```

The `DrawIcon` method of the `Graphics` class is used to draw the icon to the form. To it, you can pass the icon and either just the upper-left x and y coordinates or a bounding rectangle. If you pass a `Rectangle` instance, the icon will be scaled based on the bounding rectangle. The following line of code draws an icon object into a bounding rectangle.

```
myGraphics.DrawIcon(icon:=myIcon, _
    rectangle:=New Rectangle(x:=5, y:=5, width:=32, height:=32))
```

The `Graphics` class also gives us the `DrawIconUnstretched` method that allows us to specify a bounding rectangle without actually scaling the icon. In fact, if the icon is larger than the bounding rectangle, it will be cropped to fit from the left corner down and to the right.

 Suggestions for Further Exploration

- To animate images, take a look at the `ImageAnimator` class.
- Check out the `SmoothingMode` property of the `Graphics` class and the `SmoothingMode` enumeration members. This method allows you to set things like `antialiasing` to make your graphics look "smoother."

Transformations

In the previous section, we saw how we could enlarge an image based on the dimensions of a rectangle. This was a kind of a transformation. Transformations not only allow us to scale images, but also rotate, flip, and skew them. In drawing applications, you oftentimes need to enlarge an image to fill an area. Or you may have to rotate an arrow in a flow chart to point at a given process. This is all done through transformation.

Origins

As we stated earlier, by default GDI+ sets the upper-left corner of our drawing surface as the origin. But suppose that we want items stored in the world coordinate space to be output to a different section of the screen. For instance, suppose you have three line segments stored in a `GraphicsPath` object and want the `DrawPath` to interpret the origin of the form as 50, 0 instead of 0, 0. To do so, you would use the `TranslateTransform` method of the `Graphics` class. In its simplest form you pass the amount of pixels to transform in the x direction and the y direction. In our example, the code would look as follows:

```
MyGraphics.TranslateTransform(dx:=50, dy:=0)
```

This is an example of a *global transformation*. That is, it applies to the `Graphics` instance as a whole. Now all items drawn with this instance will have an origin of 50, 0. To reset the origin back to the default state, you can simply call the `ResetTransform` method. There is also a *local transformation*. Local transformations apply to a single object or collected set of shapes. For example, we could have achieved the same results by calling the `Transform` method of the `GraphicsPath` class. Like the `Tranform` property of the `Graphics` class, the `GraphicsPath.Transform` method requires a matrix object to set its value.

Unit of Measurement

Tired of working with pixels? Are you more comfortable with inches or centimeters? You can reset the graphics unit used by the `Graphics` class by setting the `PageUnit` property. This property takes a valid member of the `GraphicsUnit` enumeration. Members include `Inch`, `Millimeter`, `Pixel`, `Point`, and so on. After setting the `PageUnit` property, subsequent calls to the `Graphics` object will interpret your values as the new unit of measurement. For instance, the following code sets the unit to inches and creates a rectangle one inch wide and a half inch high:

```
myGraphics.PageUnit = GraphicsUnit.Inch
myGraphics.DrawRectangle(pen:=New Pen(Color.Red, Width:=0.1F), _
    x:=0, y:=0, Width:=1, Height:=0.5F)
```

Rotating, Scaling, Skewing, and Flipping

Transformation in GDI+—rotating, scaling, skewing, and flipping—happens with the aid of matrices. A matrix is a set of numbers arranged in rows and columns. For instance, the point (2, 3) on a 2D plane can be represented as a 1×2 matrix. That is, there is one row of data (2 and 3) and a column for both x and y.

Why do we care? Well, through matrix math, we can transform objects. For instance, suppose you have a point at (2, 3) and you wish to rotate that point 90°. Well, you would multiply the matrix [2 3] by the matrix [0 1 | -1 0]. The result would be the rotated point at (-2, 3). The math is: (2*0)+(2*-1) = x and (3*1) + (3*0) = y.

The namespace library provides the `Matrix` class for working with these transformations. It exposes the methods `Multiply`, `Rotate`, `Scale`, and `Shear`. Each of these applies its intended effect on the `Matrix` instance. The `Graphics` class also has similar methods like `RotateTransform`, `ScaleTransform`, and `MultiplyTransform`. Table 9.10 demonstrates transformations and their effects.

TABLE 9.10   Transformation Examples

Transformation Code	
`myGraphics.RotateTransform(angle:=45)`	
Effect	
Description	This example uses the `RotateTransform` method to rotate an image at a 45° angle.

Transformation Code	
`myGraphics.ScaleTransform(sx:=2, sy:=0.5F)`	
Effect	
Description	This example uses the `ScaleTransform` method to stretch the image out to twice its width but compress it to half of its height.

Transformation Code	
`Dim myMatrix As New System.Drawing.Drawing2D.Matrix( _` `    m11:=1.5F, m12:=0, m21:=1.5F, m22:=0.75F, dx:=0, dy:=0)`	
`myGraphics.MultiplyTransform(matrix:=myMatrix)`	
Effect	
Description	This example creates a `Matrix` instance and multiplies the output by the supplied matrix. The result is an image that is stretched along the x axis (m11:=1.5) and condensed along the y axis (m22:=.75) and skewed along the y axis (m21:=1.5).

9

DRAWING
FUNCTIONS

TABLE 9.10   Continued

Transformation Code

```
myBitmap.RotateFlip(RotateFlipType.RotateNoneFlipX)
```

Effect

.ɹǝu

Description   This example uses the `RotateFlip` method of the `Bitmap` class to flip the image on its x axis. Notice that we use the `FlipType` enumeration. There are a number of additional members to this enumeration to produce more flipping and rotating results.

Transformation Code

```
Dim myMatrix As New System.Drawing.Drawing2D.Matrix( _
    m11:=1, m12:=0, m21:=0, m22:=1, dx:=0, dy:=0)


myMatrix.Shear(shearX:=-0.75F, shearY:=0)


myGraphics.MultiplyTransform(matrix:=myMatrix)
```

Effect   *Microsoft* .net

Description   In this example we create a basic `Matrix` object that has no effect on the object. We then call the `Shear` method to indicate that the x-axis should be sheared by -.75. The result is a "faster .NET."

 ## Suggestions for Further Exploration

⊃ For more information on working with matrices, read MSDN: Visual Studio .NET/.NET Framework/Programming with the .NET Framework/Drawing and Editing Images/About GDI+ Managed Code/Coordinate Systems and Transformations.

Learning by Example: A Forms-Based Drawing Application

In this example, we build upon what you've learned throughout the chapter to create a simple, forms-based drawing application. As an application, it is not very useful; the Paint application that ships with all copies of Windows has more features. However, as a learning tool, it should give you a nice test harness in which to experiment with writing your own code and to watch code execute.

Key Concepts Covered

The following represents the key concepts covered by this sample application:

- Creating an MDI application
- Managing a drawing surface
- Maintaining drawing state with the `GraphicsState` class
- Using the `Color` structure
- Drawing, filling, and transforming shapes with the `Graphics` class

MDI Parent and Child Forms

To define the drawing surface in our application, we will use the multiple document interface (MDI) paradigm. This paradigm includes a parent, or container, form that provides the events and management of child forms. This is similar to Microsoft Word or Excel. The MDI form has a simple menu bar that provides the basic functionality for the form. Figure 9.6 shows the MDI form and its child form in their initial state.

FIGURE 9.6
`System.Drawing` *MDI form.*

Code Walkthrough

The code for the MDI form (see Listing 9.9) is rather basic. There is code to control the menu events, to load the form, and to reset the form when users click on the "New" menu item.

The code starts with form-level declarations and basic form building code.

LISTING 9.9   The Code for the MDI Form

```
Public Class frmMDI

    Inherits System.Windows.Forms.Form

    Private WithEvents menuItemDraw As System.Windows.Forms.MenuItem
    Private WithEvents menuItemSurface As System.Windows.Forms.MenuItem
    Private WithEvents menuItemExit As System.Windows.Forms.MenuItem
    Private WithEvents menuItemNew As System.Windows.Forms.MenuItem

#Region " Windows Form Designer generated code "

    Public Sub New()
        MyBase.New()

        'This call is required by the Windows Form Designer.
        InitializeComponent()

        'Add any initialization after the InitializeComponent() call

    End Sub

    'Form overrides dispose to clean up the component list.
    Protected Overloads Overrides Sub Dispose(ByVal disposing As Boolean)
        If disposing Then
            If Not (components Is Nothing) Then
                components.Dispose()
            End If
        End If
        MyBase.Dispose(disposing)
    End Sub

    Private WithEvents menuItem1 As System.Windows.Forms.MenuItem
    Private WithEvents menuItem2 As System.Windows.Forms.MenuItem
    Private WithEvents menuItem3 As System.Windows.Forms.MenuItem
    Private WithEvents menuItem4 As System.Windows.Forms.MenuItem
    Private WithEvents mainMenu1 As System.Windows.Forms.MainMenu

    'Required by the Windows Form Designer
    Private components As System.ComponentModel.Container

    'NOTE: The following procedure is required by the Windows Form Designer
    'It can be modified using the Windows Form Designer.
    'Do not modify it using the code editor.
```

LISTING 9.9 Continued

```
<System.Diagnostics.DebuggerStepThrough()> Private Sub _
    InitializeComponent()
    Me.mainMenu1 = New System.Windows.Forms.MainMenu()
    Me.menuItemSurface = New System.Windows.Forms.MenuItem()
    Me.menuItemExit = New System.Windows.Forms.MenuItem()
    Me.menuItemDraw = New System.Windows.Forms.MenuItem()
    Me.menuItemNew = New System.Windows.Forms.MenuItem()
    Me.mainMenu1.MenuItems.AddRange(New System.Windows.Forms.MenuItem() _
        {Me.menuItemNew, Me.menuItemSurface, Me.menuItemDraw, _
        Me.menuItemExit})
    Me.menuItemSurface.Index = 1
    Me.menuItemSurface.Text = "&Surface"
    Me.menuItemExit.Index = 3
    Me.menuItemExit.Text = "&Exit"
    Me.menuItemDraw.Index = 2
    Me.menuItemDraw.Text = "&Draw"
    Me.menuItemNew.Index = 0
    Me.menuItemNew.Text = "&New"
    Me.AutoScaleBaseSize = New System.Drawing.Size(5, 13)
    Me.ClientSize = New System.Drawing.Size(395, 288)
    Me.IsMdiContainer = True
    Me.Menu = Me.mainMenu1
    Me.Text = "System.Drawing Example"

End Sub
```

The form load event, formMDI_Load, is where we initialize the application and set a global reference to both the child form (m_myChild) and a Graphics object that references it (m_myGraphics). This allows us to maintain a reference to the drawing surface at all times.

```
Private Sub frmMDI_Load(ByVal sender As System.Object, _
    ByVal e As System.EventArgs) Handles MyBase.Load

    'purpose: initialize the application, create the child form

    'create a new instance of the child form
    m_myChild = New frmChild()

    'set the parent of the child form to the MDI form
    m_myChild.MdiParent = Me

    'show the form to the user
    m_myChild.Show()
```

```
'set form to default values
Call resetChildForm()

'instantiate a graphics object with the child's handle
m_myGraphics = Graphics.FromHwnd(m_myChild.Handle)

End Sub
```

The resetChildForm procedure allows us to create new forms based on the default values for the application.

```
Private Sub resetChildForm()

    'purpose: clear the child form

    'set the form back to default values
    m_myChild.Left = m_LeftPos
    m_myChild.Top = m_TopPos
    m_myChild.Width = m_Width
    m_myChild.Height = m_Height

    'set the background and foreground colors of the child form
    '        to their defaults
    m_myChild.BackColor = Color.FromName(m_ChildColor)
    m_myChild.ForeColor = Color.FromName(m_ChildColor)

    'refresh the form
    m_myChild.Refresh()

End Sub
```

The following sub routines are the click events for the various menu items:

- menuItemNew_Click creates a new drawing surface
- menuItemExit_Click exits the application
- menuSuface_Click loads the surface dialog
- menuItemDraw_Click loads the drawing form

```
Private Sub menuItemNew_Click(ByVal sender As System.Object, _
    ByVal e As System.EventArgs) Handles menuItemNew.Click
    'purpose: user clicks the NEW item on the menu bar to create a new
    '           drawing surface

    'note: no new form is actually created, we simply clear and reset
    '        current form
```

```
        'call the method used to reset the child form to its defaults
        Call resetChildForm()

End Sub

Private Sub menuItemExit_Click(ByVal sender As System.Object, _
    ByVal e As System.EventArgs) Handles menuItemExit.Click

        'purpose: close the app. when the user clicks the EXIT menu item

        'kill the application
        End

End Sub

Private Sub menuSuface_Click(ByVal sender As System.Object, _
    ByVal e As System.EventArgs) Handles menuItemSurface.Click

        'purpose:   show the surface dialog when the user clicks the
        '           SURFACE menu item

        'local scope
        Dim mySurface As frmSuface

        'create new suface form
        mySurface = New frmSuface()

        'set the start position of the modal dialog to the center position
        ' of its parent
        mySurface.StartPosition = FormStartPosition.CenterParent

        'show the form as modal
        mySurface.ShowDialog(Me)

End Sub

Private Sub menuItemDraw_Click(ByVal sender As System.Object, _
    ByVal e As System.EventArgs) Handles menuItemDraw.Click

        'purpose:   show the draw dialog when the user clicks
        '           the DRAW menu item

        'local scope
        Dim myDraw As frmDraw
```

```
             'create new suface form
             myDraw = New frmDraw()

             'set the start position of the modal dialog to the center
             '  positions of its parent
             myDraw.StartPosition = FormStartPosition.CenterParent

             'show the form as modal
             myDraw.ShowDialog(Me)

        End Sub

#End Region

End Class
```

Even though the parent form is of the type MDI, our code restricts the number of child windows to just one. We do not allow users to create more than one child form. This simplifies the example. Microsoft Paint has a similar design pattern. With very little additional effort, you can modify the code to manage multiple drawing surfaces.

The child form itself contains no additional code. Listing 9.10 shows the default code generated by Visual Studio .NET. The only items of interest are the form's property settings. The form's BorderStyle is set to None and the ShowInTaskBar property is set to False. This provides users with the illusion of working on a document, when in reality, all documents in Windows are simply versions of forms.

LISTING 9.10 System.Drawing Child Form (formChild.vb)

```
Public Class formChild
    Inherits System.Windows.Forms.Form

#Region " Windows Form Designer generated code "

    Public Sub New()
        MyBase.New()

        'This call is required by the Windows Form Designer.
        InitializeComponent()

        'Add any initialization after the InitializeComponent() call

    End Sub
```

```
    'Form overrides dispose to clean up the component list.
    Public Overrides Sub Dispose()
        MyBase.Dispose()
        If Not (components Is Nothing) Then
            components.Dispose()
        End If
    End Sub


    'Required by the Windows Form Designer
    Private components As System.ComponentModel.Container

    'NOTE: The following procedure is required by the Windows Form Designer
    'It can be modified using the Windows Form Designer.
    'Do not modify it using the code editor.
    Private Sub <System.Diagnostics.DebuggerStepThrough()> _
        InitializeComponent()

        'the following are key properties of the child form that were
        '  changed to make the form look more like a painting surface
        Me.AutoScaleBaseSize = New System.Drawing.Size(5, 13)
        Me.BackColor = System.Drawing.Color.White
        Me.BorderStyle = System.Windows.Forms.FormBorderStyle.None
        Me.MaximizeBox = False
        Me.MinimizeBox = False
        Me.ShowInTaskbar = False
        Me.Text = "formChild"

    End Sub

#End Region

End Class
```

Surface Form

The surface form demonstrates the Color structure. It allows users to manage properties of the drawing surface. Users can change the background color of the child form and its height and width. Figure 9.7 is a screen shot of the surface dialog.

Code Walkthrough

Listing 9.11 is long for such a simple form, but much of the code is simply default property overrides for the form and its controls. The key procedures in this listing are the form load event, the Defaults button event, and the OK button event.

FIGURE 9.7

System.Drawing *drawing surface form.*

LISTING 9.11   System.Drawing Surface Form (formSurface.vb)

The listing starts by defining the form.

```
Public Class frmSuface
    Inherits System.Windows.Forms.Form

#Region " Windows Form Designer generated code "

    Public Sub New()
        MyBase.New()

        'This call is required by the Windows Form Designer.
        InitializeComponent()

        'Add any initialization after the InitializeComponent() call

    End Sub

    'Form overrides dispose to clean up the component list.
    Protected Overloads Overrides Sub Dispose(ByVal disposing As Boolean)
        If disposing Then
            If Not (components Is Nothing) Then
                components.Dispose()
            End If
        End If
        MyBase.Dispose(disposing)
    End Sub

    Private WithEvents groupBox1 As System.Windows.Forms.GroupBox
    Private WithEvents groupBox2 As System.Windows.Forms.GroupBox
    Private WithEvents label1 As System.Windows.Forms.Label
    Private WithEvents label2 As System.Windows.Forms.Label
    Private WithEvents label3 As System.Windows.Forms.Label
    Private WithEvents label4 As System.Windows.Forms.Label
```

LISTING 9.11 Continued

```
Private WithEvents comboBoxColors As System.Windows.Forms.ComboBox
Private WithEvents buttonCancel As System.Windows.Forms.Button
Private WithEvents textBoxWidth As System.Windows.Forms.TextBox
Private WithEvents textBoxHeight As System.Windows.Forms.TextBox
Private WithEvents buttonOk As System.Windows.Forms.Button
Private WithEvents buttonDefaults As System.Windows.Forms.Button


'Required by the Windows Form Designer
Private components As System.ComponentModel.Container


'NOTE: The following procedure is required by the Windows Form Designer
'It can be modified using the Windows Form Designer.
'Do not modify it using the code editor.
<System.Diagnostics.DebuggerStepThrough()> Private Sub _
    InitializeComponent()
    Me.groupBox2 = New System.Windows.Forms.GroupBox()
    Me.comboBoxColors = New System.Windows.Forms.ComboBox()
    Me.buttonCancel = New System.Windows.Forms.Button()
    Me.buttonDefaults = New System.Windows.Forms.Button()
    Me.textBoxHeight = New System.Windows.Forms.TextBox()
    Me.buttonOk = New System.Windows.Forms.Button()
    Me.label4 = New System.Windows.Forms.Label()
    Me.groupBox1 = New System.Windows.Forms.GroupBox()
    Me.textBoxWidth = New System.Windows.Forms.TextBox()
    Me.label1 = New System.Windows.Forms.Label()
    Me.label2 = New System.Windows.Forms.Label()
    Me.label3 = New System.Windows.Forms.Label()
    Me.groupBox2.Controls.AddRange(New System.Windows.Forms.Control() _
        {Me.comboBoxColors})
    Me.groupBox2.Location = New System.Drawing.Point(8, 12)
    Me.groupBox2.Size = New System.Drawing.Size(176, 68)
    Me.groupBox2.TabIndex = 0
    Me.groupBox2.TabStop = False
    Me.groupBox2.Text = "Background Color"
    Me.comboBoxColors.DropDownStyle = _
        System.Windows.Forms.ComboBoxStyle.DropDownList
    Me.comboBoxColors.DropDownWidth = 121
    Me.comboBoxColors.Location = New System.Drawing.Point(12, 28)
    Me.comboBoxColors.MaxDropDownItems = 10
    Me.comboBoxColors.Size = New System.Drawing.Size(156, 21)
    Me.comboBoxColors.Sorted = True
    Me.comboBoxColors.TabIndex = 1
    Me.buttonCancel.DialogResult = System.Windows.Forms.DialogResult.Cancel
    Me.buttonCancel.Location = New System.Drawing.Point(196, 44)
    Me.buttonCancel.TabIndex = 5
```

LISTING 9.11   Continued

```
Me.buttonCancel.Text = "Cancel"
Me.buttonDefaults.Location = New System.Drawing.Point(196, 76)
Me.buttonDefaults.TabIndex = 6
Me.buttonDefaults.Text = "Defaults"
Me.textBoxHeight.Location = New System.Drawing.Point(56, 56)
Me.textBoxHeight.MaxLength = 4
Me.textBoxHeight.Size = New System.Drawing.Size(56, 20)
Me.textBoxHeight.TabIndex = 3
Me.textBoxHeight.Text = "textBoxHeight"
Me.buttonOk.Location = New System.Drawing.Point(196, 12)
Me.buttonOk.TabIndex = 4
Me.buttonOk.Text = "Ok"
Me.label4.Location = New System.Drawing.Point(116, 30)
Me.label4.Size = New System.Drawing.Size(48, 16)
Me.label4.TabIndex = 7
Me.label4.Text = "pixels"
Me.groupBox1.Controls.AddRange(New System.Windows.Forms.Control() _
    {Me.label4, Me.label3, Me.label2, Me.label1, Me.textBoxHeight, _
    Me.textBoxWidth})
Me.groupBox1.Location = New System.Drawing.Point(8, 92)
Me.groupBox1.Size = New System.Drawing.Size(176, 92)
Me.groupBox1.TabIndex = 0
Me.groupBox1.TabStop = False
Me.groupBox1.Text = "Dimensions"
Me.textBoxWidth.Location = New System.Drawing.Point(56, 24)
Me.textBoxWidth.MaxLength = 4
Me.textBoxWidth.Size = New System.Drawing.Size(56, 20)
Me.textBoxWidth.TabIndex = 2
Me.textBoxWidth.Text = "textBoxWidth"
Me.label1.Location = New System.Drawing.Point(8, 28)
Me.label1.Size = New System.Drawing.Size(48, 16)
Me.label1.TabIndex = 6
Me.label1.Text = "Width"
Me.label2.Location = New System.Drawing.Point(8, 60)
Me.label2.Size = New System.Drawing.Size(48, 16)
Me.label2.TabIndex = 7
Me.label2.Text = "Height"
Me.label3.Location = New System.Drawing.Point(116, 62)
Me.label3.Size = New System.Drawing.Size(48, 16)
Me.label3.TabIndex = 7
Me.label3.Text = "pixels"
Me.AcceptButton = Me.buttonOk
Me.AutoScaleBaseSize = New System.Drawing.Size(5, 13)
Me.FormBorderStyle = System.Windows.Forms.FormBorderStyle.FixedSingle
Me.CancelButton = Me.buttonCancel
```

LISTING 9.11 Continued

```
    Me.ClientSize = New System.Drawing.Size(283, 192)
    Me.Controls.AddRange(New System.Windows.Forms.Control() _
        {Me.groupBox2, Me.buttonOk, Me.buttonCancel, Me.buttonDefaults, _
        Me.groupBox1})
    Me.MaximizeBox = False
    Me.MinimizeBox = False
    Me.ShowInTaskbar = False
    Me.Text = "Drawing Surface"

End Sub
```

The form load event (formSurface_Load) uses the Reflection namespace to load a drop-down box with the names of the properties of the Color structure. The load event then initializes the remaining fields on the form to match the current state of the child form.

NOTE

The System.Reflection namespace is a very powerful set of classes. While they are beyond the scope of this book, you are encouraged to browse the MSDN reference to see what can be accomplished with this namespace.

```
Private Sub frmSuface_Load(ByVal sender As System.Object, _
    ByVal e As System.EventArgs) Handles MyBase.Load

    'purpose:   load the drawing surface form whose purpose is
    '               to set the properties of the drawing suface (child form)

    'local scope
    Dim myColor As System.Drawing.Color
    Dim myProps() As System.Reflection.PropertyInfo
    Dim myType As System.Type
    Dim count As Integer

    'return the type of the color structure
    myType = myColor.GetType()

    'return the property information of the structure
    myProps = myType.GetProperties()

    'iterate the properties and add to the combo box
    For count = 0 To UBound(myProps)
```

9

```
                    'make sure we only get valid colors
                    If myProps(count).PropertyType.ToString() = "System.Drawing.Color" _
                        And myProps(count).Name <> "Transparent" Then

                        'add the property name (color) to the combo box
                        comboBoxColors().Items.Add(myProps(count).Name)

                    End If
             Next

             'select the current child bg color in the properties dialog
             comboBoxColors().SelectedIndex = comboBoxColors().FindString( _
                 m_myChild.BackColor.Name())

             'set the current values of the active drawing surface
             textBoxWidth().Text = CStr(m_myChild.Width())
             textBoxHeight().Text = CStr(m_myChild.Height())

             'set the ok button as the default button
             Me.AcceptButton = buttonOk()
             Me.CancelButton = buttonCancel()

     End Sub
```

The Cancel button click event closes the form without applying any updates.

```
     Private Sub buttonCancel_Click(ByVal sender As System.Object, _
         ByVal e As System.EventArgs) Handles buttonCancel.Click

         'purpose:    respond the the cancel button's click event and close the
         '                form without the applying the changes

         'kill the form
         Me.Close()

     End Sub
```

The Defaults button event simply loads the form fields with the application's default values.

```
     Private Sub buttonDefaults_Click(ByVal sender As System.Object, _
         ByVal e As System.EventArgs) Handles buttonDefaults.Click

         'purpose:    set the properties of the drawing surface
         '                equal to the application's default values

         'set drawing surface property boxes to their defaults
         textBoxWidth().Text = CStr(m_Width)
         textBoxHeight().Text = CStr(m_Height)
```

```
        'select the default color of white
        comboBoxColors().SelectedIndex = _
            comboBoxColors().FindString(m_ChildColor)

    End Sub
```

When users click the OK button, the properties of the child form are set to these new values. The key piece here is that after changing properties of the child form, we have to get a new reference to it for the Graphics object to function properly. If we do not rereference the form, the graphics object is unaware of the changes to the drawing surface, which results in shapes getting cut off at the window's old size and other undesirable behavior.

```
    Private Sub buttonOk_Click(ByVal sender As System.Object, _
        ByVal e As System.EventArgs) Handles buttonOk.Click

        'purpose:   reset the properties of the drawing suface

        'validate the textBox myects befor submission
        If Not IsNumeric(textBoxWidth().Text) Or _
            Not IsNumeric(textBoxHeight().Text) Then

            'we would want to do more if this were a production app ...
            Beep()

        Else

            'set the dimensions of the drawing surface
            m_myChild.Width = CInt(textBoxWidth().Text)
            m_myChild.Height = CInt(textBoxHeight().Text)

            'set the background color
            m_SurfaceBackground = comboBoxColors().SelectedItem.ToString
            m_myChild.BackColor = Color.FromName(m_SurfaceBackground)
            m_myChild.Refresh()

            'settings applied, close form and return processing back to MDI
            Me.Close()

            're-get the form to the graphics object
            m_myGraphics = Graphics.FromHwnd(m_myChild.Handle)

        End If

    End Sub

#End Region

End Class
```

Draw Form

The draw form allows users to draw shapes onto the child form. Obviously, this is not the ideal way to create graphics; mouse or pen-based input is much easier. Nevertheless, for the clarity of this example and in the interest of simplicity, we'll define shapes by text boxes and drop-downs.

The features of the draw form allow users to create basic shapes (line, rectangle, and ellipse). They can set the color and width of the shape outline. Shapes can be filled with a solid color, a blend, or a pattern. The form also allows users to rotate the shape prior to drawing it to the surface. The Apply and Clear buttons were added so that you could create multiple shapes onto the child form without leaving the draw dialog. Figure 9.8 is a screen capture of the draw form.

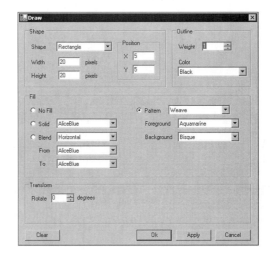

FIGURE 9.8

System.Drawing *draw form.*

Code Walkthrough

Listing 9.12 represents the code behind the draw form. Again, much of the code is form and control property settings.

LISTING 9.12   System.Drawing Draw Form (formDraw)

```
Public Class frmDraw
    Inherits System.Windows.Forms.Form

#Region " Windows Form Designer generated code "
```

LISTING 9.12 Continued

```vb
Public Sub New()
    MyBase.New()

    'This call is required by the Windows Form Designer.
    InitializeComponent()

    'Add any initialization after the InitializeComponent() call

End Sub

'Form overrides dispose to clean up the component list.
Protected Overloads Overrides Sub Dispose(ByVal disposing As Boolean)
    If disposing Then
        If Not (components Is Nothing) Then
            components.Dispose()
        End If
    End If
    MyBase.Dispose(disposing)
End Sub

'form and control property assigments
Private WithEvents groupBox1 As System.Windows.Forms.GroupBox
Private WithEvents groupBox2 As System.Windows.Forms.GroupBox
Private WithEvents groupBox3 As System.Windows.Forms.GroupBox
Private WithEvents groupBox4 As System.Windows.Forms.GroupBox
Private WithEvents comboBoxShape As System.Windows.Forms.ComboBox
Private WithEvents label1 As System.Windows.Forms.Label
Private WithEvents label2 As System.Windows.Forms.Label
Private WithEvents label3 As System.Windows.Forms.Label
Private WithEvents label4 As System.Windows.Forms.Label
Private WithEvents label5 As System.Windows.Forms.Label
Private WithEvents groupBox5 As System.Windows.Forms.GroupBox
Private WithEvents label6 As System.Windows.Forms.Label
Private WithEvents label7 As System.Windows.Forms.Label
Private WithEvents textBoxHeight As System.Windows.Forms.TextBox
Private WithEvents textBoxWidth As System.Windows.Forms.TextBox
Private WithEvents textBoxX As System.Windows.Forms.TextBox
Private WithEvents textBoxY As System.Windows.Forms.TextBox
Private WithEvents label8 As System.Windows.Forms.Label
Private WithEvents buttonCancel As System.Windows.Forms.Button
Private WithEvents buttonOk As System.Windows.Forms.Button
Private WithEvents label9 As System.Windows.Forms.Label
Private WithEvents label10 As System.Windows.Forms.Label
Private WithEvents comboBoxBlendTo As System.Windows.Forms.ComboBox
Private WithEvents comboBoxBlendFrom As System.Windows.Forms.ComboBox
```

LISTING 9.12   Continued

```vb
    Private WithEvents comboBoxPattern As System.Windows.Forms.ComboBox
    Private WithEvents comboBoxSolidColor As System.Windows.Forms.ComboBox
    Private WithEvents comboBoxOutlineColor As System.Windows.Forms.ComboBox
    Private WithEvents buttonApply As System.Windows.Forms.Button
    Private WithEvents numericUpDownWeight As _
        System.Windows.Forms.NumericUpDown
    Private WithEvents radioButtonSolid As System.Windows.Forms.RadioButton
    Private WithEvents radioButtonBlend As System.Windows.Forms.RadioButton
    Private WithEvents radioButtonNone As System.Windows.Forms.RadioButton
    Private WithEvents radioButtonPattern As System.Windows.Forms.RadioButton
    Private WithEvents label11 As System.Windows.Forms.Label
    Private WithEvents label12 As System.Windows.Forms.Label
    Private WithEvents comboBoxPattFore As System.Windows.Forms.ComboBox
    Private WithEvents comboBoxBackFore As System.Windows.Forms.ComboBox
    Private WithEvents label13 As System.Windows.Forms.Label
    Private WithEvents comboBoxBlendStyle As System.Windows.Forms.ComboBox
    Private WithEvents comboBoxPattBack As System.Windows.Forms.ComboBox
    Private WithEvents label14 As System.Windows.Forms.Label
    Private WithEvents numericUpDownRotate As _
        System.Windows.Forms.NumericUpDown
    Private WithEvents buttonClear As System.Windows.Forms.Button
    Private WithEvents label15 As System.Windows.Forms.Label


    'Required by the Windows Form Designer
    Private components As System.ComponentModel.Container

    'NOTE: The following procedure is required by the Windows Form Designer
    'It can be modified using the Windows Form Designer.
    'Do not modify it using the code editor.
    <System.Diagnostics.DebuggerStepThrough()> Private Sub _
        InitializeComponent()
        Me.buttonApply = New System.Windows.Forms.Button()
        Me.radioButtonNone = New System.Windows.Forms.RadioButton()
        Me.numericUpDownRotate = New System.Windows.Forms.NumericUpDown()
        Me.textBoxHeight = New System.Windows.Forms.TextBox()
        Me.radioButtonSolid = New System.Windows.Forms.RadioButton()
        Me.comboBoxBlendTo = New System.Windows.Forms.ComboBox()
        Me.textBoxY = New System.Windows.Forms.TextBox()
        Me.textBoxWidth = New System.Windows.Forms.TextBox()
        Me.buttonClear = New System.Windows.Forms.Button()
        Me.radioButtonBlend = New System.Windows.Forms.RadioButton()
        Me.comboBoxShape = New System.Windows.Forms.ComboBox()
        Me.comboBoxPattern = New System.Windows.Forms.ComboBox()
        Me.comboBoxPattBack = New System.Windows.Forms.ComboBox()
        Me.comboBoxBlendStyle = New System.Windows.Forms.ComboBox()
```

LISTING 9.12 Continued

```
Me.label15 = New System.Windows.Forms.Label()
Me.label14 = New System.Windows.Forms.Label()
Me.label11 = New System.Windows.Forms.Label()
Me.label10 = New System.Windows.Forms.Label()
Me.label13 = New System.Windows.Forms.Label()
Me.label12 = New System.Windows.Forms.Label()
Me.comboBoxOutlineColor = New System.Windows.Forms.ComboBox()
Me.buttonOk = New System.Windows.Forms.Button()
Me.label8 = New System.Windows.Forms.Label()
Me.label9 = New System.Windows.Forms.Label()
Me.comboBoxSolidColor = New System.Windows.Forms.ComboBox()
Me.buttonCancel = New System.Windows.Forms.Button()
Me.label4 = New System.Windows.Forms.Label()
Me.label5 = New System.Windows.Forms.Label()
Me.label6 = New System.Windows.Forms.Label()
Me.label7 = New System.Windows.Forms.Label()
Me.label2 = New System.Windows.Forms.Label()
Me.label3 = New System.Windows.Forms.Label()
Me.comboBoxBlendFrom = New System.Windows.Forms.ComboBox()
Me.radioButtonPattern = New System.Windows.Forms.RadioButton()
Me.textBoxX = New System.Windows.Forms.TextBox()
Me.comboBoxPattFore = New System.Windows.Forms.ComboBox()
Me.groupBox1 = New System.Windows.Forms.GroupBox()
Me.groupBox2 = New System.Windows.Forms.GroupBox()
Me.groupBox3 = New System.Windows.Forms.GroupBox()
Me.groupBox4 = New System.Windows.Forms.GroupBox()
Me.groupBox5 = New System.Windows.Forms.GroupBox()
Me.numericUpDownWeight = New System.Windows.Forms.NumericUpDown()
Me.label1 = New System.Windows.Forms.Label()
CType(Me.numericUpDownRotate, _
    System.ComponentModel.ISupportInitialize).BeginInit()
CType(Me.numericUpDownWeight, _
    System.ComponentModel.ISupportInitialize).BeginInit()
Me.buttonApply.Location = New System.Drawing.Point(336, 432)
Me.buttonApply.TabIndex = 5
Me.buttonApply.Text = "Apply"
Me.radioButtonNone.Checked = True
Me.radioButtonNone.Location = New System.Drawing.Point(12, 24)
Me.radioButtonNone.TabIndex = 0
Me.radioButtonNone.TabStop = True
Me.radioButtonNone.Text = "No Fill"
Me.numericUpDownRotate.Location = New System.Drawing.Point(56, 24)
Me.numericUpDownRotate.Maximum = New Decimal(New Integer() _
    {360, 0, 0, 0})
```

LISTING 9.12   Continued

```
Me.numericUpDownRotate.Minimum = New Decimal(New Integer() _
    {360, 0, 0, -2147483648})
Me.numericUpDownRotate.Size = New System.Drawing.Size(52, 20)
Me.numericUpDownRotate.TabIndex = 1
Me.textBoxHeight.Location = New System.Drawing.Point(72, 88)
Me.textBoxHeight.MaxLength = 4
Me.textBoxHeight.Size = New System.Drawing.Size(48, 20)
Me.textBoxHeight.TabIndex = 3
Me.radioButtonSolid.Location = New System.Drawing.Point(12, 52)
Me.radioButtonSolid.TabIndex = 1
Me.radioButtonSolid.Text = "Solid"
Me.comboBoxBlendTo.DropDownStyle = _
    System.Windows.Forms.ComboBoxStyle.DropDownList
Me.comboBoxBlendTo.DropDownWidth = 132
Me.comboBoxBlendTo.Location = New System.Drawing.Point(68, 136)
Me.comboBoxBlendTo.Size = New System.Drawing.Size(132, 21)
Me.comboBoxBlendTo.TabIndex = 8
Me.textBoxY.Location = New System.Drawing.Point(32, 52)
Me.textBoxY.MaxLength = 4
Me.textBoxY.Size = New System.Drawing.Size(48, 20)
Me.textBoxY.TabIndex = 5
Me.textBoxWidth.Location = New System.Drawing.Point(72, 60)
Me.textBoxWidth.MaxLength = 4
Me.textBoxWidth.Size = New System.Drawing.Size(48, 20)
Me.textBoxWidth.TabIndex = 2
Me.buttonClear.Location = New System.Drawing.Point(12, 432)
Me.buttonClear.TabIndex = 7
Me.buttonClear.Text = "Clear"
Me.radioButtonBlend.Location = New System.Drawing.Point(12, 80)
Me.radioButtonBlend.TabIndex = 3
Me.radioButtonBlend.Text = "Blend"
Me.comboBoxShape.AllowDrop = True
Me.comboBoxShape.DropDownStyle = _
    System.Windows.Forms.ComboBoxStyle.DropDownList
Me.comboBoxShape.DropDownWidth = 121
Me.comboBoxShape.Location = New System.Drawing.Point(68, 28)
Me.comboBoxShape.Size = New System.Drawing.Size(121, 21)
Me.comboBoxShape.TabIndex = 1
Me.comboBoxPattern.DropDownStyle = _
    System.Windows.Forms.ComboBoxStyle.DropDownList
Me.comboBoxPattern.DropDownWidth = 132
Me.comboBoxPattern.Location = New System.Drawing.Point(308, 24)
Me.comboBoxPattern.Size = New System.Drawing.Size(132, 21)
Me.comboBoxPattern.TabIndex = 10
```

LISTING 9.12   Continued

```
Me.comboBoxPattBack.DropDownStyle = _
    System.Windows.Forms.ComboBoxStyle.DropDownList
Me.comboBoxPattBack.DropDownWidth = 132
Me.comboBoxPattBack.Location = New System.Drawing.Point(328, 80)
Me.comboBoxPattBack.Size = New System.Drawing.Size(132, 21)
Me.comboBoxPattBack.TabIndex = 14
Me.comboBoxBlendStyle.DropDownStyle = _
    System.Windows.Forms.ComboBoxStyle.DropDownList
Me.comboBoxBlendStyle.DropDownWidth = 132
Me.comboBoxBlendStyle.Location = New System.Drawing.Point(68, 80)
Me.comboBoxBlendStyle.Size = New System.Drawing.Size(132, 21)
Me.comboBoxBlendStyle.TabIndex = 4
Me.label15.Location = New System.Drawing.Point(110, 26)
Me.label15.TabIndex = 0
Me.label15.Text = "degrees"
Me.label14.Location = New System.Drawing.Point(12, 28)
Me.label14.TabIndex = 0
Me.label14.Text = "Rotate"
Me.label11.Location = New System.Drawing.Point(256, 56)
Me.label11.TabIndex = 11
Me.label11.Text = "Foreground"
Me.label10.Location = New System.Drawing.Point(12, 64)
Me.label10.TabIndex = 1
Me.label10.Text = "Color"
Me.label13.Location = New System.Drawing.Point(28, 140)
Me.label13.Size = New System.Drawing.Size(40, 23)
Me.label13.TabIndex = 7
Me.label13.Text = "To"
Me.label12.Location = New System.Drawing.Point(256, 84)
Me.label12.TabIndex = 13
Me.label12.Text = "Background"
Me.comboBoxOutlineColor.DropDownStyle = _
    System.Windows.Forms.ComboBoxStyle.DropDownList
Me.comboBoxOutlineColor.DropDownWidth = 121
Me.comboBoxOutlineColor.Location = New System.Drawing.Point(12, 80)
Me.comboBoxOutlineColor.Size = New System.Drawing.Size(148, 21)
Me.comboBoxOutlineColor.TabIndex = 2
Me.buttonOk.Location = New System.Drawing.Point(252, 432)
Me.buttonOk.TabIndex = 4
Me.buttonOk.Text = "Ok"
Me.label8.Location = New System.Drawing.Point(28, 112)
Me.label8.Size = New System.Drawing.Size(48, 23)
Me.label8.TabIndex = 5
Me.label8.Text = "From"
Me.label9.Location = New System.Drawing.Point(12, 32)
```

9

LISTING 9.12   Continued

```
        Me.label9.Size = New System.Drawing.Size(52, 16)
        Me.label9.TabIndex = 0
        Me.label9.Text = "Weight"
        Me.comboBoxSolidColor.DropDownStyle = _
            System.Windows.Forms.ComboBoxStyle.DropDownList
        Me.comboBoxSolidColor.DropDownWidth = 132
        Me.comboBoxSolidColor.Location = New System.Drawing.Point(68, 52)
        Me.comboBoxSolidColor.Size = New System.Drawing.Size(132, 21)
        Me.comboBoxSolidColor.TabIndex = 2
        Me.buttonCancel.DialogResult = System.Windows.Forms.DialogResult.Cancel
        Me.buttonCancel.Location = New System.Drawing.Point(420, 432)
        Me.buttonCancel.TabIndex = 6
        Me.buttonCancel.Text = "Cancel"
        Me.label4.Location = New System.Drawing.Point(128, 64)
        Me.label4.Size = New System.Drawing.Size(52, 16)
        Me.label4.TabIndex = 2
        Me.label4.Text = "pixels"
        Me.label5.Location = New System.Drawing.Point(128, 92)
        Me.label5.Size = New System.Drawing.Size(52, 16)
        Me.label5.TabIndex = 2
        Me.label5.Text = "pixels"
        Me.label6.Location = New System.Drawing.Point(12, 28)
        Me.label6.Size = New System.Drawing.Size(52, 16)
        Me.label6.TabIndex = 2
        Me.label6.Text = "X"
        Me.label7.Location = New System.Drawing.Point(12, 56)
        Me.label7.Size = New System.Drawing.Size(52, 16)
        Me.label7.TabIndex = 2
        Me.label7.Text = "Y"
        Me.label2.Location = New System.Drawing.Point(12, 92)
        Me.label2.Size = New System.Drawing.Size(52, 16)
        Me.label2.TabIndex = 2
        Me.label2.Text = "Height"
        Me.label3.Location = New System.Drawing.Point(12, 64)
        Me.label3.Size = New System.Drawing.Size(52, 16)
        Me.label3.TabIndex = 2
        Me.label3.Text = "Width"
        Me.comboBoxBlendFrom.DropDownStyle = _
            System.Windows.Forms.ComboBoxStyle.DropDownList
        Me.comboBoxBlendFrom.DropDownWidth = 132
        Me.comboBoxBlendFrom.Location = New System.Drawing.Point(68, 108)
        Me.comboBoxBlendFrom.Size = New System.Drawing.Size(132, 21)
        Me.comboBoxBlendFrom.TabIndex = 6
        Me.radioButtonPattern.Location = New System.Drawing.Point(240, 24)
        Me.radioButtonPattern.TabIndex = 9
```

LISTING 9.12 Continued

```
Me.radioButtonPattern.Text = "Pattern"
Me.textBoxX.Location = New System.Drawing.Point(32, 24)
Me.textBoxX.MaxLength = 4
Me.textBoxX.Size = New System.Drawing.Size(48, 20)
Me.textBoxX.TabIndex = 4
Me.comboBoxPattFore.DropDownStyle = _
    System.Windows.Forms.ComboBoxStyle.DropDownList
Me.comboBoxPattFore.DropDownWidth = 132
Me.comboBoxPattFore.Location = New System.Drawing.Point(328, 52)
Me.comboBoxPattFore.Size = New System.Drawing.Size(132, 21)
Me.comboBoxPattFore.TabIndex = 12
Me.groupBox1.Controls.AddRange(New System.Windows.Forms.Control() _
    {Me.groupBox5, Me.label5, Me.label4, Me.textBoxHeight, _
    Me.textBoxWidth, Me.label3, Me.label2, Me.label1, _
    Me.comboBoxShape})
Me.groupBox1.Location = New System.Drawing.Point(12, 12)
Me.groupBox1.Size = New System.Drawing.Size(304, 124)
Me.groupBox1.TabIndex = 0
Me.groupBox1.TabStop = False
Me.groupBox1.Text = "Shape"
Me.groupBox2.Controls.AddRange(New System.Windows.Forms.Control() _
    {Me.comboBoxBlendStyle, Me.label13, Me.comboBoxBlendTo, _
    Me.comboBoxBlendFrom, Me.comboBoxPattBack, Me.comboBoxPattFore, _
    Me.label12, Me.label11, Me.label8, Me.comboBoxPattern, _
    Me.comboBoxSolidColor, Me.radioButtonBlend, Me.radioButtonSolid, _
    Me.radioButtonPattern, Me.radioButtonNone})
Me.groupBox2.Location = New System.Drawing.Point(12, 148)
Me.groupBox2.Size = New System.Drawing.Size(484, 176)
Me.groupBox2.TabIndex = 2
Me.groupBox2.TabStop = False
Me.groupBox2.Text = "Fill"
Me.groupBox3.Controls.AddRange(New System.Windows.Forms.Control() _
    {Me.numericUpDownWeight, Me.comboBoxOutlineColor, Me.label10, _
    Me.label9})
Me.groupBox3.Location = New System.Drawing.Point(328, 12)
Me.groupBox3.Size = New System.Drawing.Size(168, 124)
Me.groupBox3.TabIndex = 1
Me.groupBox3.TabStop = False
Me.groupBox3.Text = "Outline"
Me.groupBox4.Controls.AddRange(New System.Windows.Forms.Control() _
    {Me.label15, Me.numericUpDownRotate, Me.label14})
Me.groupBox4.Location = New System.Drawing.Point(12, 332)
Me.groupBox4.Size = New System.Drawing.Size(484, 88)
Me.groupBox4.TabIndex = 3
Me.groupBox4.TabStop = False
```

LISTING 9.12 Continued

```
            Me.groupBox4.Text = "Transform"
            Me.groupBox5.Controls.AddRange(New System.Windows.Forms.Control() _
                {Me.textBoxX, Me.textBoxY, Me.label7, Me.label6})
            Me.groupBox5.Location = New System.Drawing.Point(200, 24)
            Me.groupBox5.Size = New System.Drawing.Size(92, 84)
            Me.groupBox5.TabIndex = 4
            Me.groupBox5.TabStop = False
            Me.groupBox5.Text = "Position"
            Me.numericUpDownWeight.Location = New System.Drawing.Point(64, 28)
            Me.numericUpDownWeight.Maximum = New Decimal(New Integer() _
                {999, 0, 0, 0})
            Me.numericUpDownWeight.Size = New System.Drawing.Size(64, 20)
            Me.numericUpDownWeight.TabIndex = 1
            Me.label1.Location = New System.Drawing.Point(12, 32)
            Me.label1.Size = New System.Drawing.Size(52, 16)
            Me.label1.TabIndex = 2
            Me.label1.Text = "Shape"
            Me.AcceptButton = Me.buttonOk
            Me.AutoScaleBaseSize = New System.Drawing.Size(5, 13)
            Me.FormBorderStyle = System.Windows.Forms.FormBorderStyle.FixedSingle
            Me.CancelButton = Me.buttonCancel
            Me.ClientSize = New System.Drawing.Size(509, 462)
            Me.Controls.AddRange(New System.Windows.Forms.Control() _
                {Me.buttonClear, Me.buttonApply, Me.buttonCancel, Me.buttonOk, _
                Me.groupBox2, Me.groupBox3, Me.groupBox4, Me.groupBox1})
            Me.MaximizeBox = False
            Me.MinimizeBox = False
            Me.Text = "Draw"
            CType(Me.numericUpDownRotate, _
                System.ComponentModel.ISupportInitialize).EndInit()
            CType(Me.numericUpDownWeight, _
                System.ComponentModel.ISupportInitialize).EndInit()

End Sub
```

The Cancel button click event simply closes the form without applying the current form values. Of course, if you've already pressed the Apply button, then the Cancel button just closes the form.

```
    Private Sub buttonCancel_Click(ByVal sender As System.Object, _
        ByVal e As System.EventArgs) Handles buttonCancel.Click

        'purpose: close the form, cancel any pending actions
```

```
        'cancel the form
        Me.Close()

    End Sub
```

The `formDraw_Load` procedure initializes the controls on the form. In it, we fill the various combo boxes directly from enumeration and structure members using the `Reflection` namespace.

Note that at the end of the form load event, we set the `AcceptButton` and `CancelButton` properties of the form to the OK and Cancel buttons, respectively. The `AcceptButton` property indicates what button on the form should respond to the Enter key being pressed (default button). The `CancelButton` property indicates the button that is fired when users click the Escape key. This is new in .NET. In past versions of VB, in order to implement a button that responds to the Enter or Cancel keys you would set properties of the button; now, you set properties of the form.

```
    Private Sub frmDraw_Load(ByVal sender As System.Object, _
        ByVal e As System.EventArgs) Handles MyBase.Load

        'purpose:    initialize the form, set the initial values of controls

        'local scope
        Dim myColor As System.Drawing.Color
        Dim myProps() As System.Reflection.PropertyInfo
        Dim myType As System.Type
        Dim count As Integer
        Dim colorName As String
        Dim myHatchStyle As Drawing.Drawing2D.HatchStyle
        Dim myArray() As String
        Dim myLinGradMode As Drawing2D.LinearGradientMode

        'return the type of the color structure
        myType = myColor.GetType()

        'return the property information of the structure
        myProps = myType.GetProperties()

        'iterate the properties and add to the combo box
        For count = 0 To UBound(myProps)

            'make sure we only get valid colors
            If myProps(count).PropertyType.ToString() = "System.Drawing.Color" _
                And myProps(count).Name <> "Transparent" Then
```

9

```
                    'get the color's name
                    colorName = myProps(count).Name

                    'add the property name (color) to the color combo boxes
                    comboBoxOutlineColor().Items.Add(colorName)
                    comboBoxBlendFrom().Items.Add(colorName)
                    comboBoxBlendTo().Items.Add(colorName)
                    comboBoxSolidColor().Items.Add(colorName)
                    comboBoxPattFore().Items.Add(colorName)
                    comboBoxPattBack().Items.Add(colorName)

            End If

        Next

        'get a type object that represents the hatchStyle enum
        myType = myHatchStyle.GetType()

        'fill an array with the hatchStyle's member names
        myArray = myHatchStyle.GetNames(myType)

        'loop through the array
        For count = 0 To UBound(myArray)

            'fill the pattern dialog
            comboBoxPattern().Items.Add(myArray(count))

        Next

        'get a type object based on the linear gradient enumeration
        myType = myLinGradMode.GetType()

        'fill an array with the linear gradient's member names
        myArray = myLinGradMode.GetNames(myType)

        'loop through the array
        For count = 0 To UBound(myArray)

            'fill the blend style drop-down
            comboBoxBlendStyle().Items.Add(myArray(count))

        Next

        'add some basic shape values for users to select from
        comboBoxShape().Items.Add("Line")
        comboBoxShape().Items.Add("Rectangle")
        comboBoxShape().Items.Add("Ellipse")
```

```
        'select first item in each list by default
        '(saves enabling and disabling controls)
        comboBoxPattern().SelectedIndex = 0
        comboBoxShape().SelectedIndex = 0
        comboBoxOutlineColor().SelectedIndex = 0
        comboBoxBlendFrom().SelectedIndex = 0
        comboBoxBlendTo().SelectedIndex = 0
        comboBoxSolidColor().SelectedIndex = 0
        comboBoxPattFore().SelectedIndex = 0
        comboBoxPattBack().SelectedIndex = 0
        comboBoxBlendStyle().SelectedIndex = 0

        'set the ok button on the form to respond to the enter key
        Me.AcceptButton = buttonOk()

        'set the cancel button on the form to respond to the escape key
        Me.CancelButton = buttonCancel()

    End Sub
dialog
```

The Apply button's click event simply validates the form by calling `validateForm`. If no validation rules were broken, it calls the `submitForm` method to apply the shape to the child form.

```
    Private Sub buttonApply_Click(ByVal sender As System.Object, _
        ByVal e As System.EventArgs) Handles buttonApply.Click

        'purpose:  allow users to draw items to the form without closing the
        'dialog before drawing can happen the form fields must be validated
        If Not validateForm() Then

            'of course we would want to do more than beep ...
            'I assume a production application would capture user keystrokes
            ' and disallow invalid entries ...
            Beep()

        Else

            'call the centralized routine that call the drawing module
            Call submitForm()

        End If

    End Sub
```

The `validateForm` function checks for valid entries in our text boxes and returns either `True` to indicate all fields are valid or `False` to indicate one or more are invalid.

```
Private Function validateForm() As Boolean

    'purpose:   quick check of field values (IsNumeric)

    'validate some of the form fields
    If Not IsNumeric(textBoxWidth().Text) Or _
        Not IsNumeric(textBoxHeight().Text) Or _
        Not IsNumeric(textBoxX().Text) Or _
        Not IsNumeric(textBoxY().Text) Then

        Return False

    Else

        Return True

    End If

End Function
```

The submitForm method simply calls the draw method contained in our module. Of course, it passes all the form values as parameters.

```
Private Sub submitForm()

    'purpose:   send the form values to the draw method of modDrawing

    'local scope
    Dim strFillType As String

    'set the fill pattern selected
    If radioButtonBlend().Checked = True Then
        strFillType = "BLEND"
    ElseIf radioButtonSolid().Checked = True Then
        strFillType = "SOLID"
    ElseIf radioButtonPattern().Checked = True Then
        strFillType = "PATTERN"
    Else
        strFillType = "NONE"
    End If

    'call the draw method
    Call draw(shape:=comboBoxShape().SelectedItem.ToString, _
        Width:=CInt(textBoxWidth().Text), _
        Height:=CInt(textBoxHeight().Text), _
        x:=CInt(textBoxX().Text), _
        y:=CInt(textBoxY().Text), _
```

```
            fillType:=strFillType, _
            outlineWeight:=CSng(numericUpDownWeight().Value), _
            outlineColor:=comboBoxOutlineColor().SelectedItem.ToString, _
            solidColor:=comboBoxSolidColor().SelectedItem.ToString, _
            blendFrom:=comboBoxBlendFrom().SelectedItem.ToString, _
            blendTo:=comboBoxBlendTo().SelectedItem.ToString, _
            pattern:=comboBoxPattern().SelectedItem.ToString, _
            patternForeColor:=comboBoxPattFore().SelectedItem.ToString, _
            patternBackColor:=comboBoxPattBack().SelectedItem.ToString, _
            blendStyle:=comboBoxBlendStyle().SelectedItem.ToString, _
            rotateAngle:=numericUpDownRotate().Value)

End Sub
```

The OK button's click event checks the field entries for validity using validateForm. It then calls submitForm to apply the shape to the child form. Finally, it closes the dialog.

```
Private Sub buttonOk_Click(ByVal sender As System.Object, _
    ByVal e As System.EventArgs) Handles buttonOk.Click

    'purpose:   event triggered when users click the ok button
    '           draw the item and close the form

    'validate the form
    If Not validateForm() Then

        'of course we would want to do more than beep ...
        Beep()

    Else

        'call the centralized routine that call the drawing module
        Call submitForm()

        'close the form
        Me.Close()

    End If

End Sub

Private Sub buttonClear_Click(ByVal sender As System.Object, _
    ByVal e As System.EventArgs) Handles buttonClear.Click

    'purpose:  provide the illusion of clearing the form
    '          this allows users to keep drawing without closing the dialog
```

```
        'set the background color to the default
        m_myChild.BackColor = Color.FromName(m_SurfaceBackground)
        m_myChild.Refresh()

    End Sub


#End Region

End Class
```

Drawing Module

The drawing module contains the application's global variables and the actual draw procedure.

Code Walkthrough

We first set the application's default values including the drawing surface settings. We then declare the global objects that reference the child form and the associated graphics objects. The drawing module is presented in Listing 9.13.

LISTING 9.13   Drawing Module (modDrawing)

```
Option Strict Off

Module modDrawing

    'set defaults for child form
    Public m_LeftPos As Integer = 5
    Public m_TopPos As Integer = 5
    Public m_Width As Integer = 256
    Public m_Height As Integer = 256
    Public m_ChildColor As String = "White"
    Public m_SurfaceBackground As String = "White"

    'set a reference to a graphics object to be used globally
    Public m_myGraphics As Graphics

    'set a reference to the child form to be used by the application
    Public m_myChild As frmChild
```

The draw method takes all of the necessary values from the draw form as parameters. It uses the Graphics class to render shapes onto the surface. You can see that most of the code is just simple logic to determine the type of shape to draw, the shape's outline, and its fill type. One interesting method call is myState = m_myGraphics.Save(), where myState is declared as

`Dim myState As Drawing2D.GraphicsState`. The `GraphicsState` class allows you to save, or maintain, a copy of the `Graphics` object at a point in time. You do this by calling its `save` method.

This becomes important as you apply transforms to the `Graphics` object. Each call to a transform method sets the `Graphics` object's state to the given value. Therefore, subsequent calls to a transform method actually transform the already-transformed object. For instance, the line `m_myGraphics.RotateTransform(angle:=rotateAngle)`, where `rotateAngle` is 5°, sets the graphics object to rotate shapes that it draws by 5°. A subsequent call to the `RotateTranform` property, where `rotateAngle` is 10°, actually results in a rotation of 15° from the base shape. You can see why the `Save` method is so important. Of course we could also call `Graphics.ResetTransform`. Finally, after the transforms are complete and the objects are drawn to the screen, you call `m_myGraphics.Restore(myState)`. This restores the `Graphics` object to its original state.

```
Public Sub draw( _
    ByVal shape As String, _
    ByVal width As Integer, _
    ByVal height As Integer, _
    ByVal x As Integer, _
    ByVal y As Integer, _
    ByVal fillType As String, _
    ByVal outlineWeight As Single, _
    ByVal outlineColor As String, _
    ByVal solidColor As String, _
    ByVal blendFrom As String, _
    ByVal blendTo As String, _
    ByVal pattern As String, _
    ByVal patternForeColor As String, _
    ByVal patternBackColor As String, _
    ByVal blendStyle As String, _
    ByVal rotateAngle As Single)

    'purpose: draw a shape to the drawing surface (frmChild)

    'local scope
    Dim myPen As Pen
    Dim myRectangle As Rectangle
    Dim myBrush As Brush
    Dim myHatchStyle As Drawing2D.HatchStyle
    Dim myType As System.Type
    Dim myBlendStyle As Drawing2D.LinearGradientMode
    Dim myState As Drawing2D.GraphicsState

    'get the current state of the graphics object (pre-tranform)
    myState = m_myGraphics.Save()
```

9

```
'set the rotation transformation value
m_myGraphics.RotateTransform(angle:=rotateAngle)

'check what shape to draw
Select Case shape
    Case "Line"

        'create a new pen instance
        myPen = New Pen(color.FromName(name:=outlineColor), _
            width:=outlineWeight)

        'draw the line to the surface
        m_myGraphics.DrawLine(pen:=myPen, x1:=x, y1:=y, _
            x2:=x + width, y2:=y + height)

    Case "Rectangle", "Ellipse"

        'note: the rectangle and ellipse are very similar
        '      they can use the same code

        'create a new pen myect for the outline of the shape
        myPen = New Pen(color.FromName(name:=outlineColor), _
            width:=outlineWeight)

        'create the rectangle object
        myRectangle = New Rectangle(x:=x, y:=y, width:=width, _
            height:=height)

        'draw the rectangle to the surface
        If shape = "Ellipse" Then

            'draw the ellipse
            m_myGraphics.DrawEllipse(pen:=myPen, _
                rect:=myRectangle)

        Else

            'draw a rectangle
            m_myGraphics.DrawRectangle(pen:=myPen, _
                rect:=myRectangle)

        End If

        'fill the rectangle/ellipse
        If fillType <> "NONE" Then
```

```
                        'determine brush type to create
                    Select Case fillType
                        Case "SOLID"

                                'create a new solid brush
                                myBrush = New SolidBrush( _
                                    color:=color.FromName(name:=solidColor))

                        Case "PATTERN"

                                'create the hatch brush
                                'note:  we use the type object and the parse
                                '          method of the enum to return the
                                '          value of the enum's member from its
                                '          name (string)
                                myType = myHatchStyle.GetType()
                                myBrush = New System.Drawing.Drawing2D.HatchBrush _
                                (myHatchStyle.Parse(enumType:=myType, _
                                    value:=pattern),
➡foreColor:=Color.FromName(name:=patternForeColor),
➡backColor:=color.FromName(name:=patternBackColor))

                        Case "BLEND"

                                'create a blend brush
                                'note:  we use the type object and the parse
                                '          method of the enum to return the
                                '          value of the enum's member from its
                                '          name (string)
                                myType = myBlendStyle.GetType
                                myBrush = New _
                                    System.Drawing.Drawing2D.LinearGradientBrush( _
                                    rect:=myRectangle, _
                                    color1:=color.FromName(name:=blendFrom), _
                                    color2:=color.FromName(name:=blendTo), _
                                    LinearGradientMode:=myBlendStyle.Parse( _
                                    enumType:=myType, value:=blendStyle))

                    End Select

                    'fill the shape
                    If shape = "Ellipse" Then

                            'draw the ellipse with the correct brush
                            m_myGraphics.FillEllipse(brush:=myBrush, _
                                rect:=myRectangle)
```

```
        Else

            'fill the rectangle with the correct brush
            m_myGraphics.FillRectangle(brush:=myBrush, _
                rect:=myRectangle)

        End If

    End If

End Select

'reset the state of the graphics object
m_myGraphics.Restore(myState)

End Sub

End Module
```

Summary

In this chapter, we walked through the key classes related to drawing using managed code. The following is a summary of some of the key points related to executing common programming tasks with the .NET Framework Class Library:

- GDI+ is the underlying technology used by the managed code to execute drawing tasks.
- By default, a graphic's surface has its origin in the upper-left corner.
- The Graphics class is used to execute nearly all drawing tasks. You use its methods like DrawLine, DrawEllipse, and FillRectangle to render shapes and colors to the drawing surface.
- Classes derived from Brush can be used to fill the interior of shapes. Brush classes include SolidBrush, TextureBrush, and HatchBrush.
- The GraphicsPath class is used to group shapes. This allows you to manipulate various shapes as a whole.
- The Region class allows you to define areas of your drawing surface for clipping and hit testing.
- The Bitmap class encapsulates an image. You can use the DrawImage method of the Graphics class to render it to the surface.
- The Matrix class provides a number of ways to transform images and shapes.
- The following methods of the Graphics class can be used to transform shapes: RotateTransform, ScaleTransform, MultiplyTransform.

Reading and Writing XML

IN THIS CHAPTER

If you think of the .NET Framework as a multilayered technology, then the eXtensible Markup Language (XML) is the glue that binds those layers together. The .NET Framework provides unprecedented functionality for the VB programmer to natively interact with and use XML inside applications. As a storage mechanism, XML is the common denominator for storing data and persisting objects. As a communications mechanism, XML forms the underpinnings for how the .NET classes talk to one another. It is the default way that objects in .NET express and exchange data. For these reasons alone, an understanding of XML is necessary to be productive in the .NET runtime. But the real story is not how the Framework uses XML, but how the Framework enables you, the developer, to speak the universal XML language.

This chapter introduces the XML class libraries, `System.XML` and `System.Xml.Schema`, that .NET uses as an API for parsing, validating, and manipulating XML. First, we'll establish some baseline definitions and summaries for XML concepts. Then we will talk about the XML-related industry standards that the .NET Framework supports. Finally, we get to the meat of the chapter: an in-depth look at the classes that constitute the `System.Xml` and `System.Xml.Schema` namespaces.

Key Classes Related to XML

This chapter covers the classes and related structures listed in Table 10.1.

TABLE 10.1   Key Classes of the `System.Xml` and `System.Xml.Schema` Namespaces

Class/Structure	Description
System.Xml	The `System.Xml` namespace is used to process XML files in accordance with published World Wide Web Consortium standards.
XmlDocument	The `XmlDocument` class is used as an abstract of an entire XML document.
XmlException	The `XmlException` class is used to encapsulate and return information specifically related to XML exceptions that can occur while reading, writing, or validating XML documents.
XmlNode	The `XmlNode` class represents a node in an XML document.
XmlNodeReader	The `XmlNodeReader` class provides a way to parse XML data inside an XML node.
XmlReader	The `XmlReader` abstract class provides a basis for concrete implementations of classes designed to read XML documents.
XmlTextReader	The `XmlTextReader` class provides a way to parse XML data stored inside a file or stream.

TABLE 10.1 Continued

Class/Structure	Description
XmlTextWriter	The XmlTextWriter class provides ways to programmatically write well-formed XML.
XmlValidatingReader	The XmlValidatingReader class is used to simultaneously parse and validate XML documents against a predefined schema (either DTD, XDR, or XSD).
System.Xml.Schema	The System.Xml.Schema namespace exposes a variety of objects that can be used to construct and process XML schema documents.
ValidationEventArgs	The ValidationEventArgs class is used in conjunction with the XmlValidatingReader class to provide validation-specific information to event handlers.
XmlSchema	The XmlSchema class represents an instance of an XML schema document.
XmlSchemaAttribute	The XmlSchemaAttribute class represents a schema attribute element.
XmlSchemaComplexType	The XmlSchemaComplexType class represents a schema complex type element.
XmlSchemaElement	The XmlSchemaElement class is used as a parent or container object for XML schema elements.
XmlSchemaSequence	The XmlSchemaSequence class represents an XML schema sequence element.
XmlSchemaSimpleType	The XmlSchemaSimpleType class represents an instance of an XML schema simple type element.

Markup Languages

XML is a language that is used to *describe* data. This stands in contrast to a language such as the Hypertext Markup Language (HTML), which is a language used to *display* data. To fully appreciate what XML is and what it does, it is useful to have a baseline understanding of markup languages in general.

What Is a Markup Language?

Markup languages exist to add meaning or formatting to documents. *Rich Text Format* (RTF) is one example of a markup language. It consists of a defined set of *tags* or tokens that lend instruction on how to display a piece of a document. Figure 10.1 shows a formatted sentence typed into WordPad.

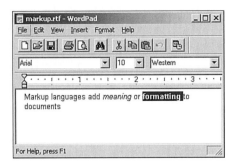

FIGURE 10.1
An RTF document in WordPad.

When the document is saved with the RTF format, the following code results:

```
{\rtf1\ansi\ansicpg1252\deff0\deflang1033
{\fonttbl{\f0\fswiss\fcharset0 Arial;}}
\viewkind4\uc1\pard\f0\fs20\par
Markup languages add \i meaning \i0 or \b formatting \b0 to documents.
\par}
```

In this example, you can see that the \i tag indicates that the piece of the document between the \i and \i0 tags should be italicized. The \b and \b0 tags indicate that the text between them should be displayed in bold text. The RTF format and others like it do their job well, but they are ill suited to the Web. For one thing, they don't generate the most readable of documents; their syntax can be confusing and awkward to the human eye. For another, there is little to the document that actually looks like it has structure. For programmers, who rely on structure, this is anathema.

Markups with HTML

HTML is also a markup language. HTML attempts to fix some of the problems of earlier markup languages by enforcing structure onto a document. If you glance at the following HTML code, it is immediately obvious that there are some standard structural rules being used. Each "tag" has a beginning and an end to it, some tags are nested inside of others, and each tag has a specific, designated place in the document with header tags coming first, followed by body tags. Figure 10.2 shows the previously formatted RTF document as HTML inside Internet Explorer.

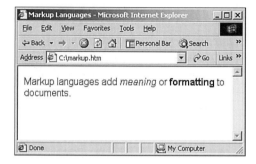

Figure 10.2
Formatted HTML inside Internet Explorer.

This is what the HTML code needed to generate the previous document looks like:

```
<html>

<head>
    <title>Markup Languages</title>
</head>

<body>

    <p>
    <font face="Arial">Markup languages add <i>meaning</i> or
    <b>formatting</b> to documents.</font>
    </p>

</body>

</html>
```

HTML and other markup languages follow a set of rules, which usually are explained inside a specification. For XML (and HTML), this specification is maintained by the World Wide Web Consortium (W3C). The language specification defines the actual syntax rules of the document. The HTML specification, for instance, defines a rule that says that each HTML document must begin with an `<html>` tag and end with an `</html>` tag. Typically, these language specifications define general syntax rules, the order in which the various tags can appear, whether different tags are dependent upon other tags, and so on.

In the next section, we look at the structure of XML documents specifically.

Suggestions for Further Exploration

⊃ Although the site is dense and not easy to digest, it will be worth your time to visit http://www.w3.org to view the actual specifications, proposals, and standards that describe some of the languages that we have talked about in this section, including HTML and XML.

⊃ A group portal on the Web for understanding all things related to XML is http://www.xml.com. The articles at this site will help the casual XML developer understand the role of XML in a deeper context and also will help answer questions on XML's origin and uses.

The Anatomy of an XML Document

An XML document is a text document. It has readable characters that are arranged in a way that causes the document to conform to the W3C specifications for an XML document. The fact that an XML document is readable to humans as well as computers is important; data that doesn't require a machine to be understood helps to alleviate needless complexity in a system. To better understand the XML functionality inside the System.XML namespace and its children namespaces, this section briefly discusses the various components of XML documents.

So that you have something concrete to refer back to as we discuss the various pieces of an XML document, Listing 10.1 shows a piece of an XML document intended to hold guest registrations for a hotel.

LISTING 10.1 XML Hotel Registration File

```
<?xml version="1.0" encoding="utf-8" ?>
<guests>
    <guest id="jlk0910211">
        <firstname>Jim</firstname>
        <middlename>L</middlename>
        <lastname>Kelley</lastname>
        <roomnbr>295</roomnbr>
        <checkindate>6/17/2001</checkindate>
        <numnights>4</numnights>
        <preferred>No</preferred>
    </guest>
</guests>
```

Nodes

An XML document consists of various discrete chunks of information called *nodes*. Nodes are the lowest level of informational unit contained in an XML document. When you read an

XML document using some of the XML reader classes in `System.XML`, they will read those documents one node at a time. If you started listing the nodes of the XML document in Listing 10.1, this is what the list would look like:

- Node 1: `<?xml version="1.0" encoding="utf-8" ?>`
- Node 2: `<guests>`
- Node 3: `<guest id="jlk0910211">`
- Node 4: `<firstname>`
- Node 5: `Jim`
- Node 6: `</firstname>`

...and so on. Nodes are useful for low-level parsing, but they don't carry enough context with them to be ultimately useful for understanding the data in an XML document. Consider the fifth node containing the text `Jim`. What does this node mean? We can guess, based on the nodes before (`<firstname>`) and after (`</firstname>`), that this is the first name of a hotel guest, but, taken by itself, the node doesn't offer up a whole lot of meaning. When people look at or create an XML document, they typically think in terms of *elements*, not nodes.

Elements

An *element* is used to describe and contain data. As such, it is the real power behind an XML document's structure. Elements are named and can encapsulate data through values or attributes. The syntax for an element is as follows:

```
<elementname attrib1="value1" attrib2="value2" ...>Data</elementname>
```

Attributes and data are all optional with elements, but the starting tags and ending tags are required. For instance, this is also a valid element:

```
<MyElement></MyElement>
```

If the element in question does not have any data associated with it, the ending tag can be short-circuited by closing out the starting tag with a / character, like this:

```
<MyElement someAttrib="Yes"/>
```

or like this:

```
<MyElement/>
```

Elements are very useful because, unlike nodes, they provide you with enough contextual information to evaluate the data that they contain. The following is an element from the hotel register XML document:

```
<firstname>Jim</firstname>
```

Because elements are said to include the starting tag, the ending tag, and everything in between, the following is also an element from our hotel example:

```
<guests>
    <guest id="jlk0910211">
        <firstname>Jim</firstname>
        <middlename>L</middlename>
        <lastname>Kelley</lastname>
        <roomnbr>295</roomnbr>
        <checkindate>6/17/2001</checkindate>
        <numnights>4</numnights>
        <preferred>No</preferred>
    </guest>
</guests>
```

The <guests> element, in this case, happens to be the outermost element in the XML document, and it is referred to as the *document element* or the root element. You can see that nested elements set up a parent-child relationship between different pieces of data. The <guest> element is a child of the <guests> element and has several child elements of its own, such as <firstname>, <roomnbr>, and <preferred>. Because of their capability to contain other elements, elements form the basis for data relationships inside an XML document.

Now let's take a further step back and examine the different sections to an XML document.

Each XML document has two major sections, the *prolog* and the *document elements*.

The Prolog

The *prolog* section of an XML document is used to specify document-wide settings or attributes. Typically, this includes the version of XML that the document adheres to, the character set that it was encoded with, and any external resource references, such as style sheets or schemas (more on these later in the chapter). The tags and structure of this section are controlled by the actual XML specification. This stands in sharp contrast to the document elements section, whose structure and tag content are entirely up to the XML document author. The prolog consists of the XML declaration, processing instructions, and comments.

The XML Declaration

The hotel register XML file that we have been looking at has only one of the items allowed in a prolog, the XML declaration:

```
<?xml version="1.0" encoding="utf-8" ?>
```

The XML declaration must be the very first line in the document. The XML declaration consists of three parts: the XML version number, the encoding type, and a "standalone" declaration. The XML version number is required. This references which version of the XML specification was used to construct the document. The encoding type is optional; if specified, it identifies which character set was used to encode the document.

> **NOTE**
>
> Utf-8 encoding is the most common type of encoding supported by XML parsers and writers. If the XML document is encoded with Utf-8 or Utf-16, the parser should be capable of figuring this out automatically, without it being specified in the XML declaration. If the encoding is not Utf-8 or Utf-16, definitely be sure to include it in the encoding type. Other encoding types that you might run into include ISO-8859-1, Big-5, and Shift-JIS. For a good description of XML encoding, see the article "Character Encodings in XML and Perl," by Michel Rodriguez, currently available at `http://www.xml.com/pub/a/2000/04/26/encodings/index.htm`.

The standalone declaration is also optional. If we had used one in the hotel register XML file, it would appear like this:

```
<?xml version="1.0" encoding="utf-8" standalone="no"?>
```

The standalone value can be set to either Yes or No. A value of Yes indicates that the document will not reference any external files. That is, no external files will be needed to correctly parse or understand the document's content. If an external resource is indicated (such as a style sheet) and the value is set to Yes, the parser will throw an error. A standalone value of No indicates that external resources may be used to parse and understand the document. No is the default value if no standalone declaration is made.

Processing Instructions

Processing instructions are a very loosely defined set of statements, typically used for referencing style sheets from within an XML document. Processing instructions really are meant to be instructions that are passed directly through to applications; it is up to the application how to handle the instruction. While these processing instructions typically are contained in the document prolog, they also may appear at the end of the document or even inside the document. Here is an example of a processing instruction:

```
<?xml-stylesheet type="text/xsl" href="register_display.xsl"?>
```

The DOCTYPE Declaration

The purpose of the DOCTYPE declaration is twofold: It provides a way for you to explicitly identify the root element of the XML document, and it allows a way for you to relate the XML document to a *Document Type Definition* file (DTD). (DTDs are covered in much greater detail in the section titled "XML Schemas.") DOCTYPE declarations are not required; when used, the root element parameter is the only one required (DTD references are optional). The following is an example of a DOCTYPE declaration:

```
<!DOCTYPE guests SYSTEM "URIToDTD">
```

The DTD reference can be of type SYSTEM (as shown previously) or of type PUBLIC. Again, we will cover this topic in more detail during our actual discussion of DTDs later in this chapter (again, in the "XML Schemas" section).

Comments

Comments also are allowed in the document prolog. Comments look like this:

```
<!--This is a test-->
```

Comments also may appear inside the document proper or at the end of the document, although they cannot be contained within element tags.

Document Elements

All the nodes following the prolog are document elements. This is the actual meat of the document. The tag definitions here can be completely customized to structure data exactly the way that it needs to be structured for the particular application or process that will consume or write it. Document elements must follow the syntax for *well-formed* XML, something we will talk about in detail in the section, "Validating XML Documents." Essentially, this means that the elements must follow certain basic rules: They must have a starting tag and an ending tag, and parent elements must wholly contain their child elements. That is, this is correct:

```
<parent>
        <child></child>
</parent>
```

This is not:

```
<parent>
        <child>
</parent>
</child>
```

 ## Suggestions for Further Exploration

➲ Many more intricacies are involved with the XML structure than we have been able to cover in this chapter. Again, for a complete review, refer to the W3C's XML standards, located at http://www.w3.org.

➲ Technically, XML is actually a subset of another specification called the Standard Generalized Markup Language (SGML). So is HTML. For an authoritative treatment of SGML and its various implementations, see http://www.oasis-open.org/cover/general.html.

Parsing XML Documents

The System.XML namespace has a variety of classes dedicated to implementing read and write functions for XML documents. This section discusses those classes that are capable of reading and parsing XML documents, tells how they are used, and shows in which situations they are most useful.

The Reader and Writer Base Classes

The System.XML namespace established two very important base classes, XMLReader and XMLWriter (see Figure 10.3). These base classes are inherited from to provide three classes dedicated to reading XML: XmlTextReader, XmlNodeReader, and XmlValidatingReader. There is only one concrete implementation of the XmlWriter base class: XmlTextWriter.

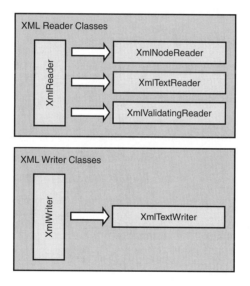

FIGURE 10.3
The XML reader and writer classes.

The XMLReader class implements functions that can read in an XML text file or stream and then navigate through the different attributes contained in that file. It also implements properties that enable you to programmatically determine the current node that is being processed and the content of that node. The XMLWriter class provides functionality to output XML as a stream. It enables you to generate well-formed XML and manage the progress and status of the output.

You can choose from two major design patterns when parsing an XML document. One involves processing XML text in a forward-only manner, node by node. The other way involves building a "tree" of an XML document in memory and then hopping from node to node (or element to element) on the tree. Both approaches are supported by different classes in the System.XML namespace, and both have their advantages and disadvantages. We'll start by examining the first approach: forward-only parsing of nodes.

Forward-Only XML Text Parsing

The XMLTextReader is a specific implementation of the XMLReader abstract class. Its sole purpose is to provide programmers with the capability to quickly read in XML from a file, stream, or URL. It does not attempt to validate the source XML document against a schema.

The simplest way to start down the road of reading in an XML document is to specify its name in the XmlTextReader constructor, like this:

```
reader = New XmlTextReader(fileName)
```

Quite a few different overloaded constructors are available with the XmlTextReader class. Supplying a string (as we previously did with fileName) enables you to load a file either from a local file path or from a URL, as you see in the following two lines of code:

```
'read from a local file-path
reader = New XmlTextReader("C:\xml documents\transcript.xml")

'read from a URL
reader = New XmlTextReader("http://www.brilliantstorm/transcript.xml")
```

You also can provide a stream object, instead of a string, to the constructor to parse in an XML document sitting inside of a stream object. Likewise, you can specify a TextReader object. For now, let's concentrate on parsing XML from a local file.

The XmlTextReader exposes a Read method that is used to actually start the parsing. When you use the Read method, you actually are moving a virtual "viewport" across the document. This viewport can look at one node at a time; calling the Read method advances it to the next node, enabling you to examine that node's properties. Listing 10.2 shows a simple console application that reads in an XML file (hotel_register.xml) and then prints its content to the console window.

LISTING 10.2   Reading in an XML File

```
Imports System.Xml

Module dataReader
```

LISTING 10.2 Continued

```vb
Sub Main()
    Const fileName = "hotel_register.xml"

    Dim reader As XmlTextReader

    Try
        'Read in an XML file (location stored in fileName)
        reader = New XmlTextReader(fileName)

        reader.WhitespaceHandling = WhitespaceHandling.None

        'Write each node in the file out to the console window:
        'The Read method tells the class to read in the next node
        'in the document; if there are no more nodes, it will return
        'false
        While reader.Read()
            Console.WriteLine(reader.ReadOuterXml())
        End While

        'Catch any thrown exceptions and display an error dialog...

    Catch xmlErr As XmlException
        MsgBox("An XML error has occurred (" & xmlErr.Message & ")." & _
            vbCrLf & vbCrLf & "      Xml Source Line Nbr: " & _
            reader.LineNumber & vbCrLf & "      Xml Source Position: " & _
            reader.LinePosition)

    Catch appErr As Exception
        MsgBox("An error occurred (" & appErr.Message & "). Stack info:" & _
        appErr.StackTrace)

    Finally
        If Not (reader Is Nothing) Then
            reader.Close()
        End If

    End Try

    Console.WriteLine("<hit 'Enter' to exit>")
    Console.ReadLine()
End Sub

End Module
```

In this example, we are setting up a while loop based on the value returned from the Read method. The Read method has a few different overloaded definitions. The one that we are using here takes no parameters and simply tells the Reader object to read in the next node from the target file. If there are no nodes left in the file, it will return a value of false.

Inside the while loop, we execute a second method XmlTextReader.ReadOuterXML. The ReadOuterXML method returns all the XML content of the current node *and* all its children as a string. Because we have just issued the Read command once at this point, the current node would be the very outermost node (<hotel>). That means that we would expect this method to return the entire file, with the exception of the XML version spec. In other words, it should return all the document elements. In fact, this is just what it does (see Listing 10.3).

LISTING 10.3   The hotel_register.xml File

```xml
<?xml version="1.0" encoding="utf-8" ?>
<hotel id="DC-4RIVERS">
    <guests>
        <guest id="jlk0910211">
            <firstname>Jim</firstname>
            <middlename>L</middlename>
            <lastname>Kelley</lastname>
            <roomnbr>295</roomnbr>
            <checkindate>6/17/2001</checkindate>
            <numnights>4</numnights>
            <preferred>No</preferred>
        </guest>
        <guest id="nlt0000704">
            <firstname>Nadia</firstname>
            <middlename>L</middlename>
            <lastname>Tatonovich</lastname>
            <roomnbr>615</roomnbr>
            <checkindate>6/17/2001</checkindate>
            <numnights>4</numnights>
            <preferred>No</preferred>
        </guest>
        <guest id="d b6620103">
            <firstname>Dorsa</firstname>
            <middlename></middlename>
            <lastname>Brevia</lastname>
            <roomnbr>408</roomnbr>
            <checkindate>6/18/2001</checkindate>
            <numnights>1</numnights>
            <preferred>Yes</preferred>
        </guest>
        <guest id="jgm9111447">
```

LISTING 10.3 Continued

```
            <firstname>Jackie</firstname>
            <middlename>G</middlename>
            <lastname>Mendelin</lastname>
            <roomnbr>223</roomnbr>
            <checkindate>6/15/2001</checkindate>
            <numnights>5</numnights>
            <preferred>No</preferred>
        </guest>
    </guests>
</hotel>
```

Compare the actual XML source, Listing 10.3, to the output in Figure 10.4.

FIGURE 10.4

XML file output to the console.

The XmlTextReader.ReadState property is a handy way to tell exactly what state the reader is currently in. You can use it to tell whether the reader has reached the end of the file, to see whether it is currently reading a node, or even whether it has been closed. The ReadState property returns an instance of a ReadState enumeration (see Table 10.2).

TABLE 10.2 The ReadState Enumeration

Name	Description
Closed	The reader has been closed through the XmlTextReader.Close method.
EndofFile	The reader has reached the end of the file (there are no more nodes to be processed).
Error	An error has occurred during a read; the read operation has been halted.
Initial	The reader has been instantiated but has not been primed with an initial Read call.
Interactive	The reader is currently reading a node (the Read method has been called).

This example gets us started. You have seen how to reference an XML document into our XmlTextReader through its class constructor. You also have seen how to use the Read method to advance through the document one node at a time, and how to use the ReadState property to interpret exactly what the reader is currently doing. Now, let's see what type of information we can retrieve about the specific node that we have read in.

Let's make a few modifications to the code.

Instead of using the ReadOuterXml method, let's truly parse this document node by node, printing out the pertinent node properties to the console along the way. Because the XmlTextReader class is constructed entirely around node-by-node access, many of its properties return information about the current node that has been read in through the Read method. Table 10.3 shows all the properties of the XmlTextReader class that are specific to the current node.

TABLE 10.3 XmlTextReader Properties Specific to the Current Node

Name	Description
AttributeCount	Returns the number of attributes defined on the current node
BaseURI	Returns the base URI string for the current node
Depth	Returns the depth of the current node in the overall XML document structure
Encoding	Returns the encoding attribute for the current node
HasAttributes	Returns a Boolean value indicating whether the current node has any attributes
HasValue	Returns a Boolean value indicating whether the current node has a value
IsDefault	Returns a Boolean value indicating whether the current node's value was derived as the result of using a default value specified in a DTD or XSD file

TABLE 10.3   Continued

Name	Description
IsEmptyElement	Returns a Boolean value indicating whether the current node is empty (devoid of data)
LocalName	Returns the name of the current node, minus any namespace prefixes (if any)
Name	Returns the fully qualified name of the current node, including any namespace prefixes (if any)
NodeType	Returns the type of the current node (XmlNodeType enumeration)
Prefix	Returns the namespace prefix of the current node
Value	Returns the text value of the current node

By including code inside our while loop (which is based on the Read method), we can examine the value of each of these properties and then write that value to the console. The new, revised code appears in Listing 10.4.

LISTING 10.4   Examining Node Properties

```
Imports System.Xml

Module dataReader

    Sub Main()
        Const fileName = "hotel_register.xml"

        Dim reader As XmlTextReader
        Dim keyPressed As Integer

        Try
            'Read in an XML file (location stored in fileName)
            reader = New XmlTextReader(fileName)
            Dim nodeType As XmlNodeType

            reader.WhitespaceHandling = WhitespaceHandling.None

            'Write each node in the file out to the console window:
            'The Read method tells the class to read in the next node
            'in the document; if there are no more nodes, it will return
            'false
            While reader.Read()

                Console.WriteLine("-------->Node: " & reader.Name)
```

LISTING 10.4   Continued

```
                Console.WriteLine("Type: " & _
                    nodeType.GetName(nodeType.GetType(), _
                reader.NodeType()))
                Console.WriteLine("Number of Attributes: " & _
                    reader.AttributeCount)
                Console.WriteLine("Depth in Document: " & reader.Depth)
                Console.WriteLine("Attributes?: " & reader.HasAttributes)
                Console.WriteLine("Value?: " & reader.HasValue)
                Console.WriteLine("Empty?: " & reader.IsEmptyElement)
                Console.WriteLine("Name: " & reader.Name)
                Console.WriteLine("Value: " & reader.Value)

            End While

        Catch xmlErr As XmlException
            'Catch instances of XmlException

            MsgBox("An XML error has occurred (" & xmlErr.Message & ")." & _
                vbCrLf & vbCrLf & "      Xml Source Line Nbr: " & _
                reader.LineNumber & vbCrLf & "      Xml Source Position: " & _
                reader.LinePosition)

        Catch appErr As Exception
            'Catch generic application exceptions

            MsgBox("An error occurred (" & appErr.Message & "). Stack info:" & _
                    appErr.StackTrace)

        End Try

        Console.WriteLine("<hit 'Enter' to exit>")
        Console.ReadLine()
    End Sub

End Module
```

When you run this code, you will get output similar to that shown in Figure 10.5. In this screenshot, you can see the start of a <guest> node.

In the code, you will notice that we use an enumeration to determine the element type. The XmlNodeType enumeration (documented for you in Table 10.4) is often a useful branching indicator when parsing a document. For instance, our parser might not care about comments, XML declarations, or processing instructions; we could choose to just ignore those types of nodes and process only nodes of type Element or CDATA. It also comes in handy in understanding how nodes are pieced together to form elements and other constructs. Peruse the output generated by the code in Listing 10.4—it will give you a much better understanding of how parsers view and treat each node.

FIGURE 10.5

Node properties output.

TABLE 10.4   The XmlNodeType Enumeration

Name	Description
Attribute	The node is an XML attribute. An Attribute node can have the following child node types: Text and EntityReference. The Attribute node does not appear as the child node of any other node type; note that it is not considered a child node of an Element.
CDATA	The node is a CDATA section. CDATA sections are used to escape blocks of text that would otherwise be recognized as markup. A CDATASection node cannot have any child nodes. The CDATASection node can appear as the child of the DocumentFragment, EntityReference, and Element nodes.
Comment	The node is a comment. A Comment node cannot have any child nodes. The Comment node can appear as the child of the Document, DocumentFragment, Element, and EntityReference nodes.

TABLE 10.4   Continued

Name	Description
Document	The node is a document object, which, as the root of the document tree, provides access to the entire XML document. A Document node can have the following child node types: Element (maximum of one), ProcessingInstruction, Comment, and DocumentType. The Document node cannot appear as the child of any node types.
DocumentFragment	The node is a document fragment. The DocumentFragment node associates a node or subtree with a document without actually being contained within the document. A DocumentFragment node can have the following child node types: Element, ProcessingInstruction, Comment, Text, CDATASection, and EntityReference. The DocumentFragment node cannot appear as the child of any node types.
DocumentType	The node is a document type declaration. A DocumentType node can have the following child node types: Notation and Entity. The DocumentType node can appear as the child of the Document node.
Element	The node is an Element. An Element node can have the following child node types: Element, Text, Comment, ProcessingInstruction, CDATA, and EntityReference. The Element node can be the child of the Document, DocumentFragment, EntityReference, and Element nodes.
EndElement	The node is an end-of-element node (such as </item>).
EndEntity	The node is an end-of-entity node (could be returned when XmlReader gets to the end of the entity replacement as a result of a call to ResolveEntity).
Entity	The node is an entity declaration. An Entity node can have child nodes that represent the expanded entity (for example, Text and EntityReference nodes). The Entity node can appear as the child of the DocumentType node.
EntityReference	The node is a reference to an entity. An EntityReference node can have the following child node types: Element, ProcessingInstruction, Comment, Text, CDATASection, and EntityReference. The EntityReference node can appear as the child of the Attribute, DocumentFragment, Element, and EntityReference nodes.

TABLE 10.4 Continued

Name	Description
None	The node is returned by the XmlReader if a Read method has not been called.
Notation	The node is a notation in the document type declaration. A Notation node cannot have any child nodes. The Notation node can appear as the child of the DocumentType node.
ProcessingInstruction	The node is a processing instruction (PI). A PI node cannot have any child nodes. The PI node can appear as the child of the Document, DocumentFragment, Element, and EntityReference nodes.
SignificantWhitespace	The node is whitespace between markup in a mixed-content model or whitespace within the xml:space= "preserve" scope.
Text	The node is the text content of an element. A Text node cannot have any child nodes. The Text node can appear as the child node of the Attribute, DocumentFragment, Element, and EntityReference nodes.
Whitespace	The node is whitespace between markup.
XmlDeclaration	The node is an XML declaration node. This has to be the first node in the document. It can have no children. It is a child of the root node. It can have attributes that provide version and encoding information.

Parsing Only the Important Stuff

The process of reading in XML documents a node at a time and then examining each node's XmlNodeType to see if it is relevant to the parsing activity is a laborious process. The XmlReader base class establishes two methods specifically designed to help ease the task of pinpointing actual data that you are interested in parsing.

The MoveToContent method is the first of these methods. It enables you to quickly move the scrolling node viewport to the next occurrence of a significant content node. In other words, it skips over and does not read the following types of nodes:

- Comments
- Processing instructions
- XML declarations
- DOCTYPE declarations

Because these items are rarely needed by your actual parsing algorithm, ignoring them automatically by using the MoveToContent method is an efficient way to get at core data in the XML document.

The second way that you can efficiently ignore irrelevant XML markups is through the use of XmlReader.Skip. The Skip method enables you to jump from element to element instead of from node to node. Let's examine a snippet from our hotel_register.xml file:

```xml
<guest id="jlk0910211">
    <firstname>Jim</firstname>
    <middlename>L</middlename>
    <lastname>Kelley</lastname>
    <roomnbr>295</roomnbr>
    <checkindate>6/17/2001</checkindate>
    <numnights>4</numnights>
    <preferred>No</preferred>
</guest>
<guest id="nlt0000704">
    <firstname>Nadia</firstname>
    <middlename>L</middlename>
    <lastname>Tatonovich</lastname>
    <roomnbr>615</roomnbr>
    <checkindate>6/17/2001</checkindate>
    <numnights>4</numnights>
    <preferred>No</preferred>
</guest>
```

If we were reading in this file using XmlTextReader.Read, we would visit each node in turn until the end of the document. If we wanted only a certain guest, however, it would be easier to skip over the entire <guest> element to get to the next one if the guest doesn't have the ID we are looking for. If we were specifically interested only in the guest record with the ID of nlt0000704 and we had just read in the node <guest id="jlk0910211">, we could immediately skip to the next guest record by calling Skip. Listing 10.5 shows a revision to our previous code that iterated through each node. By using the Skip method, we jump over entire elements at a time until we arrive at the specific node that we want, which is then printed to the console (see Figure 10.6).

LISTING 10.5   Skipping Nodes

```vb
Imports System.Xml

Module dataReader

    Sub Main()
        Const fileName = "hotel_register.xml"
```

LISTING 10.5 Continued

```
Dim reader As XmlTextReader
Dim keyPressed As Integer

Try
    'Read in an XML file (location stored in fileName)
    reader = New XmlTextReader(fileName)
    Dim nodeType As XmlNodeType

    reader.WhitespaceHandling = WhitespaceHandling.None

    'Write each node in the file out to the console window:
    'The Read method tells the class to read in the next node
    'in the document; if there are no more nodes, it will return
    'false

    'Move to the content nodes
    reader.MoveToContent()

    'Parse the file starting with the second book node.
    While reader.Read()
        'We are only interested in element start tags...
        If reader.NodeType = XmlNodeType.Element And reader.Name = _
            "guest" Then
            Do
                If reader.GetAttribute("id") = "d b6620103" Then
                    Console.WriteLine("Guest record found at line " _
                    & reader.LineNumber & "...")
                    Console.WriteLine("Type: " & _
                    nodeType.GetName(nodeType.GetType(), _
                        reader.NodeType()))
                    Console.WriteLine("Number of Attributes: " & _
                    reader.AttributeCount)
                    Console.WriteLine("Depth in Document: " & _
                        reader.Depth)
                    Console.WriteLine("Attributes?: " & _
                        reader.HasAttributes)
                    Console.WriteLine("Value?: " & reader.HasValue)
                    Console.WriteLine("Empty?: " & _
                        reader.IsEmptyElement)
                    Console.WriteLine("Name: " & reader.Name)
                    Exit While
                Else
                    reader.Skip()
```

Listing 10.5 Continued

```
                End If
            Loop
        End If
    End While

Catch xmlErr As XmlException
    'Catch instances of XmlException

    MsgBox("An XML error has occurred (" & xmlErr.Message & ")." & _
        vbCrLf & vbCrLf & "      Xml Source Line Nbr: " & _
        reader.LineNumber & vbCrLf & "      Xml Source Position: " & _
        reader.LinePosition)

Catch appErr As Exception
    'Catch generic application exceptions

    MsgBox("An error occurred (" & appErr.Message & "). Stack info:" & _
            appErr.StackTrace)

Finally
    If Not (reader Is Nothing) Then
        reader.Close()
    End If

End Try

Console.WriteLine("<hit 'Enter' to exit>")
Console.ReadLine()
    End Sub

End Module
```

Using the XmlTextReader is a great way to quickly run through an XML document because it is specifically optimized for speed. Its disadvantage lies in its forward-only nature. It doesn't facilitate hopping around an XML document, forward and backward. An alternative approach to parsing XML documents revolves around the XmlDocument class.

FIGURE 10.6
The Skip *output.*

Parsing XML Document Trees

The XmlDocument class abstracts XML documents through a tree representation in memory. You can traverse this tree in a forward or backward manner, or you can jump to any node directly. Let's look at how you would go about reading an XML file into this in-memory tree. In the code that follows, we create our XmlTextReader and then immediately pass it into an XmlDocument object through the XmlDocument.Load method:

```
Dim reader As XmlTextReader
reader = New XmlTextReader("test.xml")
Dim document As XmlDataDocument = New XmlDocument()
document.Load(reader)
```

When the XML file is loaded into the XmlDocument object, you can traverse the nodes by using instances of the XmlNode class. The XmlNode class represents individual nodes in a document and has methods available to move from node to node. If we wanted to process the tree from the top down, we would first set our current node to the document's root. This is called the document element, and a reference to it is returned through the XmlDocument.DocumentElement property (we touched on the concept of a document element earlier in the chapter in our discussion of elements).

```
Dim startNode As XmlNode
startNode = document.DocumentElement
```

Now, we can set up a loop to run through all the children of the document root. If we are careful in the way we approach this, we can even set up a recursive routine to parse through the nodes like this:

```
Public Sub RecurseNodes(currNode As XmlNode)
    If node.HasChildNodes Then
        currNode = currNode.FirstChild
```

```
        While Not IsNothing(currNode)
            RecurseNodes(currNode)
            currNode  = currNode.NextSibling
        End While
    End If
End sub
```

In this code, we accept an instance of the XmlNode class and first determine whether it has any
children nodes. We then assign the current node instance to be the first child of itself. Now the
recursive part comes into play: We then pass this new node reference into the RecurseNodes
routine again. Finally, we move on to the next sibling node by using the XmlNode.NextSibling
method call.

> **NOTE**
>
> A node is said to be a sibling to another node if they are both immediate children of
> the same parent node in the tree structure of the document. In our hotel_register.xml
> file, all the <guest> nodes are siblings to one another.

By using the FirstChild, ParentNode, and NextSibling properties on the XmlNode class, we
can navigate through the document using the parent and child relationships inherent in its
structure. See Listing 10.6 for an example of navigating through nodes. The following revision
of the previous console application displays the parent-child relationships in the XML
document.

LISTING 10.6   Navigating Nodes

```
Imports System.Xml

Module dataReader

    Sub Main()
        'Path and name of the XML file to parse
        Const fileName = "..\hotel_register.xml"

        'XmlTextReader is our principal engine to read
        'the XML file
        Dim reader As XmlTextReader

        Try
            'Read in an XML file (location stored in fileName)
            reader = New XmlTextReader(fileName)
```

LISTING 10.6 Continued

```vb
        'don't want any whitespace processed
        reader.WhitespaceHandling = WhitespaceHandling.None

        'This is the object that builds an in-memory tree
        'of the XML document
        Dim document As XmlDataDocument = New XmlDataDocument()

        'The XmlDocument object is loaded by using the reader
        'object
        document.Load(reader)

        'We want to explicitly start at the outermost "root"
        'node of the document
        Dim startNode As XmlNode
        startNode = document.DocumentElement

        'Recurse through all of the nodes
        RecurseNodes(startNode)

    Catch xmlErr As XmlException
        'Catch instances of XmlException

        MsgBox("An XML error has occurred (" & xmlErr.Message & ")." & _
            vbCrLf & vbCrLf & "      Xml Source Line Nbr: " & _
            reader.LineNumber & vbCrLf & "      Xml Source Position: " & _
            reader.LinePosition)

    Catch appErr As Exception
        'Catch generic application exceptions

        MsgBox("An error occurred (" & appErr.Message & "). Stack info:" & _
                appErr.StackTrace)
    Finally
        If Not (reader Is Nothing) Then
            reader.Close()
        End If

        Console.ReadLine()
    End Try


End Sub
```

LISTING 10.6   Continued

```
Public Sub RecurseNodes(ByVal currNode As XmlNode)

    'this holds the lineage for each element
    Dim tree As String

    'temp storage of the currNode
    Dim tempNode As XmlNode
    tempNode = currNode

    'If there is a parent node to the current node...
    If Not IsNothing(tempNode.ParentNode) Then

        'Reach back through all of its parents,
        'building a string that shows us the
        'lineage
        While Not IsNothing(tempNode.ParentNode)
            tree = GetLineage(tempNode) & tree
            tempNode = tempNode.ParentNode
        End While

        'Write the lineage out to the console
        Console.WriteLine(tree)
    Else
        'If there are not parents, just write out the
        'name of the current node
        Console.WriteLine(tempNode.Name)
    End If

    'If the current node has children...
    If currNode.HasChildNodes Then

        'go to the first child...
        currNode = currNode.FirstChild

        'While we still have nodes to work with,
        'call back into this sub
        While Not IsNothing(currNode)
            RecurseNodes(currNode)

            'Move to the next sibling node
            currNode = currNode.NextSibling

        End While
    End If
```

LISTING 10.6 Continued

```
    End Sub

    Public Function GetLineage(ByVal currNode As XmlNode) As String

        'Get the name of the node that is a parent to the current
        'node and return it through the function
        GetLineage = "->" & currNode.ParentNode.Name
    End Function
End Module
```

Figure 10.7 shows the output from this applet. Each node in the document is displayed along with its ancestry (a list of all the parent nodes).

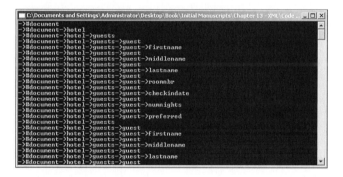

FIGURE 10.7
Parent-child lineage from the XmlDocument *class.*

Just like the XmlTextReader class, the XmlNode class exposes a NodeType property that can tell you which type of node you are dealing with (in conjunction with the XmlNodeType enumeration—refer back to Table 10.4).

There is also a way to return nodes by name by using the GetElementsByTagName method. The XmlDocument.GetElementsByTagName method is handy because it returns an instance of an XmlNodeList class, which has a list of node entities matching a tag name (which you pass to the method). The following code returns a node list of all nodes matching the tag name product. It then processes each of the nodes contained in the XmlNodeList object and writes out their XML content:

```
Dim doc As New XmlDocument()
doc.Load("inventory.xml")
```

```
Dim nodes As XmlNodeList = doc.GetElementsByTagName("product")
Dim i As Integer
For i = 0 To nodes.Count - 1
   Console.WriteLine(nodes(i).InnerXml)
Next I
```

If we had a requirement to extract all the <guest> elements from the hotel_register.xml document, this would be quite easy to implement using the XmlNodeList returned by this method. In Listing 10.7, we first load our familiar hotel_register.xml file into an XmlDocument instance, and then we place a call to GetElementsByTagName, passing in the tag name of guest. The application then writes out the XML contained by each of the guest elements to the console.

LISTING 10.7   Parsing Elements by Their Tag Name

```
Imports System.Xml

Module dataReader

    Sub Main()
        Const fileName = "hotel_register.xml"
        Dim xmlDoc As New XmlDocument()

        Try
            'simple var for our loop into the node list
            Dim i As Integer

            'to do "pretty-printing" of the element XML, we will
            'want the XmlDocument instance to preserve the whitespace
            'of the source document
            xmlDoc.PreserveWhitespace = True

            'load the XML file into the XmlDocument instance
            xmlDoc.Load(fileName)

            'get the node list of all nodes matching the tag name "guest"
            Dim nodes As XmlNodeList = xmlDoc.GetElementsByTagName("guest")

            'For each node returned in the XmlNodeList instance,
            'write out its XML content to the console
            For i = 0 To nodes.Count - 1
                Console.WriteLine(nodes(i).InnerXml)
            Next i

            'Catch any thrown exceptions and display an error dialog...
        Catch e As Exception
```

LISTING 10.7 Continued

```
        MsgBox("An error occurred (" & e.Message & "). Stack info:" & _
            e.StackTrace)
    End Try

    Console.WriteLine("<hit 'Enter' to exit>")
    Console.ReadLine()
  End Sub

End Module
```

The console output is presented in Figure 10.8.

FIGURE 10.8

Parsing elements by their tag name.

Mapping to the W3C DOM

The XmlNodeList class is a part of what the W3C considers a fundamental base class for XML support. The XmlDocument class and its brethren are actually a fairly direct implementation of the W3C concept of the XML Document Object Model (DOM). The W3C DOM specification breaks up XML functionality into two categories: those things that are absolutely needed to parse and write XML, and those that aren't needed but are helpful (that is, they make the developer's job easier). These two categories are referred to as *fundamental* and *extended*, respectively. The .NET Framework Class Library has support for both fundamental structures and extended structures. Table 10.5 lists the Framework classes considered to be fundamental;

Table 10.6 lists those considered to be extended. Developers already familiar with programming against the W3C DOM should be very comfortable with using these classes.

TABLE 10.5 DOM Fundamental Classes in the Framework

Class Name	Description
XmlNode	A representation of a node in an XML document
XmlNodeList	A representation of a collection of nodes in an XML document
XmlNamedNodeMap	A representation of a collection of nodes in an XML document; can be accessed directly by node name

TABLE 10.6 DOM Extended Classes in the Framework

Class Name	Description
XmlDocument	A representation of the top node and all children nodes of an XML document
XmlAttribute	A representation of an XML element attribute
XmlAttributeCollection	A representation of a collection of attributes associated with an XML element
XmlCDataSection	A representation of a CDATA section in an XML document
XmlCharacterData	A class used to support various text-manipulation operations; principally a utility class used by other classes in the System.Xml namespace
XmlComment	A representation of a comment in an XML document
XmlDeclaration	A representation of an XML declaration in an XML document
XmlDocumentFragment	A representation of a portion of an XML document
XmlDocumentType	A representation of a DOCTYPE declaration in an XML document
XmlElement	A representation of an element in an XML document
XmlEntity	—
XmlEntityReference	—
XmlImplementation	—
XmlLinkedNode	A representation of a node in an XML document that immediately precedes or follows the referenced node
XmlNotation	A representation of a notation declaration inside a DTD or XSD file

Table 10.6 Continued

Class Name	Description
XmlNamedNodeMap	A representation of a collection of nodes in an XML document; can be accessed directly by node name
XmlProcessingInstruction	A representation of a processing instruction in an XML document
XmlSignificantWhitespace	A representation of whitespace in an element or attribute
XmlText	A representation of the text content of an element or attribute

Introducing the XmlNodeReader Class

The XmlNodeReader class is very similar to the XmlTextReader class—something that isn't so surprising when you consider that they share the same parent class. Like XmlTextReader, the XmlNodeReader class allows for forward-only, noncached traversal of XML; where they differ is in their source. The XmlNodeReader is implemented across the node of an existing XmlDocument instance. Creating a node reader instance will look familiar to you. First, we instance an XmlDocument object and load a file into it. Then we pass the XmlDocument instance into the constructor for the XmlNodeReader object:

```
'Create an XmlNodeReader to read the XmlDocument.
Dim doc As New XmlDocument()
doc.Load(filename)
reader = New XmlNodeReader(doc)
```

There is a fairly even match between the properties and methods supported on both the XmlTextReader class and the XmlNodeReader class—so why would you use XmlNodeReader objects? Remember that instances of XmlDocument are in-memory representations of XML documents. If you have an extremely large XML document, this can prove to be problematic in terms of resource usage. In those cases, the XmlTextReader is the optimal solution because the XML document is not represented in memory at all; operations are conducted as straight read operations from a file or a stream.

 Suggestions for Further Exploration

⟳ The XmlReader class, while serving as a base class for the .NET Framework, can also serve as a base class for your own code constructs. Investigate the Framework documentation on the actual XmlReader class to see what it provides you in terms of base functionality; you might want to implement your own class to deal with XML that is not coming from a source that the .NET classes recognize.

10

➲ We have talked about parsing discrete pieces from an XML document, but if you need to actually query an XML document, you will need to dig into the System.Xml.Xpath namespace. It supports the XPath standards for querying XML documents and returning nodes as data.

Writing XML Documents

To programmatically create and write XML documents, the System.XML namespace provides the XmlTextWriter class.

Reader and Writer Similarities

Before we dig into the guts of writing XML, let's first quickly visit the similarities between the writer class and its reader siblings.

For one, XmlTextWriter is a concrete class that inherits from an abstract parent class called XmlWriter (refer back to Figure 10.3). In a similar manner to XmlReader, the XmlWriter class implements a base set of functionality that can be aggregated through inheritance to implement specialized writers.

Like XmlTextReader, the XmlTextWriter exposes a state property, WriteState, which you can use to query the current state of the writer. XmlTextWriter.WriteState returns a WriteState enumeration. Table 10.7 shows the possible WriteState values.

TABLE 10.7   The WriteState Enumeration

Name	Description
Attribute	The writer currently is writing an element attribute.
Closed	The writer has been closed through a call to the Close method.
Content	The writer currently is writing the content of an element.
Element	The writer currently is writing an element start tag.
Prolog	The writer currently is writing the XML document's prolog section.
Start	The writer has been instantiated, but none of the write methods have been called yet.

Now that the stage is set, let's see how to write a simple XML file.

Creating a Simple XML Document

The first step in writing an XML document is to determine where the document will go. In other words, will you be writing the document to a file? To a stream? The XmlTextWriter constructor is overloaded to give you three different options for specifying the output channel for the XML document. Here are their definitions:

```
Public Sub New(ByVal filename As String, encoding As Encoding)
Public Sub New(ByVal w As Stream, encoding As Encoding)
Public Sub New(ByVal w As TextWriter)
```

You can see that, in addition to the file and stream outputs, you have the option to specify a `TextWriter` instance. This turns out to be a very powerful feature. The `TextWriter` class, in the `System.IO` namespace, is an abstract class designed to allow for any possible text output. The Framework already implements a few customized writers for HTTP and HTML; others can be created from the `TextWriter` base class. In this way, the options for XML output are bound only by what can be implemented using the `TextWriter` class. See Chapter 6, "Font, Text, and Printing Operations," for more information.

After you have specified what form the output will take, you can begin to write into that output channel. As expected, `XmlTextWriter` exposes a vast spectrum of write methods to handle all the different node types. In fact, out of the 30 different methods implemented in the class (whether inherited from `XmlWriter` or newly implemented), all but three of them are actual methods that write XML. Most of these write methods are specialized to write specific XML nodes or elements. In addition to these dedicated tag writers, one method enables you to write raw text into the XML document (`WriteRaw`), and one enables you to "copy" a node from an instance of an XML reader (`WriteNode`). Table 10.8 presents all the pertinent methods and their descriptions.

TABLE 10.8 `XmlTextWriter` Methods for Generation of XML

Name	Description
WriteAttributes	Writes out any attributes located at the current node of an associated reader object
WriteAttributeString	Writes out an attribute and value
WriteBase64	Encodes bytes in Base64 and then writes out the result
WriteBinHex	Encodes bytes as binhex and then writes out the result
WriteCData	Writes out a CDATA block with the supplied text
WriteCharEntity	Writes out a character entity with the supplied text
WriteChars	Writes out characters to the output channel
WriteComment	Writes out a comment containing the supplied text
WriteDocType	Writes out a DOCTYPE declaration with the supplied name and attributes
WriteElementString	Writes out an element with the supplied text
WriteEndAttribute	Writes out the end of an attribute (used in conjunction with WriteStartAttribute)

TABLE 10.8   Continued

Name	Description
WriteEndDocument	Writes out closing tags for any currently open tags, leaving the writer in the Start state
WriteEndElement	Writes out the closing tags for an element (used in conjunction with WriteStartElement)
WriteEntityRef	Writes out an entity reference
WriteFullEndElement	Same as WriteEndElement
WriteName	Writes out the supplied text as a name that corresponds to the XML specification
WriteNmToken	Same as WriteName
WriteNode	Copies an entire node from an associated reader; advances the reader to the next sibling
WriteProcessingInstruction	Writes out a processing instruction
WriteQualifiedName	Writes out a namespace qualified name
WriteRaw	Writes raw XML into the output channel
WriteStartAttribute	Writes out the start of an attribute
WriteStartDocument	Writes out the XML declaration
WriteStartElement	Writes out an opening tag for an element (used in conjunction with WriteEndElement)
WriteString	Writes out the supplied text to the output channel
WriteSurrogateCharEntity	Generates and writes out the surrogate character entity for the surrogate character pair (see http://www.w3.org/TR/REC-xml#charsets)
WriteWhitespace	Writes out whitespace

To see this in action, let's write a simple (but slightly meaningless) program that reads in an XML file using XmlTextReader and then writes it back out, a node at a time, using XmlTextWriter (see Listing 10.8).

The first step is to set up a loop that runs through the entire source XML file. For each node encountered, the program will examine the type of node and its various properties and will execute the appropriate write method. After having processed the file, it should be easy to tell whether we have gotten the XmlTextWriter code right: The files should be visibly identical to one another.

LISTING 10.8   Writing an XML File

```
Imports System.Xml

Module dataReaderWriter

    Sub Main()
        Const FILE_NAME_IN = "..\hotel_register.xml"
        Const FILE_NAME_OUT = "..\hotel_register_out.xml"

        Dim reader As XmlTextReader
        Dim writer As XmlTextWriter

        'Used in the For loop to get attributes...
        Dim i As System.Int32

        Try
            'Read in an XML file (location stored in fileName)
            reader = New XmlTextReader(FILE_NAME_IN)

            'Spin up a new writer, pointed at the file in FILE_NAME_OUT;
            'the same encoding sensed by the reader will be used to write
            'the new file
            writer = New XmlTextWriter(FILE_NAME_OUT, reader.Encoding)

            'Ignore whitespaces
            reader.WhitespaceHandling = WhitespaceHandling.None

            'Not necessary, but this will make the resulting XML
            'file easier on the eyes...
            writer.Formatting = Formatting.Indented

            Console.WriteLine("Starting read operations on " & FILE_NAME_IN _
                & "...")

            'Loop through the source file; for each different node type
            'encountered, call the corresponding write method off the writer
            'object. The goal here is a carbon copy of the source file. If a
            'node type is encountered, the user will be notified via the
            'console. Try experimenting on your own XML documents. Where the
            'code encounters a node type that isn't handled in the Select Case,
            'try adding it in with the appropriate writer method.
            While reader.Read()
```

LISTING 10.8   Continued

```
        Select Case reader.NodeType
            Case XmlNodeType.XmlDeclaration
                Console.WriteLine("Writing: start of document")
                writer.WriteStartDocument(False)

            Case XmlNodeType.Comment
                writer.WriteComment(reader.Value)

            Case XmlNodeType.Element
                Console.WriteLine("Writing: start of element -> '" _
                    & reader.Name & "'")
                writer.WriteStartElement(reader.Name)

                If reader.HasAttributes Then
                    For i = 0 To reader.AttributeCount - 1
                        reader.MoveToAttribute(i)
                        writer.WriteAttributeString(reader.Name, _
                            reader.Value)
                    Next
                End If

            Case XmlNodeType.Text
                Console.WriteLine("Writing: element content -> '" _
                    & reader.Value & "'")
                writer.WriteString(reader.Value)

            Case XmlNodeType.EndElement
                Console.WriteLine("Writing: end of element -> '" & _
                    reader.Name _
                    & "'")
                writer.WriteEndElement()

            Case Else
                Console.WriteLine("!!!An un-handled node type was _
                    encountered:" & reader.NodeType)
        End Select

    End While

    'Close the reader
    reader.Close()

    'Close up the writer
```

LISTING 10.8 Continued

```
            writer.WriteEndDocument()
            writer.Close()

        Catch xmlErr As XmlException
            'Catch instances of XmlException

            MsgBox("An XML error has occurred (" & xmlErr.Message & ")." & _
                vbCrLf & vbCrLf & "       Xml Source Line Nbr: " & _
                reader.LineNumber & vbCrLf & "      Xml Source Position: " & _
                reader.LinePosition)

        Catch appErr As Exception
            'Catch generic application exceptions

            MsgBox("An error occurred (" & appErr.Message & "). Stack info:" & _
                      appErr.StackTrace)

        End Try

        Console.WriteLine("<hit 'Enter' to exit>")
        Console.ReadLine()
    End Sub

End Module
```

Most of this code should be self-explanatory. However, a few pieces deserve a closer look.

In the `Select Case` statement, if the node is a start element node, we also have to deal with the possibility that the start element tag will have attributes that we must write out. There are two ways of doing this. In Listing 10.8, we have used the `WriteAttribute` method. This writes out a textual name value pair to the specified document. An alternative, and arguably easier, way is to use the `WriteAttributes` method. The `WriteAttributes` method is designed to work in conjunction with a reader object, and it behaves in different ways depending on where the reader is currently positioned. If the reader is positioned at a start element tag, it will write out any and all attributes and then close the tag. In other words, we would have replaced that `Select Case` element with this:

```
Case XmlNodeType.Element
    Console.WriteLine("Writing: start of element -> '" & reader.Name _
        & "'")
    writer.WriteStartElement(reader.Name)
```

10

```
    If reader.HasAttributes Then
        writer.WriteAttributes(reader, False)
    End If

.

.

.
```

The second parameter supplied to the reader is a Boolean value that indicates whether to write any default attributes that might be attached to the XML document.

The second item that can't be discerned from a simple examination of the code is how the `XmlTextWriter.Close` method works. This method closes out the document (and thus the file, stream, and so on) that the writer was working on. But you should know that it also automatically closes out any open-ended tags by writing out their end element tags for you. That means that if you left the document in a state like this

```
<parent>
    <child>
```

and then called `Close`, the document would actually look like this:

```
<parent>
    <child>
    </child>
</parent>
```

Now that we have a grasp of the mechanics for reading and writing XML documents, we can move on to examining how XML documents can be validated. Validation implies that a schema exists that will describe the content of a particular XML document, so that is where we will start our discussion.

XML Schemas

Because XML documents adhere to a specific schema, or layout, it is often desirable to verify that a particular XML document remains true to the schema that it is supposed to follow. Having the capability to define a schema externally to an XML document allows XML as a technology and a language to continue further than other markup languages such as HTML.

What do we mean when we say that schemas can be defined externally? Well, one of the things that makes XML so well suited to data descriptions is this: The actual tags for XML are not defined in the XML specification. This means that XML can behave as a *metalanguage*. Metalanguages can be used to define other languages. This neatly side-steps the problem of being locked into a specific tag set. Regardless of how large a predefined tag set is, it will never satisfy everyone's needs regarding structuring data.

The capability for XML documents to define their own multiple tag sets is an important differentiator from the other markup languages that we have discussed. XML documents can define their tags through yet another document—this second document contains the schema to which the first document must adhere. A few different standards define what this schema document does and what its syntax looks like.

The XML classes in the .NET Framework support Document Type Definitions (DTD), XML Schema Documents (XSDs), and XML-Data Reduced Language schemas (XDRs). This section examines each of these in turn and then walks through the Framework support for validating XML documents against each.

DTD Documents

We'll start our look at XML schema descriptions with the DTD. Here, we have assembled a short DTD file:

```
<!ELEMENT books (book)*>
<!ELEMENT book (title, chapters, summary, price)>
<!ELEMENT title (#PCDATA)>
<!ELEMENT chapters (chapter)*>
<!ELEMENT chapter (#PCDATA)>
<!ELEMENT summary (#PCDATA)>
<!ELEMENT price (#PCDATA)>
```

This is a DTD that a publishing company might use. It defines the structure for an XML document that will describe books. The syntax might look a little strange, but it should be easy to see what the intent of the different pieces is. Of course, the DTD—which is just a plain text file—follows rules of its own. The DTD rules are part of the actual W3C XML specification.

An XML document that adheres to the previous DTD (let's call it books.dtd) would look something like this:

```
<!DOCTYPE books SYSTEM "book.dtd">
<books>
    <book>
        <title>VB.NET Unleashed</title>
        <chapters>
            <chapter>Introduction</chapter>
            <chapter>The New IDE</chapter>
            <chapter>...</chapter>
        </chapters>
        <summary> blah blah blah </summary>
        <price>59.99</price>
    </book>
</books>
```

If you closely examine this XML document, you can start to make a tie back to the concepts of specifications versus tag usage rules. The XML specification says that we must enclose our tags in < and > characters (as you can see with <books>); the DTD tells us that the <name>, <chapters>, <summary>, and <price> tags are contained within the <book> tag.

Because the DTD used in a particular XML document can vary from document to document, the XML specification provides syntax for indicating which DTD defines the structure of the XML document. This is the DOCTYPE declaration that we visited earlier in this chapter when we discussed the anatomy of an XML document—and that we now see as the first line in our XML document snippet.

XSD and XDR Documents

DTDs, while powerful enough in their capability to impose structure, do have their limitations. For one thing, you can't specify a data type for attributes. You cannot, for instance, specify that "price" should be a decimal number, or that "title" should be a string. DTDs also introduce an element of complexity into the design of XML applications because they require you to know yet another set of rules—those that define the actually allowed syntax inside a DTD file.

There is a solution to this: XML schemas. XML schemas are meant to replace DTDs as a mechanism for specifying structure in an XML document. They offer a few advantages over DTDs because they allow for the typing of attributes and because they are expressed, themselves, in XML.

XSD files share the same goal as DTDs: They are used to describe a schema used by XML documents. But XSDs offer a much cleaner approach to the problem of describing XML structure: Instead of using a "custom" syntax (as we have seen in the DTD), the XSD is itself XML. Listing 10.9 shows the same DTD that you glimpsed previously, this time in XSD format.

LISTING 10.9   books.dtd Expressed as an XSD Document

```
<?xml version="1.0" encoding="utf-8"?>
<xsd:schema id="Schema" targetNamespace="" xmlns="" _
    xmlns:xsd="http://www.w3.org/2001/XMLSchema" _
    xmlns:msdata="urn:schemas-microsoft-com:xml-msdata">
  <xsd:element name="Schema">
    <xsd:complexType>
      <xsd:choice maxOccurs="unbounded">
        <xsd:element name="books">
          <xsd:complexType>
            <xsd:sequence>
              <xsd:element name="book" minOccurs="0" maxOccurs="unbounded">
                <xsd:complexType>
```

LISTING 10.9 Continued

```
                    <xsd:sequence>
                      <xsd:element name="title" type="xsd:string" _
                          minOccurs="0" msdata:Ordinal="0" />
                      <xsd:element name="summary" type="xsd:string" _
                          minOccurs="0" msdata:Ordinal="1" />
                      <xsd:element name="price" type="xsd:string" _
                          minOccurs="0" msdata:Ordinal="2" />
                      <xsd:element name="chapters" minOccurs="0" _
                          maxOccurs="unbounded">
                        <xsd:complexType>
                          <xsd:sequence>
                            <xsd:element name="chapter" maxOccurs="unbounded" _
                                minOccurs="0">
                              <xsd:complexType>
                                <xsd:attribute name="chapters_Id" _
                                    type="xsd:int" use="prohibited" />
                              </xsd:complexType>
                            </xsd:element>
                          </xsd:sequence>
                          <xsd:attribute name="chapters_Id" _
                              msdata:AutoIncrement="true" type="xsd:int" _
                              msdata:AllowDBNull="false" use="prohibited" />
                          <xsd:attribute name="book_Id" type="xsd:int" _
                              use="prohibited" />
                        </xsd:complexType>
                      </xsd:element>
                    </xsd:sequence>
                    <xsd:attribute name="book_Id" msdata:AutoIncrement="true" _
                        type="xsd:int" msdata:AllowDBNull="false" _
                        use="prohibited" />
                    <xsd:attribute name="books_Id" type="xsd:int" _
                        use="prohibited" />
                  </xsd:complexType>
                </xsd:element>
              </xsd:sequence>
              <xsd:attribute name="books_Id" msdata:AutoIncrement="true" _
                  type="xsd:int" msdata:AllowDBNull="false" use="prohibited" />
          </xsd:complexType>
        </xsd:element>
      </xsd:choice>
    </xsd:complexType>
  </xsd:element>
</xsd:schema>
```

XSD commonly is referred to simply as XML schemas.

The XSD specification is a more sophisticated descendant of the XDR specification. The XDR format started life at Microsoft. It was this format that was later adopted and extensively extended by the W3C to create the XSD format standard. In principle, the XDR format most likely will be phased out in favor of the XSD format, but the XML classes are "aware" of both. As a reference point, Listing 10.10 again shows our book DTD document. In this incarnation, it follows the XDR format.

LISTING 10.10   books.dtd as an XDR Document

```
<Schema name="BOOKS" xmlns="urn:schemas-microsoft-com:xml-data">
    <ElementType name="name" content="textOnly"/>
        <ElementType name="chapter" content="textOnly"/>
        <ElementType name="chapters" content="eltOnly" model="closed">
            <element type="chapter" maxOccurs="*"/>
        </ElementType>
         <ElementType name="summary" content="textOnly"/>
        <ElementType name="price" content="textOnly"/>
        <ElementType name="book" content="eltOnly" model="closed"/>
            <element type="title"/>
            <element type="chapters"/>
            <element type="summary"/>
            <element type="price"/>
        </ElementType>
        <ElementType name="books" content="eltOnly" model="closed">
            <element type="book" maxOccurs="*"/>
        </ElementType>
    </ElementType>
</Schema>
```

> **NOTE**
>
> Although we can't recommend using XDR as your schema format, you might have some significant work already invested in that precursor to the XSD format. Microsoft provides a utility—distributed along with the .NET Framework SDK—called XSD.exe. It accepts an XDR file as input and writes out an equivalent XSD file:
>
> ```
> xsd.exe <schema.xdr> [/outputdir:]
> ```
>
> This handy utility also can generate XSD schemas from .NET assemblies and XML documents.

In an XML file, you can reference an XDR or XSD schema by using the following syntax:

```
<HeadCount xmlns='x-schema:books.xdr'>
```

This directs any schema-aware parser to the source schema document used to structure the XML document.

Both XSD files and XDR files enable you to define new attribute types in addition to just specifying the order and relationship between elements of an XML file. Consider this revised XML file that describes a book. Note that, in the line where we begin the actual book node, we have added an attribute to the node called ISBN.

```
<books>
    <book ISBN="xxxxxxxx">
        <title>VB.NET Unleashed</name>
        <chapter>Introduction</chapter>
        <chapter>The New IDE</chapter>
        <chapter>...</chapter>
        <abstract> blah blah blah </summary>
        <price>59.99</price>
    </book>
</books>
```

We now can define this attribute, which lives inside the book tag, by doing this inside our XSD:

```
<AttributeType name="ISBN" dt:type="string" required="yes"/>
```

We have just created a brand new attribute type; this new attribute type is of the string data type, and must be included everywhere that it is referenced in association with an element. Integrating this into our XSD results in this:

```
<Schema name="BOOK" xmlns="urn:schemas-microsoft-com:xml-data">
    <AttributeType name="ISBN" dt:type="string" required="yes"/>
    <ElementType name="name" content="textOnly"/>
    <ElementType name="chapter" content="textOnly"/>
    <ElementType name="chapters" content="eltOnly" model="closed">
        <element type="chapter" maxOccurs="*"/>
    </ElementType>
    <ElementType name="summary" content="textOnly"/>
    <ElementType name="price" content="textOnly"/>
    <ElementType name="book" content="eltOnly" model="closed"/>
        <attribute type="ISBN"/>
        <element type="title"/>
        <element type="chapters"/>
        <element type="summary"/>
        <element type="price"/>
    </ElementType>
    <ElementType name="books" content="eltOnly" model="closed">
        <element type="book" maxOccurs="*"/>
    </ElementType>
</Schema>
```

Programmatically Building Schemas

The System.Xml.Schema namespace contains classes that enable you to build, edit, read, and write XML schema files. At the core of this namespace lies the XmlSchema class. This class encapsulates the definition of a schema. The namespace also contains a bevy of classes used to represent the different types of XML elements that can exist inside an XML schema document (such as complex types, sequences, and groups).

> **NOTE**
>
> The System.Xml.Schema namespace implements .NET's XML Schema Object Model (SOM). The SOM is essentially a Document Object Model specifically designed to implement XML Schemas. The classes in the SOM directly correspond to the specifications laid out in the W3C's XML Schema Recommendation (visit http://www.w3.org for more information).

To explore the capabilities of the schema classes that the .NET Framework Class Library provides, let's revisit our hotel registration scenario. An XSD that would describe the hotel_register.xml document is presented in Listing 10.11. To refresh your memory on what the hotel registration XML document looks like, refer back to Listing 10.3.

LISTING 10.11   An XSD Schema for the Hotel Register XML Document

```
<xsd:schema xmlns:xsd="http://www.w3.org/2001/XMLSchema" _
    attributeFormDefault="qualified" elementFormDefault="qualified">
  <xsd:element name="hotel">
    <xsd:complexType>
      <xsd:sequence>
        <xsd:element name="guests" minOccurs="0" maxOccurs="unbounded">
          <xsd:complexType>
            <xsd:sequence>
              <xsd:element name="guest" minOccurs="0" maxOccurs="unbounded">
                <xsd:complexType>
                  <xsd:sequence>
                    <xsd:element name="firstname" type="xsd:string"
                            minOccurs="0" />
                        <xsd:element name="middlename" _
                            type="xsd:string"
                          minOccurs="0" />
                        <xsd:element name="lastname" _
                            type="xsd:string"
                          minOccurs="0" />
                        <xsd:element name="roomnbr" type="xsd:string"
```

LISTING 10.11 Continued

```
                        minOccurs="0" />
                        <xsd:element name="checkindate" _
                              type="xsd:string"
                        minOccurs="0" />
                        <xsd:element name="numnights" _
                              type="xsd:string"
                        minOccurs="0" />
                        <xsd:element name="preferred" _
                              type="xsd:string"
                        minOccurs="0" />
                </xsd:sequence>
                <xsd:attribute name="id" form="unqualified"
                              type="xsd:string" />
              </xsd:complexType>
                </xsd:element>
            </xsd:sequence>
              </xsd:complexType>
        </xsd:element>
          </xsd:sequence>
    <xsd:attribute name="id" form="unqualified" type="xsd:string" />
        </xsd:complexType>
  </xsd:element>
</xsd:schema>
```

This XSD seems dense and complicated, but it really isn't. Let's walk through the pieces. First, what do we know about the hotel_register.xml document itself?

- It contains a container element for the hotel itself.

- The hotel element contains a guests element, which, in turn, contains all the guest elements.

- Each guest element contains a firstname, middlename, lastname, roomnbr, checkindate, numnights, and preferred element.

- There may be many guest elements and many hotel elements (although we have shown examples with only one hotel instance, to keep things simple).

The XSD file should be a straightforward replay of this information. The first thing that the XSD does is set up a bunch of header information, such as the name of the XSD, the namespace it belongs to, and so on. Then it identifies the root document element, hotel, like this:

```
<xsd:element name="hotel">
```

The hotel element is considered a *complex type* because its subnodes are nontextual and because it has attributes. *Simple types* can hold only values and may not have element or attribute subnodes. Everything inside this complex type is described by a *sequence* schema element. A sequence element simply defines an order to the child elements. After this, the document matches up to our next XML element: the guests element.

```
<xsd:complexType>
  <xsd:sequence>
    <xsd:element name="guests" minOccurs="0" maxOccurs="unbounded">
```

Just as with the hotel element, the guests element is also a complex type, with a sequence of subnodes below it. Our next element up for description is the guest element. This element is contained inside the guests element and thus appears nested inside it. As usual, this element is described using a complex type.

```
<xsd:element name="guest" minOccurs="0" maxOccurs="unbounded">
  <xsd:complexType>
    <xsd:sequence>
      <xsd:element name="firstname" type="xsd:string" minOccurs="0" />
      <xsd:element name="middlename" type="xsd:string" minOccurs="0" />
      <xsd:element name="lastname" type="xsd:string" minOccurs="0" />
      <xsd:element name="roomnbr" type="xsd:string" minOccurs="0" />
      <xsd:element name="checkindate" type="xsd:string" minOccurs="0" />
      <xsd:element name="numnights" type="xsd:string" minOccurs="0" />
      <xsd:element name="preferred" type="xsd:string" minOccurs="0" />
    </xsd:sequence>
    <xsd:attribute name="id" form="unqualified" type="xsd:string" />
  </xsd:complexType>
</xsd:element>
```

We also can see that the guest ID attribute is defined inside the guest element schema. The rest of the document consists of just the closing tags for all these elements that we have discussed. So, you can see that the XSD might be confusing at first glance, but it is very easy to read and understand when looked at from the vantage point of the XML file that it is supposed to define.

Adding Elements into the Schema Document

We have already said that the XmlSchema class is used to contain XSDs. Now let's see how we can use this class to create the schema presented in Listing 10.11. To start creating your own schema, you would first start out with a new instance of XmlSchema:

```
Dim mySchema As New XmlSchema()
```

To add the schema elements into the overall schema document, we use the XmlSchemaElement class. This class encapsulates XSD elements. To create our hotel "root" element, the code would look like this:

```
'----create the schema element for "hotel"
Dim elementHotel As New XmlSchemaElement()
elementHotel.Name = "hotel"
```

To create the complex type and sequence groupings, we need to use the
XmlSchemaComplexType class and the XmlSchemaSequence class:

```
'Hotel is a complex type
Dim complexTypeHotel As New XmlSchemaComplexType()
elementHotel.SchemaType = complexTypeHotel

'Hotel is also a sequence
Dim seqHotel As New XmlSchemaSequence()
complexTypeHotel.Particle = seqHotel
```

Setting the SchemaType property of the elementHotel object to the previously created
complex type object tells the schema generator that the hotel element is a complex type. The
XmlSchemaComplexType.Particle property then is used to identify whether this complex type
element contains a choice (represented by XmlSchemaChoice), a sequence (represented by
XmlSchemaSequence), or a nonsequenced grouping of child nodes (XmlSchemaAll).

We now have created the opening pieces of the hotel element. To add it to the schema, we simply write this:

```
'Add the element to the schema
mySchema.Items.Add(elementHotel)
```

This adds the elementHotel object to the root schema document. To add more child nodes to
the hotel element itself, we can just execute the same Add method. Keep in mind, however,
that these child elements are being added to the sequence grouping and not directly to the
elementHotel node:

```
'Add the element to the schema
seqHotel.Items.Add(elementGuests)
```

Listing 10.12 shows a console application that builds the XSD file that we witnessed in
Listing 10.11.

LISTING 10.12   Building the Hotel Register XSD File

```
Imports System.Xml
Imports System.Xml.Schema

Module SchemaBuilder

    Sub Main()
        Try
```

LISTING 10.12 Continued

```
'mySchema represents the root XSD document
Dim mySchema As New XmlSchema()

'----create the schema element for "hotel"
Dim elementHotel As New XmlSchemaElement()
elementHotel.Name = "hotel"

'Hotel is a complex type
Dim complexTypeHotel As New XmlSchemaComplexType()
elementHotel.SchemaType = complexTypeHotel

'Hotel is also a sequence
Dim seqHotel As New XmlSchemaSequence()
complexTypeHotel.Particle = seqHotel

'Add the element to the schema
mySchema.Items.Add(elementHotel)

'----create the schema element for "guests"
Dim elementGuests As New XmlSchemaElement()
elementGuests.Name = "guests"

'Guests is a complex type
Dim complexTypeGuests As New XmlSchemaComplexType()
elementGuests.SchemaType = complexTypeGuests

'Guests is also a sequence
Dim seqGuests As New XmlSchemaSequence()
complexTypeGuests.Particle = seqGuests

'Add the guests element to the hotel sequence element
seqHotel.Items.Add(elementGuests)

'----create the schema element for "guest"
Dim elementGuest As New XmlSchemaElement()
elementGuest.Name = "guest"

'Guests is a complex type
Dim complexTypeGuest As New XmlSchemaComplexType()
elementGuest.SchemaType = complexTypeGuest

'Guests is also a sequence
Dim seqGuest As New XmlSchemaSequence()
complexTypeGuest.Particle = seqGuest
```

LISTING 10.12 Continued

```
                'Add the guest element to the guests sequence element
                seqGuests.Items.Add(elementGuest)

                '----create the schema element for "firstname"
                Dim elementFirstName As New XmlSchemaElement()
                elementFirstName.Name = "firstname"
                elementFirstName.SchemaTypeName = New XmlQualifiedName("string", _
                    "http://www.w3.org/2001/XMLSchema")

                'Add the element to the guest sequence
                seqGuest.Items.Add(elementFirstName)


                '----create the schema element for "middlename"
                Dim elementMiddleName As New XmlSchemaElement()
                elementMiddleName.Name = "middlename"
                elementMiddleName.SchemaTypeName = New XmlQualifiedName("string", _
                    "http://www.w3.org/2001/XMLSchema")

                'Add the element to the guest sequence
                seqGuest.Items.Add(elementMiddleName)

                '----create the schema element for "lastname"
                Dim elementLastName As New XmlSchemaElement()
                elementLastName.Name = "lastname"
                elementLastName.SchemaTypeName = New XmlQualifiedName("string", _
                    "http://www.w3.org/2001/XMLSchema")

                'Add the element to the guest sequence
                seqGuest.Items.Add(elementLastName)

                '----create the schema element for "roomnbr"
                Dim elementRoomNbr As New XmlSchemaElement()
                elementRoomNbr.Name = "roomnbr"
                elementRoomNbr.SchemaTypeName = New XmlQualifiedName("int", _
                    "http://www.w3.org/2001/XMLSchema")

                'Add the element to the guest sequence
                seqGuest.Items.Add(elementRoomNbr)

                '----create the schema element for "checkindate"
                Dim elementCheckInDate As New XmlSchemaElement()
                elementCheckInDate.Name = "checkindate"
                elementCheckInDate.SchemaTypeName = New XmlQualifiedName("string", _
                    "http://www.w3.org/2001/XMLSchema")
```

LISTING 10.12   Continued

```
                'Add the element to the guest sequence
                seqGuest.Items.Add(elementCheckInDate)

                '----create the schema element for "numnights"
                Dim elementNumNights As New XmlSchemaElement()
                elementNumNights.Name = "numnights"
                elementNumNights.SchemaTypeName = New XmlQualifiedName("int", _
                    "http://www.w3.org/2001/XMLSchema")

                'Add the element to the guest sequence
                seqGuest.Items.Add(elementNumNights)


                '----create the schema element for "checkindate"
                Dim elementPreferred As New XmlSchemaElement()
                elementPreferred.Name = "preferred"
                elementPreferred.SchemaTypeName = New XmlQualifiedName("string", _
                    "http://www.w3.org/2001/XMLSchema")

                'Add the element to the guest sequence
                seqGuest.Items.Add(elementPreferred)

                mySchema.Write(Console.Out)

            Catch schemaErr As XmlSchemaException
                MsgBox("An error with the schema occurred with the following _
                    object: " & schemaErr.SourceSchemaObject.ToString)


            Catch appErr As Exception
                MsgBox("An error was encountered generating the schema: " & _
                    appErr.Message & vbCrLf & vbCrLf & "Stack trace: " & _
                    appErr.StackTrace)


            Finally

                Console.WriteLine()
                Console.WriteLine("Hit 'Enter' to exit.")
                Console.ReadLine()

            End Try

    End Sub
```

Suggestions for Further Exploration

⊃ A great way to research the various schema elements supported by XSD documents is to quickly run through all the XmlSchemaXXX classes in the MSDN Framework documentation. Each one represents a unique element type.

⊃ Visit http://www.w3.org/XML/Schema for a detailed explanation of the W3C's work on schemas and also an index of schema materials.

Validating XML Documents

When you deal with XML in your code, you are concerned with two primary processes: reading XML and writing XML. When reading an XML document, you might be concerned about whether the XML that you are consuming is "correct." That is, is the XML compliant with the W3C XML specification, and does it correctly implement the defined grammar and vocabulary delineated by a DTD, XDR, or XSD document? XML documents that correctly adhere to the XML specification are said to be *well formed*. XML documents that adhere to the structure described in a schema document are said to be *valid*.

This section examines the System.Xml support for validating XML documents against a specific schema by using the XmlValidatingReader class.

Creating Validation Event Handlers

The XmlValidatingReader class looks very similar to the XmlTextReader class. It still processes an XML document one node at a time through its Read method. However, instead of pointing the validating reader directly at the physical XML document as we do with the text reader, the XmlValidatingReader expects to leverage an existing reader instance to act as its source like this:

```
Dim reader As XmlTextReader = New XmlTextReader(fileName)
Dim validator As XmlValidatingReader = New XmlValidatingReader(reader)
```

After creating an XmlValidatingRead instance, the first task is to tell it which type of validation needs to be done. As mentioned before, the .NET Framework Class Library currently supports XSDs, XDRs, and DTDs for XML validation. To indicate which of these formats the validating reader should use, set the ValidationType property. This property is used in conjunction with the ValidationType enumeration to specify exactly how the validation should be performed. The ValidationType enumeration is documented in Table 10.9.

TABLE 10.9   The ValidationType Enumeration

Member Name	Description
Auto	Validates the XML document against either DTD or XML schema information, depending on the schema or DOCTYPE specified in the source XML document.
DTD	Validates the XML document against the DTD specified in the DOC-TYPE directive.
None	Performs no validation. (Essentially creates a reader that has the capability to use default attributes and general entities that may be specified in a schema, but no actual validation is performed.)
Schema	Validates the XML document according to the schema pointed at by the xmlns URI.
XDR	Validates the XML document according to the XDR schema pointed at by any referenced x-schema namespaces.

If we were targeting XSD validation specifically, we would set the property like this:

```
validator.ValidationType = ValidationType.Schema
```

> **NOTE**
>
> You must set the ValidationType property before the first call to
> XmlValidatingReader.Read.

The source XML document should specify its attendant schema document, but you also have the option of building up a collection of schemas and then validating XML documents against that collection. The XmlSchemaCollection class can contain both XSD and XDR schemas for this purpose. An XmlSchemaCollection instance then can be assigned through the XmlValidatingReader.Schemas property. When the document is parsed by calling the validating reader's Read, ReadInnerXml, ReadOuterXml, or Skip methods, the document is compared and analyzed against the schema defined inside the XmlSchemaCollection instance:

```
'create a new schema collection object
Dim schemaCollection as XmlSchemaCollection = new XmlSchemaCollection()

'create a validating reader object
Dim reader As XmlTextReader = New XmlTextReader(fileName)
Dim validator as XmlValidatingReader = new XmlValidatingReader(reader)
```

```
'add a previously created XmlSchema object to the schema collection
schemaCollection.Add(mySchema)

'now, add the schema collection through the validating reader's schemas
'property
reader.ValidationType = ValidationType.Schema
reader.Schemas.Add(schemaCollection)
```

If you are validating multiple XML documents against the same XML schema, using an XML schema collection object will help improve application performance because the actual schema is loaded only once and then is cached for further references.

Now that we have indicated the type of schema validation that we want performed and exactly what schema we want to validate against, we can start parsing through the XML document using the validating reader. As the validating reader encounters XML elements that do not conform to the specified schema and schema type, it flags a validation issue. It may do so by raising either exceptions or events.

Handling Validation Errors with Events

To set up an event-handler design pattern for use with XmlValidatingReader, you use the ValidationEventHandler delegate (defined in System.Xml.Schema) and add an event handler in your code that maps to that delegate. Here is a quick example. First, write a subroutine to handle the event callback:

```
'Display the validation error.
Public Sub HandleValidationError(sender As Object, args As _
    ValidationEventArgs)

    MsgBox("Error validating source XML document: " & args.Message))
End Sub
```

There are a few things to note about the event handler. For one, its signature needs to match that of the ValidationEventHandler delegate (this means that we need the sender object and the ValidationEventArgs object as parameters). The second thing to note is how the actual validation issue is carried into the event handler: through the ValidationEventArgs instance. The ValidationEventArgs, also defined in System.Xml.Schema, carries three properties useful for specifying the exact validation failure that occurred. The Message property returns the actual description of the failed validation, the Exception property returns an instance of the XmlSchemaException class associated with the validation failure, and the Severity property returns a value from the XmlSeverityType enumeration (documented in Table 10.10).

10

TABLE 10.10   The `XmlSeverityType` Enumeration

Member Name	Description
Error	An error occurred indicating that the XML document does not conform to the supplied DTD, XDR, or XSD Schema document.
Warning	The validator was incapable of locating a corresponding schema element for the current XML document element. In other words, no schema item exists that will validate the current XML document element. The `Warning` value can be returned only if the `ValidationType` is set to `Schemas`.

Because the actual validation error event is defined on the `XmlValidatingReader` class (it is called `ValidationEventHandler`), the next step is easy: Use the `AddHandler` command to tell the runtime that our `HandleValidationError` sub should handle any `ValidationEventHandler` events:

```
AddHandler validator.ValidationEventHandler, AddressOf _
    HandleValidationError
```

With these two pieces in place, we can start the read of the XML document. This happens in an identical way to the read design pattern of the `XmlTextReader` class.

Handling Validation Errors with Exceptions

If you do not define any event handler and attach it to `XmlValidatingRead.ValidationEventHandler`, the reader instead raises exceptions of `XmlException` type. The caveat here is that the first time the exception is thrown, the read process essentially is terminated and cannot be restarted.

Here is an example of a validating reader that relies on exception handling:

```
Try
    reader = New XmlTextReader(fileName)
    validator = New XmlValidatingReader(reader)

    While validator.Read()
        .
        .
        .
    End While
```

```
Catch validationErr As XmlException
    'deal with the validation error here

Finally
    'Close the reader.
    If Not (validator Is Nothing) Then
        validator.Close()
    End If
End Try
```

In general, it is preferable to handle validation issues using events instead of exceptions. Using the event handler gives you access to more information about the error, allows the validator to continue or to be restarted, and enables you to differentiate between actual errors and validation discrepancies.

Suggestions for Further Exploration

⮑ We have only touched on instantiating validating readers from other XML readers. However, you can create a validating reader that will read over an XML fragment. For more information, consult the Framework SDK documentation on the `XmlValidatingReader` class and examine the different overloaded constructors available to you.

⮑ The `XmlDocument` class can "load" a validating reader object, enabling you to validate in-memory representations of XML documents. See the `XmlDocument.Load` method documentation for more information.

Learning by Example: The Hotel Reservations Desk

To reinforce the topics discussed in this chapter, this "learning by example" application presents an XML reading "wrapper" for a fictitious hotel chain. The application's goal is to allow customer service representatives to look up current hotel reservations in a data store (an XML file). The program first forces you to constrain your search to a specific hotel and then allows searching by last name, first name, or check-in date.

After the search is executed, a list of guest IDs that match the supplied criteria will show up in a list box. The user can then select one of these guests to view detailed information.

Figure 10.9 shows the application in action.

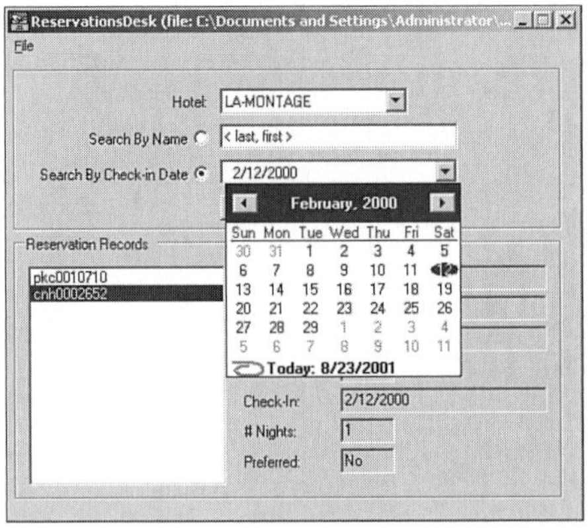

FIGURE 10.9
The main window.

Key Concepts Covered

This program showcases the following:

- Use of the `XmlValidatingReader` to validate an XML document against a schema
- Loading XML documents into memory
- Parsing XML documents using the `XmlNodeReader` class

Code Walkthrough

Listing 10.13 shows a sample XML file that you can use for testing the ReservationsDesk application.

LISTING 10.13   XML Document for Testing

```xml
<?xml version="1.0" standalone="no" ?>
<register>
    <hotel id="DC-4RIVERS">
        <guests>
            <guest id="jlk0910211">
                <firstname>Jim</firstname>
                <middlename>L</middlename>
                <lastname>Kelley</lastname>
                <roomnbr>295</roomnbr>
                <checkindate>6/17/2001</checkindate>
                <numnights>4</numnights>
                <preferred>No</preferred>
            </guest>
```

LISTING 10.13 Continued

```xml
            <guest id="nlt0000704">
                <firstname>Nadia</firstname>
                <middlename>L</middlename>
                <lastname>Tatonovich</lastname>
                <roomnbr>615</roomnbr>
                <checkindate>6/17/2001</checkindate>
                <numnights>4</numnights>
                <preferred>No</preferred>
            </guest>
            <guest id="d b6620103">
                <firstname>Dorsa</firstname>
                <middlename />
                <lastname>Brevia</lastname>
                <roomnbr>408</roomnbr>
                <checkindate>6/18/2001</checkindate>
                <numnights>1</numnights>
                <preferred>Yes</preferred>
            </guest>
            <guest id="jgm9111447">
                <firstname>Jackie</firstname>
                <middlename>G</middlename>
                <lastname>Mendelin</lastname>
                <roomnbr>223</roomnbr>
                <checkindate>6/15/2001</checkindate>
                <numnights>5</numnights>
                <preferred>No</preferred>
            </guest>
        </guests>
</hotel>
<hotel id="LA-MONTAGE">
    <guests>
            <guest id="pkc0010710">
                <firstname>Peter</firstname>
                <middlename>K</middlename>
                <lastname>Ceton</lastname>
                <roomnbr>107</roomnbr>
                <checkindate>2/12/2000</checkindate>
                <numnights>1</numnights>
                <preferred>No</preferred>
            </guest>
            <guest id="cnh0002652">
                <firstname>Casper</firstname>
                <middlename>N</middlename>
                <lastname>Houston</lastname>
                <roomnbr>109</roomnbr>
```

LISTING 10.13   Continued

```
            <checkindate>2/12/2000</checkindate>
            <numnights>1</numnights>
            <preferred>No</preferred>
         </guest>
       </guests>
    </hotel>
</register>
```

Only two items have been added into the global class scope: resFile (a string pointing to the currently selected XML document) and xmlDoc (an XmlDocument instance holding the XML file pointed at by resFile). Listing 10.14 shows the ReservationsDesk application source code.

LISTING 10.14   ReservationsDesk

```
Imports System.Xml

Public Class Main
    Inherits System.Windows.Forms.Form

    Public resFile As String
    Public xmlDoc As XmlDocument

    Friend WithEvents buttonSearch As System.Windows.Forms.Button
    Friend WithEvents Label2 As System.Windows.Forms.Label
    Friend WithEvents Label3 As System.Windows.Forms.Label
    Friend WithEvents Label4 As System.Windows.Forms.Label
    Friend WithEvents Label5 As System.Windows.Forms.Label
    Friend WithEvents Label6 As System.Windows.Forms.Label
    Friend WithEvents Label7 As System.Windows.Forms.Label
    Friend WithEvents Label8 As System.Windows.Forms.Label
    Friend WithEvents RadioButtonByName As System.Windows.Forms.RadioButton
    Friend WithEvents RadioButtonByDate As System.Windows.Forms.RadioButton
    Friend WithEvents TextBoxName As System.Windows.Forms.TextBox
    Friend WithEvents DateTimeCheckin As System.Windows.Forms.DateTimePicker
    Friend WithEvents ListBoxGuests As System.Windows.Forms.ListBox
    Friend WithEvents ComboHotel As System.Windows.Forms.ComboBox
    Friend WithEvents TextBoxPreferred As System.Windows.Forms.TextBox
    Friend WithEvents TextBoxNumNights As System.Windows.Forms.TextBox
    Friend WithEvents TextBoxCheckinDate As System.Windows.Forms.TextBox
    Friend WithEvents TextBoxRoomNbr As System.Windows.Forms.TextBox
    Friend WithEvents TextBoxLastName As System.Windows.Forms.TextBox
    Friend WithEvents TextBoxMiddleName As System.Windows.Forms.TextBox
    Friend WithEvents TextBoxFirstName As System.Windows.Forms.TextBox
```

LISTING 10.14 Continued

```vb
#Region " Windows Form Designer generated code "

    Public Sub New()
        MyBase.New()

        'This call is required by the Windows Form Designer.
        InitializeComponent()

        'Add any initialization after the InitializeComponent() call
        xmlDoc = New XmlDataDocument()
    End Sub


    'Form overrides dispose to clean up the component list.
    Protected Overloads Overrides Sub Dispose(ByVal disposing As Boolean)
        If disposing Then
            If Not (components Is Nothing) Then
                components.Dispose()
            End If
        End If
        MyBase.Dispose(disposing)
    End Sub
    Friend WithEvents MainMenu1 As System.Windows.Forms.MainMenu
    Friend WithEvents MenuItem1 As System.Windows.Forms.MenuItem
    Friend WithEvents MenuItem2 As System.Windows.Forms.MenuItem
    Friend WithEvents MenuItem3 As System.Windows.Forms.MenuItem
    Friend WithEvents OpenFileDialog1 As System.Windows.Forms.OpenFileDialog
    Friend WithEvents GroupBox1 As System.Windows.Forms.GroupBox
    Friend WithEvents GroupBox2 As System.Windows.Forms.GroupBox
    Friend WithEvents Label1 As System.Windows.Forms.Label


    'Required by the Windows Form Designer
    Private components As System.ComponentModel.Container

    'NOTE: The following procedure is required by the Windows Form Designer
    'It can be modified using the Windows Form Designer.
    'Do not modify it using the code editor.
    <System.Diagnostics.DebuggerStepThrough()> Private Sub _
        InitializeComponent()
        Dim resources As System.Resources.ResourceManager = New _
            System.Resources.ResourceManager(GetType(Main))
        Me.Label4 = New System.Windows.Forms.Label()
        Me.Label5 = New System.Windows.Forms.Label()
        Me.Label7 = New System.Windows.Forms.Label()
        Me.Label1 = New System.Windows.Forms.Label()
        Me.Label2 = New System.Windows.Forms.Label()
```

LISTING 10.14   Continued

```
Me.Label3 = New System.Windows.Forms.Label()
Me.Label6 = New System.Windows.Forms.Label()
Me.TextBoxMiddleName = New System.Windows.Forms.TextBox()
Me.ListBoxGuests = New System.Windows.Forms.ListBox()
Me.OpenFileDialog1 = New System.Windows.Forms.OpenFileDialog()
Me.GroupBox2 = New System.Windows.Forms.GroupBox()
Me.Label8 = New System.Windows.Forms.Label()
Me.TextBoxPreferred = New System.Windows.Forms.TextBox()
Me.TextBoxNumNights = New System.Windows.Forms.TextBox()
Me.TextBoxCheckinDate = New System.Windows.Forms.TextBox()
Me.TextBoxRoomNbr = New System.Windows.Forms.TextBox()
Me.TextBoxLastName = New System.Windows.Forms.TextBox()
Me.TextBoxFirstName = New System.Windows.Forms.TextBox()
Me.ComboHotel = New System.Windows.Forms.ComboBox()
Me.MenuItem1 = New System.Windows.Forms.MenuItem()
Me.MenuItem2 = New System.Windows.Forms.MenuItem()
Me.MenuItem3 = New System.Windows.Forms.MenuItem()
Me.RadioButtonByName = New System.Windows.Forms.RadioButton()
Me.DateTimeCheckin = New System.Windows.Forms.DateTimePicker()
Me.RadioButtonByDate = New System.Windows.Forms.RadioButton()
Me.TextBoxName = New System.Windows.Forms.TextBox()
Me.buttonSearch = New System.Windows.Forms.Button()
Me.MainMenu1 = New System.Windows.Forms.MainMenu()
Me.GroupBox1 = New System.Windows.Forms.GroupBox()
Me.GroupBox2.SuspendLayout()
Me.GroupBox1.SuspendLayout()
Me.SuspendLayout()
'
'Label4
'
Me.Label4.Location = New System.Drawing.Point(184, 76)
Me.Label4.Name = "Label4"
Me.Label4.Size = New System.Drawing.Size(76, 16)
Me.Label4.TabIndex = 4
Me.Label4.Text = "Last Name:"
'
'Label5
'
Me.Label5.Location = New System.Drawing.Point(184, 100)
Me.Label5.Name = "Label5"
Me.Label5.Size = New System.Drawing.Size(76, 16)
Me.Label5.TabIndex = 4
Me.Label5.Text = "Room Nbr:"
'
'Label7
'
```

LISTING 10.14   Continued

```
Me.Label7.Location = New System.Drawing.Point(184, 148)
Me.Label7.Name = "Label7"
Me.Label7.Size = New System.Drawing.Size(76, 16)
Me.Label7.TabIndex = 4
Me.Label7.Text = "# Nights:"
'
'Label1
'
Me.Label1.Location = New System.Drawing.Point(128, 24)
Me.Label1.Name = "Label1"
Me.Label1.Size = New System.Drawing.Size(40, 12)
Me.Label1.TabIndex = 0
Me.Label1.Text = "Hotel:"
'
'Label2
'
Me.Label2.Location = New System.Drawing.Point(184, 28)
Me.Label2.Name = "Label2"
Me.Label2.Size = New System.Drawing.Size(76, 16)
Me.Label2.TabIndex = 4
Me.Label2.Text = "First Name:"
'
'Label3
'
Me.Label3.Location = New System.Drawing.Point(184, 52)
Me.Label3.Name = "Label3"
Me.Label3.Size = New System.Drawing.Size(76, 16)
Me.Label3.TabIndex = 4
Me.Label3.Text = "Middle Name:"
'
'Label6
'
Me.Label6.Location = New System.Drawing.Point(184, 124)
Me.Label6.Name = "Label6"
Me.Label6.Size = New System.Drawing.Size(76, 16)
Me.Label6.TabIndex = 4
Me.Label6.Text = "Check-In:"
'
'TextBoxMiddleName
'
Me.TextBoxMiddleName.Location = New System.Drawing.Point(264, 48)
Me.TextBoxMiddleName.Name = "TextBoxMiddleName"
Me.TextBoxMiddleName.ReadOnly = True
Me.TextBoxMiddleName.Size = New System.Drawing.Size(168, 20)
Me.TextBoxMiddleName.TabIndex = 3
```

LISTING 10.14   Continued

```
        Me.TextBoxMiddleName.Text = ""
        '
        'ListBoxGuests
        '
        Me.ListBoxGuests.Enabled = False
        Me.ListBoxGuests.Location = New System.Drawing.Point(12, 24)
        Me.ListBoxGuests.Name = "ListBoxGuests"
        Me.ListBoxGuests.Size = New System.Drawing.Size(160, 173)
        Me.ListBoxGuests.TabIndex = 0
        '
        'GroupBox2
        '
        Me.GroupBox2.Controls.AddRange(New System.Windows.Forms.Control() _
            {Me.Label8, Me.TextBoxPreferred, Me.TextBoxNumNights, Me.Label7, _
            Me.TextBoxCheckinDate, Me.Label6, Me.TextBoxRoomNbr, Me.Label5, _
            Me.TextBoxLastName, Me.Label4, Me.TextBoxMiddleName, Me.Label3, _
            Me.Label2, Me.TextBoxFirstName, Me.ListBoxGuests})
        Me.GroupBox2.Location = New System.Drawing.Point(4, 140)
        Me.GroupBox2.Name = "GroupBox2"
        Me.GroupBox2.Size = New System.Drawing.Size(444, 208)
        Me.GroupBox2.TabIndex = 1
        Me.GroupBox2.TabStop = False
        Me.GroupBox2.Text = "Reservation Records"
        '
        'Label8
        '
        Me.Label8.Location = New System.Drawing.Point(184, 172)
        Me.Label8.Name = "Label8"
        Me.Label8.Size = New System.Drawing.Size(76, 16)
        Me.Label8.TabIndex = 4
        Me.Label8.Text = "Preferred:"
        '
        'TextBoxPreferred
        '
        Me.TextBoxPreferred.Location = New System.Drawing.Point(264, 168)
        Me.TextBoxPreferred.Name = "TextBoxPreferred"
        Me.TextBoxPreferred.ReadOnly = True
        Me.TextBoxPreferred.Size = New System.Drawing.Size(44, 20)
        Me.TextBoxPreferred.TabIndex = 3
        Me.TextBoxPreferred.Text = ""
        '
        'TextBoxNumNights
        '
        Me.TextBoxNumNights.Location = New System.Drawing.Point(264, 144)
        Me.TextBoxNumNights.Name = "TextBoxNumNights"
```

LISTING 10.14   Continued

```
Me.TextBoxNumNights.ReadOnly = True
Me.TextBoxNumNights.Size = New System.Drawing.Size(44, 20)
Me.TextBoxNumNights.TabIndex = 3
Me.TextBoxNumNights.Text = ""
'
'TextBoxCheckinDate
'
Me.TextBoxCheckinDate.Location = New System.Drawing.Point(264, 120)
Me.TextBoxCheckinDate.Name = "TextBoxCheckinDate"
Me.TextBoxCheckinDate.ReadOnly = True
Me.TextBoxCheckinDate.Size = New System.Drawing.Size(168, 20)
Me.TextBoxCheckinDate.TabIndex = 3
Me.TextBoxCheckinDate.Text = ""
'
'TextBoxRoomNbr
'
Me.TextBoxRoomNbr.Location = New System.Drawing.Point(264, 96)
Me.TextBoxRoomNbr.Name = "TextBoxRoomNbr"
Me.TextBoxRoomNbr.ReadOnly = True
Me.TextBoxRoomNbr.Size = New System.Drawing.Size(44, 20)
Me.TextBoxRoomNbr.TabIndex = 3
Me.TextBoxRoomNbr.Text = ""
'
'TextBoxLastName
'
Me.TextBoxLastName.Location = New System.Drawing.Point(264, 72)
Me.TextBoxLastName.Name = "TextBoxLastName"
Me.TextBoxLastName.ReadOnly = True
Me.TextBoxLastName.Size = New System.Drawing.Size(168, 20)
Me.TextBoxLastName.TabIndex = 3
Me.TextBoxLastName.Text = ""
'
'TextBoxFirstName
'
Me.TextBoxFirstName.Location = New System.Drawing.Point(264, 24)
Me.TextBoxFirstName.Name = "TextBoxFirstName"
Me.TextBoxFirstName.ReadOnly = True
Me.TextBoxFirstName.Size = New System.Drawing.Size(168, 20)
Me.TextBoxFirstName.TabIndex = 3
Me.TextBoxFirstName.Text = ""
'
'ComboHotel
'
Me.ComboHotel.DropDownStyle = _
    System.Windows.Forms.ComboBoxStyle.DropDownList
```

LISTING 10.14 Continued

```
Me.ComboHotel.DropDownWidth = 152
Me.ComboHotel.Enabled = False
Me.ComboHotel.Location = New System.Drawing.Point(168, 20)
Me.ComboHotel.Name = "ComboHotel"
Me.ComboHotel.Size = New System.Drawing.Size(152, 21)
Me.ComboHotel.TabIndex = 1
'
'MenuItem1
'
Me.MenuItem1.Index = 0
Me.MenuItem1.MenuItems.AddRange(New System.Windows.Forms.MenuItem() _
    {Me.MenuItem2, Me.MenuItem3})
Me.MenuItem1.Text = "&File"
'
'MenuItem2
'
Me.MenuItem2.Index = 0
Me.MenuItem2.Text = "&Open"
'
'MenuItem3
'
Me.MenuItem3.Index = 1
Me.MenuItem3.Text = "E&xit"
'
'RadioButtonByName
'
Me.RadioButtonByName.Location = New System.Drawing.Point(32, 52)
Me.RadioButtonByName.Name = "RadioButtonByName"
Me.RadioButtonByName.RightToLeft = System.Windows.Forms.RightToLeft.Yes
Me.RadioButtonByName.Size = New System.Drawing.Size(128, 16)
Me.RadioButtonByName.TabIndex = 2
Me.RadioButtonByName.Text = "Search By Name"
'
'DateTimeCheckin
'
Me.DateTimeCheckin.CustomFormat = ""
Me.DateTimeCheckin.Format = _
    System.Windows.Forms.DateTimePickerFormat.Custom
Me.DateTimeCheckin.Location = New System.Drawing.Point(168, 76)
Me.DateTimeCheckin.Name = "DateTimeCheckin"
Me.DateTimeCheckin.Size = New System.Drawing.Size(192, 20)
Me.DateTimeCheckin.TabIndex = 4
Me.DateTimeCheckin.Value = New Date(2000, 2, 12, 0, 0, 0, 0)
'
'RadioButtonByDate
'
```

LISTING 10.14 Continued

```
Me.RadioButtonByDate.Checked = True
Me.RadioButtonByDate.Location = New System.Drawing.Point(8, 80)
Me.RadioButtonByDate.Name = "RadioButtonByDate"
Me.RadioButtonByDate.RightToLeft = System.Windows.Forms.RightToLeft.Yes
Me.RadioButtonByDate.Size = New System.Drawing.Size(152, 16)
Me.RadioButtonByDate.TabIndex = 2
Me.RadioButtonByDate.TabStop = True
Me.RadioButtonByDate.Text = "Search By Check-in Date"
'
'TextBoxName
'
Me.TextBoxName.Location = New System.Drawing.Point(168, 48)
Me.TextBoxName.Name = "TextBoxName"
Me.TextBoxName.Size = New System.Drawing.Size(192, 20)
Me.TextBoxName.TabIndex = 3
Me.TextBoxName.Text = "< last, first >"
'
'buttonSearch
'
Me.buttonSearch.Enabled = False
Me.buttonSearch.Location = New System.Drawing.Point(168, 104)
Me.buttonSearch.Name = "buttonSearch"
Me.buttonSearch.Size = New System.Drawing.Size(76, 20)
Me.buttonSearch.TabIndex = 5
Me.buttonSearch.Text = "&Search"
'
'MainMenu1
'
Me.MainMenu1.MenuItems.AddRange(New System.Windows.Forms.MenuItem() _
    {Me.MenuItem1})
'
'GroupBox1
'
Me.GroupBox1.Controls.AddRange(New System.Windows.Forms.Control() _
    {Me.buttonSearch, Me.DateTimeCheckin, Me.TextBoxName, _
    Me.RadioButtonByDate, Me.RadioButtonByName, Me.ComboHotel, _
    Me.Label1})
Me.GroupBox1.Location = New System.Drawing.Point(4, 4)
Me.GroupBox1.Name = "GroupBox1"
Me.GroupBox1.Size = New System.Drawing.Size(444, 132)
Me.GroupBox1.TabIndex = 0
Me.GroupBox1.TabStop = False
'
'Main
'
Me.AutoScaleBaseSize = New System.Drawing.Size(5, 13)
```

LISTING 10.14 Continued

```
        Me.ClientSize = New System.Drawing.Size(460, 361)
        Me.Controls.AddRange(New System.Windows.Forms.Control() _
            {Me.GroupBox2, Me.GroupBox1})
        Me.FormBorderStyle = System.Windows.Forms.FormBorderStyle.FixedDialog
        Me.Icon = CType(resources.GetObject("$this.Icon"), System.Drawing.Icon)
        Me.MaximizeBox = False
        Me.Menu = Me.MainMenu1
        Me.Name = "Main"
        Me.Text = "ReservationsDesk (no file loaded)"
        Me.GroupBox2.ResumeLayout(False)
        Me.GroupBox1.ResumeLayout(False)
        Me.ResumeLayout(False)

    End Sub

#End Region
```

This menu event handler launched the Open File dialog box to allow users to "load" an XML document (this needs to be a document that specifically follows the correct schema). After loading the XML document, it parses the hotel nodes to get a list of unique hotel IDs.

```
    Private Sub MenuItem2_Click(ByVal sender As System.Object, ByVal e As _
        System.EventArgs) Handles MenuItem2.Click

        'Show a File Open dialog; this is for selecting the source
        'XML document...
        OpenFileDialog1.AddExtension = True

        OpenFileDialog1.DefaultExt = ".xml"
        OpenFileDialog1.Filter = "Reservation files (*.xml)|*.xml"
        OpenFileDialog1.InitialDirectory = _
            System.Reflection.Assembly.GetExecutingAssembly.Location

        OpenFileDialog1.ShowDialog()

        resFile = OpenFileDialog1.FileName

        If resFile = "" Then
            Me.Text = "ReservationsDesk (no file loaded)"
        Else
            Me.Text = "ReservationsDesk (file: " & resFile & ")"
            LoadResFile(resFile)
            ListHotels()
```

Listing 10.14   Continued

```
            buttonSearch.Enabled = True
            ComboHotel.Enabled = True
            ListBoxGuests.Enabled = True
        End If

    End Sub
```

This is the routine that performs the actual load of the XML document from a file:

```
Public Sub LoadResFile(ByVal file As String)
        Dim str As String
        Dim i As Integer
        Dim reader As XmlTextReader
        Dim validator As XmlValidatingReader

        Try

            'First, create a XmlTextReader against the supplied file
            reader = New XmlTextReader(file)

            'Then, use the XmlTextReader to create a XmlValidatingReader
            validator = New XmlValidatingReader(reader)
            validator.ValidationType = ValidationType.Auto

            'And finally, load up our global XmlDocument
            xmlDoc.Load(validator)

            'We are done with the validator, so close it
            If Not IsNothing(validator) Then
                validator.Close()
            End If

            'If the file didn't validate, this handler should catch that...
        Catch validationErr As XmlException
            MsgBox("The reservation file '" & resFile & "' has failed to _
                validate against the corporate data schema standard. The file _
                may be corrupt, or may be from an invalid source. Please _
                select a new file.")

        Catch appErr As XmlException
            MsgBox("The application was unable to load the specified XML file _
                '" & resFile & "'. The file may be corrupt, or may be from an _
                invalid source. Please select a new file.")
```

LISTING 10.14   Continued

```
    Finally
        If Not IsNothing(validator) Then
            validator.Close()
        End If

    End Try

End Sub


Private Sub buttonSearch_Click(ByVal sender As System.Object, ByVal e As _
System.EventArgs) Handles buttonSearch.Click
    ExecuteQuery()
End Sub
```

The `ExecuteQuery` routine takes the supplied search criteria and processes each node in the document, one by one, until it finds the correct match. These matches are returned in the form of guest IDs that show up in the list box to the lower left of the screen.

```
Private Sub ExecuteQuery()
    Dim nodeReader As XmlNodeReader
    Dim currID As String
    Dim fullName() As String
    Dim firstName As String
    Dim lastName As String
    Dim nodeLastName As String
    Dim nodeFirstName As String

    Try
        'We use an XmlNodeReader here to navigate the document
        nodeReader = New XmlNodeReader(xmlDoc)

        ListBoxGuests.Items.Clear()

        'skip the document prolog stuff
        nodeReader.MoveToContent()

        'This branch handles searching by last, first name
        If RadioButtonByName.Checked Then
            fullName = Split(TextBoxName.Text, ",")

            lastName = Trim(fullName(0))
            firstName = Trim(fullName(1))

            'This outer while loop keeps the cursor moving until it finds
            'a "hotel"
```

LISTING 10.14 Continued

```
While nodeReader.Read()
    If nodeReader.NodeType = XmlNodeType.Element And _
    nodeReader.Name = "hotel" Then
        'If we are on a hotel node, figure out if it is the
        'right one by looking at its ID attribute
        If nodeReader.GetAttribute("id") = ComboHotel.Text Then

            'If this is the right hotel, move through its child
            'elements
            While nodeReader.Read()

                'We cache the id of the last guest node
                'encountered
                If nodeReader.NodeType = _
                    XmlNodeType.Element And _
                    nodeReader.Name = "guest" Then
                    'nodeReader.MoveToAttribute("id")
                    currID = nodeReader.GetAttribute("id")
                End If

                'If we hit a first name node, advance the
                'cursor into the node and store the value in
                'our temp var nodeFirstName
                If nodeReader.NodeType = _
                    XmlNodeType.Element And _
                    nodeReader.Name = "firstname" Then
                    nodeReader.Read()
                    nodeFirstName = nodeReader.Value
                Else
                    'The cursor will keep going unless we
                    'terminate the loop with 'Exit While' once
                    'we hit the closing node of the hotel
                    'element
                    If nodeReader.NodeType = _
                        XmlNodeType.EndElement And _
                        nodeReader.Name = "hotel" Then
                        Exit While
                    End If

                End If

                'If we hit a last name node, advance the cursor
                'into the node and store the value in our temp
                'var nodeLastName
```

LISTING 10.14   Continued

```
                     If nodeReader.NodeType = _
                         XmlNodeType.Element And _
                         nodeReader.Name = "lastname" Then
                         nodeReader.Read()
                         nodeLastName = nodeReader.Value
                     End If

                     'If we have encountered the right match of
                     'first and last name, add the cached guest ID
                     'to the list box, and then clear out the temp
                     'nodeFirstName and nodeLastName vars
                     If (nodeFirstName = firstName) And _
                         (nodeLastName = lastName) Then
                         ListBoxGuests.Items.Add(currID)
                         nodeFirstName = ""
                         nodeLastName = ""
                     End If
                 End While

                 Exit While

             End If
         End If
     End While

 Else
     'This branch handles searching by check-in date

     'This outer while loop keeps the cursor moving until it finds
     'a "hotel"
     While nodeReader.Read()
         If nodeReader.NodeType = XmlNodeType.Element And _
         nodeReader.Name = "hotel" Then

             'If we are on a hotel node, figure out if it is the
             'right one by looking at its ID attribute
             If nodeReader.GetAttribute("id") = ComboHotel.Text Then

                 'If this is the right hotel, move through its child
                 'elements
                 While nodeReader.Read()
```

LISTING 10.14   Continued

```
                              'We cache the id of the last guest node
                              'encountered
                              If nodeReader.NodeType = _
                                  XmlNodeType.Element And _
                                  nodeReader.Name = "guest" Then
                                  'nodeReader.MoveToAttribute("id")
                                  currID = nodeReader.GetAttribute("id")
                              Else
                                  'The cursor will keep going unless we
                                  'terminate the loop with 'Exit While' once
                                  'we hit the closing node of the hotel
                                  'element
                                  If nodeReader.NodeType = _
                                      XmlNodeType.EndElement And _
                                      nodeReader.Name = "hotel" Then
                                      Exit While
                                  End If
                              End If

                              'If the checkindate value matches, add the
                              'cached guest ID to the listbox
                              If nodeReader.NodeType = _
                                  XmlNodeType.Element And _
                                  nodeReader.Name = "checkindate" Then
                                  nodeReader.Read()
                                  If nodeReader.Value = _
                                      Trim(DateTimeCheckin.Text) Then
                                      ListBoxGuests.Items.Add(currID)
                                  End If
                              End If

                          End While

                          Exit While

                  End If
              End If
          End While

      End If
```

LISTING 10.14 Continued

```
        Catch appErr As Exception
            MsgBox("An error occurred while querying the source XML _
                document." & vbCrLf & vbCrLf & "Error: " & appErr.Message)
        End Try

End Sub
```

`ListHotels` is responsible for parsing the hotel node information out of the document and into the hotel drop-down control.

```
Public Sub ListHotels()

    Try
        Dim reader As XmlNodeReader = New XmlNodeReader(xmlDoc)

        'Skip the document prolog information
        reader.MoveToContent()

        'Move the read cursor through the file
        While reader.Read()
            'If we have found a hotel, put its ID into the combo-box
            If reader.NodeType = XmlNodeType.Element And reader.Name = _
                "hotel" Then
                ComboHotel.Items.Add(reader.GetAttribute("id"))
            End If

        End While

    Catch appErr As Exception
        MsgBox("An error occurred while retrieving the hotel elements." & _
            vbCrLf & vbCrLf & "Error: " & appErr.Message)
    End Try

End Sub
```

Finally, this is the routine that goes after a specific guest node, displaying its information on the screen. The selection of the guest node is based on the selected guest ID in the list box.

```
Public Sub DisplayGuestInfo(ByVal id As String)
    Dim nodeReader As XmlNodeReader

    Try
        nodeReader = New XmlNodeReader(xmlDoc)

        'Skip the document prolog info
        nodeReader.MoveToContent()
```

LISTING 10.14 Continued

Because guest IDs are supposed to be unique, we just want to loop through the entire `xmlDoc` looking for guest nodes; when we find one, we then read through all its child elements, extracting their values for display to the screen.

```
                'Move cursor through document
            While nodeReader.Read()

                'Are we on a "guest" node?
                If nodeReader.NodeType = XmlNodeType.Element And _
                nodeReader.Name = "guest" Then

                    'Does its ID attribute match?
                    If nodeReader.GetAttribute("id") = id Then

                        'Move the reader through the elements, writing each out
                        'to the screen
                        While nodeReader.Read()
                            If nodeReader.NodeType = XmlNodeType.Element And _
                            nodeReader.Name = "firstname" Then
                                nodeReader.Read()
                                TextBoxFirstName.Text = nodeReader.Value
                            End If

                            If nodeReader.NodeType = XmlNodeType.Element And _
                            nodeReader.Name = "middlename" Then
                                nodeReader.Read()
                                TextBoxMiddleName.Text = nodeReader.Value
                            End If

                            If nodeReader.NodeType = XmlNodeType.Element And _
                            nodeReader.Name = "lastname" Then
                                nodeReader.Read()
                                TextBoxLastName.Text = nodeReader.Value
                            End If

                            If nodeReader.NodeType = XmlNodeType.Element And _
                            nodeReader.Name = "roomnbr" Then
                                nodeReader.Read()
                                TextBoxRoomNbr.Text = nodeReader.Value
                            End If

                            If nodeReader.NodeType = XmlNodeType.Element And _
                            nodeReader.Name = "checkindate" Then
                                nodeReader.Read()
                                TextBoxCheckinDate.Text = nodeReader.Value
                            End If
```

LISTING 10.14 Continued

```
                                    If nodeReader.NodeType = XmlNodeType.Element And _
                                    nodeReader.Name = "numnights" Then
                                        nodeReader.Read()
                                        TextBoxNumNights.Text = nodeReader.Value
                                    End If

                                    If nodeReader.NodeType = XmlNodeType.Element And _
                                    nodeReader.Name = "preferred" Then
                                        nodeReader.Read()
                                        TextBoxPreferred.Text = nodeReader.Value
                                    End If

                                    'If we have reached the end of the "guest" element,
                                    'exit loop
                                    If nodeReader.NodeType = XmlNodeType.EndElement _
                                    And nodeReader.Name = "guest" Then
                                        Exit While
                                    End If
                                End While
                            End If
                        End If
                    End While

            Catch appErr As Exception
                MsgBox("An error occurred while retrieving the guest node _
                    elements" & vbCrLf & vbCrLf & "Error: " & appErr.Message)
            End Try

        End Sub

        Private Sub ListBoxGuests_Click(ByVal sender As Object, ByVal e As _
            System.EventArgs) Handles ListBoxGuests.Click
            DisplayGuestInfo(ListBoxGuests.SelectedItem)
        End Sub

        Private Sub MenuItem3_Click(ByVal sender As System.Object, ByVal e As _
            System.EventArgs) Handles MenuItem3.Click
            Me.Close()
        End Sub
End Class
```

Summary

In this chapter, we discussed the importance of XML and how its characteristics as a data-description language can be put to good use with the .NET Framework.

Specifically, you learned how to leverage the `System.Xml` and `System.Xml.Schema` classes to do the following:

- Read and parse XML documents from files and streams using the `XmlTextReader` class
- Write well-formed XML documents using the `XmlTextWriter` class
- Validate XML documents with the `XmlValidatingReader` class
- Create well-formed schemas, element by element, using the `XmlSchema` class and its attendant element classes, such as `XmlComplexType` and `XmlSequence`

After reading this chapter, you should have a good understanding of not only how to interact with XML using the Framework Class Library, but also how to best deploy XML as a technology in your applications.

XSLT and XPath

IN THIS CHAPTER

This chapter continues our discussion of the `System.Xml` namespaces by delving into the .NET Framework support for XSL transformations (XSLT) and XPath queries.

Although the `System.Xml` namespace exposes objects uniquely suited to navigating and reading XML documents, the power offered by XPath expressions in that realm is unparalleled. XSL style sheets and their attendant transformation capabilities also bring much to the XML developer's bag of tricks.

We'll start off this chapter by giving a beginner's introduction to XSLT and XPath. Then we'll explore the namespace support for style sheet transformations, navigation of XML documents using XPath, and finally, the process of querying XML documents for matching node sets using XPath expressions.

By the end of this chapter, you should be able to:

- Transform an XML document into another structured document format (including HTML) using the `System.Xsl` classes
- Navigate XML documents, forward or backward, by using the features of the `XPathNavigator` class and its "helper" classes
- Construct complicated XPath expressions, issue them against an XML data store, and then process the results

Key Classes Related to XSLT and XPath

Every application, image, database, message, and document is stored as some form of a file. Directories and files are the warehouses and boxes of our applications. All our applications spend time interacting with the file system at some level. And most of our applications require us to read, write, or manipulate files and directories.

The .NET `System.IO` namespace provides us with a rich set of tools to write effective file I/O code in a productive manner. This namespace encapsulates functionality related to both synchronous and asynchronous reading and writing to files and streams. Table 11.1 presents the key classes contained in the namespaces. These classes represent those primarily used by developers when implementing features based on directories, files, and streams.

The `System.Xsl` namespace exposes a feature-rich set of components for document transformations. The System.XPath namespace works hand in hand with the transformation components by providing classes for building and encapsulating XPath queries. Table 11.1 itemizes the Xsl and XPath classes and related structures that are covered in this chapter.

TABLE 11.1 Key Classes in the `System.Xsl` Namespace

Class/Structure	Description
XSLT Transformations	
`IXsltContextFunction` Interface	This is an interface to an XSLT function in an XSLT style sheet.
`IXsltContextVariable` Interface	This is an interface to an XSLT variable in an XSLT style sheet.
`XsltArgumentList` Class	The `XsltArgumentList` Class encapsulates a collection of XSLT-defined parameters.
`XsltCompileException` Class	This class encapsulates a collection of XSLT compiler exceptions.
`XsltContext` Class	This class represents the current context of the XSLT processor. It is used primarily to allow resolution of functions, parameters, and namespaces.
`XsltException` Class	This class is used to represent any errors thrown during an XSLT transformation.
`XslTransform` Class	This class is the primary class for performing XSL transformations.
XPath Functions	
`IXPathNavigable` Interface	This interface provides the capability to create `XPathNavigator` objects.
`XPathDocument` Class	This class is used to cache XML documents in an XPath model.
`XPathExpression` Class	This class holds compiled XPath expressions.
`XPathNavigator` Class	The `XPathNavigator` class implements a cursor over a data store for XPath parsing.
`XPathNodeIterator` Class	This class allows enumeration over a specific set of XML nodes.

XSLT—Document Transformation

XSLT, or eXtensible Stylesheet Language Transformations, is a W3C-defined mechanism for taking an XML document and transforming it into another structured document. The resulting document could be XML, HTML, PDF, and so on. As we have mentioned in the previous chapter, XML is an extensible language that is used to structure information inside of a document. XSLT documents are actually written with XML syntax; if you understand XML, XSLT documents should look familiar to you. Let's look at one right now:

```
<xsl:template match="product">
     <p>
            <xsl:apply-templates />
     </p>
</xsl:template>
```

You can see that we are still dealing with nodes, elements, and the like. Some syntax may look foreign (such as `<xsl:template match="product">` and `<xsl:apply-templates />`), but the structure of the document should be easy to understand because it is really a well-formed XML document. Let's first look at why you would want to transform XML documents to begin with, and then study the exact process for doing so. Next, we will focus on the actual XSLT-specific commands that are available.

The Transformation Process

When we say "transformation," we are really talking about taking XML documents that are in one format, doing something to them, and creating an entirely different document instance in a different format. From an XSLT perspective, this involves four major items:

- The source document—The term for the source XML document.
- An XSLT style sheet—An XML document that contains XSLT instructions; the style sheet indicates how to transform the source document.
- The result document—The resulting structured document that was created from the source document using the XSLT style sheet.
- The XSLT processor—The piece of technology that understands XSLT commands and applies them to the source document to create the result document.

To help put this all into place, look at Figure 11.1, which shows a high-level view of the transformation process.

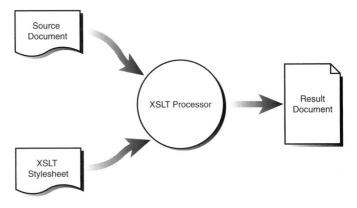

FIGURE 11.1

The XSLT transformation process.

Let's look at a simple example of how we can affect an XML document. The three listings that follow demonstrate how a real transformation might work (we'll explain the specifics of the XSL syntax in the next section).

The Source Document

First up, in Listing 11.1, is our source XML document. It is a brief and very simple XML document that describes two products.

LISTING 11.1 Source Document in XML

```
<?xml version="1.0" encoding="utf-8" ?>
<products>
      <product>
              <commonname>Garden Hose</commonname>
              <price>$13.50</price>

      </product>
      <product>
              <commonname>Garden Caddy</commonname>
              <price>$19.99</price>

      </product>
      <product>
              <commonname>Mosquito Trap</commonname>
              <price>$229.00</price>

      </product>
      <product>
              <commonname>Hammock (Cotton)</commonname>
              <price>$129.95</price>

      </product>
      <product>
              <commonname>Hammock (Polyester)</commonname>
              <price>$179.95</price>

      </product>
      <product>
              <commonname>Hammock Stand</commonname>
              <price>$125.00</price>

      </product>
</products>
```

The Style Sheet

Next, in Listing 11.2, is a sample XSLT style sheet. This style sheet is meant to interact with our source document using XSL commands.

LISTING 11.2   The XSLT Style Sheet

```xml
<?xml version="1.0" ?>
<xsl:stylesheet version="1.0" xmlns:xsl="http://www.w3.org/1999/XSL/Transform">
<xsl:output method="html" />
<xsl:template match="products">
        <table>
                <xsl:apply-templates />
        </table>
</xsl:template>
<xsl:template match="product">
        <tr>
                <xsl:apply-templates />
                </tr>
</xsl:template>
<xsl:template match="commonname">
        <td>
                <xsl:apply-templates />
        </td>
</xsl:template>
<xsl:template match="price">
        <td>
                <xsl:apply-templates />
        </td>
</xsl:template>
</xsl:stylesheet>
```

The Result Document

Third, in Listing 11.3, we have the result document. Note that our result document is an HTML document. It is the direct result of applying the style sheet against the source document.

LISTING 11.3   The Result Document

```html
<table>
        <tr>
                <td>
                        Garden Hose
                </td>
                <td>
                        $13.50
```

LISTING 11.3 Continued

```
                </td>
        </tr>
        <tr>
                <td>
                        Garden Caddy
                </td>
                <td>
                        $19.99
                </td>
        </tr>
        <tr>
                <td>
                        Mosquito Trap
                </td>
                <td>
                        $229.00
                </td>
        </tr>
        <tr>
                <td>
                        Hammock (Cotton)
                </td>
                <td>
                        $129.95
                </td>
        </tr>
        <tr>
                <td>
                        Hammock (Polyester)
                </td>
                <td>
                        $179.95
                </td>
        </tr>
        <tr>
                <td>
                        Hammock (Polyester)
                </td>
                <td>
                        $125.00
                </td>
        </tr>
</table>
```

The HTML in Listing 11.3 doesn't represent the ideally structured HTML document. It is missing header information and has only rudimentary formatting instructions, but you can see that the HTML works just well enough for most browsers to read it. Figure 11.2 shows the result document displayed inside a browser:

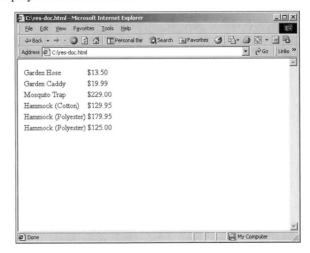

FIGURE 11.2

The result document in a browser.

This process of taking an XML and transforming it into HTML is probably one of the more common uses of XSLT transformations. But as we have said, our result document can really be any sort of structured document.

Now that we know what XSLT transformations are, it's time to dig into the meat of XSLT style sheets.

Anatomy of an XSLT Style Sheet

We can see from Listing 11.2 that an XSLT style sheet has components similar to a plain XML document. We start out with the following XML declaration statement:

```
<?xml version="1.0" ?>
```

Then we move onto our first XSLT-specific element:

```
<xsl:stylesheet version="1.0" xmlns:xsl="http://www.w3.org/1999/XSL/Transform">
```

This is the root document element for an XSLT style sheet. It is this element that contains all the other XSL elements in the document; it is the ultimate parent to all other XSL nodes. It can specify, with its attributes, a version, an ID, and namespaces.

> **NOTE**
>
> XSLT documents can also use the `<xsl:transform>` element as their root document element. For all practical intents and purposes, xsl:stylesheet and xsl:transform are identical in everything but their name.

The other XSLT elements concern themselves with one of the following:

- Formatting and setting up attributes and directives
- Selecting a portion of the source document to process
- Processing and logical comparison of document elements

The first set of elements encountered inside the document element will be the formatting and attribute elements. These elements are responsible for specifying miscellaneous instructions to the XSLT processor. For example, the `<xsl:output>` element indicates whether the result document will be in a format other than XML. In our previous example, we set this value to HTML to indicate that we were outputting an HTML document.

At the heart of XSLT functionality is the `<xsl:template>` directive. This selects portions of the source document by using pattern matching. If you again refer back to our previous example in which we transformed an XML document into an HTML document, you will see that we used the `<xsl:template>` element to specify which nodes of our source document we wanted to transform.

You also have the capability to execute simple logic in an XSLT document by using `if-then` statements, looping statements, and formatting statements.

Table 11.2 lists all the currently defined XSLT elements.

TABLE 11.2 XSLT Elements

Data Type	Description
xsl:apply-imports	Used to reference an external style sheet so that its elements will be brought into the current style sheet. Similar to the xsl:include element.
xsl:apply-templates	Works in conjunction with the xsl:template element to actually perform a transform; has a select attribute that can be used to select a set of nodes from the source document, and a mode attribute that is used to select specific xml:template elements to process.
xsl:attribute	Used to write element attributes out to the result document.

TABLE 11.2 Continued

Data Type	Description
xsl:attribute-set	Sets up a group of xsl:attribute elements that can be referenced by name.
xsl:call-template	Allows you to programmatically "call" an xsl:template element by its name.
xsl:choose	Similar to a case statement in Visual Basic; allows for a logic test that can deal with multiple conditions.
xsl:comment	Writes a comment element out to the result document.
xsl:copy	Copies the currently selected node from the source document into the result document.
xsl:copy-of	Similar to the xsl:copy element, capable of inserting entire subtrees of nodes into the result document.
xsl:decimal-format	Declares a format for decimal numbers; works in conjunction with the xsl:format-number element.
xsl:element	Used to explicitly create an element in the result document.
xsl:fallback	Used to specify "alternative" content in the result document in the event that the XSLT processor encounters an XSL element it doesn't recognize.
xsl:for-each	Supplies the capability to iterate through a node set while applying a template on each pass.
xsl:if	Performs a logical IF test.
xsl:import	Imports the contents of another XSLT style sheet.
xsl:include	Performs a wholesale include of another XSLT style sheet.
xsl:key	Sets up a named key that can then be used with the XPath key() function.
xsl:message	Sends a message to the XSLT processor for display; depending on the processor being used, this could result in a message box being displayed to the screen or an entry being written to a log file.
xsl:namespace-alias	Replaces one namespace reference with another through an alias.
xsl:number	Inserts a number into the result document.
xsl:otherwise	Branching logic for use with the xsl:choose and xsl:when elements.
xsl:output	Directs the processor on options for creating the result document.

TABLE 11.2 Continued

Data Type	Description
xsl:param	Supplies a way to create named parameters for use with an xsl:stylesheet element.
xsl:preserve-space	Allows text nodes that contain only whitespace.
xsl:processing-instruction	Writes a processing instruction element to the result document.
xsl:sort	Provides the sort criteria for sorting nodes selected by an xsl:for-each or xsl:apply-templates element.
xsl:strip-space	Tells the processor to remove any nodes that only contain whitespace.
xsl:stylesheet	The root document element; contains all other XSLT elements in a style sheet.
xsl:template	Used to define a series of commands and the nodes that they should apply to.
xsl:text	Writes raw text to the result document.
xsl:transform	See xsl:stylesheet.
xsl:value-of	Creates a string expression for evaluation by the processor; primarily used to return the text value of nodes returned by some other function.
xsl:variable	Creates a variable (and value) that can be referenced in the style sheet.
xsl:when	Used with the xsl:choose and xsl:otherwise elements to test for multiple conditions.
xsl:with-param	Used to override parameters supplied to a template.

The Transformation Process in Summary

We have already presented a high-level overview of how source documents are combined with style sheets to create a result document. We have also touched on the basics of XSLT syntax. Armed with these two pieces of knowledge, we can dig into the transformation process in more detail. Following is the detailed sequence of steps that the XSLT processor takes when transforming documents. It might be helpful for you to refer back to Listings 11.2, 11.3, and 11.4 as you read through the various steps of the transform process; you should be able to clearly see how our HTML result document is built by following the transform process closely:

- Everything starts with the `<xsl:template>` tag. The processor will look at this element's match attribute and locate all the nodes that correspond to the identified match. In our example, the first template tag tries to match against "products." This means that the XSLT processor will be looking for nodes with the name "products." Each node matched to the match attribute is passed into the template.

- The processor now processes each element in the template. A template is considered to be all the content located inside of the `xsl:template` element. As each part of the template is processed, the processor will start to build the result document. The template will essentially hold two types of content: XSLT instructions and literals. XSLT instructions are the elements that we have documented in Table 11.2. Literals are non-XSLT instructions that are passed verbatim to the result document. This occurs in fragments, which will all be pulled together at the end of the process to create the whole result document. If we again refer back to Listing 11.3, the first template processed would include the following (note the `<table>` `</table>` literals, and the `<xsl:apply-templates>` instruction):

```
<table>
        <xsl:apply-templates />
</table>
```

- While the processor executes the XSLT instructions, it generates actual content for the result document. These fragments are inserted into their correct location in the working result document (really just an in-memory representation of the final result document).

- The final step occurs when the XSLT processor actually processes the template for the source documents root. This causes all the previously generated result fragments to be assembled in the correct order. Typically, at this point, the result document is complete and is streamed out to its final destination.

This whole process is best understood as one of substitution: The XML document content (element content) is substituted in for `xsl:apply-templates` tags, matching specifically on the element identified by the `xsl:template match` attribute.

The preceding is a quick tour of what XSLT is and what it does. At this point, your basic understanding of XML document transforms is almost complete. However, we have to touch on one more set of concepts before diving into the .NET XSLT namespace particulars: XPath.

NOTE

Any element in a style sheet that does not have the xsl: prefix is considered to be a *literal result element* (LRE). LREs are simply shoved into the result document as is. This is what lets us get away with embedding HTML tags into a style sheet. The style sheet is not HTML aware; it simply writes the tags into the result document (which, in our examples, is an HTML document).

Suggestions for Further Exploration

⊃ There are two great resources for obtaining exact details on the syntax of each XSL element (including all their possible attributes): the Microsoft XML SDK documentation and the actual W3C XSLT specification at http://www.w3.org/TR/xslt.

⊃ We've mentioned this Web site in Chapter 10, "Reading and Writing XML," but it deserves to be repeated here: http://www.xml.com is a great site for gathering information about all things XML, including XSLT and XPath.

XPath Basics

A discussion of XSLT is not complete without a discussion of XPath. They are part and parcel of the larger transformation features provided for XML documents.

XPath, *XML Path Language*, is a specific XML-based vocabulary designed to uniquely specify portions of an XML document. That is, XPath enables you to select certain pieces of an XML document that are of interest to you. It does this through a standard syntax similar to a query language.

XSLT and XPath: Partners in the Transform Process

Consider the xml:template element again. From following the entire transform process, you know that the xml:template element is really running the show. Consider, too, how you "match" XML document nodes for template processing by using the match attribute. The examples we have shown simply match on an element's name. If this were all we could do to select nodes for template processing, XSLT would be a fairly brittle solution. Another XML sample proves this point; Listing 11.4 shows an XML document that describes manufactured assemblies in terms of their constituent parts.

LISTING 11.4   XML Document Describing Part Assemblies

```
<?xml version="1.0" encoding="utf-8" ?>
<assemblies>
        <assembly>
                <part>seal gasket</part>
                <part>3/4 star fastener</part>
                <part>connecting flange</part>
                <part>bolt</part>
                <part>bolt</part>
        </assembly>
        <assembly>
                <part>type T compressor </part>
                <part>front right elbow joint</part>
```

LISTING 11.4 Continued

```
                <part>connecting flange</part>
                <part>bolt</part>
                <part>bolt</part>
                <part>vertical swash plate</part>
        </assembly>
        <assembly>
                <part>float valve</part>
                <part>distribution valve</part>
                <part>agitator</part>
                <part>dipole switch</part>
        </assembly>
</assemblies>
```

What if your assignment as a programmer was to take that XML document and transform it, using XSLT, into an HTML document that would display the name of the third part in the second assembly?

You could loop through the document using some sort of XSLT-specified loop, perhaps setting up a counter variable so that you would know how many "assembly" nodes deep you were and how many "part" nodes deep you were, but the solution really cries out for some way to specify a path through the XML document to the exact node or nodes that you want. XPath makes this task trivial. Listing 11.5 shows one possible solution that uses an `xsl-template` element that matches XML nodes using something called an XPath *expression*. An XPath expression is a series of one or more functions that resolve to a specific location in an XML document.

LISTING 11.5 XSLT Style Sheet Matching with an XPath Expression

```
<?xml version="1.0" ?>
<xsl:stylesheet version="1.0" xmlns:xsl="http://www.w3.org/1999/XSL/Transform">
<xsl:output method="html" />
<xsl:template match="/assemblies/assembly[position()=2]/part[position()=3]">
        <table>
                <tr>
                        <td>
                                <xsl:apply-templates />
                        </td>
                </tr>
        </table>
</xsl:template>
</xsl:stylesheet>
```

Transforming the XML document in Listing 11.4 with the style sheet in Listing 11.5 would result in the HTML code in Listing 11.6:

LISTING 11.6   HTML Result Document

```
<table>
        <tr>
                <td>
                        connecting flange
                </td>
        </tr>
</table>
```

XPath Expressions

XPath expressions are meant to verbalize a path into an XML document, reaching down to a specific node or set of nodes. This is a successful method of navigating through an XML document because of XML's hierarchical nature. Just as you would navigate to a specific file in a file store using a path like this:

```
c:\my documents\work stuff\financials\cash flow.xls
```

you can specify a path to a document node like this:

```
/rootnode/somechildnode/adeeperchildnode/targetnode
```

Each XPath expression can consist of a variety of operators, each with its own specific relevance to the path. In addition, XPath expressions can contain functions, such as the `Position()` function we used in the preceding example.

Table 11.3 shows some of the more common operators (also known as *tokens*) in an XPath expression.

TABLE 11.3   XPath Expression Operators

Operator	Description
( )	Establishes groupings of operators
[ ]	Either applies a filter pattern or identifies an element through its subscript
.	Indicates the current element
..	Indicates the parent element
@	Identifies an attribute's name; if used without an attribute name, identifies all attributes (wildcard)
*	Wildcard for selecting all elements
:	Separator

TABLE 11.3 Continued

Operator	Description
/	Either indicates the start of the XML document or the immediate children of the preceding element
//	Specifies a recursive search for an element (digs down any number of tree levels to find the element)

Table 11.4 shows all the currently defined XPath functions with their descriptions. Each function is grouped within one of five categories. The *node-set functions* provide the capability to query or return nodes, the *string functions* provide string manipulation and formatting functionality, the *Boolean functions* provide true/false condition testing, the *number functions* provide numerical and arithmetic operations, and the *XSLT functions* provide information about nodes encapsulated in a collection. Like the XSLT elements, the best place for detailed documentation on each of these functions is the Microsoft XML SDK documentation or the W3C at http://www.w3.org/TR/xpath.

TABLE 11.4 XPath Functions

Function	Description
Node-Set Functions	
count	Returns the number of nodes in the supplied node set
document	Returns nodes contained in an externally referenced document
id	Returns an element based on its ID
key	Returns all nodes that match the passed-in key and key value
last	Returns the number of the last node in the referenced node set
local-name	Returns the local name (the part after the namespace separator) for the first node in the referenced node set
name	Returns the entire expanded name of the reference node set
namespace-uri	Returns the URI to the namespace
position	Returns the position (index) of the currently referenced node inside to the parent node
String Functions	
concat	Returns a string that is a concatenation of the passed-in strings
contains	Returns a Boolean indicating whether the first referenced string contains the second referenced string
normalize-space	Returns the passed-in string with whitespaces removed
starts-with	Returns a Boolean indicating whether the first referenced string starts with the second referenced string

TABLE 11.4 Continued

Function	Description
	String Functions
string	Converts the supplied parameter to a string and returns it
string-length	Returns the number of characters in the reference string
substring	Returns a substring of the references string, as indicated by the supplied offset position value and the supplied length value
substring-after	Returns a substring of the first referenced string that follows the first occurrence of the second referenced string
substring-before	Returns a substring of the first referenced string that occurs before the first occurrence of the second referenced string
translate	Returns a version of a string with the characters replaced by any matching characters supplied in the arguments to the function
	Boolean Functions
boolean	Converts the supplied parameter to a Boolean value
false	Returns the value `false`
lang	Returns a Boolean indicating whether the xml:lang attribute matches the supplied parameter
not	Returns the opposite of the supplied Boolean parameter
true	Returns the value `true`
	Number Functions
ceiling	Returns the integer that is closest in value and larger than the supplied integer
floor	Returns the integer that is closest in value and smaller than the supplied integer
number	Returns the supplied parameter as a number
round	Returns the integer closest in value to the supplied parameter
sum	Returns the sum of all nodes in the referenced node set
	XSLT Functions
current	Returns the current node that is being processed
element-available	Returns a Boolean value indicating whether the processor supports the instruction element specified in the parameter
format-number	Returns a string representation of the supplied number parameter
function-available	Returns a Boolean value indicating whether the processor supports the function specified in the parameter
generate-id	Generates a unique ID for the first node in the identified node set

TABLE 11.4   Continued

Function	Description
	XSLT Functions
node-set	Converts a result tree fragment to a node set
system-property	Returns the value of the specified system property
unparsed-entity-uri	Returns the PUBLIC or SYSTEM value of an entity's URI

XPath expressions themselves can contain a mixture of path identifiers and functions. Our example interspersed both:

```
/assemblies/assembly[position()=2]/part[position()=3]
```

When XPath expressions are evaluated by the XSLT processor, they can result in one of the following:

- A set of nodes
- A Boolean value
- A numeric value
- A string value

With a summary of both XSLT and XPath concepts under our belt, we are now prepared to examine the `System.Xml.Xslt` and `System.Xml.XPath` namespaces.

XSLT Processing with .NET

The `System.Xml.Xsl` namespace houses .NET's XSLT processor: the `XslTransform` class. This class is responsible for performing, with the assistance of other utility classes, XSLT-compliant parsing. To understand its capabilities, it is probably best to jump right in and see it in action.

Loading a Style Sheet

If you think back to the high-level view of the XSLT transformation process, you can easily see the steps that we will have to take to perform such a transform programmatically. We will want to specify a style sheet to use for the transform. We will also want to specify the source document. The `XslTransform` class handles both tasks.

We need to first instantiate an instance of the class:

```
Dim xslt As New XslTransform()
```

Then we need to specify the style sheet we want to use for our transform. This is done through the `XslTransform.Load` method. We have a variety of options on how to actually use the Load method; it is overloaded in several forms because the `XslTransform` class supports many types of sources for the style sheet. We'll talk about the different varieties of inputs in a moment. For now, let's assume we want to specify a local file as the style sheet:

```
xslt.Load("xform.xsl")
```

We now need an instance of the source document. Let's assume our source XML document is the "assemblies.xml" document that we constructed in Listing 11.4 and that it is available to us as a local file:

```
sourceDoc = "assemblies.xml"
resultDoc = "out.html"
xslt.Transform(sourceDoc, resultDoc)
```

Let's look at a simple console application that brings all this together. We will reuse the general structure of the files that we detailed at the beginning of this chapter in Listings 11.1 and 11.2. This time through, we have added some more data fields to the XML source document (which we call garden_catalog.xml; see Listing 11.7).

LISTING 11.7   The Garden Catalog XML Document

```xml
<?xml version="1.0" encoding="utf-8" ?>
<products>
        <product>
                <commonname>Garden Hose</commonname>
                <price>$13.50</price>
                <SKU>77809132</SKU>
                <instock>yes</instock>
                <mfr>Trevarney</mfr>
        </product>
        <product>
                <commonname>Garden Caddy</commonname>
                <price>$19.99</price>
                <SKU>76700032</SKU>
                <instock>yes</instock>
                <mfr>Trevarney</mfr>
        </product>
        <product>
                <commonname>Mosquito Trap</commonname>
                <price>$229.00</price>
                <SKU>42911732</SKU>
                <instock>yes</instock>
                <mfr>Dasher</mfr>
        </product>
        <product>
```

LISTING 11.7   Continued

```
                <commonname>Hammock (Cotton)</commonname>
                <price>$129.95</price>
                <SKU>43260632</SKU>
                <instock>yes</instock>
                <mfr>Herrington</mfr>
        </product>
        <product>
                <commonname>Hammock (Polyester)</commonname>
                <price>$179.95</price>
                <SKU>44478732</SKU>
                <instock>yes</instock>
                <mfr>Herrington</mfr>
        </product>
        <product>
                <commonname>Hammock Stand</commonname>
                <price>$125.00</price>
                <SKU>44478032</SKU>
                <instock>yes</instock>
                <mfr>Herrington</mfr>
        </product>
</products>
```

In Listing 11.8 we have added some more HTML formatting elements in the style sheet (xform.xsl), but everything is still basic in content.

LISTING 11.8   The Garden Catalog Style Sheet

```
<?xml version="1.0" encoding="utf-8" ?>
<xsl:stylesheet version="1.0" xmlns:xsl="http://www.w3.org/1999/XSL/Transform">
        <xsl:output method="html" />
        <xsl:template match="products">
                <table>
                        <xsl:apply-templates />
                </table>
        </xsl:template>
        <xsl:template match="product">
                <table>
                        <xsl:apply-templates />
                </table>
        </xsl:template>
        <xsl:template match="commonname">
                <tr>
                        <td>
                                <b>
                                        <xsl:apply-templates />
```

LISTING 11.8   Continued

```
                                </b>
                        </td>
                </tr>
        </xsl:template>
        <xsl:template match="price">
                <tr>
                        <td>
                                Price:
                        </td>
                        <td>
                                <xsl:apply-templates />
                        </td>
                </tr>
        </xsl:template>
        <xsl:template match="SKU">
                <tr>
                        <td>
                                SKU:
                        </td>
                        <td>
                                <xsl:apply-templates />
                        </td>
                </tr>
        </xsl:template>
        <xsl:template match="instock">
                <tr>
                        <td>
                                In Stock?
                        </td>
                        <td>
                                <xsl:apply-templates />
                        </td>
                </tr>
        </xsl:template>
        <xsl:template match="mfr">
                <tr>
                        <td>
                                Made By:
                        </td>
                        <td>
                                <xsl:apply-templates />
                        </td>
                </tr>
        </xsl:template>
</xsl:stylesheet>
```

Finally, the console app that brings everything together is in Listing 11.9.

LISTING 11.9   Console Application: A Simple Transform

```
Imports System.Xml.Xsl

Module Module1

    Sub Main()
        Try
            Dim xslt As New XslTransform()
            Dim sourceDoc As String
            Dim resultDoc As String
            Dim xformDoc As String

            sourceDoc = "garden_catalog.xml"
            resultDoc = "display_catalog.html"
            xformDoc = "xform.xsl"

            Console.WriteLine("Source document: " & sourceDoc)
            Console.WriteLine("Style sheet: " & xformDoc)
            Console.WriteLine("Result document: " & resultDoc)

            Console.WriteLine()
            Console.WriteLine("Loading style sheet...")
            xslt.Load(xformDoc)

            Console.WriteLine("Processing transformation...")
            xslt.Transform(sourceDoc, resultDoc)

            Console.WriteLine("Processing complete.")
            Console.WriteLine("Hit ENTER to exit.")
            Console.ReadLine()

        Catch appErr As Exception
            MsgBox("An error was encountered." & vbCrLf & appErr.Message)
        End Try

    End Sub

End Module
```

If everything goes well, after running the console application you should end up with an HTML document (display_catalog.html) in the applications execution directory. Figure 11.3 shows what the resulting HTML looks like in a browser.

NOTE

Don't forget that for the program to work as written, these XML and XSL documents need to be in the same directory as the application executable.

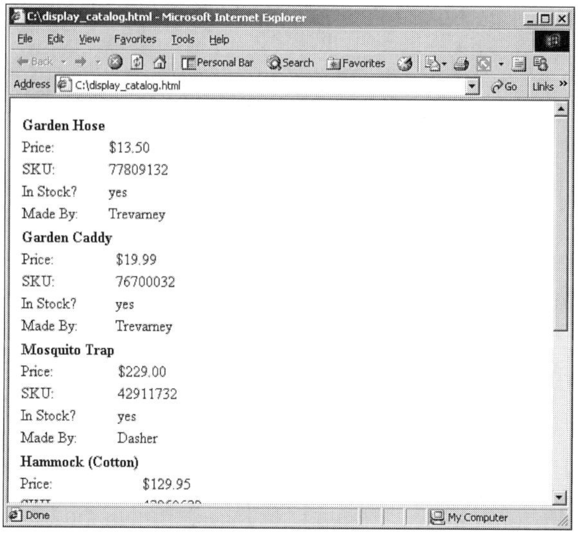

FIGURE 11.3
Display_Catalog.html in a browser.

Sources of Input

The capability of the `XslTransform` class to support many varieties of input and output is its key strength. The possibilities are represented through the different overloaded versions of both the `Load` method and the `Transform` method. Each version supports a different design pattern for XSLT transforms.

Here are the different definitions of the `Load` method:

```
Overloads Public Sub Load(ByVal stylesheet As IXPathNavigable)

Overloads Public Sub Load(ByVal url As String)

Overloads Public Sub Load(ByVal stylesheet As XmlReader)
```

```
Overloads Public Sub Load(ByVal stylesheet As XPathNavigator)

Overloads Public Sub Load(ByVal stylesheet As IXPathNavigable, _
    ByVal resolver As XmlResolver)

Overloads Public Sub Load(ByVal url As String, ByVal resolver As _
    XmlResolver)

Overloads Public Sub Load(ByVal stylesheet As XmlReader, ByVal resolver _
    As XmlResolver)

Overloads Public Sub Load(ByVal stylesheet As XPathNavigator, ByVal _
    resolver As XmlResolver)
```

We can see that the class supports URLs for referencing style sheets on the Internet, XmlReader instances, and XPathNavigator instances. It also enables you to reference an IXPathNavigable interface—and that interface is implemented by the XmlNode class, the XmlDocument class, and the XmlDataDocument class. In essence, we can implement a transform over nearly any type of data store by using one of these four sources.

As an example of the flexibility, consider some of the following code snippets:

```
'Load the style sheet from a web adddress...
xslt.Load("http://someserver/xform.xsl")


'Load the style sheet from a file
xslt.Load("c:\my documents\style sheets\xform.xsl")


'Load the style sheet from an XPathNavigator
Dim xpathDoc As XPathDocument = New XPathDocument("xform.xsl")
Dim xpathNav As XPathNavigator = xpathDoc.CreateNavigator()
xslt.Load(xpathNav)


'Load the style sheet from an XmlReader
Dim reader As XmlTextReader = New XmlTextReader("xform.xsl")
xslt.Load(reader)
```

Figure 11.4 shows us the various supported inputs to the transform process.

The XPathNavigator is an interesting option to use because it has been specifically designed and optimized for style sheet parsing. Before we get into the specifics of the XPathNavigator and related classes, let's study the different types of outputs possible with the XslTransform.Transform method.

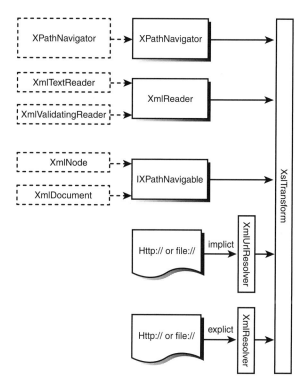

FIGURE 11.4
Supported inputs to the transform process.

Types of Output

Like the Load method, the XslTransform.Transform method is supported in a multitude of overloaded versions. Following are their function signatures:

```
Overloads Public Function Transform(ByVal input As IXPathNavigable, _
    ByVal args As XsltArgumentList) As XmlReader

Overloads Public Sub Transform(ByVal inputfile As String, _
    ByVal outputfile As String)

Overloads Public Function Transform(ByVal input As XPathNavigator, _
    ByVal args As XsltArgumentList) As XmlReader

Overloads Public Sub Transform(ByVal input As IXPathNavigable, _
    ByVal args As XsltArgumentList, ByVal output As Stream)

Overloads Public Sub Transform(ByVal input As IXPathNavigable, _
    ByVal args As XsltArgumentList, ByVal output As TextWriter)
```

```
Overloads Public Sub Transform(ByVal input As IXPathNavigable, _
    ByVal args As XsltArgumentList, ByVal output As XmlWriter)

Overloads Public Sub Transform(ByVal input As XPathNavigator, _
    ByVal args As XsltArgumentList, ByVal output As Stream)

Overloads Public Sub Transform(ByVal input As XPathNavigator, _
    ByVal args As XsltArgumentList, ByVal output As TextWriter)

Overloads Public Sub Transform(ByVal input As XPathNavigator, _
    ByVal args As XsltArgumentList, ByVal output As XmlWriter)
```

You can see that some of the Transform methods specify the result document instance as a parameter, and others will actually return an instance by defining Transform as a function call. For instance, we can do the following to get an XmlReader instance as the result of the transform:

```
Dim reader As XmlTextReader = xslt.Transform(xpathNavigable, argList)
```

Figure 11.5 represents a combined picture of the supported inputs and outputs of the XslTransform class.

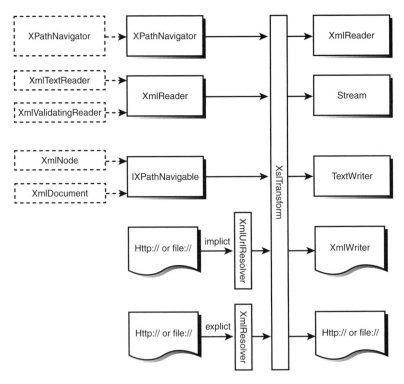

FIGURE 11.5

Supported inputs to the transform process.

Handling Exceptions

An XsltException instance will be thrown if an error is encountered while applying a style sheet through the XslTransform class. The XsltException class provides three specialized properties to help you diagnose and deal with the error:

- LineNumber Property—The line number in which the processing error occurred
- LinePosition Property—The exact position in the document line where the error occurred
- SourceUri Property—Returns the URI pointing to the loaded style sheet

All this works as expected in a Try-Catch block:

```
Try
    Dim xslt As New XslTransform()
    .
    .
    .
    xslt.Load(xformDoc)
    xslt.Transform(sourceDoc, resultDoc)
    .
    .
    .
Catch xslErr As XsltException
    MsgBox("An error was encountered (" & xslErr.Message & _
        ")in the XSLT document at line " & xslErr.LineNumber & _
        ", position " & xslErr.LinePosition)
Catch appErr As Exception
    MsgBox("A general application error was encountered." & vbCrLf & _
        vbCrLf & appErr.Message)
End Try
```

 Suggestions for Further Exploration

⊃ To specifically resolve a variable or function contained in a style sheet, investigate the use of the XsltContext class. It is an abstract class that provides a ResolveFunction method and a ResolveVariable method which both return interfaces, allowing access to the references function or variable.

Working with XPath

The System.Xml.Xpath namespace provides several classes designed to provide programming support for evaluating XPath expressions against XML data stores. In this section, we'll examine how to leverage these classes to query XML documents and evaluate build XPath expressions.

Navigating XML Documents

The XPathNavigator class is designed to enable you to quickly and easily traverse the attribute nodes of an XML document. The class uses XPath expressions and implements a cursor-based reader over a variety of different data stores. Unlike the XmlTextReader, XPathNavigator objects exist to provide random access. You instantiate an instance of an XPathNavigator by calling the CreateNavigator class on either the XmlNode class, the XPathDocument class, or the XmlDataDocument class:

```
Dim xmlNav As XPathNavigator

'Read in an XML file (location stored in fileName)
Dim xmlDoc As XmlDocument = New XmlDocument()

xmlDoc.Load(fileName)

'Create a navigator object from the XmlDocument instance
xmlNav = xmlDoc.CreateNavigator()
```

There are really two approaches supported by the XpathNavigator class to document navigation. The first is a simple, node-based series of "move to" methods. By using these methods in conjunction with the HasChildren property, it is relatively easy to hop around nodes by navigating up and down the XML element tree.

For instance, we can position the XPath cursor to the root node and then, using this pattern, recursively examine all the child nodes.

```
Dim xmlNav As XPathNavigator

'Read in an XML file (location stored in fileName)
Dim xmlDoc As XmlDocument = New XmlDocument()

xmlDoc.Load(fileName)

'Create a navigator object from the XmlDocument instance
xmlNav = xmlDoc.CreateNavigator()

xmlNav.MoveToRoot()

RecurseNodes(xmlNav)

Public Sub RecurseNodes(ByVal xmlNav As XPathNavigator)

    If xmlNav.HasChildren Then
        'child nodes detected
        'move to the first child...
        xmlNav.MoveToFirstChild()
```

```
        'now pass a new XPathNavigator instance into the
        'RecurseNodes sub
        RecurseNodes(xmlNav)

        'and finally, position the navigator back node
        'we started at
        xmlNav.MoveToParent()
    End If

    'We can now loop through the other nodes at the same
    'level as the current node
    While xmlNav.MoveToNext()
        '(do some processing)
        RecurseNodes(xmlNav)
    End While


End Sub
```

You will note that this is very similar to the code that we wrote in the previous chapter to recursively process nodes in an XML document using the `XmlDocument` class.

By querying the `NodeType` property (which returns an `XpathNodeType` instance, as shown in Table 11.5), we can figure out the type of element on which the cursor is currently positioned.

TABLE 11.5   The `XpathNodeType` Enumeration

Member	Description
All	All node types
Attribute	An element attribute
Comment	A comment
Element	An element
Namespace	A namespace
ProcessingInstruction	A processing instruction (PI)
Root	The root node
SignificantWhitespace	A node containing whitespace
Text	A text node (contained text of an element)
Whitespace	A node containing only whitespace

If you need to examine an element's attributes, you can first determine if the current element has attributes and, if it does, walk through those attributes the same as you walk node sets. To do this, you would query the HasAttributes property, using the MoveToNextAttribute to process each one individually:

```
If xmlNav.HasAttributes Then
    While xmlNav.MoveToNextAttribute()
        '(do some processing)

        'Reset the cursor to the parent
        xmlNav.MovetoParent()
    End While
End If
```

All the "move to" methods are documented in Table 11.6.

TABLE 11.6   XPathNavigator Cursor-Positioning Methods

Method	Description
MoveToAttribute	Moves the XPathNavigator to the attribute with the passed-in name
MoveToFirstAttribute	Moves the XPathNavigator to the first attribute of the current node
MoveToFirstChild	Moves the XPathNavigator to the first child node of the current node
MoveToFirstNamespace	Moves the XPathNavigator to the first namespace of the current node
MoveToId	Moves the XPathNavigator to the first attribute with the specified ID value
MoveToNamespace	Moves the XPathNavigator to the namespace node with the specified name
MoveToNext	Moves the XPathNavigator to the next sibling of the current node
MoveToNextAttribute	Moves the XPathNavigator to the next attribute of the current node
MoveToNextNamespace	Moves the XPathNavigator to the next namespace of the current node
MoveToParent	Moves the XPathNavigator to the parent of the current node
MoveToPrevious	Moves the XPathNavigator to the previous sibling of the current node
MoveToRoot	Moves the XPathNavigator to the root node

Of course, the real power of XML document addressing lies with XPath expressions and queries.

Querying XML Documents

The basic functionality of XPath queries begins with the `XPathNavigator.Select` method. This method takes in an XPath expression as either a string or as an actual `XPathExpression` instance. To illustrate programmatically specifying an XPath expression, let's revisit the scenario we set up in Listing 11.5. Specifically, we have an XML source document that contains assembly elements. Each assembly will have one or more part elements assigned to it.

To start off, let's write a simple console application that duplicates a solution to our prior requirement of selecting the third part from the second assembly. We have already presented the XPath expression necessary to retrieve that portion of the XML document:

```
"/assemblies/assembly[position()=2]/part[position()=3]"
```

Recall that this expression consists of both path information and function calls. Issuing this as a query command should be as simple as pumping this expression in as a string to the `XPathNavigator.Select` method:

```
xmlNav.Select("/assemblies/assembly[position()=2]/part[position()=3]")
```

The last piece of the puzzle falls into place when the `Select` method returns an `XPathNodeIterator` instance. We will have to deal with this iterator instance when we call the `Select` method:

```
Dim nodeIterator As XPathNodeIterator

nodeIterator = _
    xmlNav.Select("/assemblies/assembly[position()=2]/part[position()=3]"
```

The `XPathNodeIterator`, as its name suggests, is used to provide an iteration mechanism over a specific set of nodes. In this case, it is used to iterate through the node set returned as a result of our `Select` method call. As an iterator object, it provides the expected methods and properties necessary to count the nodes in the node set (through the `Count` property), retrieve the current node as an `XPathNavigator` instance (through the `Current` property), and move to the next node (by using the `MoveNext` method).

To see this in action, let's modify our initial XPath expression slightly:

```
"/assemblies/assembly[position()=2]/part"
```

Instead of selecting the third part from the second assembly, this revised expression should give us all the parts contained in the second assembly. Because we are expecting multiple nodes returned to us, this will allow us to see the iteration object visiting multiple nodes.

Listing 11.10 presents a console application that displays the name of each part contained in assembly #2 using the preceding XPath expression, and Figure 11.6 shows the output:

LISTING 11.10   Executing an XPath Query

```vb
Imports System.Xml
Imports System.Xml.XPath

Module Module1

    Sub Main()
        Try
            Dim xmlNav As XPathNavigator
            Dim xmlDoc As XmlDocument = New XmlDocument()
            Dim expression As String

            'First, load up an XMLDocument instance
            xmlDoc.Load("assemblies.xml")

            'Create an XPathNavigator from the XMLDocument
            xmlNav = xmlDoc.CreateNavigator()

            'This is the XPath expression we will send in;
            'will path down to the second assembly element in the
            'assemblies element and select all part elements
            expression = "/assemblies/assembly[position()=2]/part"

            'An XPathNodeIterator is returned to allow us to
            'explore the node-set selected as a result of the expression
            Dim iterator As XPathNodeIterator = xmlNav.Select(expression)

            'Using .MoveNext, we visit all of the return nodes, writing
            'their value out to the console
            While iterator.MoveNext()
                Console.WriteLine("Part: " & iterator.Current.Value)
            End While

            Console.WriteLine()
            Console.WriteLine("Hit Enter to Exit...")
            Console.ReadLine()

        Catch appErr As Exception
            MsgBox("An error occurred: " & appErr.Message)

        End Try


    End Sub

End Module
```

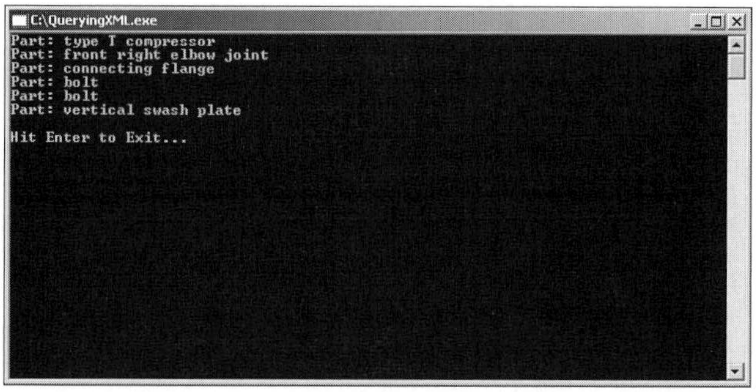

FIGURE 11.6
Results of the XPath query.

You can see that all the part elements inside the targeted assembly have been returned with one concise XPath expression. To demonstrate some more of the power of XPath, we'll tweak the console application a little bit to let you interactively specify an expression (see Listing 11.11):

LISTING 11.11 Executing an XPath Query

```
Imports System.Xml
Imports System.Xml.XPath

Module Module1
    Dim boolContinue As Boolean

    Sub Main()
        Try
            Dim xmlNav As XPathNavigator
            Dim xmlDoc As XmlDocument = New XmlDocument()
            Dim expression As String

            'First, load up an XMLDocument instance
            Console.WriteLine("Enter the full path/name of the target XML _
                doc:")
            Dim fileName As String = Console.ReadLine()

            xmlDoc.Load(fileName)

            'Create an XPathNavigator from the XMLDocument
            xmlNav = xmlDoc.CreateNavigator()


            boolContinue = True

            'Keep going until the user types 'EXIT'
```

LISTING 11.11 Continued

```
            While boolContinue
                Console.WriteLine("To exit, type 'EXIT' and hit ENTER...")
                Console.WriteLine()

                expression = PromptForQuery()

                'An XPathNodeIterator is returned to allow us to
                'explore the node-set selected as a result of the expression
                Dim iterator As XPathNodeIterator = xmlNav.Select(expression)

                'Using .MoveNext, we visit all of the return nodes, writing
                'their value out to the console. For clarity, we are also
                'writing out the type of node returned
                While iterator.MoveNext()
                    Console.WriteLine("Node Type: " & _
                        iterator.Current.NodeType.ToString)
                    Console.WriteLine(iterator.Current.Name & ": " & _
                        iterator.Current.Value)
                    Console.WriteLine()
                End While

                Console.WriteLine()
                Console.WriteLine()
            End While


        Catch appErr As Exception
            MsgBox("An error occurred: " & appErr.Message)

        End Try


    End Sub
    Public Function PromptForQuery() As String
        Dim expr As String

        Console.WriteLine("Type a valid XPath expression, then hit ENTER:")
        expr = Console.ReadLine()

        If Trim(expr) = "EXIT" Then
            boolContinue = False
        End If

        PromptForQuery = Trim(expr)

    End Function

End Module
```

Figure 11.7 shows the results of a few queries made against the same assemblies.xml file.

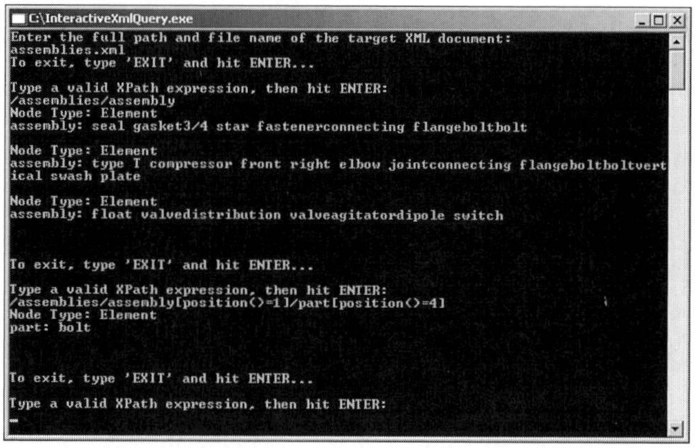

FIGURE 11.7
More XPath queries.

There is also the option of encapsulating XPath expressions in an XPathExpression class. The XPathExpression class is actually a precompiled representation of an XPath expression and, as such, may offer performance benefits for static queries.

XPathExpression objects are generated by calling the XpathNavigator.Compile method; after retrieving an XPathExpression instance, this can be passed into the XPathNavigator.Select method:

```
Dim xpathExpr As XPathExpression

xpathExpr = xmlNav.Compile("assemblies.xml")

xmlNav.Select(xpathExpr)
```

We had previously mentioned that an XPath expression could evaluate to a node set, a Boolean, a number, or a string. The XPathExpression class lets you query its ReturnType property to determine exactly what type of value was returned as a result of the query. Table 11.7 shows the possible XpathResultType enumerations.

TABLE 11.7 The XpathResultType Enumeration

Member	Description
Any	Any of the possible XPath return types.
Boolean	The XPath expression has evaluated to a True or False value.
Error	There was an error matching the result to an XPath result type.

TABLE 11.7   Continued

Member	Description
Navigator	The XPath expression has evaluated to a tree fragment.
NodeSet	The XPath expression has evaluated to a node set.
Numeric	The XPath expression has evaluated to a numerical value.
String	The XPath expression has evaluated to a string value.

 Suggestions for Further Exploration

⊃ If you are curious about XPath schemas, consult the .NET Framework documentation on the XmlSchemaXPath class.

⊃ Because XPath seems so well suited to data retrieval from structured documents, you may be wondering if any sort of integration is offered with Microsoft SQL Server 2000. The short answer is, "Yes!" See the Microsoft SQL Server 2000 documentation for more information on how you can use XPath with your relational database solutions.

Learning by Example: ReservationsDesk 2

This application is a revision of the sample application discussed in the previous chapter; we have essentially reprogrammed the ReservationsDesk program to use XPath queries for information retrieval. You can still query the guests.xml file either by a check-in date or the guests' first and last names. Each search is constrained to a specific hotel, which is selected from the hotel drop-down list.

Figure 11.8 shows the main form of the application.

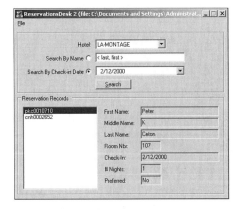

FIGURE 11.8

ReservationsDesk 2 main form.

Key Concepts Covered

Key concepts covered by the OrderQuery application are the following:

- Use of the XPathNavigator and XPathNodeIterator classes to "Walk" nodes in an XML document
- Dynamically querying an XML document using XPath expressions

Listing 11.12 shows all of the usual form setup for the user interface. We have added two declarations that are global to the Main class: resFile contains the full file path and name for the source XML document, and xmlDoc is our global XmlDocument instance that represents that file.

LISTING 11.12 ReservationsDesk 2

```
Imports System.Xml
Imports System.Xml.XPath

Public Class Main
    Inherits System.Windows.Forms.Form

    Public resFile As String
    Public xmlDoc As XmlDocument

    Friend WithEvents buttonSearch As System.Windows.Forms.Button
    Friend WithEvents Label2 As System.Windows.Forms.Label
    Friend WithEvents Label3 As System.Windows.Forms.Label
    Friend WithEvents Label4 As System.Windows.Forms.Label
    Friend WithEvents Label5 As System.Windows.Forms.Label
    Friend WithEvents Label6 As System.Windows.Forms.Label
    Friend WithEvents Label7 As System.Windows.Forms.Label
    Friend WithEvents Label8 As System.Windows.Forms.Label
    Friend WithEvents RadioButtonByName As System.Windows.Forms.RadioButton
    Friend WithEvents RadioButtonByDate As System.Windows.Forms.RadioButton
    Friend WithEvents TextBoxName As System.Windows.Forms.TextBox
    Friend WithEvents DateTimeCheckin As System.Windows.Forms.DateTimePicker
    Friend WithEvents ListBoxGuests As System.Windows.Forms.ListBox
    Friend WithEvents ComboHotel As System.Windows.Forms.ComboBox
    Friend WithEvents TextBoxPreferred As System.Windows.Forms.TextBox
    Friend WithEvents TextBoxNumNights As System.Windows.Forms.TextBox
    Friend WithEvents TextBoxCheckinDate As System.Windows.Forms.TextBox
    Friend WithEvents TextBoxRoomNbr As System.Windows.Forms.TextBox
    Friend WithEvents TextBoxLastName As System.Windows.Forms.TextBox
    Friend WithEvents TextBoxMiddleName As System.Windows.Forms.TextBox
    Friend WithEvents TextBoxFirstName As System.Windows.Forms.TextBox
```

LISTING 11.12   Continued

```
#Region " Windows Form Designer generated code "

    Public Sub New()
        MyBase.New()

        'This call is required by the Windows Form Designer.
        InitializeComponent()

        'Add any initialization after the InitializeComponent() call
        xmlDoc = New XmlDataDocument()
    End Sub

    'Form overrides dispose to clean up the component list.
    Protected Overloads Overrides Sub Dispose(ByVal disposing As Boolean)
        If disposing Then
            If Not (components Is Nothing) Then
                components.Dispose()
            End If
        End If
        MyBase.Dispose(disposing)
    End Sub
    Friend WithEvents MainMenu1 As System.Windows.Forms.MainMenu
    Friend WithEvents MenuItem1 As System.Windows.Forms.MenuItem
    Friend WithEvents MenuItem2 As System.Windows.Forms.MenuItem
    Friend WithEvents MenuItem3 As System.Windows.Forms.MenuItem
    Friend WithEvents OpenFileDialog1 As System.Windows.Forms.OpenFileDialog
    Friend WithEvents GroupBox1 As System.Windows.Forms.GroupBox
    Friend WithEvents GroupBox2 As System.Windows.Forms.GroupBox
    Friend WithEvents Label1 As System.Windows.Forms.Label

    'Required by the Windows Form Designer
    Private components As System.ComponentModel.Container

    'NOTE: The following procedure is required by the Windows Form Designer
    'It can be modified using the Windows Form Designer.
    'Do not modify it using the code editor.
    <System.Diagnostics.DebuggerStepThrough()> _
        Private Sub InitializeComponent()
        Dim resources As System.Resources.ResourceManager = New _
            System.Resources.ResourceManager(GetType(Main))
        Me.TextBoxCheckinDate = New System.Windows.Forms.TextBox()
        Me.TextBoxNumNights = New System.Windows.Forms.TextBox()
        Me.RadioButtonByDate = New System.Windows.Forms.RadioButton()
        Me.GroupBox2 = New System.Windows.Forms.GroupBox()
        Me.Label8 = New System.Windows.Forms.Label()
```

LISTING 11.12 Continued

```
Me.TextBoxPreferred = New System.Windows.Forms.TextBox()
Me.Label7 = New System.Windows.Forms.Label()
Me.Label6 = New System.Windows.Forms.Label()
Me.TextBoxRoomNbr = New System.Windows.Forms.TextBox()
Me.Label5 = New System.Windows.Forms.Label()
Me.TextBoxLastName = New System.Windows.Forms.TextBox()
Me.Label4 = New System.Windows.Forms.Label()
Me.TextBoxMiddleName = New System.Windows.Forms.TextBox()
Me.Label3 = New System.Windows.Forms.Label()
Me.Label2 = New System.Windows.Forms.Label()
Me.TextBoxFirstName = New System.Windows.Forms.TextBox()
Me.ListBoxGuests = New System.Windows.Forms.ListBox()
Me.MainMenu1 = New System.Windows.Forms.MainMenu()
Me.MenuItem1 = New System.Windows.Forms.MenuItem()
Me.MenuItem2 = New System.Windows.Forms.MenuItem()
Me.MenuItem3 = New System.Windows.Forms.MenuItem()
Me.OpenFileDialog1 = New System.Windows.Forms.OpenFileDialog()
Me.DateTimeCheckin = New System.Windows.Forms.DateTimePicker()
Me.RadioButtonByName = New System.Windows.Forms.RadioButton()
Me.TextBoxName = New System.Windows.Forms.TextBox()
Me.Label1 = New System.Windows.Forms.Label()
Me.buttonSearch = New System.Windows.Forms.Button()
Me.ComboHotel = New System.Windows.Forms.ComboBox()
Me.GroupBox1 = New System.Windows.Forms.GroupBox()
Me.GroupBox2.SuspendLayout()
Me.GroupBox1.SuspendLayout()
Me.SuspendLayout()
'
'TextBoxCheckinDate
'
Me.TextBoxCheckinDate.Location = New System.Drawing.Point(264, 120)
Me.TextBoxCheckinDate.Name = "TextBoxCheckinDate"
Me.TextBoxCheckinDate.ReadOnly = True
Me.TextBoxCheckinDate.Size = New System.Drawing.Size(168, 20)
Me.TextBoxCheckinDate.TabIndex = 3
Me.TextBoxCheckinDate.Text = ""
'
'TextBoxNumNights
'
Me.TextBoxNumNights.Location = New System.Drawing.Point(264, 144)
Me.TextBoxNumNights.Name = "TextBoxNumNights"
Me.TextBoxNumNights.ReadOnly = True
Me.TextBoxNumNights.Size = New System.Drawing.Size(44, 20)
Me.TextBoxNumNights.TabIndex = 3
Me.TextBoxNumNights.Text = ""
```

LISTING 11.12 Continued

```
'
'RadioButtonByDate
'
Me.RadioButtonByDate.Checked = True
Me.RadioButtonByDate.Location = New System.Drawing.Point(8, 80)
Me.RadioButtonByDate.Name = "RadioButtonByDate"
Me.RadioButtonByDate.RightToLeft = _
    System.Windows.Forms.RightToLeft.Yes
Me.RadioButtonByDate.Size = New System.Drawing.Size(152, 16)
Me.RadioButtonByDate.TabIndex = 2
Me.RadioButtonByDate.TabStop = True
Me.RadioButtonByDate.Text = "Search By Check-in Date"
'
'GroupBox2
'
Me.GroupBox2.Controls.AddRange(New System.Windows.Forms.Control() _
{Me.Label8, Me.TextBoxPreferred, Me.TextBoxNumNights, Me.Label7, _
Me.TextBoxCheckinDate, Me.Label6, Me.TextBoxRoomNbr, Me.Label5, _
Me.TextBoxLastName, Me.Label4, Me.TextBoxMiddleName, Me.Label3, _
Me.Label2, Me.TextBoxFirstName, Me.ListBoxGuests})
Me.GroupBox2.Location = New System.Drawing.Point(4, 140)
Me.GroupBox2.Name = "GroupBox2"
Me.GroupBox2.Size = New System.Drawing.Size(444, 208)
Me.GroupBox2.TabIndex = 1
Me.GroupBox2.TabStop = False
Me.GroupBox2.Text = "Reservation Records"
'
'Label8
'
Me.Label8.Location = New System.Drawing.Point(184, 172)
Me.Label8.Name = "Label8"
Me.Label8.Size = New System.Drawing.Size(76, 16)
Me.Label8.TabIndex = 4
Me.Label8.Text = "Preferred:"
'
'TextBoxPreferred
'
Me.TextBoxPreferred.Location = New System.Drawing.Point(264, 168)
Me.TextBoxPreferred.Name = "TextBoxPreferred"
Me.TextBoxPreferred.ReadOnly = True
Me.TextBoxPreferred.Size = New System.Drawing.Size(44, 20)
Me.TextBoxPreferred.TabIndex = 3
Me.TextBoxPreferred.Text = ""
'
'Label7
'
```

LISTING 11.12   Continued

```
    Me.Label7.Location = New System.Drawing.Point(184, 148)
    Me.Label7.Name = "Label7"
    Me.Label7.Size = New System.Drawing.Size(76, 16)
    Me.Label7.TabIndex = 4
    Me.Label7.Text = "# Nights:"
    '
    'Label6
    '
    Me.Label6.Location = New System.Drawing.Point(184, 124)
    Me.Label6.Name = "Label6"
    Me.Label6.Size = New System.Drawing.Size(76, 16)
    Me.Label6.TabIndex = 4
    Me.Label6.Text = "Check-In:"
    '
    'TextBoxRoomNbr
    '
    Me.TextBoxRoomNbr.Location = New System.Drawing.Point(264, 96)
    Me.TextBoxRoomNbr.Name = "TextBoxRoomNbr"
    Me.TextBoxRoomNbr.ReadOnly = True
    Me.TextBoxRoomNbr.Size = New System.Drawing.Size(44, 20)
    Me.TextBoxRoomNbr.TabIndex = 3
    Me.TextBoxRoomNbr.Text = ""
    '
    'Label5
    '
    Me.Label5.Location = New System.Drawing.Point(184, 100)
    Me.Label5.Name = "Label5"
    Me.Label5.Size = New System.Drawing.Size(76, 16)
    Me.Label5.TabIndex = 4
    Me.Label5.Text = "Room Nbr:"
    '
    'TextBoxLastName
    '
    Me.TextBoxLastName.Location = New System.Drawing.Point(264, 72)
    Me.TextBoxLastName.Name = "TextBoxLastName"
    Me.TextBoxLastName.ReadOnly = True
    Me.TextBoxLastName.Size = New System.Drawing.Size(168, 20)
    Me.TextBoxLastName.TabIndex = 3
    Me.TextBoxLastName.Text = ""
    '
    'Label4
    '
    Me.Label4.Location = New System.Drawing.Point(184, 76)
    Me.Label4.Name = "Label4"
    Me.Label4.Size = New System.Drawing.Size(76, 16)
```

LISTING 11.12   Continued

```
Me.Label4.TabIndex = 4
Me.Label4.Text = "Last Name:"
'
'TextBoxMiddleName
'
Me.TextBoxMiddleName.Location = New System.Drawing.Point(264, 48)
Me.TextBoxMiddleName.Name = "TextBoxMiddleName"
Me.TextBoxMiddleName.ReadOnly = True
Me.TextBoxMiddleName.Size = New System.Drawing.Size(168, 20)
Me.TextBoxMiddleName.TabIndex = 3
Me.TextBoxMiddleName.Text = ""
'
'Label3
'
Me.Label3.Location = New System.Drawing.Point(184, 52)
Me.Label3.Name = "Label3"
Me.Label3.Size = New System.Drawing.Size(76, 16)
Me.Label3.TabIndex = 4
Me.Label3.Text = "Middle Name:"
'
'Label2
'
Me.Label2.Location = New System.Drawing.Point(184, 28)
Me.Label2.Name = "Label2"
Me.Label2.Size = New System.Drawing.Size(76, 16)
Me.Label2.TabIndex = 4
Me.Label2.Text = "First Name:"
'
'TextBoxFirstName
'
Me.TextBoxFirstName.Location = New System.Drawing.Point(264, 24)
Me.TextBoxFirstName.Name = "TextBoxFirstName"
Me.TextBoxFirstName.ReadOnly = True
Me.TextBoxFirstName.Size = New System.Drawing.Size(168, 20)
Me.TextBoxFirstName.TabIndex = 3
Me.TextBoxFirstName.Text = ""
'
'ListBoxGuests
'
Me.ListBoxGuests.Enabled = False
Me.ListBoxGuests.Location = New System.Drawing.Point(12, 24)
Me.ListBoxGuests.Name = "ListBoxGuests"
Me.ListBoxGuests.Size = New System.Drawing.Size(160, 173)
Me.ListBoxGuests.TabIndex = 0
'
```

LISTING 11.12 Continued

```vb
    'MainMenu1
    '
    Me.MainMenu1.MenuItems.AddRange(New System.Windows.Forms.MenuItem()_
    {Me.MenuItem1})
    '
    'MenuItem1
    '
    Me.MenuItem1.Index = 0
    Me.MenuItem1.MenuItems.AddRange(New System.Windows.Forms.MenuItem()_
    {Me.MenuItem2, Me.MenuItem3})
    Me.MenuItem1.Text = "&File"
    '
    'MenuItem2
    '
    Me.MenuItem2.Index = 0
    Me.MenuItem2.Text = "&Open"
    '
    'MenuItem3
    '
    Me.MenuItem3.Index = 1
    Me.MenuItem3.Text = "E&xit"
    '
    'DateTimeCheckin
    '
    Me.DateTimeCheckin.CustomFormat = ""
    Me.DateTimeCheckin.Format = _
       System.Windows.Forms.DateTimePickerFormat.Custom
    Me.DateTimeCheckin.Location = New System.Drawing.Point(168, 76)
    Me.DateTimeCheckin.Name = "DateTimeCheckin"
    Me.DateTimeCheckin.Size = New System.Drawing.Size(192, 20)
    Me.DateTimeCheckin.TabIndex = 4
    Me.DateTimeCheckin.Value = New Date(2000, 2, 12, 0, 0, 0, 0)
    '
    'RadioButtonByName
    '
    Me.RadioButtonByName.Location = New System.Drawing.Point(32, 52)
    Me.RadioButtonByName.Name = "RadioButtonByName"
    Me.RadioButtonByName.RightToLeft = System.Windows.Forms.RightToLeft.Yes
    Me.RadioButtonByName.Size = New System.Drawing.Size(128, 16)
    Me.RadioButtonByName.TabIndex = 2
    Me.RadioButtonByName.Text = "Search By Name"
    '
    'TextBoxName
    '
    Me.TextBoxName.Location = New System.Drawing.Point(168, 48)
```

LISTING 11.12   Continued

```vb
Me.TextBoxName.Name = "TextBoxName"
Me.TextBoxName.Size = New System.Drawing.Size(192, 20)
Me.TextBoxName.TabIndex = 3
Me.TextBoxName.Text = "< last, first >"
'
'Label1
'
Me.Label1.Location = New System.Drawing.Point(128, 24)
Me.Label1.Name = "Label1"
Me.Label1.Size = New System.Drawing.Size(40, 12)
Me.Label1.TabIndex = 0
Me.Label1.Text = "Hotel:"
'
'buttonSearch
'
Me.buttonSearch.Enabled = False
Me.buttonSearch.Location = New System.Drawing.Point(168, 104)
Me.buttonSearch.Name = "buttonSearch"
Me.buttonSearch.Size = New System.Drawing.Size(76, 20)
Me.buttonSearch.TabIndex = 5
Me.buttonSearch.Text = "&Search"
'
'ComboHotel
'
Me.ComboHotel.DropDownStyle = _
    System.Windows.Forms.ComboBoxStyle.DropDownList
Me.ComboHotel.DropDownWidth = 152
Me.ComboHotel.Enabled = False
Me.ComboHotel.Location = New System.Drawing.Point(168, 20)
Me.ComboHotel.Name = "ComboHotel"
Me.ComboHotel.Size = New System.Drawing.Size(152, 21)
Me.ComboHotel.TabIndex = 1
'
'GroupBox1
'
Me.GroupBox1.Controls.AddRange(New System.Windows.Forms.Control() _
{Me.buttonSearch, Me.DateTimeCheckin, Me.TextBoxName, _
Me.RadioButtonByDate, Me.RadioButtonByName, Me.ComboHotel, Me.Label1})
Me.GroupBox1.Location = New System.Drawing.Point(4, 4)
Me.GroupBox1.Name = "GroupBox1"
Me.GroupBox1.Size = New System.Drawing.Size(444, 132)
Me.GroupBox1.TabIndex = 0
Me.GroupBox1.TabStop = False
'
'Main
'
```

LISTING 11.12 Continued

```
        Me.AutoScaleBaseSize = New System.Drawing.Size(5, 13)
        Me.ClientSize = New System.Drawing.Size(454, 355)
        Me.Controls.AddRange(New System.Windows.Forms.Control() _
          {Me.GroupBox2, Me.GroupBox1})
        Me.FormBorderStyle = System.Windows.Forms.FormBorderStyle.FixedDialog
        Me.Icon = CType(resources.GetObject("$this.Icon"), System.Drawing.Icon)
        Me.MaximizeBox = False
        Me.Menu = Me.MainMenu1
        Me.Name = "Main"
        Me.Text = "ReservationsDesk 2 (no file loaded)"
        Me.GroupBox2.ResumeLayout(False)
        Me.GroupBox1.ResumeLayout(False)
        Me.ResumeLayout(False)

    End Sub

#End Region
```

This click event handler is responsible for displaying the File Open box, which lets the user select the input XML file.

```
    Private Sub MenuItem2_Click(ByVal sender As System.Object, _
        ByVal e As System.EventArgs) Handles MenuItem2.Click

        'Show a File Open dialog; this is for selecting the source
        'XML document...
        OpenFileDialog1.AddExtension = True

        OpenFileDialog1.DefaultExt = ".xml"
        OpenFileDialog1.Filter = "Reservation files (*.xml)|*.xml"
        OpenFileDialog1.InitialDirectory = _
            System.Reflection.Assembly.GetExecutingAssembly.Location

        OpenFileDialog1.ShowDialog()

        resFile = OpenFileDialog1.FileName

        If resFile = "" Then
            Me.Text = "ReservationsDesk 2 (no file loaded)"
        Else
            Me.Text = "ReservationsDesk 2 (file: " & resFile & ")"
            LoadResFile(resFile)
            ListHotels()
            buttonSearch.Enabled = True
            ComboHotel.Enabled = True
```

LISTING 11.12   Continued

```
        ListBoxGuests.Enabled = True
    End If

End Sub
```

The `LoadResFile` routine takes care of loading up our global `xmlDoc` object. All our XPath queries will be made against that object.

```
Public Sub LoadResFile(ByVal file As String)

    Try
        xmlDoc.Load(file)

    Catch appErr As XmlException
        MsgBox("The application was unable to load the XML file '" _
        & resFile & "'. The file may be corrupt, or may be from an _
        invalid " & "source. Please select a new file.")

    End Try

End Sub
```

This event handler kicks off the whole query process by calling the `ExecuteQuery` routine.

```
Private Sub buttonSearch_Click(ByVal sender As System.Object, _
    ByVal e As System.EventArgs) Handles buttonSearch.Click
    ExecuteQuery()
End Sub
```

Two major queries happen in this application. The first one pulls back all the guest nodes that match the criteria. `ExecuteQuery` is responsible for that, adding the guest IDs to the list box as it iterates through the node set returned by the XPath expression.

```
Private Sub ExecuteQuery()


    Try
        Dim expression As String
        Dim xmlHotel As XmlDocumentFragment
        Dim xpathNavGlobal As XPathNavigator
        Dim xpathIterator As XPathNodeIterator
        Dim firstName As String
        Dim lastName As String
        Dim fullName As String()
        Dim checkinDate As String
```

LISTING 11.12 Continued

```
Dim guestID As String

'Create the XPathNavigator object
xpathNavGlobal = xmlDoc.CreateNavigator

' If we are searching by name, build the appropriate
' XPath expression...
If RadioButtonByName.Checked Then
    'split the first/last name out
    fullName = Split(TextBoxName.Text, ",")

    lastName = Trim(fullName(0))
    firstName = Trim(fullName(1))

    'start to build up the string based on the user selections
    expression = "/register/hotel[@id = """ & _
        Me.ComboHotel.Text & """]"
    expression = expression & "/guests/guest[firstname = """ & _
        firstName & _
        """"
    expression = expression & " and lastname = """ & _
        lastName & """]"

    'Otherwise, search by check-in date
Else
    checkinDate = DateTimeCheckin.Text

    'start to build up the string based on the user selections
    expression = "/register/hotel[@id = """ & _
        Me.ComboHotel.Text & """]"
    expression = expression & "/guests/guest[checkindate = """ & _
        checkinDate & """]"
End If

'Execute the XPath query
xpathIterator = xpathNavGlobal.Select(expression)

ListBoxGuests.Items.Clear()

If xpathIterator.Count = 0 Then
    MsgBox("No guest records were found.", _
        , "No Records Found")

Else
```

LISTING 11.12 Continued

```
                'Iterate through the node-set returned by the XPath expression
                While xpathIterator.MoveNext()
                    guestID = ReturnGuestID(xpathIterator)
                    ListBoxGuests.Items.Add(guestID)
                End While
            End If

        Catch appErr As Exception
            MsgBox("An error occurred." & _
                vbCrLf & vbCrLf & "Error: " & appErr.Message)
        End Try
    End Sub
```

ReturnGuestID is a helper function; it takes the current XPathNodeIterator instance and uses it to retrieve the ID attribute for the current node. This is then used to fill the guest ID list box.

```
    Public Function ReturnGuestID(ByVal iterator As XPathNodeIterator) _
        As String
        Try
            iterator.Current.MoveToFirstAttribute()

            ReturnGuestID = iterator.Current.Value

            iterator.Current.MoveToPrevious()

        Catch appErr As Exception
            MsgBox("An error occurred while retrieving the id attribute" & _
            " of the guest _element." & vbCrLf & vbCrLf & "Error: " & _
                appErr.Message)
        End Try

    End Function
```

ListHotels is another helper function. It preloads the hotel drop-down list as soon as the XML source document is loaded into our global xmlDoc object.

```
Public Sub ListHotels()

        Try
            Dim xpathNavGlobal As XPathNavigator
            Dim xpathIterator As XPathNodeIterator

            xpathNavGlobal = xmlDoc.CreateNavigator

            xpathIterator = xpathNavGlobal.Select("/register/hotel/@id")
```

LISTING 11.12 Continued

```
            While xpathIterator.MoveNext()
                ComboHotel.Items.Add(xpathIterator.Current.Value)
            End While

            If ComboHotel.Items.Count <> 0 Then
                ComboHotel.Select(1, 1)
            End If

        Catch appErr As Exception
            MsgBox("An error occurred while retrieving the hotel elements." & _
                vbCrLf & vbCrLf & "Error: " & appErr.Message)
        End Try

    End Sub
```

This is where our second major query takes place. Operating from the guest ID attribute, DisplayGuestInfo pulls back a pointer to that entire guest element and then walks the child elements to retrieve the guest record data (such as first name, last name, check-in date, and so on). This is all then displayed out to the screen.

```
    Public Sub DisplayGuestInfo(ByVal id As String)
        Try
            Dim iterator As XPathNodeIterator
            Dim nav As XPathNavigator
            Dim childNav As XPathNavigator
            Dim childIterator As XPathNodeIterator

            nav = xmlDoc.CreateNavigator()

            iterator = nav.Select("/register/hotel/guests/guest[@id = """ & _
                id & """]")

            iterator.MoveNext()

            iterator.Current.MoveToFirstChild()
            TextBoxFirstName.Text = iterator.Current.Value

            iterator.Current.MoveToNext()
            TextBoxMiddleName.Text = iterator.Current.Value

            iterator.Current.MoveToNext()
            TextBoxLastName.Text = iterator.Current.Value

            iterator.Current.MoveToNext()
            TextBoxRoomNbr.Text = iterator.Current.Value
```

LISTING 11.12   Continued

```
            iterator.Current.MoveToNext()
            TextBoxCheckinDate.Text = iterator.Current.Value

            iterator.Current.MoveToNext()
            TextBoxNumNights.Text = iterator.Current.Value

            iterator.Current.MoveToNext()
            TextBoxPreferred.Text = iterator.Current.Value

        Catch appErr As Exception
            MsgBox("An error occurred retrieving the guest node elements" & _
                vbCrLf & vbCrLf & "Error: " & appErr.Message)
        End Try
    End Sub


    Private Sub ListBoxGuests_Click(ByVal sender As Object, _
        ByVal e As System.EventArgs)
          Handles ListBoxGuests.Click
        DisplayGuestInfo(ListBoxGuests.SelectedItem)
    End Sub
End Class
```

Summary

XPath and XSLT are two powerful technologies that can be put to some fantastic use for querying XML documents and transforming XML documents. We have seen the powerful support offered in .NET for XML document reading, writing, and validating: the `System.Xml.Xsl` and `System.Xml.XPath` namespaces further enrich that functionality.

In this chapter, we investigated the following:

- The concepts of XSLT and style sheets
- XPath expressions
- Transforming XML documents into HTML documents by using the `XslTransform` class and an XSL style sheet
- Selecting nodes out of an XML document using XPath expressions
- Navigating XML documents using the cursor-based `XpathNavigator` class

Working with Threads

IN THIS CHAPTER

In this chapter, we'll discuss how to leverage the Framework Class Library's support for threads. Due to the previous lack of support in Visual Basic for easily generating and managing threads, the topic of threading and multithreaded application design is not one that Visual Basic developers are typically familiar with. So, first on tap is a brief discussion of why you would want to develop multithreaded applications in the first place. Multithreaded applications are not a cure-all, but they are certainly one more tool that you can use to solve application design problems.

Then, we'll introduce some of the basic concepts of threading that will enable you to digest and understand how Microsoft has structured the threading classes in the .NET Framework. There is a very rich threading library exposed to you, and Visual Basic .NET also has some intrinsic language support for threads.

Finally, we will dive into programming with threads at both an introductory level and a more advanced level.

After reading this chapter, you should be able to:

- Apply threading concepts in your application design
- Create and use thread objects to execute code
- Understand how and why threads transition from state to state
- Discuss ways to prevent contention between threads
- Store and retrieve data within a thread and across threads

Key Classes Related to Threading

Table 12.1 shows some key classes related to threading.

TABLE 12.1   Key Classes of the `System.Threading` Namespace

Element/Namespace	Description
System.Threading	This namespace acts as an interface for developers to create and manage threads.
AutoResetEvent	A "signaling" class used to indicate when a specific thread has been released.
Interlocked	The `Interlocked` class synchronizes access to a variable, allowing more than one thread to safely access the variable without encountering concurrency problems.
ManualResetEvent	Similar to the `AutoResetEvent` class, this class is a "signaling" class used to indicate when a specific thread has been released. The signal can be manually set.
Monitor	The `Monitor` class is a synchronization class used to avoid concurrency and contention issues through the use of locks.
Mutex	The `Mutex` class is a synchronization class, which enforces mutually exclusive access to a resource between threads.

TABLE 12.1 Continued

Element/Namespace	Description
ReaderWriterLock	The ReaderWriterLock class is used to manage thread synchronization in scenarios that require multiple reader threads to access a resource while only allowing one writer thread access.
Thread	The Thread class represents a thread running in the context of a process. This class provides thread state management services.
ThreadAbortException	The ThreadAbortException class is generated whenever a thread object is aborted.
ThreadPool	The ThreadPool class allows developers to spawn threads from a common, framework-maintained pool of threads.

Understanding and Applying Threads

Before we can examine how to use threads in our code, we need a crash-course in what a thread is and how threading is supported by the Windows operating system.

Microsoft Windows Threading Support

Microsoft Windows is a *pre-emptive multitasking* operating system. That means that the operating system, by means of a program called the task scheduler, doles out processor time to programs that are running.

All of these running programs are demanding attention from the CPU to perform their code instructions. Windows, based on a few different parameters that we will talk about later, lets a program run for a period of time (called *a time slice*) before interrupting it so that another program can get processor time—the term pre-emptive. The task scheduler forces programs to yield their processing slot regardless of whether they have indicated that it is acceptable to do so. These time slices are measured in microseconds. For single-processor machines, this provides us with the illusion of multiple operations happening at once. Because these time slices are so small, the operating system is able to interleave one program's execution with another so quickly that it appears that more than one program is executing at the same exact time. For machines that have more than one processor, the illusion is replaced by fact: Program A can be running at the same physical time as program B, provided that the operating system has "placed" them on different processors.

Splitting available work into time-slices and across processors is the essence of multitasking; this is what allows us to watch a streaming video feed while we are typing a document in Microsoft Word. In the world of threading, what we typically think of as a program (such as Microsoft Word, Notepad, and so on) is called a *process*. A process is a body of code along with all of its attendant baggage such as assigned memory, data storage, and assigned system resources. Processes can create other processes: Launching MS Word from its executable inside of Windows Explorer causes Windows Explorer (a process) to launch MS Word (also a process). So where do threads come in? *Threads* are the basic unit of work for a multitasking operating system. The task scheduler doesn't schedule processes to run, it schedules threads to run.

Threads are actually a very simple construct. There are just a few things that you need to know to get started:

1. A process is a discrete body of code that operates inside of a context (think program).

2. A thread is a path of execution through a body of code. Every process has at least one thread, created by default.

3. Microsoft Windows, as a multitasking operating system, allocates processor time by threads (thus the need for number two).

4. There may be certain technical challenges that are best solved by creating new threads inside of a process (thus creating a multithreaded program).

Let's move on and try to answer the question of why you, as a developer, should care about threads.

Multithreaded Application Design Goals

It could very well be that you may never need or want to worry about threads as you write your applications. The operating system and Visual Basic itself do a good job of managing threads for you, and certainly there are more than a few Visual Basic programmers who have no trouble solving real business problems without ever even considering threads.

But threads are a useful construct in certain scenarios. In general, threads can help you:

- Increase an application's performance level
- Increase the responsiveness of an application to user input
- Scale system use

We should discuss each of these in turn.

Increasing Performance

Multithreaded applications do not necessarily lead to performance increases. It is false to think that you can increase your application's performance in any meaningful way if the application is running on a single processor machine. The reason for this should be obvious: The processor still has the same amount of work to do, regardless of how you have designed your threads. In a multiprocessor machine, however, the ability to increase performance is a very real and intended result of multithreaded application design. Because the scheduler can place threads onto any one of the CPUs for execution, you could have two threads—thus, two pieces of work—executing simultaneously. Figure 12.1 shows an approximation of how one such multi-threaded program might run on a single processor machine versus a dual processor machine.

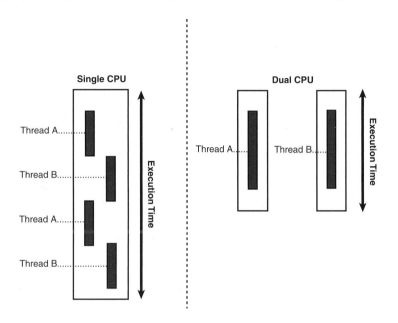

FIGURE 12.1
Single versus dual CPU processing.

Concurrent processing can lead to large performance gains.

> **NOTE**
>
> An interesting question is raised about the use of processes versus threads. If the operating system allocates time to threads, and each process by definition has at least one thread, couldn't we just create multiple processes to achieve our goal of multi-tasked, concurrently executing code? The short answer is yes. So why turn to multiple threads instead of multiple processes? Threads represent a halfway point between having no concurrency at all in our application designs and using processes to achieve concurrency. Threads offer a few unique benefits over processes. For one, their over-all context is much smaller, making it faster for the OS to switch between threads instead of between processes. It is also much easier to share data between threads than it is between processes. And lastly, threads have a much lower resource over-head than processes.

One common design pattern you will see with multithreaded applications is the "divide and conquer" pattern. If a program has a long and complex series of computations that it must perform, and if those calculations do not have to be performed in serial, it should be possible to break the atomic sections of that computation apart and place their execution on their own thread. Again, if the application is run on a multiprocessor system, this design pattern should lead to quantifiable performance increases; simply put, it should reach the end of the computation faster.

Just because measurable performance increases won't occur on a single-processor machine is not a reason to abandon the concept of multithreaded applications.

There is always the illusion of speed—we can increase an application's responsiveness lending the appearance of speed.

Increasing Responsiveness

Many times, it is sufficient to create the illusion of speed in your applications by simply increasing how fast your user interface responds to user input. This leads us to another common design pattern found in multithreaded applications: the UI versus worker threads pattern. Applications designed around this pattern place their computational work onto one or more "background" threads that execute at the same time that another thread monitors the user interface for events. An excellent example of this approach can be found in the way that many applications handle printing to a physical printer. In MS Word, for instance, the print job is spooled and then handled by a completely separate worker thread. This means that control is returned back to the application almost as soon as you click the Print button; you are free to continue typing your document at the same time that it is running off your printer.

Another good example of this is found with the way that Windows Explorer allows you to search for files on your hard drive. Take a look at Figure 12.2, which shows the familiar Windows 2000 Search for Files and Folders window. In this figure, we have just entered a filename pattern to search for, and pressed the Search button.

Figure 12.3 shows that, while the application is busy performing the search, we can still interact with the dialog. In this case, we have entered a new filename pattern. We can also quite easily stop the search because of this worker thread approach. The Stop Search button is available and ready.

Being able to respond to user input quickly, without forcing users to wait for the application to finish whatever it is doing, leads to a snappy program that users tend to like. Having to stare at an hourglass pointer is often frustrating for users. The hourglass is a sign to users that the software can't keep up with their ability to interact with it—a definite problem that can be easily rectified in many cases.

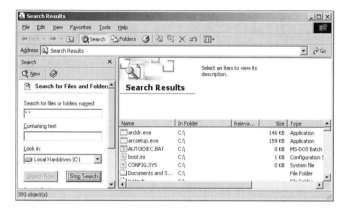

FIGURE 12.2

Searching for a file (*.*).

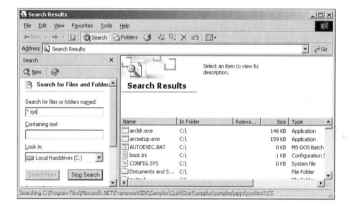

FIGURE 12.3

Still searching.

Application Scalability

Threads can help applications reach higher levels of *scalability*. By scalability, we mean the capability of an application to efficiently use operating system and hardware resources to handle increased demand or load. A scalable application allows you to add software or hardware resources in order to accommodate increasing demands. There are many different ways to implement threads to enhance scalability. One approach would be to implement a thread pool (or use the class library's `ThreadPool` class) to handle user computations. As users (or load) are added to the system, threads are spooled up to handle the workload. As users leave the system, the threads are returned back to the thread pool. This is an example of front-end scaling. We can also scale applications on the back-end. For instance, we might choose to spawn a thread for each network connection available on the system to listen for specific requests coming across the network. In other words, our software intelligently recognizes when resources are added or subtracted from the system and adjusts accordingly through thread instantiation or destruction.

Threads Are Not a Panacea

Like everything else, threads are not likely to simply make application deficiencies disappear. A word of caution: If your application doesn't require threads, don't implement them just for their own sake. Threads carry with them their own set of unique (and often frustrating) problems that programmers have to deal with. If you aren't aware of the myriad of ways that threads can interfere with one another, and if you don't carefully design your code with this in mind, threads can cause some difficult-to-diagnose contention problems when they try to run the same block of code. We talk about threading contention and ways to avoid it later in this chapter.

In addition to threading contention issues, you can also end up *hurting* your application's performance and scalability. Creating and working with threads creates overhead that a single-threaded application doesn't have to deal with.

 Suggestions for Further Exploration

⊃ If you are used to developing COM or COM+ applications under Microsoft Transaction Server, you are probably familiar with the terms Multithreaded Apartments (MTAs) and Single Threaded Apartments (STAs). The .NET Framework deals with threads in a sufficiently abstract method so you won't need to worry about these different threading models anymore. If you need more background on exactly what MTAs and STAs are, please see the MSDN knowledgebase article Q150777—*INFO: Descriptions and Workings of OLE Threading Models*.

⊃ For an excellent treatment on multithreaded programming in general, pick up a copy of *Multithreaded Programming with Win32*, by Thuan Q. Pham and Pankaj K. Garg. While the book doesn't cover Visual Basic (or .NET) at all, it is a useful primer for understanding threading concepts.

Basic Operations with Threads

If the concept of a thread is still not clear to you, our next discussion on programming basic thread operations with Visual Basic .NET will likely cement the concept in your mind.

Starting and Stopping Threads

Our exploration of the System.Threading namespace will start with the Thread class and its capability to create, start, and stop new threads.

The `Thread` class is the primary worker class in the `System.Threading` namespace. It is a sealed, non-inheritable class. To create a thread and start executing some code on it, you have to understand the `Thread` class constructor and the `Start` method. First, a quick glance at the constructor. It is defined like this:

```
Public Sub New(ByVal start As ThreadStart)
```

The `ThreadStart` object required in this constructor is actually a delegate. It is responsible for pointing at the block of code that the thread will run. The `Start` method, which will actually start the thread on its code path, is a simple, parameterless method, defined like this:

```
Public Sub Start()
```

To try to flesh these items out a bit, let's look at some self-contained code. In the following example, we'll kick a new thread off to deal with some computations (contained in the `SomeCode` routine).

First, we'll import the namespace.

```
Imports System.Threading

Module Module1
```

Now, we'll write a short dummy routine that will represent the code that we want to run on our new thread.

```
Sub SomeCode()
    Dim x As Integer
    Dim loopIndex As Integer

    For loopIndex = 1 To 10
        x = x * x + 2
    Next
End Sub
```

Our `Sub Main` represents the core, primary thread of our application. It's here that we will create our new thread object and then start it running the `SomeCode` routine. As we have already seen, the thread constructor accepts an instance of a `ThreadStart` object, which is simply a delegate to the piece of code that we want to run on our new thread (remember that a delegate is just a pointer to a subroutine). After creating the thread object, we need to "start" it. Calling the `Start` method simply tells the thread to begin running the code pointed to by the `ThreadStart` delegate that was used when we created the thread object.

```
Sub Main()
    Dim ourThread As Thread = New Thread(New ThreadStart(AddressOf SomeCode))
    'do some stuff

    'create a new thread and start it up
    ourThread.Start()
```

At this point in our code, we have created and started our new thread. The operating system has taken over management of the thread's execution and has returned control back to our application—in other words, our path of execution in our application has now been split. We have one thread (the intrinsic thread) that was automatically created along with our application, running parallel to the thread that we explicitly created.

```
        'continue on with our main code


    End Sub
End Module
```

That's it! We have now looked at a process that spawned two threads. Both of these threads will run to completion (in other words, execute until they reach the end of their code path) and then die. When all of the threads in a process have completed, the process itself will complete.

> **NOTE**
>
> The `Application.ThreadExit` event will be fired just prior to a thread completing. In the case of the preceding code snippet, we would expect this event to fire twice: once for the explicit thread we created and once for the main thread of the application. When the main thread of the application finishes, the `ThreadExit` event will be followed immediately by the `ApplicationExit` event. Of course, any code in the `ThreadExit` event that actually requires more computation by the thread will keep the thread alive—the thread may never die!

Prioritizing Threads

All threads are not created equal. When writing multithreaded applications, it is often useful to indicate to the system that more attention should be spent on one thread over another. The Windows operating system uses a priority ranking system to decide how often it will give processor attention to a particular thread. This whole scheduling process works something like this:

1. Each thread is allocated a certain time slice in which it will run; at the end of that time slice, the system will wrest control back from the thread.

2. The scheduler now needs to figure out which of the waiting threads will get the next time slice.

3. The waiting threads are all categorized by their priority; those with a higher priority relative to another will receive their time slice first.

4. Where multiple waiting threads exist with the same priority level, the scheduler will deal with each of them in the order that they were entered into the waiting thread queue.

5. After a thread has had its time slice expired it is placed in the back of the waiting thread queue for its particular priority level.

Thread priorities range across five different levels: lowest, below normal, normal, above normal, and highest. Naturally, there is an enumeration (`ThreadPriority`) that can be used to represent these values (see Table 12.2).

TABLE 12.2   `ThreadPriority` Enumeration

Name	Description
AboveNormal	A thread somewhere between normal and highest priority.
BelowNormal	A thread somewhere between normal and lowest priority.
Highest	A thread of the highest priority; use sparingly if at all.
Lowest	A thread of the lowest possible priority. Do not use this for timing dependent threads.
Normal	A thread of normal priority; this is the default value for a thread.

Changing a thread's priority is straightforward:

```
workerThread.Priority = ThreadPriority.AboveNormal
```

Of course, you can also use the `Priority` property to query the thread for its currently indicated priority level:

```
If workerThread.Priority = ThreadPriority.Lowest Then …
```

Using the `Thread.Priority` property, you can explicitly set or view the priority level of the thread that you have created. Setting thread priorities is useful when you need to leverage process from one thread relative to another. For instance, a thread that is running code that needs to be responsive and snappy should be running at a higher priority level than a thread that only needs to crunch some numbers during the system's idle time. In fact, this is a fairly typical pattern used by multithreaded applications: One thread is used to react to user interface operations (leading to a snappy and responsive program, something users love), while another worker thread is used to conduct its non–time-critical business in the background (during whatever lulls may occur on the user interface side of things).

> **NOTE**
>
> In addition to a priority, a thread is also assigned as either a background thread or a foreground thread. Surprisingly, these have nothing to do with the actual priority or urgency of a thread. The difference is in the way that they affect the current running

> instance of the .NET runtime. The .NET runtime will shut itself down when the last
> foreground thread expires (for example, reaches the aborted or stopped state). Any
> background threads still running will be issued ThreadAbortException exceptions. You
> can set or query this attribute by using the IsBackground property (a boolean prop-
> erty). As long as there is a foreground thread running, the runtime will stay alive.

When playing around with thread priority levels, you need to exercise a certain amount of
restraint and act responsibly. For one thing, your code needs to share the processor with other
programs. It isn't fair or responsible to users to simply assume that your application can or
should supercede the processing of everything else in the system. You also need to remember
that these priorities are only useful if there is a relative difference between threads. Simply
setting all of your threads to the highest priority defeats the purpose of having a priority scale
in the first place. If you need to bump up the responsiveness of some code, try using the
AboveNormal priority level. Reserve the use of Highest for those threads that have to respond
to critical events or timings (perhaps these are code routines that need to react to hardware
events such as disc changes, keyboard input, and so on). Likewise, setting thread priority
to Lowest should be reserved for those operations that can truly be executed whenever
time permits.

NOTE

> Actually, the whole issue of thread priority is slightly more complicated than this. The
> scheduler, in addition to looking at the priority level of the thread, also considers the
> priority level of the process that the thread is running in. In addition, the scheduler
> allows for dynamic prioritization of threads. A thread, for instance, may have its pri-
> ority boosted for a time slice because of a system event, such as a user typing on the
> keyboard. For the most part, however, you won't need to concern yourself with these
> intricacies.

Pausing a Thread

From time to time, you may need to tell a thread to stop what it is doing and wait. There are
actually two ways that you can accomplish this: You can sleep a thread or you can suspend a
thread. Both are similar in effect with some key differences that we should touch on. Let's first
examine putting a thread to sleep.

When you issue a Sleep message to a thread, you are basically telling it to stop executing for a
fixed period of time—in this case, milliseconds. Execution will be frozen (or blocked) until the

specified timeout has transpired. Why would you want to do this? If your thread is processing data being returned from another thread, you may want to put it to sleep for brief chunks of time to allow its data buffer to fill up. Or, you may have a polling operation working in a thread that needs to wake up, examine some data, and then go back to sleep if there hasn't been a change. Whatever the reason, issuing the Sleep method call requires only one parameter that specifies how long the thread should sleep (in milliseconds). The following code would sleep the referenced thread for approximately 5 seconds:

```
workerThread.Sleep(5000)
```

Specifying zero milliseconds invokes a special case: The thread scheduler will take away any remaining time from the thread on its current time slice. In effect, you are telling the scheduler to cancel the thread out of its current slot and place it back in the queue for execution.

We can also tell the thread to sleep indefinitely, waking up only when another thread interrupts it. You can interrupt a sleeping thread, causing it to continue execution, by calling the Interrupt method:

```
workerThread.Interrupt()
```

The other way that we can pause a thread is through the Suspend method. Instead of pausing a thread for a specific period of time, the Suspend method will pause the thread indefinitely until a Resume call is made to the thread. The Suspend method does not take any parameters. There is also another key difference: Suspending a thread will not cause the thread to freeze immediately. Instead, the thread will keep running until it reaches something called a *safe point*. A safe point is a runtime term; it refers to a point in time when the garbage collector can safely interrupt a thread.

Stopping a Thread

So far, we have seen how to start a thread and then pause, or block, a thread while running. The last basic thread operation that we will pursue is the simple concept of stopping a thread. Of course, once your thread runs out of code to execute, it will die on its own. To explicitly stop a thread, you have to turn to the Abort method. Like the Suspend method, the Abort method doesn't accept any parameters:

```
workerThread.Abort()
```

In addition, the Abort method does not immediately stop a thread in its tracks. Again, the runtime will wait for the thread to reach a safe point before actually terminating it. As straightforward as its use seems, there are a few peculiar twists to using the Abort method that you need to be aware of. For one, calling the Abort method causes an exception—a ThreadAbortException—to be thrown. This exception is unique from any of the other exceptions that you will deal with in .NET—it can't be caught! In other words, if you have a structured exception handler, the Catch block will never fire even in the face of a thrown ThreadAbortException. Any Finally blocks you have written, however, *will* be fired.

> **TIP**
>
> If for some reason a thread has its Abort method called twice, the second abort call and any subsequent abort calls will cause a DuplicateThreadAbort exception to be thrown. The first abort will still throw the ThreadAbortException, which will be the call ultimately responsible for its death.

If you abort a thread that is in a state where it *can't* be aborted, the general rule of thumb is that the abort message is delayed until the thread reaches a state where it can be stopped. This causes a few situations that might run contrary to your expectations on how the thread should behave. For instance, you might expect that aborting a thread that hasn't been started would throw an exception. After all, how can you stop something that isn't started? The other plausible expectation would be for the method to just do nothing. Unfortunately, it does neither. Aborting a thread that hasn't started will actually have the effect of queuing an abort call to the thread. If the thread ever does get started, the abort will be immediately applied to it.

In some cases, the runtime will actually push the thread to a state where it can be stopped. If you abort a suspended thread, the thread will first be resumed and then stopped. Aborting a thread that is sleeping will cause the thread to be interrupted before being stopped.

Working with the Thread Pool

We have now touched on the basics of creating your own threads, and managing them to a certain extent. If, however, you don't require the degree of control and flexibility that is offered by creating and managing your own threads, there is an alternative: the thread pool. The thread pool contains a worker queue of idle threads. If you need to spin some code onto a thread, you can simply place a request into this pool. The runtime will allocate a thread to your task, and then return the thread back to the pool when it is done. This offers a few advantages over rolling your own threads. For one, it relieves you of the responsibility of worrying about thread creation, startup, management, and deconstruction. For another, it maximizes system resources; if there are threads sitting around idle, there is no sense in creating new ones. The thread pool allows these resources to be consolidated in one place and then doled out when needed to call processes.

You use the thread pool through the ThreadPool class; it's a static class, so there is no instantiation required. To request some work to be done by the thread pool, we queue a work item into it using the QueueUserWorkItem method. Here is its prototype:

```
Overloads Public Shared Function QueueUserWorkItem(ByVal callback As _
    WaitCallBack) As Boolean
```

With the `ThreadPool`, instead of using a `ThreadStart` delegate to point at the code we want to run, we use a `WaitCallBack` delegate. The effect is the same, but the `WaitCallBack` delegate accepts an object parameter to carry state between method calls. If you don't need to use it, you don't have to, but the subroutine that is pointed at by the `WaitCallBack` delegate must match its function prototype. The `WaitCallBack` delegate definition looks like this:

```
Public Delegate Sub WaitCallBack(ByVal state As Object)
```

Therefore, our `SomeCode` subroutine from our example has to be changed to look like this:

```
Public Sub SomeCode(ByVal state As Object)
```

Note that we aren't actually using the state object for anything (at least in this example); it is just there to synchronize the function definitions, allowing the `WaitCallBack` delegate to work correctly.

If we revisit our prior code sample for starting a new thread, we can see the changes made to work with the `ThreadPool` class:

```
Imports System.Threading

Module Module1

    Sub SomeCode()
        Dim x As Integer
        Dim loopIndex As Integer

        For loopIndex = 1 To 5
            x = x * x + 2
        Next
    End Sub


    Sub Main()
        'do some stuff

        'queue our work item into the thread pool
        ThreadPool.QueueUserWorkItem(New WaitCallback(AddressOf _
        SomeCode)

        'continue on with our main code

    End Sub
End Module
```

12

WORKING WITH
THREADS

Working with the `ThreadPool` is a particularly useful and quick way to delegate a work item (function or subroutine) onto its own thread, without worrying about the inherent housekeeping and overhead yourself.

Threading Basics—A Summary

- To explicitly create a thread, you first need to create a thread instance (which points to some block of code that will run on the thread).

- To put a thread to sleep for a specified amount of time, use the `Thread.Sleep` method.

- After creating a thread, you can alter the amount of attention that the OS will give to it by altering its priority level. Use the `Thread.Priority` property (and the `ThreadPriority` enumeration) to alter your thread's relative priority.

- To temporarily stop a thread, use the `Thread.Sleep` method. You can specify the number of milliseconds that the thread should block until continuing with its execution.

- To stop a thread until you tell it to start up again, use the `Thread.Suspend` and `Thread.Resume` methods, respectively.

- To kill a thread, use the `Thread.Abort` method.

Understanding Thread States

Starting threads, stopping threads, pausing them—these are all acts that conspire to change the state of a thread. That is, it is in a particular state before we interact with it and another state when we are done. As you might imagine, the issue of what thread is in what state can quickly become an important piece of information for you to know. It's probably time to examine all of the possible thread states. Then we'll see what we can do to affect a thread in any given state.

Querying for State Information

To find out what state any particular thread is currently in, we need to examine the `ThreadState` property. This property will return a bit-masked `ThreadState` enumeration (see Table 12.3). Why does this property return a bit-mask instead of just a direct enumeration? The answer—threads can be in more than one state at a time. Consider a thread that has had its `Sleep` method called, and then its `Abort` method called. For that brief time period where it is still sleeping, it will be in the state `WaitJoinSleep` *and* `AbortRequested`. Once it comes out of its sleep, it will start to process the `Abort` command, eventually ending up in the `Aborted` state.

TABLE 12.3 The `ThreadState` Enumeration

Name	Description
Aborted	Thread has stopped execution due to an Abort request.
AbortRequested	Thread is waiting until a safe point has been reached before transitioning to Aborted.
Running	Thread is currently executing code.
Stopped	Thread has stopped execution (final state).
StopRequested	Thread is awaiting a safe point in order to cease execution.
Suspended	Thread is suspended, awaiting Resume.
SuspendRequested	Thread is waiting until a safe point has been reached before transitioning to Suspended.
Unstarted	Thread has been created, but not started.
WaitSleepJoin	Thread is waiting.

You can't affect a thread's state by simply assigning it through this property; it is read-only. The only way that you can affect a thread's state is through an action method call (such as the `Start` and `Stop` methods that we just went over). Figure 12.4 shows a state diagram representing all of the possible thread states, and the actual transitions that are responsible for moving a thread from one state to another.

You can see by looking at the graphic that there is only one initial state for a thread, `Unstarted`, and two possible "ending" states or final states: `Aborted` and `Stopped`. These last final states are final in the sense that once a thread enters either of those two states, it cannot leave the state. Likewise, there is no way to place a thread back into the `Unstarted` states.

Most of these states are self-explanatory, but there are a few that deserve some attention.

The `WaitSleepJoin` state may be a little confusing to you at first glance. It doesn't sound like a state that we can place with any degree of certainty—what does it mean to wait-sleep-join? The property enumeration itself is really just a concatenation of the three different states that it represents. In other words, a thread could be waiting, sleeping, or joined. Any of these states will be indicated as `WaitSleepJoin`. We now know what a sleeping thread is all about, but waiting threads and joined threads require some more background.

Joining Threads

If you recall our discussion about the `Abort` method, you will remember that the thread isn't actually aborted until it reaches a safe point. This could be a problem if you have some code that depended on the thread actually reaching the end state that you want it to be in. You might, for instance, have some global cleanup code that needs to be executed as soon as the thread has died. It isn't good enough to know that it will *eventually* abort; you need to know the second that it *has* aborted. This is where the concept of joining a thread comes in. Essentially, one thread may join another as a form of software eavesdropping. The thread that has called the Join method (the calling thread) on another thread (the joined thread) will block its execution until the targeted thread has been actually aborted. Then, its execution will continue.

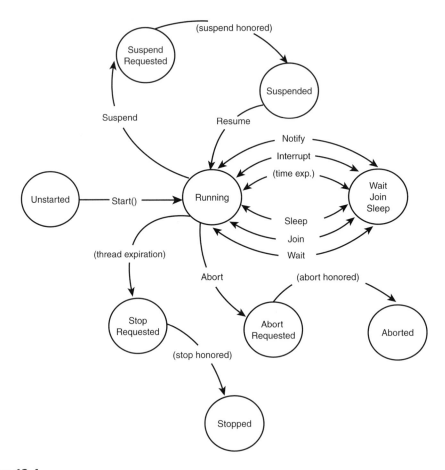

FIGURE 12.4

Thread state transitions.

Just so we don't get confused, let's examine a specific scenario. Suppose that you had a simple forms-based application that, when activated, would spool a thread to perform some background operations. When the form is deactivated (by, say, the user minimizing it to the task bar), we want to abort the thread. The trick here is that we don't want the form to become deactivated until we are guaranteed that the thread has aborted. We could handle this scenario by hooking the Activated and Deactivated events, and popping in our threading code. It might look something like this:

```
Private Sub Form1_Activate(ByVal sender As System.Object, ByVal e As _
    System.EventArgs) Handles MyBase.Activated          workerThread.Start()
End Sub

Private Sub Form1_Deactivate(ByVal sender As System.Object, ByVal e As _
    System.EventArgs) Handles MyBase.Deactivate
        workerThread.Abort()
        workerThread.Join()
End Sub
```

In the deactivate event, we first issue the Abort command, and then we join our worker thread. Our code will block on this line of code—workerThread.Join()—preventing the form from deactivating until the workerThread object has actually transitioned into the aborted state.

 ## Suggestions for Further Exploration

In addition to examining the current state of a thread, you may want to examine various aspects of the context in which it is running. See the CurrentContext, CurrentCulture, CurrentPrincipal, and CurrenUICulture properties on the Thread class for more information on how to obtain this information.

Avoiding Contention Issues

One big design problem exists with multithreaded applications: thread contention. When you start creating threads, you are simultaneously creating the potential for a conflict any time two or more threads try to access a resource like a file, area of memory, object, and so on. Sharing resources and running threads concurrently are certainly two of the reasons why you would choose to multithread your application in the first place; you just need to be aware of the potential problems this introduces, and actively work to mitigate or eliminate these problems in your code.

Races and Deadlocks

To give us a background for discussing the kinds of problems you can experience with ill-behaved resource access, let's consider a scenario that involves two threads. We'll call them Thread A and Thread B. Thread A, the primary thread, is responsible for reading some values in and placing them into an array. It will then create and start a new thread, Thread B, to perform some computations on those values. Specifically, Thread B will write each value into a file, compute their average, and then write this average into the file as well. While this is happening, Thread A will continue on its path of execution, performing some heavy-duty computations. (Maybe its computing a re-entry trajectory or amortizing a 1,000 year loan!) Once Thread A is at the end of its code, it will open the file that was created by Thread B and read the last value in. This value should, at this point, hold the average of the numbers that we started with.

Just so we can visually picture this flow, here is a "timeline" of how things are supposed to work:

Thread A	Thread B
(Program started)	
Read int vals into array (9,73,11,99,1024)	
Create Thread B	(state: unstarted)
Start Thread B	(state: running)
>Perform some additional calcs<	Create file
.	Write value into file (9)
.	Write value into file (73)
.	Write value into file (11)
.	Write value into file (99)
.	Write value into file (1024)
.	Compute avg. of the values
.	Write avg. into file (243.2)
>Calcs done<	(state: stopped)
Open file and read in last value (243.2)	

The problem here is that we don't know how long either thread will take to run. You may be lulled into a false sense of safety, knowing that Thread A has some pretty intensive calculations to do, while Thread B should be fairly speedy with its stuff. Working with asynchronous concepts like threads can be dangerous work; you need to start challenging these assumptions. If Thread A finishes up before Thread B has had a chance to write the average value into the file, Thread A will be picking up what it thinks is the average value but really isn't. This could happen if Thread A is abnormally speedy with its calculations, or if the file system is busy with other things and is taking a while to honor Thread B's file requests, thus slowing Thread B down.

Here is our ideal world turned upside down. Thread A reads in the final average before Thread B has finished:

Thread A	Thread B
(Program started)	
Read int vals into array (9,73,11,99,1024)	
Create Thread B	(state: unstarted)
Start Thread B	(state: running)
>Perform some additional calcs<	Create file
.	Write value into file (9)
.	Write value into file (73)
.	Write value into file (11)
.	Write value into file (99)
>Calcs done<	Write value into file (1024)
Open file and read in last value (1024)	Compute avg. of the values
.	Write avg. into file (243.2)
.	(state: stopped)

This problem is called a *race condition*. In a race condition, one of the threads is actually racing the other to the finish line—a real problem if your code assumes who the winner will be.

Running multiple threads also introduces the specter of *deadlocks*. A deadlock exists when two or more threads are each waiting for something to happen before they will continue with their execution. Let's look at another scenario. We'll use a hardware resource backdrop for this example. Consider an application that writes a file out via the modem port. The application is designed such that, while a thread is using the modem port, it will lock it for its use only—likewise with accessing the file. If you have one thread that locked the modem port and then tried to lock the file, while another thread had locked the file and was trying to lock the modem port, you would have a deadlock or stalemate between the two threads. Each thread is waiting on the other to release its lock before processing. See Figure 12.5.

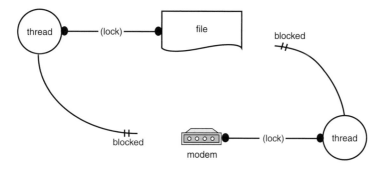

FIGURE 12.5

A deadlock between threads.

Deadlocks and race conditions are notoriously difficult to diagnose and debug, and the problem gets exponentially worse with each thread that you create.

Hopefully, as you were reading through and thinking about these simple examples of thread contention, you realized that if you could just force the threads to communicate their current intentions and actions to one another, you could eliminate or reduce the likelihood of these contentions occurring. This act of coordinating the actions of two or more threads is what we call *synchronization*. In fact, we have already talked about one primitive form of synchronization when we discussed the use of the Join method. By joining one thread to another, we were able to effectively coordinate their actions. In the following sections, we'll tackle the issue of synchronizing threads head on. We'll learn how to write well-behaved threads that leverage the synchronization objects exposed by the System.Threading namespace to avoid contentions.

If poor thread coordination is the problem, synchronization is the cure.

> **NOTE**
>
> The "cure" can introduce problems of its own. That is, it is better to not get sick in the first place! Try to design your applications so that issues like deadlocks and race conditions are not possible instead of relying on synchronization to take care of them. Solving a race condition might cause a deadlock, and each synchronization object you use consumes application resources and can decrease application performance.

Serialization and the Mutex Class

Sometimes, the solution to the thread contention problem is to serialize thread execution. By this, we mean forcing threads to access a particular resource one thread at a time. Typically, you will see this scenario with shared data. You won't want to invite data corruption by having one thread writing data at the same time as another thread.

A *mutex* is a synchronization object that helps to serialize thread execution. Its name comes from the fact that it enforces *mut*ually *ex*clusive operations between processes or threads. Simply put, you can use a mutex as a sort of access pass. If a thread holds the pass, it can access the resource or execute the block of code that has been identified as concurrently unsafe. As long as the thread "holds" the mutex, no other threads can use it (see Figure 12.6). The mutex is then cycled among the threads that need it in various ways. The Mutex class in .NET is an abstraction of this synchronization primitive.

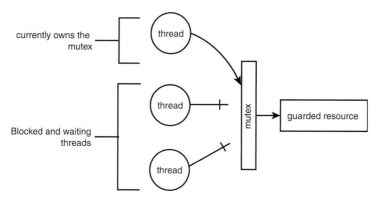

FIGURE 12.6
Serializing access through a mutex.

To see this in action, read through the following sample code in Listing 12.1. You can run the code by simply creating a new console application project in Visual Studio .NET and then pasting the code listing into the Module1 module. In this console application, we are protecting a simulated file from thread contention by serializing write access to the file. The simplest way to achieve this is to write a wrapper class to represent the write operation. This class (appropriately called `FileWrapper`) will be responsible for implementing a mutex to guard its concurrent use. Because we write out to the console when we enter our threaded code and leave it, you can see quite easily that the threads are serialized: You will never see multiple "Thread started" messages in a row. Each thread must finish before the next one can begin. To prove this, try removing all of the mutex code and then run the program. You should see instances of thread overlap as evidenced by two or more "Threads started" messages in a row.

LISTING 12.1   Example of a Mutex Guarding a Resource

```
Imports System
Imports System.Threading

Module Module1
    Dim numThreads As Integer
    Public threadsAreDone As New AutoResetEvent(False)
    Public targetFile As New FileWrapper()

    Sub Main()
        Dim loopIndex As Integer

        numThreads = 5

        'Queue up 5 threads for execution
```

Listing 12.1 Continued

```vb
        For loopIndex = 0 To numThreads - 1
            ThreadPool.QueueUserWorkItem(New WaitCallback(AddressOf _
                AccessFile), loopIndex)
            Console.WriteLine("Thread #{0} queued...", loopIndex)
        Next loopIndex

        threadsAreDone.WaitOne()

        Console.WriteLine("Hit ENTER to exit...")
        Console.ReadLine()
    End Sub

    Public Sub AccessFile(ByVal state As Object)
        targetFile.WriteToFile(CType(state, Integer))
        If Interlocked.Decrement(numThreads) = 0 Then
            threadsAreDone.Set()
        End If
    End Sub
End Sub

End Module

Class FileWrapper
    'Instance our mutex
    Private lockMutex As New Mutex()

    Public Sub WriteToFile(ByVal threadNum As Integer)

        'This code actually requests ownership of the mutex
        lockMutex.WaitOne()

        Try
            'this is where our code would go to do the actual file I/O

            'we'll just simulate work by sleeping the thread for a bit
            '(note that we are using the static Thread object to represent
            'the currently executing thread)
            Console.WriteLine("Thread started. {0}", threadNum)
            Thread.Sleep(2000)
            Console.WriteLine("Thread stopped. {0}", threadNum)

        Catch
            'We would want to catch any system or file i/o specific exceptions
            'here
```

LISTING 12.1 Continued

```
        Finally
            'When all is done, we need to release the mutex so the next queued
            'thread can use it
            lockMutex.ReleaseMutex()
        End Try

    End Sub

End Class
```

You can see that we only used two methods from the `Mutex` class: `WaitOne` and `ReleaseMutex`.

The `WaitOne` method signals the mutex that a thread is waiting to use it. The `ReleaseMutex` signals that a thread has completed its interaction and is through with the mutex. The runtime can now pass the mutex on to the next thread that needs it.

> **NOTE**
>
> In the correct threading vernacular, a mutex is said to be *signaled* when it is free, and *non-signaled* when it belongs to a thread.

If our thread dies before calling `ReleaseMutex`, the mutex will still be released.

In our `FileWrappper` class, we deal exclusively with file write operations through our `WriteToFile` subroutine. What if we intended to also wrap read operations? A `ReadFromFile` would be easy enough to write:

```
Public Sub ReadFromFile()

        'This code actually requests ownership of the mutex
        lockMutex.WaitOne()

        Try
            'this is where our code would go to do the actual file I/O

            'we'll just simulate work by sleeping the thread for a bit
            '(note that we are using the static Thread object to represent
            'the currently executing thread)
            Thread.Sleep(2000)
```

```
      Catch
          'We would want to catch any system or file i/o specific
          'exceptions here

      Finally
          'When all is done, we need to release the mutex so the next
          'queued thread can use it

          lockMutex.ReleaseMutex()
      End Try

  End Sub
```

Our original premise for the use of a mutex was serializing write access to a file. But, is this really something we would need to do with a read operation? Two threads reading from a file at the same time wouldn't be in contention; this is a fairly safe operation to conduct in parallel. A mutex in this scenario is overkill. In the next section, we will discuss another synchronization object: the ReaderWriterLock class. The ReaderWriteLock class serializes write access while allowing multiple read threads inside of the code at once.

The ReaderWriterLock Class

The ReaderWriterLock class works in a similar fashion to the Mutex class; however, it is custom tailored for read/write scenarios in which you want to serialize threads that are accessing write operations, but allow multiple threads accessing read operations inside of your code.

If we modify our FileWrapper class once more, we can see how the ReaderWriterLock code plays a part:

```
Class FileWrapper
    'Instance our mutex
    Private lockRW As New Mutex()

    Public Sub WriteToFile()

        'This code actually requests ownership of the mutex
        lockRW.AcquireWriterLock()

        Try
            'this is where our code would go to do the actual file I/O

            'we'll just simulate work by sleeping the thread for a bit
            '(note that we are using the static Thread object to represent
            'the currently executing thread)
            Thread.Sleep(2000)
```

```
        Catch
            'We would want to catch any system or file i/o specific
            'exceptions here

        Finally
            'When all is done, we need to release the mutex so the next
            'queued thread
            'can use it
            lockRW.ReleaseWriterLock()
        End Try

    End Sub

Public Sub ReadFromFile()

        'This code actually requests ownership of the mutex
        lockRW.AcquireReaderLock()

        Try
            'this is where our code would go to do the actual file I/O

            'we'll just simulate work by sleeping the thread for a bit
            '(note that we are using the static Thread object to represent
            'the currently executing thread)
            Thread.Sleep(2000)

        Catch
            'We would want to catch any system or file i/o specific
            'exceptions here

        Finally
            'When all is done, we need to release the mutex so the next
            'queued thread can use it

            lockRW.ReleaseReaderLock()
        End Try

    End Sub

End Class
```

The overall design pattern is the same as the one we used with the Mutex class. Inside of each block of code, where we access the resource, we first request a lock for our thread. Then, when we are done, we release the lock.

Let's see what our previous mutex console application looks like using the ReaderWriterLock class. In Listing 12.2, we have implemented two separate methods in our FileWrapper class:

One simulates reading from the file, and the other simulates writing to the file. We spool threads just as before. This time, however, every fourth thread will be assigned to run the WriteToFile code. The other threads will run the ReadFromFile method.

LISTING 12.2   Using the ReaderWriterLock Class

```
Imports System
Imports System.Threading

Module Module1
    Public numThreads As Integer = 10
    Public threadsAreDone As New AutoResetEvent(False)
    Public targetFile As New FileWrapper()

    Public Sub Main()
        Dim loopIndex As Integer

        'Queue up 5 threads for execution
        For loopIndex = 0 To 9
            ThreadPool.QueueUserWorkItem(New WaitCallback(AddressOf _
                AccessFile), loopIndex)
        Next loopIndex

        threadsAreDone.WaitOne()

        Console.WriteLine("Hit ENTER to exit...")
        Console.ReadLine()
    End Sub


    ' The callback method's signature MUST match that of a
    ' System.Threading.TimerCallback delegate (it takes an Object parameter and
    ' returns void)
    Public Sub AccessFile(ByVal state As Object)
        Dim threadNum As Integer

        threadNum = CType(state, Integer)

        'Every 4th thread, will simulate a write to the file;
        'all other threads will simulate a read from the file
        If threadNum Mod 4 Then
            targetFile.ReadFromFile(state)
        Else
            targetFile.WriteToFile(state)
        End If
```

LISTING 12.2   Continued

```
        Interlocked.Decrement(numThreads)
        If numThreads = 0 Then
            threadsAreDone.Set()
        End If
    End Sub
End Module

Class FileWrapper
    'Instance our ReaderWriterLock
    Private lockRW As New ReaderWriterLock()

    Public Sub ReadFromFile(ByVal threadNum As Integer)
        'This code actually requests ownership of the lock
        lockRW.AcquireReaderLock(Timeout.Infinite)

        Try
            'this is where our code would go to do the actual file I/O

            'we'll just simulate work by sleeping the thread for a bit
            '(note that we are using the static Thread object to represent
            'the currently executing thread)
            Console.WriteLine("Thread started (reading from file). {0}", _
                threadNum)
            Thread.Sleep(2000)
            Console.WriteLine("Thread stopped (reading from file). {0}", _
                threadNum)

        Catch
            'We would want to catch any system or file i/o specific exceptions
            'here

        Finally
            'When all is done, we need to release the mutex so the next queued
            'thread can use it
            lockRW.ReleaseReaderLock()
        End Try
    End Sub

    Public Sub WriteToFile(ByVal threadNum As Integer)

        'This code actually requests ownership of the mutex
        lockRW.AcquireWriterLock(Timeout.Infinite)
```

LISTING 12.2   Continued

```
        Try
            'this is where our code would go to do the actual file I/O

            'we'll just simulate work by sleeping the thread for a bit
            '(note that we are using the static Thread object to represent
            'the currently executing thread)
            Console.WriteLine("Thread started (writing to file). {0}", _
                threadNum)
            Thread.Sleep(2000)
            Console.WriteLine("Thread stopped (writing to file). {0}", _
                threadNum)

        Catch
            'We would want to catch any system or file i/o specific exceptions
            'here

        Finally
            'When all is done, we need to release the mutex so the next queued
            'thread can use it
            lockRW.ReleaseWriterLock()
        End Try

    End Sub

End Class
```

Locks with the Monitor Class

The third and final synchronization mechanism that we will talk about is the `Monitor` class.
The `Monitor` class is used to synchronize thread access down to the line of code by using the
`Enter` and `Exit` methods. The `Enter` method requests the lock on the block of code, and the
`Exit` releases the lock.

You are free to use the `Monitor` class just like the other synchronization primitives that we
have discussed. If we revisit our `FileWrapper` example, we can see again that our design pattern for synchronization remains essentially unchanged.

```
Public Sub WriteToFile()

    'This code actually requests ownership of the mutex
    Monitor.Enter()

    'this is where our code would go to do the actual file I/O
```

```
        'we'll just simulate work by sleeping the thread for a bit
        '(note that we are using the static Thread object to represent
        'the currently executing thread)
        Thread.Sleep(2000)

        Monitor.Exit()

    End Sub
```

This is where Visual Basic .NET provides us with some intrinsic locking support. Consider the following code, and compare it carefully to our previous `Monitor` code:

```
    Public Sub WriteToFile()

        'This code actually requests ownership of the mutex
        SyncLock(Me)

            'this is where our code would go to do the actual file I/O

            'we'll just simulate work by sleeping the thread for a bit
            '(note that we are using the static Thread object to
            'represent the currently executing thread)

            Thread.Sleep(2000)

        End SyncLock

    End Sub
```

Visual Basic .NET's one contribution to thread synchronization is the `SyncLock` statement. It allows you to block out some code that then requires exclusive locking by threads or processes; a thread, for instance, will block on the `SyncLock(Me)` until the lock has been released.

The `SyncLock` statement simply calls out to the `Monitor` class in much the same fashion that we have shown previously: The beginning of the statement, `SyncLock(Me)` is the equivalent to calling `Monitor.Enter`, and the `End SyncLock` statement causes `Monitor.Exit` to be called.

Synchronizing Access to Variables

Threads that access a global, common variable can also introduce contention problems. One way that threads typically run into problems is when they try to increment or decrement a globally shared variable.

Consider the following code:

```
someVar = someVar + 1
```

What if the preceding statement is run in a block of code that multiple threads are running? An unseen problem lurks here: To the runtime, our one line of code is actually two operations—an increment and an assignment. First, the value of someVar is incremented, and then the result is stored into someVar. What happens if, between the increment and the assignment operation, another thread executes this line of code? The variable someVar will have actually been incremented twice instead of the expected once.

There is a specialized synchronization object that specifically handles incrementing and decrementing variables like this: the Interlocked class.

```
'Interlocked class definition
NotInheritable Public Class Interlocked
```

It exposes an Increment and a Decrement method that guard against this type of contention by forcing the code to behave as if the increment and assignment operations occur in one single, atomic operation. Here are their definitions:

```
Overloads Public Shared Function Increment(ByRef location As Integer) As _
    Integer

Overloads Public Shared Function Decrement(ByRef location As Integer) As _
    Integer
```

The Interlocked class only exposes static, shared methods so there is no need to instance an object of its class. It is used like this:

```
newValue = Interlocked.Increment(someVar)
```

The location parameter is the variable that you want to increment or decrement. These methods are really targeted at variable operations that involve keeping a count of items. You will notice that you cannot pass the increment value into these methods; they always add or subtract 1 to the integer specified by location, making these items fairly useless for computational arithmetic on variables. Some design patterns require your application to maintain a count of the number of threads that are currently executing. In the case of an application that delegates some processing to a number of worker threads, the application will want to know when all of the threads have completed their work. We can do this easily enough by having each thread decrement a global "thread count" variable when it is done, like this:

```
Class ThreadOp
    Public Sub DoSomething()
        'Perform some calculations…
        Thread.Sleep(500)
        numRunningThreads = Interlocked.Decrement(numRunningThreads)
    End Sub
End Class
```

Suggestions for Further Exploration

⊃ Examine the `UpgradeToWriterLock` method on the `ReaderWriterLock` class for a way to transition a read operation to a write operation after you have already obtained a read lock on the resource.

⊃ We have been using the `AutoResetEvent` class to indicate to our application when all of the threads have completed. For more information on how to use this class, as well as the `ManualResetEvent` class, please see the .NET Framework documentation.

Variables and Their Scope

The last topic that we will tackle with regards to threads is that of variable access and scope. What happens when more than one thread is executing a body of code where a variable is defined? Is that variable's value unique across the instances of the thread, or is it shared? In this section, we will look at how variables interoperate between threads. We will then look at ways that we can explicitly tell VB .NET to create variables that are private to a specific thread.

General Scope Rules

Consider if we had a class that defined the following variables:

```
Class ourClass
    Private a As Integer
    Private Shared b As Integer
    Shared c As Integer

    Sub ourMethod()
            Dim d As Integer
    End Sub
End Class
```

How would you expect these different variables to react given multiple threads? The answer is this: Threads, because they share the same virtual address space as any other thread in their process, also share any global variables that have been defined. For VB .NET developers, that means that any variable you have defined as static or instance members will persist across any and all threads. Any local variables that are marked as such will remain local to each thread. So, looking back to the code snippet above, we should expect variables a, b, and c to exist globally across all threads that, say, run the `ourMethod` method. Variable d, because it is local in scope, would be unique to each thread.

Thread-Private Variables

From time to time, you may run across the need to explicitly tell the compiler that a specific variable should remain private and specific to a given thread. To declare a variable in such a fashion, we can use a *declarative attribute* class. A declarative attribute is a special modifier to a variable declaration. The .NET runtime defines a few declarative attribute classes; you can also define your own. To use a declarative attribute class, you simply specify the class and its constructor like this:

```
<SomeDeclAttrib()> Private someVar As Integer
```

The one we are interested in at the moment is the ThreadStaticAttribute class. Specifically, to use ThreadStaticAttribute, we would write

```
<ThreadStaticAttribute()> Shared someVar as Integer
```

By including this syntax, we are telling the compiler that the someVar variable should be maintained on each thread, not globally across threads. That's really all there is to it. If two threads started to run a body of code where we had someVar defined previously, they would not overwrite each other's copy of the someVar variable.

Thread Local Storage

Each time a thread is started, the .NET runtime allocates a storage mechanism to it known as *thread local storage*. Thread local storage is really just a bucket, into which you can place values that won't change from thread to thread. They are thread specific. You access this local storage through *data slots*. You can think of data slots as an un-initialized array carried around by every thread. That is, each thread has its own potential array of data slots. You can choose to create new slots, store data in them, and retrieve data out of them. All of this is made possible through a series of methods available on the Thread class. The AllocateDataSlot method creates a new data slot for you to use. The SetData method actually stores a value into a data slot. And the GetData method will retrieve whatever is sitting inside of a previously created data slot. Data slots can be named to allow them to be referenced easily. To create a named data slot, you would use the AllocateNamedDataSlot method. Their function definitions are shown here:

```
Public Shared Function AllocateDataSlot() As LocalDataStoreSlot

Public Shared Function AllocateNamedDataSlot( ByVal name As String) As _
    LocalDataStoreSlot

Public Shared Function GetData(ByVal slot As LocalDataStoreSlot) As Object
```

So, to store something in a data slot, we would first allocate a new data slot, store something in it, and then retrieve it like this:

```
'create the data slot
Dim tls As LocalDataStoreSlot = Thread.AllocateDataSlot()

'store something in it
Thread.SetData(tls, "test")

'retrieve it
Dim var As String = Thread.GetData(tls)
```

To try and illustrate further the concept of thread-private variables, see Listing 12.3. This simple console application declares a few different types of variables inside a class, and then spawns a few threads to run a method off that class. Each variable is randomly assigned a value. As the threads run, they will write the content of each variable out to the console window.

LISTING 12.3   Examining Variables Across Threads

```
Imports System.Threading

Module Module1
    Sub Main()
        'Our startup routine

        'Create new instances of the VarTester class; start a thread running on
        'the SomeMethod method...
        Dim ourClass1 As New VarTester(1)
        Dim thread1 As New Thread(New ThreadStart(AddressOf _
            ourClass1.SomeMethod))
        thread1.Start()

        Dim ourClass2 As New VarTester(2)
        Dim thread2 As New Thread(New ThreadStart(AddressOf _
            ourClass2.SomeMethod))
        thread2.Start()

        Dim ourClass3 As New VarTester(3)
        Dim thread3 As New Thread(New ThreadStart(AddressOf _
            ourClass3.SomeMethod))
        thread3.Start()

        'Wait for the threads to finish...
        thread1.Join()
        thread2.Join()
        thread3.Join()
```

LISTING 12.3   Continued

```
        Console.WriteLine()
        Console.WriteLine("Hit ENTER to re-run.")

        Console.ReadLine()
        Main()
    End Sub

End Module
Class VarTester
    'Dim a variety of data types for us to use

    'First, a private var
    Private a As Integer

    'Second, a shared var
    Private Shared b As Integer

    'Third, a var specific to the current thread
    <ThreadStaticAttribute()> Private Shared c As Integer

    'Fourth, a "public" shared var
    Shared d As Integer

    'Fifth, a data slot (using thread local storage) specific to
    'the current thread
    Public myTLS As LocalDataStoreSlot = Thread.AllocateDataSlot()

    'This holds the "number" of our thread so we can tell
    'which thread we are dealing with when we write values
    'out to the console.
    Private threadId As Int32

    Sub New(ByVal ID As Integer)

        'To prove the point, we will randomize all of the numbers
        'we assign to our variables (somewhere in between 10 and
        '1)

        '"Reset" the randomizer used by the Rnd() function
        Randomize()

        'Set all vars to a random number between 10 and 1
        a = Int((100 - 1 + 1) * Rnd() + 1)
        b = Int((100 - 1 + 1) * Rnd() + 1)
        c = Int((100 - 1 + 1) * Rnd() + 1)
```

LISTING 12.3 Continued

```
        d = Int((100 - 1 + 1) * Rnd() + 1)

        'We have passed in our thread number to this constructor
        Me.threadId = ID

    End Sub

    Sub SomeMethod()
        'This bogus method just writes out variable values out to a
        'console window. We have wrapped everything in a SyncLock
        'statement so it is easier to read the output (in other
        'words, thread 2 won't write its values out until thread 1
        'is done, etc.)

        Dim e As Integer
        SyncLock GetType(VarTester)
            Randomize()
            Thread.SetData(myTLS, Int((100 - 1 + 1) * Rnd() + 1))
            e = Int((100 - 1 + 1) * Rnd() + 1)

            'create the data slot
            Dim tls As LocalDataStoreSlot = Thread.AllocateDataSlot()
            'store something in it
            Thread.SetData(tls, "test")
            'retrieve it
            Dim var As String = Thread.GetData(tls)


            Console.WriteLine("Thread {0}, a = {1}", threadId, a)
            Console.WriteLine("Thread {0}, b = {1}", threadId, b)
            Console.WriteLine("Thread {0}, c = {1}", threadId, c)
            Console.WriteLine("Thread {0}, d = {1}", threadId, d)
            Console.WriteLine("Thread {0}, e = {1}", threadId, e)
            Console.WriteLine("Thread {0}, TLS slot = {1}", threadId, _
            Thread.GetData(myTLS))
            Console.WriteLine("----------------------------------------")
        End SyncLock
    End Sub
End Class
```

Notice the output in Figure 12.7. We see that variables a, e, and something we call "TLS slot" change between each thread. The other variables remain the same. Variables a and e should both be thread specific, variable a because of our use of the ThreadStaticAttribute modifier, and variable e because it is a locally declared variable. The "TLS slot" is a data slot created on the thread (again, thread specific). Therefore, the code behaves as expected: Each of these should be private and unique to the individual threads.

```
C:\Documents and Settings\Administrator\Desktop\Book\Chapter 10 - Processes and Threads\Threa...

Thread 1, a = 85
Thread 1, b = 42
Thread 1, c = 0
Thread 1, d = 5
Thread 1, e = 18
Thread 1, TLS slot = 41

Thread 2, a = 44
Thread 2, b = 42
Thread 2, c = 0
Thread 2, d = 5
Thread 2, e = 58
Thread 2, TLS slot = 34

Thread 3, a = 8
Thread 3, b = 42
Thread 3, c = 0
Thread 3, d = 5
Thread 3, e = 98
Thread 3, TLS slot = 77

Hit ENTER to re-run.
```

FIGURE 12.7
Console output—thread local storage.

The other variables are all static or instance member variables. These are shared across all of the threads. Their values will be the same across each thread instance. Try running the program a few times (just press the Enter key) to satisfy yourself that things are working as you expect them to.

Learning by Example—ThreadedTimer

This sample application is simple in nature. It illustrates some of the basic threading concepts that we have talked about to this point by creating two explicit threads. One thread continuously displays the current system time onto the form. The other thread continuously "monitors" the timer thread, reporting its current state out to a list box. The form also exposes a few buttons that allow you to play with the timer thread by starting it, sleeping it, suspending it, or aborting it (see Figure 12.8).

FIGURE 12.8
Window—ThreadedTimer application.

This program is primarily an educational exercise to see how the timer thread progresses from state to state based on the user clicking one of the method buttons.

With this application, we are also showing a common design pattern for threads: using a "background" worker thread in conjunction with a user interface thread. In our case, the threadUI object constantly runs to poll the threadTimer on its current state. The threadTimer, of course, is subject to your control by using the buttons on the left-hand side. In an actual business application, our UI thread would be running code to accept user input, repaint the form, fill list boxes with data, and so on, thus allowing users to continuously interact with the application. All the while, the background worker thread is working on the problem at hand: calculating payroll, interest payments, and so on. Again, in our case here the worker thread is represented by threadTimer. This thread obviously does nothing useful for us. We could have easily used a timer control to do the same thing, but it shows us the possibility.

Key Concepts Covered

Key concepts covered by the ThreadTimer application (see Listing 12.4):

- Thread state management
- UI versus worker thread design patterns
- Basic thread operations: starting, sleeping, suspending, and aborting threads

LISTING 12.4   ThreadedTimer Application

```
Imports System.Threading

Public Class Form1
    Inherits System.Windows.Forms.Form

    'global thread objects
    'threadTimer displays current time
    Private threadTimer As Thread

    'threadUI queries threadTimer for current state
    Private threadUI As Thread

    'currentState will hold the current state of the timer thread
    Private currentState As String

    Private WithEvents GroupBox2 As System.Windows.Forms.GroupBox
    Private WithEvents ListBox1 As System.Windows.Forms.ListBox
    Private WithEvents Button1 As System.Windows.Forms.Button
```

LISTING 12.4   Continued

```vb
#Region " Windows Form Designer generated code "

    Public Sub New()
        MyBase.New()

        'This call is required by the Windows Form Designer.
        InitializeComponent()

        'Add any initialization after the InitializeComponent() call

    End Sub

    'Form overrides dispose to clean up the component list.
    Public Overrides Sub Dispose()
        MyBase.Dispose()
        If Not (components Is Nothing) Then
            components.Dispose()
        End If
    End Sub
    Private WithEvents GroupBox1 As System.Windows.Forms.GroupBox
    Private WithEvents StartThread As System.Windows.Forms.Button
    Private WithEvents PauseThread As System.Windows.Forms.Button
    Private WithEvents SleepThread As System.Windows.Forms.Button
    Private WithEvents StopThread As System.Windows.Forms.Button
    Private WithEvents TextBox1 As System.Windows.Forms.TextBox
    Private WithEvents TextBox2 As System.Windows.Forms.TextBox
    Private WithEvents Label5 As System.Windows.Forms.Label

    'Required by the Windows Form Designer
    Private components As System.ComponentModel.Container

    'NOTE: The following procedure is required by the Windows Form Designer
    'It can be modified using the Windows Form Designer.
    'Do not modify it using the code editor.
    <System.Diagnostics.DebuggerStepThrough()> Private Sub _
        InitializeComponent()
        Me.PauseThread = New System.Windows.Forms.Button()
        Me.GroupBox2 = New System.Windows.Forms.GroupBox()
        Me.ListBox1 = New System.Windows.Forms.ListBox()
        Me.Label5 = New System.Windows.Forms.Label()
        Me.StartThread = New System.Windows.Forms.Button()
        Me.GroupBox1 = New System.Windows.Forms.GroupBox()
        Me.StopThread = New System.Windows.Forms.Button()
        Me.SleepThread = New System.Windows.Forms.Button()
        Me.Button1 = New System.Windows.Forms.Button()
```

LISTING 12.4 Continued

```
Me.GroupBox2.SuspendLayout()
Me.GroupBox1.SuspendLayout()
Me.SuspendLayout()
'
'PauseThread
'
Me.PauseThread.Location = New System.Drawing.Point(24, 84)
Me.PauseThread.Name = "PauseThread"
Me.PauseThread.Size = New System.Drawing.Size(104, 24)
Me.PauseThread.TabIndex = 1
Me.PauseThread.Text = "Suspend"
'
'GroupBox2
'
Me.GroupBox2.Controls.AddRange(New System.Windows.Forms.Control() _
    {Me.Button1, Me.ListBox1})
Me.GroupBox2.Location = New System.Drawing.Point(160, 48)
Me.GroupBox2.Name = "GroupBox2"
Me.GroupBox2.Size = New System.Drawing.Size(156, 176)
Me.GroupBox2.TabIndex = 3
Me.GroupBox2.TabStop = False
Me.GroupBox2.Text = "Thread State History"
'
'ListBox1
'
Me.ListBox1.Location = New System.Drawing.Point(8, 24)
Me.ListBox1.Name = "ListBox1"
Me.ListBox1.Size = New System.Drawing.Size(140, 121)
Me.ListBox1.TabIndex = 0
'
'Label5
'
Me.Label5.Location = New System.Drawing.Point(104, 4)
Me.Label5.Name = "Label5"
Me.Label5.Size = New System.Drawing.Size(124, 36)
Me.Label5.TabIndex = 2
Me.Label5.Text = "00:00:00"
'
'StartThread
'
Me.StartThread.Location = New System.Drawing.Point(24, 28)
Me.StartThread.Name = "StartThread"
Me.StartThread.Size = New System.Drawing.Size(104, 24)
Me.StartThread.TabIndex = 1
Me.StartThread.Text = "Start"
'
```

LISTING 12.4   Continued

```
'GroupBox1
'
Me.GroupBox1.Controls.AddRange(New System.Windows.Forms.Control() _
    {Me.StopThread, Me.SleepThread, Me.PauseThread, Me.StartThread})
Me.GroupBox1.Location = New System.Drawing.Point(4, 48)
Me.GroupBox1.Name = "GroupBox1"
Me.GroupBox1.Size = New System.Drawing.Size(152, 176)
Me.GroupBox1.TabIndex = 0
Me.GroupBox1.TabStop = False
Me.GroupBox1.Text = "Thread Ops"
'
'StopThread
'
Me.StopThread.Location = New System.Drawing.Point(24, 112)
Me.StopThread.Name = "StopThread"
Me.StopThread.Size = New System.Drawing.Size(104, 24)
Me.StopThread.TabIndex = 1
Me.StopThread.Text = "Abort"
'
'SleepThread
'
Me.SleepThread.Location = New System.Drawing.Point(24, 56)
Me.SleepThread.Name = "SleepThread"
Me.SleepThread.Size = New System.Drawing.Size(104, 24)
Me.SleepThread.TabIndex = 1
Me.SleepThread.Text = "Sleep"
'
'Button1
'
Me.Button1.Location = New System.Drawing.Point(84, 152)
Me.Button1.Name = "Button1"
Me.Button1.Size = New System.Drawing.Size(64, 20)
Me.Button1.TabIndex = 1
Me.Button1.Text = "Clear"
'
'Form1
'
Me.AutoScaleBaseSize = New System.Drawing.Size(5, 13)
Me.ClientSize = New System.Drawing.Size(320, 229)
Me.Controls.AddRange(New System.Windows.Forms.Control() _
    {Me.GroupBox2, Me.Label5, Me.GroupBox1})
Me.MaximizeBox = False
Me.MinimizeBox = False
Me.Name = "Form1"
Me.Text = "ThreadedTimer"
```

LISTING 12.4   Continued

```
        Me.GroupBox2.ResumeLayout(False)
        Me.GroupBox1.ResumeLayout(False)
        Me.ResumeLayout(False)

    End Sub

#End Region

    Private Sub Form1_Load(ByVal sender As System.Object, ByVal e As _
        System.EventArgs) Handles MyBase.Load
        InitForm()
    End Sub

    Private Sub InitForm()
        'This routine just does some UI housekeeping,
        'disabling buttons that aren't valid at launch
        StopThread.Enabled = False
        PauseThread.Enabled = False
        SleepThread.Enabled = False

    End Sub

    Private Sub TimerCode()
        'This is the code our timer thread will run; this thread
        'is responsible for updating the "label5" control
        'on the dialog with the current time (to the millisecond)

        'Continuous loop; only way out is to abort the thread
        Do
            Label5.Text = Format(Now(), "hh:mm:ss")

            'Sleep the thread for a little bit
            Thread.Sleep(500)
        Loop
    End Sub

    Private Sub UICode()
        'This is the code that our ui thread will run; this thread
        'queries the threadTimer object to get its current state.
        'If its state has changed from the last poll (i.e., is different
        'than what is stored in currentState), add it to the listbox
        'control. The state history listbox control lets you see the exact
        'state progression that threadTimer has gone through.

        'stateEnum is an interim object needed to get the actual
```

12

WORKING WITH
THREADS

LISTING 12.4   Continued

```
        'name of the ThreadState enum value
        Dim stateEnum As ThreadState

        Do
            If Trim(stateEnum.GetName(enumType:=stateEnum.GetType(), _
                value:=threadTimer.ThreadState)) <> Trim(currentState) Then
                currentState = _
                    Trim(stateEnum.GetName(enumType:=stateEnum.GetType(), _
                    value:=threadTimer.ThreadState))
                ListBox1.Items.Add(item:=currentState)
            End If
        Loop
    End Sub

    Private Sub StartThread_Click(ByVal sender As System.Object, ByVal e As _
        System.EventArgs) Handles StartThread.Click
        'This kicks everything off...

        'Point the threadUI object at the UI code
        threadUI = New Thread(start:=New ThreadStart(AddressOf UICode))

        'Point the threadTimer object at the timer code
        threadTimer = New Thread(start:=New ThreadStart(AddressOf TimerCode))

        'First, start the UI thread; we'll sleep it for a bit to let
        'it write out the first threadTimer state before threadTimer
        'has had a chance to start.
        threadUI.Start()
        Thread.Sleep(millisecondsTimeout:=500)

        'Start the timer thread
        threadTimer.Start()

        'Set the form buttons to an appropriate state
        StopThread.Enabled = True
        PauseThread.Enabled = True
        SleepThread.Enabled = True
        StartThread.Enabled = False

    End Sub

    Private Sub StopThread_Click(ByVal sender As System.Object, ByVal e As _
        System.EventArgs) Handles StopThread.Click
        'This routine stops our timer thread by aborting it.
        threadTimer.Abort()
```

LISTING 12.4 Continued

```vb
          'Set the form buttons to an appropriate state
          StopThread.Enabled = False
          PauseThread.Enabled = False
          SleepThread.Enabled = False
          StartThread.Enabled = False

      End Sub

      Private Sub SleepThread_Click(ByVal sender As System.Object, ByVal e As _
          System.EventArgs) Handles SleepThread.Click
          'This routine sleeps the timer thread for roughly 2 seconds;
          'experiment with different times by replacing the constant...
          Const SLEEP_INTERVAL = 2000

          threadTimer.Sleep(millisecondsTimeout:=SLEEP_INTERVAL)

      End Sub

      Private Sub PauseThread_Click(ByVal sender As System.Object, ByVal e As _
          System.EventArgs) Handles PauseThread.Click
          'This routine either suspends or resumes a suspended thread;
          'we look at the button text to determine the appropriate
          'action.
          If PauseThread.Text = "Suspend" Then
              PauseThread.Text = "Resume"
              threadTimer.Suspend()
          Else
              PauseThread.Text = "Suspend"
              threadTimer.Resume()
          End If
      End Sub

      Private Sub Button1_Click(ByVal sender As System.Object, ByVal e As _
          System.EventArgs) Handles Button1.Click
          'This routine clears our state history listbox...
          ListBox1.Items.Clear()
      End Sub
End Class
```

 ## Suggestions for Further Exploration

The threading library actually contains a `Timer` class that we could have easily used for this sample. Research how you can use the `Timer` class to periodically execute code pointed at by a delegate.

Learning by Example: Divide and Conquer

The Divide and Conquer application is a monolithic forms-based application. It reads in a sample file of decimal values and then computes the average for all of the values in the file. You can tell the application whether to use two threads (created from the thread pool) to process the file or to simply use the application's primary thread to process the file. If you elect to multithread the processing, the application will split the file content into two. One thread will process the "front half," and one will process the "back half."

Each thread will be responsible for updating two global variables that hold the running total and the current count of values processed. They will also update a count variable holding the number of currently executing threads. When this thread count variable drops to zero, the application will perform the final calculation (by dividing the running total by the running count) and then display it to the form.

The application also attempts to compute how long it has taken to compute the average. If you have the opportunity, try comparing the time to finish on a single-processor machine and a dual-processor machine. You should see a noticeable performance increase on the multiprocessor machine if you select multithreaded. Don't be surprised if the multithreaded times come out longer than the single-threaded times on a single processor system!

We have included a very large test file for use with this application (decvalues.txt). It contains a repeating group of decimal values that are space delimited.

Key Concepts Covered

Divide and Conquer in Listing 12.5 showcases the following:

- Using the `ThreadPool` class to assign work items to a thread
- Synchronizing variable access using the `Interlock` class and the `Synclock` statement
- Indicating thread completion with the `AutoResetEvent` class

Code Walkthrough

LISTING 12.5   Divide and Conquer Code Listing

The application starts out with the typical `Imports` statements. Here, we are using the IO library and the threading library.

```
Imports System.IO
Imports System.Threading

Public Class Form1
    Inherits System.Windows.Forms.Form
```

LISTING 12.5   Continued

This is where we set up all of our global, forms-level variables. Note the use of the
AutoResetEvent. This is a class that we haven't talked about yet. See the comments in the
"Suggestions for Further Exploration" section after this code listing.

```
'threadsAreDone is an AutoResetEvent;
Shared threadsAreDone As New AutoResetEvent(False)
Shared numThreads As Integer

'holds the total (sum) of values in the file
Private runningTotal As Decimal

'holds the count of values found in the file
Private runningCount As Integer

'holds the final computed average (total / count)
Private average As Decimal
```

This is all of the form designer code. We haven't added anything to this; it is included for the
sake of being complete.

```
#Region " Windows Form Designer generated code "

    Public Sub New()
        MyBase.New()

        'This call is required by the Windows Form Designer.
        InitializeComponent()

        'Add any initialization after the InitializeComponent() call

    End Sub

    'Form overrides dispose to clean up the component list.
    Public Overrides Sub Dispose()
        MyBase.Dispose()
        If Not (components Is Nothing) Then
            components.Dispose()
        End If
    End Sub
    Private WithEvents Label1 As System.Windows.Forms.Label
    Private WithEvents Start As System.Windows.Forms.Button
    Private WithEvents GroupBox1 As System.Windows.Forms.GroupBox
    Private WithEvents Label2 As System.Windows.Forms.Label
    Private WithEvents Label3 As System.Windows.Forms.Label
    Private WithEvents ElapsedTime As System.Windows.Forms.Label
```

LISTING 12.5   Continued

```
Private WithEvents ComputedAverage As System.Windows.Forms.Label
Private WithEvents ActivityList As System.Windows.Forms.ListBox
Private WithEvents Label4 As System.Windows.Forms.Label
Private WithEvents UseThreadPool As System.Windows.Forms.CheckBox
Private WithEvents FileName As System.Windows.Forms.TextBox

'Required by the Windows Form Designer
Private components As System.ComponentModel.Container

'NOTE: The following procedure is required by the Windows Form Designer
'It can be modified using the Windows Form Designer.
'Do not modify it using the code editor.
<System.Diagnostics.DebuggerStepThroughAttribute()> Private Sub _
    InitializeComponent()
    Me.GroupBox1 = New System.Windows.Forms.GroupBox()
    Me.Label4 = New System.Windows.Forms.Label()
    Me.ActivityList = New System.Windows.Forms.ListBox()
    Me.ComputedAverage = New System.Windows.Forms.Label()
    Me.ElapsedTime = New System.Windows.Forms.Label()
    Me.Label3 = New System.Windows.Forms.Label()
    Me.Label2 = New System.Windows.Forms.Label()
    Me.UseThreadPool = New System.Windows.Forms.CheckBox()
    Me.Label1 = New System.Windows.Forms.Label()
    Me.FileName = New System.Windows.Forms.TextBox()
    Me.Start = New System.Windows.Forms.Button()
    Me.GroupBox1.SuspendLayout()
    Me.SuspendLayout()
    '
    'GroupBox1
    '
    Me.GroupBox1.Controls.AddRange(New System.Windows.Forms.Control() _
        {Me.Label4, Me.ActivityList, Me.ComputedAverage, Me.ElapsedTime, _
        Me.Label3, Me.Label2})
    Me.GroupBox1.Location = New System.Drawing.Point(4, 88)
    Me.GroupBox1.Name = "GroupBox1"
    Me.GroupBox1.Size = New System.Drawing.Size(308, 112)
    Me.GroupBox1.TabIndex = 4
    Me.GroupBox1.TabStop = False
    '
    'Label4
    '
    Me.Label4.Location = New System.Drawing.Point(180, 12)
    Me.Label4.Name = "Label4"
    Me.Label4.Size = New System.Drawing.Size(84, 16)
    Me.Label4.TabIndex = 5
```

LISTING 12.5 Continued

```
        Me.Label4.Text = "Activity Log:"
        '
        'ActivityList
        '
        Me.ActivityList.Location = New System.Drawing.Point(180, 32)
        Me.ActivityList.Name = "ActivityList"
        Me.ActivityList.Size = New System.Drawing.Size(120, 69)
        Me.ActivityList.TabIndex = 4
        '
        'ComputedAverage
        '
        Me.ComputedAverage.Location = New System.Drawing.Point(92, 52)
        Me.ComputedAverage.Name = "ComputedAverage"
        Me.ComputedAverage.Size = New System.Drawing.Size(84, 16)
        Me.ComputedAverage.TabIndex = 3
        Me.ComputedAverage.Text = "---"
        '
        'ElapsedTime
        '
        Me.ElapsedTime.Location = New System.Drawing.Point(92, 32)
        Me.ElapsedTime.Name = "ElapsedTime"
        Me.ElapsedTime.Size = New System.Drawing.Size(84, 16)
        Me.ElapsedTime.TabIndex = 2
        Me.ElapsedTime.Text = "---"
        '
        'Label3
        '
        Me.Label3.Location = New System.Drawing.Point(8, 52)
        Me.Label3.Name = "Label3"
        Me.Label3.Size = New System.Drawing.Size(80, 16)
        Me.Label3.TabIndex = 1
        Me.Label3.Text = "Average:"
        '
        'Label2
        '
        Me.Label2.Location = New System.Drawing.Point(8, 32)
        Me.Label2.Name = "Label2"
        Me.Label2.Size = New System.Drawing.Size(80, 16)
        Me.Label2.TabIndex = 0
        Me.Label2.Text = "Elapsed Time:"
        '
        'UseThreadPool
        '
        Me.UseThreadPool.Location = New System.Drawing.Point(76, 32)
        Me.UseThreadPool.Name = "UseThreadPool"
```

Listing 12.5 Continued

```
        Me.UseThreadPool.Size = New System.Drawing.Size(104, 16)
        Me.UseThreadPool.TabIndex = 2
        Me.UseThreadPool.Text = "Use ThreadPool"
        '
        'Label1
        '
        Me.Label1.Location = New System.Drawing.Point(4, 8)
        Me.Label1.Name = "Label1"
        Me.Label1.Size = New System.Drawing.Size(72, 16)
        Me.Label1.TabIndex = 0
        Me.Label1.Text = "File Name:"
        '
        'FileName
        '
        Me.FileName.Location = New System.Drawing.Point(76, 4)
        Me.FileName.Name = "FileName"
        Me.FileName.Size = New System.Drawing.Size(236, 20)
        Me.FileName.TabIndex = 1
        Me.FileName.Text = "c:\decvalues.txt"
        '
        'Start
        '
        Me.Start.Location = New System.Drawing.Point(76, 56)
        Me.Start.Name = "Start"
        Me.Start.Size = New System.Drawing.Size(88, 24)
        Me.Start.TabIndex = 3
        Me.Start.Text = "Compute Avg."
        '
        'Form1
        '
        Me.AutoScaleBaseSize = New System.Drawing.Size(5, 13)
        Me.ClientSize = New System.Drawing.Size(314, 203)
        Me.Controls.AddRange(New System.Windows.Forms.Control() _
            {Me.GroupBox1, Me.Start, Me.UseThreadPool, Me.FileName, Me.Label1})
        Me.FormBorderStyle = System.Windows.Forms.FormBorderStyle.FixedDialog
        Me.MaximizeBox = False
        Me.MinimizeBox = False
        Me.Name = "Form1"
        Me.Text = "Divide and Conquer"
        Me.GroupBox1.ResumeLayout(False)
        Me.ResumeLayout(False)

    End Sub

#End Region
```

LISTING 12.5 Continued

`WorkFileSingle` is the routine that will compute the average of values in the target file without using threads; this is how you would do it if threads weren't available in VB .NET. This sub-routine accepts a single parameter, `fileString`, which represents the contents of our target file in string format.

```
Private Sub WorkFileSingle(ByVal fileString As String)
    'Holds our starting time tick-count
    Dim startTime As Integer

    'Holds our ending time tick-count
    Dim endTime As Integer

    'Looping variable for our for loops...
    Dim loopIndex As Long

    'This is an array of values from the target file;
    'stored as string to let us do a split easily
    Dim fileStringValues() As String
```

If you recall, the specific format of file that this application deals with is a straight-text format with decimal values space delimited. This allows us to use the `Split` method off the string to easily generate an array of the values we need to process.

```
    'Split the values out into an array for easier
    'processing.
    fileStringValues = fileString.Split(" ")
```

Here we use a class from the `System` library: `Environment`. The `Environment` class has a useful property, `TickCount`, which returns the number of milliseconds since the operating system started. We will use this to compute our elapsed time.

```
    'set our start time
    startTime = Environment.TickCount

    'Loop through our array of values; increment the count and re-sum
    'the total each time through
    For loopIndex = 0 To fileStringValues.GetUpperBound(0)
        runningTotal = runningTotal + CType(fileStringValues(loopIndex), _
            Decimal)
        runningCount = runningCount + 1
    Next loopIndex

    'We're done; compute the average and store in "average"
    average = runningTotal / runningCount
```

LISTING 12.5   Continued

```
        'Set the end time
        endTime = Environment.TickCount

        'Write out the elapsed time to the form
        ElapsedTime.Text = (endTime - startTime) & " ms"

    End Sub
```

The `ReadFile` function is responsible for our file I/O operations. It opens the file pointed to by `fileName`, reads the entire length of the file using a `StreamReader` object and then assigns it to a string (`fileString`). This is then returned through the function.

```
    Private Function ReadFile(ByVal fileName As String) As String
        Dim targetFile As FileInfo = New FileInfo(filename:=fileName)
        Dim fileContent As StreamReader = targetFile.OpenText()
        Dim fileString As String = fileContent.ReadToEnd()

        fileContent.Close()

        ReadFile = fileString
    End Function
```

`WorkFileMulti` is the routine that will compute the average of values in the target file by using two threads requested from the `ThreadPool` object. Like `WorkFileSingle`, this subroutine accepts a single parameter, `fileString`, which represents the contents of our target file in string format.

```
    Private Sub WorkFileMulti(ByVal fileString As String)
        'Holds our starting time tick-count
        Dim startTime As Integer

        'Holds our ending time tick-count
        Dim endTime As Integer

        'Looping variable for our for loops...
        Dim loopIndex As Long

        'Holds the first half of the file string in an array
        Dim frontValues() As String

        'Holds the second hald of the file string in an array
        Dim backValues() As String

        'Holds how many values to chunk into each array
        Dim chunkLength As Integer
```

Listing 12.5 Continued

```
    'Used to set lower bound for the array copy
    Dim currLowerBound As Integer

    'This is an array of values from the target file;
    'stored as string to let us do a split easily
    Dim fileStringValues() As String

    'Split the values out into an array for easier
    'processing.
    fileStringValues = fileString.Split(" ")

    'We will use two threads from the ThreadPool
    numThreads = 2

    'Here we are essentially set the length of each array
    'equal to half of the total file length
    chunkLength = fileStringValues.GetLength(0) / numThreads

    'Start at the bottom of the array for our array copy
    currLowerBound = 0

    'Setup our array to hold the front half of the file
    ReDim frontValues(chunkLength - 1)

    'Setup our array to hold the back half of the file
    ReDim backValues((fileStringValues.GetLength(0) - chunkLength) - 1)

    'copy the front half of our original array into a new array
    fileStringValues.Copy(fileStringValues, currLowerBound, frontValues, 0, _
        chunkLength)

    'copy the back half of our original array into a new array
    fileStringValues.Copy(fileStringValues, currLowerBound + chunkLength, _
        backValues, 0, backValues.Length)

    'Set our start time
    startTime = Environment.TickCount
```

This is where our application execution will start to branch across two separate threads. We are passing in a delegate for each thread, as well as a state object which, in this case, is the array of values we want that particular thread to work on.

```
    'Request two threads from the thread pool; note that we pass in a
    'different half of the array to divide and conquer the average
    'computation
```

LISTING 12.5   Continued

```
        ThreadPool.QueueUserWorkItem(New WaitCallback(AddressOf _
            ThreadCallBack), _
            frontValues)
        ThreadPool.QueueUserWorkItem(New WaitCallback(AddressOf _
            ThreadCallBack), _
            backValues)
```

The program will actually block out this next line of code until the AutoResetEvent object that we created (threadsAreDone) signals.

```
        'Wait for threads to complete
        threadsAreDone.WaitOne()

        'Threads are done; compute the average and assign into "average"
        average = runningTotal / runningCount

        'Set our end time
        endTime = Environment.TickCount

        'Write out the elapsed time to the form
        Me.ElapsedTime.Text = (endTime - startTime) & " ms"

    End Sub
```

This subroutine is the element of code that we will run on each of our two threads from the thread pool. Because this is the one piece of code in the application that can be entered by more than one thread at a time, we use the Interlocked class and the Synclock statement to help serialize the threads during access to global variables. This subroutine accepts a string array; this is a piece of the target file for the thread to work on.

```
    Private Sub ComputeAverage(ByVal valueArray() As String)
        'just a variable to use in our For loop
        Dim loopIndex As Long

        'Write out to the form that this thread is done.
        ActivityList.Items.Add("Starting thread.")

        'Process through the supplied array
        For loopIndex = 0 To valueArray.GetUpperBound(0)

            'Keep adding to the runningTotal; protected by the
            'SyncLock statement to avoid data corruption
            SyncLock (Me)
                runningTotal = runningTotal + CType(valueArray(loopIndex), _
                    Decimal)
```

LISTING 12.5 Continued

```
      End SyncLock

      'Increment the runningCount by 1; protected by the
      'Interlocked.Increment method to avoid data
      'corruption
      Interlocked.Increment(runningCount)
  Next loopIndex

      'Write out to the form that this thread is done.
      ActivityList.Items.Add("Ending thread.")

  End Sub
```

This is our delegate for our threads; this is required by the `QueueUserWorkItem` method on the `ThreadPool` class. We are using the `state` parameter to pass around the array that each thread needs to work on.

```
  Private Sub ThreadCallBack(ByVal state As Object)


      'ComputeAverage is the actual routine that will compute the
      'averages.
      ComputeAverage(CType(state, String()))
```

After the thread has completed `ComputeAverage()`, it will fall back into the delegate `ThreadCallBack`. We neeed to decrement the global `numThreads` var; when we reach zero, we know that both threads are done executing. We can then indicate this to the application by calling the `Set` method off of our global `AutoResetEvent` object (called `threadsAreDone`).

```
      If Interlocked.Decrement(numThreads) = 0 Then
          threadsAreDone.Set()
      End If
  End Sub
```

Of course, clicking on the Start button sets it all in motion. This is where we hook the click event and respond accordingly.

```
  Private Sub Start_Click(ByVal sender As System.Object, _
      ByVal e As System.EventArgs) Handles Start.Click

      'visually indicate that the system is working...
      Me.Cursor = System.Windows.Forms.Cursors.WaitCursor

      'disable the start button; don't want to re-enter this
      'multiple times while we are crunching...
      Start.Enabled = False
```

12

LISTING 12.5   Continued

```
        ActivityList.Items.Clear()

        'zero out our running total
        runningTotal = 0

        'zero out our running count
        runningCount = 0

        'zero out our average value
        average = 0

        'check to see if we need to run single
        'threaded or with the thread pool; both
        'routines expect a file stream object as
        'an input parameter... we return this from
        'our ReadFile() routine
        If UseThreadPool.Checked = True Then
            WorkFileMulti(ReadFile(FileName.Text))
        Else
            WorkFileSingle(ReadFile(FileName.Text))
        End If

        'display the computed average to the form
        ComputedAverage.Text = average

        're-enable the start button
        Start.Enabled = True

        'we're done; give the UI back its pointer
        Me.Cursor = System.Windows.Forms.Cursors.Default
    End Sub
End Class
```

 ## Suggestions for Further Exploration

⊃   In this sample application, we have hardcoded the number of worker threads to two. Try
    rewriting the WorkFileMulti routine to accept any number of threads. You will need to
    break the file up evenly among the threads, and keep track of them through the
    numThreads variable. Once you have that done, you can add a NumericUpDown
    control to the form to let users specify how many threads to create.

⊃ To signal to the application that our threads are done executing, we use the `AutoResetEvent` class. Research this class in the .NET documentation: What is the difference between the `WaitOne`, `WaitAny`, and `WaitAll` methods?

⊃ How would you approach this application's design if the `ThreadPool` class didn't exist? In other words, how might you go about implementing your own `ThreadPool` class?

Summary

In this chapter, we had a look at how the .NET Framework supports thread concepts. We saw how:

- We can use the `Thread` class to create and manage our own threads.
- We can leverage the `ThreadPool` class to quickly and easily dispatch work onto multiple threads.
- The various synchronization mechanisms help programmers avoid thread contention.
- Variables can be created that are specific and local to individual threads.

The ability to control threads represents a very large step forward for Visual Basic developers, and the rich threading support in the .NET Framework makes syntax easy to understand and clear to implement.

Messaging

IN THIS CHAPTER

Most business applications today require some form of distributed processing. At its core, that's what .NET is all about—the capability to easily create highly distributed applications. Architects and developers alike need technologies analogous to message queuing to help bridge the gap between these distributed environments and dissimilar networks.

This chapter illustrates the System.Messaging namespace and demonstrates how you can leverage it to add Message Queuing to your applications. We start by introducing Messaging, including key concepts and design considerations. We then quickly move into the classes and related example code—all designed to get you writing code.

The chapter is rounded out with a Web-based Messaging application using ASP.NET. The application allows users to explore queues and their messages; it also supports transactional Messaging.

We think that you'll find Messaging to be an indispensable paradigm for application architecture. Moreover, .NET offers a complete set of components to make you effective in leveraging this tool in your applications.

After reading this chapter, you will be able to

- Know when, where, and why to use Messaging
- Connect to a queue
- Enumerate queues on a server
- Send a message to a queue
- Receive a message from a queue both synchronously and asynchronously
- Execute priority-based Messaging
- Enumerate messages within a queue
- Send and receive messages in various formats (serialization)
- Execute a Messaging transaction
- Control access to queues and queue objects
- Encrypt messages
- Authenticate message senders

Key Classes Related to Messaging

The System.Messaging namespace provides .NET with its Messaging capabilities. This library is designed specifically to work with Microsoft Message Queuing.

Table 13.1 lists the key classes that this chapter will discuss. At first glance, the library seems small, and, in fact, it is very manageable. However, the MessageQueue and Message classes make up the bulk of functionality exposed by the Messaging framework. The size of these classes more than makes up for the relatively small namespace.

TABLE 13.1 Key Classes in the `System.Messaging` Namespace

Class	Description
Messages and Queues	
Message	The `Message` class provides access to message-queuing messages. It can be used to read a message's body, check its posted time and priority, find its sender and authentication, and so on.
MessageEnumerator	The `MessageEnumerator` class gives you access to a cursor that enumerates (loops) through messages in a message queue. Think of this as similar to an ADO recordset's forward-only cursor, complete with a `moveNext` method.
MessagePropertyFilter	The `MessagePropertyFilter` class is used to control (filter) the properties that are returned when peeking or receiving messages from a queue. A large number of properties are associated with a `Message`. This class allows you to limit this list to only the ones that are of interest, and thus reduce network traffic and increase performance.
MessageQueue	The `MessageQueue` class is used to provide access to a message queue on a server (think MSMQ). Message queues are typically servers that allow disparate applications to exchange data in an asynchronous and transactional manner.
MessageQueueEnumerator	The `MessageQueueEnumerator` class can be used to enumerate (loop) through message queues on a server or network.
MessageQueueTransaction	The `MessageQueueTransaction` class provides a transaction context in which to execute a message-queuing transaction. This class provides methods for committing (`Commit`) and rolling back (`Abort`) transactions.
Security	
Trustee	The `Trustee` class represents a person or service with a set of access rights that is trying to access an item.

TABLE 13.1   Continued

Class	Description
	Security
MessageQueueAccessControlEntry	The MessageQueueAccessControlEntry class is used to encapsulate the access rights for a given trustee on a specific message queue.
AccessControlList	The AccessControlList class provides a collection of AccessControlEntry instances that can be used to set or return permissions on a queue.
	Message Formatters
ActiveXMessengerFormatter	The ActiveXMessengerFormatter class is used to format objects made with previous versions of MSMQ into and out of MessageQueue messages.
BinaryMessageFormatter	The BinaryMessageFormatter class is used to serialize and deserialize objects into and out of message-queue messages using the binary format.
XmlMessageFormatter	The XmlMessageFormatter class uses the XML format to serialize and deserialize messages into and out of message queues. This is the default formatter used by both the MessageQueue and the Message classes.
	Exceptions
MessageQueueException	The MessageQueueException class is used to manage errors thrown by the message queue (MSMQ). These exceptions are passed to your code and must be trapped and handled.
	Event Arguments
PeekCompletedEventArgs	The PeekCompletedEventArgs class provides information (instance of the Message class) regarding the peek for the PeekCompleted event.
ReceiveCompletedEventArgs	The ReceiveCompletedEventArgs class provides information (instance of the Message class) regarding the results of the message received.

Messaging

To help better understand Message Queuing, consider the following analogy of Instant Messaging (IM) and e-mail. Although each technology is very similar (bits from one user to another across a wire), each tool's actual use is quite different. IM is more conversational—a short burst followed by a reply, and so on. The communication is synchronous, real-time, and usually light. We use e-mail for our more important communications. E-mail guarantees delivery or sends an undeliverable message, notifies us of delivery (read receipt), stores a record of the message, can secure a message, and continues to communicate when the other user is "down." As users, we understand the ramifications and instinctively choose the appropriate tool for the job.

As programmers and system architects, we have to make the same kinds of choices. We use a simple solution similar to IM when we have a reliable network, are less concerned when processing goes down, and are communicating only with our own, known systems. Processing messages in real-time with a database connection to a server gives us a simple solution but provides a single point of failure: the database server. We do what we can to keep this thing up by creating backups and emergency measures, but when it goes down (and it will), all processing stops. Applications at the enterprise level need to do everything to guarantee that processing continues without the database. Better yet, they must *message* with disparate systems on varied networks, even if the systems are not running at the same time. These cases require an e-mail-like paradigm: *Message Queuing*.

Messaging Design Pattern

Messaging is a design strategy to help us deal with issues related to application integration and distribution. It can be thought of as a kind of *middleware*, or software that is used to mediate communications and transactions between applications. The design pattern is simple in concept. Messages (orders, invoices, credit card transactions, and so on) are sent by one or more parties to a central queue. The message is stored in its native format (XML, text, binary, and so on) in the Active Directory. The sending application hands off the message and returns to other business. A receiving application is either triggered by the message drop or set to check the queue for messages at various intervals. When it finds messages that belong to it, they are picked up and processed accordingly. If the sending application requests a response or receipt that the message was retrieved, the receiving application places a response message in a special response queue. That's Messaging.

Figure 13.1 illustrates a simple message-queuing design. Orders are sent by various systems to an order queue. Orders can be in EDI format, XML, text—whatever. The important thing to note is that orders are sent to the queue and are not *blocked,* waiting for a response. The order-processing application is not taxed, either. It can wait until downtime to pick up its orders. All this processing is *asynchronous*, or not concurrent.

Of course, Messaging in .NET provides more than simple queuing. The Messaging service built into Windows provides guaranteed delivery of messages, efficient routing, security and encryption, priority-based Messaging—just to name a few features. We also can implement both asynchronous and synchronous transactional Messaging. This functionality is exposed to our application through the Framework Class Library.

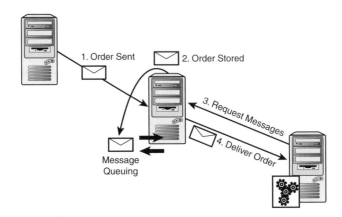

FIGURE 13.1

Typical message-queuing scenario.

Practical Applications

Message queuing is used primarily in enterprise-level, mission-critical applications as a fail-safe way to execute business processes. Message queuing is a compelling design strategy for multiple scenarios, for many reasons. We will walk through various application scenarios and demonstrate how Message Queuing can be leveraged to solve particular challenges.

Applications whose users work remotely, such as applications used by a sales force, are solid candidates for Message Queuing. Users out in the field might not have a reliable network connection, if they have one at all. These users still need to be capable of processing customer requests—and not on paper. Enter Microsoft Message Queuing. It can be configured to work offline. When these users are not connected, they still can execute orders, create invoices, do their timesheet, and so on. When their network connection is restored, the messages are delivered from their internal private queue to the central application-processing queue. Message queuing works to guarantee delivery and the transaction.

Applications with a high degree of concurrent requests need a message-like solution. When bursts of user requests flood a server, they begin to pile up synchronously. If everyone wants the same resource (such as a database connection or an object), the resource becomes blocked. Requests will time out or be rejected by the server. The server's capability to process requests will rapidly degrade. We've seen this repeatedly when a "dotcom" gets an unexpected article in a major newspaper or magazine. One solution is to put a queue in front of the requests. That way, each is stored and processed in turn. The queue might get large, but the server maintains its capability to process, and everybody waits in line; nobody is rejected.

Applications that need to allocate resources (bandwidth and processing power) based on priority can benefit from a message-queuing strategy. The concept of priority-based Messaging allows those messages with a higher level of priority to be executed ahead of those with lower priority. Suppose that you want to process new orders ahead of cancellations, or, for certain customers, you want to guarantee a response time. By implementing priority Messaging, you can make sure that you handle the urgent requests first.

e-Commerce applications that process credit card transactions can benefit from Message Queuing. If the credit card processor goes down, users should still be capable of entering orders. If the processor is blocked, users will just move on to another site whose processor is up and running. When the credit processor comes back up, the transactions are committed. If there is an error, your code suspends the order and notifies the user of the problem. Overall, a Messaging strategy is less affected by typical failures because the transactions are persisted. If an error occurs when the message is received, the message still sits until the problem is fixed.

There are a number of other creative ways to leverage Messaging in your applications. One involves using message queues to implement workflow. Suppose that the entities (timesheets, invoices, purchase orders, and so on) in a corporation need to be tracked by various departments, external suppliers, and disparate systems. Users throughout need to know the item's status as it's handed back and forth for revisions, approvals, payment, and so on. The systems themselves are in constant flux, always being modified or upgraded. It almost seems impossible to manage. With Message Queuing, you can create various agents that interact with each system to learn the status of an item. Messages that update status can be posted to a queue, where receiving applications can use an agent to read an entity's status. This loose coupling between systems provides the flexibility for each system to be managed independently of the collective.

As you can see, a message-queue design strategy affords applications stable, reliable, and flexible communication between the various layers and different systems that make up enterprise infrastructure. The remainder of this chapter is dedicated to writing Messaging code using the .NET Framework.

13

MESSAGING

NOTE

The current version of Microsoft Message Queuing is 2.0. At the time of this writing, Microsoft has announced 3.0 as part of Windows 2002. .NET will have full support for Microsoft Message Queuing 3.0.

Microsoft Message Queuing is installed as part of Windows 2000 (Professional or Server). To view queue information, go to Administrative Tools/Computer Management and expand the Services and Applications node. You also can explore queues on your network to which you have access using the Server Explorer in the Visual Studio development environment.

Message Queues

Without message queues, you can't have Messaging. Message queues are required to send and receive messages. (For this section, all you need to know about messages is that they are units of information in text or binary form. We will delve into more detail on messages later in the chapter.)

A *message queue* is a file structure (similar to a folder) that stores messages in transit. It can be thought of as a mediator between a sender and a receiver, similar to your mailbox. A letter is sent by the power company, and it is stored at the post office. The message is picked up by the mail carrier, who takes it to your mailbox. The message is again stored; finally, you pick it up. The message queues in this analogy are the post office and your mailbox. They store messages until the receiver is ready to pick them up.

Messaging applications send messages to queues, read from queues, and create and delete queues. System administrators browse queues to gather information and troubleshoot issues. The Messaging service itself uses queues for logging and writing out acknowledgements and responses.

Two primary types of message queues exist: user created queues and system queues. Users (administrators, applications, developers, and end users) can create public, private, administration, and response queues. System queues fall into the categories of journal, dead-letter, report, and private system. Most applications are built around public queues. Table 13.2 provides more information on the types of queues.

TABLE 13.2 Message Queue Types

Type	Description
Public	Public queues provide functionality for most Messaging applications. This is where you will most likely create your order, invoice, or purchase order queues. Public queues can be browsed on the network.
Private User	A private user-defined queue exists only on local machines. Applications that know the full name of the queue can access private queues. You will use these for offline processing storage.
Administration	The administration queue contains message acknowledgement and receipts. This is essentially the event log for Message Queuing.
Response	Response queues are used to store the response message for sending applications. When the destination application receives a message, a response can be left for the sending application inside a response queue.
Journal	The journal queue can be configured as the queue's historical record. It contains copies of messages that were sent and received.

TABLE 13.2   Continued

Type	Description
Dead-letter	The system discards messages when they expire or, for some reason, cannot be delivered. The dead-letter queue stores a copy of these messages.
Report	The report queue contains information on the route that a message took to its destination. This queue can be very handy for troubleshooting.
Private system	The system needs a series of private queues to store administrative information and notification messages.

Managing Queues

When working with message queues, we are primarily concerned with the methods and properties of the `MessageQueue` class. This class allows us to explore existing queues, create and delete queues, as well as send and receive messages. This class provides us a wrapper for Microsoft Message Queuing. With the class, we can obtain a reference to a specific message queue on a server or manipulate queues using the object's static members.

To reference a queue on a server, we have two basic options: path or format name reference. To use the path paradigm, we must follow some basic syntax conventions. Public queues are referenced by the queue name—for example, `MyComputer\MyQueue`. Private queues are referred to using a dollar sign ($), as in `MyComputer\Private$\MyQueue`. Two kinds of journal queues exist. One is specific to a single queue and is referred to with the syntax `MyComputer\MyQueue\Journal$`. The other is a journal queue for a server. You access it in the following manner: `MyComputer\Journal$`. The last queue type is the dead-letter queue. You refer to it with `MyComputer\Deadletter$` or `MyComputer\XactDeadletter$`. The latter refers to the transactional dead-letter queue. Transactional queues are explained later in the chapter.

The format name method allows you to reference a queue based on a queue or machine GUID on the network and a string value to indicate whether the queue is public or private. The syntax should look familiar to those who are accustomed to creating SQLOLEDB connection strings. For example, `FORMATNAME:PUBLIC=QueueGUID`, `FORMATNAME:PUBLIC=QueueGUID;JOURNAL`, and `FORMATNAME:PRIVATE=MachineGUID\QueueNumber;Journal` are all ways to access a queue based on a formatted name. Format names are sometimes preferred because they do not require the domain controller on the network to resolve the path. The `FormatName` property of the `MessageQueue` class returns a queue's format name.

The `MessageQueue` class supports both static and instance instantiation. Static versions of the object allow us to call methods that manipulate queues without actually equating our object instance to an actual queue. This allows us to do things such as create, delete, and verify the existence of queues without loading the queue's properties into our object instance.

Listing 13.1 gets us started with some sample code that demonstrates some of the static methods of the `MessageQueue` class. It is designed as a console application with one class and a module that calls the class's functions. Both functions use the `Exists` method to verify a queue's existence based on the `Path` parameter. Provided that the queue exists, one method creates a new queue, and the other deletes a queue. Note that, when using the namespace, you must set a reference to `System.Messaging`.

LISTING 13.1   Exists, Create, and Delete

```
'import the Messaging namespace for easier syntax
Imports System.Messaging

Public Class StaticExamples

    Public Shared Function CreateQueue( _
        ByVal queuePath As String) As Boolean

        'purpose: create a new queue based on a given path
        '         returns true if queue created, else false

        'instantiate a static (has no queue reference) queue object
        Dim queue As New MessageQueue()

        'verify the queue doesn't already exist prior to creation
        If Not queue.Exists(path:=queuePath) Then

            Try

                'create the queue
                queue.Create(path:=queuePath)

                Return True

            Catch

                Return False

            End Try

        Else
            'raise a message that queue already exists ...
        End If

    End Function
```

LISTING 13.1 Continued

```
    Public Shared Function DeleteQueue( _
        ByVal queuePath As String) As Boolean

        'purpose: delete a queue based on a given path
        '         returns true if queue deleted, else false

        'instantiate a static (has no queue reference) queue object
        Dim queue As New MessageQueue()

        'verify queue exists prior to deleting
        If queue.Exists(path:=queuePath) Then

            Try

                'delete the queue
                queue.Delete(path:=queuePath)

                Return True

            Catch

                Return False

            End Try

        Else
            'could raise a message that there is no queue to delete
        End If

    End Function

End Class

Module Module1

    Sub main()

        'purpose: call the functions & write the result to the console

        Console.WriteLine( _
                staticExamples.CreateQueue(".\Private$\TestQueue"))

        Console.WriteLine( _
                staticExamples.DeleteQueue(".\Private$\TestQueue"))
```

LISTING 13.1   Continued

```
        'wait for the user to stop the console application
        'this allows you to view the results
        Console.WriteLine("Enter 's' to stop the application.")

        'loop until users presses s key
        Do While Console.ReadLine <> "s" : Loop

    End Sub

End Module
```

This example assumes that you have access rights to the machine and queues. We specifically use the private queues to help ensure this. Security and permission are discussed later in the chapter.

The Delete method deletes the queue and all its messages. Messages are *not* sent to a dead-letter queue. They are gone and cannot be retrieved.

These examples are straightforward, with just a few method calls. However, we can use a static version of the object to do other things, such as return an array of public queues on the server. The next section describes different strategies for accessing and managing queues as a group.

Enumerating Queues

The MessageQueue class provides us with a number of methods to return groups of queues. Two prime strategies exist for accessing queues. One is to return a static snapshot of the queues in a given moment in time. Methods such as GetPublicQueues and GetPrivateQueuesByMachine return an array of MessageQueue objects at the time of the method call. This is useful if you need the queue information over a short period of time or if the queues on your network do not frequently change.

The other strategy for accessing queues is to maintain a more dynamic view of the queues on a server or network. The MessageQueueEnumerator class gives us this functionality. As you cycle through the queue objects, the object reflects queues that have been added or removed since the method call. This can be very useful if your queues are constantly changing or if you need a real-time depiction of the queues on a network or machine.

It is important to remember that MessageQueueEnumerator represents a forward-only cursor. This means that any queue appended or deleted beyond the cursor's current position will be reflected by the object. This is the concept of a forward-only cursor. A queue that is deleted or added before the current position, however, will not be reflected by the object. Again, "forward-only" implies that you cannot look back on queues that you've already accessed. The class does offer us a method that refreshes its view of the queues. By calling the `Reset` method, we return the object's cursor to the beginning and get a fresh look at the queues. One caveat of using this class is that its access to queues is completely random. We can never be sure when iterating queues that they will be accessed in a logical order, such as by name or ID.

To loop through and access the message queues of the enumerator, we use the `MoveNext` method and the `Current` property. `MoveNext` moves the cursor forward to the next queue member. Calls to the method return `true` if a new queue was found and return `false` if the cursor could not advance beyond the current queue. When a new `MessageQueueEnumerator` is instantiated, the cursor is positioned before the first member of the enumeration. Therefore, the first call to `MoveNext` accesses the first message queue. After the cursor is positioned on valid queue, accessing its `Current` property returns a `MessageQueue` object representing the current queue. Calls to the property when no current queues exist throw an exception.

Table 13.3 lists the methods of the `MessageQueue` class that provide us the capability to return groups of queues. Additionally, queue properties such as category, label, and machine name are described.

TABLE 13.3 `MessageQueue` Grouping Methods

`GetPrivateQueuesByMachine(ByVal machineName as String) As MessageQueue()`	Returns a static snapshot of queues on a server as an array of `MessageQueue` objects. Filters the result set by the server's name.
`GetPublicQueues() As MessageQueue()`	Returns a static snapshot of all public queues on the network as an array of `MessageQueue` objects.
`GetPublicQueues(ByVal criteria As MessageQueueCriteria) As MessageQueue()`	Returns a static snapshot of public queues on the network based on a specified set of criteria. The criteria are defined by an instance of the `MessageQueueCriteria` class explained later in the chapter.
`GetPublicQueuesByCategory(ByVal category as GUID) As MessageQueue()`	Returns a static snapshot of all public queues on the network that belong to a specific category. Categories in message queue terms allow us to categorize a set of queues. For example, we might have a group of public queues for orders and another for invoices.
`GetPublicQueuesByLabel(ByVal label As String) As MessageQueue()`	Returns a static snapshot of all public queues on the network that have a specific label. A message queue label represents the queue's description. By default, message queues have no label (empty string). Labels are not necessarily unique across queues; hence, we get an array of objects back from the method.

13

MESSAGING

TABLE 13.3 Continued

`GetPublicQueuesByMachine(ByVal machineName As String) As MessageQueue()`	Returns a static snapshot of all public queues on a specified machine. The `machineName` parameter represents the actual name of the computer on which the queue(s) reside.
`GetMessageQueueEnumerator() As MessageQueueEnumerator`	Returns a dynamic listing of all public message queues on the network. The `MessageQueueEnumerator` class is discussed in detail in the following section.
`GetMessageQueueEnumerator(ByVal criteria As MessageQueueCriteria)As MessageQueueEnumerator`	Returns a dynamic listing of all public message queues on the network based on a set of filter criteria defined by an instance of the `MessageQueueCriteria` class. Both `MessageQueueEnumerator` and `MessageQueueCriteria` are discussed in detail in the following section.

Notice that when returning groups of queues, we often want only those on a specific machine or of a particular type, such as public or private. The capability to access only those queues to which we have interest is paramount. In fact, `System.Messaging` provides us another class intended to help further refine our filtering. `MessageQueueCriteria` exposes properties designed for this specific purpose. Some filter properties include: `Category`, `CreatedAfter`, `CreatedBefore`, `Label`, `MachineName`, `ModifiedAfter`, and `ModifiedBefore`. To use the class, we simply set as many of its properties as apply to our needs and pass it as a parameter to method's such as `GetPublicQueues` and `GetMessageQueueEnumerator`. The following code illustrates this concept:

```
'local scope
Dim queues As MessageQueueEnumerator
Dim queueCriteria As New MessageQueueCriteria()

'set criteria of message queues to return
queueCriteria.MachineName = machineName
queueCriteria.CreatedBefore = DateTime.Now

'return an cursor of MessageQueue objects that meet the criteria
'note: this is a dynamic, forward-only view of the queues
queues = MessageQueue.GetMessageQueueEnumerator( _
    criteria:=queueCriteria)
```

In Listing 13.2, we write code that demonstrates access to all the private queues on a machine. We return the queues as an array of `MessageQueue` objects using the static method `GetPrivateQueuesByMachine`. We then loop through the array and output `QueueName` to the console window.

LISTING 13.2 Return Private Queues

```
Imports System.Messaging

Module Module1

    Sub main()

        'purpose: return a collection of private queues

        'local scope
        Dim privateQueues() As MessageQueue
        Dim queue As MessageQueue

        'return an array of MessageQueue objects that represent the
        '   private queues on the machine
        'note: this is a static snapshot of the queues
        privateQueues = MessageQueue.GetPrivateQueuesByMachine( _
            machineName:="myMachineName")

        'iterate the queue objects
        For Each queue In privateQueues

            'write the queue name to the console
            Console.WriteLine(queue.QueueName)

        Next

        'wait for the user to stop the console application
        Console.WriteLine("Enter 's' to stop the application.")
        Do While Console.ReadLine <> "s" : Loop

    End Sub
End Module
```

> **NOTE**
>
> You might have already figured this one out, but a Windows 2000 Professional (or workgroup) installation supports only private queues. Attempts to access a public queue will raise an exception. This is one reason why most examples were written for private queues. To work with public queues, install Message Queuing under Windows 2000 Server.

So far, we've seen how to access our message queues and garner some control over them. Now we will delve into some actual Messaging functionality. For now, all messages should be assumed to be text-based. Additional message types are discussed in the "Messages" section later in this chapter.

Sending Messages

Before a message can be sent, received, or even peeked at, we must have a reference to a physical queue on a server. We've already looked at a few ways to accomplish this in the preceding "Enumerating Queues" section. Remember, the methods presented returned a group of `MessageQueue` instances. Each instance represented an actual queue rather than simply a static object. In fact, properties such as `Category`, `Label`, and `MachineName` are available only to physical queue instances.

The easiest way to reference a single queue is to create an instance of the `MessageQueue` class and pass the queue's path on the constructor—for example, `Dim queue As New MessageQueue(path:=myPath)`. Sometimes, however, you need to convert a static instance of the object into a physical reference. This is useful if you need to do some preprocessing, such as checking whether the queue actually exists. In this case, you can create the queue object, do your preprocessing, and then set its `Path` property to actually reference the physical queue. The following is a quick example:

```
Dim queue As New MessageQueue()

If (queue.Exists(path:=myPath)) Then
    queue.Path = myPath
End If
```

Now that we have a physical queue reference, let's send a message. To do so, we use (you guessed it!) the `Send` method of the `MessageQueue` class. This method has a number of overloads, most of which will be discussed in the chapter. Each version of the method contains the `obj` parameter. We use this to define the message (object) that should be sent to the queue. Of course, messages can be simple text, a data object, a structure, or any other managed object. Message types other than text will be discussed in the "Messages" section.

It is often important to set the Label property of the message when sending. This can be done on the function call. The message label is yours to use for your application. It can serve several purposes. Primarily, it helps identify messages in human-readable terms. Additionally, it can be used to group, sort, or selectively process messages. Suppose that you create a queue that received messages from several suppliers. Perhaps each supplier's messages are processed differently or on different days. You might not want to read each message to determine the supplier. You might instead use the Label property to filter messages for a given supplier. This saves your application valuable processing resources and allows you to quickly access messages from a given supplier when browsing your queue.

Code for sending a simple message along with its label is presented in Listing 13.3. This code can be pasted into a console application and stepped through in the IDE.

LISTING 13.3   Sending a Message

```
Public Class sendExample

    Public Shared Sub sendMessage( _
        ByVal queuePath As String, _
        ByVal msg As object, _
        ByVal msgLabel As String)

        'purpose:   send a message to a queue

        'local scope
        Dim queue As New MessageQueue()

        'check to see if the queue exists
        If queue.Exists(path:=queuePath) Then

            'reference the physical queue
            queue.Path = queuePath

            'send the message to the queue
            queue.Send(obj:=msg, label:=msgLabel)

        Else
            'raise some exception
        End If

    End Sub

End Class

Module Module1
```

LISTING 13.3   Continued

```
Sub main()

    'purpose: call the function(s) & write the result to the console

    'send a message
    'note: the dot (.) in the path is a shortcut to indicate you are
    '       referencing the same server on which the code is executing
    sendExample.sendMessage( _
        queuePath:=".\Private$\myqueue", msg:="This is a test", _
        msgLabel:="TEST MESSAGE")

    'wait for the user to stop the console application
    'this allows you to view the results
    Console.WriteLine("Enter 's' to stop the application.")

    'loop until users presses s key
    Do While Console.ReadLine <> "s" : Loop

End Sub

End Module
```

Receiving Messages with `MessageQueue`

In the previous example, we sent a message to a queue. How do we retrieve that message? We call the `Receive` method, of course. This method has a number of overloads mostly dealing with transactional and asynchronous issues. We will save these for later in the chapter. For now, we just want to pluck our message from the queue.

`Receive` returns the first message in the queue. The method call is synchronous; it blocks processing until a message is received. If no message is available, it waits. At first glance, this seems odd. However, it does allow our applications to watch and wait on a queue. When a message comes in, the application can grab it, process it, and return its eyes on the queue. Of course, this is not the only strategy that .NET gives us for receiving messages. It's simply the most basic. We'll look at asynchronous and transactional Messaging later in the chapter.

You might wonder how we access other messages in the queue if `Receive` returns only the first message. The answer is simple: Calls to `Receive` actually remove the message from the queue. Therefore, subsequent calls look at the next "first message" in the queue. But what if we want to check the message before we actually remove it? For instance, let's say that a queue is shared by multiple modules in an application and that each module processes different message types. How then can we make sure that a module only reads its messages? We could create separate queues for each module (preferred in this case), or we could call the `Peek` method before receiving the message.

Peek allows our code to read the message without removing it from the server. The method is again synchronous and returns only the first message in the queue. It is often necessary to look beyond the Peek, beyond the first message in the queue. For more information on this, see the section "Enumerating Messages," later in the chapter.

A couple other methods allow us direct access to a message. ReceiveById and PeekById return a Message object from a known, unique identifier. Identifiers are generated by the Messaging application. These methods are most useful when your application allows users to dynamically read and process messages, or in similar cases when the message's Id property is known. If no message is found with the given identifier, the method immediately throws an exception. We'll use these methods in our "Learning by Example" sample application later in this chapter.

Now let's look at some code. Listing 13.4 presents a simple paradigm for message reading. First, in Sub Main, we use the previous send example to create a few messages in the queue. Next, we call our custom function, peekAndWait. As messages arrive in the queue (in this case they are already there), they are examined (Peek) for content. If they do not match the correct content, they are deleted (received without processing) and we continue to wait. If we find a message that we do want, it is returned by the function.

LISTING 13.4 Peeking and Receiving a Message

```
Public Class ReceiveExample

    Public Shared Function peekAndWait( _
        ByVal queuePath As String, _
        ByVal msgLabel As String) As Message

        'purpose:   peek at messages as the arrive in the queue
        '           if they contain the label (msgLabel) return the
        '           message, else remove the message from the queue
        '           and continue to wait

        'local scope
        Dim queue As New MessageQueue(path:=queuePath)
        Dim msg As Message

        'set the message properties that we are interested in reading
        With queue.MessageReadPropertyFilter

            'clear the filter (sets all to false)
            .ClearAll()

            'indicate that we want to read the label property
            .Label = True
```

LISTING 13.4 Continued

```
        End With

        'call the peak method
        'note: processing is blocked until a message arrives in the queue
        msg = queue.Peek

        'we have a message, read its label
        If msg.Label <> msgLabel Then

            'write the label to the console
            Console.WriteLine(msg.Label)

            'pull the message from the server
            queue.Receive()

            'use recursion to wait for a valid message
            msg = peekAndWait(queuePath:=queuePath, msgLabel:=msgLabel)

        Else

            'return a valid message
            queue.MessageReadPropertyFilter.SetAll()
            msg = queue.Receive

        End If

        'function return
        Return msg

    End Function

End Class

Module Module1

    Sub Main()

        'purpose: call the function(s) & write the result to the console

        'purge the queue
        Dim queue As MessageQueue
        queue = New MessageQueue(path:=".\Private$\myqueue")
        queue.Purge()
        queue.Close()
```

LISTING 13.4 Continued

```
        'add a few messages to the queue
        sendExample.sendMessage( _
            queuePath:=".\Private$\myqueue", msg:="Test", _
            msgLabel:="NOT ORDER 1")

        sendExample.sendMessage( _
            queuePath:=".\Private$\myqueue", msg:="Test", _
            msgLabel:="NOT ORDER 2")

        sendExample.sendMessage( _
            queuePath:=".\Private$\myqueue", msg:="Test", _
            msgLabel:="ORDER")

        sendExample.sendMessage( _
            queuePath:=".\Private$\myqueue", msg:="Test", _
            msgLabel:="NOT ORDER 3")

        'peek at messages and return the correct one
        Console.WriteLine( _
            receiveExample.peekAndWait( _
            queuePath:=".\Private$\myqueue", msgLabel:="ORDER").Label)

        'wait for the user to stop the console application
        'this allows you to view the results
        Console.WriteLine("Enter 's' to stop the application.")

        'loop until users presses s key
        Do While Console.ReadLine <> "s" : Loop

    End Sub

End Module
```

The preceding code presented a couple of new concepts. First, in Sub Main, we called the Purge method of the MessageQueue class to empty the queue of all messages. This helped to ensure that we were looking at only our test messages. Next, when reading the messages in the peekAndWait function, we used the MessageReadPropertyFilter to peek at only message labels. This can be useful when processing large messages or working with low bandwidth. It allows us to read only the items of which we have interest. Note that when we found a valid message, we called the SetAll method to make sure that we returned all properties of the message.

13

MESSAGING

Figure 13.2 represents the output of our console application. Remember, we created three nonorders and only one order. Where is the other nonorder? Well, our method returns processing to the module after an order has been found. In a real-world scenario, we would process the message and call the peekAndWait function again.

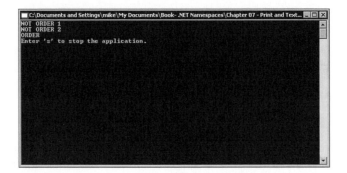

FIGURE 13.2

Output of peekAndWait.

Asynchronous Messaging

Messaging is inherently asynchronous; messages are sent to a queue and received in a separate process. Asynchronous Messaging is the capability for our applications to be notified of an incoming message without blocking or waiting on the message queue. Asynchronous Messaging is useful for retrieving messages without tying up application processing. The best analogy is Microsoft's Outlook e-mail client. When active, it receives messages as they arrive, but it does not block access to other features when waiting to receive a message.

Standard implementation of asynchronous Messaging is straightforward. The following details the basic steps involved in coding asynchronous Messaging:

1. We tell the queue that we want to be notified of all incoming messages by making a call to the BeginReceive method of the MessageQueue class. This method immediately returns processing to our application; there is no blocking as in the MessageQueue.Receive method.

2. BeginReceive has a corresponding event, ReceiveCompleted. We add an event delegate to our application to handle this event. The event is raised when a message is available to be retrieved. It passes the ReceiveCompletedEventArgs class to our application. These arguments represent the associated message data. Our application uses this information to retrieve the message.

3. We call `EndReceive` to end the operation. `EndReceive` actually returns the message to our application. At this point, we will no longer be notified of additional incoming messages. If we want to continue to listen to the queue, we must again call `BeginReceive`.

That is the basic overview. Two more methods, `BeginPeek` and `EndPeek`, allow us to asynchronously peek at messages rather than receive. These methods work identically to the receive methods. They have a corresponding `PeekCompleted` event and `PeekCompletedEventArgs` class.

In Listing 13.5, we set up an asynchronous message receiver. This console application does other processing (writes text to the console) while waiting for a message to arrive in the queue. (To put messages in the queue, simply execute some additional send code from another example.) When a message arrives, the application retrieves the message and goes back to work.

LISTING 13.5 Asynchronous Messaging

```
Imports System.Messaging

Module Module1

    'module-level scope
    Private msgReceived As Boolean = False

    Sub Main()

        'purpose: provide an example of asynch. Messaging

        'local scope
        Dim queue As New MessageQueue(path:=".\private$\myqueue")

        'add event delegate.
        AddHandler queue.ReceiveCompleted, AddressOf ReceiveCompletedEvent

        'purge the queue
        queue.Purge()

        'tell the queue that we want to listen for messages
        queue.BeginReceive()

        'execute code to demo. asych
        Do While Not msgReceived
            Console.WriteLine("Doing something else ...")
        Loop
```

LISTING 13.5 Continued

```
        'pause the application to read the demo. text
        Console.WriteLine("Enter 's' to stop")
        Do While Not Console.ReadLine = "s" : Loop

    End Sub

    Sub ReceiveCompletedEvent( _
        ByVal source As Object, _
        ByVal result As ReceiveCompletedEventArgs)

        'purpose: process the asynch event

        'local scope
        Dim msg As Message
        Dim queue As MessageQueue

        Console.WriteLine("ReceiveCompletedEvent Fired")

        'return the queue information
        queue = CType(source, MessageQueue)

        Console.WriteLine(queue.QueueName)

        'return the message
        msg = queue.EndReceive(result.AsyncResult)

        Console.WriteLine(msg.Label)

        'indicate that we want the processing to stop
        msgReceived = True

        'tell the queue that we want to listen again
        'queue.BeginReceive()

    End Sub

End Module
```

In the example, we created the Boolean value `msgReceived` to indicate when the processing should stop. This is solely for reading the example text in the console. If we don't pause the application, the message is read and processing continues so fast that you can hardly see it in the console.

The peek methods work the same way. In fact, inside both event handlers we have the option to peek or receive the message. The events just tell us that there is a message in the queue. Because we get a reference the queue from within the event, all queue methods and properties are still valid.

By now, you should be familiar with the MessageQueue basics. This class is the backbone of the components that make up Messaging in .NET. As such, it will be referred to often in the remainder of the chapter. The next sections explore the details of messages and how to work with them in your applications.

Suggestions for Further Exploration

MessageQueue is a very involved class. A number of additional methods and properties are key to your writing successful code. To get a full understanding of just what the class can do, we present the following methods and properties for your own exploration:

- ⊃ **Refresh**—Refreshes the instance's properties to reflect any changes that might have occurred to the queue since the object was created

- ⊃ **ReceiveByCorrelationId**—Allows you to receive a message based on a correlation ID found in an associated acknowledgement or response message

- ⊃ **BasePriority**—Allows you to specify how a message is treated as it moves across the network

- ⊃ **WriteHandle**—Provides a Windows handle for the message queue

Messages

Applications send messages to one another to indicate status, execute transactions (orders, credit cards, and so on), submit invoices, and generally update data. A message is a unit of information (text or binary) sent from one computer to another. A message can be a simple string, formatted XML, or even an embedded object of executable code. .NET gives us the Message class for working with messages.

The Message class, through its properties, gives us granular control over sending and receiving messages to and from queues. In fact, the Message class has no methods. All manipulation (sending, receiving, formatting, deleting, and so on) of messages is done through associated classes. Remember, when we peeked at and received messages in the previous section, the MessageQueue instance used the Message class for these operations.

The Message class contains two types of properties. Those that are read-only are designed to work with receiving messages. The read/write properties apply to both sending and receiving messages. These properties will be discussed in context throughout the remainder of this chapter.

Timeouts and Expirations

Applications often require that messages reach their destination and be received within a given time period. For instance, if an order sits in a queue for two days and you've guaranteed a customer that his items will ship within two days, then you have a problem. Or perhaps the messages contain timely information that is updated on a regular basis, such as a report or entity status in which each day's message is meant to override the previous day's messages. If not acted on within a set time frame, the message should expire itself and your application should take appropriate actions.

The Message class provides us two properties for dealing with message timeouts: TimeToReachQueue and TimeToBeReceived. TimeToReachQueue allows us to indicate how much time a message has to reach its destination. This is important when sending the message or relaying a message. TimeToBeReceived allows us to specify how much time a message can be in the system, from time sent to time received. Essentially, this is the message's lifetime.

Both properties use the TimeSpan structure for their data. TimeSpan indicates a time interval. There is no equivalent in VB6 to this very useful structure. It allows us to set days, hours, minutes, seconds, and milliseconds using its numerous constructors. You can return TotalDays, TotalHours, and so on from its many properties. TimeSpan is part of System, not System.Messaging.

If either interval expires, the message will be discarded. Message Queuing provides a few options for handling discarded messages. A copy of the message can be sent to a specified dead-letter queue. To do so, we must first set the message's UseDeadLetterQueue property to true. Additionally, we can have Message Queuing send us a negative acknowledgement message to indicate that the message was discarded. Acknowledgements are discussed in detail later in this section. In either case, our code should be trained on the dead-letter queue or a similar acknowledgement queue to intercept expired messages and process them accordingly.

Listing 13.6 illustrates expired messages. We first create a message and set its TimeToBeReceived property to 15 seconds. We then watch the dead-letter queue and wait for MSMQ to expire the message. Finally, we process the message upon its arrival in the dead-letter queue.

LISTING 13.6 Message Timeouts

```
Imports System.Messaging

Module Module1

    Sub Main()

        'purpose:   demonstrate the message timeout features
```

LISTING 13.6   Continued

```
        'local scope
        Dim msg As New Message()
        Dim queue As MessageQueue = _
            New MessageQueue(path:=".\Private$\myqueue")
        Dim deadQueue As MessageQueue = _
            New MessageQueue(path:=".\Deadletter$")

        'purge both queues
        queue.Purge()
        Try
            deadQueue.Purge()
        Catch
            MsgBox(Err.Description)
        End Try

        'tell the message to use the dead letter queue
        msg.UseDeadLetterQueue = True

        'set the expiration using a TimeSpan instance
        msg.TimeToBeReceived = _
            New TimeSpan(hours:=0, minutes:=0, seconds:=15)

        'set the message body
        msg.Body = "Expiring message test"

        'send the message
        queue.Send(obj:=msg)

        'indicate we are watching the dead-letter queue
        Console.WriteLine("Message sent. Waiting ...")

        'grab message from dead letter queue (blocks until there)
        Try
            Console.WriteLine(deadQueue.Receive().Body)
        Catch
            MsgBox(Err.Description)
        End Try

        'wait to continue
        Console.WriteLine("Enter 's' to stop")
        Do While Not Console.ReadLine = "s" : Loop

    End Sub

End Module
```

13

MESSAGING

Notice the error handling around each attempt to access the dead-letter queue. Attempts to access this information on a professional installation of Windows throw an exception. You must have Window Server installed to access this queue through code. However, you can still run the code and navigate to the queue to see the results.

Acknowledgement and Response

It can be important for our applications to understand when a message has arrived at its destination and when it was received by the destination application. The application might simply verify all messages sent, as an extra level of safety. For example, an application might have the business rule that states, "After a message is sent, it must be verified as received within three business days." Additionally, we might have a new business process that kicks off based on a message being received. For instance, suppose that an application sends a purchase order message. It then receives acknowledgement that the message was received by its destination. At that point, the application might trigger a process to generate a request for payment to the billing department.

Message Queuing provides two types of message verification: acknowledgement and response. Acknowledgements are generated by Message Queuing; responses are generated by the receiving application. The acknowledgement strategy has the following application benefits:

- Message Queuing manages acknowledgement for our applications.
- Acknowledgements automatically are generated and sent.
- Acknowledgements are based on conditions (received, failed, timeout, and so on).
- Acknowledgements have a preset type (received, failed, and so on).
- There is no information in the body of the message. The entire acknowledgement is contained in the message header.

Responses provide our applications the capability to receive a custom message directly from the receiver. Responses are not automatic; it is up to the receiving application to send a response back to the sender. This can be useful when the response contains more information than a simple acknowledgement. An application might send the order ID back as part of its response, for instance. The choice on which verification strategy to implement depends on the context of your application. In fact, sometimes you will want to employ both strategies.

To indicate acknowledgement with `System.Message`, we use the `Message.AdministrationQueue` and `Message.AcknowledgmentType` properties. `AdministrationQueue` is used to indicate the queue that receives the acknowledgement. Its type is an instance of the class `MessageQueue`. We can use any nontransactional queue to receive our acknowledgements. We set `AcknowledgmentType` to tell the receiving system what types of acknowledgements we want to receive back. This property is of the type `AcknowledgmentTypes` enumeration. Its values can be combined using a bitwise operator. Table 13.4 describes the values of the enumeration.

TABLE 13.4 `AcknowledgeTypes` Enumeration Value

Value	Description
`FullReachQueue`	`FullReachQueue` indicates that we want both positive and negative (full) acknowledgement on messages arriving to their destination (reaching the queue).
`FullReceive`	`FullReceive` indicates that we want both positive and negative (full) acknowledgement on messages being received by the destination application.
`NegativeReceive`	`NegativeReceive` indicates that we want acknowledgement when messages fail (negative) to be received by the destination application.
`None`	`None` indicates that we want no acknowledgement whatsoever. This is the default value of `Message` objects.
`NotAcknowledgeReachQueue`	`NotAcknowledgeReachQueue` indicates that we want acknowledgement when messages fail (not) to reach their intended destination queue.
`NotAcknowledgeReceive`	`NotAcknowledgeReceive` indicates that we want acknowledgement when messages fail (not) to be received by the destination application.
`PositiveArrival`	`PositiveArrival` indicates that we want acknowledgement when messages succeed (positive) in reaching their intended destination queue.
`PositiveReceive`	`PositiveReceive` indicates that we want acknowledgement when messages succeed (positive) in being received by the destination application.

We tell destination applications where to send responses by setting the `Message.ResponseQueue` property. This property takes a valid instance of `MessageQueue`. Again, it is up to the destination application to read this property and send the appropriate message to the given response queue.

Listing 13.7 demonstrates acknowledgements by first creating two identical messages. We then receive one message and let the other time out. Lastly, we read the acknowledgement queue for messages and output them to the console.

LISTING 13.7   Acknowledgements

```vb
Imports system.Messaging

Module Module1

    Sub Main()

        'purpose:   demonstrate the acknow. and response
        '           properties of the Message class

        'local scope
        Dim msg As New Message()
        Dim queue As New MessageQueue(path:=".\private$\myQueue")
        Dim ackQueue As New MessageQueue(path:=".\private$\myQueueAckn")
        Dim ackMsg As Message

        'purge the queues
        queue.Purge()
        ackQueue.Purge()

        'set the admin. queue to which ack. should be set
        msg.AdministrationQueue = ackQueue

        'set the type of ack. we want to receive
        msg.AcknowledgeType = AcknowledgeTypes.FullReceive

        'set a timeout value for the message (10 seconds)
        msg.TimeToBeReceived = New TimeSpan(ticks:=100000000)

        'send the message twice
        msg.Label = "Ack example 1"
        queue.Send(obj:=msg)
        msg.Label = "Ack example 2"
        queue.Send(obj:=msg)

        'receive the 1st message
        Console.WriteLine(queue.Receive().Label)

        'retrieve the positive ack. message
        ackMsg = ackQueue.Receive()

        'write out the ack. information
        Console.WriteLine(value:=ackMsg.Acknowledgment.ToString)

        'retrieve the negative ack. message (timeout)
        ackMsg = ackQueue.Receive()

        'write out the ack. information
```

LISTING 13.7 Continued

```
        Console.WriteLine(value:=ackMsg.Acknowledgment.ToString)

        'wait to continue
        Console.WriteLine("Enter 's' to stop")
        Do While Not Console.ReadLine = "s" : Loop

    End Sub

End Module
```

Note that we used the `Acknowledgement` property of `Message` to retrieve the type of acknowledgement that the acknowledgement message represented. This is our only indication of exactly what the message represents. Figure 13.3 illustrates the routine's output. You can see that the first acknowledgement is telling us that the message was received, and the second indicates that the message timed out.

FIGURE 13.3
Output of acknowledgements example.

Setting Priority

Message Queuing supports the concept of priority-based Messaging. This design dictates that messages will have an associated priority level relative to one another. Those with the higher priority are processed (received or routed) first. Messages that have identical priority levels are processed based on their arrival time in the queue. This allows our applications to respond faster to the special customer or to put new orders ahead of information requests.

We use `Message.Priority` to set a message's priority using the namespace. The `Priority` property is of the type `MessagePriority` enumeration. This enumeration has the following values (from high to low priority): `Highest`, `VeryHigh`, `High`, `AboveNormal`, `Normal`, `Low`, `VeryLow`, `Lowest`.

Listing 13.8 sends four messages with varying degrees of priority. Each message then is read back from the queue in turn, to illustrate priority-based Messaging.

LISTING 13.8   Priorities

```vb
Imports System.Messaging

Module Module1

    Sub Main()

        'purpose:    demonstrate priority based Messaging

        'local scope
        Dim queue As MessageQueue = _
            New MessageQueue(path:=".\Private$\myqueue")
        Dim msg(3) As Message
        Dim cnt As Short

        'create new messages
        For cnt = 0 To 3 : msg(cnt) = New Message() : Next

        'set message priorities
        msg(0).Priority = MessagePriority.Normal
        msg(1).Priority = MessagePriority.Highest
        msg(2).Priority = MessagePriority.AboveNormal
        msg(3).Priority = MessagePriority.High

        'clear the queue
        queue.Purge()

        'set the message body and send
        For cnt = 0 To 3
            msg(cnt).Formatter = New BinaryMessageFormatter()
            msg(cnt).Body = CStr(msg(cnt).Priority.ToString)
            queue.Send(obj:=msg(cnt))
        Next

        'receive the messages based on priority
        queue.Formatter = New BinaryMessageFormatter()
        For cnt = 0 To 3
            Console.WriteLine(queue.Receive.Body)
        Next

        'wait to continue
        Console.WriteLine("Enter 's' to stop")
        Do While Not Console.ReadLine = "s" : Loop

    End Sub

End Module
```

The console's output is provided in Figure 13.4. Notice the difference in the output compared to the order in which the messages were sent to the system.

FIGURE 13.4
Priority example output.

Default Properties

.NET provides us with a shortcut for sending similar messages in bulk. We might want to set all messages to generate an acknowledgement message or to time out in the same specified time. To do so, we use the `DefaultPropertiesToSend` property of `MessageQueue`; this takes an instance of the `DefaultPropertiesToSend` class. To use the class, we simply set its various properties.

Listing 13.9 illustrates the concepts with some basic code. We start by setting a number of default properties. We then send 10 messages to the queue. When you run the application, use a message explorer to watch the messages spool into the queue and then time out after a minute and send an acknowledgement to that effect.

LISTING 13.9   Default Properties to Send

```
Imports System.Messaging

Module Module1

    Sub Main()

        'purpose:    illustrate defaultPropertiesToSend class

        'lcoal scope
        Dim queue As New MessageQueue(path:=".\private$\myQueue")
        Dim cnt As Short
```

LISTING 13.9   Continued

```
        'purge the queue
        queue.Purge()

        'set some default properties
        queue.DefaultPropertiesToSend.AcknowledgeType = _
            AcknowledgeTypes.FullReceive
        queue.DefaultPropertiesToSend.AdministrationQueue = _
            New MessageQueue(path:=".\private$\myQueueAckn")
        queue.DefaultPropertiesToSend.TimeToBeReceived = _
            New TimeSpan(hours:=0, minutes:=1, seconds:=0)
        queue.DefaultPropertiesToSend.Label = "EXAMPLE"
        queue.DefaultPropertiesToSend.Priority = MessagePriority.Highest

        'send some messages
        For cnt = 1 To 10
            queue.Send(obj:=cnt)
        Next

    End Sub

End Module
```

Enumerating Messages

Similar to enumerating queues, the MessageQueue class provides us with a number of methods to return groups of messages. There are again two primary strategies: return a static snapshot of the messages, or maintain a dynamic connection to the messages in queue.

To obtain a snapshot of all messages in a queue at a given moment in time, we use the MessageQueue.GetAllMessages method. This method returns an array of Message objects. GetAllMessages does not remove messages from the queue. It is equivalent to peeking at all the messages in the queue.

We use the MessageQueue.GetEnumerator method to maintain a more dynamic relationship with the messages in a queue. This method returns a valid IEnumerator interface. We can set this interface to an instance of the class MessageEnumerator. This class allows us to access all messages in the queue.

Listing 13.10 shows how to use the GetAllMessages and GetEnumerator methods.

LISTING 13.10   Enumerating Messages

```
Imports System.Messaging

Module Module1

    Sub Main()

        'purpose:    illustrate enumerating messages

        'local scope
        Dim queue As New MessageQueue(path:=".\private$\myQueue")
        Dim cnt As Short
        Dim msg() As Message
        Dim cursor As MessageEnumerator

        'purge the queue
        queue.Purge()

        'send some messages for GetAllMessages
        For cnt = 1 To 5 : queue.Send(cnt) : Next

        'return the messages as a snapshot
        msg = queue.GetAllMessages()

        'loop the array and write out to console
        For cnt = 0 To UBound(msg) - 1
            Console.WriteLine(value:=msg(cnt).Body)
        Next

        'send some messages for the enumerator
        For cnt = 1 To 5 : queue.Send(cnt) : Next

        'return an emumerator hooked to the queue's messages
        cursor = queue.GetMessageEnumerator

        'loop the cursor
        While (cursor.MoveNext())
            Console.WriteLine(cursor.Current.Body)
        End While

        'wait to continue
        Console.WriteLine("Enter 's' to stop")
        Do While Not Console.ReadLine = "s" : Loop

    End Sub

End Module
```

Note that the MoveNext method does not actually remove the message from the queue. Instead, it allows you to examine its contents and decide what you would like to do. If you decide that you want to remove the message, you can use the RemoveCurrent method. This method returns the current Message object and removes the item from the queue. MoveNext also provides another overload that allows you to pass it a TimeSpan value. This value indicates how long the method should wait if it finds no additional messages.

 ## Suggestions for Further Exploration

System.TimeSpan can be an indispensable structure when writing interval and time-related code. You are encouraged to check out its many properties and methods.

Serialization

Earlier, we used an instance of MessageQueue to send a message composed of a string. We will now look at other ways to format messages using the Message class and associated formatting classes (XMLMessageFormatter, BinaryMessageFormatter, ActiveXMessageFormatter). These classes are responsible for serializing and deserializing our messages when sending and receiving from queues.

Message Body

When we discuss message formatting, we are primarily concerned with the contents, or *body*, of the message. When we specify a format for a message or encrypt a message, only its body is affected. The message body can consist of nearly any type of information. It can contain a simple string value, a date, a currency, an array of bytes, or even a managed object. Listing 13.11 sends a message, receives it, and writes its body out to the console.

LISTING 13.11   Return Message Body

```
'import the Messaging namespace for easier syntax
Imports System.Messaging

Module Module1

    Sub Main()

        'purpose:   display message body and body type properties

        'local scope
        Dim queue As MessageQueue
        Dim msg As Message
```

LISTING 13.11   Continued

```
        'get a reference to the queue
        queue = New MessageQueue(path:=".\Private$\myqueue")

        'purge any unwanted messages
        queue.Purge()

        'add a new message to the queue
        queue.Send(obj:=Now)

        'retrieve the message
        msg = queue.Receive

        'write the XML contents to the console
        Console.WriteLine(value:="Body:=" & msg.Body)

        'close the queue
        queue.Close()

        'wait for the user to stop the console application
        'this allows you to view the results
        Console.WriteLine("Enter 's' to stop the application.")

        'loop until users presses s key
        Do While Console.ReadLine <> "s" : Loop

    End Sub

End Module
```

The output is captured in Figure 13.5.

FIGURE 13.5

Return message body output.

Note that the message's format was output as a simple string. However, if we view the body of the message using the queue explorer, we see that the message is stored as XML with some surrounding binary data (see Figure 13.6).

FIGURE 13.6
Message queue explorer output.

How did the message get stored as XML, and how was it returned as a string? Well, when we send messages, we must specify a special formatting class to dictate the message's format. These classes *serialize* data into the correct format when sending messages and *deserialize* messages when receiving. Of course, we didn't explicitly set a formatter class. However, the .NET Messaging components use XML, by default, to send and receive messages. This should-n't come as a surprise because Microsoft has publicized .NET's XML capabilities. In fact, the messages that we sent in the previous section using the MessageQueue class also were sent with XML. This is the default formatter used by MessageQueue.

In our example, MessageQueue.Send created an instance of a Message object and used the XmlMessageFormatter class to serialize our string into XML before sending the message to the queue. When we read back the message, MessageQueue.Receive used the same class to deserialize the body of the message into a Message instance. In fact, you can use MessageQueue.Send to send any object whose type is not Message. The object is simply serial-ized by the XmlMessageFormatter and is stored in the message body. For simple Messaging, this works great. We don't have to set many properties or create additional objects; it just works. When we want to control our message format, however, .NET gives us that capability as well. We will cover this in more detail in the coming sections.

NOTE	

There is a limit to message size in Microsoft Message Queuing. Messages must be less than 4MB. This includes the properties and all contents.

When we set the `Message.Body` property, the `Message` instance uses a formatter class to format and serialize our contents out to the `BodyStream` property. Sometimes it is not convenient to write the body contents to the `Body` property and let the formatter do the work for us. Instead, we might want to stream the contents of an object or file directly to the `BodyStream` property. Listing 13.12 demonstrates this use of the `BodyStream` property.

LISTING 13.12   BodyStream Example

```
Imports System.Messaging

Module Module1

    Sub Main()

        'purpose:   stream a file into a message body and send the message

        'local scope
        Dim fileStream As IO.FileStream
        Dim queue As MessageQueue
        Dim msg As Message
        Dim fileByte As Integer

        'create new fileStream object based on file
        fileStream = New IO.FileStream(path:="c:\test.txt", _
            mode:=IO.FileMode.Open, access:=IO.FileAccess.Read)

        'create new message object
        msg = New Message()

        'set the stream location to the start
        msg.BodyStream.Seek(offset:=0, _
            origin:=IO.SeekOrigin.Begin)

        'read the contents of the file and write to the message as bytes
        fileByte = fileStream.ReadByte()
        Do While fileByte <> -1
            msg.BodyStream.WriteByte(value:=fileByte)
            fileByte = fileStream.ReadByte()
        Loop
```

LISTING 13.12   Continued

```
        'get a reference to the queue
        queue = New MessageQueue(path:=".\Private$\myqueue")

        'send the message to the queue
        queue.Send(obj:=msg)

    End Sub

End Module
```

In the code example, we created the contents of a message 1 byte at a time. We read bytes from a file using the FileStream object (for more information on System.IO, see Chapter 7, "Stream and File Operations") and output those bytes directly to our Message object by calling Message.BodyStream.WriteByte. We then sent the message to the queue. If you look at the message, you will notice that there is no XML formatting. Because we are streaming the message, the message formatter is skipped and the message is written to the queue byte by byte. No additional serialization is done by a formatter class. This can be useful in situations that require streaming or when you need more granular control over message contents and format.

XML Format (XmlMessageFormatter)

We already know that the XmlMessageFormatter class is the default setting in .NET Messaging. When you create a new MessageQueue instance, an instance of XmlMessageFormatter is created and applied to the Formatter property. This class is responsible for serializing message contents when writing to a queue. Of course, messages must be retrieved in the same format that was used to write them to the queue. When receiving messages, the MessageQueue class again defers to XmlMessageFormatter to deserialize message content.

There are two key properties of XmlMessageFormatter: TargetTypeNames and TargetType. These properties provide similar functionality. They define the schemas (types) that XmlMessageFormatter must match when deserializing message contents. A schema type can be thought of as anything that can be an object in .NET. TargetTypeNames is used when you have type names that are string values. You use TargetType when you want to set the actual type and not its name. Setting either property automatically updates the other property.

When the XmlMessageFormatter deserializes a message, it matches a schema type with the message contents. If it cannot find a corresponding type, it throws an exception. If it does find a match, the formatter creates an instance of the type and deserializes the contents directly to the object. This can be very useful. For instance, let's say that we store a timesheet record in our message body as an instance of the type CTimesheet, where CTimesheet is a custom class we create. We then send the message across the wire to our central office. When an application reads the message from the queue, the XmlMessageFormatter class automatically triggers an instance of CTimesheet whose properties are set based on the message body. The CTimesheet instance could contain code to write its contents directly to the database. Remember, the queue-reading application simply made a call to receive the message. Listing 13.13 further defines our timesheet example.

LISTING 13.13 TargetType: CTimesheet

```
Imports System.Messaging

Public Class CTimesheet

    'purpose:   represent a timesheet object

    'property declarations
    Public employeeId As String
    Public hours As Short
    Public periodStart As Date
    Public periodEnd As Date

    Public Sub recordTimesheet()

        'purpose:   record the timesheet to the database

        'add code to write to the database

        Console.WriteLine(value:="Timesheet recorded.")

    End Sub

End Class

Module Module1

    Sub Main()

        'purpose:   illustrate TargetType property of
        '           XmlMessageFormatter class

        'local scope
        Dim queue As MessageQueue
        Dim timeSheetWrite As CTimesheet
        Dim timeSheetRead As CTimesheet

        '-------send the message
```

LISTING 13.13   Continued

```
       'create a timesheet instance, set its properties
       timeSheetWrite = New CTimesheet()
       timeSheetWrite.employeeId = "5001-00"
       timeSheetWrite.hours = 80
       timeSheetWrite.periodStart = "5/1/2001"
       timeSheetWrite.periodEnd = "5/15/2001"

       'get a reference to the queue
       'note: by default we are using XmlMessageFormatter
       queue = New MessageQueue(path:=".\Private$\myqueue")

       'purge any items in the queue
       queue.Purge()

       'send the message to the queue
       queue.Send(obj:=timeSheetWrite)

       '-------receive the message

       'get an instance of CTimesheet by simply receiving the message
       '  and converting the type
       timeSheetRead = CType(queue.Receive().Body, CTimesheet)

       'call the record method
       timeSheetRead.recordTimesheet()

       '-------wait for input

       'wait for the user to stop the console application
       'this allows you to view the results
       Console.WriteLine("Enter 's' to stop the application.")

       'loop until users presses s key
       Do While Console.ReadLine <> "s" : Loop

    End Sub

End Module
```

In the code example, we demonstrated how to use the XmlMessageFormatter class to serialize a custom class into a message, receive that message, and deserialize it back into a usable object. You can see from Figure 13.7 that the formatter actually wrote the message contents to human-readable XML. Suppose that something happened to your application and you could no longer deserialize messages. If they were formatted as XML, you could at least view their contents and get a better understanding of what went wrong. It gives the application a lot of flexibility when sending messages, reading their contents, and triggering business rules directly from a message based solely on its type. We do not have to create any wrapper code to write and read our objects as messages; it is all done for us by the formatter.

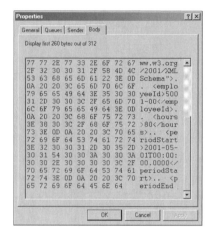

FIGURE 13.7
CTimesheet *message.*

Binary Messages (`BinaryMessageFormatter`)

Suppose that we don't want to use the default formatter. The namespace gives us a couple more options. To change the format that a `MessageQueue` instance uses to read from and write to queues, we set its `Formatter` property. This property applies only to messages sent using the default properties (`DefaultPropertiesToSend`), however. Messages sent using a `Message` instance rely on the `Message.Formatter` property. Both properties take an instance of a class that implements the `IMessageFormatter` interface. One such class, `BinaryMessageFormatter`, provides us binary serialization of messages.

Unlike the XML-formatted messages, binary-formatted message are not human-readable. Nevertheless, they do offer us very compact messages that the system can parse quickly. Binary-formatted messages are useful for sending files or data of different types. For instance, suppose that your message was a Visio drawing or an image, perhaps a customer's receipt. With the binary formatter class, this information can be stored and sent as a message and then deserialized back into its binary form.

Listing 13.14 writes a bitmap to a message, reads the bitmap message, and deserializes the contents out to a new bitmap file. In the example, we first set the `Formatter` property of the `Message` instance to a new instance of `BinaryMessageFormatter`. We then use some of our `BodyStream` code to read the file into the message, receive it, and write it back out as a new message.

LISTING 13.14   Binary Formatter

```
Imports System.Messaging

Module Module1

    Sub Main()

        'purpose:    demonstrate binary formatter
        '            application opens a bitmap file, streams the contents
        '                to a message. The message is then received from the
        '                queue where it is stream back out into a new file

        'local scope
        Dim fileStream As IO.FileStream
        Dim queue As MessageQueue = _
            New MessageQueue(path:=".\Private$\myqueue")
        Dim msg As New Message()
        Dim fileByte As Integer

        'tell the formatter object to use the binary formatter
        msg.Formatter = New BinaryMessageFormatter()

        'set the stream location to the start
        msg.BodyStream.Seek(offset:=0, _
            origin:=IO.SeekOrigin.Begin)

        'create new fileStream object based on a bitmap file
        fileStream = New IO.FileStream(path:="c:\figure 11-1.bmp", _
            mode:=IO.FileMode.Open, access:=IO.FileAccess.Read)

        'read the contents of the file and write to the message as bytes
        fileByte = fileStream.ReadByte()
        Do While fileByte <> -1
            msg.BodyStream.WriteByte(value:=fileByte)
            fileByte = fileStream.ReadByte()
        Loop
        fileStream.Close()
```

LISTING 13.14 Continued

```
        'purge the queue
        queue.Purge()

        'send the message to the queue
        queue.Send(obj:=msg)

        '----allows you to check the message
        'wait for you to continue the app.
        Console.WriteLine("Message Sent.")
        Console.WriteLine("Enter 'c' to continue the application.")
        Do While Console.ReadLine <> "c" : Loop

        'receive the message
        msg = queue.Receive()

        'create a new fileStream object and file
        fileStream = New IO.FileStream(path:="c:\figure 11-1-2.bmp", _
            mode:=IO.FileMode.Create, access:=IO.FileAccess.Write)

        'set the stream location to the start
        msg.BodyStream.Seek(offset:=0, _
            origin:=IO.SeekOrigin.Begin)

        'read the contents of the message and write to the new file
        fileByte = msg.BodyStream.ReadByte()
        Do While fileByte <> -1
            fileStream.WriteByte(value:=fileByte)
            fileByte = msg.BodyStream.ReadByte()
        Loop
        fileStream.Close()

    End Sub

End Module
```

Transactional Messaging

Transactional Messaging is the bundling of one or more messages into a cohesive set that can be processed as a single transaction. A transaction, in the Messaging sense, is simply the sending or receiving of one or more messages. Transactional messages are grouped inside a *transaction context*. The transaction context stores the state of the transaction independent of the state of a given message.

Transactional Messaging provides our applications the capability to cancel or *abort* the sending or receiving of multiple messages. Suppose that we have an application that sends three messages to a queue. The three messages are part of an order transaction. One is the request from the buyer, the second is the approval by the bank, and the third is the confirmation from our inventory application. Let's say that the first two messages send just fine, but the third encounters a problem. We are out of stock and cannot fulfill the order. Our business rules state that the transaction is not complete without all three messages. If we wrap each `Send` call inside a transaction context, we can just tell the context that we want to abort the operation. At this time, all three messages are cancelled; the transaction is *aborted*. This includes the first two messages that already were sent. Suppose that we did have stock. We simply tell the transaction context to finish or *commit* the transaction. At this time, the transaction is finished and the messages are sent to the queue. This process of committing or aborting is said to be *atomic*—that is, the transaction succeeds or fails as a whole.

Of course, the same holds true for receiving messages. If the valid transaction represents multiple messages, we wrap the `Receive` calls inside a transaction context. If all messages are received without incidence, we commit the transaction. If there is an error, we abort.

To implement transactional Messaging with the .NET components, we use the `MessageQueue` class and the `MessageQueueTransaction` class. The remainder of this section explores these classes and gets you started sending and receiving transactional messages.

Transactional Queues

A transactional queue is any queue inside Microsoft's Messaging Queuing that is marked as having the capability to receive transactional messages. All queues in MSMQ can be marked transactional. Transactional queues also can receive nontransactional messages. Of course, these messages cannot make use of the fact that the queue is transactional.

To use the transactional features of Messaging, you first must make sure that you are using a transactional queue. Probably the easiest way to create a transactional queue is to check the Transactional check box on the management interface dialog box used to create a queue. If you create a queue programmatically, you can call this overloaded method:

```
MessageQueue.Create(ByVal path as string, ByVal transactional as Boolean)
```

In this version of the `Create` method, you simply set the `transactional` property to `True`.

You can read the `MessageQueue.Transactional` property to make sure that your application is communicating with a transactional queue. This property returns a `Boolean` value of `True` if the queue supports transactions.

Transactional Sending

The `MessageQueueTransaction` class is used to wrap a transaction context for our use. Each instance of the class represents one transaction. We use one property and three methods from this class. Its property, `Status`, is used to indicate the transaction's current status. Status is of the type `MessageQueueTransactionStatus` enumeration. The possible values that this read-only property can return are as follows:

- **Aborted**—Indicates that the transaction was cancelled
- **Committed**—Indicates that the transaction is complete and has been committed
- **Initialized**—Indicates that the transaction has begun
- **Pending**—Indicates that the object is in mid-transaction

The methods of this class are `Begin`, `Abort`, and `Commit`. `Begin` tells the context to initialize the transaction. `Abort` cancels all pending activity within the transaction context. `Commit` tells the context that all is okay and that we want to finish the transaction.

We use an overload of the `MessageQueue.Send` method to actually send transactional messages. This overload, as you might expect, takes an instance of `MessageQueueTransaction` as one of its parameters. The full function signature is as follows:

```
Send(ByVal obj As Object, ByVal transaction As MessageQueueTransaction)
```

All messages sent using this transaction context are wrapped as part of the same transaction. The rest of the sending operation is the same; you can still pick a formatter for your messages, for instance.

Listing 13.15 provides an example of how to send messages as a grouped transaction. It also demonstrates the `Transactional` property of `MessagQueue` and the `Status` property of `MessageQueueTransaction`.

LISTING 13.15 Transactional Send

```
Imports System.Messaging

Module Module1

    Sub Main()

        'purpose: transaction sending example

        'local scope
        Dim queue As New MessageQueue(path:=".\private$\myqueue")
```

LISTING 13.15   Continued

```
    Dim trx As New MessageQueueTransaction()
    Dim cnt As Short
    Dim msg() As Message

    'make sure the queue is transactional
    If Not (queue.Transactional) Then
        MsgBox(prompt:="Please mark queue as transactional")
        End
    End If

    'purge the queue
    queue.Purge()

    'begin the transaction
    Console.WriteLine("Trx Status: " & trx.Status.ToString)
    trx.Begin()
    Console.WriteLine("Trx Status: " & trx.Status.ToString)

    'send a couple messages
    For cnt = 1 To 4
        'send the message and pass the transaction
        '  context on the function signature
        queue.Send(obj:="Transaction test " & cnt, _
            transaction:=trx)
    Next

    'check the queue for messages
    msg = queue.GetAllMessages
    Console.WriteLine("Messages prior to commit: " & UBound(msg) + 1)

    'commit the transaction
    trx.Commit()
    Console.WriteLine("Trx Status: " & trx.Status.ToString)

    'check the queue again for messages
    msg = queue.GetAllMessages
    Console.WriteLine("Messages after to commit: " & UBound(msg) + 1)

    'pause the app. to read the console
    Console.WriteLine("Press 's' to stop the application")
    Do While Console.ReadLine <> "s" : Loop

    End Sub

End Module
```

Within the listing, we write out a number of interesting details of the executing code. The output is provided in Figure 13.8 for you to follow along. Notice that the messages are not even in the queue until the Commit method is called. Try changing Commit to Abort. You will notice that no messages are written to the queue. Thus, the entire set of messages was cancelled and the transaction rolled back. Also notice the Status of the transaction within the various sections of our code. It moves from Initialized to Pending and finally to Committed.

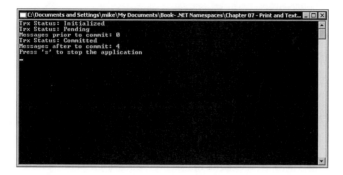

FIGURE 13.8

Transactional send output.

Transactional Receiving

Receiving messages within a transaction context is very similar to sending. We use the MessageQueueTransaction class, except that this time we pass a parameter of the Receive method. The Begin, Abort, and Commit methods are all the same. However, now when you call Abort, the messages that you had previously received are returned to the queue, untouched. Messages are not permanently removed from the queue until we call Commit.

Message Queuing does guarantee our applications that messages can be identified as being part of a set transaction. We use the TransactionId property of the Message instance to identify those messages that are part of the same transaction. Each message in the transaction will have the identical TransactionId. The TransactionId property is not guaranteed unique by MSMQ. However, it is guaranteed to be sequentially different. This ensures that a transaction that follows another transaction will not have the same ID as the previous transaction.

Additionally, we can be assured by Message Queuing that messages can be received in the same order that they were sent. To check the bounds of a transaction, we use the IsFirstInTransaction and IsLastInTransaction properties of the Message instance. These read-only properties allow us to know when a transaction starts and when it ends. The messages in between will be received in the order of the transaction.

13

MESSAGING

Listing 13.16 sends a set of four messages to the queue as a transaction. To prove some of the features that we've been discussing, we stuck a nontransactional message in the middle of the send operation. We then start a `Receive` transaction, call `Commit`, and write the results to the screen.

LISTING 13.16   Transactional Receiving

```
Imports System.Messaging

Module Module1

    Sub Main()

        'purpose: transaction sending example

        'local scope
        Dim queue As New MessageQueue(path:=".\private$\myqueue")
        Dim trxSend As New MessageQueueTransaction()
        Dim trxRec As New MessageQueueTransaction()
        Dim cnt As Short
        Dim msg(4) As Message

        'make sure the queue is transactional
        If Not (queue.Transactional) Then
            MsgBox(prompt:="Please mark queue as transactional") : End
        End If

        'purge the queue
        queue.Purge()

        'begin the send transaction
        trxSend.Begin()

        'send a couple messages
        For cnt = 1 To 4

            'send the message and pass the transaction
            '  context on the function signature
            queue.Send(obj:="Transaction test " & cnt, _
                transaction:=trxSend)

            If cnt = 2 Then

                'send a non-transactional message in the sequence
                queue.Send(obj:="Non-Transactional")
```

LISTING 13.16 Continued

```
        End If

    Next

    'commit the transaction
    trxSend.Commit()

    '----Receive transaction------

    'begin the receive transaction
    trxRec.Begin()

    'set the queue's formatter to xml
    queue.Formatter = New XmlMessageFormatter( _
        targetTypeNames:=New String() {"System.String"})

    'tell the queue to read all message properties
    queue.MessageReadPropertyFilter.SetAll()

    'receive the messages
    'note: the messages are not actually received until we call commit
    For cnt = 0 To 3
        msg(cnt) = queue.Receive(transaction:=trxRec)
    Next

    'commit the receive
    trxRec.Commit()

    'loop through the messages and display the results
    For cnt = 0 To 3

        'write the message's trx id
        Console.WriteLine("TransactionId: " & msg(cnt).TransactionId)

        'indicate if the message is the first in a transaction
        Console.WriteLine("Is First: " & _
            msg(cnt).IsFirstInTransaction)

        'indicate if the message is the last in a transaction
        Console.WriteLine("Is Last: " & _
            msg(cnt).IsLastInTransaction)

        'write the message body
        Console.WriteLine("Receive " & cnt & " Body: " _
            & msg(cnt).Body)
```

13

MESSAGING

Listing **13.16**   Continued

```
            'add some space between messages
        Console.WriteLine()
    Next

        'pause the app. to read the console
        Console.WriteLine("Press 's' to stop the application")
        Do While Console.ReadLine <> "s" : Loop

    End Sub

End Module
```

Figure 13.9 represents our output. Notice that we did not return all four messages in our transaction. At first glance, this might look like a bug. After all, we sent a group of four messages into the queue as a transaction. We want to receive the same four messages back as a transaction. Remember, Messaging guarantees only that we will receive transactional messages in the order that they were sent to the queue. If we look closely, the messages were received in the correct order. It just sent us the nontransactional message first (which was actually sent as the third message). The remaining messages were delivered in their correct order.

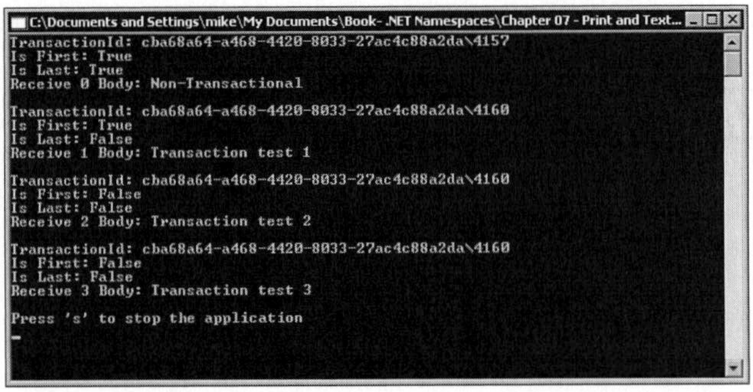

Figure **13.9**

Transactional receive output.

It is up to our application to determine whether a message is part of a transaction and how many messages make up a transaction. Of course, Messaging provides us with this information as well. Notice the TransactionId of each message. Those that are part of the same transaction have the same ID. Also note the value of IsFirstInTransaction. Our application clearly can delineate between the start and end of a given transaction.

Security and Encryption

Messaging applications typically are deployed over large networks, including the Internet. Additionally, Messaging is a mission-critical piece of an application's design. As such, it is important to use message-queuing security as another layer of protection to help our applications guarantee safety.

Message-queuing security is implemented using built-in security features of Windows 2000. These include auditing, access control, encryption, and authentication. This section explores each strategy in turn. The intent is to provide you with the tools to implement the various security strategies found inside the System.Messaging namespace.

Managing Permissions

Our applications need the capability to control permissions that users have to our Messaging objects. For instance, if you have a half-dozen suppliers sending shipping confirmations, you do not want them reading each other's queues. Perhaps they are allowed only to send messages and not receive, or they can only retrieve their acknowledgements. Additionally, when your application runs, it should have rights to view and manipulate all Messaging objects on the server. Rules such as these must be enforced through permission management.

Permission management (also called *access control*) allows us to lock down various Messaging objects to individual users or groups. Messaging objects that we can target for controlling access include servers, queues, routing links, and message-queuing settings objects. Permission management has two discrete levels. The first allows us to control a user's access to a given object. The second manages the user's actual permissions after they've been granted access. User permissions can include peek, receive, send, and many others.

Table 13.5 lists items with System.Messaging that pertain to permission management.

TABLE 13.5   System.Messaging Permission-Management Items

Item	Description
AccessControlEntry	The AccessControlEntry class is used to manage rights on a given object.
AccessControlEntryType	The AccessControlEntryType enumeration maintains values for security access actions. Values include Allow, Deny, Revoke, and Set.

13

MESSAGING

TABLE 13.5 Continued

Item	Description
AccessControlList	The `AccessControlList` class provides a collection of `AccessControlEntry` instances that can be used to set or return permissions on a queue.
GenericAccessRights	The `GenericAccessRights` enumeration represents a common set of access values. Values include `All`, `Execute`, `None`, `Read`, and `Write`.
MessageQueueAccessControlEntry	The `MessageQueueAccessControlEntry` class is used to encapsulate the access rights for a given trustee on a specific message queue.
MessageQueueAccessRights	The `MessageQueueAccessRights` enumeration represents security values that apply specifically to message queues. Values include `ChangeQueuePermissions`, `DeleteJournalMessage`, `DeleteMessage`, `DeleteQueue`, `FullControl`, `GenericRead`, `GenericWrite`, `GetQueuePermissions`, `GetQueueProperties`, `PeekMessage`, `ReceiveJournalMessage`, `SetQueueProperties`, `TakeQueueOwnership`, and `WriteMessage`.
MessageQueuePermission	The `MessageQueuePermission` class is used to encapsulate the permissions on a given queue.
MessageQueuePermissionAccess	The `MessageQueuePermissionAccess` enumeration indicates a set of access values that apply to a message queue. Values include `Administer`, `Browse`, `None`, `Peek`, `Receive`, and `Send`.
MessageQueuePermissionAttribute	The `MessageQueuePermissionAttribute` class allows you to set Messaging permissions within your code using attributes.
MessageQueuePermissionEntry	The `MessageQueuePermissionEntry` class manages rights on a given message queue.

TABLE 13.5 Continued

Item	Description
MessageQueuePermissionEntryCollection	The MessageQueuePermissionEntryCollection class represents a collection of MessageQueuePermissionEntry objects.
StandardAccessRights	The StandardAccessRights enumeration indicates the basic values for security rights. Values include All, Execute, ModifyOwner, None, Read, ReadSecurity, Required, Synchronize, WriteSecurity, Write, and Delete.
Trustee	The Trustee class represents a set of credentials that are being used to access a resource.
TrusteeType	The TrusteeType enumeration indicates the various types of trustees. Values include User, Group, Computer, Alias, Domain, and Unknown.

Although this list is a little long, the classes and enumerations actually work quite well together to provide your application flexibility when managing and accessing security. For instance, to grant, deny, or revoke permissions on a queue, you use the SetPermissions method of a MessageQueue instance. This method takes an instance of MessageQueueAccessControlEntry. This class defines the access that you want to set for the given message queue. Before you do anything, however, you must create a valid Trustee object. A trustee represents a computer, a group, or an individual user with which you want to set rights. Now, when creating the MessageQueueAccessControlEntry instance, we both pass the Trustee instance and set the trustee's rights with the MessageQueueAccessRights enumeration. Rights can be any combination of things, such as DeleteMessage, PeekMessage, and WriteMessage. You then use the AccessControlEntryType enumeration to indicate the type of access that is being applied for the trustee and right. Types can include Allow, which allows user access with the specified rights, Deny, which denies the user the specified rights, and Revoke, which revokes specified rights for the user. Listing 13.17 illustrates this further.

LISTING 13.17   Manage Permissions

```vb
Imports System.Messaging

Module Module1

    Sub Main()

        'purpose: creates a access control entry
        '    and uses it to set the permissions on a given queue

        'local scope
        Dim myAccessEntry As MessageQueueAccessControlEntry
        Dim myTrustee As Trustee
        Dim queue As New MessageQueue(path:=".\private$\myqueue")

        'create a trustee ("." = localmachine)
        myTrustee = New Trustee(name:="mike", systemName:=".", _
            TrusteeType:=TrusteeType.User)

        'create an instance of the access control entry
        myAccessEntry = New MessageQueueAccessControlEntry( _
            trustee:=myTrustee, _
            rights:=MessageQueueAccessRights.FullControl, _
            entryType:=AccessControlEntryType.Allow)

        'set the rights on the queue
        queue.SetPermissions(ace:=myAccessEntry)

    End Sub

End Module
```

The code simply applies full control access to myQueue for the user mike. Figure 13.10 shows the Security tab inside the Message Queue management interface.

Authentication

Depending on your application's design, it is often imperative that you know who is sending a message. Applications should not blindly accept messages—even if they are properly formatted. Incoming messages should be verified, or authenticated, against a list of acceptable senders. Authentication is yet another layer of protection that your applications can use to thwart undesirable behavior and ensure security.

FIGURE 13.10
myQueue *permissions.*

To authenticate a message, you must use some type of a security certificate. A certificate contains the sender's information and the public signature key of the sender. Messaging provides *internal* certificates automatically. These can be used from within a Windows 2000 environment. To authenticate outside Windows 2000, you must create (or purchase) an *external* certificate from a certified certificate authority.

> **NOTE**
>
> Workgroup installations of Windows do not allow for authentication. You must have MSMQ Server installed to use authentication.

Table 13.6 lists the items in the namespace that correspond directly to message and message-queue authentication.

TABLE 13.6 System.Messaging Authentication Items

Item	Description
CryptographicProviderType	The CryptographicProviderType enumeration indicates the type of cryptographic provider used by the digital signature. This enum typically is used when working with foreign (non-MSMQ) queues. Some types include Ssl, RsaFull, MicrosoftExchange, and Fortezza.

TABLE 13.6 Continued

Class	Description
Message Class Properties	
Authenticated	The Authenticated property returns a Boolean value that indicates whether the message was authenticated. Messages are authenticated by the receiving queue. If the property is marked True, the receiving queue requested authentication and the message passed. If the property returns False, the queue did not request authentication. *You cannot determine whether a message failed authentication by looking at its properties.* The message queue discards messages that fail authentication.
AuthenticationProviderName	The AuthenticationProviderName property is used to return or set the name of the cryptographic provider used to generate the digital signature of the message. The default value for this property is Microsoft Base Cryptographic Provider, Ver. 1.0.
AuthenticationProviderType	The AuthenticationProviderType property is used to return or set the type of the cryptographic provider used to generate the digital signature of the message. The property is of the type CryptographicProviderType enumeration. The default value for this property is RSA_FULL.
UseAuthentication	The UseAuthentication property returns a Boolean value that indicates whether the sending application requested authentication. Set this value to True to request authentication before sending a message.
HashAlgorithm	The HashAlgorithm property is of the type HashAlgorithm enumeration. It indicates the hash algorithm used to authenticate a message. Hash algorithms are used to create the digital signature for the message. Both the sender and the receiver use the same hash algorithm to authenticate a message. Values include Mac, Md2, Md4, Md5 (default), None, and Sha.
DigitalSignature	The DigitalSignature property is used to return or set the digital signature that Message Queuing uses to authenticate a message. The property is of the type byte array.

TABLE 13.6 Continued

Class	Description
	Message *Class Properties*
SenderCertificate	The SenderCertificate property is used to return or set the security certificate that Message Queuing uses to authenticate a message. The property is of the type byte array.
ConnectorType	The ConnectorType property is used when sending messages to and receiving messages from connector applications. A connector application is an application that allows you to communicate between Message Queuing and other queuing systems.
AttachSenderId	The AttachSenderId property is used to indicate whether the sender's ID should be attached to the message.
SenderId	The SenderId property is used to return the identifier (as an array of bytes) of the message sender. The Boolean property is True if you want to attach the sender ID.
	MessageQueue *Class Properties*
Authenticate	The Authenticate property is used to read and to indicate that a message queue on the server (not simply an instance of the object) accepts only authenticated messages. If this value is set to True or returns True, then only authenticated messages will be accepted by the queue.

You set the Authenticate property of the MessageQueue instance to True to indicate that a message queue requires authentication. If a queue requires authentication, messages that appear in the queue are considered, by default, to be authenticated. If the message fails authentication, it is discarded by MSMQ or ends up in the dead-letter queue (provided that the UseDeadLetter queue property has been set to True). External messages require you to set the SenderCertificate property of your message object. External certificates must be registered with the domain of the receiving queue. External certificates can be used by your receiving application to identify the sender and the certificate authority, as well as provide other information.

To indicate that you want Messaging to create an internal certificate, you mark a Message object's properties UseAuthentication and AttachSenderId to True. This forces Messaging to create a digital signature and use it to sign your message. This signature then is used by the receiving queue to authenticate the message. Internal certificates have no value to your receiving application. They simply are used as a means for the queue to authenticate the message.

Listing 13.18 demonstrates the use of internal authentication. We first indicate that the queue requires authentication by setting `queue.Authenticate = True`. Note that this setting applies to the queue, not just the object instance. We then create a message and mark `UseAuthentication` and `AttachSenderId` as `True`. Next, we write out some of the default values that the message uses to sign the object using the properties `AuthenticationProviderName`, `AuthenticationProviderType`, and `HashAlgorithm`. Finally, we send the message to the queue.

LISTING 13.18   Authenticate Messages

```
Imports System.Messaging

Module Module1

    Sub Main()

        'purpose:   provide a message authentication example

        'local scope
        Dim queue As New MessageQueue(path:="myServer\myPublicQueue")
        Dim msg As New Message()

        'purge the queue
        queue.Purge()

        'indicate that the queue only accepts authenticated messages
        queue.Authenticate = True

        'set message properties
        msg.UseDeadLetterQueue = True
        msg.UseAuthentication = True
        msg.AttachSenderId = True
        msg.Body = "My Authentication Example"

        'display auth. info.
        Console.WriteLine(msg.AuthenticationProviderName())
        Console.WriteLine(msg.AuthenticationProviderType().ToString)
        Console.WriteLine(msg.HashAlgorithm().ToString)

        'send the message
        Try
            queue.Send(obj:=msg)
        Catch
```

LISTING 13.18   Continued

```
            MsgBox(Err.Description)
        End Try

    End Sub

End Module
```

Taking a look at the message (see Figure 13.11) we can see that the sender identification (SID) has an algorithm (MD5) and that the message was indeed authenticated.

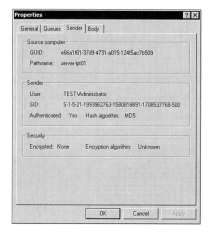

FIGURE 13.11
Authenticated message.

Auditing

Auditing allows us to record events inside MSMQ. You may implement an auditing strategy whenever you or your application needs to know when queues have been accessed and when messages were sent or received. For instance, suppose that you have a process that generates an invoice after an order has been received by the application. If orders are messages inside your queue, your invoicing application can use the journal queue to know when the order messages were received.

By default, every queue created inside MSMQ has an associated journal queue. This queue is used to track messages as they are received. Both the `Message` and the `MessageQueue` classes provide the property `UseJournalQueue`. This property indicates that Messaging should write a copy of the message to the journal queue after the message has been received. The following code snippet can be used to test this principle. Copy it into a console application and check the journal queue for `myQueue` after its execution.

```
Dim queue As New MessageQueue(path:=".\private$\myQueue")
Dim msg As Message

queue.UseJournalQueue = True

queue.Send("test message")

msg = queue.Receive()
```

You can do additional auditing to see that your message is routed to its destination. The `UseTracing` property of the `Message` class can be set to `True` if you want Messaging to generate a report message each time that your message is moved through a MSMQ server. To use tracing, you must have Active Directory installed and must specify a report queue for the enterprise.

Encrypting Messages

The contents of your messages are private. They can contain credit card information, ordering information, Social Security numbers, and so on. As they move across a network, it's important to make sure that only the intended audience can view their contents. You would not want the message intercepted, read, modified, or resent. Encryption ensures that only those with the private key can unlock the message contents.

Table 13.7 lists the items in the namespace that pertain to enforcing encryption.

TABLE 13.7   System.Messaging Encryption Items

Item	Description
Message Class Properties	
DestinationSymmetricKey	You set the DestinationSymmetricKey property when you want to encrypt the message yourself.
EncryptionAlgorithm	The EncryptionAlgorithm property returns or sets the algorithm used to encrypt the body of the message.
	The property is of the type EncryptionAlgorithm enumeration. The possible values are None, Rc2 (default), and Rc4.
UseEncryption	The UseEncryption property is used to return or set a Boolean value indicating whether the message should use encryption.

TABLE 13.7 Continued

Item	Description
	MessageQueue *Class Properties*
EncryptionRequired	The EncryptionRequired property is used to return or set a value indicating whether a given queue requires encryption.
	The property is of the type EncryptionRequired enumeration. Possible values: Queues can accept only encrypted messages (Body), only nonencrypted messages (None), or both (Optional).

You can encrypt the message yourself using the DestinationSymmetricKey property, or you can let Messaging encrypt the message for you. To use automatic Messaging encryption, you must be running a version of MSMQ Server with access to a domain's directory services. Messaging uses the directory services to encrypt the message before it is sent and again to automatically decrypt the message when it reaches its destination. Encryption differs from authentication in that it does not verify the sender of the message; instead, it protects the contents of the message itself from being read by anyone without the capability to decrypt.

Listing 13.19 sends an encrypted message to a public queue on a domain. We first indicate that the queue accepts only encrypted messages by setting the EncryptionRequired property of the MessageQueue instance to True. Then we indicate that the message must use encryption by setting our Message object's UseEncryption property to True. Finally, we set the algorithm used to encrypt the message by assigning the EncryptionAlgorithm property a value from the EncryptionRequired enumeration.

LISTING 13.19 Encrypting Messages

```
Imports System.Messaging

Module Module1

    Sub Main()

        'local scope
        Dim queue As New MessageQueue(path:="myServer\myPublicQueue")
        Dim msg As New Message()

        'indicate that the queue requires encryption
        queue.EncryptionRequired = EncryptionRequired.Body
```

LISTING 13.19   Continued

```
        'indicate that the message uses encryption
        msg.UseEncryption = True

        'set the encryption algorithm
        msg.EncryptionAlgorithm = EncryptionAlgorithm.Rc4

        'set the body of the message
        msg.Body = "Encryption"

        'send the message
        Try
            queue.Send(msg)
        Catch
            MsgBox(Err.Description)
        End Try

    End Sub

End Module
```

Learning by Example: qManager

In this example, we will create a Web-based MSMQ manager, called qManager. Users then will be capable of selecting a server on which to view queues. The queues will be exposed via a user interface designed to allow access to queue properties and actual messages. Lastly, users will be capable of accepting or rejecting—with full support for message transactions—the exposed messages.

NOTE

Of course, this is a Web-based example, and, as a result, the code is written inside ASP.NET. We used the Web Forms engine to build our forms. Longtime VB developers will appreciate this new model—we did. There is now a complete separation of code and UI, just like in Windows Forms. This made coding a lot easier (once we got used to it). If you've been working with ASP for a while, you'll need some time to poke around and figure things out. But don't worry—the Request and Response objects are still there and work much the same as before.

For the sake of clarity and brevity, we eliminated the HTML and style sheet information from the code listings. To ASP.NET's credit, the HTML is no longer very interesting. You can get the gist of the form just by looking at the corresponding figures.

Key Concepts Covered

The following represents the key class and concepts demonstrated with this sample application:

- Enumerating queues and messages
- Accessing the properties of a message queue
- Working with transactional messages
- Writing an ASP.NET application

Selecting a Machine

The Machine Select page allows users to query a machine on the network for public and private queues. Users are required to indicate a machine name, select Private or Public, and submit the form to return a list of queues on a given machine. Figure 13.12 captures an example of this ASP.NET page.

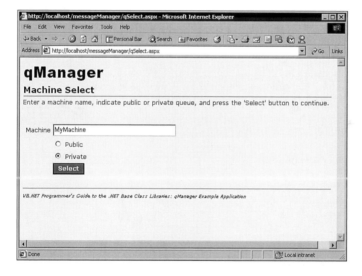

FIGURE 13.12
Machine Select page.

Code Walkthrough

The Web page's code is used to initialize the page and to process the Select button's click event. Listing 13.20 is an output of the form's code.

LISTING 13.20 qSelect.aspx

```
Public Class qSelect
    Inherits System.Web.UI.Page
    Protected WithEvents userMsg As _
        System.Web.UI.HtmlControls.HtmlGenericControl
    Protected WithEvents publicQueues As _
        System.Web.UI.HtmlControls.HtmlInputRadioButton
    Protected WithEvents privateQueues As _
        System.Web.UI.HtmlControls.HtmlInputRadioButton
    Protected WithEvents machineText As _
        System.Web.UI.HtmlControls.HtmlInputText
    Protected WithEvents selectButton As _
        System.Web.UI.HtmlControls.HtmlInputButton

#Region " Web Form Designer Generated Code "

    'This call is required by the Web Form Designer.
    <System.Diagnostics.DebuggerStepThrough()> Private Sub _
        InitializeComponent()

    End Sub

    Private Sub Page_Init(ByVal sender As System.Object, _
        ByVal e As System.EventArgs) Handles MyBase.Init

        'CODEGEN: This method call is required by the Web Form Designer
        'Do not modify it using the code editor.

        InitializeComponent()

    End Sub

#End Region

    Private Sub Page_Load(ByVal sender As System.Object, _
        ByVal e As System.EventArgs) Handles MyBase.Load

        'purpose: init. the form

        'set a default machine name
        machineText.Value = "myMachine"

    End Sub
```

The click event for the Select button creates a new instance of our CExplore class. This class returns a list of queues based on machine name and public versus private. If no queues are

LISTING 13.20 Continued

found, the method raises an error. This event traps for errors and displays the message to the client by setting the InnerHtml attribute of a DIV tag equal to the error message.

```
Private Sub selectButton_ServerClick(ByVal sender As System.Object, _
    ByVal e As System.EventArgs) Handles selectButton.ServerClick

    'purpose: control the select button click event

    'local scope
    Dim explore As CExplore

    'create a new instance of the explore class
    explore = New CExplore(machineName:=machineText.Value)

    'make sure user can browse before passing them on
    Try

        'return queue information
        explore.returnQueues(isPublic:=publicQueues.Checked)

        'all is well, pass user on
        Response.Redirect(url:="qExplore.aspx?machine=" _
            & machineText.Value & _
            "&isPublic=" & CStr(publicQueues.Checked))

    Catch

        'error getting queue information
        userMsg.InnerHtml = Err.Description

    End Try

End Sub

End Class
```

Exploring Queues

We created the class CExplore to handle all things related to exploring queues and their message contents.

Code Walkthrough

Listing 13.21 details the contents of the CExplore class.

The class starts by importing the `System.Messaging` library to make our calls to the Messaging objects easier. Next, we set a global-level variable to maintain the name of the machine (`c_machineName`) containing the message queue that the user is browsing. We created the required constructor `Public Sub New` to allow users to set the machine name upon object instantiation.

Listing 13.21 CExplore

```
Imports System.Messaging

Public Class CExplore

    'purpose:   expose methods revolving around exploring msmq

    'class-level scope
    Private c_machineName As String

    Public Sub New(ByVal machineName As String)

        'purpose:   constructor, req. a machine name to explore

        'set internal variables
        c_machineName = machineName

    End Sub
```

The `returnQueues` method is used to return an array of `MessageQueue` objects for the given machine. We pass the variable `isPublic` as Boolean to indicate whether the user has requested to browse public or private queues. If the function cannot return queues, it simply raises an error to the calling client.

```
    Public Function returnQueues(ByVal isPublic As Boolean) As MessageQueue()

        'purpose: return an array of messageQueue objects for the local machine

        'determine if browsing public or private queues
        If isPublic Then

            Try

                'return public queues by machine name
                Return MessageQueue.GetPublicQueuesByMachine
➥(machineName:=c_machineName)
```

LISTING 13.21   Continued

```
            Catch

                'can't get public queues
                Err.Raise(number:=Err.Number, source:=Err.Source, _
                    description:=Err.Description)

            End Try

        Else

            Try

                'return private queues by machine name
                Return MessageQueue.GetPrivateQueuesByMachine
➡(machineName:=c_machineName)

            Catch

                'can't get private queues
                Err.Raise(number:=Err.Number, source:=Err.Source, _
                    description:=Err.Description)

            End Try

        End If

    End Function
```

The `returnQueue` function returns a `MessageQueue` object from a queue path (`qPath`). If no queue is found at the path, an error is raised to the calling application.

```
    Public Function returnQueue(ByVal qPath As String) As MessageQueue

        'purpose: return queue object based on guid

        Try

            'return the requested queue
            Return New MessageQueue(path:=c_machineName & "\" & qPath)

        Catch

            'can't get queue, raise error
            Err.Raise(number:=Err.Number, source:=Err.Source, _
                description:=Err.Description)
```

LISTING 13.21 Continued

```
      End Try

  End Function
```

The `returnMessages` method returns an array of `Message` objects for a given queue. Note that the function takes a snapshot of the messages in the queue. It does not receive the messages. To do so, we call the `GetAllMessages` method.

```
Public Function returnMessages(ByVal qPath As String) As Message()

    'purpose: return a snapshot of all the messages in a given queue

    'local scope
    Dim queue As MessageQueue

    Try

        'get a reference to the queue
        queue = New MessageQueue(path:=c_machineName & "\" & qPath)

        'set the property read filter to return all properties
        queue.MessageReadPropertyFilter.SetAll()

        'tell the queue the message format to return
        CType(queue.Formatter, XmlMessageFormatter).TargetTypeNames = _
            New String() {"System.String"}

        'return the messages
        Return queue.GetAllMessages()

    Catch

        'raise error to calling client
        Err.Raise(number:=Err.Number, source:=Err.Source, _
            description:=Err.Description)

    End Try

End Function
```

The `returnMessage` function returns a `Message` instance from a queue path (`qPath`) and message ID (`msgId`). We set the `MessageReadPropertyFilter` to `SetAll` to indicate that we want to return all properties of the message. To get the message without actually receiving it, we call the `PeekById` method of the `MessageQueue` class.

LISTING 13.21 Continued

```
    Public Function returnMessage(ByVal qPath As String, _
        ByVal msgId As String) As Message

        'purpose: return a snapshot of a given message

        'local scope
        Dim queue As MessageQueue

        Try

            'get a reference to the queue
            queue = New MessageQueue(path:=c_machineName & "\" & qPath)

            'tell the queue the message format to return
            CType(queue.Formatter, XmlMessageFormatter).TargetTypeNames = _
                New String() {"System.String"}

            'set the property read filter to return all properties
            queue.MessageReadPropertyFilter.SetAll()

            'return the messages
            Return queue.PeekById(id:=msgId)

        Catch

            'raise error to calling client
            Err.Raise(number:=Err.Number, source:=Err.Source, _
                description:=Err.Description)

        End Try

    End Function

End Class
```

Queue Properties

The Queue Properties screen allows users to view the various properties of their selected queue. Message queues on the selected server are listed to the left. When a user clicks a given queue's properties link, the Queue Properties table within the form is updated. This screen also provides users access to a queue's messages and journal contents. Figure 13.13 shows this Web page.

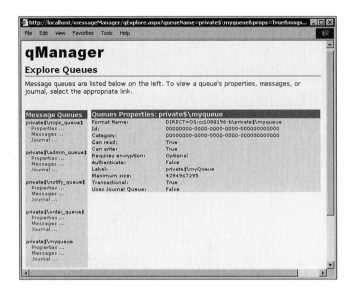

FIGURE 13.13
Queue Properties page.

The same page is used to display the queue's contents. When users click on the "Messages" link, the main table to the right of the left message queue list is updated to display the messages contained inside the queue. Similarly, when users select the "Journal" link, this table is updated to display the message contents of the queue's journal.

If a queue is transactional and the messages in the queue are transactional, the page displays this using color banding. A green message indicates a message that is first in the transaction sequence. Single message transactions are simply green. A gray band is used to display messages that are in the middle of the transaction (not first or last). A red-coded message indicates the last message in the transaction set.

The page allows users to accept or reject messages in the queue. Next to each green-banded message (gray for nontransactional queues) is a check box for either Accept or Reject. Users click the appropriate check box next to the message and press their Select button to either reject or accept messages as a transactional unit.

Figure 13.14 displays transactional messages in a private queue.

Code Walkthrough

Listing 13.22 details the code used to build the Web page.

The code starts by declaring a number of page-level variables for storing user settings and such. These variables are set in the Page_Load event via the query string and hidden form field variables.

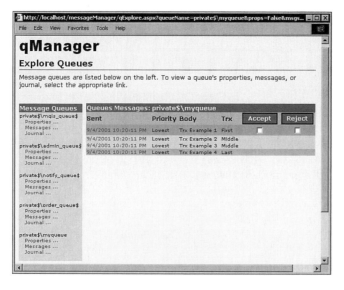

FIGURE 13.14
Messages and Transactions page.

LISTING 13.22   qExplore.aspx.vb

```
Imports System.Messaging

Public Class qExplore
    Inherits System.Web.UI.Page
    Protected WithEvents userMsg As _
        System.Web.UI.HtmlControls.HtmlGenericControl

    'form-level scope
    Private machineName As String
    Protected WithEvents queueList As _
        System.Web.UI.HtmlControls.HtmlGenericControl
    Private isPublic As Boolean
    Private qPath As String
    Private showMsg As String
    Private showJournal As String
    Protected WithEvents qDetails As _
        System.Web.UI.HtmlControls.HtmlGenericControl
    Private showProps As String

    Private Enum msgProcessing
        accept = 1
        reject = 2
    End Enum
```

LISTING 13.22   Continued

```vb
#Region " Web Form Designer Generated Code "

    'This call is required by the Web Form Designer.
    <System.Diagnostics.DebuggerStepThrough()> Private Sub _
        InitializeComponent()

    End Sub

    Private Sub Page_Init(ByVal sender As System.Object, _
        ByVal e As System.EventArgs) Handles MyBase.Init

        'CODEGEN: This method call is required by the Web Form Designer
        'Do not modify it using the code editor.

        InitializeComponent()

    End Sub

#End Region

    Private Sub Page_Load(ByVal sender As System.Object, _
        ByVal e As System.EventArgs) Handles MyBase.Load

        'purpose: init the page, control flow

        'check if the user is submitting the form (post) or requesting the page
        '(get)
        If Request.ServerVariables("REQUEST_METHOD") = "GET" Then

            'return q-string values
            machineName = Request.QueryString(name:="machine")
            isPublic = Request.QueryString(name:="isPublic")
            qPath = Request.QueryString(name:="queueName")
            showMsg = Request.QueryString(name:="msgs")
            showJournal = Request.QueryString(name:="jrnl")
            showProps = Request.QueryString(name:="props")

            'display the q-information
            Call displayQueueInfo()

            'check if user has selected to view messages,
            ' properties, or journal of a given queue
            If qPath <> "" Then
```

LISTING 13.22   Continued

```
            If showProps = "True" Then
                Call displayQueueProperties()

            ElseIf showMsg = "True" Then
                Call displayQueueMessages()

            ElseIf showJournal = "True" Then
                Call displayQueueJournal()

            End If
        Else
            qDetails.InnerHtml = ""
        End If

    Else

        'set machine and qPath based on hidden values
        machineName = Request.Form("machineName")
        qPath = Request.Form("qPath")
        isPublic = Request.Form("isPublic")

        'determine the button the user clicked
        Select Case Request.Form("subMsg")

            Case "Accept"

                'receive messages that are checked
                Call processMessages(msgProcessing.accept)

            Case "Reject"

                'receive messages that are checked
                Call processMessages(msgProcessing.reject)

        End Select

        Call displayQueueMessages()

    End If

End Sub

Private Sub processMessages(ByVal processType As msgProcessing)
```

LISTING 13.22 Continued

```
'purpose:    process messages based on type (accept or reject)

'local scope
Dim messageIds() As String
Dim i As Int16
Dim trx As New CTrx(machineName:=machineName, qPath:=qPath)

Try
    'get messages to process
    Select Case processType

        Case msgProcessing.accept

            'get an array of message ids to process
            messageIds = Request.Form("accept").Split

            'loop through each message
            For i = 0 To UBound(messageIds)

                'determine if message is transactional
                If Request.Form(messageIds(i)) <> "" Then

                    'call receiveTrxMsg
                    trx.receiveTrxMsg(trxId:=Request.Form(messageIds(i)))

                Else

                    'call receiveMsg
                    trx.receiveMsg(msgId:=messageIds(i))

                End If
            Next

        Case msgProcessing.reject

            'get an array of message ids to process
            messageIds = Request.Form("reject").Split

            'loop through each message
            For i = 0 To UBound(messageIds)

                'determine if message is transactional
                If Request.Form(messageIds(i)) <> "" Then
```

LISTING 13.22 Continued

```
                            'call rejectTrxMsg
                            trx.rejectTrxMsg(trxId:=Request.Form(messageIds(i)))

                    Else

                            'call rejectMsg
                            trx.rejectMsg(msgId:=messageIds(i))

                    End If

            Next

        End Select
    Catch

        'write out error information
        userMsg.InnerHtml = Err.Description

    End Try

End Sub
```

The displayQueueInfo procedure writes each queue to the left queue selection bar on the page. We create an instance of CExplore to use to return the various queues on the selected server. We then loop through the array of MessageQueue objects and write the queue name to the screen. Along with the name, we set a number of query string variables to be used when refreshing the page after a user has selected a queue link.

```
    Private Sub displayQueueInfo()

        'purpose: show queue information

        'local scope
        Dim explore As CExplore
        Dim queues() As MessageQueue
        Dim i As Int16
        Dim display As String

        'create a new instance of the explore class
        explore = New CExplore(machineName:=machineName)

        Try

            'return queue information
            queues = explore.returnQueues(isPublic:=CBool(isPublic))
```

LISTING 13.22   Continued

```
Catch

    'error getting queue information
    userMsg.InnerHtml = Err.Description
    Exit Sub

End Try

'display queue information
display = "<table border=0 cellpadding=1 cellspacing=0>"
display = display & "<tr><td class=tableTitle>Message Queues</td></tr>"

'loop queues and write out to text string
For i = 0 To UBound(array:=queues)

    'write the name of the queue
    display = display & "<tr><td class=queueCell>"
    display = display & queues(i).QueueName

    'write the properties link
    display = display & "<br>   <a href=qExplore.aspx?"
    display = display & "queueName=" & queues(i).QueueName & _
        "&props=True"
    display = display & "&msgs=False&jrnl=False&machine=" & machineName
    display = display & "&isPublic=" & CStr(isPublic) & ">Properties _
        ...</a>"

    'write the messages link
    display = display & "<br>   <a href=qExplore.aspx?"
    display = display & "queueName=" & queues(i).QueueName & _
        "&props=False"
    display = display & "&msgs=True&jrnl=False&machine=" & machineName
    display = display & "&isPublic=" & CStr(isPublic) & ">Messages _
        ...</a>"

    'write the journal link
    display = display & "<br>   <a href=qExplore.aspx?"
    display = display & "queueName=" & queues(i).QueueName
    display = display & "&props=False&msgs=False&jrnl=True&machine="
    display = display & machineName & "&isPublic=" & CStr(isPublic)
    display = display & ">Journal ...</a>"

    'close the row
    display = display & "<br> </td></tr>"
```

LISTING 13.22 Continued

```
        Next
        display = display & "</table>"

        'write display contents to the label control
        queueList.InnerHtml = display

    End Sub
```

The displayQueueProperties procedure writes properties of the selected queue to the main
table on the page. We again create an instance of the CExplore class and, with it, return a valid
MessageQueue object. We then read the various properties of the queue and write them to the
Web page.

```
    Private Sub displayQueueProperties()

        'purpose: update property information for the given queue

        'local scope
        Dim display As String
        Dim mq As MessageQueue

        'create a new instance of the explore class
        Dim explore As New CExplore(machineName:=machineName)

        Try

            'return selected queue information
            mq = explore.returnQueue(qPath:=qPath)

        Catch

            'error getting queue information
            userMsg.InnerHtml = Err.Description
            Exit Sub

        End Try

        'show q properties
        display = "<table border=0 cellpadding=1 cellspacing=0 width=100%>"

        display = display & "<tr><td class=tableTitle colspan=2>Queues _
            Properties: "
        display = display & qPath & "</td></tr>"

        display = display & "<tr><td class=queueCell>" & "Format Name: "
```

LISTING 13.22   Continued

```
    display = display & "</td><td class=queueCell>" & mq.FormatName & _
        "</td></tr>"

    display = display & "<tr><td class=queueCell>" & "Id: "
    display = display & "</td><td class=queueCell>" & mq.Id.ToString & _
        "</td></tr>"

    display = display & "<tr><td class=queueCell>" & "Category: "
    display = display & "</td><td class=queueCell>" & mq.Category.ToString
    display = display & "</td></tr>"

    display = display & "<tr><td class=queueCell>" & "Can read: "
    display = display & "</td><td class=queueCell>" & mq.CanRead & _
        "</td></tr>"

    display = display & "<tr><td class=queueCell>" & "Can write: "
    display = display & "</td><td class=queueCell>" & mq.CanWrite & _
        "</td></tr>"

    display = display & "<tr><td class=queueCell>" & "Requires encryption: "
    display = display & "</td><td class=queueCell>" '
    display = display & mq.EncryptionRequired.ToString & "</td></tr>"

    display = display & "<tr><td class=queueCell>" & "Authenticate: "
    display = display & "</td><td class=queueCell>" & _
        mq.Authenticate.ToString
    display = display & "</td></tr>"

    display = display & "<tr><td class=queueCell>" & "Label: "
    display = display & "</td><td class=queueCell>" & mq.Label & _
        "</td></tr>"

    display = display & "<tr><td class=queueCell>" & "Maximum size: "
    display = display & "</td><td class=queueCell>" & mq.MaximumQueueSize
    display = display & "</td></tr>"

    display = display & "<tr><td class=queueCell>" & "Transactional: "
    display = display & "</td><td class=queueCell>" & mq.Transactional
    display = display & "</td></tr>"

    display = display & "<tr><td class=queueCell>" & "Uses Journal Queue: "
    display = display & "</td><td class=queueCell>" & mq.UseJournalQueue
    display = display & "</td></tr>"
```

LISTING 13.22 Continued

```
        display = display & "</table>"

        qDetails.InnerHtml = display

    End Sub
```

The `displayQueueMessages` subroutine returns all the messages using the `returnMessages` method of the `CExplore` class. We then loop through the message array and use each `Message` instance's properties to build the Message Details table. This includes transactional messages.

```
    Private Sub displayQueueMessages()

        'purpose: update message list for the given queue

        'local scope
        Dim display As String
        Dim mq As MessageQueue
        Dim msg() As Message
        Dim i As Int16
        Dim trxPos As String

        'create a new instance of the explore class
        Dim explore As New CExplore(machineName:=machineName)

        Try

            'return all messages for the given queue
            msg = explore.returnMessages(qPath:=qPath)

            'get the queue information to determine trx level
            mq = explore.returnQueue(qPath:=qPath)

        Catch

            'display error if any
            userMsg.InnerHtml = Err.Description
            Exit Sub

        End Try

        'set hidden values (machine name, qPath, and public/private)
        display = display & "<input type=hidden name=machineName "
        display = display & "value=" & machineName & ">"
        display = display & "<input type=hidden name=qPath value= " & qPath & ">"
```

LISTING 13.22   Continued

```
display = display & "<input type=hidden name=isPublic value= " & _
    isPublic & ">"

'display message detail headings
display = display & "<table border=0 cellpadding=1 cellspacing=0 _
    width=100%>"

display = display & "<tr><td class=tableTitle colspan=10>"
display = display & "Queues Messages: " & qPath & "</td></tr>"

display = display & "<tr><td class=colTitle>Sent</td>"
'display = display & "<td class=colTitle>Label</td>"
display = display & "<td class=colTitle>Priority</td>"
display = display & "<td class=colTitle>Body</td>"

'add trx col if transactional
If mq.Transactional Then display = display & "<td _
    class=colTitle>Trx</td>"

'check for messages to decide if buttons should show
If UBound(msg) >= 0 Then

    'add accept and reject buttons
    display = display & "<td class=colTitle align=center>"
    display = display & "<input type=submit value=Accept class=bttn _
        name=subMsg>"
    display = display & "</td>"

    display = display & "<td class=colTitle align=center>"
    display = display & "<input type=submit value=Reject class=bttn _
        name=subMsg>"
    display = display & "</td>"

End If

'close row
display = display & "</tr>"

'determine if messages exist
If UBound(msg) >= 0 Then

    'loop messages and display
    For i = 0 To UBound(msg)
```

LISTING 13.22   Continued

```
                    'indicate transactional information through colors
            If mq.Transactional Then

                    'check if the message is the first in the trx.
                    If msg(i).IsFirstInTransaction Then

                            'note: all messages sent to a trx. queue have a
                            '        transaction id and we therefore assume
                            '        transactional also, messages that are both first
                            '        and last in trx are single message trx. we set
                            '        them to first-level
                            display = display & "<tr class=trxFirst>"
                            trxPos = "First"

                    ElseIf msg(i).IsLastInTransaction And _
                            Not msg(i).IsFirstInTransaction Then

                            'messages last in the trx and not also first
                            ' (single trx. message)
                            display = display & "<tr class=trxLast>"
                            trxPos = "Last"

                    Else

                            'messages in middle of trx
                            display = display & "<tr class=queueCell>"
                            trxPos = "Middle"

                    End If

            Else

                    'non-trx queue
                    display = display & "<tr class=queueCell>"

            End If

            'list message details: sent time link
            display = display & "<td><a href=qMessage.aspx?id="
            display = display & msg(i).Id & "&queueName=" & mq.QueueName
            display = display & "&machine=" & machineName & ">"
            display = display & msg(i).SentTime & "</a></td>"

            'display = display & "<td>" & msg(i).Label & "</td>"
            display = display & "<td>" & msg(i).Priority.ToString & "</td>"
```

LISTING 13.22   Continued

```
'translate body if possible (only reads XML, string messages)
Try

    'add msg body to display string
    display = display & "<td>" & msg(i).Body & "</td>"

Catch

    'cannot translate msg body
    display = display & "<tr class=queueCell><td>Body:</td>"
    display = display & "<td>--NOT XML STRING--</td></tr>"
    Err.Clear()

End Try

'check if queue is transactional to display checkboxes
If mq.Transactional Then

    'indicate the msg's position in the trx
    display = display & "<td>" & trxPos & "</td>"

    'allow user to only accept or reject trx as a group
    If trxPos = "First" Then

        'show accept checkbox
        display = display & "<td align=center><input _
            type=checkbox "
        display = display & "name=accept value=" & msg(i).Id _
            & "></td>"

        'show reject checkbox
        display = display & "<td align=center><input _
            type=checkbox "
        display = display & "name=reject value=" & msg(i).Id _
            & "></td>"

        'add hidden value to indicate to post that this is
        ' part of a transaction
        display = display & "<input type=hidden name=" _
            & msg(i).Id
        display = display & " value=" & msg(i).TransactionId _
            & ">"

    Else
```

LISTING 13.22 Continued

```
                           'no check boxes
                           display = display & "<td> </td><td> </td>"

                   End If

            Else

                   'queue is not transactional (checkboxes for each message)

                   'show accept checkbox
                   display = display & "<td align=center><input type=checkbox "
                   display = display & "name=accept value=" & msg(i).Id _
                       & "></td>"

                   'show reject checkbox
                   display = display & "<td align=center><input type=checkbox "
                   display = display & "name=reject value=" & msg(i).Id _
                       & "></td>"

            End If

            'close the row
            display = display & "</tr>"

        Next
    Else

        'no messages in the queue
        display = display & "<tr class=queueCell><td colspan=10>"
        display = display & "There are no messages in the queue.</td></tr>"

    End If

    'close the table
    display = display & "</table>"

    'write the table to the label (div) control
    qDetails.InnerHtml = display

End Sub
```

The displayQueueJournal procedure outputs the queue's journal messages to the main table
in the Web page. It uses the returnMessages method of the MessageQueue object to get an
array of journal messages. It then loops through the array and outputs the messages to the
screen.

LISTING 13.22   Continued

```
    Private Sub displayQueueJournal()

        'purpose: display journal information for the given queue

        'local scope
        Dim display As String
        Dim mq As MessageQueue
        Dim msg() As Message
        Dim i As Int16
        Dim trxPos As String

        'create a new instance of the explore class
        Dim explore As New CExplore(machineName:=machineName)

        'append journal to the path
        qPath = qPath & "\journal$"

        Try

            'return selected queue information
            msg = explore.returnMessages(qPath:=qPath)

            'get queue information to pass on q-string
            mq = explore.returnQueue(qPath:=qPath)

        Catch

            'error getting queue information
            userMsg.InnerHtml = Err.Description
            Exit Sub

        End Try

        'display messages
        display = "<table border=0 cellpadding=1 cellspacing=0 width=100%>"
        display = display & "<tr><td class=tableTitle colspan=4>"
        display = display & "Queues Messages: " & qPath & "</td></tr>"
        display = display & "<tr><td class=colTitle>Sent</td>"
        display = display & "<td class=colTitle>Label</td></tr>"

        'determine if messages exist
If UBound(msg) >= 0 Then
```

LISTING 13.22 Continued

```
          'loop messages and display
          For i = 0 To UBound(msg)

                display = display & "<tr class=queueCell><td>"
                display = display & "<a href=qMessage.aspx?id=" & msg(i).Id
                display = display & "&queueName=" & mq.QueueName
                display = display & "&machine=" & machineName & ">"
                display = display & msg(i).SentTime & "</a></td>"
                display = display & "<td>" & msg(i).Label & "</td></tr>"

          Next

       Else

          'no messages in queue
          display = display & "<tr class=queueCell><td colspan=10>"
          display = display & "There are no messages in the queue.</td></tr>"

       End If

       'close the table
       display = display & "</table>"

       'write the table to the label (div) control
       qDetails.InnerHtml = display

    End Sub

End Class
```

Transaction Management

The CTrx class is used to receive and reject messages. Its methods are called by the click event for the given Accept or Reject button. You might extend this class to enforce specific business rules or call other classes that enforce these rules. Additionally, you might log information to the event log, send special messages to other queues, and so on. Currently, the code simply receives messages and writes them to the event log.

Code Walkthrough

Listing 13.23 shows the output of the code for CTrx.

LISTING 13.23   CTrx

We declare a global-level queue variable to maintain a reference to the queue for the class. The class has a constructor that is used to set this global queue value.

```
Imports System.Messaging
Imports System.Diagnostics

Public Class CTrx

    'class-level scope
    Private queue As MessageQueue

    Public Sub New(ByVal machineName As String, ByVal qPath As String)

        'purpose:   constructor, req. a machine name and queue

        'get a class-level reference to a the queue
        Try
            queue = New MessageQueue(path:=machineName & "\" & qPath)
        Catch
            Err.Raise(number:=Err.Number, description:=Err.Description)
        End Try

        'set the property read filter to return all properties
        queue.MessageReadPropertyFilter.SetAll()

        'set the formatter for the queue to use
        CType(queue.Formatter, XmlMessageFormatter).TargetTypeNames = _
            New String() {"System.String"}

    End Sub
```

The `receiveTrxMsg` routine receives a transactional set of messages based on the parameter `trxId` (transaction identifier). The method starts a transaction with the line `trx.Begin`. Messages then are received and written to the event log. If an error occurs, `trx.Abort` is called and all messages received as part of the transaction are rolled back to their original state (not received). Upon success, we call `trx.Commit`.

```
    Public Sub receiveTrxMsg(ByVal trxId As String)

        'purpose: receive messages as a transaction

        'local scope
        Dim msg() As Message
        Dim trx As New MessageQueueTransaction()
        Dim i As Integer
        Dim msgRec As Message
```

LISTING 13.23 Continued

```
    'get a snapshot of messages in the queue as an array
    'note: the array is in the same order as msgs in the queue
    '      therefore, trx can be assumed sequential as they were written
    msg = queue.GetAllMessages

    'start a transaction
    trx.Begin()

    'loop through our snapshot of messages and pull out the transaction
    For i = 0 To UBound(msg)

        'check the transaction id property
        If msg(i).TransactionId = trxId Then

            Try

                'receive the message as part of a transaction
                msgRec = queue.ReceiveById(id:=msg(i).Id, transaction:=trx)

            Catch

                'error, abort the transaction
                trx.Abort()
                Err.Raise(number:=Err.Number, description:=Err.Description)

            End Try

            'do something with the message, business rules, write to db, etc.
            'write the item to the event log
            EventLog.WriteEntry(source:="messageManager", _
                Message:="Message Received: " & msgRec.Body, _
                type:=EventLogEntryType.Information)

            'short-circuit the loop if end of trx
            If msg(i).IsLastInTransaction Then Exit For

        End If

    Next

    'commit the transaction
    trx.Commit()

End Sub
```

LISTING 13.23   Continued

The `rejectTrxMsg` procedure is identical to the `receiveTrxMsg` procedure. It simply receives the message and then writes it to the event log as rejected. Of course, you would want to modify this procedure to process your own set of rejection rules.

```
Public Sub rejectTrxMsg(ByVal trxId As String)

    'purpose: reject a group of messages as trx

    'local scope
    Dim msg() As Message
    Dim trx As New MessageQueueTransaction()
    Dim i As Integer
    Dim msgRec As Message

    'get a snapshot of messages in the queue as an array
    'note: the array is in the same order as msgs in the queue
    '      therefore, trx can be assumed sequential as they were written
    msg = queue.GetAllMessages

    'start a transaction
    trx.Begin()

    'loop through our snapshot of messages and pull out the transaction
    For i = 0 To UBound(msg)

        'check the transaction id property
        If msg(i).TransactionId = trxId Then

            Try

                'receive the message as part of a transaction
                msgRec = queue.ReceiveById(id:=msg(i).Id, transaction:=trx)

            Catch

                'error, abort the transaction
                trx.Abort()
                Err.Raise(number:=Err.Number, description:=Err.Description)

            End Try

            'do something with the message, business rules, write to db, etc.
            'write the item to the event log
            EventLog.WriteEntry(source:="messageManager", _
                Message:="Message Rejected: " & msgRec.Body, _
                type:=EventLogEntryType.Information)
```

LISTING 13.23 Continued

```
                    'short-circuit the loop if end of trx
                    If msg(i).IsLastInTransaction Then Exit For

            End If

    Next

    'commit the transaction
    trx.Commit()

End Sub
```

The receiveMsg procedure is used for receiving nontransactional messages. It takes a message ID as its one parameter. It uses the ReceiveById method of the MessageQueue object to pull the message from the queue and write its contents to the event log. The following routine, rejectMsg, is identical except that it writes a rejection notice to the event log.

```
Public Sub receiveMsg(ByVal msgId As String)

    'purpose: receive single message

    'local scope
    Dim msg As Message
    Dim eventLog As New EventLog()

    'get the message
    msg = queue.ReceiveById(id:=msgId)

    'do something with the message, business rules, write to db, etc.
    'write the item to the event log
    eventLog.WriteEntry(source:="messageManager", _
        Message:="Message Received: " & msg.Body, _
        type:=EventLogEntryType.Information)

End Sub

Public Sub rejectMsg(ByVal msgId As String)

    'purpose: reject a single message

    'local scope
    Dim msg As Message
    Dim eventLog As New EventLog()

    'get the message
    msg = queue.ReceiveById(id:=msgId)
```

```
        'do something with the message, business rules, write to db, etc.

        'write the item to the event log
        eventLog.WriteEntry(source:="messageManager", _
            Message:="Message Rejected: " & msg.Body, _
            type:=EventLogEntryType.Information)

    End Sub

End Class
```

Summary

The items we've covered in this chapter represent the foundation of Messaging. Because the topic is such a large one, with so many features available, there are undoubtedly details that you will uncover as you write your applications and continue to explore the library. These details should be easily learned because they complement and extend your foundation.

The following are key points regarding Messaging with the .NET Class Library:

- The Messaging design pattern provides our applications with guaranteed delivery, security, encryption, priority-based Messaging, and transactional Messaging.

- The MessageQueue class is used to connect to a message queue, set and return its many properties, and send and receive messages.

- You can return a static snapshot of all queues on a machine using the GetPublicQueues or GetPrivateQueuesByMachine methods of the MessageQueue class, or you can maintain dynamic connection to the queues on a machine using the MessageQueueEnumerator class.

- You use MessageQueue.Send to send messages to a given queue.

- MessageQueue.Peek allows you to view the contents of a message without actually removing it from the queue.

- MessageQueue.Receive is used to receive a message and pull it off the queue.

- Asynchronous Messaging is accomplished via the MessageQueue class's BeginReceive and EndReceive methods and corresponding ReceiveCompleted event.

- You can receive message acknowledgements by setting Message.ResponseQueue, provided that the receiving message queue supports this feature.

- Setting the Message.Priority property forces a queue to process a message with a higher priority first, regardless of the order in which it was received.

- You can return a snapshot of all messages on a queue using `MessageQueue.GetAllMessages`, or you can maintain a dynamic connection to a queue's messages using the `MessageEnumerator` class and the `MessageQueue.GetEnumerator` method.

- The formatter objects `XMLMessageFormatter`, `BinaryMessageFormatter`, and `ActiveXMessageFormatter` allow you to serialize messages into varying formats.

- The `MessageQueueTransaction` class is used to manage queue-based transactional Messaging.

- You can manage permissions on a queue using the classes `MessageQueueAccessControlEntry`, `MessageQueueAccessRights`, and `Trustee`.

- Message authentication can be accomplished by setting the `UseAuthentication` and `AttachSenderId` properties of the `Message` class to `True`.

- To audit messages in and out of queue, set the `MessageQueue.UseJournalQueue` property to `True`.

- To use MSMQ encryption, set the `UseEncryption` property of the `Message` class.

 ## Suggestions for Further Exploration

➲ Check out Microsoft Message Queuing for Windows CE. You can download the SDK at `http://www.microsoft.com/msmq/downloads/MSMQ_CE.zip`.

➲ Trigger business rules as messages arrive in the queue—without additional programming. MSMQ Triggers is a very cool add-on that allows you to create rules that invoke COM components based on a message. We hope that Microsoft will extend this application for managed code under .NET. Check out `http://www.microsoft.com/msmq` for details, or download the documentation at `http://www.microsoft.com/ntserver/zipdocs/msmqtriggersdoc.zip`.

➲ Microsoft Message Queuing interoperates with the IBM MQSeries products through the Microsoft MSMQ-MQSeries Bridge. Check out `http://www.microsoft.com/msmq/interop.htm` for more information on MSMQ interoperability.

➲ Check out `http://www.microsoft.com/msmq/developer.htm` for even more interesting downloads and MSMQ resources for developers.

13

MESSAGING

Browser/Server Communications

IN THIS CHAPTER

ASP.NET evolved out of Microsoft's original Active Server Pages, but that is where the similarities end. Sure, some of the objects are still named the same, but the capabilities and programming paradigms that ASP.NET offers have really grown up. VB developers will be pleased to know that it is often difficult to distinguish in which environment you are programming—VB or ASP!

This chapter starts by detailing `System.Web`, the namespace related to Web development and ASP.NET. We then present a number of key classes in the namespace, each related to Web development basics. Our discussion then moves to handling client requests and issuing responses. We also talk about why proper state management within your application is so critical and illustrate how to use ASP.NET new features related to managing Web application state. Finally, we finish the chapter with a sample ASP.NET application that lets users indicate where they are, when they'll be back, and how they can be reached.

After reading this chapter, you should

- Understand how to handle form data submitted to your ASP.NET page
- Be able to verify whether a Web client can accept cookies, write a cookie value out to the client, and retrieve it at a later date
- Manage client-side and server-side user data (aka state) between page requests

Key Classes Used for Browser/Server Communication

Handling browser-to-server communication is the principal responsibility of the ASP.NET technology. In the past, ASP meant embedded script inside of HTML—script that got translated through an ISAPI filter on an IIS server. ASP was a very different model from Windows application development or client server. .NET blurs the line between development for the Web world and creating Windows applications.

ASP.NET is the combination of a Web Forms engine and the .NET CLR. This new forms engine allows developers to create event-driven applications the same way they would create them using the Windows Forms engine. In fact, with code behind classes that work in conjunction with an HTML Web Form, developers are free to write code in any .NET language—not only VBA.

Of course, the classes and objects that make up ASP.NET can be found in the .NET Framework Class Library. `System.Web` and its associated third-level namespaces wrap a great deal of the ASP functionality. These namespaces are described briefly in the following list:

- `System.Web`—Provides the principal classes that wrap communication between browsers and servers. This namespace is the focus of this chapter.

- `System.Web.Caching`—Provides classes used to cache resources (Web pages, controls, Web services) on the server. This class is presented in this chapter.

- `System.Web.Configuration`—Provides classes that can be used to set up and manage ASP.NET configurations.

- `System.Web.Hosting`—Provides classes that can be used to host ASP.NET applications outside of IIS.

- `System.Web.Mail`—Provides classes that allow you to send mail to your Web application via SMTP. This namespace replaces CDO. It wraps a message with the `MailMessage` class and an attachment with the `MailAttachment` class. Developers will use the `SmtpMail` class to send messages.

- `System.Web.Security`—Provides classes that allow you to manage the security in your ASP.NET application. The namespace includes classes for working with the Microsoft Passport system.

- `System.Web.Services`—Provides classes used to create and consume Web services. The `WebService` base class can be used to create an XML Web service that has access to the ASP.NET objects. The `WebMethodAttribute` class is used to tag methods in your service as available to remote clients.

- `System.Web.Services.Configuration`—Provides attribute classes that indicate how an ASP.NET Web service will execute.

- `System.Web.Services.Description`—Provides classes that enable you to publicly describe an XML Web service using Web Services Description Language (WSDL).

- `System.Web.Services.Discovery`—Provides classes that help you discover Web services on a server using the XML Web Service Discovery process.

- `System.Web.Services.Protocols`—Provides classes that are used to define the protocols (HTTP, MIME, SOAP) when transmitting data between a Web service and its clients.

- `System.Web.SessionState`—Provides classes that enable you to manage user state (on the Web server) between requests. This namespace is covered within this chapter.

- `System.Web.UI`—Provides classes that are used to create ASP.NET HTML, Web, User, and Server controls.

- `System.Web.UI.Design`—Provides classes that are used to support design-time functionality for Web Forms.

- `System.Web.UI.Design.WebControls`—Provides designer classes that are used to support design-time functionality for Web controls.

- `System.Web.UI.HtmlControls`—Provides classes that are used to create and control HTML controls on your ASP.NET form.

- `System.Web.UI.WebControls`—Provides classes that wrap Web controls. These are controls that run on the server and provide easier management than HTML controls.

As you can see, Web development is well represented in the .NET Framework Class Library. Indeed, entire books are dedicated to the subject. For our purposes, we are going to focus on those classes you will most commonly access. Table 14.1 lists the key classes we will be discussing.

TABLE 14.1   Key Classes in the `System.Web` Namespace

Class	Description
	Request and Response
HttpRequest	The `HttpRequest` class is used to read the contents of an HTTP request sent by a client requesting an ASP.NET page. The methods and properties of this object are exposed through ASP.NET's intrinsic `Request` object.
HttpResponse	The `HttpResponse` class is used to read the contents of an HTTP response. The methods and properties of this object are exposed through ASP.NET's intrinsic `Response` object.
HttpContext	The `HttpContext` class is used to gather all HTTP-specific information regarding an HTTP request. This class is accessed through the ASP intrinsic object `Page`.
	Browser Capabilities
HttpBrowserCapabilities	The `HttpBrowserCapabilities` class returns information about a user's browser.
	State Management
HttpApplicationState	The `HttpApplicationState` class is used to share application-specific information across user sessions.
SessionState	The `SessionState` class is used to store client-specific information on the server. This class is in the `System.Web.SessionState` namespace.
HttpCookie	The `HttpCookie` class is used to create and manage individual client cookies.
HttpCookieCollection	The `HttpCookieCollection` class wraps individual `HttpCookie` objects into a collection.
	Caching Resources
HttpCachePolicy	The `HttpCachePolicy` is used to control the ASP.NET page output cache.
Cache	The `Cache` class is used to control the items in the server's cache on a per application basis. This class is in the `System.Web.Caching` namespace.

Client Request and Server Response

In a typical Web application, clients request pages and the server sends a response to the client. Managing the content of this request-and-response transaction is the subject of this section. Those that have worked with earlier versions of ASP should use this section as a refresher. You'll find that a lot of what you know about the old object models still holds true in ASP.NET. We think you'll also be pleasantly surprised by some new features, the way the object model has been cleaned up, and the new structure of ASP.NET pages.

Managing User Requests

When users request an ASP.NET page from your Web server, their browsers send data that details the specifics of their request. This request gets wrapped by an instance of the `HttpRequest` class. This class is accessible by calling the intrinsic `Request` object inside your ASP.NET page. `Request` is actually a property of the `Page` object, which does not have to be explicitly referenced in your code. The `Request` property is of the type `HttpRequest` class. Developers can, however, simply reference the `Request` property, which allows for backward compatibility.

Key Properties and Methods of `HttpRequest`

Table 14.2 lists properties and methods developers will use to execute common programming tasks using the `HttpRequest` object. Note that the properties dealing with paths and URLs have been grouped for easy reference.

TABLE 14.2   Key Properties and Methods of `HttpRequest`

Properties	Description
ApplicationPath	Suppose you are requesting the page `http://localhost/Chapter14/WebForm1.aspx/temp`. The `ApplicationPath` property returns the virtual path of the request (/Chapter14).
CurrentExecutionFilePath FilePath	Both the `FilePath` and the `CurrentExecutionFilePath` property return the virtual path and the filename of the current request (/Chapter14/WebForm1.aspx).
Path	The `Path` property returns the virtual path, filename, and trailing information (/Chapter14/WebForm1.aspx/temp).
PathInfo	The `PathInfo` property returns only the trailing information (/temp).
PhysicalApplicationPath	The `PhysicalApplicationPath` returns the physical path on your server to your application's directory (c:\inetpub\wwwroot\Chapter14\).

TABLE 14.2   Continued

Properties	Description
PhysicalPath	The PhysicalPath property returns the physical path to the requested file (c:\inetpub\wwwroot\Chapter14\ WebForm2.aspx).
RawUrl	The RawUrl property returns the portion of the URL following the domain information, including query string information (/Chapter14/WebForm2.aspx/temp).
Url	The Url property returns the full URL of the request (http://localhost/Chapter14/WebForm2.aspx/temp).
Browser	The Browser property returns an HttpBrowserCapabilities object that provides details about the requesting client's browser.
	For more information, see "Determining Browser Capabilities" later in this chapter.
ClientCertificate	The ClientCertificate returns an HttpClientCertificate object that wraps the requesting client's security certificate.
ContentLength	The ContentLength property returns the size (in bytes) of the content sent by the requesting client.
ContentType	The ContentType property returns the MIME content type of the current request.
Cookies	The Cookies property returns an HttpCookieCollection object that represents the cookies sent by the client.
	For more information, see "State Management" later in this chapter.
Files	The Files property returns an HttpFileCollection object that represents a collection of files uploaded by a user.
Form	The Form property returns a NameValueCollection that is a collection of form values.
Headers	The Headers property returns a NameValueCollection that is a collection of request headers.
HttpMethod RequestType	The HttpMethod property returns the data transfer method of the request. Values can be Get, Post, or Head.
	The RequestType property returns similar information.

TABLE 14.2 Continued

Properties	Description
IsAuthenticated	The IsAuthenticated property returns True if the user making the request has been authenticated.
IsSecureConnection	The IsSecureConnection property returns True if the connection is using Secure Sockets Layer SSL (HTTPs).
QueryString	The QueryString property returns a NameValueCollection containing a collection of the query string values sent in the request.
ServerVariables	The ServerVariables property returns a collection of type NameValueCollection that represents all the server variables available to your application.
	You access a server variable by passing it a key. For example, to get the request method of the current request, you would call the following:
	`Request.ServerVariables("REQUEST_METHOD")`
	This class allows you to access server variables in the same manner as the prior version of ASP.
TotalBytes	The TotalBytes property returns the total number of bytes in the input stream.
UrlReferrer	The UrlReferrer property returns a URI object that provides information about any URL that referred (linked) the client to your site.
UserHostAddress	The UserHostAddress property returns the IP address of the requesting client.
UserHostName	The UserHostName property returns the DNS name of the requesting client.
Methods	
BinaryRead	The BinaryRead method is used to read portions of the input stream.
MapPath	The MapPath method is used to map the requested URL to a physical path on your server.
SaveAs	SaveAs property allows you to save the request to disk.

Reading Data from the Request

Users enter data on your page using controls, including text boxes and the like. This data is then sent to your site (as part of the HTTP request) when a user clicks a button on your form. How this data is packaged in the request depends on how you've defined the page's form tag.

The HTML <form> tag has two key attributes: Method and Action. The Method attribute indicates the request method used to package and send the data to your site. There are two HTTP request methods, GET and POST. The Action attribute is used to indicate to which page the request should be sent. Typically, a request for a page is sent to the server as a GET method. This is when a user types in a URL or links to your page using a hyperlink. The POST method is reserved for when users submit form data to one of your pages.

After you've defined your form's properties, you create an <input> control whose Type attribute is Submit. This control defines your button. When users click this button, your form will be submitted to the target of your Action attribute using the request method defined by the form's Method attribute.

If the form is submitted using the GET method, all your data is appended to the URL of the target page on what is called the query string. The query string is indicated by a question mark (?) and contains name/value pairs separated by the "&" sign. The names of each item in the query string are equivalent to the names of all your form elements. Each item's value is either the data entered (or selected) by the user or the value attribute of the given control. The query string names and values are packaged into a collection accessible from the QueryString property of the HttpRequest object. The query string, however, is typically reserved for passing data from page to page using a hyperlink rather than submitting form data.

Many times you'll pass hidden fields and other sensitive data as part of the request. For this reason, you should use the POST method when submitting data as part of a request. In this scenario, data is hidden from the user; it does not appear on the URL. This has the added benefit of preventing users from *hacking* at your URL and producing unwanted results. When a Web Form submits or "posts" its information, the submitted data is accessible via the Form property of the HttpRequest object.

Both the QueryString and the Form property are of the type NameValueCollection. This collection class enables you to access items using a key value (or name). You simply pass the name of the query string element or name of the form control to the class, and it returns the value.

To demonstrate reading the query string and form values using these objects, we'll create a simple ASP.NET form with two text boxes and a submit button. When a user clicks the button, the request is sent to the server in the type defined by the form's method. The HttpRequest object (ASP's Page.Request property) is accessible inside the button's server-side click event.

Listing 14.1 represents this event. In this code we, check the request type and then write out the contents of the form using either the QueryString or the Form property's collection (depending on GET or POST). Note that we've eliminated the form definition code for clarity; full source code is available from the Web site.

LISTING 14.1 The QueryString and Form Properties

```vb
Private Sub Button1_Click(ByVal sender As System.Object, _
  ByVal e As System.EventArgs) Handles Button1.Click

  'check the request type
  If Request.RequestType = "GET" Then

    'write form values out from querystring
    Response.Write("GET" & "<br>")
    Response.Write(Request.QueryString("TextBox1") & "<br>")
    Response.Write(Request.QueryString("TextBox2"))

  ElseIf Request.RequestType = "POST" Then

    'write form values out from form
    Response.Write("POST" & "<br>")
    Response.Write(Request.Form("TextBox1") & "<br>")
    Response.Write(Request.Form("TextBox2"))

  End If

End Sub
```

Now, simply toggling the Method of the form definition between the GET and POST values produces different results.

Figure 14.1 shows the results for a GET method; notice the highlighted query string.

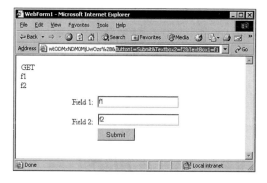

FIGURE 14.1

Results of the QueryString *code example.*

Responding to Requests

Data is sent to the server (and to your page) as a client request. You respond to these requests by processing information and sending data back to the client. This information (also called the response) is managed by an instance of the `HttpResponse` class. This class is accessible by calling the ASP.NET intrinsic `Response` object (`Page.Response` property) from within your ASP.NET page. Developers can simply reference the `Response` property as you did in the ASP of old. This allows for backward compatibility. However, the property is of the type `HttpResponse` class.

Key Properties and Methods of `HttpResponse`

Table 14.3 lists properties and methods developers use to execute common programming tasks using the `HttpResponse` object.

TABLE 14.3   Key Properties and Methods of `HttpResponse`

Properties	Description
BufferOutput	The `BufferOutput` property is a `Boolean` value that you can return or set to indicate whether the output to the client should be buffered on the server before being sent to the client. The default value is `True`.
Cache	The `Cache` property is used to return the caching policy for a given Web page as part of the current response.
ContentType	The `ContentType` property is used to return or set the HTTP MIME type of the response stream.
Cookies	The `Cookies` property returns an `HttpCookiesCollection` object that can be used to add cookies to the client as part of the response.
	See the "State Management" section later in this chapter for more details.
IsClientConnected	The `IsClientConnected` property returns `True` if the client is still connected to the server; that is, an open and active session is still on the server.
Output	The `Output` property returns a `TextWriter` instance that enables you to send custom text output to the client.
OutputStream	The `OutputStream` property returns a `Stream` instance that enables you to send custom binary output to the client.
SuppressContent	The `SuppressContent` property is used to return or set a Boolean value indicating whether to suppress the HTTP output to the client.

TABLE 14.3 Continued

Properties	Description
	Methods
AddCacheItemDependencies	The AddCacheItemDependencies method enables you to create dependencies between a group of items (an array of keys) in the cache.
AddCacheItemDependency	The AddCacheItemDependency method enables you to create a dependency between two items in the cache.
AppendToLog	The AppendToLog method enables you to write your own custom information into the IIS log file.
BinaryWrite	The BinaryWrite method enables you to write binary data to the HTTP output response.
Clear	The Clear method is used to clear the entire HTTP output response.
Close	The Close method is used to close the socket connection to the client.
End	The End method is used to stop the execution of the response. When called, this method sends all buffered output down to the client and raises the Application_EndRequest event.
Flush	The Flush method is used to force the current buffered content to be sent directly to the client. Note that Flush can be called multiple times during a long response.
Pics	The Pics method is used to append a "PICS-Label" header to the output stream. The acronym, PICS, stands for Platform for Internet Content Selection. It is a W3C standard for content labeling and rating.
Redirect	The Redirect method is used to send the client to a different URL.
Write	The Write method is used to write information to the HTTP content that gets sent to the client as part of the response.
WriteFile	The WriteFile method is used to write the contents of a file directly to the HTTP content stream.

Writing Data to the Client

A response to a client's request can be as simple as processing its information and then redirecting that information to another page within your site. In this case, if users have submitted a form, you might write some of that information off to a data store and then direct the user on to another menu page or the like. To do so, you simply call the Redirect method, as in the following:

```
Response.Redirect("WebForm2.aspx")
```

Often, however, you'll make decisions in your code that require you to change content sent to the client. The simplest example of this is when returning data from a data store that is intended for users. In this case, you'll want to use the Write method to embed this information into the response. This method is accessed as follows:

```
Response.Write(someVariable)
```

To write binary data into the response content, you use the BinaryWrite method. This can be useful if you store binary objects, such as graphics, in your data store. As an example, we'll create a binary stream based on a JPEG file. We'll send this stream down to the client using the BinaryWrite method.

Listing 14.2 represents the click event of a button defined on a Web Form. When users click the button, they are presented with graphics streamed to them using BinaryWrite.

LISTING 14.2 BinaryWrite Example

```
Private Sub Button1_Click(ByVal sender As System.Object, _
    ByVal e As System.EventArgs) Handles Button1.Click

    'local scope
    Dim myFileSize As Long

    'create a file stream object based on a graphics file
    Dim myFileStream As New FileStream( _
      Path:="c:\temp\myGraphic.jpg", mode:=FileMode.Open, _
      access:=FileAccess.Read)

    'set the file size
    myFileSize = myFileStream.Length

    'create a byte array for the buffer
    Dim myBuffer(CInt(myFileSize)) As Byte

    'read the stream into the buffer
    myFileStream.Read(myBuffer, 0, CInt(myFileSize))

    'close the stream
    myFileStream.Close()
```

LISTING 14.2 Continued

```
    'write the file as part of the response
    Response.BinaryWrite(myBuffer)

End Sub
```

You can also write the contents of a file directly to the output response. To do so, you use the `WriteFile` method. This is a new feature specific to ASP.NET. The method works with both text and binary file data. For instance, in the preceding example, we could use `WriteFile` to output the same image to the response.

```
Response.WriteFile(fileName:="c:\temp\myGraphic.jpg")
```

 Suggestions for Further Exploration

For information on how users can upload (post) files to your server, check out the `HttpPostedFile` class and the `HttpFileCollection` class.

Determining Browser Capabilities

Web browser compatibility has been a thorn in the side of many developers. Typically, you'll write code that executes perfectly in one browser, only to watch it blow up in another (or worse, the same browser but different versions). Additionally, you may choose to offer users personalization by storing their user IDs inside a client-side cookie. This feature should not work the same for those users with browsers that do not support cookies (or that have cookies turned off). To trap this information, the .NET Framework Class Library gives us the `HttpBrowserCapabilities` class.

Detecting Browser Information

Browsers are classified into the two groups: uplevel and downlevel. Downlevel browsers provide support for HTML 3.2. Uplevel browsers are those that support HTML 4.0 and later, JavaScript 1.2, and Cascading Style Sheets (CSS).

To determine the capabilities of a requesting client's browser, you use the `Request` object's `Browser` property. For example, to determine whether a browser supports cookies, you can use the following code:

```
If Request.Browser.Cookies then
    ...
End If
```

The Browser property returns an instance of the HttpBrowserCapabilities class. This class is made up of a number of Boolean properties that indicate whether the requesting browser supports a given capability. A majority of these properties are listed in Table 14.4.

TABLE 14.4   Key Properties of HttpBrowserCapabilities

Property	*Description*
ActiveXControls	The ActiveXControls property returns True if the browser supports ActiveX controls.
AOL	The AOL property returns True if the browser is an America Online browser.
BackgroundSounds	The BackgroundSounds property returns True if the browser supports background sounds.
Beta	The Beta property returns True if the browser is a beta release version.
Browser	The Browser property returns the browser type from the user-agent header ("IE" for example).
CDF	The CDF property returns True if the browser supports channel definition format.
ClrVersion	The ClrVersion property returns the version number of the Common Language Runtime (CLR) installed on the given client.
Cookies	The Cookies property returns True if the browser supports cookies.
Crawler	The Crawler property returns True if the browser is a Web crawler.
Frames	The Frames property returns True if the browser supports frames.
JavaApplets	The JavaApplets property returns True if the browser supports Java applets.
JavaScript	The JavaScript property returns True if the browser supports JavaScript.
MajorVersion	The MajorVersion property returns the major version number of the browser (6, for example).
MinorVersion	The MinorVersion property returns the minor version number of the browser (.05, for example).
MSDomVersion	The MSDomVersion property returns the version number of the Microsoft Document Object Model that the browser supports.
Platform	The Platform property returns the name of the operating system of the requesting client (WinNT, for example).

TABLE 14.4 Continued

Property	Description
Tables	The Tables property returns True if the client browser supports HTML tables.
Type	The Type property returns the name and major version number of the client browser.
VBScript	The VBScript property returns True if the browser supports VBScript.
Version	The Version property returns the full version number of the browser (5.5, for example).
W3CDomVersion	The W3CDomVersion property returns the W3C DOM version number.
Win16	The Win16 property returns True if the browser is on a Win16 platform.
Win32	The Win32 property returns True if the browser is on a Win32 platform.

State Management

How you manage the storage and retrieval of global, local, and user data is one of the most important design considerations you can make when writing Web applications. Three areas where your application will typically store state are the client, your Web server, or your database server. Getting the right mix of state management for your application will lead to scalable and fast ASP.NET applications.

Storing Global State

Values that are used globally by your Web application are referred to as *application state*. A Web application is defined by all the ASP files and classes in your domain. When your application is started (or restarted), IIS creates an application-scoped area inside your server's memory space to store data. Effective use of globally scoped data can speed page requests and trim development time. However, mismanagement can severely limit the scalability of your application. Let's look at how to use, and how not to use, application state.

Application state is stored in memory on your server. This can be great because a page is no longer required to make a trip to a data store to retrieve data. At the same time, the data is eating up a precious memory on your server. This memory is not recovered until the application data is removed or the site is stopped and started. When you decide whether to store data within application state, it is important to be sure of the following:

- All users of your application will be accessing the same data.

- The data is accessed by a large number of pages in your site.

- Your server has enough memory to handle the data.

After you've addressed these issues, application state might be your answer. For instance, suppose an e-commerce site's catalog is made up from a 5MB data set retrieved from the database on every request. Perhaps the catalog items change only once a day, or even once an hour. Nearly every page in the site needs to access this data. To speed customer requests and limit the toll on your database server, you should consider storing this data within the global scope of your application (check out ASP.NET's new caching features for an alternative). Of course, if this data was more transient and was used by only a few, infrequently accessed pages, this strategy wouldn't solve much of a problem and instead would consume resources on your server.

If you do decide to store application state on your server, you need to be aware of a few technical issues:

- Data is not durable—Application state does not survive a Web server (or system) restart; instead, your application state is wiped out when the application is ended. To handle this, developers typically will use the `Application_Start` event from within the `global.asax` file to load their application state from a database or object. Similarly, the `Application_End` event can be used to persist this data back to a data store.

- ASP is multithreaded—Most of the time this is a huge advantage. Multiple worker threads can safely access the global data simultaneously. However, to prevent race conditions, developers must be sure to lock the application state prior to updating its data. Data that is frequently updated can be problematic for application state. In this situation, all pages that are requesting application data are blocked until the current thread doing the update finishes. This is typically fine provided your data is updated only every 15 minutes or so and that the update is relatively fast.

- Web farms—When working with Web farm environments (multiple IIS servers running the same application and load-balanced), it is important to understand that application state is per server. For this reason, a change to the application's state on one server is not necessarily reflected on the other servers in the "garden." To handle this problem, application state is typically updated in the database and then reloaded by each server at appropriate intervals.

HttpApplicationState

To store application state on the server, you use the `HttpApplicationState` class. This is a collection class containing name/value pairs. To access this class, you use the `Application` property of the `Page` instance. The following code demonstrates adding a value to the `HttpApplicationState` object inside the `global.asax` when the application starts:

```
Sub Application_Start(ByVal sender As Object, ByVal e As EventArgs)

   'purpose: fires when the application is started

   'add an item to the application scope
   Application.Add(name:="myAppScope", _
             value:="This value is used by all pages!")

End Sub
```

This application scoped value is available to any page (or class) from within your ASP.NET application. To access the value, you simply pass the key to the collection and it returns the value. For example:

```
Private Sub Page_Load(ByVal sender As System.Object, _
   ByVal e As System.EventArgs) Handles MyBase.Load

   'get application value and write to screen
   Response.Write(Page.Application("myAppScope").ToString)

End Sub
```

Storing User-Specific State

HTTP is, by design, a stateless protocol. That is, with HTTP, after a Web page is requested or a response is made, there is no way to remember previous user requests or even to know if the user's browser is still open. Applications, however, need a mechanism to identify users, their requests, and their data. It is not practical to ask users to resupply their credentials and data with every request. Therefore, working in this model requires you to understand the various user-state storage options that are available.

Hidden Fields and the Query String

HTTP and HTML try to solve some of the issues with user state by providing the query string (discussed previously) and the concept of hidden fields. Query strings are ideal if you are working only with page requests (and not posts) and you are not sending sensitive data to the client or sending information a user might tamper with. How many sites can be messed with just by altering some of the values in the query string? How many developer hours have been spent trapping for this case? Query strings do serve a purpose in a limited, well-planned role—they are, however, only part of the solution.

Hidden fields are a little better in that they are "hidden" from the user. A hidden field is sent as part of the request in the form of <input> tags whose type attribute is set to the value of hidden. Of course, they are hidden only from the browser window. They are still sent to the client, and as such, can be viewed by a user. Simply right-clicking the browser window and choosing View Source exposes all the hidden fields. Of course, this is still a viable option for data that is not too sensitive.

ASP.NET provides a new object for managing hidden form fields. This object is accessed from the `ViewState` property, which derives from `IStateManager`. This object is easy to use and provides for object-oriented development instead of HTML coding when managing hidden form fields. Additionally, items added to the `ViewState` collection are hashed, compressed, and encoded before being sent to the client. This severely limits the likelihood of nefarious users manipulating your form input. (`ViewState` is also used by Web controls for the same effects.)

> **NOTE**
>
> All client data can be tampered with by mischievous developers sending posts to your pages and embedding their own input values or cookies in the request. You need to make sure you are aware of this and be sure to trap for it if you consider it a likely occurrence.

To add a hidden form field to your response, you call the `Add` method of `ViewState` and pass both the item's name and its value as follows:

```
ViewState.Add(key:="HiddenValue", value:="Some hidden value")
```

When the input field is sent to the client, the field's hidden value looks like the following:

```
<input type="hidden" name="__VIEWSTATE"
  value="dDwtNTMwNzcxMzI0O3Q8cDxsPEhpZGRlblZhb
  HVlOz47bDxTb21lIGhpZGRlbiB2YWx1ZTs+Pjs7Pjs+" />
```

To read the hidden form field from the posted request, you simply call the `Item` method of the `ViewState` collection. The following writes this value to the screen:

```
Response.Write(ViewState.Item(key:="HiddenValue"))
```

HttpCookie

Another option available for storing client-based state information is inside the user's cookie. A cookie is a small, text-based file or an area in memory that you can use to place information onto the client's machine. Cookies are specific to your application and are sent along with every page request. Typically, these are used for applications that remember your settings. When you log in, a cookie containing your user ID might get written to your machine for later retrieval. Cookies work well in this scenario, provided the user hasn't turned them off on the browser.

Cookies in ASP.NET are wrapped by the HttpCookie class. Cookies are accessed using the Cookies property of the Request object. Cookies are written using the same property of the Response object. Both properties use the HttpCookieCollection class to add and retrieve items from the cookie collection.

To write a cookie as part of the HTTP response, you call the Add method of HttpCookieCollection and pass the cookie's name and its value. For example:

```
'add a cookie value to the response
Response.Cookies.Add( _
        New HttpCookie(name:="myCookies", value:="cookie value"))
```

To read a cookie from the client request, you simply access an item from the collection using the cookie's key as follows:

```
'retrieve a cookie value from the request
'  and write out its value to the response
Response.Write(Request.Cookies.Item(name:="myCookies").Value)
```

It is generally good form to make sure your cookies expire. The Expires property of the HttpCookie class is useful for setting (and returning) an expiration date and time for the cookie. Depending on your site's traffic patterns, if a user hasn't visited your site in more than a month, he should expect that his cookie has expired.

HttpSessionState

The last weapon in your client-state arsenal is the client's session state. When users request a page from your server, each user is assigned a session—provided the server is configured in this manner—and a session identifier. This information is used by the server to store client-specific information for the lifetime of the session, and even beyond. Again, depending on how you use this tool, you can either end up optimizing your application for performance and easing your development effort—or crippling your application's scalability. Because session state is managed by the server, it consumes valuable memory for every client with an active session (an active session is one that has yet to time out because of user inactivity).

The session identifier can either be written to the user's cookie (provided the user's browser supports cookies) or sent with each request on the URL as a query string value. The ID is a 120-bit ASCII string generated by an algorithm that guarantees uniqueness and randomness.

To access a user's session ID, you can call Session.SessionID. To determine whether the session ID came from a URL or a cookie, call the Session.IsCookieless property. This property returns True if the session ID is in the URL.

ASP developers will be happy to know that ASP.NET's Session object has little in common with the Session object of old. ASP.NET's Page.Session property is of the type

`HttpSessionState` class found in the `System.Web.SessionState` namespace. This class, and namespace, provides a whole host of new, robust capabilities.

To add items to the session, you call the `Add` method of the `HttpSessionState` object and pass the name of the item and its value. For example:

```
Session.Add(name:="SessionItem", value:="Some client-specific value")
```

To read items from the session state, you simply access the session collection's `Item` property and pass the name of the element you want to access. For example:

```
Response.Write(Session.Item(name:="SessionItem"))
```

Most of the new session state features revolve around where the session state gets managed. Session state can be configured to work in one of four modes. You can return the mode your application is running under by calling the `Mode` property of the `SessionState` class. This class returns a value of the type `SessionStateMode` enumeration. The possible modes are as follows:

- InProc—The `InProc` mode indicates that the server manages user sessions in the same process in which your application runs. This is the default mode configuration. This provides fast access to session state because items are in the same memory space as your application. However, the `InProc` configuration is problematic if your application stops, is restarted, if the user gets redirected to another server based on a load-balancing situation, or if the machine is restarted. In any of these cases, this session state is lost. `InProc` is equivalent to how IIS managed session state in past versions.

- SqlServer—In the `SqlServer` mode, session state is persisted to and managed from a SQL Server database. This provides the capability for your application to live beyond users closing their browsers or even in the event of a server shutdown or reboot.

- StateServer—With the `StateServer` mode, session state is stored out-of-process from your IIS server. This ensures that it survives service restarts. The `StateServer` mode can be used in a Web farm to share states between servers.

- Off—Many developers choose to manage their state themselves using cookies or a SQL server. In this case, it's best to turn session management off to free resources.

You can alter the mode in which your application manages state by setting the special tag `<SessionState>` in your application's configuration file. This file is stored in the root of your ASP.NET application and is called `Web.config`. The following is an example of the default settings for this tag:

```
<sessionState
    mode="InProc"
    stateConnectionString="tcpip=xxx.x.x.x:42424"
    sqlConnectionString="data source=xxx.x.x.x;user id=sa;password="
```

```
        cookieless="false"
        timeout="20"
/>
```

When a user's session is created, an event is fired on the server. You can easily trap this event inside the `global.asax` file. To do so, you create a `Session_Start` event as follows:

```
Sub Session_Start(ByVal sender As Object, _
   ByVal e As EventArgs)

   'purpose: event that fires when the session is started

   'set the session's timeout value
   Session.Timeout = 2

   'add items to the user's session ...

End Sub
```

Notice that in the example, we set the session's `Timeout` property to the value 2. This value indicates the number of minutes that the session can stay dormant on the server before it is destroyed.

You can trap a similar event when the session is torn down. You create a `Session_End` event. This can be useful to clear any session-level resources you might have been consuming, or even to persist information from the session out to a data store. An example follows:

```
Sub Session_End(ByVal sender As Object, _
   ByVal e As EventArgs)

   'purpose: an event that fires when the session ends

   'persist some session data to the database
   ' or release some session-level resources ...

End Sub
```

 ## Suggestions for Further Exploration

- The `System.Web.Caching.Cache` class makes it easy to cache pages, partial pages, and other data on your Web server. Also, check out the related `HttpCachePolicy` class of `System.Web`.

- For more information on creating scalable ASP.NET applications, see the document "Developing High-Performance ASP.NET Applications" in MSDN.

Learning by Example: MyStatus Indicator

Suppose that you are ready to check in your code and, of course, you're working from home, when you notice another developer has checked out a shared DLL. You need the latest versions of this DLL to compile your application against and meet your deadline. You call this guy at the office: no answer. You try at home: no answer. You call around and nobody can find him. In this sample, we'll create a simple Web application that can help solve this frustration—a form that can be used to indicate a user's current status as it relates to how the user can be reached. In the application, users navigate to a form that enables them to change their current status. This includes indicating where they are and how to contact them. The form persists its data into a client-specific XML file stored on the server. When users return to the site, their information is loaded from the XML file and is displayed for them to edit.

Note that the HTML has been excluded from the code samples because it is not relevant to our discussion.

Key Concepts Covered

The following concepts are demonstrated with this sample application:

- Handling client requests with the Request object, including the submission of the form
- Loading a Web Form from an XML data store
- Storing submitted data back to the XML data store
- Remembering users with the HttpCookie object

Home Page

The MyStatus application's home page could not be much simpler. We've added two hyperlinks: one for users to change their current status and the other to view the status of everyone else in the data store. We'll leave the View Others' Status page for you to implement because this is XML coding and unrelated to our System.Web demonstration. A screenshot of the home page is provided in Figure 14.2.

Code Walkthrough

There is not much code behind this page; the only code is that which is generated by ASP.NET. In a production application, we would suggest building this page in simple HTML. The code is presented in Listing 14.3.

Note: There is no code in the global.asax file for this application.

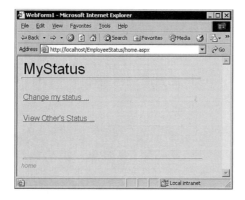

FIGURE 14.2

MyStatus home page.

LISTING 14.3   Code for the MyStatus Home Page

```
Public Class WebForm1

  Inherits System.Web.UI.Page

  Protected WithEvents HyperLink1 As System.Web.UI.WebControls.HyperLink
  Protected WithEvents HyperLink2 As System.Web.UI.WebControls.HyperLink
  Protected WithEvents Label2 As System.Web.UI.WebControls.Label
  Protected WithEvents Label1 As System.Web.UI.WebControls.Label

#Region " Web Form Designer Generated Code "

    'This call is required by the Web Form Designer.
    <System.Diagnostics.DebuggerStepThrough()> _
        Private Sub InitializeComponent()

  End Sub

  Private Sub Page_Init(ByVal sender As System.Object, _
    ByVal e As System.EventArgs) Handles MyBase.Init
    'CODEGEN: This method call is required by the Web Form Designer
    'Do not modify it using the code editor.
    InitializeComponent()
  End Sub

#End Region

End Class
```

MyStatus Page

The MyStatus page represents all the functionality in our sample application. Here, the users enter their current status. Notice that we store and indicate the last time current status was updated. This ensures that users will know the accuracy of the information. Figure 14.3 is a capture of the MyStatus page.

FIGURE 14.3

MyStatus screenshot.

Code Walkthrough

The code behind the MyStatus page is straightforward. We start by importing the `System.Xml` namespace to make our coding easier and clearer. The basic form code is then presented; this is automatically generated by ASP.NET. This is shown in Listing 14.4.

LISTING 14.4   Code for the MyStatus Page

```
Imports System.Xml

Public Class myStatus

  Inherits System.Web.UI.Page

  Protected WithEvents Label2 As System.Web.UI.WebControls.Label
  Protected WithEvents Label3 As System.Web.UI.WebControls.Label
  Protected WithEvents Label1 As System.Web.UI.WebControls.Label
  Protected WithEvents LastUpdatedLabel As System.Web.UI.WebControls.Label
```

LISTING 14.4 Continued

```
Protected WithEvents TextBoxName As System.Web.UI.WebControls.TextBox
Protected WithEvents TextBoxBack As System.Web.UI.WebControls.TextBox
Protected WithEvents TextBoxReach As System.Web.UI.WebControls.TextBox
Protected WithEvents DropDownListCurrently _
  As System.Web.UI.WebControls.DropDownList
Protected WithEvents TextBoxEmergency As System.Web.UI.WebControls.TextBox
Protected WithEvents Button1 As System.Web.UI.WebControls.Button

#Region " Web Form Designer Generated Code "

 'This call is required by the Web Form Designer.
 <System.Diagnostics.DebuggerStepThrough()> Private Sub InitializeComponent()

 End Sub

 Private Sub Page_Init(ByVal sender As System.Object, _
   ByVal e As System.EventArgs) Handles MyBase.Init
   'CODEGEN: This method call is required by the Web Form Designer
   'Do not modify it using the code editor.
   InitializeComponent()
 End Sub

#End Region
```

Inside the page load event, we try to load the user's XML data. This data is stored to a folder within our Web domain. The filename is made up of the user's original session ID when the user came to the site. This session ID was written out to the user's browser and returned each time as part of the request. If the user's session ID doesn't exist, we simply present a blank form.

In the event that the user has saved data on our server and the cookie has not expired, we create an instance of `XmlTextReader` class to read the user's last status from a file. Notice that we use the `Request.PhysicalApplicationPath` property to point the text reader at the appropriate file. We then loop through the elements in this data file and trap for the ones related to our Web page controls. When found, we set the `Text` property of the appropriate control to the string value of the XML element. For the drop-down box, we have to call the `FindByValue` method of the control and mark the found value as selected.

```
Private Sub Page_Load(ByVal sender As System.Object, _
  ByVal e As System.EventArgs) Handles MyBase.Load

  'purpose: check if the user has a valid cookie from a prior visit
  '         if so, grab their XML file and fill form fields
  '         if not, simply display the form
```

14

LISTING 14.4   Continued

```vb
'local scope
Dim userSessionId As String

'get the session id (if any)
If Not IsNothing(Request.Cookies("UserSession")) Then
  userSessionId = Request.Cookies("UserSession").Value
End If

'check for cookie
If userSessionId <> "" Then

  'block scope
  Dim xReader As XmlTextReader

  'get xml file, parse, and write to form field values
  'create new xml reader object
  xReader = New XmlTextReader( _
    url:=Request.PhysicalApplicationPath & _
    "\fileStore\" & userSessionId & ".xml")

  'read items out of the file and update set values on the form
  xReader.WhitespaceHandling = WhitespaceHandling.None
  While xReader.Read()

    'check for element nodes
    Select Case xReader.NodeType
      Case XmlNodeType.Element

        'check for each element and update control
        Select Case xReader.Name
          Case "TextBoxName"
            TextBoxName.Text = xReader.ReadString()

          Case "TextBoxBack"
            TextBoxBack.Text = xReader.ReadString()

          Case "TextBoxReach"
            TextBoxReach.Text = xReader.ReadString()

          Case "DropDownListCurrently"
            DropDownListCurrently.Items.FindByValue( _
            xReader.ReadString()).Selected = True

          Case "TextBoxEmergency"
            TextBoxEmergency.Text = xReader.ReadString()
```

LISTING 14.4 Continued

```
                Case "LastUpdated"
                    LastUpdatedLabel.Text = xReader.ReadString()

            End Select

        End Select

    End While

    'close the reader
    xReader.Close()

    Else

        'set the last updated text box to nothing
        LastUpdatedLabel.Text = ""

    End If

End Sub
```

When users submit their status data, we must write it out to the file store, which is simply a directory in our application. The first thing we do is check the user's cookie for an original session ID. If the user has no cookie—whether it is because it is the user's first time accessing the page or because the cookie has expired—we write one out using the Response object. We set the cookie's expiration date to be one month from the current date.

After we have a valid cookie, we are ready to write our XML stream. We use the session ID taken from the cookie value as the filename. We first create an instance of the XmlTextWriter class. This class allows us to write XML elements directly to the file. We pass the element name and the string value on the method call WriteElementString.

Finally, we close the XmlTextWriter instance and redirect the user back to the home page.

```
Private Sub Button1_Click(ByVal sender As System.Object, _
    ByVal e As System.EventArgs) Handles Button1.Click

    'purpose: respond to update button (user submit)
    '         update the user's XML data file

    'local scope
    Dim origSessionId As String

    'check for the user's cookie, if not write out
    If Not IsNothing(Request.Cookies("UserSession")) Then
```

LISTING 14.4 Continued

```
    origSessionId = Request.Cookies.Item("UserSession").Value.ToString
End If

'check for a cookie value
If origSessionId = "" Then

  'block scope
  Dim myCookie As HttpCookie

  'no cookie exists, write one out
  origSessionId = Session.SessionID

  'create a cookie
  myCookie = New HttpCookie( _
    name:="UserSession", _
    value:=origSessionId)

  'set the cookie's expiration date to be one month from now
  myCookie.Expires = DateAdd(DateInterval.Month, 1, Now)

  'add the cookie to the response
  Response.Cookies.Add(cookie:=myCookie)

End If

'add each form element to the xml stream
Dim xWriter As XmlTextWriter

'creates a new xml text writer object
'if the file exists it will write over it (nothing=UTF-8)
xWriter = New XmlTextWriter( _
  filename:=(Request.PhysicalApplicationPath & _
  "\fileStore\" & origSessionId & ".xml"), _
  encoding:=Nothing)

'write the xml out to the file
'start the xml element
xWriter.WriteStartElement(localName:="Status")

'add the sessionid to the status element as an attribute
xWriter.WriteAttributeString( _
  localName:="UserSession", _
  value:=origSessionId)
```

LISTING 14.4 Continued

```
   'write each form field as an xml element
   xWriter.WriteElementString( _
     localName:="TextBoxName", _
     value:=Request.Form("TextBoxName").ToString)

   xWriter.WriteElementString( _
     localName:="TextBoxBack", _
     value:=Request.Form("TextBoxBack").ToString)

   xWriter.WriteElementString( _
     localName:="TextBoxReach", _
     value:=Request.Form("TextBoxReach").ToString)

   xWriter.WriteElementString( _
     localName:="DropDownListCurrently", _
     value:=Request.Form("DropDownListCurrently").ToString)

   xWriter.WriteElementString( _
     localName:="TextBoxEmergency", _
     value:=Request.Form("TextBoxEmergency").ToString)

   xWriter.WriteElementString( _
     localName:="LastUpdated", _
     value:=Now.ToString)

   'end the element
   xWriter.WriteEndElement()

   'close the xml stream
   xWriter.Close()

   'redirect the user back to the home page
   Response.Redirect("home.aspx")

 End Sub

End Class
```

The XML

An example of the XML that gets written to the file is presented in Figure 14.4.

FIGURE 14.4

XML data file.

Summary

ASP.NET, although still familiar, represents a radical upgrade from previous versions. This chapter simply scratched the surface of what is available. The use of the .NET Framework Class Library ensures consistent object-oriented development rather than the spaghetti code of old. We think that as you explore more of its features, you'll soon find ASP.NET and the System.Web namespace as indispensable as VB .NET itself.

The following are key points presented in this chapter:

- The System.Web namespace exposes the HttpRequest and HttpResponse objects used when working with HTTP.

- Data can be passed on the URL using a query string. This data is accessible as a collection from the Request object.

- Forms get posted to a Web page. This data is exposed to the Request object using the Form collection.

- The HttpBrowserCapabilities class enables you to ascertain a client's capabilities.

- You can store and retrieve application-level state information (accessible to all ASP.NET pages in your site) using the HttpApplicationState class.

- User-specific state can be managed in a number of ways, including using hidden form fields with the ViewState object, cookies, and session state using the HttpSessionState class.

Data Storage and Access

IN THIS CHAPTER

Some of the fundamental questions that developers ask during system design are: Should the application persist its data somewhere? If so, where and how? Persisting, or storing, data for later use is such a core concept that many of us simply take it as a "given" when we write our applications. Whether we store state in a database, in an INI file, or in the registry, we are forced to employ design patterns ranging from simple data queries and record inserts, to complicated transactional programming and schema manipulation.

Visual Basic traditionally has had very rich support for implementing data storage, particularly with relational databases. Although in the history of Visual Basic it is a relatively recent "invention," ADO (ActiveX Data Objects) is a cornerstone technology for allowing developers to abstract data storage concepts in their code. ADO has been extended into the .NET world with the `System.Data`, `System.Data.Common`, `System.Data.OleDb`, `System.Data.SqlClient`, and `System.Data.SqlTypes` namespaces. Collectively, the `System.Data.*` namespaces are often referred to as ADO.NET—a clear indication of its technical legacy.

In this chapter, we examine common programming tasks related to the storage and access of data, primarily with relational databases.

We'll begin by providing a brief introduction to ADO.NET and examining the several paradigm changes it brings. Then, we discuss how to connect to a database, issue SQL commands to a database, and work with stored procedures. Finally, we examine how to handle errors, work with transactions, and examine relational schemas.

After reading this chapter, you should have a firm grasp of the following:

- Connecting to a database
- Querying a database for data, and then processing the data that has been returned
- Programming SQL commands in a transactional environment

Key Classes Related to Data

The .NET namespaces concerned with data access are organized into three categories: a namespace that holds common functionality to be shared among the different .NET data providers (the `System.Data.Common` namespace), a namespace that holds generic components for data manipulation (the `System.Data` namespace), and separate namespaces for each .NET data provider (at the time of this writing, the `System.Data.OleDb` namespace and the `System.Data.SqlClient` namespace).

Table 15.1 itemizes the classes and related structures that are covered in this chapter across the referenced namespaces.

TABLE 15.1 Key Classes Covered

Class/Structure	Description
System.Data Namespace	This namespace houses the core classes necessary for persisting data.
Constraint	This class represents a relational constraint that can be imposed on a DataColumn object.
ConstraintCollection	This class represents a collection of Constraint objects applied against a DataTable object.
ConstraintException	This exception class represents a violation of a Constraint object.
DataColumn	This class encapsulates a column schema.
DataColumnCollection	This class represents a collection of DataColumn objects associated to a DataTable.
DataException	This is the primary exception class, used to indicate errors encountered when accessing a data source.
DataRelation	This class defines a parent-to-child relationship between two or more tables.
DataRelationCollection	This class represents a collection of DataRelation objects.
DataRow	This class encapsulates a row of data stored in a DataTable object.
DataRowCollection	This class holds a collection of DataRow objects associated with a DataTable object.
DataSet	This class is used to encapsulate and organize data from a database; it wraps a set of DataTable objects.
DataTable	This class represents a table from a database.
DataTableCollection	This class holds a collection of DataTable instances.
ForeignKeyConstraint	This class inherits from the Constraint class and is used to represent a foreign-key relationship between two tables.
PropertyCollection	This class is used to define properties for a DataSet, a DataColumn, or a DataTable object.
System.Data.Common Namespace	This namespace holds classes that are shared among data providers.
DataAdapter	A DataAdapter is used to encapsulate commands and connection information for a particular data source.

TABLE 15.1   Continued

Class/Structure	Description
DataColumnMapping	This class is used to link columns in a DataTable with an actual data store column.
DataColumnMappingCollection	This class holds a collection of DataColumnMapping objects.
DataTableMapping	This class is used to map a DataTable with an actual data store table.
DataTableMappingCollection	This class holds a collection of DataTableMapping objects.
DBDataPermission	This class represents security levels and permissions used to control communication through a .NET data provider.
DBDataPermissionAttribute	This class associates a particular action with a security attribute.
System.Data.OleDb	This namespace houses classes used to access OLE DB data sources.
OleDbCommand	This class encapsulates a SQL command (or stored procedure).
OleDbCommandBuilder	This class is used to automatically generate SQL commands to reconcile changes made in a DataSet with the underlying data store.
OleDbConnection	This class wraps a connection to an OLE DB data store.
OleDbDataReader	This class is used to implement forward-only streams of data (DataRows) from a data source.
OleDbError	This class represents an error returned from a database.
OleDbErrorCollection	This class is a collection of OleDbError objects.
OleDbParameter	This class represents a parameter to an OleDbCommand object.
OleDbTransaction	This class represents a transaction constructed against a specific data source.
System.Data.SqlClient	This namespace holds classes used to access SQL Server databases.
SqlClientPermission	This class represents security levels and permissions used to control communication to a SQL Server database (inherits from DBDataPermission).

TABLE 15.1 Continued

Class/Structure	Description
SqlCommand	This class encapsulates a SQL command (or stored procedure) specific to SQL Server.
SqlCommandBuilder	This class is used to automatically generate SQL commands to reconcile changes made in a DataSet with the underlying data store.
SqlConnection	This class wraps a connection to a SQL Server database.

An Overview of ADO.NET

In ADO.NET, components are categorized into one of two categories: data manipulation and access through direct communication to a database, and data manipulation and access against in-memory copies of data (generated from a variety of different sources). *Data providers* supply the direct communication pipeline; they function as a data manipulation layer that sits between your code and a specific underlying data source. The DataSet component is responsible for allowing in-memory representations of both data and data schema.

Data Manipulation with Data Providers

As we have said, a data provider implements a layer of technology between your code and a database. Data providers are actually supplied by the .NET Framework and work to encapsulate the code necessary to connect to a specific database and issue commands to that database. The .NET Framework currently has two data providers: one for SQL Server (the SQL Server .NET Data Provider) and one for any OLE DB–compliant data source (the OLE DB .NET Data Provider).

The SQL Server .NET Data Provider is designed and optimized to work specifically with SQL Server 7.0 or later. In general, if you can be assured that your application will be working solely against SQL Server as its data store, you should use this data provider. It gives you support for Transact-SQL, and other SQL Server–specific functionality. Functionality for this data provider is exposed through the System.Data.SqlClient namespace.

The OLE DB .NET Data Provider actually works with OLE DB data sources by directly talking to the OLE DB COM library. If your application requires a certain degree of database agnosticism, this is the provider you should use. Although it currently supports only OLE DB Provider for SQL Server, Oracle, and Microsoft Jet, other OLE DB providers will be added as they become available. This data provider fully supports transactions.

Its functionality is exposed through the `System.Data.OleDb` namespace.

Each data provider is implemented in a separate namespace that will contain:

- A `Connection` object to handle database connections
- A `Command` object to issue commands to a database and return data
- A `DataReader` object to access data streams from the database
- A `DataAdapter` object that connects `DataSet` objects with the underlying data in the data source.

These objects are all based on different interfaces defined in the `System.Data` namespace. The interfaces are inherited by different classes (such as `System.Data.SqlClient`) inside the data provider namespaces to implement base functionality while providing functionality enhanced and targeted at a specific data source.

To understand exactly how data providers expose functionality, it will be helpful to examine the generic intent, properties, and methods of each of these interfaces.

The `Connection` Object

The `Connection` object is implemented by the individual data providers through the `IDbConnection` interface. For instance, the SQL Server Data Provider defines its connection class like this:

```
NotInheritable Public Class SqlConnection
    Inherits Component
    Implements ICloneable, IDbConnection
```

Whereas the OLE DB Data Provider defines its connection class like this:

```
NotInheritable Public Class OleDbConnection
    Inherits Component
    Implements ICloneable, IDbConnection
```

The naming convention that is used by data providers for their specific connection class follows this format: `<provider_tag><Connection>`, in which `<provider_tag>` is the unique class prefix shared by that particular provider's classes. This naming standard is actually applied to all the classes in a given data provider's namespace—thus, we have `SqlConnection` versus `OleDbConnection`, and `SqlCommand` versus `OleDbCommand`, and so on.

The `IDbConnection` interface supports the properties and methods shown in Tables 15.2 and 15.3. We look at the specific implementations of each of these later in the chapter when we deal with code actually written for a selected data provider.

TABLE 15.2 Properties and Methods of the `IDbConnection` Interface

Property	Description
ConnectionString	A connection string identifying the parameters necessary to establish a connection to a database
ConnectionTimeout	An `Integer` value indicating how long a connection class should wait before abandoning a nonresponding connection request
Database	A `String` identifying the name of the database to be used after a successful connection
State	A `ConnectionState` value representing the current state of the connection

Method	Description
BeginTransaction	Starts a database transaction
ChangeDatabase	Changes the database for the current connection
Close	Closes the connection to the database
CreateCommand	Creates an `IDbCommand` object
Open	Opens a database connection using the parameters supplied in the `ConnectionString` property

The `Command` Object

Command objects have their core functions defined through the `IDbCommand` interface. The following are the SQL Server and OLE DB Data Provider implementations for their respective Command objects:

```
NotInheritable Public Class SqlCommand
    Inherits Component
    Implements ICloneable, IDbCommand


NotInheritable Public Class OleDbCommand
    Inherits Component
    Implements ICloneable, IDbCommand
```

Command objects are responsible for encapsulating SQL statements and conveying them to a data source for processing. Table 15.3 shows the properties and methods supported by the `IDbCommand` interface.

15

TABLE 15.3   Properties and Methods of the `IDbCommand` Interface

Property	Description
CommandText	A `String` representing the command to be issued to the database
CommandTimeout	An `Integer` value indicating how long the command object should wait before abandoning a nonresponsive command
CommandType	A `CommandType` value indicating the type of command being issued
Connection	The `IDbConnection` interface through which the command should be issued
Parameters	Returns an `IDataParameterCollection` instance representing the parameters used for the SQL command or stored procedure
Transaction	The `IDbTransaction` interface representing a transaction instance that the SQL command should execute within
UpdatedRowSource	An `UpdateRowSource` value that specifies how results of the SQL command are applied to the row being updated

Method	Description
Cancel	Cancels the execution of the current command
CreateParameter	Creates a new `IDataParameter` instance
ExecuteNonQuery	Executes a SQL command against the data source and returns the number of rows affected (designed to be used with queries that don't return data)
ExecuteReader	Executes a SQL command and creates an `IDataReader` instance to deal with the returned data
ExecuteScalar	Executes a SQL command and returns the first column in the resultset (all other columns are ignored)
Prepare	Prepares a compiled version of the SQL command

The `DataReader` Object

The `IDataReader` interface provides the base level of functionality for a data provider's `DataReader` object. The SQL Server provider defines the `SqlDataReader` class, whereas the OLE DB provider defines the `OleDbDataReader` class.

`DataReader` classes provide a way to access resultsets returned from a database as streams. `DataReader` objects are not created directly; they are created by calling the `ExecuteReader` method from a data provider's `Command` object implementation.

The stream exposed by the `DataReader` is used for forward-only processing through the resultset.

Table 15.4 shows the properties and methods of the IDataReader interface.

TABLE 15.4 Properties and Methods of the IDataReader Interface

Property	Description
Depth	An Integer that indicates how many levels deep in a hierarchy the current row sits
IsClosed	A Boolean value indicating whether the data reader is closed
RecordsAffected	An Integer count of the rows affected by execution of a SQL command

Method	Description
Close	Closes the data reader
GetSchemaTable	Returns a DataTable instance containing the metadata for the data reader content
NextResult	Moves the data reader one resultset forward in the resultset stream
Read	Moves the data reader one record forward in the resultset stream

The DataAdapter Object

Data adapters are implemented by inheriting the IDataAdapter interface. The SQL Server Data Provider gives us the SqlDataAdapter class, and the OLE DB Data Provider provides the OleDbDataAdapter class.

Data adapters primarily exist to fill DataSet objects with data from a data source and act as the link between in-memory data representations and a selected data source. The properties and methods of the IDataAdapter interface are documented in Table 15.5.

TABLE 15.5 Properties and Methods of the IDataAdapter Interface

Property	Description
MissingMappingAction	A MissingMappingAction enumeration value that tells the data adapter what to do in the event of a missing mapping
MissingSchemaAction	A MissingSchemaAction enumeration value that tells the data adapter what to do if data is being added to a DataSet and a required DataTable or DataColumn is missing
TableMappings	An ITableMappingCollection instance that tells the data adapter how a particular source table is mapped to a data set table

TABLE 15.5 Continued

Method	Description
Fill	Creates a DataTable inside a DataSet whose rows match those of the corresponding table in the data source
FillSchema	Creates a DataTable inside a DataSet and configures its schema to match that of a specific data source
GetFillParameters	Moves the data reader one resultset forward in the resultset stream
Update	Causes SQL commands to be generated that will cause the data source data to change to resemble the current data in the data set

Data Access with the DataSet Class

The second mechanism by which .NET supports data storage and access is through in-memory representations of data. The DataSet class is a representation of data that is actually stored in a data source. With its collection of DataTable objects and DataRelation objects, it really represents a virtual, in-memory database (or subset of a database).

DataSet objects are inherently "disconnected"—that is, they operate and exist without needing an active connection to a database. As a result, they are a perfect mechanism to be employed in tiered applications that must scale well.

Schema Representation

DataTable objects manifest their schema through their DataColumn objects (referenced from the DataTable's Columns property, which returns a DataColumnCollection instance). Column objects will store their name and data type and can also contain "expression" formulas for computing column values.

Data Representation

Inside of each data set, data is represented as DataRow objects. Each DataRow object will conform to a specific schema for a specific table; for this reason, you can't directly create a DataRow instance. It must be created using the NewRow method on a DataTable object. Each DataRow object will specify a value for each DataColumn instance represented in a DataTable's schema.

Figure 15.1 shows how all the different ADO.NET building blocks interact with one another.

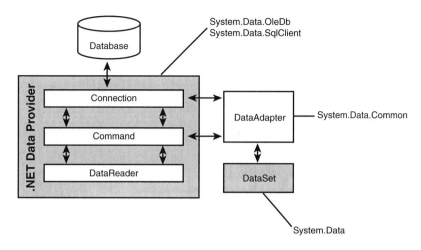

Figure 15.1
ADO.NET architecture.

Now that we have examined some of the core building blocks for ADO, let's look at how to exercise them through code. We will use the OLE DB Data Provider in most of the examples; where significant or interesting items of note exist with the SQL Server Data Provider, we cover those as well.

You can query and affect data stored in a database by two principle means: The first involves SQL commands issued through a command object. The second involves populating and manipulating data sets in memory. In the next two sections, we examine each of these methods.

Queries and Resultsets

One of the simplest actions you can perform against a database is to retrieve data from a table. Let's assume you are writing an interface into a Human Resources database and need to retrieve a list of employees' last names from the employee table.

Establishing a Connection

Using ADO.NET, how would you approach this relatively simple task? Normally, the first step is to establish a connection to the desired database. For this example, we make the following assumptions: the HR database we are interested in resides inside a Microsoft SQL Server 2000 database, on a server called HR-DB01. The database itself is called "dbHumanRes," and the table that holds all the employee records is called "employee."

We also assume that a design goal requires us to use the OLE DB Data Provider instead of the SQL Server Data Provider. That means that we will want to reference the `System.Data.OleDb` namespace:

```
Imports System.Data
Imports System.Data.OleDb
```

Next, we need to create our connection string. We can assign this to a string variable that we will then use to create the connection object:

```
Dim connStr As String

connStr = "Provider=SQLOLEDB;Data Source=HR-DB01;" & _
          "Integrated Security=SSPI;Initial Catalog=dbHumanRes"
```

Note that the actual syntax and elements required for a connection string can and will change, depending on the data source you are going after and on the particulars of the particular database installation you are programming against. See the MSDN Platform SDK documentation for the complete definition of OLE DB and native SQL Server connection strings.

After we have the connection string set up the way we need it, we can create our connection object (in this case, an `OleDbConnection` object) by passing the string into the object's constructor, like this:

```
Dim dbConn As OleDbConnection = New OleDbConnection(connStr)
```

Now, the only thing left to do is to actually open the connection. This is done with the `Open` method:

```
bConn.Open()
```

Let's leave the topic of error handling alone for the time being and assume that the connection works. With a valid and working connection to the database, we can now create the SQL command and issue it through the open connection.

Constructing and Issuing a SQL Command

Because at this point we are interested only in retrieving a resultset from a `SELECT` statement, we need to concern ourselves only with the command object and a `DataReader` object. A `DataSet` class at this point would be overkill. To create the command object that will wrap our `SELECT` query, we first put the SQL query into a string and then pass it into an `OleDbCommand` object's constructor (along with the previously created connection object). We also indicate to the `command` object that the command text (assigned to the string 'query') is just that: simple text. We are not executing a stored procedure.

```
'Create a string with our command text
Dim query As String = "SELECT last_name FROM employee"

'Create a new command object using the command text and
```

```
'the previously created connection object
Dim selectQry As New OleDbCommand(query, dbConn)

'Flag the nature of the command text...
selectQry.CommandType = CommandType.Text
```

The `OleDbCommand.CommandType` property equates to one of the `CommandType` enumeration values (shown in Table 15.6). If we were calling a stored procedure, we would have used the `CommandType.StoredProcedure` value.

TABLE 15.6 The `CommandType` Enumeration

Member	Description
StoredProcedure	The `CommandText` property contains the name of a stored procedure.
TableDirect	The `CommandText` property contains the name of a table; the Command object will return all rows and all columns for the identified table.
Text	The `CommandText` property contains a SQL text command.

After setting the `Command` object's `CommandText` property (which we have done implicitly by supplying the command text in the constructor), and after setting the `OleDbCommand.CommandType` property, we are ready to issue the command to the database. There are three ways to actually issue the command to the database: with the `ExecuteNonQuery` method, the `ExecuteReader` method, and the `ExecuteScalar` method. If we think back to the definitions that we have provided for each of these (back in our discussion of `Command` objects and the `IDbCommand` interface), we can see that only one option exists for us: the `ExecuteReader` method. The `ExecuteScalar` method won't work, because it is designed to return only the first column of the first row in the resultset. The `ExecuteNonQuery` method won't work, because it won't actually return a resultset; it simply returns a count of the number of rows affected by the issued command.

The `ExecuteReader` method will send our `SELECT` query through the associated database connection object and create an `OleDbDataReader` instance to deal with the returning resultset:

```
Dim dataReader As OleDbDataReader = selectQry.ExecuteReader()
```

Normally, calling the `ExecuteReader` with no parameters is sufficient; it certainly does the job that it was needed to do for this example. But an overloaded version of `ExecuteReader` exists, which accepts a `CommandBehavior` enumeration value as a parameter. To see some of the options that are available when using this version of the `ExecuteReader` method, see Table 15.7, which documents the different values of the `CommandBehavior` enumeration. Note that these `CommandBehavior` values can be combined bitwise.

TABLE 15.7   The `CommandBehavior` Enumeration

Member	Description
CloseConnection	Automatically closes the data reader's associated connection object when the data reader is closed.
KeyInfo	Primary key info is returned along with the column data; no locks are placed on the returned rows or columns (for applicability, see the Browse Mode documentation in the SQL Server Books Online).
SchemaOnly	Query returns column metadata only.
SequentialAccess	The resultset is read sequentially, column by column.
SingleResult	The query returns a single result.
SingleRow	The query returns a single row.

Working with the Resultset

At this point, our `dataReader` object will expose a data stream mapped to the resultset generated by our `SELECT` query. If we wanted to enumerate that resultset and write its values out to a console window, we can set up a very simple loop based on the `OleDbDataReader.Read` method:

```
While dataReader.Read()
    Console.WriteLine(dataReader.GetString(0))
End While
```

We can use two methods to extract information from the data reader: the `Read` method advances the read cursor through the resultset record by record. When it reaches the end of the resultset, it will return `False` (thus ending our `While` loop). Inside the `While` loop, we are calling the `GetString` method off our `dataReader` object. The `OleDbDataReader` class adds quite a few `Get` methods to the default roster of methods defined by the `IDbDataReader` interface. Each of these `Get` methods is designed to return a resultset value for a specific column, in a specific format. Because we know that we are going after a "last name" value with our query, we are explicitly asking for values back from the resultset as strings. The zero that we pass into the `GetString` method simply identifies the column that we want the data from (columns are numbered with a zero-based system).

Table 15.8 identifies some of the `Get` methods supported by the `OleDbDataReader` class.

TABLE 15.8 Partial List of Methods of the `OleDbDataReader` Class

Member	Description
GetBoolean	Returns the value contained in the specified column as a Boolean
GetByte	Returns the value contained in the specified column as a Boolean
GetChar	Returns the value contained in the specified column as a Boolean
GetDataTypeName	Returns the name of the underlying data type for the data contained in the specified column
GetDateTime	Returns the value contained in the specified column as a Boolean
GetDecimal	Returns the value contained in the specified column as a Boolean
GetDouble	Returns the value contained in the specified column as a Boolean
GetFieldType	Returns the `Type` value of the data contained in the specified column
GetFloat	Returns the value contained in the specified column as a Boolean
GetGuid	Returns the value contained in the specified column as a Boolean
GetInt16	Returns the value contained in the specified column as a Boolean
GetInt32	Returns the value contained in the specified column as a Boolean
GetInt64	Returns the value contained in the specified column as a Boolean
GetName	Returns the name of the specified column
GetOrdinal	Returns the ordinal of the specified column
GetSchemaTable	Returns a `DataTable` instance containing the metadata of the specified column
GetString	Returns the value contained in the specified column as a Boolean
GetTimeSpan	Returns the value contained in the specified column as a `TimeSpan` object
GetValue	Returns the value contained in the specified column as an `Object` instance

Now that you have seen a simple example of connecting to a database, issuing a SELECT statement, and processing the returned data, we can look at a slightly more complicated scenario through which we can explore the concepts of data updates.

 Suggestions for Further Exploration

➲ Cases can occur in which multiple resultsets are returned to a DataReader (consider a command or stored procedure that issues two SELECT commands). For information on how to move the DataReader from one resultset to another, investigate the DataReader.NextResult method.

⊃ Working with hierarchical resultsets (also known as chapters) is possible by specifying the MSDataShape provider in your connection string. For more information on working with chapters in ADO.NET, search the .NET Framework documentation for OLE DB chapters.

Updating Data Directly to a Database

You have already seen how to issue queries directly to a database—now let's see how we can issue SQL commands that will perform record inserts or updates. To do this, we'll need to explore a little more of the fictional HR database that we have touched on previously. Let's suppose that the HR database holds, in addition to the employee table, a division table: Each employee belongs to a division of the company, and a division will have one or more employees working for it. The relationship, for those familiar with entity-relationship diagrams, is shown in Figure 15.2.

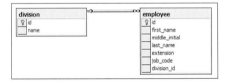

FIGURE 15.2
Entity relationship diagram: employee and division tables.

We should also go ahead and define the full schema for both the employee table (shown in Table 15.9) and the division table (shown in Table 15.10).

TABLE 15.9   The Employee Table Schema

Field	Description
Id	SQL Server Data type: int
	Length: 4
	Notes: primary key for this table; uniquely identifies employee records. This is an auto-incrementing identity column.
first_name	SQL Server Data type: varchar
	Length: 25
	Notes: employee's first name
middle_initial	SQL Server Data type: char
	Length: 1
	Notes: first initial of employee's middle name

TABLE 15.9 Continued

Field	Description
last_name	SQL Server Data type: varchar
	Length: 25
	Notes: employee's last name
extension	SQL Server Data type: char
	Length: 4
	Notes: employee's 4-digit extension
job_code	SQL Server Data type: char
	Length: 4
	Notes: employee's HR job code classification
division_id	SQL Server Data type: int
	Length: 4
	Notes: foreign key to the division table; represents the division the employee belongs to

TABLE 15.10 The Division Table Schema

Field	Description
Id	SQL Server Data type: int
	Length: 4
	Notes: primary key for this table; uniquely identifies division records. This is an auto-incrementing identity column.
name	SQL Server Data type: varchar
	Length: 25
	Notes: division's name

Suppose that we want to build a simple SQL statement that inserts the data for a new employee into the employee table. Let's assume, for instance, that we want to process the following INSERT statement:

```
INSERT INTO employee (first_name, middle_initial, last_name,
extension, job_code, division_id)
VALUES ('Burton', 'John', 'M', '5001', 'DEV', 3)
```

The first parameter provides the last name, the second parameter provides the first name, and so on (per the schema discussed in Table 15.9), closing out with the ID of the division record related to this employee (3).

15

Issuing this INSERT statement involves some of the same steps as our previous example that issued a SELECT statement against the database. We must first open a connection to the database and then issue a command across that connection. Finally, we want to be able to respond to any data returned from the database as a result of the SQL command.

Assuming that we have previously captured all the pertinent employee information in variables, we have a choice in this case. We can either build up a string containing the whole of the SQL command, or we can build up a basic SQL command with placeholders for the actual record values and then pass in these values in a second step using parameters.

SQL Commands with Static Strings

Listing 15.1 shows one possible code path that will build up the required SQL string and then issue it for execution to the database.

LISTING 15.1   A Record Insert Through String Concatenation

```
Imports System.Data
Imports System.Data.OleDb
Imports System.Text

Module Module1

    Sub Main()
        Dim dbConn As OleDbConnection
        Dim connStr As String

        Dim firstName As String = "John"
        Dim middleInitial As String = "M"
        Dim lastName As String = "Burton"
        Dim extension As String = "5001"
        Dim jobCode As String = "DEV"
        Dim divID As Integer = 3

        Try

            connStr = "Provider=SQLOLEDB;Data Source=HR-DB01;" & _
                      "Integrated Security=SSPI;Initial Catalog=dbHumanRes"

            dbConn = New OleDbConnection(connStr)

            Console.WriteLine("Trying db connect with -> {0}", connStr)
            dbConn.Open()

            Dim query As StringBuilder = _
                New StringBuilder("INSERT INTO employee VALUES")
```

LISTING 15.1 Continued

```
            'build up the SQL command through concatenation of variable values
            query = query.Append("(")
            query = query.Append("'" & firstName & "',")
            query = query.Append("'" & middleInitial & "',")
            query = query.Append("'" & lastName & "',")
            query = query.Append("'" & extension & "',")
            query = query.Append("'" & jobCode & "',")
            query = query.Append(divID)
            query = query.Append(")")

            'Create a new command object using the command text and
            'the previously created connection object
            Dim insertQry As New OleDbCommand(query.ToString, dbConn)

            'Flag the nature of the command text...
            insertQry.CommandType = CommandType.Text

            Console.WriteLine("Trying command -> {0}", query.ToString)
            Dim rowsAffected As Integer = insertQry.ExecuteNonQuery()

            Console.WriteLine("{0} rows inserted.", rowsAffected)

        Catch appErr As Exception
            Console.WriteLine("An error occurred with the INSERT command.")
        Finally
            dbConn.Close()
        End Try

    End Sub

End Module
```

To run this code sample, you will need to create your own database schema in a local SQL Server database and change the connection string accordingly.

We have done a few things of note here. For one, because we are building up a SQL command string by concatenating variables, we are using the `StringBuilder` class instead of the `String` class to avoid performance penalties dealing with the immutable characteristic of `String` values. Second, we are using the `ExecuteNonQuery` method instead of the `ExecuteReader` method because we don't expect our SQL to return data. The `ExecuteNonQuery` method returns a count of the rows affected, providing us with a convenient way to determine if the insert worked as expected. Notice that we have also implemented a rudimentary error handler.

SQL Commands with Parameters

Another possible way to process the employee insert command would be to use a parameterized SQL command. This involves building a SQL string with tokens or placeholders for the actual values required. The Command object will attempt to replace the placeholders in the SQL string with values specified in its Parameters property.

Listing 15.2 shows code that performs an identical task to Listing 15.1, but this time we are passing in the employee values as parameters instead of static text. This way might be preferred if you need to generalize the routine so that it can handle any data passed to it (instead of just the hard-coded variables we are showing here).

Nothing else changes in the code.

LISTING 15.2   A Record Insert with Parameters

```
Imports System.Data
Imports System.Data.OleDb
Imports System.Text

Module Module1

    Sub Main()
        Dim dbConn As OleDbConnection
        Dim connStr As String

        Dim firstName As String = "John"
        Dim middleInitial As String = "M"
        Dim lastName As String = "Burton"
        Dim extension As String = "5001"
        Dim jobCode As String = "DEV"
        Dim divID As Integer = 3

        Try

            connStr = "Provider=SQLOLEDB;Data Source=DB01;" & _
                      "Integrated Security=SSPI;Initial Catalog=test"

            dbConn = New OleDbConnection(connStr)

            Console.WriteLine("Trying db connect with -> {0}", connStr)
            dbConn.Open()

            Dim query As StringBuilder = _
                New StringBuilder("INSERT INTO employee VALUES")

            'build up the SQL command with placeholders
```

LISTING 15.2 Continued

```
        query = query.Append("(")
        query = query.Append("?,")
        query = query.Append("?,")
        query = query.Append("?,")
        query = query.Append("?,")
        query = query.Append("?,")
        query = query.Append("?")
        query = query.Append(")")

        'Create a new command object using the command text and
        'the previously created connection object
        Dim insertQry As New OleDbCommand(query.ToString, dbConn)

        insertQry.Parameters.Add("lastname", lastName)
        insertQry.Parameters.Add("firstname", firstName)
        insertQry.Parameters.Add("mi", middleInitial)
        insertQry.Parameters.Add("ext", extension)
        insertQry.Parameters.Add("jobcode", jobCode)
        insertQry.Parameters.Add("div", divID)

        'Flag the nature of the command text...
        insertQry.CommandType = CommandType.Text

        Console.WriteLine("Trying command -> {0}", query.ToString)
        Dim rowsAffected As Integer = insertQry.ExecuteNonQuery()

        Console.WriteLine("{0} rows inserted.", rowsAffected)

    Catch appErr As Exception
        Console.WriteLine("An error occurred: {0}", appErr.Message)
        Console.ReadLine()
    Finally
        dbConn.Close()
    End Try

End Sub

End ModuleEnd Module
```

Note that we have simply substituted question marks for values in the SQL statement. The OLE DB .NET Data Provider will resolve these placeholders to actual values taken, in order, from the Parameters collection. The SQL Server .NET Data Provider enables you to specify parameters by name, thereby eliminating the need to add parameters to the Parameters collection in the exact order that they will be used in the SQL statement.

Placing SQL Commands in Transactions

ADO.NET supports transactions through the `Connection` object and an associated `Transaction` object. The `Connection` object exposes a `BeginTransaction` method that in turn returns a transaction object (type specific to the actual data provider). With the OLE DB provider, for instance, the following code will produce a transaction object that can be used to provide transactional context for SQL queries:

```
Dim cmd As New SqlCommand()
Dim trans As OleDbTransaction

'Spawn a transaction on the current connection (dbConn)
trans = dbConn.BeginTransaction(IsolationLevel.ReadCommitted, "Test")
cmd.Transaction = trans
```

First, the transaction is created from the connection object and assigned to an `OleDbTransaction` object. Then, the transaction object is assigned to a command component (represented here by the cmd object) so that each command issued is enrolled in the transaction. Note that the `BeginTransaction` method accepts an `IsolationLevel` enumeration value and a name for the transaction. Table 15.11 shows the different `IsolationLevel` enumeration values.

TABLE 15.11 The `IsolationLevel` Enumeration

Member	Description
Chaos	If there are pending changes from another transaction that is more highly isolated, the transactions will not be overwritten.
ReadCommitted	Shared locks are issued to prevent dirty reads, but data can be changed before the end of the transaction.
ReadUncommitted	No shared locks are issued (dirty reads are not prevented).
RepeatableRead	Locks are placed on all query-related data elements.
Serializable	For `DataSet` objects, places a range lock on the `DataSet`; the dataset will be locked until the transaction has completed.
Unspecified	The isolation level cannot be determined.

The transaction object enables you to complete the transaction through its `Commit` method or roll back any current changes in the transaction with its Rollback command.

In the code shown in Listing 15.3, the intent is to insert all three divisions into the division table or fail the insert operation altogether. Notice that we leverage the `Try Catch` block to determine whether we should issue a `Commit` command or a `Rollback` command.

LISTING 15.3 Commands Issued Inside a Transaction

```vb
Imports System.Data
Imports System.Data.OleDb

Module Module1

    Sub Main()
        Dim dbConn As OleDbConnection
        Dim connStr As String
        Dim trans As OleDbTransaction
        Dim rowsAffected As Integer
        Dim query As String

        connStr = "Provider=SQLOLEDB;Data Source=HR-DB01;" & _
            "Integrated Security=SSPI;Initial Catalog=dbHumanRes"

        Try

            dbConn = New OleDbConnection(connStr)

            Console.WriteLine("Trying db connect with -> {0}", connStr)
            dbConn.Open()

            Console.WriteLine("Starting transaction...")

            'Start the transaction
            trans = dbConn.BeginTransaction(IsolationLevel.ReadCommitted)

            'Create the command object and assign the transaction
            'context
            Dim insertQry As New OleDbCommand()
            insertQry.Connection = dbConn
            insertQry.Transaction = trans

            'First insert
            query = "INSERT INTO division VALUES ('Operations')"
            insertQry.CommandType = CommandType.Text
            insertQry.CommandText = query
            insertQry.ExecuteNonQuery()

            'Second insert
            query = "INSERT INTO division VALUES ('Administration')"
            insertQry.CommandType = CommandType.Text
            insertQry.CommandText = query
            insertQry.ExecuteNonQuery()
```

LISTING 15.3   Continued

```
                'Third, and final, insert
                query = "INSERT INTO division VALUES ('Administration')"
                insertQry.CommandType = CommandType.Text
                insertQry.CommandText = query
                insertQry.ExecuteNonQuery()

                'Finalize the transaction
                trans.Commit()

                Console.WriteLine("Transaction committed.")

        Catch appErr As Exception
            trans.Rollback()
            MsgBox("An error occurred while processing SQL commands: " & _
                appErr.Message)

        Finally
            Console.WriteLine("Hit the ENTER key to exit...")
            Console.ReadLine()
            dbConn.Close()

        End Try

    End Sub

End Module
```

Executing Stored Procedures

Stored procedures are a performance-optimized, robust way to encapsulate and compile queries on a database server. In this section, you see how to execute stored procedures using the SQL Server .NET Data Provider and the classes in the System.Data.SqlClient namespace.

Supplying Input Parameters

If we were to revisit our SQL code responsible for inserting employee records and place that code into a stored procedure, we would end up with something like the SQL code shown in Listing 15.4.

LISTING 15.4 A Record Insert with Parameters

```
USE dbHumanRes
GO
CREATE PROCEDURE insert_employee
            (@id                     int,
             @first_name             varchar(25),
             @middle_initial    char(1),
             @last_name         varchar(25),
             @extension         char(4),
             @job_code          char(4),
             @division_id            int)

AS INSERT INTO [dbHumanRes].[dbo].[employee]
            (id,
             first_name,
             middle_initial,
             last_name,
             extension,
             job_code,
             division_id)

VALUES
            ( @id,
             @first_name,
             @middle_initial,
             @last_name,
             @extension,
             @job_code,
          @division_id)
```

This SQL code can be directly compiled as a stored procedure in SQL Server. Notice that the insert_employee stored procedure accepts seven input parameters. Because parameters are parameters in ADO.NET, regardless of whether we are talking about plain SQL commands or stored procedures, our design pattern established with Listing 15.2 doesn't need to change much. Listing 15.5 shows how we can rework our previous parameterized query code to work with a stored procedure.

To help illustrate the differences and similarities between the OLE DB Data Provider and the SQL Server Data Provider, we have written the code this time around using the components from the System.Data.SqlClient namespace and not the System.Data.OleDb namespace.

LISTING 15.5   A Record Insert Using a Stored Procedure

```vb
Imports System.Data
Imports System.Data.SqlClient
Imports System.Text

Module Module1

    Sub Main()
        Dim dbConn As SqlConnection
        Dim connStr As String

        Dim firstName As String = "John"
        Dim middleInitial As String = "M"
        Dim lastName As String = "Burton"
        Dim extension As String = "5001"
        Dim jobCode As String = "DEV"
        Dim divID As Integer = 3

        Try

            connStr = "Provider=SQLOLEDB;Data Source=HR-DB01;" & _
                    "Integrated Security=SSPI;Initial Catalog=dbHumanRes"

            dbConn = New SqlConnection(connStr)

            Console.WriteLine("Trying db connect with -> {0}", connStr)
            dbConn.Open()

            Dim query As StringBuilder = New StringBuilder("insert_employee")

            'Create a new command object using the command text and
            'the previously created connection object
            Dim insertQry As New SqlCommand(query.ToString, dbConn)

            insertQry.Parameters.Add("@last_name", SqlDbType.VarChar, 25)
            insertQry.Parameters.Add("@first_name", SqlDbType.VarChar, 25)
            insertQry.Parameters.Add("@middle_initial", SqlDbType.Char, 1)
            insertQry.Parameters.Add("@extension", SqlDbType.Char, 4)
            insertQry.Parameters.Add("@job_code", SqlDbType.Char, 4)
            insertQry.Parameters.Add("@division_id", SqlDbType.Int, 4)

            'Flag the nature of the command text...
            insertQry.CommandType = CommandType.StoredProcedure

            Console.WriteLine("Trying command -> {0}", query.ToString)
```

LISTING 15.5 Continued

```
            Dim rowsAffected As Integer = insertQry.ExecuteNonQuery()

            Console.WriteLine("{0} rows inserted.", rowsAffected)

        Catch appErr As Exception
            Console.WriteLine("An error occurred: {0}", appErr.Message)

        Finally
            dbConn.Close()

        End Try

    End Sub

End Module
```

The parameter statements look a bit different from our previous example, as well. Notice that we are free to use named parameters when working with the SqlClient namespace. That is, we can actually identify a parameter by its name (as defined and declared inside the target stored procedure). We don't have to pass parameters in along a fixed order. We are also specifying the data type and size. These should match the parameter declarations in the stored procedures as well. Table 15.12 shows the possible SqlDbType enumeration values.

TABLE 15.12 The SqlDbTypes Enumeration

Member	Description
BigInt	A 64-bit signed integer (equivalent to System.Int64)
Binary	A fixed-length stream of binary data ranging between 1 and 8,000 bytes
Bit	A bit value that can be 0, 1, or null (equivalent to System.Boolean)
Char	A fixed-length stream with a minimum of 1 and a maximum of 8,000 characters (equivalent to System.String)
DateTime	A date and time value (equivalent to System.DateTime)
Decimal	A numeric value with fixed precision and scale (equivalent to System.Decimal)
Float	A floating-point value (equivalent to System.Double)
Image	A stream of binary data, variable in length
Int	A 32-bit signed integer (equivalent to System.Int32)

15

**DATA STORAGE
AND ACCESS**

TABLE 15.12 Continued

Member	Description
Money	A floating-point currency value; has an accuracy to the ten-thousandth of a currency unit (equivalent to `System.Decimal`)
NChar	A fixed-length stream of 1 to 4,000 Unicode characters (data type equivalent: `System.String`)
NText	A variable-length stream of 1 to 1,073,741,823 characters (data type equivalent: `System.String`)
NVarChar	A variable-length stream of 1 to 4,000 Unicode characters (data type equivalent: `System.String`)
Real	A floating-point value (data type equivalent: `System.Single`)
SmallDateTime	A date and time data value (data type equivalent: `System.DateTime`)
SmallInt	A 16-bit signed integer (data type equivalent: `System.Int16`)
SmallMoney	A currency value with an accuracy to the ten-thousandth of a currency unit (data type equivalent: `System.Decimal`)
Text	A variable-length stream of 1 to 2,147,483,647 non-Unicode characters (data type equivalent: `System.String`)
Timestamp	A date and time value in the format of yyyymmddhhmmss (data type equivalent: `System.DateTime`)
TinyInt	An 8-bit unsigned integer (data type equivalent: `System.Byte`)
UniqueIdentifier	A globally unique identifier (data type equivalent: `System.GUID`)
VarBinary	A variable-length stream of binary data of 1 to 8,000 bytes
VarChar	A variable-length stream of 1 to 8,000 non-Unicode characters (data type equivalent: `System.String`)
Variant	A data type that can accommodate varying data formats, including numeric, string, and binary data (data type equivalent: `System.Object`)

Stored procedures also have the capability to place values in output parameters.

Capturing Output Parameters

Listing 15.6 shows a new version of the stored procedure from Listing 15.5. In this version, we have decided to return the ID of the recently inserted row as an output parameter. To do this, we have added one more parameter, `@new_id`, which is identified in the parameters list as an OUTPUT parameter. We have also added a SELECT statement at the end of the stored procedure, which assigns the current value of `@@IDENTITY` (a SQL Server system function) into the `@new_id` parameter. The `@@IDENTITY` function will return the last assigned identity value used by SQL Server. Because the primary key ID column for the employee table is defined as an identity column, the value we see returned here should be the assigned ID value for the employee record that we have just inserted.

LISTING 15.6   Insert Stored Procedure with an Output Parameter

```
USE dbHumanRes
GO
CREATE PROCEDURE insert_employee
            (@id                        int,
             @first_name                varchar(25),
             @middle_initial    char(1),
             @last_name         varchar(25),
             @extension         char(4),
             @job_code          char(4),
             @division_id               int,
 @new_id        int OUTPUT)

AS INSERT INTO [dbHumanRes].[dbo].[employee]
            (id,
             first_name,
             middle_initial,
             last_name,
             extension,
             job_code,
             division_id)

VALUES
            ( @id,
             @first_name,
             @middle_initial,
             @last_name,
             @extension,
             @job_code,
             @division_id)

SET @new_id = @@IDENTITY
```

With this stored procedure in mind, let's consider the changes that we would have to make to our applet. First, we would need another addition to our parameters collection to account for the new @new_id parameter:

```
insertQry.Parameters.Add("@new_id", SqlDbType.Int, 4)
```

There is a problem here: The Add method doesn't allow you to specify a "direction" to the parameter. In other words, there is no way for you to indicate that the @new_id parameter is not an input parameter but is instead an output parameter. However, a property is available on the `SqlParameter` and `OleDbParameter` classes that enables you to specify a direction. The `Direction` property returns or accepts a `ParameterDirection` enumeration value. All the possible `ParameterDirection` values are listed in Table 15.13.

TABLE 15.13   The `ParameterDirection` Enumeration

Member	Description
Input	The parameter is an input parameter.
InputOutput	The parameter can function both as an input parameter and an output parameter.
Output	The parameter is an output parameter.
ReturnValue	The parameter is a return value.

The `Parameters.Add` method actually returns a parameter instance (in this case, `SqlParameter`). With all our previous parameter additions, we have not worried about "catching" this returned parameter object. Here, because we need to set the `Parameter.Direction` property, we do need to worry about it. The code change is simple:

```
Dim parm As SqlParameter
parm = insertQry.Parameters.Add("@new_id", SqlDbType.Int, 4)
parm.Direction = ParameterDirection.Output
```

To examine the contents of the output parameter after the stored procedure has been executed, you would just reference the Value property of the appropriate `SqlParameter` object like this:

```
Console.WriteLine("Assigned ID: {0}", _
    insertQry.Parameters("@new_id").Value)
```

Stored procedures also have the capability to return values outside the parameters interface with a `Return` statement.

Capturing Return Values

To see return values in action, let's take one more pass at our stored procedure. This time, we will be adding code that checks for a special value of 9999 for the employee's extension (perhaps an extension of 9999 is an indication to an operations group that the employee has a phone but still needs his extension configured). Put aside the question of whether or not the stored procedure is the correct place to place logic like this—this example will at least let us verify the syntax for capturing the return value.

Listing 15.7 shows our insert procedure, revised yet again.

LISTING 15.7 Insert Stored Procedure with a `Return` Statement

```
CREATE PROCEDURE insert_employee
        (@id                    int,
         @first_name            varchar(25),
         @middle_initial    char(1),
         @last_name         varchar(25),
         @extension         char(4),
         @job_code          char(4),
         @division_id           int,
         @new_id            int OUTPUT)

AS INSERT INTO [dbHumanRes].[dbo].[employee]
        (id,
         first_name,
         middle_initial,
         last_name,
         extension,
         job_code,
         division_id)

VALUES
        ( @id,
         @first_name,
         @middle_initial,
         @last_name,
         @extension,
         @job_code,
         @division_id)

SET @new_id = @@IDENTITY

IF (SELECT (@extension)) = '9999'
        Return 1
Else
        Return 0
```

Even though return values aren't technically treated as part of the parameters collection by SQL Server, they are lumped into that category by the `SqlClient` namespace. In fact, they are treated the same way as all other parameters with the exception of their `Direction` property, which should be set to `ParameterDirection.ReturnValue`:

```
parm = insertQry.Parameters.Add("@ext_flag", SqlDbType.Int, 4)
parm.Direction = ParameterDirection.ReturnValue
```

> **NOTE**
>
> The OLE DB .NET Data Provider requires that any return parameters be added to the parameters collection first. The SQL Server provider does not suffer from this limitation.

You can examine the return value in an identical fashion to the way that we examined the contents of the output parameter:

```
If insertQry.Parameters("ext_flag").Value <> 0 Then
    Console.WriteLine("Phone needs configuration")
End If
```

Listing 15.8 pulls all these concepts together.

LISTING 15.8   Working with Output from a Stored Procedure

```
Imports System.Data
Imports System.Data.SqlClient
Imports System.Text

Module Module1

    Sub Main()
        Dim dbConn As SqlConnection
        Dim connStr As String

        Dim firstName As String = "John"
        Dim middleInitial As String = "M"
        Dim lastName As String = "Burton"
        Dim extension As String = "5001"
        Dim jobCode As String = "DEV"
        Dim divID As Integer = 3

        Try

            connStr = "Provider=SQLOLEDB;Data Source=HR-DB01;" & _
                      "Integrated Security=SSPI;Initial Catalog=dbHumanRes"

            dbConn = New SqlConnection(connStr)

            Console.WriteLine("Trying db connect with -> {0}", connStr)
            dbConn.Open()

            Dim query As StringBuilder = New StringBuilder("insert_employee")
```

LISTING 15.8 Continued

```vbnet
            'Create a new command object using the command text and
            'the previously created connection object
            Dim insertQry As New SqlCommand(query.ToString, dbConn)

            insertQry.Parameters.Add("@last_name", SqlDbType.VarChar, 25)
            insertQry.Parameters.Add("@first_name", SqlDbType.VarChar, 25)
            insertQry.Parameters.Add("@middle_initial", SqlDbType.Char, 1)
            insertQry.Parameters.Add("@extension", SqlDbType.Char, 4)
            insertQry.Parameters.Add("@job_code", SqlDbType.Char, 4)
            insertQry.Parameters.Add("@division_id", SqlDbType.Int, 4)

            Dim parm As SqlParameter
            parm = insertQry.Parameters.Add("@new_id", SqlDbType.Int, 4)
            parm.Direction = ParameterDirection.Output

            parm = insertQry.Parameters.Add("@ext_flag", SqlDbType.Int, 4)
            parm.Direction = ParameterDirection.ReturnValue

            insertQry.CommandType = CommandType.StoredProcedure

            Console.WriteLine("Trying command -> {0}", query.ToString)

            Dim rowsAffected As Integer = insertQry.ExecuteNonQuery()

            Console.WriteLine("{0} rows inserted.", rowsAffected)
            Console.WriteLine("Assigned ID: {0}", _
                insertQry.Parameters("@new_id").Value)

            If insertQry.Parameters("ext_flag").Value <> 0 Then
                Console.WriteLine("Phone needs configuration")
            End If

        Catch appErr As Exception
            Console.WriteLine("An error occurred: {0}", appErr.Message)

        Finally
            dbConn.Close()

        End Try

    End Sub

End Module
```

Managing Cached Data and Schemas

At the start of this chapter, we mentioned that the ADO.NET classes support two ways of interacting with a database: direct access and cached access. We have already seen how we can issue commands to a database through the OLE DB and SQL Server .NET Data Providers. In this section, we illustrate the use of the DataSet class and its related classes.

The Anatomy of a DataSet

The DataSet class, in the System.Data namespace, enables you to programmatically create your own virtual database in memory. This virtual database can be fashioned complete with data, tables, table relationships, constraints, and so on. From a software design perspective, datasets are a great mechanism both for storage of data internal to an application and for representing a disconnected view of data stored externally in a database. Therefore, DataSet objects are a good candidate for communicating data across the different tiers of a multitiered application.

DataSet objects consist of the following:

- DataTable objects that hold table schema information and data
- DataRelation objects that represent relationships between the various DataTable objects
- Constraint objects that encapsulate table and relationship constraints, such as those for foreign keys and unique values

See Figure 15.3 to see how all these items relate to one another.

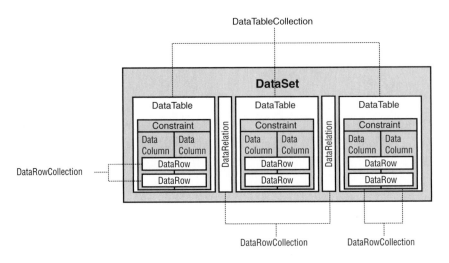

FIGURE 15.3

Composition of a DataSet *object.*

Creating a `DataSet`

To create a `DataSet`, you first physically instance a new `DataSet` object:

```
Dim hrDataSet As DataSet = New DataSet("dbHumanResources")
```

The constructor accepts a name for the `DataSet` object (this is optional; if you don't provide a name, the runtime will assign `NewDataSet` as its name).

Adding Tables to the `DataSet`

After creating the `DataSet` object, you would add `DataTable` objects, along with their `DataColumns`. If we wanted to replicate our employee table from previous examples, we would write the following:

```
Dim employee As DataTable = hrDataSet.Tables.Add("employee")
```

Notice that we are calling the `Tables.Add` method to create a new `DataTable` instance. The `Tables` property on the `DataSet` class is used to manage the collection of tables (this is actually a `DataTableCollection` class instance). The `Add` method returns a new instance of a `DataTable` object that we have assigned into our employee object.

Adding Columns to a `DataTable`

Next, we will need to define the columns that the employee object will have. Just as the `DataSet` class has a `Tables` property, the `DataTable` class has a `Columns` property (which returns a reference to a `DataColumnsCollection` instance). We can use this collection class, and its `Add` method, to define and add our columns to the virtual table. The `Add` method enables us to specify a column name and a data type. We can even specify an expression for that column, such as an expression to filter rows or compute values. With the following code, we have added the ID column to the employee `DataTable` object:

```
employee.Columns.Add("id", GetType(System.Int32))
```

Assigning a Primary Key to the `DataTable`

After adding the columns into the table, we can specify the column or columns that should act as the primary key for the table. This is done with the `DataTable.PrimaryKey` property. This property will accept or return an array of `DataColumn` objects that represent the primary key for the table. Because our ID column is our primary key, we can specify this by simply assigning its `DataColumn` object into the `PrimaryKey` property, like this:

```
employee.PrimaryKey = New DataColumn() {employee.Columns("id")}
```

If that code looks confusing to you, remember that Visual Basic .NET allows you to initialize elements of an array using the braces {} after the array name. We are just creating a new array of type `DataColumn` and assigning the "id" `DataColumn` object as its first element.

Adding Table Relationships to a `DataSet`

The `DataSet` class also supports table relationships. These are maintained through the `DataSet.Relationships` property (which accepts/returns a `DataRelationCollection` instance). Assuming we have implemented a division table in the same way that we added our employee table to the data set, we could set up the relationship between the two like this:

```
'add the division to employee relationship
hrDataSet.Relations.Add("EmpToDivision", _
   hrDataSet.Tables("division").Columns("id"), _
   hrDataSet.Tables("employee").Columns("division_id"))
```

Manually Adding Data to a `DataSet`

At this point, we have added all the database schema items that we need to create a shell database. To manually add data into the virtual database, you use the `DataTable.Rows` property and the `DataTable.NewRow` method.

The `NewRow` method will create a new `DataRow` object that has the same schema as the `DataTable`'s schema. After assigning values to each column in the new `DataRow` instance, it can be added to the `DataRowCollection` by using the `Rows` property.

The following code illustrates adding a row of data into the employee `DataTable` object:

```
Dim empRow As DataRow = employee.NewRow()

empRow("first_name") = "Sandy"
empRow("middle_initial") = "K"
empRow("last_name") = "Cartmann"
    .
    .
    .

employee.Rows.Add(empRow)
```

Listing 15.9 consolidates all the `DataSet` code we have talked about up to this point. In this console application, we build up a `DataSet` that matches the human resource database we have been using for our coding examples. After the `DataSet` is built, a few rows of data are added into the employee and division table and are redisplayed to the screen for confirmation.

LISTING 15.9   Manually Adding Data to a `DataSet`

```
Imports System.Data
Imports System.Text

Module Module1
    Dim id As System.Int32 = 1  'identity seed (used for primary keys)
```

LISTING 15.9   Continued

```
Sub Main()
    Try
        Console.WriteLine("Creating DataSet 'dbHumanResources'...")
        Dim hrDataSet As Data.DataSet = _
            New Data.DataSet("dbHumanResources")

        'Create the table schemas inside of the DataSet
        CreateDivisionTable(hrDataSet)
        CreateEmployeeTable(hrDataSet)

        Console.WriteLine()

        Console.WriteLine("Adding 'division' to 'employee' _
            relationship...")
        'add the division to employee relationship
        hrDataSet.Relations.Add("EmpToDivision", _
            hrDataSet.Tables("division").Columns("id"), _
            hrDataSet.Tables("employee").Columns("division_id"))

        Console.WriteLine()

        Dim divID As Integer

        'Add some data to the division table, then
        'add the employees for that division
        divID = AddDivRecord(hrDataSet, "System Administration")
        AddEmpRecord(hrDataSet, "Sandy", "J", "Cartman", "2379", "ADM", _
            divID)
        AddEmpRecord(hrDataSet, "Talim", "D", "Dahlabbi", "2381", "ADM", _
            divID)


        divID = AddDivisionRecord(hrDataSet, "Operations")
        AddEmpRecord(hrDataSet, "Amy", "L", "DeLisle", "1020", "OPS", _
            divID)

        divID = AddDivisionRecord(hrDataSet, "Marketing")
        AddEmpRecord(hrDataSet, "Jim", "J", "Chapman", "5008", "GEN", _
            divID)
        AddEmpRecord(hrDataSet, "Craig", "X", "Wahlmer", "5001", "MGR", _
            divID)

        Console.WriteLine()

        'Add some data to the employee table
```

LISTING 15.9 Continued

```
        Console.WriteLine()

        'Write out rows and column values to the console
        DisplayData(hrDataSet)

    Catch appErr As Exception
        MsgBox("An error occured: " & appErr.Message)

    Finally
        Console.WriteLine("Hit the ENTER key to exit...")
        Console.ReadLine()

    End Try

End Sub

Private Sub CreateDivisionTable(ByVal ds As Data.DataSet)
    'Create the new table object and add it to the DataTable
    'Tables collection

    Console.WriteLine(" -- creating employee table...")

    Dim employee As DataTable = ds.Tables.Add("employee")

    'Create and define the columns in the employee table
    employee.Columns.Add("id", GetType(System.Int32))
    employee.Columns.Add("first_name", GetType(System.String))
    employee.Columns.Add("middle_initial", GetType(System.String))
    employee.Columns.Add("last_name", GetType(System.String))
    employee.Columns.Add("extension", GetType(System.String))
    employee.Columns.Add("job_code", GetType(System.String))
    employee.Columns.Add("division_id", GetType(System.Int32))

    'Indicate the primary key column(s)
    employee.PrimaryKey = New DataColumn() {employee.Columns("id")}

End Sub

Private Sub CreateEmployeeTable(ByVal ds As Data.DataSet)
    'Create the new table object and add it to the DataTable
    'Tables collection

    Console.WriteLine(" -- creating division table...")

    Dim division As DataTable = ds.Tables.Add("division")
```

LISTING 15.9 Continued

```
      'Create and define the columns in the employee table
      division.Columns.Add("id", GetType(System.Int32))
      division.Columns.Add("name", GetType(System.String))

      'Indicate the primary key column(s)
      division.PrimaryKey = New DataColumn() {division.Columns("id")}
End Sub

Private Sub AddEmpRecord(ByVal ds As Data.DataSet, _
   ByVal firstName As String, ByVal midInit As String, _
   ByVal lastName As String, ByVal extension As String, _
   ByVal jobCode As String, ByVal divID As Integer)

      Console.WriteLine("Adding record to employee table...")

      Dim empRecord = ds.Tables("employee").NewRow()

      'Assign the column values
      id = id + 1
      empRecord("id") = id
      empRecord("first_name") = firstName
      empRecord("middle_initial") = midInit
      empRecord("last_name") = lastName
      empRecord("extension") = extension
      empRecord("job_code") = jobCode
      empRecord("division_id") = divID

      'Add the row to the Rows collection
      ds.Tables("employee").Rows.Add(empRecord)

End Sub

Private Function AddDivRecord(ByVal ds As Data.DataSet, _
   ByVal name As String) As Integer

      Console.WriteLine("Adding record to division table...")

      Dim empDiv = ds.Tables("division").NewRow()

      'Assign the column values
      id = id + 1
      empDiv("id") = id
      empDiv("name") = name
```

LISTING 15.9   Continued

```
        'Add the row to the Rows collection
        ds.Tables("division").Rows.Add(empDiv)

        'Pass the id that was used back out through the function
        'signature
        AddDivisionRecord = id

    End Function

    Private Sub DisplayData(ByVal ds As Data.DataSet)
        Dim table As DataTable
        Dim rowOut As StringBuilder

        'For every table in the DataSet...
        For Each table In ds.Tables
            Dim row As DataRow
            Dim col As DataColumn

            Console.WriteLine(table.Rows.Count & " rows in table '" & _
                table.TableName & "'")

            'And for every row in the table...
            For Each row In table.Rows
                rowOut = New StringBuilder()

                'Write out all of the column values
                For Each col In table.Columns
                    rowOut = rowOut.Append(row(col.ColumnName) & ",")
                Next

                Console.WriteLine(rowOut)
            Next

            Console.WriteLine()
            Console.WriteLine()

        Next

    End Sub
```

Connecting `DataSets` to Databases

You also have the option of using `DataSets` as virtual caches of data stored in a database. You can populate a `DataSet` with data from a data store, make changes to it, and then reconcile those changes to the actual database.

Filling `DataSets` from a Database

`DataSet` objects work through the `DataAdapter` class to grab data out of a particular data source. Each .NET Data Provider will implement its own version of the `DataAdapter` class. If we again use the SQL Server Provider as a basis for our walkthrough, we would be referencing a `SqlDataAdapter` class. This class has an overloaded constructor with the following defined interfaces:

```
Public Sub New()
Public Sub New(SqlCommand)
Public Sub New(String, SqlConnection)
Public Sub New(String, String)
```

For a complete description of each of these constructors, consult the MSDN documentation; for now, just know that the constructor is typically used to tie the `DataAdapter` to a specific SQL command, whether that exists as a string SQL statement or as a `SqlCommand` object. The following code creates a `SqlDataAdapter` object that references our employee table:

```
Dim hrAdapter As SqlDataAdapter = _
   New SqlDataAdapter("SELECT * FROM employee", dbConn)
```

By supplying a SQL command and a connection, the adapter is made aware of the underlying data source and subset of data with which we want to populate the `DataSet` object. To actually transfer the data from the data store into the `DataSet`, we use the `DataAdapter.Fill` method. The `Fill` method also has a variety of overloaded variants; in this example, we are supplying it with a `DataSet` instance and a table name:

```
workDA.Fill(workDS, "employee")
```

Calling the `Fill` method will immediately cause the `DataSet` to conform to the data selected from the data source. If columns or rows have been added or changed, those changes will be reflected inside the `DataSet` object.

Updating Data from the `DataSet` Object

The `DataAdapter.Update` method takes care of updating data and schema in the opposite direction: *from* the `DataSet` *to* the database. If you were to add rows to the employee table inside the `DataSet` object and then call the `Update` method, those rows would be processed into the database—likewise for record deletes and updates.

15

**DATA STORAGE
AND ACCESS**

> **NOTE**
>
> The process of mapping actual data store elements to `DataSet` elements can be a tedious chore for mid- to large-size databases. Thankfully, Visual Studio .NET supports a way to do this in a drag-and-drop fashion. Consult the MSDN Visual Studio documentation (specifically, the topic "Mapping Data Source Tables to Dataset Tables") for more information on this and other aids present in the IDE for `DataSet` design and development.

The `Update` method is overloaded to enable you to update data for a specific `DataRow` object, a `DataTable` object, or even across an entire `DataSet`.

 ## Suggestions for Further Exploration

We haven't touched on the `DataSet` class's capability to work against XML data in addition to true relational data. To see how this is done, see the MSDN documentation on the `DataSet.ReadXML` method, the `GetXML` method, and the `WriteXML` method. You will also find it useful to read the topics that discuss DiffGrams—a format for XML serialization of data changes in a resultset.

The `DataSet` class defines a `MergeFailed` event that will be fired whenever primary key values violate their constraint rules. This is a useful event to trap while performing updates. See the `DataSet.MergedFailed` event documentation for more information.

Learning by Example: DatabaseExplorer

This application enables you to investigate the schema and data contained in an OLE DB– or SQL Server–compliant database. By specifying a connection string, the application will attempt to connect to the targeted database and then return a list of all the tables present. By using the Tree View control, you can expand each table to examine its column schema information or the actual data present in the table. You can also write SQL queries, issue them against the database, and view the resultsets in a different pane. The DatabaseExplorer application is shown in Figure 15.4.

Key Concepts Covered

Key concepts covered by the DatabaseExplorer application include the following:

- Establishing a connection to a database using the OLE DB .NET Data Provider
- Issuing `SELECT` queries via the `OleDbCommand` object

- Using the `DataReader` class to process resultsets
- Filling `DataSet` objects from a valid `DatabaseConnection`
- Querying an OLE DB data source for schema and catalog information

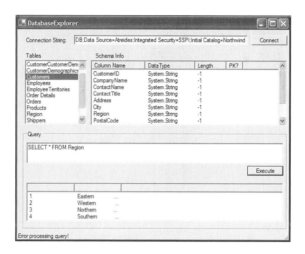

Figure 15.4

The DatabaseExplorer application.

Listing 15.10 details the DatabaseExplorer. This application starts with the typical form setup code. We have created an `OleDbConnection` object of global scope to maintain a constant connection to the targeted database.

Listing 15.10   The DatabaseExplorer

```
Imports System.Data
Imports System.Data.SqlClient
Imports System.Data.OleDb

Public Class Form1
    Inherits System.Windows.Forms.Form

    'Global connection object
    Dim dbConn As OleDbConnection


#Region " Windows Form Designer generated code "

    Public Sub New()
        MyBase.New()
```

LISTING 15.10 Continued

```
        'This call is required by the Windows Form Designer.
        InitializeComponent()

        'Add any initialization after the InitializeComponent() call
        dbConn = New OleDbConnection()

    End Sub

    'Form overrides dispose to clean up the component list.
    Protected Overloads Overrides Sub Dispose(ByVal disposing As Boolean)
        If disposing Then
            If Not (components Is Nothing) Then
                components.Dispose()
            End If
        End If
        MyBase.Dispose(disposing)
    End Sub
    Friend WithEvents TextConnStr As System.Windows.Forms.TextBox
    Friend WithEvents Label1 As System.Windows.Forms.Label
    Friend WithEvents Button1 As System.Windows.Forms.Button
    Friend WithEvents ListBox1 As System.Windows.Forms.ListBox
    Friend WithEvents StatusBar1 As System.Windows.Forms.StatusBar
    Friend WithEvents Label2 As System.Windows.Forms.Label
    Friend WithEvents Label3 As System.Windows.Forms.Label
    Friend WithEvents ListView1 As System.Windows.Forms.ListView
    Friend WithEvents GroupBox1 As System.Windows.Forms.GroupBox
    Friend WithEvents Button2 As System.Windows.Forms.Button
    Friend WithEvents ColumnHeader1 As System.Windows.Forms.ColumnHeader
    Friend WithEvents ColumnHeader2 As System.Windows.Forms.ColumnHeader
    Friend WithEvents ColumnHeader3 As System.Windows.Forms.ColumnHeader
    Friend WithEvents ColumnHeader4 As System.Windows.Forms.ColumnHeader
    Friend WithEvents ListView2 As System.Windows.Forms.ListView
    Friend WithEvents TextSql As System.Windows.Forms.TextBox

    'Required by the Windows Form Designer
    Private components As System.ComponentModel.Container

    'NOTE: The following procedure is required by the Windows Form Designer
    'It can be modified using the Windows Form Designer.
    'Do not modify it using the code editor.
    <System.Diagnostics.DebuggerStepThrough()> _
    Private Sub InitializeComponent()
        Me.Label3 = New System.Windows.Forms.Label()
        Me.Label1 = New System.Windows.Forms.Label()
```

Listing 15.10   Continued

```
Me.TextConnStr = New System.Windows.Forms.TextBox()
Me.StatusBar1 = New System.Windows.Forms.StatusBar()
Me.Button1 = New System.Windows.Forms.Button()
Me.Button2 = New System.Windows.Forms.Button()
Me.TextSql = New System.Windows.Forms.TextBox()
Me.ListBox1 = New System.Windows.Forms.ListBox()
Me.GroupBox1 = New System.Windows.Forms.GroupBox()
Me.ListView2 = New System.Windows.Forms.ListView()
Me.ListView1 = New System.Windows.Forms.ListView()
Me.ColumnHeader1 = New System.Windows.Forms.ColumnHeader()
Me.ColumnHeader2 = New System.Windows.Forms.ColumnHeader()
Me.ColumnHeader3 = New System.Windows.Forms.ColumnHeader()
Me.ColumnHeader4 = New System.Windows.Forms.ColumnHeader()
Me.Label2 = New System.Windows.Forms.Label()
Me.GroupBox1.SuspendLayout()
Me.SuspendLayout()
'
'Label3
'
Me.Label3.Location = New System.Drawing.Point(164, 48)
Me.Label3.Name = "Label3"
Me.Label3.Size = New System.Drawing.Size(120, 12)
Me.Label3.TabIndex = 6
Me.Label3.Text = "Schema Info"
'
'Label1
'
Me.Label1.Location = New System.Drawing.Point(16, 16)
Me.Label1.Name = "Label1"
Me.Label1.Size = New System.Drawing.Size(100, 16)
Me.Label1.TabIndex = 1
Me.Label1.Text = "Connection String:"
'
'TextConnStr
'
Me.TextConnStr.Anchor = ((System.Windows.Forms.AnchorStyles.Top Or _
    System.Windows.Forms.AnchorStyles.Left) _
        Or System.Windows.Forms.AnchorStyles.Right)
Me.TextConnStr.Location = New System.Drawing.Point(120, 12)
Me.TextConnStr.Name = "TextConnStr"
Me.TextConnStr.Size = New System.Drawing.Size(372, 20)
Me.TextConnStr.TabIndex = 0
Me.TextConnStr.Text = _
"Provider=SQLOLEDB;Data Source=Atreides;Integrated _
    Security=SSPI;Initial Catalog=N" & "Northwind"
```

15

Data Storage and Access

LISTING 15.10   Continued

```
'
'StatusBar1
'
Me.StatusBar1.Location = New System.Drawing.Point(0, 422)
Me.StatusBar1.Name = "StatusBar1"
Me.StatusBar1.Size = New System.Drawing.Size(580, 16)
Me.StatusBar1.TabIndex = 4
'
'Button1
'
Me.Button1.Anchor = ((System.Windows.Forms.AnchorStyles.Top Or _
    System.Windows.Forms.AnchorStyles.Left) _
            Or System.Windows.Forms.AnchorStyles.Right)
Me.Button1.Location = New System.Drawing.Point(500, 12)
Me.Button1.Name = "Button1"
Me.Button1.Size = New System.Drawing.Size(76, 20)
Me.Button1.TabIndex = 2
Me.Button1.Text = "Connect"
'
'Button2
'
Me.Button2.Anchor = (System.Windows.Forms.AnchorStyles.Top Or _
    System.Windows.Forms.AnchorStyles.Right)
Me.Button2.Enabled = False
Me.Button2.Location = New System.Drawing.Point(480, 72)
Me.Button2.Name = "Button2"
Me.Button2.Size = New System.Drawing.Size(76, 20)
Me.Button2.TabIndex = 2
Me.Button2.Text = "Execute"
'
'TextSql
'
Me.TextSql.Anchor = ((System.Windows.Forms.AnchorStyles.Top Or _
    System.Windows.Forms.AnchorStyles.Left) _
            Or System.Windows.Forms.AnchorStyles.Right)
Me.TextSql.Location = New System.Drawing.Point(8, 24)
Me.TextSql.Multiline = True
Me.TextSql.Name = "TextSql"
Me.TextSql.Size = New System.Drawing.Size(548, 44)
Me.TextSql.TabIndex = 0
Me.TextSql.Text = ""
'
'ListBox1
'
```

LISTING 15.10   Continued

```
    Me.ListBox1.Enabled = False
    Me.ListBox1.Location = New System.Drawing.Point(16, 64)
    Me.ListBox1.Name = "ListBox1"
    Me.ListBox1.Size = New System.Drawing.Size(132, 134)
    Me.ListBox1.TabIndex = 3
    '
    'GroupBox1
    '
    Me.GroupBox1.Anchor = (((System.Windows.Forms.AnchorStyles.Top Or _
        System.Windows.Forms.AnchorStyles.Bottom) _
            Or System.Windows.Forms.AnchorStyles.Left) _
            Or System.Windows.Forms.AnchorStyles.Right)
    Me.GroupBox1.Controls.AddRange(New System.Windows.Forms.Control() _
     {Me.ListView2, Me.Button2, Me.TextSql})
    Me.GroupBox1.Location = New System.Drawing.Point(12, 212)
    Me.GroupBox1.Name = "GroupBox1"
    Me.GroupBox1.Size = New System.Drawing.Size(564, 204)
    Me.GroupBox1.TabIndex = 8
    Me.GroupBox1.TabStop = False
    Me.GroupBox1.Text = "Query"
    '
    'ListView2
    '
    Me.ListView2.Anchor = (((System.Windows.Forms.AnchorStyles.Top Or _
        System.Windows.Forms.AnchorStyles.Bottom) _
            Or System.Windows.Forms.AnchorStyles.Left) _
            Or System.Windows.Forms.AnchorStyles.Right)
    Me.ListView2.Location = New System.Drawing.Point(8, 108)
    Me.ListView2.Name = "ListView2"
    Me.ListView2.Size = New System.Drawing.Size(548, 80)
    Me.ListView2.TabIndex = 3
    Me.ListView2.View = System.Windows.Forms.View.Details
    '
    'ListView1
    '
    Me.ListView1.Anchor = ((System.Windows.Forms.AnchorStyles.Top Or _
        System.Windows.Forms.AnchorStyles.Left) _
            Or System.Windows.Forms.AnchorStyles.Right)
    Me.ListView1.Columns.AddRange(New System.Windows.Forms.ColumnHeader() _
     {Me.ColumnHeader1, Me.ColumnHeader2, Me.ColumnHeader3, _
     Me.ColumnHeader4})
    Me.ListView1.Location = New System.Drawing.Point(156, 64)
    Me.ListView1.Name = "ListView1"
    Me.ListView1.Size = New System.Drawing.Size(420, 136)
    Me.ListView1.TabIndex = 7
```

LISTING 15.10   Continued

```
        Me.ListView1.View = System.Windows.Forms.View.Details
        '
        'ColumnHeader1
        '
        Me.ColumnHeader1.Text = "Column Name"
        Me.ColumnHeader1.Width = 114
        '
        'ColumnHeader2
        '
        Me.ColumnHeader2.Text = "DataType"
        Me.ColumnHeader2.Width = 107
        '
        'ColumnHeader3
        '
        Me.ColumnHeader3.Text = "Length"
        Me.ColumnHeader3.Width = 67
        '
        'ColumnHeader4
        '
        Me.ColumnHeader4.Text = "PK?"
        Me.ColumnHeader4.Width = 36
        '
        'Label2
        '
        Me.Label2.Location = New System.Drawing.Point(16, 48)
        Me.Label2.Name = "Label2"
        Me.Label2.Size = New System.Drawing.Size(96, 12)
        Me.Label2.TabIndex = 5
        Me.Label2.Text = "Tables"
        '
        'Form1
        '
        Me.AutoScaleBaseSize = New System.Drawing.Size(5, 13)
        Me.ClientSize = New System.Drawing.Size(580, 438)
        Me.Controls.AddRange(New System.Windows.Forms.Control() _
        {Me.GroupBox1, Me.ListView1, Me.Label3, Me.Label2, Me.StatusBar1, _
        Me.ListBox1, Me.Button1, Me.Label1, Me.TextConnStr})
        Me.Name = "Form1"
        Me.Text = "DatabaseExplorer"
        Me.GroupBox1.ResumeLayout(False)
        Me.ResumeLayout(False)

    End Sub

#End Region
```

LISTING 15.10 Continued

```vb
Private Sub Form1_Load(ByVal sender As System.Object, _
    ByVal e As System.EventArgs) Handles MyBase.Load

End Sub

Private Sub ListTables()
    'DataTable object to hold schema
    Dim schemaTable As DataTable

    Try

        'Call into connection for OLE DB schema info
        schemaTable = dbConn.GetOleDbSchemaTable(OleDbSchemaGuid.Tables, _
        New Object() {Nothing, Nothing, Nothing, "TABLE"})

        Dim row As DataRow

        'Retrieve all of the table names returned
        For Each row In schemaTable.Rows
            'Column 2 should be the table name
            ListBox1.Items.Add(row.Item(2))
        Next

    Catch appErr As System.Exception
        MsgBox("An error occurred: {0}", appErr.Message)

        StatusBar1.Text = "Unable to enumerate tables!"

        Me.Cursor.Current = System.Windows.Forms.Cursors.Default
    End Try

End Sub

Private Sub ListColumns(ByVal tableName As String)
    Dim ds As DataSet
    Dim da As OleDbDataAdapter
    Dim table As DataTable
    Dim itm As ListViewItem

    Try
        ListView1.Items.Clear()

        'We use a DataSet here to get a collection of
        'DataColumn objects
        ds = New DataSet()
```

LISTING 15.10   Continued

```
            'Add a table to the DataSet
            table = ds.Tables.Add(tableName)

            'Retrieve all of the rows (and columns) from the
            'identified table
            da = New OleDbDataAdapter("SELECT * FROM " & tableName, dbConn)

            'Fill the dataset with the rows from the
            'DataAdapter
            da.Fill(ds, tableName)

            Dim col As DataColumn

            'Display column schema info in the ListView
            For Each col In table.Columns
                itm = ListView1.Items.Add(col.ColumnName)

                itm.SubItems.Add(col.DataType.ToString)
                itm.SubItems.Add(col.MaxLength)

                If InPK(table, col) Then
                    itm.SubItems.Add("X")
                Else
                    itm.SubItems.Add(" ")
                End If
            Next

        Catch appErr As System.Exception
            MsgBox("An error occurred: {0}", appErr.Message)

        End Try
    End Sub

    Private Function InPK(ByVal table As DataTable, ByVal col As DataColumn) _
        As Boolean
        Dim counter As Integer

        'This routine just determines if a particular column is
        'in the PrimaryKey array
        InPK = False

        For counter = 0 To table.PrimaryKey.GetUpperBound(0)

            If table.PrimaryKey(counter).ColumnName = col.ColumnName Then
                InPK = True
```

LISTING 15.10 Continued

```
            Exit For
        End If
    Next

End Function

Private Sub IssueQuery(ByVal query As String)

    Dim i As Integer
    Dim itm As ListViewItem
    Dim colsSet As Boolean
    Dim dataReader As OleDbDataReader
    Dim cmd As OleDbCommand

    Try

        'Clear out the list view control that will handle
        'the result set
        ListView2.Items.Clear()
        ListView2.Columns.Clear()

        'Create a new command object
        cmd = New OleDbCommand(query, dbConn)

        'Flag the nature of the command text...
        cmd.CommandType = CommandType.Text

        dataReader = cmd.ExecuteReader()

        colsSet = False

        'Advance through the result set
        While dataReader.Read()

            For i = 0 To dataReader.FieldCount - 1
                If Not colsSet Then
                    ListView2.Columns.Add(" ", 100, _
                        HorizontalAlignment.Left)
                End If

                If i = 0 Then
                    itm = ListView2.Items.Add(dataReader.GetValue(i))
                Else
                    itm.SubItems.Add(dataReader.GetValue(i))
                End If
```

LISTING 15.10 Continued

```
            Next

            colsSet = True

        End While

    Catch appErr As System.Exception
        MsgBox("Unable to execute the query: " & appErr.Message)

        StatusBar1.Text = "Error processing query!"

        Me.Cursor.Current = System.Windows.Forms.Cursors.Default

    Finally
        dataReader.Close()

    End Try
End Sub

Private Sub ConnectToDb(ByVal connString As String)
    Try

        'Connect to the database using the supplied connection string
        dbConn.ConnectionString = Trim(TextConnStr.Text)
        dbConn.Open()

        StatusBar1.Text = "Connected to '" & dbConn.Database & "'."

        Button2.Enabled = True
        ListBox1.Enabled = True

    Catch appErr As System.Exception
        MsgBox("Error connecting to the database: " & appErr.Message)

        StatusBar1.Text = "Error connecting to the database!"
        Me.Cursor.Current = System.Windows.Forms.Cursors.Default
    End Try
End Sub

Private Sub Button1_Click(ByVal sender As System.Object, _
    ByVal e As System.EventArgs) Handles Button1.Click
    Me.Cursor.Current = System.Windows.Forms.Cursors.WaitCursor
    ConnectToDb(TextConnStr.Text)
    ListTables()
    Me.Cursor.Current = System.Windows.Forms.Cursors.Default
End Sub
```

LISTING 15.10 Continued

```
    Private Sub ListBox1_SelectedIndexChanged(ByVal sender As System.Object, _
        ByVal e As System.EventArgs) Handles ListBox1.SelectedIndexChanged
        Dim itm As Object = ListBox1.SelectedItem

        StatusBar1.Text = "Table: " & itm.ToString

        ListColumns(itm.ToString)

    End Sub

    Private Sub Button2_Click(ByVal sender As System.Object, _
        ByVal e As System.EventArgs) Handles Button2.Click
        Me.Cursor.Current = System.Windows.Forms.Cursors.WaitCursor
        IssueQuery(Trim(TextSql.Text))
        Me.Cursor.Current = System.Windows.Forms.Cursors.Default
    End Sub

    Protected Overrides Sub Finalize()
        MyBase.Finalize()
        dbConn.Close()
    End Sub
End Class
```

Summary

The ADO.NET components offer a variety of mechanisms for data access from Visual Basic .NET. In this chapter we have examined both .NET Data Providers and DataSet components. Specifically, we covered the following:

- Connecting to a database
- Issuing queries against a database connection and processing the resultsets
- The differences between direct database access through data providers and indirect access through data cached in a DataSet
- Creating a DataSet from scratch; adding tables, columns, relationships, and constraints to build our own in-memory database
- Executing stored procedures and dealing with input, output, and return parameters
- Placing queries inside transactions

15

Directory Services

IN THIS CHAPTER

Microsoft Windows 2000 first introduced the concept of Active Directory (AD) to the Microsoft product family. With Active Directory on the scene, Windows 2000 was capable of providing a consistent and standard way of storing and referencing network resources. This chapter focuses on the `System.DirectoryServices` namespace, which consists of classes that encapsulate and abstract Active Directory objects and operations. This namespace will allow you to query and modify directory entries through a small set of classes and enumerations. For instance, you can examine a directory object's properties, search for specific objects in the directory, and walk up or down a directory tree.

We'll start by examining the purpose of a directory and how directories are organized. Then we will move into simple programming tasks with the `System.DirectoryServices` classes, and we'll wrap up the chapter by explaining some more advanced directory query functions available to .NET programmers.

By the end of this chapter, you should be able to:

- Describe what a directory is
- Understand the key components of Active Directory
- Understand the roles of the Active Directory Services Interface (ADSI) and the Lightweight Directory Access Protocol (LDAP)
- Bind to a specific object in a directory, query its attributes, and change them
- Create collections of directory objects that represent a portion of a directory tree
- Examine a directory's schema information
- Query a directory tree

Key Classes Related to Directory Services

Table 16.1 itemizes the classes and related structures covered in this chapter.

TABLE 16.1   Key Classes of the `System.DirectoryServices` Namespace

Class/Structure	Description
Security/Permissions	
DirectoryServicesPermission	Represents access rights to the classes in the `System.DirectoryServices` namespace.
Searching	
DirectorySearcher	Provides querying capability against an LDAP directory.
SearchResult	Represents an object similar to a `DirectoryEntry`. `SearchResult` instances are returned by the `DirectorySearcher` class.

TABLE 16.1 Continued

Class/Structure	Description
Searching	
SearchResultCollection	Holds any directory entries returned by the DirectorySearcher class.
SortOption	Is a utility class used to specify how search results are sorted.
ResultPropertyCollection	Holds the list of directory entry properties for each object returned by a search using the DirectorySearcher class.
ResultPropertyValueCollection	Holds all the property values for each property in a ResultPropertyCollection instance.
Accessing Directory Entries	
DirectoryEntry	Represents an object in an Active Directory.
PropertyCollection	Stores a DirectoryEntry's properties.
PropertyValueCollection	Holds the actual values for entries in the PropertyValueCollection class.

Basics of Directory Services

Before we dig deep into the System.DirectoryServices namespace, we are going to spend some time reviewing basic information about directories—Active Directory, in particular. If you are already very familiar with directory concepts and Active Directory programming in general, feel free to skip this section. If this is your first foray into AD programming, or if you need a small refresher, this first section can be your starting point to AD programming in .NET.

What Is a Directory?

A directory is really a database specifically designed to store information about different resources that reside on a network. Directories have actually been around for a while—for instance, the Banyan VINES NOS (network operating system) incorporated a directory service called StreetTalk back in the late 1980s. A directory is supposed to make life easier on those who need to administer networks or access network resource listings in a structured way.

Network directories allow you to do all sorts of things that would otherwise be impossible (or at least extremely difficult). Take the example of locating a printer on a network. On a large, enterprise-scale network, thousands of printers might be installed—some type of facility is needed to organize these printers into a coherent list so that a user new to the network can quickly locate the one to which he wants to print. A network directory helps in this case by providing a one-stop shop for the information. By simply querying one data store (the directory), you can get to all the printer information on the network rather than querying separate print servers or domain servers, all potentially located in different offices, buildings, states, or even countries! By cataloging pertinent printer information (Is it color or black-and-white? Inkjet or laser? Is it in my current building, floor, and area?), a user can simply browse the directory for the right printer. Because directories are organized hierarchically, just like files and folders in a file system, an otherwise complex process becomes quite simple.

This is just one scenario that shows the potential benefit of network directories. There are many others, such as providing a central place to store user information, implementing a security layer to protect network resources, and so on.

Active Directory is simply Microsoft's implementation of a network directory service. Many of the Windows 2000 networking functions are centralized inside Active Directory. AD provides a secure storage for such networking resources as logins, printing services, remote connections, and so on.

Exposing Directories for Programmers

A network directory is merely a storage mechanism and, as such, doesn't provide you with many of the facilities that you need to actually get at the underlying data. This is the purpose of directory service APIs. This chapter discusses the two interfaces that are inherently supported by and relevant to the classes of the `System.DirectoryServices` namespace: LDAP and ADSI. LDAP, the *Lightweight Directory Access Protocol*, is both a protocol and an API meant to enable directory communications from inside applications. As a protocol, it defines a standard way for a directory to operate over TCP/IP. ADSI, the *Active Directory Services Interface*, is a Microsoft COM API that performs many of the same functions as LDAP, specifically against Active Directory. The `System.DirectoryServices` namespace roughly maps to ADSI in terms of functionality.

> **NOTE**
>
> As we will see later in this chapter, both LDAP and ADSI are valid and supported interfaces in the Microsoft Active Directory Service, and they are supported with the .NET Framework Class Library.

The Structure of an Active Directory

As we mentioned, an Active Directory instance is organized in a hierarchical, tree-like fashion. This tree consists of objects. Just like in the OOP world, an object in the Active Directory world represents an instance of a specific class of objects and can possess attributes as well as contain other objects. It is to look at a simple graphical representation of a directory tree, as shown in Figure 16.1. Each block in the tree is an object. You can see that certain objects are used just for organization (as in the case of user levels), and certain objects are discrete leaf-level resources (such as Administrator). These are considered *containers* and *leaf nodes*, respectively. Drawing on the file system analogy, you would say that containers are similar to file folders, and leaf nodes are similar to files.

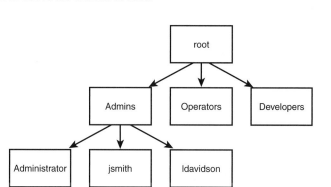

FIGURE 16.1
A directory tree.

Active Directory Schemas

Like a database, a directory tree must conform to a specific schema. Its schema dictates which types of objects are in the directory and which attributes they can have. Because Active Directory encapsulates its schema in directory objects, they can be treated in the same way you treat the other objects in the directory. This means that the schema is inherently extensible: Just add a new object with a new set of attributes, and you have effectively extended that directory's schema.

> **NOTE**
>
> In Microsoft's Active Directory, the class responsible for schema definitions is called `schemaClass`.

Classes

Your knowledge of classes from earlier discussions in this book can be put to good use with directory service programming as well. A class in a directory service is a template for an object—it defines what attributes an object can have. In this way, directory objects are instances of a specific class. The classes are defined in the schema section of the directory tree, and each class is capable of specifying which attributes an object *can* have and which attributes it *must* have.

Attributes

Attributes are the properties of a directory object. Each object has a set of name-value pairs that constitute its attribute list. For example, each object in a particular directory tree typically has a common name attribute called `Common-Name`. This attribute has a value that identifies the object's name. A user object might have the user's name assigned to its `Common-Name`; a printer object might have its manufacturer and type as its `Common-Name` value. The exact set of possible attributes for each object is defined by the class that provides the template for that object.

Active Directory ships with a default schema, but there is nothing stopping developers or others from adding to this schema, thus defining their own classes and attributes.

> **NOTE**
>
> Similar to the way that you can relate database entities to one another through keys, attributes can be used to link directory objects together as well. For more information, see the Active Directory Platform SDK documentation.

Although the schema for Active Directory is extensible, the actual types of attributes supported are not; they are hard-coded into the system. Table 16.2 shows a partial list of the different attribute data types currently supported by Active Directory.

TABLE 16.2   Attribute Data Types Supported by Active Directory

Data Type	Description
Boolean	A true or false value.
Integer	An integer value (32-bit).
INTEGER8	An integer value (64-bit).
CaseExactString	A value consisting of a string of characters (the string is case-sensitive).
CaseIgnoreString	A value consisting of a string of characters (the string is not case-sensitive).
DirectoryString	A value consisting of a string of Unicode characters (the string is not case-sensitive).

TABLE 16.2 Continued

Data Type	Description
NTSecurityDescriptor	A value consisting of an OctetString that represents a Windows 2000 security descriptor.
NumericString	A string value that consists entirely of numerical digits.
OctetString	A value consisting of an array of bytes (most commonly used to store binary data).
PrintableString	A value consisting of a string of characters. Each character is a valid, printable character.
Sid	A security identifier value.
GeneralizedTime	A time value (string format).
UTCTime	A time value (string format).
DN	A DN (distinguished name) value in string format.
DNWithBinary	A DN value with a binary value, in OctetString format.
DNWithString	A DN value with a string value.

Class Types

Each class in a directory's schema is either a structural class, an abstract class, or an auxiliary class.

- *Structural classes* are meant to encapsulate the actual content of the directory. In other words, they are the only type of class that can have actual instances in the directory.

- *Abstract classes* are abstract in the sense that you cannot directly create an object from them. They exist for other structural classes to inherit from in a very similar vein to abstract classes in the Framework Class Library.

- *Auxiliary classes* cannot be used for direct object creation either. You can think of them as being similar to interfaces in the class library: They can be included in another class's definition as a form of "code reuse" (although, in this case, we are reusing schema definitions).

> **NOTE**
>
> The actual term for the entire tree of containers is the *Directory Information Tree*, often abbreviated as DIT.

Directory Object Identities

Because you will need a way to reference a particular object sitting inside a directory tree, there are provisions for exposing attributes that can uniquely identify an object, separating it from all the other objects in the directory. In Active Directory, there are actually three ways to identify an object.

The Relative Distinguished Name (RDN)

The *relative distinguished name* of an object is simply the value of that object's name attribute. The actual attribute used to represent the object's name can vary by class, but typically you can count on this being the object's common name (represented as Common-Name). For instance, the Common-Name attribute value for a user object might be that user's first and last names. In this case, the object's RDN would be equal to the object's Common-Name attribute. RDNs are meant to uniquely identify an object within the scope of its immediate container. If you refer back to Figure 16.1, you can see that the leaf nodes inside the Admins container each have unique names such as Administrator, jsmith, and ldavidson. If these represented the object's common names, you would not be able to add another object with Common-Name equal to jsmith. These names must be unique within the Admins container. You could, however, add a user object inside the Operators container with the common name of jsmith; there would be no scope conflict with the name.

The relative distinguished name is referenced by examining the rDnAttId attribute; this points to the actual naming attribute that is assigned as the RDN.

The Distinguished Name

The distinguished name of an object uniquely identifies an object across all containers, not just the container in which the object resides. The DN does this by recursively building on the RDN with its immediate parent container's name. So, a DN for one of the Administrator user objects would incorporate the object's name (such as jsmith), the container name (Admins), its container's name (root), and so on, until reaching the beginning of the directory tree. Because you are starting with a value that is unique to a container (the RDN) and then are building on this with the unique names of all of the parent containers, you end up with a name that is globally unique.

The distinguished name is referenced through the distinguishedName attribute.

The GUID

Each object is also assigned a globally unique identifier. GUID creation and assignment is managed by the Active Directory service and is never changed after it is assigned.

Typically, simply moving an object from one container to another, you would, by definition, be changing its DN. And you certainly can change an object's RDN. GUIDs are the only object identifiers that are *not* subject to change—GUIDs alone are static and never duplicated.

An object's GUID is referenced by the `objectGUID` attribute.

Accessing Objects in the Directory

If a directory is a type of information store, then it stands to reason that one of the most common activities performed against that data store is data retrieval. In the `System.DirectoryServices` namespace, you can examine a directory object's properties by using the `DirectoryEntry` class.

Loading a Specific Directory Entry

Much like an XML tree (see Chapter 10, "Reading and Writing XML"), a directory tree can be "walked" and examined node by node. The `DirectoryEntry` class represents discrete entries in the directory structure. An entry can be either a container or an actual leaf-level object. For instance, if the directory contains employee records, the directory might be organized along department lines.

To load one of the directory objects, you must provide a path to the object. Let's use a fairly deep directory tree as a backdrop for examining paths in a directory. Figure 16.2 shows a DIT that stretches all the way down to user information. You'll use this as your test bed for this discussion on binding to directory objects.

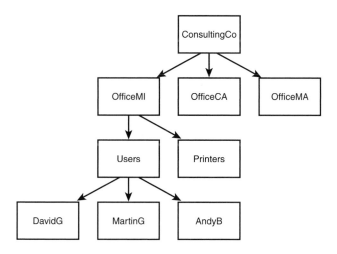

Figure 16.2

A directory tree.

You specify a path using the following syntax:

```
provider://path
```

A provider is the specific code implementation that is providing access to the directory. Common examples are LDAP, WinNT, and NDS. Each provider implements the path syntax in its own way.

As an example, an LDAP-specified path to the user DavidG might look like this:

```
LDAP://CN=DavidGraham,OU=OfficeMI,OU=Users,OU=OfficeMI,DC=ConsultingCo,DC=com
```

The code to bind to this entry looks like this:

```
Dim dirEntry As DirectoryEntry
Dim path As String

path = "LDAP://CN=David Graham,OU=OfficeMI,OU=Users,OU=OfficeMI _
,DC=ConsultingCo,DC=com"

dirEntry = New DirectoryEntry(path)
```

At this point, you would have a valid reference to the directory entry pointed to by the path, with all its attendant properties populated.

Examining Base Properties

When you have successfully bound your DirectoryEntry object to an actual directory entry, it becomes very simple to examine and change its various properties. The DirectoryEntry class supports a few basic properties that you will find useful:

- The Path property allows you to get the full path to the currently bound object.
- The Name property returns the object's name.
- The SchemaClassName property returns the name of the schema class that this object was constructed from.
- If having only the name of the object's schema class isn't enough, the SchemaEntry property goes one step further by actually returning another DirectoryEntry instance that represents the object's schema class.

Examining Hierarchical Relationships

You can also traverse up or down the directory tree from the current DirectoryEntry instance by using the Parent and Children properties. Because each DirectoryEntry object can have only one immediate parent, the Parent property returns another DirectoryEntry instance representing the current node's parent node.

The `DirectoryEntry.Children` property works in a similar manner. It returns a `DirectoryEntries` instance, containing all the child directory entry objects for the currently bound directory entry object. To look up a specific entry in the `DirectoryEntries` collection, you use the `DirectoryEntries.Find` method by passing it the name of the object that you want:

```
Dim dirNodes As DirectoryEntries
.
.
.
Dim myNode As DirectoryEntry
myNode = dirNodes.Find("DavidG")
```

The `DirectoryEntries` object also gives you the capability to identify exactly which types of objects are contained inside its collection. It does this through its `SchemaFilter` property. This property works in conjunction with another helper class, `SchemaNameCollection`, to show only those directory entries that are based on the schemas contained in the `SchemaNameCollection`. In other words, if an entry was not created from one of the identified entries in `SchemaNameCollection`, it won't show up in the `DirectoryEntries` collection. For instance, you could display the names of all the represented object types by writing code like this:

```
Dim dirNodes As DirectoryEntries
Dim schemaNames As SchemaNameCollection
Dim schemaName As Object
.
.
.
schemaNames = dirNodes.SchemaFilter

For Each schemaName In schemaNames
    Console.WriteLine(schemaName.ToString)
Next
```

> **NOTE**
>
> If the `SchemaNamesCollection` is empty, the `DirectoryEntries` collection is considered to contain all types of entries.

Examining Directory Object Attributes

Earlier we discussed the capability for directory objects to have attributes. We said that each directory object possesses a certain number of attributes that are defined in its schema class. These attribute name/value pairs are accessed through the `DirectoryEntry.Properties` property. Getting to an actual readable list of these name/value pairs will take some work:

1. You first reference the `DirectoryEntry.Properties` property. This returns an instance of a `PropertyCollection` class.

2. Next, look at the `PropertyCollection.PropertyNames` property. The `PropertyNames` property returns a collection of the property names assigned to the directory object to which you have bound your `DirectoryEntry` object.

3. These property names are half of the name/value pairs. To get the corresponding property values, you will have to use each property name as an index into the `PropertyCollection` class (referenced earlier). The values are returned in the form of yet another collection: a `PropertyValueCollection`.

> **NOTE**
>
> Keep in mind that the actual, valid list of attributes for an object can be dynamic. That is, they are based off its schema class, which can define any number of attributes and valid values. It is because of this capability to extend a directory entry's possible attributes that these are implemented in a name/value pair collection instead of statically as methods on the `DirectoryEntry` class.

This outwardly convoluted process turns out to be simple when considered at the code level. Listing 16.1 retrieves a directory object's attributes and displays them to the screen.

LISTING 16.1   Querying a Directory Object's Attributes

```
Imports System.DirectoryServices

Module Module1

    Sub Main()
        Const path As String = "LDAP://RootDSE"

        Try
            Dim dirEntry As DirectoryEntry = New DirectoryEntry(path)
            Dim indx As Long
            Dim propCollection As PropertyCollection
            Dim propValueCollection As PropertyValueCollection
            Dim prop As Object
            Dim propVal As Object

            'Assign a reference to the Properties (name/value pairs)
            'of our directory entry object
            propCollection = dirEntry.Properties

            Console.WriteLine(propCollection.Count & " properties found for " & _
```

LISTING 16.1 Continued

```
            path & ".")
        Console.WriteLine("------------------------")

        'These loops will iterate through the name/value pairs
        For Each prop In propCollection.PropertyNames

            Console.WriteLine("Property: " & prop.ToString)

            'For each property name, walk through its collection of values
            For Each propVal In propCollection.Item(prop.ToString)
                Console.WriteLine("    Value->" & propVal.ToString)
            Next

        Next

        Console.WriteLine("Hit the ENTER key to exit.")
        Console.ReadLine()

    Catch appErr As Exception
        'Catch any errors here
        MsgBox("An error binding to the " & path & " directory object." & _
            vbCrLf & vbCrLf & "Error: " & appErr.Message & vbCrLf & "Stack _
            Trace: " & appErr.StackTrace)
    End Try
End Sub

End Module
```

Figure 16.3 shows the output run against a directory path of LDAP://RootDSE.

FIGURE 16.3

Directory query output.

To change the path, simply change the path constant in `Sub Main`.

> **NOTE**
>
> You also can assign values to an object's properties. The assignment is cached until you commit it using the `DirectoryEntry.CommitChanges` method.

Object Security

By default, all the actions that you perform against a directory are done under the guise of the currently logged-in user. However, you can choose to explicitly identify a username and password when accessing directory entries. The `UserName` and `Password` properties (which are both strings) allow you to specify another set of credentials, other than those of the logged-in user, for requesting a bind to a directory object.

You also can query or set the type of authentication that the Active Directory will perform. The `DirectoryEntry.AuthenticationType` returns an `AuthenticationTypes` value (documented in Table 16.3). These authentication methods most likely will look unfamiliar to all but the most experienced ADSI developer. You likely will need to seek out in-depth information on the machinations of Active Directory before you feel comfortable with their actual uses.

TABLE 16.3   The `AuthenticationTypes` Enumeration

Member	Description
Anonymous	Allows anonymous access.
Delegation	Uses ADSI delegation of the user's security context.
Encryption	Uses encryption.
FastBind	Exposes only base object values. This will speed up directory access, at the expense of not being able to work with an object's full complement of interfaces.
None	Doesn't use authentication.
ReadonlyServer	Does not require a writeable server.
Sealing	Uses Kerberos encryption.
Secure	Forces NTLM or Kerberos authentication.
SecureSocketsLayer	Encrypts data with SSL.
ServerBind	Needed when using LDAP if the directory path contains a server name.
Signing	Uses data signing to ensure that there was no data corruption between the sent data and the received data.

Suggestions for Further Exploration

We have only lightly touched on the subject of Active Directory's mechanisms for caching write operations to a directory object. For more information on how the .NET classes deal with this, consult the .NET Platform SDK documentation on the CommitChanges method, the RefreshCache method, and the UsePropertyCache property, all available off the DirectoryEntry class.

Although not written specifically for Visual Basic developers, Gil Kirkpatrick's book *Active Directory Programming* offers a thorough treatment of Active Directory and ADSI programming concepts and techniques.

Searching a Directory

So far, we have touched on how to bind to objects inside a directory without worrying about how to find a specific object in the first place. In this section, we review the namespace support for querying directories for objects and dealing with the results.

It should be noted that the classes in this section—and, indeed, the entire concept of querying against an Active Directory—is really only directly supported by the LDAP provider.

Specifying What to Search For

The DirectorySearch class provides the actual mechanisms for searching an Active Directory. The first questions to be answered are: What are we searching for? and How do you communicate this to the directory using the DirectorySearch class? The answers to both lie in the DirectorySearch.Filter property.

This property is a string that you can set using LDAP's own search string syntax. We won't get into the specifics of this syntax, but the .NET Framework SDK does offer up some basic information:

- The filter string must begin and end with a parenthesis.
- The search criteria can be grouped and evaluated with Boolean logic by using the & (for "and") and the | (for "or") operators.
- The search criteria follows the general pattern of name=value.

If you want to search for any user in the AD with the last name of Powers, you could set the Filter property like this:

```
Dim search As DirectorySearcher

search.Filter = "(&(objectClass=user)(lastName=Powers))"
```

Specifying Where to Search

Now you can concern yourself with where to start the search and how to limit it. The two properties involved are `DirectorySearcher.SearchRoot` and `DirectorySearcher.SearchScope`.

The `SearchRoot` property tells the class which `DirectoryEntry` to use as its starting point. Supplying it with the actual tree root, for instance, will cause the directory to be searched from the very top. You can specify any valid `DirectoryEntry` as the start of the search, regardless of how deep in the tree it sits.

The `SearchScope` property uses the `SearchScope` enumeration to identify how far the search will extend. The possible values for the `SearchScope` enumeration are listed in Table 16.4.

TABLE 16.4   The `SearchScope` Enumeration

Member	Description
Base	Only the base object will be searched.
OneLevel	The immediate children of the base object will be searched, but the actual base object will not.
Subtree	The base object and all its children will be searched.

Specifying How the Results Are Sorted

You can use a helper class, `SortOption`, to tell the `DirectorySearcher` class how you want the results of the search sorted (such as ascending or descending) and which property to use when doing the sorting. The `SortOption` constructor allows you to specify a property name for the sort (such as `lastName`) and a `SortDirection` enumeration (see Table 16.5).

TABLE 16.5   The `SortDirection` Enumeration

Member	Description
Ascending	The results will be sorted in ascending order based on selected property value.
Descending	The results will be sorted in descending order based on selected property value.

After creating a `SortOption` instance, you assign it to the `DirectorySearcher.Sort` property like this:

```
Dim search As DirectorySearcher
Dim sort As SortOption = New SortOption("lastName", _
    SortDirection.Ascending)

search.Sort = sort
```

Specifying What to Return

The search that you run will, of course, return directory objects. But you can pick
and choose which object properties are returned to you in the search by using the
DirectorySearcher.PropertiesToLoad property. This property is a simple string collection of
property names. For instance, if you wanted to return only the email property, you could prime
the search accordingly:

```
search.PropertiesToLoad.Add("email")
```

If you don't select any properties at all, the search will default to return only the name and path.

NOTE

You also have the capability to not return any properties that don't have values
assigned to them. Use the DirectorySearcher.PropertyNamesOnly property. Set it to
True to indicate that the search results should contain only property names for those
properties that have actual values assigned to them. Set it to False to indicate that
the search results should contain all the property names, regardless of whether they
have assigned values.

Executing the Search

After setting up the search parameters, you are ready to actually launch the query. This is
done with one of two methods on the DirectorySearcher class: FindAll and FindOne.
Their names are self-describing: FindAll returns all matching directory objects as a
SearchResultCollection instance, while FindOne returns only the first entry found, as a
SearchResult instance.

The SearchResult class is nearly identical to the DirectoryEntry class. The difference is that
the SearchResult class is populated with only those properties returned.

Learning by Example: `DirectoryBrowser`

This application allows you to specify a provider and path root. It attempts to enumerate all the
children objects in that path and display their properties and attributes when selected.

Figure 16.4 shows the application in action; here we have enumerated the user nodes for a PC sitting on an AD Windows 2000 network.

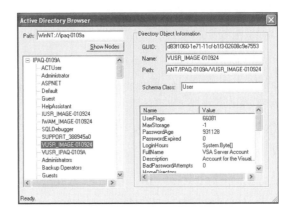

FIGURE 16.4

The DirectoryBrowser *application.*

Keep in mind that you must be connected to a network that actually can see an Active Directory for this application to work. Also, the System.DirectoryServices DLL is not normally referenced inside Visual Studio. You will need to add this to your project references for the code references to work.

Key Concepts Covered

The DirectoryBrowser application in Listing 16.2 demonstrates the following:

- Recursively examining the DirectoryEntry.Children property to fully traverse a directory tree
- Binding to a directory object
- Querying directory objects for their attribute list

Code Walkthrough

This application makes extensive use of the Children property, in a recursive manner, to display the entire directory tree. After building up the tree, you can select any one of the nodes by clicking on it. This causes the program to attempt to bind to that node and shows you all its properties in addition to all its attribute name/value pairs.

The application starts off with all the form setup. Beyond just the general control instantiation and configurations, nothing special is going on here other than the Imports statement, which references the System.DirectoryServices namespace.

16

LISTING 16.2   The `DirectoryBrowser`

```vb
Imports System.DirectoryServices

Public Class Form1
    Inherits System.Windows.Forms.Form

#Region " Windows Form Designer generated code "

    Public Sub New()
        MyBase.New()

        'This call is required by the Windows Form Designer.
        InitializeComponent()

        'Add any initialization after the InitializeComponent() call

    End Sub


    'Form overrides dispose to clean up the component list.
    Protected Overloads Overrides Sub Dispose(ByVal disposing As Boolean)
        If disposing Then
            If Not (components Is Nothing) Then
                components.Dispose()
            End If
        End If
        MyBase.Dispose(disposing)
    End Sub
    Friend WithEvents Label1 As System.Windows.Forms.Label
    Friend WithEvents TreeView1 As System.Windows.Forms.TreeView
    Friend WithEvents Button1 As System.Windows.Forms.Button
    Friend WithEvents TextBoxRoot As System.Windows.Forms.TextBox
    Friend WithEvents StatusBar1 As System.Windows.Forms.StatusBar
    Friend WithEvents GroupBox1 As System.Windows.Forms.GroupBox
    Friend WithEvents Label2 As System.Windows.Forms.Label
    Friend WithEvents Label3 As System.Windows.Forms.Label
    Friend WithEvents Label4 As System.Windows.Forms.Label
    Friend WithEvents Label5 As System.Windows.Forms.Label
    Friend WithEvents ListView1 As System.Windows.Forms.ListView
    Friend WithEvents ColumnHeader1 As System.Windows.Forms.ColumnHeader
    Friend WithEvents ColumnHeader2 As System.Windows.Forms.ColumnHeader
    Friend WithEvents TextBoxGUID As System.Windows.Forms.TextBox
        Friend WithEvents TextBoxName As System.Windows.Forms.TextBox
    Friend WithEvents TextBoxPath As System.Windows.Forms.TextBox
    Friend WithEvents TextBoxSchemaClass As System.Windows.Forms.TextBox

    'Required by the Windows Form Designer
```

Listing 16.2   Continued

```
    Private components As System.ComponentModel.Container

    'NOTE: The following procedure is required by the Windows Form Designer
    'It can be modified using the Windows Form Designer.
    'Do not modify it using the code editor.
    <System.Diagnostics.DebuggerStepThrough()> Private Sub _
        InitializeComponent()
        Dim resources As System.Resources.ResourceManager = New _
            System.Resources.ResourceManager(GetType(Form1))
        Me.Label3 = New System.Windows.Forms.Label()
        Me.TextBoxGUID = New System.Windows.Forms.TextBox()
        Me.TextBoxSchemaClass = New System.Windows.Forms.TextBox()
        Me.StatusBar1 = New System.Windows.Forms.StatusBar()
        Me.TreeView1 = New System.Windows.Forms.TreeView()
        Me.Button1 = New System.Windows.Forms.Button()
        Me.TextBoxPath = New System.Windows.Forms.TextBox()
        Me.TextBoxName = New System.Windows.Forms.TextBox()
        Me.GroupBox1 = New System.Windows.Forms.GroupBox()
        Me.ListView1 = New System.Windows.Forms.ListView()
        Me.ColumnHeader1 = New System.Windows.Forms.ColumnHeader()
        Me.ColumnHeader2 = New System.Windows.Forms.ColumnHeader()
        Me.Label5 = New System.Windows.Forms.Label()
        Me.Label4 = New System.Windows.Forms.Label()
        Me.Label2 = New System.Windows.Forms.Label()
        Me.TextBoxRoot = New System.Windows.Forms.TextBox()
        Me.Label1 = New System.Windows.Forms.Label()
        Me.GroupBox1.SuspendLayout()
        Me.SuspendLayout()
        '
        'Label3
        '
        Me.Label3.Location = New System.Drawing.Point(16, 76)
        Me.Label3.Name = "Label3"
        Me.Label3.Size = New System.Drawing.Size(48, 16)
        Me.Label3.TabIndex = 4
        Me.Label3.Text = "Path:"
        '
        'TextBoxGUID
        '
        Me.TextBoxGUID.Location = New System.Drawing.Point(68, 24)
        Me.TextBoxGUID.Name = "TextBoxGUID"
        Me.TextBoxGUID.ReadOnly = True
        Me.TextBoxGUID.Size = New System.Drawing.Size(208, 20)
        Me.TextBoxGUID.TabIndex = 1
        Me.TextBoxGUID.Text = ""
        '
```

LISTING 16.2   Continued

```
'TextBoxSchemaClass
'
Me.TextBoxSchemaClass.Location = New System.Drawing.Point(100, 108)
Me.TextBoxSchemaClass.Name = "TextBoxSchemaClass"
Me.TextBoxSchemaClass.ReadOnly = True
Me.TextBoxSchemaClass.Size = New System.Drawing.Size(176, 20)
Me.TextBoxSchemaClass.TabIndex = 7
Me.TextBoxSchemaClass.Text = ""
'
'StatusBar1
'
Me.StatusBar1.Location = New System.Drawing.Point(0, 347)
Me.StatusBar1.Name = "StatusBar1"
Me.StatusBar1.Size = New System.Drawing.Size(554, 20)
Me.StatusBar1.TabIndex = 4
'
'TreeView1
'
Me.TreeView1.ImageIndex = -1
Me.TreeView1.Location = New System.Drawing.Point(8, 60)
Me.TreeView1.Name = "TreeView1"
Me.TreeView1.SelectedImageIndex = -1
Me.TreeView1.Size = New System.Drawing.Size(220, 276)
Me.TreeView1.TabIndex = 3
'
'Button1
'
Me.Button1.Location = New System.Drawing.Point(148, 32)
Me.Button1.Name = "Button1"
Me.Button1.Size = New System.Drawing.Size(80, 20)
Me.Button1.TabIndex = 2
Me.Button1.Text = "&Show Nodes"
'
'TextBoxPath
'
Me.TextBoxPath.Location = New System.Drawing.Point(68, 72)
Me.TextBoxPath.Name = "TextBoxPath"
Me.TextBoxPath.ReadOnly = True
Me.TextBoxPath.Size = New System.Drawing.Size(208, 20)
Me.TextBoxPath.TabIndex = 5
Me.TextBoxPath.Text = ""
'
'TextBoxName
'
Me.TextBoxName.Location = New System.Drawing.Point(68, 48)
```

LISTING 16.2   Continued

```
Me.TextBoxName.Name = "TextBoxName"
Me.TextBoxName.ReadOnly = True
Me.TextBoxName.Size = New System.Drawing.Size(208, 20)
Me.TextBoxName.TabIndex = 3
Me.TextBoxName.Text = ""
'
'GroupBox1
'
Me.GroupBox1.Controls.AddRange(New System.Windows.Forms.Control() _
    {Me.TextBoxSchemaClass, Me.TextBoxPath, Me.TextBoxName, _
    Me.TextBoxGUID, Me.ListView1, Me.Label5, Me.Label4, Me.Label3, _
    Me.Label2})
Me.GroupBox1.Location = New System.Drawing.Point(248, 8)
Me.GroupBox1.Name = "GroupBox1"
Me.GroupBox1.Size = New System.Drawing.Size(288, 328)
Me.GroupBox1.TabIndex = 5
Me.GroupBox1.TabStop = False
Me.GroupBox1.Text = "Directory Object Information"
'
'ListView1
'
Me.ListView1.Columns.AddRange(New System.Windows.Forms.ColumnHeader() _
    {Me.ColumnHeader1, Me.ColumnHeader2})
Me.ListView1.Location = New System.Drawing.Point(12, 156)
Me.ListView1.Name = "ListView1"
Me.ListView1.Size = New System.Drawing.Size(264, 160)
Me.ListView1.TabIndex = 8
Me.ListView1.View = System.Windows.Forms.View.Details
'
'ColumnHeader1
'
Me.ColumnHeader1.Text = "Name"
Me.ColumnHeader1.Width = 125
'
'ColumnHeader2
'
Me.ColumnHeader2.Text = "Value"
Me.ColumnHeader2.Width = 125
'
'Label5
'
Me.Label5.Location = New System.Drawing.Point(16, 112)
Me.Label5.Name = "Label5"
Me.Label5.Size = New System.Drawing.Size(80, 16)
Me.Label5.TabIndex = 6
Me.Label5.Text = "Schema Class:"
```

LISTING 16.2 Continued

```
'Label4
'
Me.Label4.Location = New System.Drawing.Point(16, 28)
Me.Label4.Name = "Label4"
Me.Label4.Size = New System.Drawing.Size(48, 16)
Me.Label4.TabIndex = 0
Me.Label4.Text = "GUID:"
'
'Label2
'
Me.Label2.Location = New System.Drawing.Point(16, 52)
Me.Label2.Name = "Label2"
Me.Label2.Size = New System.Drawing.Size(48, 16)
Me.Label2.TabIndex = 2
Me.Label2.Text = "Name:"
'
'TextBoxRoot
'
Me.TextBoxRoot.Location = New System.Drawing.Point(40, 8)
Me.TextBoxRoot.Name = "TextBoxRoot"
Me.TextBoxRoot.Size = New System.Drawing.Size(188, 20)
Me.TextBoxRoot.TabIndex = 1
Me.TextBoxRoot.Text = "WinNT://acclaran-dgvwad"
'
'Label1
'
Me.Label1.Location = New System.Drawing.Point(8, 12)
Me.Label1.Name = "Label1"
Me.Label1.Size = New System.Drawing.Size(32, 16)
Me.Label1.TabIndex = 0
Me.Label1.Text = "Path:"
'
'Form1
'
Me.AutoScaleBaseSize = New System.Drawing.Size(5, 13)
Me.ClientSize = New System.Drawing.Size(554, 367)
Me.Controls.AddRange(New System.Windows.Forms.Control() _
    {Me.GroupBox1, Me.StatusBar1, Me.Button1, Me.TreeView1, _
    Me.TextBoxRoot, Me.Label1})
Me.FormBorderStyle = System.Windows.Forms.FormBorderStyle.FixedDialog
Me.Icon = CType(resources.GetObject("$this.Icon"), System.Drawing.Icon)
Me.MaximizeBox = False
Me.MinimizeBox = False
Me.Name = "Form1"
Me.Text = "Active Directory Browser"
Me.GroupBox1.ResumeLayout(False)
```

798

LISTING 16.2 Continued

```
        Me.ResumeLayout(False)

    End Sub

#End Region
```

This is the button click event that reacts to a user clicking the Show Nodes button. This event merely calls the OpenRoot subroutine.

```
    Private Sub Button1_Click(ByVal sender As System.Object, ByVal e As _
        System.EventArgs) Handles Button1.Click
        Cursor.Current = System.Windows.Forms.Cursors.WaitCursor
        OpenRoot(TextBoxRoot.Text)
        Cursor.Current = System.Windows.Forms.Cursors.Default
    End Sub
```

This application really consists of two macro-level features. The first one, represented by the following routine called OpenRoot, is responsible for taking the entered directory path and displaying all its containers and objects in a hierarchical fashion inside the TreeView control. Each item in the ListView control is named after the directory entry's name, and the item Tag is set to the Path property of the directory entry.

```
    Public Sub OpenRoot(ByVal root As String)
        Dim myEntry As DirectoryEntry
        Dim rootNode As TreeNode
        Dim entry As DirectoryEntry

        Try
            TreeView1.Nodes.Clear()

            'Attempt to bind to the specified directory entry
            myEntry = New DirectoryEntry(Trim(root))

            'add the root node to the treeview control
            Dim newNode As TreeNode
            newNode = TreeView1.Nodes.Add(myEntry.Name)

            'We hold the path in the Tag property of the TreeView item;
            'this will be used to actually bind to the node and view its
            'properties
            newNode.Tag = myEntry.Path

            'This is the routine that we will call recursively in order
            'to build out our view of the directory tree. It searches down
            'the child path of each entry, writing them out to the TreeView
            'as it goes...
```

LISTING 16.2 Continued

```
        AddNodes(newNode, myEntry)

        'Refresh the TreeView just in case
        TreeView1.Refresh()

        'Indicate that we are done parsing the directory tree
        StatusBar1.Text = "Ready."

    Catch appErr As Exception
        'This is where we catch any and all errors in this routine
        MsgBox("An error occurred displaying the directory tree. Please _
            verify that you have typed in a correct directory root path." _
            & vbCrLf & vbCrLf & "Error: " & appErr.Message & vbCrLf & _
            "Stack Trace: " & _
            appErr.StackTrace)
        Console.ReadLine()
    End Try

End Sub
```

The AddNodes routine is meant to be called recursively by the OpenRoot routine. It accepts a
TreeNode instance and a DirectoryEntry instance, and it takes care of both querying the
directory entry and writing its information as TreeView nodes.

```
Public Sub AddNodes(ByVal tNode As TreeNode, ByVal entry As DirectoryEntry)
    Dim childEnumerator As IEnumerator
    Dim newNode As TreeNode
    Dim newEntry As DirectoryEntry

    'Indicate what we are currently working on through the
    'StatusBar control
    StatusBar1.Text = "Recursing " & tNode.Text & " node..."

    Me.Refresh()

    'An enumerator is used to move over a collection; in this
    'case, the enumerator will allow us to walk the Children
    'collection
    childEnumerator = entry.Children.GetEnumerator

    'MoveNext, called the first time, will position the enumerator
    'on the first element of the collection, and increment it down
    'the collection on each successive call
```

LISTING 16.2 Continued

```
        While (childEnumerator.MoveNext())

            'Assign a new DirectoryEntry object to the currently enumerated
            'DirectoryEntry object from the Children collection
            newEntry = CType(childEnumerator.Current, DirectoryEntry)

            'Add another node to the TreeView to represent the current
            'directory entry
            newNode = tNode.Nodes.Add(newEntry.Name)

            'Set the Tag property of the new node with the
            'current directory entry's path
            newNode.Tag = newEntry.Path

            'Call into this routine again with the new tree view node
            'and the new directory entry object (need to find its
            'children as well)
            AddNodes(newNode, newEntry)

        End While

    End Sub

    Private Sub Label3_Click(ByVal sender As System.Object, ByVal e As _
        System.EventArgs) Handles Label3.Click

    End Sub

    Private Sub GroupBox1_Enter(ByVal sender As System.Object, ByVal e As _
        System.EventArgs) Handles GroupBox1.Enter

    End Sub

    Private Sub Form1_Load(ByVal sender As System.Object, ByVal e As _
        System.EventArgs) Handles MyBase.Load

    End Sub
```

The AfterSelect event fires when you click on one of the nodes in the TreeView control. It fires off the BindToNode routine.

```
    Private Sub TreeView1_AfterSelect(ByVal sender As System.Object, ByVal e As _
        System.Windows.Forms.TreeViewEventArgs) Handles TreeView1.AfterSelect
        Cursor.Current = System.Windows.Forms.Cursors.WaitCursor
        BindToNode(TreeView1.SelectedNode.Tag)
```

LISTING 16.2 Continued

```
        Cursor.Current = System.Windows.Forms.Cursors.Default
    End Sub
```

The `BindToNode` routine represents the second largest chunk of functionality in this application. It is responsible for binding to an indicated `DirectoryEntry` instance by using the path to that entry (previously stashed in the `ListView` item's `Tag` property). After binding to the entry, this routine then displays its class properties and its attribute list to the form.

```
Public Sub BindToNode(ByVal nodePath As String)
    Try
        Dim dirEntry As DirectoryEntry = New DirectoryEntry(nodePath)
        Dim indx As Long
        Dim propCollection As PropertyCollection
        Dim propValueCollection As PropertyValueCollection
        Dim prop As Object
        Dim propVal As Object
        Dim itm As ListViewItem


        'Populate text boxes with the basic dir entry properties
        TextBoxGUID.Text = dirEntry.Guid.ToString
        TextBoxName.Text = dirEntry.Name
        TextBoxPath.Text = dirEntry.Path
        TextBoxSchemaClass.Text = dirEntry.SchemaClassName

        ListView1.Items.Clear()

        'Assign a reference to the Properties (name/value pairs)
        'of our directory entry object
        propCollection = dirEntry.Properties


        'These loops will display the name/value pairs in the
        'ListView control
        'Walk through the collection of property names
        For Each prop In propCollection.PropertyNames

            itm = ListView1.Items.Add(prop.ToString)

            'For each property name, walk through its collection of values
            For Each propVal In propCollection.Item(prop.ToString)
                itm.SubItems.Add(propVal.ToString)
            Next

        Next
```

LISTING 16.2 Continued

```
        Catch appErr As Exception
            'Catch any errors here
            MsgBox("A problem was encountered while querying the directory _
                node for information. This may occur when querying the root _
                node using LDAP, or there may be a problem with either the _
                path you have specified or _
                the current state of the directory service." & vbCrLf & vbCrLf _
                & "Error: " & appErr.Message & vbCrLf & "Stack Trace: " & _
                appErr.StackTrace)
        End Try

    End Sub

End Class
```

Summary

Through a short series of simple classes, the System.DirectoryServices namespace is capable of exposing a rich set of features for programming Active Directory applications. In this chapter, we investigated the classes of the DirectoryServices namespace and learned how to:

- Bind to a directory object using the DirectoryEntry class
- Examine a directory object's ancestors and children in a directory tree by using the Parent and Children properties on a DirectoryEntry object
- View and change a directory object's attribute list by using the PropertyCollection and PropertyValueCollection classes
- Search for an object in a directory with the DirectorySearcher class
- Control the search results returned

ADSI programmers should be able to make a smooth transition to AD programming with .NET by just understanding these basics of directory access and control. For those of you who have never touched ADSI before, the namespace makes entry into this area of programming very attainable.

Real-World .NET Programming

PART III

Part III of this book focuses on high-level Framework design patterns and architecture considerations. The topics in Part III are not focused specifically on a given namespace. Rather, they deal with overarching design considerations and best practices for programming against the .NET Framework Class Library.

Part III explores

- Architecture decisions to be made when using the .NET namespaces
- Best practices for technical design of .NET applications
- Select advanced topics for further consideration by readers

Accessing COM+ Services

IN THIS CHAPTER

COM+ programming is still relevant in a .NET world. The services that COM+ offers enterprise-level application developers still apply to components written with .NET code. VB developers, especially, should be thrilled to know that .NET now provides full access to the services of COM+ from their favorite language. If you write .NET enterprise-level applications, you will want to take advantage of COM+ services.

A lot of misinformation and misunderstanding surround this one technology. For some reason, COM+ and its predecessor, MTS, carry a weight of complexity and are considered advanced concepts by many VB programmers. This is unfortunate because the technology has tended to be misused—or not used—for these reasons. In reality, COM+ exists to make developers' lives easier. With COM+, things such as transaction processing, loosely coupled events, and object pooling become extremely simple. Without COM+, many applications would suffer performance and scalability issues, or many developer hours would be wasted creating services similar to those that COM+ provides.

This chapter does not explain the inner workings of COM+. It is intended for developers who are familiar with COM+ programming in VB and need to understand how to create serviced components with .NET and access the new features .NET programming exposes to VB developers. Those new to COM+ development should pay close attention to the chapter content but will also want to make sure they follow up on a number of the "For Further Exploration" suggestions. The chapter's principal focus is on the .NET namespaces System.EnterpriseServices.

After reading this chapter, you should be able to do the following:

- Understand when, where, and how to use COM+ services in your applications
- Access the services of COM+ from .NET managed code
- Register your objects with the COM+ catalog
- Use COM+ role-based security
- Configure your components to take advantage of object pooling and Just-in-Time (JIT) activation
- Work with the shared property manager
- Execute Automatic Transactions with COM+ and the Distributed Transaction Coordinator (DTC)
- Incorporate loosely coupled events into your application
- Work with objects asynchronously

COM+ Services

The primary advantage COM+ provides to your application is the capability to share resources. This has a direct, positive impact on the scalability of your system. Whether you are creating applications for managing inventory or facilitating e-commerce, you can take advantage of the COM+ services to ease your burden when creating your middle tier.

> **NOTE**
>
> This chapter focuses squarely on COM+ as it exists in Windows 2000. Windows XP will introduce new services inside of COM+ 1.5.

Introduction

COM+ handles resource-management tasks such as thread allocation, object pooling, and activation. It provides services for managing security, protecting data, and executing loosely coupled events. These services directly relate to your application's capability to scale and to the amount of code you will need to write. First, scalability is built into COM+. Provided you design your application correctly, COM+ will manage your resources efficiently and increase your capability to support requests.

COM+ also offers services such as queued components that allow your application to continue to process should blocking occur or in the case when a database goes down. Transaction processing becomes rudimentary using the COM+ transaction manager.

Components that take advantage of COM+ are said to be serviced components. That is, they are managed by and take advantage of services of COM+.

Practical Application

Of course, if your application is currently using COM+ effectively, you will want to continue to do so. The key point for these applications (provided they were written in VB) is that they now can take full advantage of the COM+ services. You will want to port your most-used components over to objects written in .NET that take advantage of COM+ services (also called *serviced components*) immediately.

For applications that currently exist and that do not take advantage of COM+, you must consider your application's state-management strategy before jumping into COM+. The best-performing application architecture for COM+ is a stateless design. This design dictates that your COM+ components do not retain state information between method calls. This flies in the face of many OO design principles; however, it is one of those real-world trade-offs for increased efficiency. COM+ cannot manage your components effectively if you maintain state between method calls. To be effective, COM+ must be able to use your objects that sit idle between method calls. If your object is holding state waiting for user interaction, it is simply eating an expensive resource on the server without providing real value.

When creating new applications, you should take a long look at COM+. We suggest examining the application's requirements in relation to the services provided by COM+. Can you see the need for any or all of these services in the application? If the answer is yes, the application is a strong candidate for COM+. Another question to ask is, "How long will it take to create the service in the absence of COM+?" Don't forget to take into account support for the additional code.

Services Available to .NET

A number of services are available to you from COM+. Table 17.1 lists each of these services and provides a brief description.

TABLE 17.1   COM+ Services Available to .NET Components

Service	Brief Description
Automatic Transaction Processing	Automatic Transaction Processing is a service that enables your component to participate in COM+ transactions.
COM Transaction Integrator (COMTI)	COM Transaction Integrator (COMTI) is a service for accessing the IBM Customer Information Control System (CICS) and the IBM Information Management System (IMS). COMTI is used to wrap mainframe transactions as COM+ components.
Compensating Resource Managers (CRMs)	Compensating Resource Manager (CRM) is a service that enables you to use nontransactional objects in Microsoft Distributed Transaction Coordinator (DTC) transactions.
Just-in-Time Activation	Just-in-Time (JIT) activation (and deactivation) is a service that enables the creation of context-only objects. That is, the object is instantiated independent of its related resource locks and dependencies. The object sits in memory until a request for the object is made. At that time, COM+ creates a full version of the object from the object in memory. After its use, COM+ releases its locks on resources and returns the object to memory. The result is the advantage of cached objects without resource locks.

TABLE 17.1 Continued

Service	Brief Description
Loosely Coupled Events	Loosely Coupled Events is a service that enables your components to raise events to other components, as well as subscribe to the events of other components. This model saves you from having to repeatedly poll the server for change information. Instead, events are broadcast to all parties listening.
Object Construction	Object Construction is a service that enables you to initialize information such as a database connection string at the time of object creation. COM+ provides this service to save you from having to store this information within the code and thus recompile whenever configuration information changes.
Object Pooling	Object Pooling is a service that places (or pools) objects into memory when requested. An object that is accessed often will have a larger pool of cached objects. When an object is released, it is put back into the pool to be used again without full instantiation. This saves the overhead of re-creating objects at every request.
Queued Components	Queued Components is a service that enables you to create and execute objects asynchronously, as if they were simply messages in a queue that needed to be received.
Role-Based Security	Role-Based Security is a service that controls access to COM+ code based on Windows .NET users and roles.
Synchronization	Synchronization is a service that allows only one caller at a time to enter a component. COM+ controls access to the component from the requestors.
XA Interoperability	XA Interoperability is a service that allows access to databases that use the X/Open transaction-processing model.

Creating a Serviced Component

If you are familiar with writing MTS or COM+ applications from past versions of Visual Basic, you know that not all services were available to the VB developer. For instance, *object pooling* (the capability to hold objects in memory between requests) is a service that increases performance and scalability but was closed off to the VB developer. To make this type of programming easier for VB developers, Microsoft integrated many of the features of MTS/COM+ into the VB environment. Therefore, when object pooling arrived on the scene with COM+, nothing but a rewrite of the language would make it accessible to VB developers.

Visual Basic .NET is that rewrite. However, the architects of .NET (and VB) this time made sure that VB would support future versions of COM+. In trade for future compatibility, VB no longer has special hooks specifically for managed services. Instead, services are accessed from VB .NET the same way they are accessed from the other .NET languages—through metadata and inheritance. VB developers no longer simply set a reference and mark a couple properties on the class to make their components COM+ aware. Thankfully, however, .NET makes using COM+ services straightforward when you understand the basic steps involved.

The Basics

.NET makes accessing COM+ services mostly a new task. Developers should be familiar with COM+ services and terminology, but the code is all new. Before we discuss various services and their design implications, we will first walk you through the process of creating a simple serviced component. We present the concepts at a high level, write some code, and then delve deeper into the programming constructs. Our code will register the component with COM+ and actually call it directly from a console application.

To access the services provided to us by COM+, we must first make sure our components inherit directly from the class ServicedComponent. In doing so, we make sure that our object has the necessary interface for operating with COM+. This is done simply by calling Inherits ServicedComponent from within class-level scope.

The next important step is to mark various attributes of our class and methods as taking advantage of COM+ services. .NET uses *attributes,* a kind of metadata, to indicate this information to the compiler and pass it on to COM+. For example, to indicate that a class requires transaction, we set an attribute on the class as follows:
<System.EnterpriseServices.Transaction(TransactionOption. Required)> Public Class myServicedComponent. The code between the <> is the metadata. The compiler uses this metadata to register our component with the appropriate COM+ application.

Finally, to use COM+ services from .NET, we must register our object. To do so, we strongly name, or sign, the object.

In summary, steps required to take advantage of COM+ services include the following:

1. You must set a reference to `System.EnterpriseServices` in your application. This enables you to access the various classes in the namespace.

2. In the assembly, you should indicate the name of the COM+ application with which you want to register. This name should match an application-name setup inside Component Services. For example, `<Assembly: ApplicationName("myComApp")>`.

3. You must indicate the key pair to the compiler for signing your strong name. You should generate the key pair file using the utility sn.exe and indicate the key pair to the compiler using an attribute. For example, `<Assembly:`
   `System.Reflection.AssemblyKeyFile("keyPair.snk")>`.

4. Next, mark your classes with the appropriate transaction option. For example, our example requires transactions, so we set the attribute
   `<Transaction(TransactionOption.Required)> Public Class myServicedComponent`.

5. Classes that are hosted by COM+ must inherit directly from the `ServicedComponent` class. This class allows context sharing between COM+ and the .NET Framework. To do so, simply write, `Inherits ServicedComponent`.

6. Next, as in MTS/COM+, you must indicate each transactional method's transaction vote. In COM+, we used the enumeration values `TxCommit` and `TxAbort`. In MTS, we called `SetComplete` or `SetAbort`. Our example uses another attribute at the method level, `<AutoComplete()> Public Function test() As Boolean`. AutoComplete indicates that we want the method to call commit unless an exception is thrown, in which case we want the method to automatically call abort.

7. Finally, all that is left to do is compile the class and call it directly as you would any other .NET component. We do this in our module code.

Listing 17.1 represents a simple serviced class that gets executed from a module. It illustrates the basic steps required to write a serviced component.

LISTING 17.1 Creating a Serviced Component

```
Imports System.EnterpriseServices

'indicate the COM+ application name
<Assembly: ApplicationName("myComApp")>

'indicate the key pair used to generate the strong name for the assembly
<Assembly: System.Reflection.AssemblyKeyFile("keyPair.snk")>

'add attribute indicating transactions are required by this class
```

LISTING 17.1   Continued

```vb
<Transaction(TransactionOption.Required)> _
Public Class servicedCompTest

    'must derive from ServicedComponent
    Inherits ServicedComponent

    'indicate that .NET can manage SetComplete and SetAbort
    <AutoComplete()> _
    Public Function test() As Boolean

        'purpose: create a serviced component function

        'return the function result
        Return True

    End Function

End Class

Module Module1

    Sub Main()

        'purpose: illustrate calling a serviced component

        'local scope
        Dim sc = New servicedCompTest()

        'write function call results to screen
        Console.WriteLine(sc.test)

        'pause the output window
        Console.WriteLine("Enter 's' to stop the application")
        Do While Console.ReadLine() <> "s" : Loop

    End Sub

End Module
```

We've looked at the basic steps required to write a simple serviced component. We will now go backward and dig more deeply into each of the basic steps presented. We will then run through the namespace and indicate how and why various COM+ services can be accessed appropriately.

Using Attributes to Define Services

.NET relies on attributes to indicate that a class or method takes advantage of COM+ services. Prior to .NET, to indicate that a class supported transactions, you would set the `MtxTransactionMode` property of the class from within the VB IDE. In addition, the Component Services Microsoft Management Console (MMC) offers could be used to indicate similar things such as constructor strings and transaction mode. .NET enables us to programmatically use and set these properties via attributes.

Attributes are a new programming concept introduced with .NET. They are similar to metadata and used to annotate our programming elements with information for the compiler and, in our case, COM+. For example, if you want to indicate that a class requires transactions, you set an attribute on the class as follows:

```
<System.EnterpriseServices.Transaction(TransactionOption.Required)> _
    Public Class myClass
```

The code between the <> is the metadata or attribute. This annotation is stored with the metadata of the MSIL file. It is then used by the runtime to register our component with the appropriate COM+ application. The COM+ catalog holds this configuration information and allows us to take advantage of COM+ services.

Note that you can apply multiple attributes to a single class. This is often necessary when setting up a COM+ class. To do so, you simply separate the attributes with commas (,) as in the following:

```
<Transaction(TransactionOption.Required), _
ObjectPooling(True)> Public Class myClass
```

Additionally, that attribute syntax enables you to set properties of the class within the tag. To do so, you simply use the named parameter syntax to indicate the property and its value, as in the following:

```
<ObjectPooling(MinPoolSize:=5)> Public Class myClass
```

The attribute programming construct might seem odd at first because VB developers have been used to setting properties on their objects to access transaction services. However, the trade-off for this new model is worth the extra effort. Advantages to this model include the following:

- Our code is stored as code and not hidden from us by the IDE. This enables us to move between IDEs more easily. It also makes our programming more explicit and ensures that code is stored with code. This should reduce the chance for misunderstandings and thus, bugs.

- With metadata, the VB language can support future versions of COM+ services without a rewrite of the language.

- The attributes concept can be leveraged to access a number of similar services. For instance, to mark your component as an XML Web service, you use attributes.

- You can create your own custom attributes to be used by other developers or within your application. Custom attributes are created as classes within .NET that derive from `System.Attribute`. For example, you could create a code-versioning attribute class to be used by developers and referenced by a source safe-like application.

- Attributes unlock the VB language from Windows services and allow the programming elements written with the language to support an unlimited number of "properties."

Table 17.2 references the attributes in the `System.Enterprise` namespace. For each attribute, the level to which it applies, or scope, is indicated.

TABLE 17.2 `System.EnterpriseServices` Attributes

Attribute	Scope	Description
ApplicationActivation	Assembly	The `ApplicationActivation` attribute is used to specify whether your component runs in the process of its creator or in a server-provided process.
		The attribute is of type `ActivationOperation` enumeration. This enumeration has the following two values:
		Library, which indicates the creator's process.
		Server, which indicates server, or system-provided, process.
ApplicationID	Assembly	The `ApplicationID` attribute is used to specify a GUID for a given assembly that indicates where the components should be installed inside COM+. This is similar to `ApplicationName` but is unique because of the nature of GUIDs.
		When components in the assembly are registered with COM+, they will install in the COM+ application identified by the indicated GUID.
ApplicationName	Assembly	The `ApplicationName` attribute is used to specify the name of the COM+ application to which you intend your component in the assembly to install.

TABLE 17.2   Continued

Attribute	Scope	Description
ApplicationQueuing	Assembly	The ApplicationQueuing attribute allows a component in an assembly to participate in MSMQ transactions.
AutoComplete	Method	The AutoComplete attribute is used to indicate that if a method executes normally (does not throw an exception), the SetComplete() should automatically be called for the transaction. If, however, the method does throw an exception, SetAbort() will automatically be called to abort the transaction.
ComponentAccessControl	Class	The ComponentAccessControl attribute is used to indicate that a given class requires a security check on calls. The type of this class is Boolean. True indicates that a security check is required and False indicates it is not.
COMTIIntrinsics	Class	The COMTIntrinsics attribute indicates that a class is designed to participate in a COMTI service.
ConstructionEnabled	Class	The ContructionEnabled attribute is a Boolean value that indicates True if the class supports object construction and False if it does not. Object construction enables you to pass configuration data to a class at the time of COM+ instantiation. To use this service, your code must support the IObjectConstruct interface.
Description	Assembly Class Method Interface	The Description attribute is a String value that is used to describe the contents of the given assembly, class, method, or interface.
EventClass	Class	The EventClass attribute is used to mark a class as an event class. This allows method calls to a class marked as EventClass to be passed to other listening components as events. Note that these methods do not actually process; rather, they pass processing off to event subscribers.

TABLE 17.2   Continued

Attribute	Scope	Description
EventTrackingEnabled	Class	EventTrackingEnabled is a Boolean attribute that indicates whether a class supports event tracking. Event tracking tracks object instances and their state, such as pooled, activated, and so on. This is most commonly viewed in the components services MMC.
InterfaceQueuing	Class Interface	The InterfaceQueuing attribute enables you to set a Boolean value that indicates if calls to your class can be queued with MSMQ.
JustInTimeActivation	Class	The JustInTimeActivation class enables you to indicate whether your class uses the Just-in-Time activation service. This attribute's type is Boolean.
LoadBalancingSupported	Class	The LoadBalancingSupported class enables you to indicate whether your class supports Load-Balancing services. This attribute's type is Boolean.
MustRunInClientContext	Class	The MustRunInClientContext is used to require that object calls must run in the context of their creator. This attribute's type is Boolean.
ObjectPooling	Class	The ObjectPooling attribute is used to indicate that your class participates in the Object-Pooling service provided by COM+. It also allows you to configure at runtime the minimum and maximum number of objects that can exist in a given pool.
SecurityRole	Assembly Class Interface	The SecurityRole attribute is used to associate COM+ roles with components and to create new roles. Note: Members of a newly created role can be added to the COM+ catalog via the Component Services Explorer. By default, new roles have no members.

TABLE 17.2 Continued

Attribute	Scope	Description
Synchronization	Class	The Synchronization attribute is used to set the type of synchronization supported by a given class. The attribute is of the type SynchronizationOption Enumeration. This enumeration has the following values:
		Disabled, which indicates that synchronization is disabled for the given component.
		NotSupported, which indicates that the component does not support synchronization.
		Required, which indicates that the component requires synchronization.
		Supported, which indicates that the component does not require synchronization but supports it should the caller request it.
Transaction	Class	The Transaction attribute is used to indicate the type of transaction your object supports. The attribute is of the type TransactionOption enumeration. Values include the following:
		Disabled, which indicates that your class should ignore any transaction.
		NotSupported, which indicates that your class should be created without regard to transactions.
		Required, which indicates that your class should share a transaction should it exist. If not, it should create a transaction context for processing.
		RequiresNew, which indicates that the component should be created with a new transaction context regardless of the state/request of the caller.
		Supported, which indicates that the class should use a transaction context should it exit; otherwise, just ignore it.

A number of attributes in the namespace have a default value. In these cases, it is not necessary to add the attribute to your code; COM+ registration will automatically apply the value. Additionally, you do not always need to set the value of the attribute. Simply by adding the attribute to your code, you set what is called a *configured attribute value*. For example, if you omit the ObjectPooling attribute, the compiler assumes this is set to False (unconfigured default value). However, if you simply add <ObjectPooling> My Class and never set the value, the compiler assumes a True value. This is a nice shortcut, but we suggest you write your code as explicitly as possible and actually set the value.

Registration and Configuration

To use COM+ services from .NET, your component must comply with the registration and configuration requirements of COM+. All components running under COM+ must meet the following requirements:

- They should be strongly named.
- They must be registered in the Windows Registry.
- They must have type library definitions registered and installed into a specific COM+ application.
- They must indicate, in the COM+ catalog, any services of which they want to take advantage.

Application Identity

The ApplicationName attribute class enables you to set the name of the COM+ application to which your component should be installed. The attribute applies at the assembly scope and can be a string value or a GUID. For example, <assembly: ApplicationName("myCOMApp")> indicates that your component should be installed in the COM+ application called myCOMApp.

Note that if the component has not previously been set up, it will be created for you by .NET. Additionally, should you not provide the ApplicationName attribute, .NET will create the application based on the name of your library. For instance, myLibrary.dll would get put into an application called myLibrary; in the case of the IDE, it will create an application based on your project name.

```
[ assembly: ApplicationName("BankComponent")]
```

Strong Names

To access COM+ services, you must register your object. To do so, you strongly name, or sign, the object. COM+ applications written with .NET must be deployed in the Global Assembly Cache (GAC) and, therefore, must have a strong name. A strong name is made up from the assembly's name, version, any culture information, a public key, and a digital signature.

VS .NET supports creating strong names for our assemblies. But first, you must have a public/private key pair. To generate a key pair, we use the utility `sn.exe`. For example, the command `sn -k MyComp.snk` creates a new strong name key in the active directory. To sign our assembly, we indicate the key pair to the compiler using an attribute. For example, `<Assembly: System.Reflection. AssemblyKeyFile("keyPair.snk")>`.

Dynamic Registration

.NET automatically registers and hosts the component within the appropriate COM+ application when it is first accessed. This is considered dynamic registration. This process has the advantage of storing all your COM+ configuration information directly inside your component, so you do not need to concern yourself with the actual setup of the component with the COM+ catalog. You simply copy the file into the application.

Although this process is easy and often preferred, it does offer a couple drawbacks. COM applications will be unable to reference your component prior to registration. Therefore, your component will need to be manually registered to be accessible from COM clients. Additionally, dynamically registered components are not stored in the GAC. Again, only those manually registered make it into the GAC.

Manual Registration

Although not always preferred, manual registration of your components can offer a few advantages. For instance, the utility used to manually register components, `Regsvcs.exe`, provides direct feedback and error messages of the registration process. This can be quite helpful when trying to debug errors. The following is an example of this utility in action: `regsvcs myComp.dll /appname:myApp /tlb:myComp.tlb`.

 ## Suggestions for Further Exploration

⊃ For information on the attribute concept as it relates to VB, see MSDN/Visual Studio .NET/Visual Basic and Visual C#/Reference/Visual Basic Language Tour/Visual Basic Language Features/Visual Basic .NET and the .NET Framework/Attributes.

⊃ For even more information on attributes in VB, check out the VB .NET language specification at MSDN/Visual Studio .NET/Visual Basic and Visual C#/Reference/Visual Basic .NET Language Specification/4. General Concepts/4.8 Attributes.

⊃ For information on writing custom attributes and retrieving their information, see MSDN/Visual Studio .NET/.NET Framework/Programming with the .NET Framework/Extending Metadata Using Attributes.

Role-Based Security

COM+ offers a role-based security model that groups Windows users into COM+ roles. This model relies on the NT user accounts (tokens) associated with executing code as the basis for identity. To gain access, these users must belong to a COM+ role that has been assigned access to the class.

This simple model is used to enforce basic access to your components.

> **NOTE**
>
> Note that the .NET Framework's code access security (see Appendix C) is independent from COM+ role-based security. In fact, .NET allows only one or the other. You cannot use both models simultaneously.

Adding and Associating Roles

You can programmatically add roles to a COM+ application and associate those roles to your methods. The `SecurityRoleAttribute` attribute is used to mark your component with the appropriate role. When registered, .NET will verify that the intended role exists within the COM+ catalog. If not, .NET will add the role to the application. The following example associates the role `TestRole` with the classes in your assembly.

```
<Assembly: SecurityRole("TestRole")>
```

In addition to the assembly, you can also associate security roles at the class, method, and interface levels. Marking a method with the `SecurityRole` attribute, for instance, indicates that only those roles marked have access to the actual method. Figure 17.1 illustrates the COM+ catalog interface for setting this information. The example shown is for setting a class-level property.

Note that you can also add roles and users to those roles through the MMC interface. Figure 17.2 illustrates this interface.

Security Call Context

The `SecurityCallContext` class provides your application access to the COM+ security context. This provides you with the capability to know who is requesting the application, down to the account name and call chain.

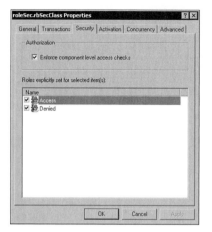

FIGURE 17.1
Enforce role access at the class level.

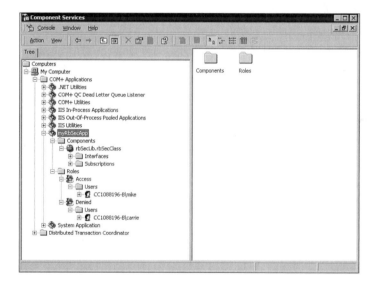

FIGURE 17.2
Roles and users setup.

To create an instance of the `SecurityCallContext`, you use the `CurrentCall` property within your serviced component. `CurrentCall` is a static property that returns a valid instance of `SecurityCallContext`. For example, the following code creates a valid `SecurityCallContext` object:

```
'local scope
Dim mySecurityContext As System.EnterpriseServices.SecurityCallContext

'call static method to get security context
mySecurityContext = _
    System.EnterpriseServices.SecurityCallContext.CurrentCall()
```

To know the principal caller (that is, the identity of the person or application that made the direct request for your method or component), you access the DirectCaller property. To return the chain of current callers, you access the Callers property, which returns an instance of the SecurityCallers class. This class is a collection of all callers in the chain leading up to the current call. You also have direct access to the first caller in the chain using the OriginalCaller property. Both DirectCaller and SecurityCallers.Item return an instance of the SecurityIdentity class. Table 17.3 lists the properties available to you through the SecurityIdentity class.

TABLE 17.3 SecurityIdentity Properties

Property	Description
AccountName	The AccountName property is a string value representing the name of the user (or account) that the SecurityIdentity instance represents.
AuthenticationLevel	The AuthenticationLevel property returns a member of the AuthenticationOption enumeration that indicates how the user was authenticated. Authentication options include Call, Connect, Default, Integrity, None, Packet, Privacy.
AuthenticationService	The AuthenticationService property returns the authentication server described by the security identity.
ImpersonationLevel	The ImpersonationLevel property returns a member of the ImpersonationLevelOption enumeration indicating the level of impersonation used in the call. Impersonation levels include Anonymous, Identify, Delegate, Impersonate, and Default.

Note that you must turn on authorization at the application level for the security context to be made available to your application. You do this from the Security tab on the Application Properties window. Figure 17.3 provides a screenshot.

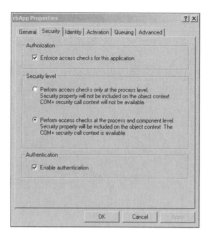

FIGURE 17.3
Security enabled.

Listing 17.2 demonstrates controlling security from within the actual method call. Suppose that all roles have access to the actual method. However, you want to block certain portions of the method to users who are not of a certain level. This example simply gets the security call context and uses it to check the `IsCallerInRole` method.

LISTING 17.2 Security Call Context

```
Imports System.EnterpriseServices

<Assembly: ApplicationName("rbApp")>
<Assembly: System.Reflection.AssemblyKeyFile("rbSec.snk")>

Public Class rbSecClass

    Inherits ServicedComponent

    <AutoComplete()> _
    Public Function execute() As Boolean

        'purpose: demonstrate COM+ role-based security

        'local scope
        Dim mySecCtx As SecurityCallContext

        'set the current security context
        mySecCtx = SecurityCallContext.CurrentCall()
```

LISTING 17.2   Continued

```
        'check to see if the caller is in the access role
        If mySecCtx.IsCallerInRole("Access") Then
            Return True
        Else
            Return False
        End If

    End Function

End Class
```

Resource Management

One of the more expensive things in any application is creating and loading objects into memory. A key way in which COM+ can help make applications work more efficiently is through resource management. COM+ provides resource management through the services of Object Pooling, Just-in-Time activation and deactivation, and State Management. These services, together with the stateless programming model COM+ enforces, can give your application better overall scalability.

Object Pooling and Construction

Object Pooling is one of the features that COM+ promised, but on which VB developers were never able to capitalize. This was the result of VB's tight integration with COM and its capability to support only the apartment-threading model. Now, with the .NET version of VB and its support for multithreading, you can use COM+ services to maintain pools of objects and thus increase your application's scalability.

Object Pooling is a service that keeps objects cached in a queue. Clients requesting these objects do not have to suffer the overhead of their creation. Instead, COM+ hands them the cached object, nearly eliminating the largest overhead involved with using COM+ objects. This provides faster access to objects and increases the number of requests that a server can process. Typically with pooling, just a few objects can handle hundreds of requests.

Objects are either loaded into the pool after a client request or can be preloaded into the pool. Preloading eliminates the lag the initial caller usually suffers because of object creation.

The class library provides the ObjectPoolingAttribute class to mark components as participants in an object pool. When tagging a component as taking advantage of Object Pooling, you are creating a new instance of this class. As such, you can set a number of properties on the class that will affect how COM+ services pool the object:

- `MinPoolSize` enables you to control the minimum number of objects that are maintained in the pool. As objects are requested or on startup of the COM+ application, the pool reaches its minimum size and COM+ maintains at least this number of objects for use by additional callers.

- `MaxPoolSize` sets the maximum number of objects that can exist in the pool. If all pool objects are in use and the pool has not reached its maximum size, COM+ creates an additional component for the caller. When the maximum pool size is reached, however, COM+ queues the client requests and each must wait in turn for an object to become available from the queue.

- `CreationTimeout` sets the number of milliseconds COM+ should wait for an object from the pool when requesting an object. If the timeout value is reached, COM+ throws an exception.

COM+ manages an object's life cycle; as such, it calls methods of the `IObjectControl` interface exposed by the `ServicedComponent` class. You can override and intercept these calls for use by your application. The following are methods of `IObjectControl` that can be overridden:

- `Activate` is called by COM+ when your object is removed from the pool (handed out to the calling client).

- `Deactivate` is called when an object is placed back into the pool (released from the client).

- When COM+ returns an object to the pool after deactivation, it first calls `CanBePooled`. This enables you to check your object to make sure it is okay to be returned to the pool. If so, you return `True` from the function call; if not, returning `False` causes COM+ to discard the object.

In Listing 17.3, we create a COM+ object called `myPooledObject`. We tag it as a pooled object and set the pooling parameters of minimum pool size to 5 and maximum pool size to 10.

LISTING 17.3   Object Pooling

```
Imports System.EnterpriseServices

'indicate the COM+ application name
<Assembly: ApplicationName("myComApp")>

'indicate the key pair used to generate the strong name for the assembly
<Assembly: System.Reflection.AssemblyKeyFile("keyPair.snk")>

<Transaction(TransactionOption.Required), _
ObjectPoolingAttribute(MinPoolSize:=5, MaxPoolSize:=10)> _
Public Class myPooledObject
```

17

ACCESSING COM+ SERVICES

LISTING 17.3   Continued

```
'purpose:   provide pooled component example

'class-level scope
Inherits ServicedComponent

<AutoComplete()> _
Public Function doTask() As Boolean

    'purpose:   simulate a function

    Return True

End Function

Public Overrides Function CanBePooled() As Boolean

    'purpose:   called by COM+ after Deactivate
    '           used to decide if the object can be returned to the
    '           queue or should be discarded

    Return True

End Function

Public Overrides Sub Activate()

    'purpose:   called when an object is handed out to a client and
    '           removed from the pool

End Sub

Public Overrides Sub Deactivate()

    'purpose:   called before placing back in the pool on deactivation

End Sub

End Class
```

How do you verify that COM+ is pooling your objects? One way is to view the components'
real-time inside the COM+ Component Services management console application. This enables
you to see the number of objects in a given pool at a specific time. Figure 17.4 is a screenshot
of this interface as it is reporting resource-management statistics.

FIGURE 17.4
Component Services monitoring.

To make sure your components are tracked by the COM+ Component Service monitor, you must set the attribute `EventTrackingEnabledAttribute` to `True`. Additionally, your component must be running in a server and not in a library application.

Of course, you can use the Component Services manager application to mark Object Pooling attributes directly or to override the attributes your component has set at the time of install. Your object should still override the `CanBePooled` method and mark this value to `True` to indicate that COM+ can pool your object. Figure 17.5 illustrates the interface.

Just-in-Time Activation

COM+ provides the service of *Just-in-Time* (JIT) activation and deactivation of components. Components that take advantage of this service are instantiated as context-only objects on request. That is, the objects are not activated (and locked) by calling the client at the time of creation. COM+ activates the JIT object on a method call from a client. When the method returns, COM+ deactivates the component. This allows COM+ to pass out these expensive resources only when they are really needed (on the method call) rather than when they are created.

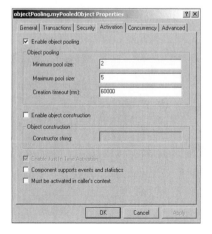

FIGURE 17.5
Object Pooling Component Services interface.

As an example of the benefits this service can provide, suppose you have an application that creates a number of COM+ objects in the declaration section at the top of your procedure. Now suppose that as your procedure executes, it uses some of the objects some of the time and deactivates all the objects after the procedure has completed. Without JIT activation, COM+ would be forced to hand your application an instance of each object on its creation. These objects would be blocked from access by other requesting applications until your application is finished with them, regardless of when or if your application actually uses them. Thus, COM+ would have to create another instance for a second requesting client. With JIT activation, COM+ knows that you may want the resource, but until you actually use it by calling one of its methods, it is available to be used by other clients. After they are used, on method call return, COM+ deactivates the object and makes it again available to others, regardless of whether your application is finished using it.

Of course, this model—and COM+ in general—requires that your object architecture is a stateless design. Stateless objects are those that do not maintain object state or data between method calls. A stateless object fires up at method call, gets its work done, passes results to the client call, and then dies. Therefore, even though your application holds a reference to a JIT object, the object does not maintain state between method calls. It is deactivated, and thus all data from the method call is wiped out. This design prevents objects from blocking or holding expensive resources open and thereby increases the scalability of your application.

To indicate that your object is ready for deactivation, you set the *doneness* bit (a flag value indicating that your method has completed). This is automatically set for you when using `AutoComplete` or calling `SetComplete` or `SetAbort` of the `ContextUtil` class. Additionally, setting `DeactivateOnReturn = True` indicates that your object is ready to be deactivated.

To mark a class as taking advantage of JIT activation and deactivation, you simply use the `JustInTimeActivationAttribute` class, as in

```
<JustInTimeActivation(True)> Public Class myJITClass
```

Note that components marked as `AutoComplete` automatically set the JIT attribute to `True`.

Shared Property Manager

Because of the stateless nature of COM+ programming, your objects cannot retain data between method calls. That is, if you set a number of property values on your object at the time of a method call, after the method completes, the object deactivates and flushes all its data—even though your application still maintains a contextual reference. Working within such a programming model requires that you design your system state management very carefully.

One solution is to push all state out to the data store. This requires your objects to constantly poll the database for state information. This solution is often very effective, provided it is designed correctly.

Sometimes it's preferable to store your user-specific state somewhere within the user-interface tier. You can push state out to the client in the form of cookies or session variables in the case of a Web application. In the case of a client/server application, you could store state out to locally executing code inside the client.

But what if you need to manage a global value between objects, and you want neither to return the data to the calling client nor store it to (or access it from) the database?

COM+ provides the Shared Property Manager (SPM) for precisely this occasion. The SPM is a resource dispenser that allows you to share state between objects executing in the same server process. The SPM state is transient—that is, shared state does not survive system failures, reboots, or application shutdowns. The SPM is meant to be accessed across a transaction and not across a process. Because of this transient nature, it is important for you to ensure the execution sequence of your methods that require shared data. Alternatively, you should implement your method in such a way that on shared property access exceptions, your method knows how to create and populate the shared property values.

Shared properties are available only to objects running in the same process. Therefore, objects that require access to global data must be installed inside the same COM+ application.

To create a shared property, you must first create a SharedPropertyGroupManager object. This object enables you to create and access property groups. One of the problems with global data that the shared property manager solves is naming collisions among global variables. For example, if Object A creates a value called mySharedValue, Object B should be restricted from creating the same shared variable or a collision will occur—or worse, Object B could simply overwrite Object A's value. Object B and Object A know nothing about each other and therefore could easily create this collision. The SharedPropertyGroup class and the SharedPropertyGroupManager solve this problem by enforcing unique namespaces for properties to use.

The CreatePropertyGroup method of SharedPropertyGroupManager is used to define a new property group and returns a SharedPropertyGroup instance. This method call requires that you indicate the following parameters:

- name—The property group name. This is a string value that you use to reference the property group when returning property values.

- dwIsoMode—The property group isolation (or lock) mode. The value is of the type PropertyLockMode enumeration, whose values include Method and SetGet. Setting the lock mode to SetGet indicates that after you set or return the value of the property group, you are finished using it and it can be released for others to share. If you make a call that sets a value, this call is atomic. Setting the value to Method indicates that the property access locking should correspond with the execution of your method. When the method is complete, you can unlock the property value.

- dwRelMode—The release mode requested. The value is of the type `PropertyReleaseMode` enumeration, whose values include `Process` and `Standard`. If the value is `Process`, the property values are maintained for the lifetime of the process. If the value `Standard` exists as the default mode for COM object, it indicates that when all objects have released their references to the shared property, the object will automatically be destroyed.

- fExist—A parameter indicating what to do if the property group already exists. You set this `Boolean` parameter to `True` if the property group already exists and you simply want access to it, or set it to `False` if you want the property group to be created by the method call.

After you have a defined `SharedProperty` group, you use its method, `CreateProperty`, to define a new property. This method call returns a `SharedProperty` instance. You pass the property `name` and `fExists` as parameters to the method call. `fExists` is a `Boolean` value that you set to `True` if you are returning a preexisting property or `False` if you are creating a new property. You use the `Value` property of the `SharedProperty` object to set the shared value.

In Listing 17.4, we create two classes: `classSet` and `classGet`. Our `classSet` creates a shared property inside the custom method `setProp`. This method uses the objects `SharedPropertyGroupManager`, `SharedPropertyGroup`, and `SharedProperty`. The property's value is set based on the method's parameter, `propVal`. Our `classGet` creates the custom function `getProp` which finds the property group and property and returns the property value from the function.

LISTING 17.4   Shared Properties

```
Imports System.EnterpriseServices

<Assembly: ApplicationName("myApp")>

'indicate the key pair used to generate the strong name for the assembly
<Assembly: System.Reflection.AssemblyKeyFile("sharedProp.snk")>

Public Class classSet

    'purpose: sets a value in the shared property group

    Inherits ServicedComponent

    <AutoComplete()> _
    Public Sub setProp(ByVal propVal As String)

        'local scope
        Dim spGroupMgr As SharedPropertyGroupManager
```

LISTING 17.4 Continued

```vb
        Dim spGroup As SharedPropertyGroup
        Dim sharedProp As SharedProperty

        'create a property group manager object
        spGroupMgr = New SharedPropertyGroupManager()

        'create a shared property group
        spGroup = spGroupMgr.CreatePropertyGroup( _
            name:="spGroup", dwIsoMode:=PropertyLockMode.SetGet, _
            dwRelMode:=PropertyReleaseMode.Standard, fExist:=False)

        'create a property
        sharedProp = spGroup.CreateProperty(name:="spProp", fExists:=True)

        'set the property value to the passed string value
        sharedProp.Value = propVal

    End Sub

End Class

Public Class classGet

    'purpose: retrieves a value in the shared property group

    Inherits ServicedComponent

    <AutoComplete()> _
    Public Function getProp() As String

        'local scope
        Dim spGroupMgr As SharedPropertyGroupManager
        Dim spGroup As SharedPropertyGroup
        Dim sharedProp As SharedProperty

        'create a property group manager object
        spGroupMgr = New SharedPropertyGroupManager()

        'find our shared property group
        spGroup = spGroupMgr.CreatePropertyGroup( _
            name:="spGroup", dwIsoMode:=PropertyLockMode.SetGet, _
            dwRelMode:=PropertyReleaseMode.Standard, fExist:=True)

        'get our property
        sharedProp = spGroup.Property(name:="spProp")
```

LISTING 17.4 Continued

```
            'return the property value
            getProp = sharedProp.Value

    End Function

End Class

Module Module1

    Sub Main()

        'local scope

        'create the class that sets the shared prop
        Dim mySet As New classSet()

        'set the shared property
        mySet.setProp(propVal:="This is a shared property!")

        'create a class that reads the property
        Dim myGet As New classGet()

        'get the property and write out to the console
        Console.WriteLine(myGet.getProp())

        'wait
        Do While Console.ReadLine <> "s" : Loop

    End Sub

End Module
```

 # Suggestions for Further Exploration

⊃ Check out the System.EnterpriseServices.CompensatingResourceManager name-space. This set of classes enables you to create resource managers that use nontransactional objects inside of a Distributed Transaction Coordinator (DTC) transaction.

⊃ For some useful content on COM+ in general and some specifics on Object Pooling and other services, read: MSDN/ MSDN Library/Component Development/COM+/Technical Articles.

Transaction Processing

A transaction is simply a group of tasks that either succeed or fail as a unit. For instance, suppose that your application runs a nightly import process to update its product-specification data. The specification data is stored in a set of six tables that are interrelated. That is, if you update one table, you must ensure that all new data makes it into the associated tables. These six tasks represent a transaction. They either all succeed (commit), or in the event of a failure, they all must fail (rollback). Imagine the chaos if you updated the model line but it still had the old colors and dimensions—or worse, prices. With proper transaction processing, no operation is permanent until all have successfully completed.

Objects created in COM+ and marked transactional automatically take advantage of the COM+ transaction service. On creation, these objects have a transactional context and can enlist or nest other objects into this context. In fact, transactions can be supported across heterogeneous data sources, computers, and networks.

> **NOTE**
>
> COM+ uses the Windows Distributed Transaction Coordinator (DTC) to provide transaction processing. From managed code you can use a manual or automatic model of transaction management. Manual transactions require that you write code directly to the given transaction manager to start, end, and roll back a transaction.

The topics of transactions and transaction processing can span many technologies. For the purpose of this chapter and book, we will focus our discussion specifically on COM+ transactions in the .NET Framework Class Library.

Transaction Management

For you to mark that your COM+ object is transactional, .NET provides the TransactionAttribute class. This class simply indicates to COM+ how your object should be managed when dealing with automatic transactions. The Timeout property of the class indicates the number of milliseconds the transaction can run before COM+ raises an exception. The class has a Value property that is of the type TransactionOption enumeration. Setting this value is the key to getting the desired behavior out of your objects and transactions. Note that when you mark a class as transactional, COM+ enforces both JIT activation and concurrency protection (also called synchronization. Table 17.4 lists the enumeration's values and a brief description of each.

TABLE 17.4 TransactionOption Enumeration Values

Member	Description
Disabled	The Disabled value disables automatic transactional support on the given object. Note: Objects marked Disabled can still manually participate in DTC transactions.
NotSupported	The NotSupported value indicates that the object does not support transactions. Instances of objects marked NotSupported are created without transaction support, regardless of the transactional nature of the creator.
Supported	The Supported value indicates that the given object can run inside (supports) a transaction context, provided one is present. If not, the object is created without regard for transactions.
Required	The Required value indicates that the given object requires a transaction context. If one is present, the object will enlist itself in the scope of the active transaction context. If no context exists, a new transaction context will be created.
RequiresNew	The RequiresNew value indicates that the given object requires a new transaction context for each request.

Each task within a transaction must indicate whether it succeeded or failed. You can indicate this with your code in a number of ways. One is to use the AutoCompleteAttribute class. AutoComplete indicates that a tagged method should automatically be considered successful (commit), provided that it does not raise an exception. On exception, however, the method will vote to abort the transaction.

COM+ also provides the ContextUtil class for this purpose. ContexUtil is available to any object running as a serviced component. Calling it returns access to the object's transaction context. With this context, you can explicitly call SetComplete or SetAbort. SetComplete indicates that the object succeeded, whereas SetAbort indicates that the transaction failed. Note, as we stated previously, COM+ transactional objects automatically are JIT enabled. Calling SetComplete also indicates that the object should be deactivated (sets the doneness bit to True) after the DeactivateOnReturn method call.

The last way you can indicate to COM+ that your object succeeded is by setting the ContextUtil.MyTransactionVote, also called the consistency bit. This property takes a TransactionVote enumeration value. Values are Commit and Abort. What is the difference between setting the transaction vote versus calling SetComplete? The MyTransactionVote property gives you finer control because it does not automatically set the doneness bit (indicated by DeactivateOnReturn = True), and it allows you to manage the two properties independently.

Transaction Example

In Listing 17.5, we create a two-part transaction. The class trxWrite writes data to the data-base. We set its TransactionOption to Required and indicate that the method writeTrx should allow COM+ to automatically manage its transaction state by setting the attribute AutoComplete. The trxManage class, on the other hand, is set to RequiresNew for its transaction option. It enlists writeTrx into its transaction context by creating the object and calling its method. Its method, manageTrx, explicitly aborts the transaction by setting MyTransactionVote to Transaction.Abort. Finally, we create a simple console-based client that calls trxManage.

LISTING 17.5   Transaction Example

```
Imports System.EnterpriseServices
Imports System.Data.OleDb

'indicate the COM+ application to use
<Assembly: ApplicationName("trx")>

'indicate the key pair used to generate the strong name for the assembly
<Assembly: System.Reflection.AssemblyKeyFile("trx.snk")>

'create interface for trxWrite
Public Interface IWrite
    Sub writeTrx(ByVal strText As String)
End Interface

'create interface for trxManage
Public Interface IManage
    Sub manageTrx()
End Interface

'set the transaction attribute
<Transaction(TransactionOption.Required)> _
Public Class trxWrite

    'indicate serviced component
    Inherits ServicedComponent

    'use the IWrite interface
    Implements IWrite

    'indicate that the transaction should setComplete on success
    '    and setAbort upon an exception
    <AutoComplete(True)> _
    Public Sub writeTrx(ByVal strText As String) Implements IWrite.writeTrx
```

LISTING 17.5   Continued

```vb
        'purpose: execute a database insert and auto commit

        'local scope
        Dim myConn As OleDbConnection
        Dim myCommand As New OleDbCommand()
        Dim sql As String

        'create a database connection
        myConn = New OleDbConnection(connectionString:= _
            "Provider=Microsoft.Jet.OLEDB.4.0;Data Source=C:\trxDb.mdb")

        'set an insert statement
        sql = "insert into trxTest (name) values('" & strText & "')"

        'set command text
        myCommand.CommandText = sql

        'set connection property of command object
        myCommand.Connection = myConn

        'open the database connection
        myConn.Open()

        'execute the sql statement
        myCommand.ExecuteNonQuery()

        'close the db connection
        myCommand.Connection.Close()

    End Sub

End Class

'indicate that the class must create a new transaction
<Transaction(TransactionOption.RequiresNew)> _
Public Class trxManage

    'purpose: manage a 2 part transaction

    'indicate serviced component
    Inherits ServicedComponent

    'use the IManage interface
    Implements IManage
```

LISTING 17.5   Continued

```
    Public Sub manageTrx() Implements IManage.manageTrx

        'local scope
        Dim myTrxEvent As New trxWrite()

        'indicate that com+ can deactivate the object upon return
        ContextUtil.DeactivateOnReturn = True

        'call the logging transaction
        myTrxEvent.writeTrx("Test Event")

        'abort the transaction
        ContextUtil.MyTransactionVote = TransactionVote.Abort

    End Sub

End Class

Module Module1

    Sub Main()

        'purpose: act as a client to the trx manager class

        'local scope
        Dim trxManage As New trx.trxManage()

        'call the transaction manage method
        trxManage.manageTrx()

    End Sub

End Module
```

 Suggestions for Further Exploration

➲ Explore the many properties and methods of the ContextUtil. VB6/COM+ programmers should feel right at home!

➲ For more on COM+ transactions inside .NET, including using XML Web services with transactions, see MSDN/Visual Studio .NET/.NET Framework/Programming with the .NET Framework/Processing Transactions.

Events

COM+ provides a service for connecting objects that transmit information with those that want to receive this information. This service can be essential in today's distributed environments. When designing components for enterprise applications, it's just not possible to know all the external or internal objects with which your new class will need to interact. Therefore, it is important to anticipate the types of access to your object's events in which other objects will have interest. The loosely coupled event model creates a programming paradigm of event publishers and event subscribers that know nothing of one another at their time of inception.

Loosely Coupled Event Model

The term *publisher* describes any component that fires events. These components indicate data or an activity to subscribers, such as user login and credit card failed validation. A *subscriber* represents those components that are interested in being notified about a publisher's event. For instance, in the event of a canceled order, your account object may want to be notified to execute a credit against the account. Of course, publishers and subscribers can be *tightly coupled*; that is, they know all about one another and are typically in the same component and run in the same process. This is the model of controls on a form. Your code subscribes to a click event and the form fires your code. Of course, this requires that both the publisher and the subscriber are running at all times and assumes that the subscriber is interested in all the events of the publisher.

The loosely coupled event model, on the other hand, assumes that publisher and subscriber are relatively unaware of each other. The model allows publishers to register events and subscribers to indicate the events in which they might have interest. When the publisher fires an event, an event service handles passing this event out to the various subscribers. This includes creating new objects and firing specific methods on the behalf of the subscriber.

COM+ stores publisher information for loosely coupled events inside the COM+ catalog. To publish an event, you create what is called an *event class*. Event classes are the communication links between publishers and subscribers. Publishers use event classes to fire their events. COM+ uses them to allow subscribers to register for the event and to actually make the calls directly to the subscribers.

Figure 17.6 illustrates the COM+ event model.

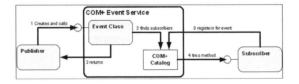

FIGURE 17.6

COM+ event model.

Accessing the COM+ Event Service

To access the event services provided by COM+, you must create an interface, an event class, a subscriber, and a publisher. This section walks you through the creation of an event class and the process of receiving subscriber notification from a published event.

The Interface

By using an interface, you ensure that your subscribers receive events the same way your publisher fires them. Inside Listing 17.6, we create an example of a simple interface called myEventInterface. This interface has one method (someEvent) that takes someData as String as a parameter. We give the interface a strong name, compile it, and register it with the COM+ catalog, mylcEventApp. We then set a reference to it from our subscriber and publisher.

LISTING 17.6 Event Interface

```
Imports System.EnterpriseServices

'indicate the COM+ application to use
<Assembly: ApplicationName("mylcEventApp")>

'set the application to a library package
<Assembly: ApplicationActivation(ActivationOption.Library)>

'indicate the key pair used to generate the strong name for the assembly
<Assembly: System.Reflection.AssemblyKeyFile("myEventI.snk")>

Public Interface myEventInterface

    'purpose: interface communication object between event
    '    publisher(s) and event subscriber(s)

    Sub someEvent(ByVal someData As String)

End Interface
```

The Event Class

The event class is used to define our event. This is the class that gets registered with the COM+ catalog and becomes available for subscription. The class can be marked with the one new .NET attribute that the COM+ events service introduces—EventClassAttribute. This attribute indicates that the class is an event class and marks it as such in the catalog.

The `EventClassAttribute` class has three properties. `AllowInprocSubscribers` indicates that the event supports in-process subscriptions. The `FireInParallel` property tells the COM+ catalog to trigger all subscriber events in parallel rather than in sequence. The `PublisherFilter` is a string value that allows you to filter out specific publishers.

To create the component, we first set a reference to `System.EnterpriseServices` and to our interface object, `myEventInterfaceLib`. The class implements this interface and its one method, `someEvent`. We then create the class and the private key `myEventSNK.snk` and register the component with COM+ services. This can be done inside the IDE, through a component services wizard called Add New Component or via the `regsvcs.exe` utility. Listing 17.7 presents an event class example.

LISTING 17.7   Event Class

```
Imports myEventInterfaceLib
Imports System.EnterpriseServices

'indicate the COM+ application to use
<Assembly: ApplicationName("mylcEventApp")>

'set the application to a library package
<Assembly: ApplicationActivation(ActivationOption.Library)>

'indicate the key pair used to generate the strong name for the assembly
<Assembly: System.Reflection.AssemblyKeyFile("myEventSNK.snk")>

<EventClass()> _
Public Class myEventClass

    'purpose: create an actual event class to be used '
    '    to pass events to subscribers

    'mark as serviced component
    Inherits ServicedComponent

    Implements myEventInterface

    Public Sub someEvent(ByVal someData As String) _
        Implements myEventInterface.someEvent

        'purpose: pass notification from publisher to subscriber

    End Sub

End Class
```

The Subscriber

The event subscriber receives notification when the event class is fired by the publisher. We again set reference to System.EnterpriseServices and myEventInterfaceLib. The class implements myEventInterface and its method, someEvent. On execution, the event data is passed to this subscriber, which logs the data to the event log (see Listing 17.8).

LISTING 17.8 Event Subscriber

```
Imports System.EnterpriseServices
Imports myEventInterfaceLib

'indicate the COM+ application to use
<Assembly: ApplicationName("my1cEventApp")>

'set the application to a library package
<Assembly: ApplicationActivation(ActivationOption.Library)>

'indicate the key pair used to generate the strong name for the assembly
<Assembly: System.Reflection.AssemblyKeyFile("myEventSub.snk")>

Public Class mySubscriberClass

    'purpose: subscribe to the event
    '    this event sink will get notice when event is fired
    '    by publisher

    'mark as serviced component
    Inherits ServicedComponent

    'implement event class
    Implements myEventInterface

    'implement event
    <AutoComplete()> _
    Public Sub someEvent(ByVal someData As String) _
        Implements myEventInterface.someEvent

        'purpose: receive notification that a publisher has sent
        '    and event. note, this routine receives notification
        '    via the myEventInterface interface

        'record the event's data
        EventLog.WriteEntry(source:="messageManager", _
            Message:=someData, _
            type:=EventLogEntryType.Information)
```

LISTING 17.8   Continued

```
    End Sub

End Class
```

No attribute tags allow us to indicate the events to which the object subscribes. These must be set through the Component Services Management application. To do so, right-click the Subscriptions folder and select the event to which you want to subscribe. Figure 17.7 illustrates this interface.

The Publisher

The publisher is any application that makes a direct call to the event class. In Listing 17.9, we create a simple module application. We first set references to `System.EnterpriseServices`, `myEventClassLib`, and `myEventInterfaceLib`. We then create the object, `fireEvent`, based on the `myEventInterface` interface and convert it to the type of `myEventClass`. This is necessary because you cannot instantiate the event class directly. Finally, we call the `someEvent` method and pass it a string value. The COM+ event system intercepts this call and doles it out to all subscribers. In our case, `mySubscriberClass` writes the data to the event log.

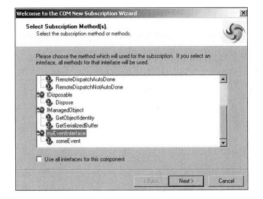

FIGURE 17.7
Subscribing to COM+ events.

LISTING 17.9   Event Publisher

```
Imports myEventClassLib
Imports myEventInterfaceLib

Module Module1
```

LISTING 17.9   Continued

```
'purpose: create an event publisher

Sub Main()

    'purpose: act as the publisher and fire the event class

    'local scope
    Dim fireEvent As myEventInterface

    'convert interface to an instance of the event class
    fireEvent = CType(New myEventClass(), myEventInterface)

    'fire the event
    fireEvent.someEvent("Event data ...")

End Sub

End Module
```

Asynchronous Components

COM+ provides our applications the capability to create and execute components asynchronously. COM+ uses Messaging and a service called Queued Components to provide this functionality. Queued Components work like this: Suppose you have an order-processing system and you want to take your database offline for a few hours every night to do backup. In the meantime, you do not want to stop your site from taking orders. Instead, you can queue your order objects and their requests inside a message queue. When the database comes back online, COM+ will play back the messages and the orders will be processed accordingly. Of course, backing up a database is one thing, but what if your database failed? Or what if your order-processing server started blocking because of high volume? In either of these events, you could code your application to queue your components in these desperate scenarios; no data would be lost and processing could continue seamlessly to the user. Queued Components are certainly not for everyone. When creating your application, you must consider the users' needs, the availability of your system, and the disconnectedness of your enterprise.

> **NOTE**
>
> Chapter 13 is entirely dedicated to Messaging. In Chapter 13, we discussed storing a class as a message using the `System.Messaging` namespace. In this section, we discuss the COM+ service (Queued Components) that provides similar functionality.

Using the COM+ Queued Component Service

You can use a number of attributes inside `System.EnterpriseService` to mark your components as taking advantage of the COM+ Queued Component service. This section defines these attributes as we walk through the process of creating a queued component. We first create a queued component and then create a simple client of the component.

The Queued Component

Queued Components are said to be *recorded* and stored in a message queue on behalf of the client when the message is originally posted. A *listener* listens to recorded messages and receives them from the queue. It then passes the message to a message player. A message *player* plays back the message. In doing so, the player actually reconstructs the object and invokes one of its methods accordingly.

To create a queued component, we must mark the COM+ application as queued. To do this, we use the `ApplicationQueueingAttribute` class. This attribute class allows us to enable both queuing on an application as well as listening. The `Enabled` property indicates that the application can participate with MSMQ queued components. The `QueueListenerEnabled` property, when set to `True`, indicates that the COM+ application will process messages that arrive in its associated queue. An application that is set to handle Queued Components will have an associated private messaging queue.

We use the `InterfaceQueueingAttribute` class to indicate queuing support for an interface. This class has two simple properties: `Enabled` and `Interface`. `Enabled` indicates that the class does support interface queuing. Interface indicates the name of the interface to which the attribute applies.

Listing 17.10 represents a basic queued component. We create one class called `qClass` and one method called `someMethod` that takes `SomeData` as a `String` parameter. The method then writes this data out to the event log.

LISTING 17.10   Queued Component

```
Imports System.EnterpriseServices

'indicate the COM+ application to use
<Assembly: ApplicationName("qc")>

'set the application to a library package
<Assembly: ApplicationActivation(ActivationOption.Server)>
```

LISTING 17.10 Continued

```
'indicate application queueing, set properties
<Assembly: ApplicationQueuing(Enabled:=True, _
    QueueListenerEnabled:=True)>

'indicate the key pair used to generate the strong name for the assembly
<Assembly: System.Reflection.AssemblyKeyFile("qc.snk")>

Namespace qCompNamespace

    Public Interface myQueuedInterface

        'purpose: interface of queued component

        Sub someMethod(ByVal someData As String)

    End Interface

    <InterfaceQueuing(Interface:="myQueuedInterface")> _
    Public Class qClass

        Inherits ServicedComponent

        Implements myQueuedInterface

        Public Sub someMethod(ByVal someData As String) _
            Implements myQueuedInterface.someMethod

            'record the method's data
            EventLog.WriteEntry(source:="messageManager", _
                Message:=someData, _
                type:=EventLogEntryType.Information)

        End Sub

    End Class

End Namespace
```

You can, of course, set the same queuing properties from within the Component Services Explorer application. Figure 17.8 illustrates enabling queuing and marking the application as a listener.

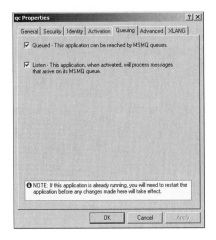

FIGURE 17.8

Queued Component MMC.

Again, you can use the Component Services MMC to mark your interfaces as queued, as illustrated in Figure 17.9. To get this dialog box, you navigate the interfaces on the component, right-click, and choose Properties.

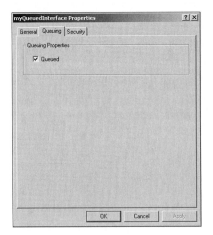

FIGURE 17.9

Queued Component MMC.

The Sender

To actually queue a component, we create a simple client application that uses our qComp namespace. We first set a reference to this namespace and then dimension a variable as the interface type myQueuedInterface. We then create an instance of the Queued Component using CType and bind the component to a message queue using Marshal.BindToMonker.

Finally, we call the method on the component, which gets recorded into the message queue. In fact, if your COM+ application is stopped, you can view the message from the Computer Management application. After you start your COM+ application, it picks up the message and plays it back—in our case, writing the data out to the event log.

Listing 17.11 presents an example that creates a queued component.

LISTING 17.11   Message Sender

```
Imports qComp.qCompNamespace
Imports System.EnterpriseServices
Imports System.Runtime.InteropServices

Module Module1

    Sub Main()

        'purpose: create a queued component

        'local scope
        Dim queuedComp As myQueuedInterface

        'create a queued component, indicate queue and comp. interface
        queuedComp = CType(Marshal.BindToMoniker( _
            "queue:/new:qComp.qCompNamespace.qClass"), _
            myQueuedInterface)

        'call the method of the queued component
        queuedComp.someMethod("Queued Component")

        'release the object
        Marshal.ReleaseComObject(queuedComp)

    End Sub

End Module
```

Summary

COM+ offers developers a number of key services. These services are still very much relevant with the advent of .NET and continue to be extended by Microsoft. As you've seen, COM+ is very accessible and makes your job easier. If your application requires you to write scalable and highly available objects, you should consider incorporating COM+ services.

The following are key points of the chapter:

- COM+ services can increase the scalability of your application and ease the burden of writing resource-management code.
- To gain the full benefit of COM+, you need to design your objects as stateless.
- To create a serviced component, you must inherit directly from System.Enterprise.ServicedComponent.
- To be accessible from other objects, serviced components should have a strong name and be registered in the global assembly cache. .NET provides the utility sn.exe for creating strong names and regsvcs.exe for manually registering managed code with COM+.
- You can assign roles-based access to assemblies, classes, methods, and interfaces using the SecurityRole attribute class.
- You can access the security context of your executing code with the SecurityCallContext class and its CurrentCall property.
- The ObjectPooling attribute class allows you to mark your class as pooled and set the minimum and maximum pool size.
- Use the JustInTimeActivation attribute class to take advantage of the JIT activation and deactivation service provided by COM+.
- The classes SharedPropertyGroupManager, SharedPropertyGroup, and SharedProperty allow you to maintain global state between otherwise stateless object calls.
- You can set your components to automatically manage transaction state by setting the AutoComplete attribute.
- To access the transaction context and call things such as SetComplete and SetAbort, use the ContexUtil class.
- The EventClass attribute class is used to mark your components as event classes that can be loosely coupled and subscribed to by other objects.
- Queued Components enable you to store a transaction for asynchronous execution at a later date. To enable queuing from your component, use the ApplicationQueueing attribute class.

.NET Interop with COM
Applications

IN THIS CHAPTER

Microsoft has devoted a number of resources to ensure that your current code base is not trashed with the advent of .NET. As a result, .NET and the CLR understand how to talk to COM, and Microsoft has provided features that make COM forward compatible with .NET! Therefore, before you fire up that porting engine or rewrite your entire middle tier, make sure that porting—and not simply interoperating—is the answer.

In this chapter, we discuss how to determine which pieces of existing applications you might migrate, as well as the task of creating new functionality in .NET while keeping your legacy code base intact. We then walk through the process of creating both a COM-to-.NET and a .NET-to-COM interop example. Finally, we detail the specifics of interoperation and illustrate some of the key classes inside the System.Runtime.InteropServices namespace.

After reading this chapter, you should be able to do the following:

- Determine when it is more feasible to interoperate, port, or write a custom wrapper
- Call a COM server component from a .NET client
- Call a .NET server object from a COM client
- Design your .NET interop components to work well with COM
- Understand how to leverage the attribute classes inside of the InteropServices namespace

.NET Interop with COM

For the most part, the CLR inside of .NET shields us from the intricacies and complexities associated with interoperating between the world of legacy COM applications and that of .NET. When making cross-boundary calls, the CLR automatically generates a wrapper for the given client to use, effectively making the call appear as native to the given client, whether it is .NET or COM. In doing so, .NET manages all of the following:

- Object binding
- Object identity
- Marshaling and translation
- Object life cycle
- Error and exception handling

Without this support, the task of accessing objects across these very different programming models would be daunting to the average developer. However, by leveraging the services the CLR provides and understanding the interoperation process and rules, you should be well equipped to preserve your current vested code base.

Interop Design Decisions

.NET and the CLR make it possible, in almost every case, to continue to leverage your current COM components. Additionally, it is very possible to co-mingle your environments—that is, run both ASP/VB, COM/ADO, and .NET alongside on the same server. The question is not then about the possible, but about the practical, cost effective, and reasonable.

Maintaining the Status Quo

Perhaps migrating or interoperation is not the right choice for your application. It is possible that simply sticking with the current COM state of your application is your best strategy. After all, thousands of applications are running very well under Windows DNA architecture and are using COM objects to encapsulate their business logic. It is no small endeavor to port these applications or to comingle them with .NET code. You must quantify the return on such an investment.

From our perspective, applications that have been effectively stabilized and that require very little maintenance or extension of features make the best candidates for maintaining the COM status quo. Unless you can point to a specific business, architecture, or performance problem that .NET solves, it is more cost effective to continue this application down its current path. That is not to say that you should not consider an upgrade to .NET during the next major over-haul of the system—in most cases, you will see the largest benefits from upgrades that take a sweeping path through the system.

Extending Your Application

When you're ready to reinvent your application, significantly enhance it, or change your business model, it is likely the best time to consider moving much of the new features to .NET. In this case, you are more than likely already rewriting the logic or creating new business objects in your application. The added cost to move to .NET during such a change is minimal compared to the benefits. This assumes that your development team is well versed in the new technology.

In such cases, an interop solution affords you the following benefits:

- Maintains business logic that did not change inside of COM
- Realizes the productivity enhancements that .NET provides project teams
- Allows your developers to progress to the new world
- Brings your application inline with the state of the art, allowing access to new features and robustness

Creating a New Application

We suggest that all new development be written inside .NET—but we also live in the real world. New development these days might mean a new project, but many times, a good portion of the code will come from existing sources. Of course, these sources are heavily entrenched in the COM world. Rather than rewrite thousands of lines of code you are used to purchasing, we believe this is where interoperation can really shine. While you await a .NET version of an existing COM object, you can create your clients and surrounding objects using .NET and make great use of interop to work with those exiting objects. And don't forget, the Framework Class Library itself often offers a managed solution that might replace the need for the third-party control or library.

Porting an Application Tier

At times, it can be ideal to migrate an entire tier of an application at one time. Your business needs might be such that you're forced to change a majority of your business logic or rewrite your user interface. This is a perfect time to consider .NET. Typically, it is much easier to migrate an entire tier rather than a few objects.

When taking on such an endeavor, it is important to understand the effects of such an integrated approach. For instance, suppose you plan to roll out a new user interface for your application and decide to use ASP.NET. Your business objects are all COM based and you know the CLR will wrap them for you, so you move ahead. However, if your interfaces to those objects are *chatty*—that is, they require a lot of property sets and gets, you may suffer a significant performance penalty for interoperating in this manner. Each call between the unmanaged and managed worlds must be marshaled by the CLR. An ideal interop application in this case would be one whose middle-tier objects are designed to closely conform to the COM stateless design guidelines. The interfaces to these objects are said to be *chunky*—that is, one call does a lot of work. In this case, the performance penalty for marshaling will probably go unnoticed.

Ultimately, you will need to test your components in their environment to make the final decision regarding how to interoperate and which portions of your code you should port and when.

For Further Exploration

For a great discussion on migration strategies, check out the whitepaper, "Microsoft .NET/COM Migration and Interoperability" available on MSDN at `http://msdn.microsoft.com/library/default.asp?url=/library/en-us/dnbda/html/cominterop.asp`.

Calling COM from .NET Clients

COM has been the standard for a very long time, at least in computer programming years. As a result, literally millions of existing COM objects and associated COM clients exist. .NET does not presuppose its programming model as a 100% solution for all functionality written for an application. .NET developers will be working with existing COM infrastructure for years to come. It is for this reason that .NET comes well equipped to deal with the heterogeneous world through predefined interop capabilities.

The Basics

Calling a COM server from a .NET client can be a very simple task in the majority of cases, but depending on your requirements, the process can quickly become complex. We'll start with the simple. In this section, we walk you through the steps involved with calling a COM server from a .NET client.

First, we create a simple COM object to act as a server for our .NET client calls. The following code creates a VB6 ActiveX dll project with one method, Add, that simply adds two numbers and returns the resulting sum.

```
Public Function add( -
    ByVal numberOne As Integer, _
    ByVal numberTwo As Integer) as Integer

    'add two numbers together and return
    add = numberOne + numberTwo

End Function
```

This project gets compiled the same way as any VB6 project does. Remember, we could just as easily use an existing COM server.

Next, inside the VS .NET IDE, we create a simple console application to act as our .NET client. We initially attempt to set a reference to our COM server from the References dialog box for our project. However, on doing so, we are presented with the warning message, as indicated in Figure 18.1.

This warning message indicates that no Primary Interop Assembly (PIA) exists for our COM server. An *interop assembly* is simply a managed code dll that wraps our COM server's interface. This allows us to work with the COM server as if it were a native .NET server and assists the CLR in translating calls between .NET and COM. To be clear, interop assemblies contain no implementation code. They are simply type definitions for the COM component's equivalent .NET types.

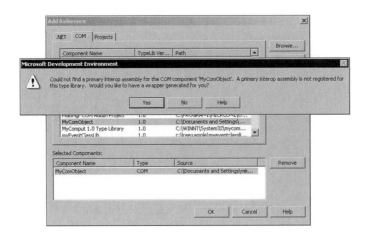

FIGURE 18.1
Setting a reference to our COM server.

The *primary* interop assembly differs from a standard (sometimes called alternate) interop assembly in that it is signed by the publisher as the unique interop source for the given COM server. This ensures that two .NET clients access a given COM server in the same manner and provides the official definition of the assembly's types. Standard interop assemblies are generated by a developer wanting to access a COM server. As a result, two developers generating two distinct interop assemblies against the same COM object result in two incompatible interop assemblies. This is fine as long as the two applications never try to pass an instance of the assembly to one another. The COM server may be identical, but its interop assembly is very different, resulting in an exception. For this reason, COM servers that are typically shared should have one primary interop assembly generated for them by the publisher.

.NET provides the tools to generate both standard and primary interop assemblies. In fact, because the PIA is managed code, you can even write them yourself. To do so, you would tag a given assembly with the `PrimaryInteropAssemblyAttribute` class located inside `System.Runtime.InteropServices`. However, it is often much simpler to use the .NET utilities.

The Type Library Importer (`TlbImp.exe`) utility is used to convert the types inside a COM server to an interop assembly. Because we are the publisher, we will use the utility to generate the PIA for our COM server. Because PIAs are strongly named, we must first create a new key pair to sign our server. We do this with the Strong Name tool (sn.exe) and create the file, `MyPIAKey.snk`. The following represents the command prompt call

```
Sn.exe –k MyPIAKey.snk
```

Next, we simply run the `TlbImp.exe` against our COM server and attach our key pair as in the following:

```
Tlbimp.exe /primary /keyfile:MyPIAKey.snk
  /out:MyComObjectPIA.dll MyComObject.dll
```

Note that we specified the option `/primary` to indicate that this was a PIA and not simply an IA. We then indicate the key file (`/keyfile:`) and finally tell the utility where to output the resulting PIA (`/out:`).

Now, from our .NET client, we can simply reference the newly created PIA file instead of the COM server library. This interop object appears to our client as any other .NET object would. You can see this by examining the PIA inside the object browser, as Figure 18.2 indicates.

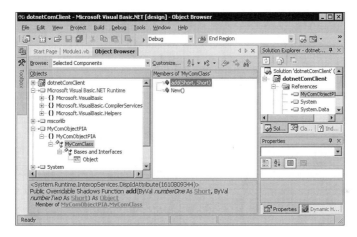

FIGURE 18.2
Our COM server PIA.

All that is left is to make our object calls to the COM server. The following code creates a new instance of the PIA and calls its method, `Add`.

```
Module Module1

  Sub Main()

    'local scope
    Dim comObject As MyComObjectPIA.MyComClass

    'create the com instance
    comObject = New MyComObjectPIA.MyComClass()
```

```
'call the com method
MsgBox(prompt:=comObject.add(numberOne:=8, numberTwo:=6))
```

```
End Sub
```

```
End Module
```

Although PIAs are a best practice, it is often necessary to allow VS .NET to generate an alternate interop assembly for you. If you choose Yes in response to the dialog box question, `Would you like to have a wrapper generated for you?`, VS .NET will generate an interop assembly whose filename in this case is `Interop.MyComObject_1_0.dll`. Again, this is a standard IA and can be used to the same result, but warnings apply. The code to access this IA and the COM server from our .NET client is as follows:

```
'local scope
Dim comObject As MyComObject.MyComClass
```

```
'create the com instance
comObject = New MyComObject.MyComClass()
```

```
'call the com method
MsgBox(prompt:=comObject.add(numberOne:=8, numberTwo:=6))
```

VB .NET developers have one more tool available to them to support interop with ActiveX COM servers—the `CreateObject` function. As in VB of old, `CreateObject` provides late binding to ActiveX COM libraries. In this case, no PIA or IA is required; the CLR handles all tasks for you. Of course, calls are late bound, which disables compiler type checking and can create undesirable effects. However, it is worth mentioning because it is a very simple method you can use to call COM servers from .NET. The following represents making a late-bound call to our `MyComObject`:

```
Dim comObject As Object
```

```
'create the com instance
comObject = CreateObject("MyComObject.MyComClass")
```

```
'call the com method
MsgBox(prompt:=comObject.add(numberOne:=8, numberTwo:=6))
```

The Runtime Callable Wrapper (RCW)

How is .NET able to call a COM server from an interop assembly? What controls marshaling of the types between COM and .NET? The answer to both these questions is a *Runtime Callable Wrapper,* or RCW. An RCW is generated by the CLR on-the-fly for your application during an interop session. The RCW acts as a proxy between the .NET client and the COM server. The RCW uses your interop assembly to understand exactly how to marshal data between the two layers. Figure 18.3 illustrates a .NET client communicating to a COM object via an RCW proxy.

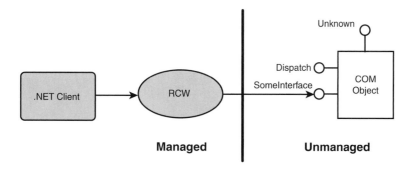

FIGURE 18.3
Runtime Callable Wrapper (RCW).

The CLR uses the interop assembly's metadata to generate the RCW and to create the COM server instance. The RCW wraps the COM server and mediates method calls and data type translations between the two environments. Its job is to make the COM server appear as a native .NET object to the CLR and make the .NET client appear as a COM client to the COM server.

The COM object is reference counted, and as such, references are maintained by the RCW. The RCW, on the other hand, is managed and therefore subject to garbage collection. It is the RCW that manages the releasing of references to the COM server.

Some limitations exist to COM servers that bleed through to your interop assembly and the RCW. These include the lack of support for parameterized constructors, inheritance, and static methods. These are features that .NET clients will come to expect from server objects, whether they are COM or .NET. To bridge these limitations, you can create a custom interop wrapper.

Custom Interop Wrapper

You can customize the way your data types are transformed by the CLR by editing your interop assembly. However, unless you've created your own interop assembly or are at ease writing Interface Definition Language (IDL) to edit type libraries, we do not suggest this. Instead, because the IA is a managed object, you can take advantage of .NET inheritance to customize your interoperation.

To illustrate this concept, consider our original VB6 COM server that did addition. For this example, we'll add a function to subtract two numbers.

```
Public Function Add(ByVal numberOne As Integer, _
    ByVal numberTwo As Integer) As Integer

    'add two numbers together and return

    Add = numberOne + numberTwo

End Function

Public Function Subtract(ByVal numberOne As Integer, _
    ByVal numberTwo As Integer) As Integer

    'subtract two numbers and return result

    Subtract = numberOne - numberTwo

End Function
```

Now suppose that our requirement is to make the add function operate with decimal values. For our .NET client, we want to continue to support the COM interface and continue to use the other logic embedded inside the COM server (the Subtract method). However, as we extend our object, we want to build our new code inside .NET.

To accomplish this, you create a wrapper class for your COM server. This wrapper class should inherit directly from the interop assembly. Your new code can be implemented as an override to the Add method while Subtract continues to interoperate with the COM server. An example of this wrapper class follows:

```
Public Class MyComObject

    Inherits MyComObjectPIA3.MyComClass

    Public Overloads Function Add( _
        ByVal numberOne As Double, _
        ByVal numberTwo As Double) As Double

        Add = numberOne + numberTwo

    End Function

End Class
```

Your .NET client now simply references your wrapper classes and makes the same calls to Add and Subtract.

```
Module Module1

  Sub Main()

    'local scope
    Dim comObject As MyComObject

    'create the com instance
    comObject = New MyComObject()

    'call the com method
    MsgBox(prompt:=comObject.Add(numberOne:=8.2, numberTwo:=6.4))
    MsgBox(prompt:=comObject.Subtract(numberOne:=8, numberTwo:=6))

  End Sub

End Module
```

The biggest advantage to creating a custom wrapper is that you can slowly replace your COM server with managed code, and clients will continue to function regardless. You can apply this design pattern to solve a number of interop issues.

Calling .NET from COM Clients

You undoubtedly will want to quickly take advantage of the benefits .NET development provides your application. Chances are, you will be extending an existing application rather than executing a complete rewrite for .NET. For this reason, Microsoft has made sure that .NET components can be written to support forward compatibility from COM.

Suppose you have the requirement to add a new component to your system that relies on a COM client application and other COM servers. You do not intend to replace the client application or rewrite your middle tier. However, you are anxious to create your new components to take advantage of .NET's features and flexibility. The CLR allows you to create a managed component that looks native to COM.

The Basics

Creating .NET servers for COM clients involves properly defining a component's architecture, understanding the constraints COM imposes, creating a type library, and registering the component. In this section, we walk through the necessary steps involved with exposing managed code to COM.

First, we create a simple .NET server object. In our case, we define two functions: Multiply and Divide.

```vb
Imports System.Reflection
Imports System.Runtime.InteropServices

<Assembly: AssemblyKeyFile("MyKey.snk")>

Public Interface IDNetServer

    'explicitly create the interface

    Function Multiply(ByVal numberOne As Integer, _
        ByVal numberTwo As Integer) As Integer

    Function Divide(ByVal numberOne As Integer, _
        ByVal numberTwo As Integer) As Integer

End Interface

<ClassInterface(ClassInterfaceType.None)> _
Public Class MyDNetClass

    Implements IDNetServer

    Public Sub New()
        'default constructor, in this case it does nothing
    End Sub

    Public Function Multiply( _
        ByVal numberOne As Integer, _
        ByVal numberTwo As Integer) As Integer _
        Implements IDNetServer.Multiply

        'multiply 2 numbers
        Return numberOne * numberTwo

    End Function

    Public Function Divide( _
        ByVal numberOne As Integer, _
        ByVal numberTwo As Integer) As Integer _
        Implements IDNetServer.Divide
```

```
        'divide 2 numbers
        Try
              Return numberOne / numberTwo
        Catch
              'do nothing
        End Try

   End Function

End Class
```

Notice that we explicitly define an interface (IDNetServer) for use by our class
(MyDNetClass). COM requires our classes to publish an interface. It is a best practice to define
interfaces explicitly. When doing so, it is best to use the ClassInterfaceAttribute class to
tag the class as not requiring an autogenerated class interface.

> **NOTE**
>
> We are free to use the default class interface that is generated by utilities such as the
> table exporter (TlbExp.exe). By default, when we export a type library, the utility cre-
> ates a class interface for each class in the .NET server. On the surface, this sounds like
> a great idea; indeed, it can be in the right situation. However, because of the inter-
> face rules COM imposes and the possible restructuring of those interfaces by a type
> library generator, it is best to define these interfaces explicitly.

Also notice that we define a default constructor for our object, even though we do not attach
any code to the routine. This is a requirement of COM. COM services cannot create the object
without a defined default constructor.

Another requirement for COM interoperation is that all members visible to COM must be
declared as public. Additionally, COM, by its nature, imposes a few restrictions on what our
components are allowed to do. For instance, parameterized constructors are not permitted, static methods are out, and COM has no idea of constant fields. Although you need to be acutely
aware of these restrictions, you undoubtedly have good reason for creating .NET servers for
COM clients. These restrictions should not dissuade you from your course; they represent features of .NET that, as VB COM developers, we're used to living without.

Finally, to register our managed server with COM, we must digitally sign it. In our case, we
create the file MyKey.snk using the strong name utility, SN.exe, and apply the attribute
AssemblyKeyFile to the assembly.

18

.NET INTEROP
WITH COM
APPLICATIONS

After compilation, we must register the .NET server with COM inside the Windows Registry to make it visible. Prior to registration, we need to create a type library. .NET provides a number of means for creating type libraries for interop purposes. Two of the most popular are the Table Exporter utility (`TlbExp.exe`) and the Assembly Registration tool (`Regasm.exe`).

In our example, we'll use the `Regasm.exe` utility. This enables us to create our type library and register it at the same time. The following creates a type library called `MyDNetServer.tlb` and registers our library (`MyDNetServer.dll`) with COM:

```
regasm MyDNetServer.dll /tlb:MyDNetServer.tlb
```

We have a couple options open to us for storing our library. When COM requests a .NET server, the CLR searches either the requesting application's directory tree for the library or the Global Assembly Cache (GAC). Public servers—those that are used by more than one application—should, as a rule, be stored in the GAC. See Chapter 22, "Deploying, Configuring, and Licensing .NET Components," for more information on the GAC.

In our example, we intend our math functions to apply to many applications, so we will install the object to the GAC. To do so, we use the `GacUtil.exe` executable as follows and the parameter "/i" to indicate that we are installing.

```
gacutil /i MyDNetServer.dll
```

Last, we create a COM client that uses our .NET server. The following list outlines the steps involved:

1. Create a simple VB6 forms application and add a button to the form.
2. Set a reference to the managed server, the same as you would any other COM server. Note that you are actually setting a reference to the type library.
3. Inside the button's click event, create a variable to reference the server. Notice that you dimension the variable as the interface to .NET server. This is useful—although not necessary—so that your code can get Intellisense on your server's methods.
4. Finally, create an instance of your .NET server (`MyDNetClass`) and call its methods.

```
Private Sub Command1_Click()

    'define the object as the interface to gain intellisense
    Dim myServer As MyDNetServer.IDNetServer

    'create an actual class instance
    Set myServer = New MyDNetServer.MyDNetClass

    'call methods
    MsgBox myServer.Divide(10, 5)
    MsgBox myServer.Multiply(10, 5)


End Sub
```

The COM Callable Wrapper (CCW)

Like the RCW generated by the CLR when calling COM from .NET, a *COM Callable Wrapper* (CCW) is created on-the-fly by the CLR when a COM client requests the use of a .NET server. This wrapper ensures that calls between the two objects appear as native to their respective environments. The wrapper, again like the RCW, is a proxy that mediates and marshals the data between the two worlds. Figure 18.4 illustrates this interop call via the CCW.

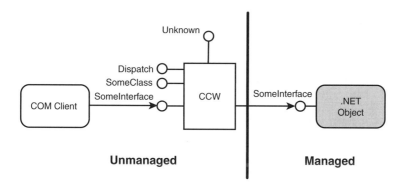

Unmanaged   **Managed**

FIGURE 18.4
COM Callable Wrapper (CCW).

The runtime uses the metadata associated with the managed class to generate the CCW. This metadata describes the types your object exposes and allows the CCW to proxy those types to and from COM. Also notice that the COM client interacts with the CCW via the traditional interfaces, IUnknown and IDispatch, which are created by the CLR. It should be noted that the runtime always provides implementation for these specific interfaces. The CCW also implements a number of additional traditional COM interfaces, all of which are available for override by the .NET server object. Some of these include IErrorInfo, ITypeInfo, IProvideClassInfo, IProvideErrorInfo.

Another key point about the CCW is that although it is created by the CLR, it is actually an unmanaged COM object. As a result, it is reference counted like any other COM object and not garbage collected. When the CCW ceases to have a reference, it is destroyed and the managed object that it wraps is marked for garbage collection.

Interop Considerations

This brief section describes some additional considerations you need to be aware of when designing and coding your application components for interoperation.

Marshaling and Translation

Fortunately, some data types are common across the interop boundary. These types are said to be *blittable*. Blittable types do not require translation or conversion between .NET and COM worlds. As a result, these types are marshaled with less overhead and a higher degree of performance. Blittable types include `byte`, `short`, `integer`, `long`, `single`, `double`.

Translated types, also called nonblittable, require conversion. A VB BSTR is an example of a nonblittable type. You should remain aware of these types and minimize their use because they do result in a performance penalty.

Object Life Cycle

As we've discussed, COM servers are reference counted, whereas their .NET counterparts rely on garbage collection to manage their life cycle. Developers need to be acutely aware of this fact because a shared system results in behavior that is not necessarily indicative of either system. For instance, a .NET client that is referencing a COM server will hold that reference long after it is finished with the object. (This is because of the nature of garbage collection, which processes only when the system requires it, not the application or server. Typically, this may not be a problem.) However, if the COM object is holding references to another expensive resource such as a data connection, this can be troublesome. In this specific example, you should either force garbage collection or explicitly release the COM object. Forcing GC is not the preferred method; it undermines the GC's effectiveness. To release a specific COM instance, when your .NET server is finished (awaiting GC), make a call to `System.Runtime.InteropServices.MarshalReleaseComObject`.

Error and Exception Handling

Traditional VB developers use the `raise` statement to send errors back to their clients. This has the same effect as returning traditional COM HRESULTs. .NET, on the other hand, handles errors by throwing and catching exception objects within the CLR. For the purpose of interoperability, each exception class within the Framework maps directly to an HRESULT. This ensures that the wrapper classes can intercept errors from both systems, can translate them, and then forward them on in the native format. If, however, you decide to create your own exceptions by extending `System.Exception`, you should always set the HRESULT field to provide this same support for interoperation.

Handling Events

The .NET event model based on delegates is very different from that of COM's connection point events. Fortunately, when you create a .NET client based on the interop assembly for a COM server, the conversion process generates a .NET delegate for each COM event. Using this method, you simply wire your event handlers to the given delegates as if they were native to .NET. Similarly, VB6 COM clients interacting with .NET events will see those events as native to COM, thanks to the exported type library.

Attribute Classes

The namespace `System.Runtime.InteropServices` provides a number of attribute classes that can be used to further refine your interop servers. These classes enable you to control marshaling, define methods that get exposed, and the like. Table 18.1 lists a number of these attribute classes.

TABLE 18.1   `InteropServices` Key Attribute Classes

Attribute Class	Applies To	Description
ClassInterface	Assemblies Classes	`ClassInterface` enables you to define the type of class interface that is created for the given class or set of classes when a .NET export utility is used to create a type library for COM. `ClassInterface` has a `Value` property that is of the type `ClassInterfaceType` enumeration. This enum's values include `AutoDispatch`, `AutoDual`, and `None`.
COMRegisterFunction	Methods	The `COMRegisterFunction` attribute class tags a given function to be run when the assembly is registered. This enables you to ensure the execution of your code during the registration process. The CLR takes care of calling the method when registering with the RegAsm.exe utility. A given assembly can have only one method marked as `COMRegisterFunction`.
		The counterpart to this attribute class is `COMUnregisterFunction`, which gets called when a .NET server is unregistered with the `RegAsm.exe` utility.

TABLE 18.1   Continued

Attribute Class	Applies To	Description
COMVisible	Assemblies Interfaces Classes Structures Delegates Enumerations Fields Methods Properties	The COMVisible attribute class is used to control which parts of your objects are made visible to COM. Of course, by default, all public types in your assembly are made visible to COM. This attribute class enables you to further refine what is visible to COM versus .NET. Note settings for COMVisible at the lowest level override those at the highest. For instance, if you set COMVisible to False at the assembly level and want to make one method visible, you can simply reset COMVisible to True for that method only.
MarshalAs	Parameters Fields Return Values	The MarshalAs attribute class enables you to control how data is marshaled between the managed world of .NET and the unmanaged world of COM. The attribute class has a Value property of the type UnmanagedType enumeration. This enumeration defines all the marshaling types available. Each type has a default marshal-as value; this class simply allows you to override those settings.
Optional	Parameters	The Optional attribute class is used to indicate to COM that a .NET parameter is optional.
PrimaryInteropAssembly	Assemblies	The PrimaryInteropAssembly attribute class allows you to indicate that your developer-defined assembly is a PIA for your .NET server.
ProgId	Classes	The ProgId attribute class allows you to explicitly define a ProgId for your .NET interop server. Note that if you do not set this attribute, the registration process uses your namespace and type name to generate a ProgId for you.

Summary

Interoperability is paramount to the success of modern application development and .NET itself. For this reason, .NET exposes a number of interop possibilities and provides the level of control that a given developer may need or can handle.

The following are key points of the chapter:

- .NET can reach into COM servers through the CLR-generated and managed Runtime Callable Wrapper.
- COM developers integrating with .NET clients should create a Primary Interop Assembly to wrap their object's interfaces.
- You can create a custom wrapper for a given COM object through inheritance and overriding methods of a COM server's PIA.
- .NET components can be called from COM clients through the CLR-generated unmanaged COM Callable Wrapper.
- .NET components shared with a number of clients (COM or .NET) should be installed in the Global Assembly Cache.

18

**.NET INTEROP
WITH COM
APPLICATIONS**

Managing Collections of Objects

IN THIS CHAPTER

As Visual Basic programmers, we have a number of new options available for managing collections of objects. The simple, but effective, collection object that we had become accustomed to as VB developers is a relic. The `System.Collections` namespace adds a number of specialized collection classes to our programmer's tool belt. This chapter focuses on those collections and on indicating when you might implement a given solution.

After reading this chapter, you should

- Understand the differences between all the collection classes in the namespace
- Decide when to implement a given type of collection class
- Be able to write code using the various collection classes
- Create custom, strongly typed collection classes

Managing Collections of Objects

Our applications often need to manage data in groups. For instance, we may have a set of similar database records that we want to iterate through, or perhaps we need to sort values in an array. To do so, we typically place this data into a collection for easy management and storage. A collection is simply a class that exposes properties and methods for working with a group of like data. Collection classes often implement standard interfaces that allow us to retrieve, count, and generally order our data in our application.

Depending on our design and requirements, a surprising number of collection strategies are available to us. The Framework Class Library exposes all-purpose collections (such as the `ArrayList`) as well as highly specialized collections (such as `BitArray`). The more specialized a given collection class, the more limited it is to its specific purpose. Because of the large variety of collections available, this section will detail a number of collections and demonstrate their usage.

System.Collections Namespace

Collections differ based on how elements are stored, sorted, searched, and compared. These are the key considerations to examine when searching for the right class for the task at hand. For example, items in collections are typically accessed by a key value or by indicating the index of the item. Additionally, classes such as `Queue` and `Stack` are used to store items you expect to remove from a collection. Table 19.1 presents the various collections in the library across these parameters.

TABLE 19.1 Collection Classes at a Glance

Collection	Sorted	Accessed	Storage	Key/Value Pair
Queue	NA	First In/First Out	Temporary	Value
Stack	NA	Last In/First Out	Temporary	Value
ArrayList	Sorts by IComparer	Index	Longer	Value
Hashtable	NA	Key	Longer	Value
SortedList	Sorts by key	Key	Longer	Key-Value
ListDictionary	NA	Key	Longer	Key-Value
StringDictionary	NA	Key	Longer	Key-Value
StringCollection	NA	Index	Longer	Key-Value
NameValueCollection	NA	Index or Key	Longer	Key-Value

Stack

The Stack collection class stores objects in the reverse order they were placed in the collection. That is, adding a tenth item to a collection with nine items makes the new item the first item in the collection and pushes each subsequent item down the "stack." One becomes two, two, three, and so on. As items are accessed or removed from the stack, they are done so sequentially. So even though item one represents the last item to be added (10), it is the first item to be accessed. This is also known as "last in, first out."

One interesting thing about a stack is that you cannot change an item's value after it has been placed on the stack. You can only remove it from the stack.

Stacks can be very useful in the right context. They offer temporary storage for data that is accessed in a particular manner. One of the most common uses of the stack collection is to store the state of an object or variable between calls.

Constructors

Three constructors are available for creating a Stack instance. The first, which takes no parameters, creates a Stack object with a default initial capacity of 10. The Stack class doubles its current size when its capacity is reached. If you have a good idea of what your Stack size will be, you can save the overhead of doubling every time the capacity is reached, or from allocating more memory than is necessary, by using the constructor, New Stack(initialCapacity as Integer). This constructor lets you initialize the Stack object to your intended size. Last, you can create a new Stack instance from an existing collection object. This constructor takes an instance of a collection object derived from the ICollection interface. Items are added to the Stack object, based on the order they are enumerated, using the IEnumerable interface. We'll discuss these interfaces in greater detail in just a minute.

Properties and Methods

The key methods for working with a Stack object are Push, Pop, and Peek. Items are said to be *pushed* onto the stack, *popped* off the stack, or *peeked* at. Table 19.2 is a reference detailing the key properties and methods of the Stack collection class.

TABLE 19.2   Key Properties and Methods of the Stack Class

Property	Description
Count	The Count property returns the actual number of elements contained inside the Stack collection—not the capacity.
IsReadOnly	The IsReadOnly property returns True if the Stack instance is read-only.
Method	
Clear	The Clear method removes all items from the Stack instance and resets the Count property to zero.
Clone	The Clone method creates a copy of the current Stack instance. The cloned Stack instance references the original Stack objects; it does not copy them. However, the cloned Stack and the Stack from which it was created can be operated on independently. That is, items can be pushed and popped on both instances without regard for the other. Cloning in this manner is also referred to as creating a shallow copy (a deep copy would actually copy items from one instance to the other).
Contains	The Contains method executes a linear search for a given object passed as a parameter. The method returns True if the object is contained by the Stack instance. Note: Because the search is linear, the execution time depends on how deep the item is within the Stack.
CopyTo	The CopyTo method enables you to output a copy of all the elements within the Stack to a one-dimensional array. Items are copied in the "last-in, first-out" order. That is, the uppermost item in the array will contain the last item pushed onto the stack. The method takes two parameters: an array to which to copy stack items and the index indicating where in the array to begin the copy procedure.
GetEnumerator	The GetEnumerator method returns an object of the type IEnumerator. This object enables you to walk through the collection without peeking or popping items off the stack.

TABLE 19.2 Continued

Property	Description
Method	

A simple example follows:

```
Dim myStack As New Collections.Stack()
Dim myEnum As IEnumerator

'add items to the stack ...

myEnum = myStack.GetEnumerator

Do While myEnum.MoveNext <> False
   Console.WriteLine(myEnum.Current)
          Loop
```

Property	Description
Peek	The Peek method returns the item at the top of the Stack object. Peek enables you to view the item without removing it from the collection.
Pop	The Pop method returns the topmost item on a Stack instance. Pop removes the item from the collection.
Push	The Push method adds an item to the top of a Stack instance. In doing so, it pushes each successive item down one level in the Stack.
ToArray	The ToArray method copies all items in the Stack instance to a one-dimensional array.

Learning by Example: Stack Collection

In Listing 19.1, we create a simple class, called StackClass, that monitors internal calls to various functions similar to a call stack. The class exposes one function, SomeFunction, which uses a random number to simulate code logic and in turn calls other internal functions. Each function pushes a value onto the stack when it is called. The resulting Stack collection is exposed as a property of the class CallStack.

Additionally, we create a console application that creates an instance of StackClass, calls its function SomeFunction, and writes the Stack contents to the command window.

LISTING 19.1 A Simple Call Stack

```
Module Module1

  Sub Main()

    'local scope
```

LISTING 19.1   Continued

```
    Dim myStackClass As New StackClass()
    Dim i As Integer

    'call the class' function
    myStackClass.SomeFunction()

    'write out the stack
    For i = 1 To myStackClass.CallStack.Count
      Console.WriteLine(myStackClass.CallStack.Pop)
    Next

    'pause
    Do While Console.ReadLine <> "s" : Loop

  End Sub

End Module

Public Class StackClass

  'global stack collection object
  Private myStack As Collections.Stack
  Private myRandom As New Random()

  Public Sub New()

    'purpose: create an instance of the stack collection
    '         within the object's constructor
    myStack = New Collections.Stack(initialCapacity:=15)

  End Sub

  Public Function SomeFunction()

    'purpose: simulate logic with random numbers, track procedure
    ' calls using a stack instance

    'push this function onto the stack
    myStack.Push(obj:="SomeFunction")

    'some logic ... random number
    If myRandom.Next(maxValue:=3) = 2 Then
      Call SomeFunction2()
    Else
      Call SomeFunctionElse()
```

LISTING 19.1 Continued

```vb
    End If

  End Function

  Private Function SomeFunction2()

    'purpose: demonstrate call stack

    'push this function onto the stack
    myStack.Push(obj:="SomeFunction2")

    'some logic ... random number
    If myRandom.Next(maxValue:=3) = 2 Then
      Exit Function
    Else
      Call SomeFunctionElse()
    End If

  End Function

  Private Function SomeFunctionElse()

    'purpose: demonstrate call stack

    'push this function onto the stack
    myStack.Push(obj:="SomeFunctionElse")

    'some logic ... random number
    If myRandom.Next(maxValue:=4) = 2 Then
      Exit Function
    Else
      Call SomeFunction2()
    End If

  End Function

  Public ReadOnly Property CallStack() As Collections.Stack

    Get
      'return the stack object for examination
      Return myStack
    End Get

  End Property

End Class
```

Queue

The Queue class is the opposite of the Stack collection and mimics the functionality most closely associated with a message queue. Items are added and removed from a queue in a "first-in, first-out" (FIFO) order. That is, the oldest item in the queue has the top priority and is removed first. Queues are best used for managing message priority and transaction order. Unlike message queues, the Queue collection class is persisted only in memory and not to disk.

Constructors

Four options are available for creating a Queue instance. The first allows us to create a Queue instance that takes no parameters. It simply creates a Queue object with an initial capacity of 32 and a growth factor of 2. The *initial capacity* defines the starting size of the queue. When this size is reached, the queue is expanded by multiplying its current size by the growth factor (in this case it, doubles the queue's size).

The second constructor enables you to indicate the initial size using the parameter capacity as Integer for the Queue collection. This can save the overhead of doubling every time the capacity is reached or from allocating more memory than is necessary.

A third constructor, capacity as Integer, growFactor as Single, enables you to indicate both the starting capacity and the value by which the capacity is multiplied when the Queue instance reaches its maximum.

Last, you can create a new Queue instance from an existing collection object. This constructor takes an instance of a collection object derived from the ICollection interface. Items are added to the Queue object based on the order in which they are enumerated using the IEnumerable interface.

Properties and Methods

The methods used most often when working with the Queue class are Enqueue and Dequeue. Table 19.3 details these and other key properties and methods of the Queue collection class.

TABLE 19.3 Key Properties and Methods of the Queue Class

Property	Description
Count	The Count property returns the actual number of elements contained inside the Queue collection—not the capacity.
IsReadOnly	The IsReadOnly property returns True if the Queue instance is read-only.
Method	
Clear	The Clear method removes all items from the Queue instance and resets the Count property to zero.

TABLE 19.3   Continued

Property	Description
	Method
Clone	The Clone method creates a copy of the current Queue instance. The cloned Queue instance references the original Queue items; it does not copy them. However, the cloned Queue and the Queue from which it was created can be operated on independently. That is, items can be added and removed on both instances without regard for the other. Cloning in this manner is also referred to as creating a shallow copy (a deep copy would actually copy items from one instance to the other).
Contains	The Contains method executes a linear search for a given object (passed as a parameter). The method returns True if the object is contained by the Queue instance.
CopyTo	The CopyTo method enables you to output a copy of all the elements within the Queue to a one-dimensional array. Items are copied in the "first-in, first-out" order.
Dequeue	The Dequeue method returns and removes the topmost (oldest) item from the queue.
Enqueue	The Enqueue method adds an item to the queue. Items are added to the end, or bottom, of the Queue collection.
GetEnumerator	The GetEnumerator method returns an object of the type IEnumerator. This object enables you to walk through the collection without removing items. Refer to "stack" for example.
Peek	The Peek method returns the item at the start of the Queue collection without removing it from the collection.
ToArray	The ToArray method copies all items in the Queue instance to a one-dimensional array.

Learning by Example: Queue Collection

Listing 19.2 is a simple console application that writes three items to a Queue collection instance using the Enqueue method. It then pulls those items out of the collection using the Dequeue method. The results are output to the console window.

LISTING 19.2   Queue Collection

```
Module Module1

  Sub Main()
```

LISTING 19.2   Continued

```vb
    'purpose: demonstrate queue collection class

    'local scope
    Dim myQueue As Collections.Queue
    Dim i As Int16

    'create new instance
    myQueue = New Collections.Queue(capacity:=3)

    'add items to the queue
    myQueue.Enqueue(obj:="Item 1")
    myQueue.Enqueue(obj:="Item 2")
    myQueue.Enqueue(obj:="Item 3")

    'write queue contents to the console
    For i = 1 To myQueue.Count

      'remove the item from the queue
      Console.WriteLine(myQueue.Dequeue())

    Next

    'pause
    Do While Not Console.ReadLine = "s" : Loop

  End Sub

End Module
```

ArrayList

The ArrayList collection class is best used for working with a group of objects after they have been added to the collection. Unlike Stack and Queue, the ArrayList collection enables you to modify the value of an item after it has been added. Additionally, you can use the Sort method to order the items in the array or the Reverse method to reverse all the items in the array. The class has strong support for working with items as a range. Methods such as AddRange, GetRange, InsertRange, and SetRange all support the manipulation of the ArrayList in chunks. A number of methods also are used to find items within the collection, including BinarySearch, Contains, IndexOf, and LastIndexOf. If you need a powerful and flexible collection object that enables you to do a lot of manipulation on the collection, rather than simple storage, you should consider an ArrayList.

Constructors

Three options are available for creating an ArrayList instance. The first, which takes no parameters, creates an ArrayList object with a default initial capacity of 16. The initial capacity defines the starting size of the queue. When the ArrayList reaches its capacity, it automatically doubles its capacity.

The second constructor enables you to indicate the initial size of the ArrayList collection, capacity as Integer. Provided that you have a good idea of the size your collection needs to support, this can save the overhead of doubling or from allocating more memory than is necessary.

Last, you can create a new ArrayList instance from an existing collection object. This constructor takes an instance of a collection object derived from the ICollection interface. Items are added to the ArrayList object based on the order in which they are enumerated using the IEnumerable interface.

Properties and Methods

Table 19.4 details key properties and methods of the ArrayList collection class.

TABLE 19.4   Key Properties and Methods of the ArrayList Class

Properties	Description
Capacity	The Capacity property enables you to set and get a value indicating the number of elements the collection is capable of storing. The default capacity of the ArrayList collection object is 16. When set to 0, the ArrayList is automatically reset to the default value of 16.
Count	The Count property returns the number of items actually contained in the collection.
IsFixedSize	The IsFixedSize property is a Boolean value that indicates if the ArrayList is of a fixed size. If True, items cannot be added or removed from the collection. See the FixedSized method for more details.
IsReadOnly	The IsReadOnly property is a Boolean value indicating True if the collection is read-only. See the ReadOnly method to create a read-only ArrayList.
Item	The Item property is used to return or to set the value of an item in the collection. The property takes the parameter index as integer and is of the type Object.
Methods	
Add	The Add method adds an item to the end of the collection. When the collection's capacity is reached, its capacity is doubled.

19

MANAGING
COLLECTIONS
OF OBJECTS

TABLE 19.4   Continued

Properties	Description
Methods	
AddRange	The AddRange method is used to add a set of items to a collection. The method takes a valid collection object (c as ICollection) as its one parameter.
BinarySearch	The BinarySearch method is used to find items within a sorted ArrayList using a binary search. The method returns the index of the found item.
Clear	The Clear method removes all items from the collection without changing its capacity.
Clone	The Clone method creates a copy of the current ArrayList instance.
Contains	The Contains method returns True if an item (passed as an Object) is found within the ArrayList.
CopyTo	The CopyTo method is used to output a copy of the ArrayList into a one-dimensional array. There are three versions of this method. The first enables you simply to specify the array to copy to. The second enables you to indicate the starting position within the array to begin copying. The third enables you to specify where to start copying from in the source array, the number of elements to copy, and where to start copying to in the target array.
FixedSize	The FixedSize method is used to fix the capacity and count of items within an ArrayList. To do so, you create an ArrayList, add items to it accordingly, and then call the FixedSize method passing your ArrayList as a parameter. The method returns another ArrayList object whose size is fixed. You can change values of the fixed ArrayList, but you cannot add or remove items.
GetEnumerator	The GetEnumerator method returns an object of the type IEnumerator. This method is overloaded and enables you to get an enumerator for the entire collection or a range within the collection.
GetRange	The GetRange method returns another ArrayList object that represents a subset of the given ArrayList. You pass the parameters index and count to the method to indicate where the range starts and the number of elements you want to return, respectively.
IndexOf	The IndexOf method performs a linear search on an array for a given object and returns the index value representing the position in the array of the found item. One overloaded parameter enables you to indicate where in the array you want to start searching (startIndex). Another allows you to indicate both the startIndex and the number of elements to search (count).

TABLE 19.4 Continued

Properties	Description
	Methods
Insert	The Insert method enables you to insert an item at the specified index within an ArrayList. This method differs from Add in that it enables you to insert items anywhere in the collection.
InsertRange	The InsertRange method is used to insert a range of items at a specified index. You indicate the range by passing a collection class derived from ICollection.
LastIndexOf	The LastIndexOf method is similar to the IndexOf method but returns the last occurrence of the object for which you are searching.
ReadOnly	The ReadOnly method is used to create an ArrayList that is read-only. To do so, you create an ArrayList, add items to it accordingly, and then call the ReadOnly method, passing your ArrayList as a parameter. The method returns another ArrayList object that is read-only.
Remove	The Remove method enables you to specify an item (as Object) to be removed from the collection. The first item found that matches the parameter value is removed.
RemoveAt	The RemoveAt method enables you to specify an index value that indicates a specific item in the collection to be removed.
RemoveRange	The RemoveRange method is used to remove a group of items from a collection. You specify the starting point of the remove operation by passing an index value. You indicate the number of items to be removed by passing a parameter called count.
Repeat	The Repeat method is used to create an ArrayList that contains multiple copies of the same value. You pass both the value to be repeated and indicate the number of times to repeat. The method returns an ArrayList object.
Reverse	The Reverse method is used to reverse the order of the elements contained within the collection. The method can apply to the entire array, or you can use an overloaded member to specify a range to reverse.
SetRange	The SetRange method is used to copy a given collection into the ArrayList, starting a specified index.
Sort	The Sort method is used to sort the array using the QuickSort algorithm.
TrimToSize	The TrimToSize method is used to set the collection's capacity to the current count of items contained in the collection. This enables you to reclaim unused memory when you are sure that the collection will no longer require additional items.

19

MANAGING
COLLECTIONS
OF OBJECTS

Learning by Example: `ArrayList` Collection

In Listing 19.3, we create an `ArrayList` collection. We add five items to the collection using the `Add` method. We then call `Sort` followed by `Reverse`. We use `GetRange` and `GetEnumerator` to display a range of items in the array list. Then, we use the `IndexOf` method to display the position of an item in the collection. Finally, we call the `RemoveRange` method to remove three items from the array list.

LISTING 19.3 ArrayList

```
Module Module1

    Sub Main()

        'local scope
        Dim myArray As New Collections.ArrayList()
        Dim myRange As Collections.ArrayList
        Dim myEnumerator As IEnumerator
        Dim i As Short

        'lower the array's capacity from default
        myArray.Capacity = 5

        'add items to the arrayList
        myArray.Add("Item R")
        myArray.Add("Item E")
        myArray.Add("Item B")
        myArray.Add("Item L")
        myArray.Add("Item F")

        'sort the array
        myArray.Sort()

        'reverse the array
        myArray.Reverse()

        'check the index of an item (array is zero-based)
        Console.WriteLine(myArray.IndexOf("Item E"))

        'pull 2 items out of the array using GetRange
        myRange = myArray.GetRange(3, 2)

        'write range items out
        myEnumerator = myRange.GetEnumerator
        Do While myEnumerator.MoveNext
            Console.WriteLine(myEnumerator.Current)
```

LISTING 19.3 Continued

```
        Loop

        'delete 3 items out of the array
        myArray.RemoveRange(2, 3)

        'write out new count
        Console.WriteLine(myArray.Count)

        'pause
        Do While Console.ReadLine() <> "s" : Loop

    End Sub

End Module
```

Hashtable

The `Hashtable` class provides fast and easy access to items based on key values. Users of VB's dictionary object will find the `Hashtable` class very familiar because it derives from the interface `IDictionary`.

Items are added to a `Hashtable` collection using a unique key value. In turn, keys are internally converted to hash codes. A *hash code* is a numeric value that represents the unique key. Hash codes are used to identify buckets inside the collection. *Buckets* are a subgroup of elements within the collection; splitting the collection into buckets makes access and retrieval of elements faster. When the collection is partitioned into buckets and each bucket is indexed by a hash code, there is no need to search the entire collection for an item. Instead, the bucket is accessed based on the key and the item returned.

The `Hashtable` class is best used when working with items that naturally contain a unique key. A row in a recordset is a good example of a candidate. Each column represents a unique key for the value it contains. Users access the values by indicating the column name or key.

Constructors

The `Hashtable` class can be created using a large variety of constructors. The quantity is simply the result of the various combinations of all the possible parameters that can be passed on the constructor. Rather than list all these constructors, we'll describe all the possible parameters and define how you might use them.

- `capacity as Integer`—Indicates the number of `Hashtable` buckets to be allocated to the collection. The default capacity for a `Hashtable` instance is zero.

- d as IDictionary—Creates an instance of a Hashtable class from a collection object derived from an IDictionary interface.

- loadFactor as Single—Indicates the ratio of items in the collection to Hashtable buckets that store the items. A smaller value provides faster lookup but consumes more memory. The default value is 1.0, indicating a ratio of one item per bucket.

- hcp as IHashCodeProvider—Indicates the class that provides the hash code. Valid classes are those that inherit from IHashCodeProvider.

- comparer as IComparer—Indicates the comparer to use when creating the Hashtable instance.

Properties and Methods

Table 19.5 details key properties and methods of the Hashtable collection class.

TABLE 19.5   Key Properties and Methods of the Hashtable Class

Properties	Description
Comparer	The Comparer property is used to get or set the class that is used to compare two objects. Valid values are classes that implement the IComparer interface. Some are CaseInsensitiveComparer, Comparer, KeyConverter.
Count	The Count property returns the number of key/value pairs contained within the collection.
hcp	The hcp (hash code provider) property gets or sets an object used to dispense hash codes.
IsFixedSize	The IsFixedSize property returns the Boolean value of True if the Hashtable has a fixed size. That is, it does not allow items to be added or removed.
IsReadOnly	The IsReadOnly property returns the Boolean value of True if the Hashtable is read only.
Item	The Item property is used to return or to set the value of a specific element within the collection. You reference an item in the collection by passing the key value as a parameter of the property.
Keys	The Keys property returns a collection object that contains all the keys within the collection. The returned collection references the original Hashtable and therefore reflects changes made to its keys.
Values	The Values property returns a collection object that contains all the values within the Hashtable instance. The Values property references the original Hashtable and therefore reflects any changes made to its values.

TABLE 19.5 Continued

Properties	Description
	Note that the Keys and Values properties do not allow you to specify an order for the collection. However, each property returns a collection in the same order as the other. This enables you to synch the two collections for key/value pairing if need be.

Methods

Properties	Description
Add	The Add method enables you to add items to the Hashtable collection. When doing so, you specify both the key and value of the item to add. The key parameter must be unique within the collection.
Clear	The Clear method removes all items from the Hashtable.
Clone	The Clone method creates a shallow copy of the current Hashtable instance.
Contains	The Contains method returns True if an item (passed as an Object) is found within the Hashtable.
ContainsKey	The ContainsKey method returns True if a specified key is found within the Hashtable.
ContainsValue	The ContainsValue method returns True if a specified value is found within the Hashtable.
CopyTo	The CopyTo method is used to output a copy of the HashTable into a one-dimensional array. The method enables you to specify where to start copying to in the target array.
GetEnumerator	The GetEnumerator method returns an object of the type IEnumerator that enables you to enumerate through the Hashtable collection.
GetHash	The GetHash method is used to return the hash code of a specified key.
GetObjectData	The GetObjectData enables you to serialize the Hashtable collection.
KeyEquals	The KeyEquals method returns a Boolean value indicating whether an item and key, both passed as parameters, are of equal value.
OnDeserialization	The OnDeserialization method is used to raise an event when a Hashtable deserialization is complete.
Remove	The Remove method enables you to remove an item from the Hashtable collection. To do so, you must specify the key of the item to be removed.

19

Learning by Example: HashTable Collection

Using the Hashtable collection class is straightforward. In Listing 19.4, we use the Add method to add four items to the collection and then reference two of those items by their keys and write their contents to the console window.

LISTING 19.4   Hashtable

```
Module Module1

 Sub Main()

   'purpose: demo hashtable collection

   'local scope
   Dim myHashtable As New Collections.Hashtable()

   'add items to the collection
   myHashtable.Add(key:=1, value:="Microsoft")
   myHashtable.Add(key:=2, value:="Visual")
   myHashtable.Add(key:=3, value:="Basic")
   myHashtable.Add(key:=4, value:=".NET")

   'return the hash code of a specific item
   Console.WriteLine(myHashtable.Item(key:=2) _
     & myHashtable.Item(key:=3))

   'pause
   Do While Console.ReadLine() <> "s" : Loop

 End Sub

End Module
```

Thread Safety and Synchronization

Thread-safe is a term that indicates whether multiple threads can access an object simultaneously; if an object does not allow this type of access, it is considered to be thread-safe. The *safe* portion of the terms connotes the many problems that can occur when two threads access—and change—the global data of an object at the same time (see Chapter 12, "Working with Threads," for more detail).

By default, the collection classes in the System.Collections namespace are not thread-safe. In fact, the majority of objects in the .NET Framework Class Library are not thread-safe. The reason has to do with performance. The process of making objects thread-safe degrades performance.

This process of ensuring thread safety is called synchronization. *Synchronization* ensures that properties and methods of a given object are accessed by only one thread at a time. Sounds good and safe, right? It is, but it requires the CLR to block threads from accessing synchronized objects while another thread is executing a method or property. However, blocking equates to a performance penalty. Therefore, thread safety via synchronization requires a performance hit.

This undesired performance hit coupled with the fact that the majority of .NET applications will execute on a single thread makes objects in the library not thread-safe by default. If, however, you need a thread-safe version of a given object, typically an appropriate synchronization method exists.

The collection classes that we've discussed thus far have an `IsSynchronized` property. This property is of the type `Boolean`. The property returns `True` if the collection class instance is synchronized. To create a synchronized version of a given collection, you use the `Synchronized` method. This method returns a synchronized wrapper for your collection class. The method takes the instance of the collection you want synchronized as its parameter.

The following code snippet creates an `ArrayList` object, adds a few items to the collection, and then outputs a thread-safe version.

```
Dim myArray As New Collections.ArrayList()
Dim mySafeArray As Collections.ArrayList

myArray.Add(value:="Test 1")
myArray.Add(value:="Test 2")
myArray.Add(value:="Test 3")
mySafeArray = myArray.Synchronized(list:=myArray)

Console.WriteLine(myArray.ToString & ": " & myArray.IsSynchronized)
Console.WriteLine(mySafeArray.ToString & ": " _
  & mySafeArray.IsSynchronized)
```

 ## Suggestions for Further Exploration

- ⊃ The `BitArray` class provides compact storage for an array of `True` and `False` values.

- ⊃ The `SortedList` class provides a collection based on key/value pairs and is sorted by the collection's keys.

- ⊃ Check out the namespace `System.Collections.Specialized` for more specialized collection classes. For example, the `ListDictionary` class provides `Hashtable`-like functionality on small groups of objects (10 or fewer). The classes `StringCollection` and `StringDictionary` are also available for manipulating collections of string values.

Strongly Typed Collections

You've seen that the .NET Framework Class Library offers a wide range of collection options. However, the collections in the Framework allow only generic elements of type Object. This is fine for most internal use, when you know what your code is doing. However, if you plan to expose your own collection objects, you'll want to strongly type them. *Strong typing* means to enforce the data type of elements within the collection. The Object data type allows anything to be added to your collection. For example, if you expose a collection of inventory objects and another developer adds a shipping notice to the collection, you will more than likely have a problem.

The good news is that the same interfaces and base classes used by the collections presented thus far are available to you to inherit and override. This section defines how to write custom collection classes using the various classes and interfaces exposed by the System.Collections namespace.

CollectionBase

The CollectionBase class is the abstract base class specifically designed for defining custom, strongly typed collections. Internally, the CollectionBase class uses an IList object for storing elements. This object is accessed through the CollectionBase.List property. The IList class should look familiar because a number of frequently used objects implement it, including ArrayList, ImageList.ImageCollection, ComboBox.ObjectCollection, and ListView.ListViewItemCollection, to name a few. IList has an Item property used to store and retrieve collection elements based on an index value. Additionally, it has the standard methods Add, Insert, Remove, Clear, Contains, IndexOf, and RemoveAt that you are familiar with from the previous section.

We'll now walk through the process of defining a custom collection class. Before we begin, we must define a class to use as our type. In our example, we define a simple order object. The object has a constructor that requires an order number to create the object. Additionally, we define two other properties: Quantity and Price.

```
Public Class MyOrder

    'private property variables
    Dim localNumber As Integer
    Dim localQuantity As Short
    Dim localPrice As Decimal

    Public Sub New(ByVal number As Integer)

        'purpose: constructor for the object
```

```
      'set the local number
      localNumber = number

  End Sub

  Public ReadOnly Property Number() As Integer
    Get
      Return localNumber
    End Get
  End Property

  Public Property Quantity() As Short
    Get
      Return localQuantity
    End Get
    Set(ByVal Value As Short)
      localQuantity = Value
    End Set
  End Property

  Public Property Price() As Decimal
    Get
      Return localPrice
    End Get
    Set(ByVal Value As Decimal)
      localPrice = Value
    End Set
  End Property

End Class
```

Next, we begin defining a custom collection class called MyOrders. We indicate that the class inherits from CollectionBase. We then create a couple of methods used for adding objects to our collection. AddFromValues enables a user of our class to add an element to the collection by passing all the appropriate values of a MyOrder object. In this method, we create a new instance of MyOrder, set its properties, and add the object to the CollectionBase class's internal IList object MyBase.List.Add. We also create a method called Add that simply takes a MyOrder instance and adds it to the underlying collection.

```
Public Class MyOrders

  Inherits CollectionBase

  Public Sub AddFromValues(ByVal number As Integer, _
    ByVal quantity As Short, ByVal price As Decimal)
```

```
        'purpose: creates an order object and adds it as an
        '           item to the underlying list collection

        'create the strongly typed class
        Dim orderInstance As New MyOrder(number:=number)
        orderInstance.Quantity = quantity
        orderInstance.Price = price

        'add the item to the base collection
        MyBase.List.Add(value:=orderInstance)

    End Sub

    Public Sub Add(ByVal value As MyOrder)

        'purpose: add an order object to the underlying collection

        'add the item to the base collection
        MyBase.List.Add(value:=value)

    End Sub
```

Next, we create an `Item` property to allow other developers to access and set items within our custom collection. We define the property as the default for our collection class. This is allowed because the property has a parameter. To access items in the base class's collection object, we call `MyBase.List.Item` and pass an `index` parameter.

```
    Default Property Item(ByVal index As Integer) As MyOrder

        'purpose: set or get items in the collection

        Get
            Return CType(MyBase.List.Item(index:=index), MyOrder)
        End Get

        Set(ByVal Value As MyOrder)
            MyBase.List.Item(index:=index) = Value
        End Set

    End Property
```

We expose a couple of additional methods for working with our collection: `IndexOf` and `Insert`. The `IndexOf` method enables users to return the index value of the given `MyOrder` instance within the collection. The `Insert` method allows users to insert a specified `MyOrder` object at a specific index position.

```
Public Function IndexOf(ByVal value As MyOrder) As Integer

   'purpose: return the index of the specified object within the array

   Return MyBase.List.IndexOf(value:=value)

End Function

Public Sub Insert(ByVal index As Integer, ByVal value As MyOrder)

   'purpose: insert an order at the specified index

   'add the item
   List.Insert(index:=index, value:=value)

End Sub
```

Finally we override three type-checking events on the base class: OnInsert, OnSet, and
OnValidate. These events are raised when items are inserted, changed, or validated. This
ensures that items added to the collection are not changed to an invalid type afterward. If the
value of the item being checked is not of the type MyOrder, we throw an exception.

```
Protected Overrides Sub OnInsert(ByVal index As Integer, _
   ByVal value As Object)

   'purpose: check the type of an object being inserted (added)

   If Not TypeOf (value) Is MyOrder Then
     Throw New ArgumentException(message:="InvalidType")
   End If

End Sub

Protected Overrides Sub OnSet(ByVal index As Integer, _
   ByVal oldValue As Object, ByVal newValue As Object)

   'purpose: check the type of an object being set

   If Not TypeOf (newValue) Is MyOrder Then
     Throw New ArgumentException(message:="InvalidType")
   End If

End Sub

Protected Overrides Sub OnValidate(ByVal value As Object)
```

```
        'purpose: check the type of an object on validation

        If Not TypeOf (value) Is MyOrder Then
          Throw New ArgumentException(message:="InvalidType")
        End If

    End Sub

End Class
```

That's it. We've just created a custom, strongly typed collection using `CollectionBase`. All that is left is to demonstrate its use by defining a simple client. The following is a console-based application that creates an instance of `MyOrders` and adds `MyOrder` objects to it.

```
Module Module1

  Sub Main()

    'purpose: act as a client for the MyOrders collection class

    'local scope
    Dim orders As New MyOrders()
    Dim order As MyOrder

    'add a couple items to the collection
    orders.AddFromValues(101, 3, 30.5)
    orders.AddFromValues(102, 2, 30.5)
    orders.AddFromValues(103, 4, 30.5)

    'insert an order
    orders.Insert(index:=2, value:=New MyOrder("104"))

    'remove an item at the specified index
    'note: we are calling the base class
    orders.RemoveAt(index:=1)

    'reset a value
    order = New MyOrder(number:=105)
    orders.Item(index:=2) = order

    'display index
    Console.WriteLine(orders.IndexOf(value:=order))

    'pause
    Do While Console.ReadLine <> "s" : Loop

  End Sub

End Module
```

DictionaryBase

The System.Collections namespace also defines the class DictionaryBase for creating custom collections based on a dictionary format (key/value pairs). Fortunately, the concepts here are the same as in CollectionBase. Instead of an underlying IList object, the DictionaryBase class has a Dictionary property that is of type IDictionary. This is the same object from which collection classes such as Hashtable and SortedList derive.

Using our preceding order example, we can create a new collection class that derives from DictionaryBase. This class accesses items in the base class's dictionary collection by a key value. In our example, we'll create an Add method that takes a key as a parameter. We will then change the Item property to access items in the collection by a key value.

```
Public Class MyOrders

  Inherits Collections.DictionaryBase

  Public Sub Add(ByVal key As String, ByVal value As MyOrder)

    'purpose: add an order object to the underlying collection

    'add the item to the base collection
    MyBase.Dictionary.Add(key:=key, value:=value)

  End Sub

  Default Property Item(ByVal key As String) As MyOrder

    'purpose: set or get items in the collection

    Get
      Return CType(MyBase.Dictionary.Item(key:=key), MyOrder)
    End Get

    Set(ByVal Value As MyOrder)
      MyBase.Dictionary.Item(key:=key) = Value
    End Set

  End Property

End Class
```

Now we'll modify our client to add and access items from the collection based on a key. In our case, we'll use the order number as our key value.

```
Module Module1

  Sub Main()

    'purpose: act as a client for the MyOrders collection class

    'local scope
    Dim orders As New MyOrders()
    Dim order As MyOrder

    'create an order object
    order = New MyOrder(number:=105)
    order.Quantity = 5
    order.Price = 3.15
    orders.Add(key:=order.Number.ToString, value:=order)

    'access the order in the collection
    Console.WriteLine(orders(key:="105").Number)

    'pause
    Do While Console.ReadLine <> "s" : Loop

  End Sub

End Module
```

 Suggestions for Further Exploration

Extend the ReadOnlyCollectionBase class to create custom, read-only collection classes.

Summary

The Framework Class Library provides a host of powerful, easy-to-use collection classes. The next time you need to manage a group of data, you should be well equipped to choose the right solution.

The following key points were presented in this chapter:

- The Stack collection class is used for last-in, first-out access.
- The Queue collection class provides first-in, first-out access.
- The ArrayList collection class is powerful when manipulating a collection in ranges.
- The Hashtable collection class provides fast access to items based on keys.
- The Synchronized method on a collection class returns a thread-safe wrapper for the given class.
- You can use classes such as CollectionBase and DictionaryBase to implement your own strongly typed collection classes.

Profiling, Debugging, and Exception Handling

IN THIS CHAPTER

In this chapter, we discuss the different methods of debugging and optimizing managed .NET applications. The task of troubleshooting and debugging software is a difficult one that begins in the design phase of the software development process. We will look at the different options open to Visual Basic .NET developers for ferreting out runtime and logic problems that may be present in your code. Starting with exception handling, we examine the different varieties of error-handling constructs available in Visual Basic .NET. Then we examine the concepts of instrumentation and tracing as an additional complement to error handling. Finally, we look at how to use various .NET components in an attempt to identify and fix performance issues with managed code.

Although this chapter does not focus on any one namespace, we will be seeing a lot of the System.Diagnostics namespace because of its tight integration in the debugging mission.

After reading this chapter, you should have a firm grasp of the following:

- Implementing structured exception handlers
- Instrumenting your code using the Debug and Trace classes from the System.Diagnostics namespace
- Creating custom performance counters to track an application's performance statistics

Handling Errors with Structured Exception Handlers

With .NET, Visual Basic now supports *structured exception handling*. Structured exception handling, or SEH, provides developers with a powerful way of protecting specific blocks of code and reacting to specific classes of errors.

> **NOTE**
>
> Unstructured exception handling is also supported through the "old style" method of using On Error commands and inline procedure blocks for handling errors.

Structured Exception Handling

Consider the following code:

```
Function SearchInFile(ByVal searchValue As String, _
    ByVal fileName As String) As Boolean

        Dim reader As StreamReader
        Dim content As String
```

```
    reader = File.OpenText(fileName)

    content = reader.ReadToEnd()

    If InStr(content, searchValue) > 0 Then
        SearchInFile = True
    Else
        SearchInFile = False
    End If

    reader.Close()

End Function
```

This is a simple function that tries to do the following:

- Open a file using the `File` class
- Search for the occurrence of a string inside of that file (using the `StreamReader` class and the `InStr` function)
- If the string is found, return `True` through the function signature
- If the string is not found, return `False` through the function signature

As it is currently written, the routine is problematic: There are a variety of places where the code could break, and the function does nothing to mitigate that risk.

This is the essence of error handling: placing code into a procedure so that errors can be detected and dealt with on the programmer's terms instead of the runtime's terms. For example, if the routine was supplied with the name of a file that doesn't exist, the `File.OpenText` instruction will fail. If this function was being called by a forms application, it would do neither the programmer nor the user any good to simply be left with a hard error raised to the screen that will cause the application to abruptly terminate. Instead, users will expect a nicely formatted message that essentially informs them that they have supplied an invalid filename and that they should try again.

SEH enables you to identify blocks of code that require protection from possible errors. Referring back to the preceding code, we can immediately see some areas that require such protection; for example, the `OpenText` and `ReadToEnd` method calls. Let's look at the different pieces of a structured exception handler and see how they might help us out in this scenario.

Anatomy of a Structured Exception Handler

Each structured exception handler consists of a `Try...Catch...Finally` statement. This statement consists of three or more blocks of code: one `Try` block, one or more `Catch` blocks, and zero or one `Finally` blocks.

The `Try` Statement

The `Try` block is the starting point for the error handler. Its purpose is to encapsulate any code that needs to have errors handled. In other words, this is the code that the error handler is designed to protect.

The `Catch` Statement

The `Catch` statement is designed to catch any errors that were thrown inside of the `Try` block. The `Catch` statement implements a form of error filtering. That is, it sets up a condition that the runtime can evaluate. If the statement is evaluated to `True`, the code inside the `Catch` block will be run. Otherwise, the runtime will keep looking for a valid `Catch` block to execute. The syntax definition of a `Catch` statement looks like this:

```
Catch [ Identifier As TypeName ] [ When BooleanExpression ]
```

`Catch` statements can actually be set up using one of two kinds of filters. The first, an exception class filter, attempts to determine the nature of the error that was encountered. When managed code in the .NET runtime encounters a runtime error, it classifies the error according to the `Exception` class it represents. In other words, each class in the Framework Class Library will typically have a documented list of exceptions that may be thrown on an error. For instance, the `StreamReader.ReadToEnd` method will throw an `IOException` when an error occurs. This thrown exception can be caught using a `Catch` statement, like this:

```
Catch ioErr As IOException
```

The second type of evaluation that can be forced with a `Catch` statement is a simple Boolean expression. You might use this to test for a specific error number or to test whether a switch has been set inside your code. The following `Catch` block will be executed only if the error number is 1001:

```
Catch When ErrNum = 1001
   'code to execute
```

Neither the exception class identifier nor the `Boolean` `When` evaluator is required. A naked `Catch` statement will simply be executed anytime an exception that derives from `System.Exception` is raised:

```
Catch
   'code to execute
```

You can specify multiple `Catch` blocks. The runtime will execute the first one that matches on the current conditions.

If an exception occurs and the runtime is unable to find a Catch statement that can handle the error, the error will get passed up through the stack of calling procedures until a valid Catch statement is found. If no Catch statements are found by the time the error reaches the outermost procedure on the stack, an actual runtime error message will be displayed to the screen. This is exactly what you don't want to happen in your applications.

The `Finally` Statement

The `Finally` statement is not required in an exception handler but, when present, will always be executed regardless of a run with or without errors. Typically, `Finally` blocks are where you would place finalization code that closes out connections, files, and the like; this is a task that is relevant whether or not an exception was thrown.

Implementing a Structured Exception Handler

If we revisit our earlier `SearchInFile` function and embed a structured exception handler, it might look something like Listing 20.1:

LISTING 20.1   A Structured Exception Handler

```
Imports System.IO

Module Module1

    Sub Main()
        SearchInFile("test", "c:\abc.txt")
    End Sub

    Function SearchInFile(ByVal searchValue As String, _
        ByVal fileName As String) _
        As Boolean

        Dim reader As StreamReader
        Dim content As String

        Try

            reader = File.OpenText(fileName)

            Try
```

LISTING 20.1   Continued

```
            content = reader.ReadToEnd()

            If InStr(content, searchValue) > 0 Then
                SearchInFile = True
            Else
                SearchInFile = False
            End If

        Catch ioErr As IOException
            MsgBox("An error occurred reading the file: " & ioErr.Message)

        Finally
            reader.Close()

        End Try

    Catch secErr As System.Security.SecurityException
        MsgBox("Unable to open the file, please check your permissions.")

    Catch fileErr As FileNotFoundException
        MsgBox("Unable to locate the specified file.")

    End Try

End Function

End Module
```

The console application in Listing 20.1 immediately fires off the SearchInFile function with the values "test" and "abc.txt". The Try...Catch...Finally blocks in the SearchInFile function are obvious.

Notice that we have actually nested two exception handlers in the code. One deals with problems calling the OpenText method, and the other deals with problems encountered issuing the ReadToEnd method call. We test explicitly for two classes of exceptions with the OpenText method: a SecurityException, which would be thrown if the application didn't have permission to access the file, and a FileNotFoundException, which would be thrown if the file could not be located at the specified location or filename.

The exception handler that deals with the reader.ReadToEnd statement explicitly catches IOException instances that are thrown. In this case, because it is almost impossible to guess the cause of the error, we write out the error message to the screen so that the user can perhaps troubleshoot the problem. A few different properties and methods implemented by the Exception class objects are useful inside of error handlers.

Variable Scope

It is important to know that each block in a `Try...Catch...Finally` statement carries its own scope. For instance, in the following code, we see a routine that is trying to open a database connection. The code is wrapped in an exception handler, complete with a `Finally` block that will close the connection:

```
Sub ConnectToDb()
    Try
        Dim dbConn As OleDbConnection = New OleDbConnection(connStr)
        .
        .
        .
    Catch
        'handle any error here

    Finally
        dbConn.Close()

    End Try

End Sub
```

This code, as written, will not even compile. Why? The `dbConn` object is declared inside the `Try` block and therefore does not exist (is out of scope) inside the `Finally` block. The `dbConn.Close` method call won't be allowed; a syntax error of `'The name dbConn is not declared'` will result. To really make this work the way it was intended, the code would have to be rewritten to place the database connection object declaration in a code block that has scope superiority over the `Finally` block:

```
Sub ConnectToDb()

    Dim dbConn As OleDbConnection

    Try
        dbConn = New OleDbConnection(connStr)
        .
        .
        .
    Catch
        'handle any error here

    Finally
        dbConn.Close()

    End Try

End Sub
```

Using Exception Objects

The .NET Framework defines several classes of exceptions. All of them derive from the System.Exception base class. They are used to provide specific error information based on the exact type of error. In some cases, for instance, an exception class will add properties to the base exception class to help deal with a specific type of error. As you can see in Figure 20.1, the hierarchy of exception classes is quite large.

In other cases, properties and methods on the System.Exception class will be overridden to provide information relevant to the context of a specific error.

Exception classes are typically used in two ways inside an exception handler. In our discussion on the Catch statement, we have seen how they can be used to filter on error types and cause a specific Catch block to be executed. The second way that they can be used is as a query mechanism to help derive more information about the circumstances that triggered the error.

Probably the most relevant member of an exception class as far as debugging is concerned is the Message property. This is a plain-text message stating exactly what the error is. The Source property is also very useful in terms of debugging. It will return a string identifying the application or object that actually triggered the error. Both the Message and Source properties can be used to present information to a user so that the user can react accordingly.

From a developer's perspective, a few other properties are useful for figuring out the root cause of an error. These are the HResult and StackTrace properties. The HResult property returns the familiar HResult value from the COM world. This is a 32-bit number that has information embedded into it including the severity of the error, a facility code, and the actual error code. Examining the HResult value is particularly valuable when you're trying to troubleshoot problems that occur as a result of interop with either COM objects or the Win32 API. The StackTrace property will identify exactly where in the code that an exception was encountered.

NOTE

You can define your own custom exception classes to deal with errors specific to your application. As a general rule, if you are going to create your own exception class, it should inherit from System.Exception (or one of its children classes).

Figure 20.2 shows a stack trace message triggered from the SearchInFile function in our sample console application. The StackTrace property will return a string that identifies the path of execution inside the application, from the latest method call through to the application module. It will also identify the line number of the offending code. This is not the sort of thing that you would want to show a user, but it is useful to a developer because of the sheer volume of technical information it presents.

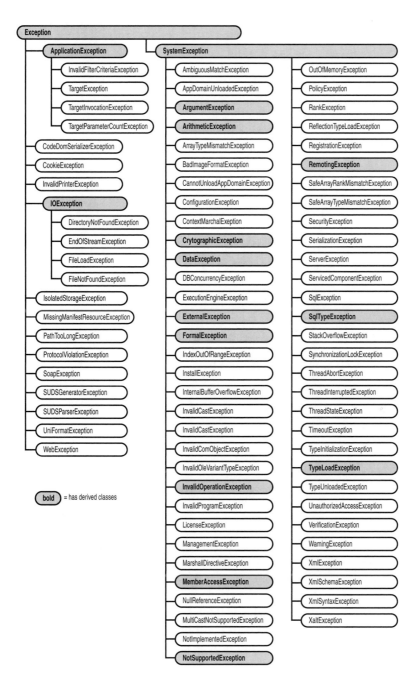

FIGURE 20.1

`System.Exception` *and derived classes.*

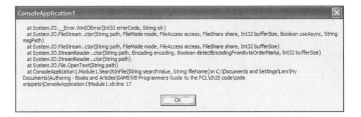

FIGURE 20.2

A StackTrace message.

Table 20.1 shows all the defined properties and methods of the System.Exception class. Keep in mind that specific classes that derive from the base System.Exception class will implement their own versions of these properties. For example, we saw in Chapter 8, "Networking Functions," that a SocketException class returns an ErrorCode property that corresponds to the error codes defined in the Winsock library.

TABLE 20.1   Properties and Methods of the System.Exception Class

Property	Description
HelpLink	A String value representing a URI of the help file resource associated with the exception.
HResult	An Integer value representing an HRESULT code for the exception.
InnerException	An Exception instance used for nesting exceptions inside one another.
Messag	A String value containing the error message.
Source	A String value that contains the name of the object that caused the exception.
StackTrace	A String value that contains a description of the entire call stack leading up to the error.
TargetSite	A MethodBase object that can be used to reference the actual method that caused the exception.

Method	Description
GetBaseException	Returns an Exception object that is the actual root exception; this is done by chaining through the InnerException properties until the base exception is reached.
GetObjectData	Populates a SerializationInfo object with information from the exception.
ToString	Returns a String with the fully qualified exception class name; may also return the error message, stack trace info, and so on.

Throwing Exceptions

So far, we have concentrated on what to do if your code encounters an exception. But what do you do if you want to throw an exception on purpose? There will certainly be times when you must develop a component that will flag to its consumers that something has gone wrong: Either an actual runtime error has occurred, or perhaps a business rule has been broken. Either way, you can infuse into your components the capability for them to throw their own exceptions, much like the Framework Class Library classes throw theirs.

The key is the Throw statement. The Throw statement enables you to instantiate a new exception object, provide it with an appropriate error message, and raise it to any listening error handlers. Consider the following code, which we could insert into the SearchInFile function:

```
If searchValue.Length = 0 Then
    Throw New ApplicationException("You must provide a search value.")
End If
```

In this case, we are checking to make sure that one of the function's input parameters, searchValue, actually has content. If it doesn't, we enforce the business rule by throwing an ApplicationException instance with the message You must provide a search value. Putting this code into Listing 20.1 doesn't make a whole lot of sense, but if we choose to compile the SearchInFile function into a class library to be consumed by other objects, it would make a whole lot of sense. It protects the function from returning a value that might be misleading; for instance, was the searchValue really not found in the file, or was a problem elsewhere causing this value to be empty by the time it makes it into the function?

In a similar fashion, we can assist an exception to bubble up with the correct information. For instance, consider this code:

```
Sub Main()
    Dim appSettings As String

    appSettings = RetrieveSettings("C:\Program Files\myApp")
End Sub

Function RetrieveSettings(ByVal path As String) As String

    Const FILENAME = "\myApp.cfg"

    Try

        reader = File.OpenText(path & FILENAME)

        .
        .
        .
```

```
    Catch fileErr As FileNotFoundException
        .
        .
        .

    End Try

End Function
```

It shows a hypothetical (albeit poorly designed) application that stores some of its startup information in a text file that it expects to find in a specific, hard-coded directory. If something happens to this file, an exception will be raised on the line that tries to read it:

```
reader = File.OpenText(path & FILENAME)
```

Because we have an exception handler to deal with this problem, this is not a complete disaster. However, the user may not be able to determine enough information to accurately troubleshoot and solve the problem, because the user has no knowledge of the internal machinations of the program.

In other words, the user possibly would be presented with an error message saying that the application could not locate the specified file, but it would be far more useful if the message stated exactly what was happening—such as, This application can't find its configuration file in its default directory. Please try to locate the file on the original CD and copy it into the directory, or reinstall the application.

To be faithful to the idea of structured exception handling, you want the calling component to be responsible for dealing in an appropriate way with any errors encountered. By extending the structured exception handling design pattern throughout all your code, you can treat each error in a consistent fashion.

Consider this small rewrite that handles the problem by throwing a new exception with more detailed information for the user or calling component:

```
Sub Main()
    Dim appSettings As String

    appSettings = RetrieveSettings("C:\Program Files\myApp")
End Sub

Function RetrieveSettings(ByVal path As String) As String

    Const FILENAME = "\myApp.cfg"

    Try
```

```
      reader = File.OpenText(path & FILENAME)

          .
          .
          .


   Catch fileErr As FileNotFoundException
      Dim errMsg As New StringBuilder("The application could not")
      errMsg.Append("  locate its configuration file, ")
      errMsg.Append( & FILENAME & ", which should be located")
      errMsg.Append(" in the directory '" & path & "'. Please")
      errMsg.Append(" reinstall the application or copy the needed ")
      errMsg.Append(" file from the installation CD.")

      Throw New ApplicationException(errMsg.ToString, fileErr)

   End Try

End Function
```

Now that you have a good handle on the mechanics of error handlers, we can look at the `System.Diagnostics` namespace support for debugging applications.

NOTE

We don't touch on the use of unstructured exception handlers in this chapter because their use is not recommended (performance and general design penalties can be involved with implementing them). However, the "old" Visual Basic style of error handling with `On Error GoTo` and `On Error Resume Next` is still supported in Visual Basic .NET. If you must use unstructured exception handlers in your code, be aware that you cannot mix structured and unstructured handlers inside the same procedure.

Debugging and Tracing

Developers who are interested in debugging their code to the fullest extent possible must become comfortable with the concept of *instrumenting* their code. This simply refers to the practice of burying various code constructs inside an application; these constructs have the capability to report on execution details and errors as they occur.

The .NET Framework Class Library has some great support for instrumentation within the `System.Diagnostics` namespace—specifically, through its `Debug` and `Trace` classes.

The Debug and Trace Classes

Both the Debug and Trace classes provide programmers with a way of inserting instrumentation code into applications for debugging assistance. They are essentially the same in terms of their supported properties and methods; they differ only in their projected use. The Debug class is designed to be used in debug builds of software, whereas the Trace class is designed to be used in actual release builds of software.

To understand what these classes do, it is easiest to first look at some code. The following code snippet shows the Debug component in action:

```
Sub Main()
      Debug.WriteLine("Main: Enter")
      Debug.Indent()

      ProcedureA()
      ProcedureB()
      ProcedureC()

      Debug.Unindent()
      Debug.WriteLine("Main: Exit")
   End Sub

   Sub ProcedureA()
      Debug.WriteLine("ProcedureA: Enter")
      '
      'Do some work here
      '
      Debug.WriteLine("ProcedureA: Exit")
   End Sub

   Sub ProcedureB()
      Debug.WriteLine("ProcedureB: Enter")
      '
      'Do some work here
      '
      Debug.WriteLine("ProcedureB: Exit")
   End Sub

   Sub ProcedureC()
      Debug.WriteLine("ProcedureC: Enter")
      '
      'Do some work here
      '
      Debug.WriteLine("ProcedureC: Exit")
   End Sub
```

In the preceding code, we are using the `Debug.WriteLine` method to log some informational messages that will be useful in terms of tracing the flow of the application. These messages are actually being broadcast to a collection of objects called listeners. (We'll get more into the concept of listeners later in the chapter.) Even without the explicit knowledge of exactly where these debug messages are going, it is easy to discern the main function of the `Debug` (and the `Trace`) class. They expose a series of methods and properties that are useful for logging information about the execution of a program.

If you are like many developers, you have probably used message boxes or event log entries to do the same thing. In .NET, the Framework provides the `Debug` and `Trace` classes to enable you to do this in a more formal and structured manner. Of course, you aren't limited to writing static messages; you could be writing out the contents of variables, whether specific conditions are present, who is logged in, and so on. This is the essence of instrumentation. Fully instrumenting your code, however, could have serious repercussions for code size and performance. Chances are that you will not want the production release of your code spewing out thousands of lines of debug information every time it is run. In the past, this has usually involved brute force maintenance of separate source-code branches in a version control system; one version has the debug code in it, the other doesn't. This is not a good way to go, because it has a lot of potential for human error. A slightly better way in Visual Basic 6.0 was the use of compiler constants. You could bracket certain blocks of code and then set a compiler flag to indicate whether that code should be executed. But this still did not address the actual presence of the debug code in the released executable.

In .NET, this process has become much more formalized. The Visual Studio .NET IDE and the command-line compilers all have the capability to specifically compile a debug or a release build of the software. Before getting more in-depth with the `Debug` class, let's quickly see how we can use the Visual Studio IDE to build a debug or a release version of a project.

Compiling a Debug Build

To compile a debug build of your software, you need to set the project Configuration to Debug. This is done through the project Property Pages dialog box (see Figure 20.3). You can access this dialog box by selecting the Project menu in the IDE, and then selecting Properties.

Notice at the top of the dialog box that a drop-down box is titled Configuration. This is where the possible build configurations will show up, enabling you to select between Release and Debug. Why is this important?

The beauty of the `Debug` and `Trace` classes is that if you have your project set to a Debug build, all the `Debug` class code you have embedded in it will be compiled into the resulting assembly and will execute. If you have your project set to a release build, the `Debug` code will not be included and will not execute. Because the .NET compilers support the capability to turn Debug and Trace code on and off individually, you have full control over the exact level of tracing that will happen in any build configuration of your application.

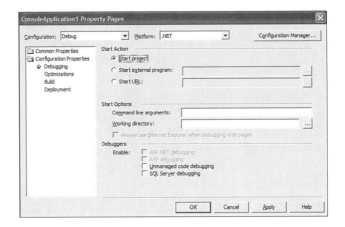

FIGURE 20.3

The Visual Studio Project Property dialog box.

To actually set the options for enabling Debug code and Trace code, you need to click the Build entry under the Configuration Properties (see Figure 20.4). Notice the two check boxes toward the center and bottom of the screen. This is where you can explicitly tell the compiler to include or not include Debug or Trace code.

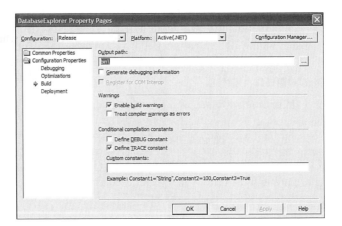

FIGURE 20.4

Compiler options for Debug and Trace code.

In practice, Debug code is for Debugging alpha or beta software; Trace code is for instrumenting production code.

Listening for Trace Messages

Both the Debug and Trace classes write messages out to a group of listener objects specified by their Listeners property. A Listener is nothing more than an object that accepts a debug message from a Debug or Trace component and then formats it for consumption. Various listener classes are defined in the Framework Class Library; they are shown, along with their targeted output, in Table 20.2.

> **NOTE**
>
> All the listener classes are derived from the base TraceListener class. This base class can also be used to create your own listener classes.

TABLE 20.2 The Available Listeners in System.Diagnostics

Class	Function
DefaultTraceListener	Default listener present in the Debug.Listeners and Trace.Listeners collection; directs debug content to the debug window and any debug monitors
EventLogTraceListener	Directs debug and trace content to the Event Log
TextWriterTraceListener	Directs debug and trace content to a TextWriter object or to a Stream object

As each Debug or Trace object issues a write command, the content of the write command is made available to each listener object identified in the Listeners property (which returns an instance of TraceListenerCollection). No difference exists between the listeners in terms of which trace messages they receive; if they are in the listeners collection, they receive the same message.

To see how all this comes together, look at the code presented in Listing 20.2. Here we are taking a simple console application that, when launched, calls two functions that manipulate an integer value. At the end of the program, the final value is written out to the console.

LISTING 20.2 Adding Listeners

```vb
Imports System.IO

Module Module1

    Sub Main()
        'This is the debug log file
        Dim logFile As Stream = File.Create("debug.log")
```

LISTING 20.2   Continued

```vb
    'Create a listener to write to the debug log
    Dim listener As New TextWriterTraceListener(logFile)
    Debug.Listeners.Add(listener)

    'Flush the listeners after every write
    Debug.AutoFlush = True

    Debug.WriteLine("Main: Enter")
    Debug.Indent()

    Dim someVal As Integer
    someVal = 1000

    someVal = ProcedureB(ProcedureA(someVal))

    Console.WriteLine("Final value: " & someVal)
    Console.WriteLine("Hit the ENTER key to exit...")
    Console.ReadLine()

    Debug.WriteLine("Final value of someVal: " & someVal)

    Debug.Unindent()
    Debug.WriteLine("Main: Exit")
End Sub

Function ProcedureA(ByVal number As Integer) As Integer
    Debug.Indent()
    Debug.WriteLine("ProcedureA: Enter")

    Dim i As Integer

    For i = 1 To 10
        Debug.Indent()
        Debug.WriteLine("Loop counter = " & i & "; number = " & number)
        Debug.Unindent()

        number = number - (i * 10)
    Next

    ProcedureA = number

    Debug.WriteLine("ProcedureA: Exit")
    Debug.Unindent()
End Function
```

LISTING 20.2 Continued

```
    Function ProcedureB(ByVal number As Integer) As Integer
        Debug.Indent()
        Debug.WriteLine("ProcedureB: Enter")

        Dim i As Integer

        For i = 10 To 1 Step -1
            Debug.Indent()
            Debug.WriteLine("Loop counter = " & i & "; number = " & number)
            Debug.Unindent()

            number = number + i
        Next

        ProcedureB = number

        Debug.WriteLine("ProcedureB: Exit")
        Debug.Unindent()
    End Function

End Module
```

To investigate the actual output of the debug code, we have littered the application with Debug statements. We have also added a TextWriterTraceListener object to our Debug.Listeners collection; this will have the effect of logging each debug message to the specified debug.log file.

Note that you can also affect the listeners in force for your application by modifying the application's configuration file. For instance, you can edit the application configuration file to add a TextWriterTraceListener, like this:

```
<configuration>
    <system.diagnostics>
        <listeners>
            <add name="listener" type="TextWriterTraceListener"
            parameter="c:\\debug.log" />
        </listeners>
    </system.diagnostics>
</configuration>
```

Figure 20.5 shows the content of the debug.log file after running the application once. Notice that the display is kept readable by using the Debug.Indent and Debug.Unindent commands to format the messages.

FIGURE 20.5
Debug output directed to a file.

To see the effect that the project build configuration has on the debug code, try creating a new console application inside Visual Studio .NET, copying the code from Listing 20.2 into it and then running the code with a debug configuration. You should notice two things: The debug output window in the IDE should show all the debug messages written out during execution, and in the application's bin directory, you should see a file that matches the file shown in Figure 20.5. Now try setting your build configuration to release, and rerun the application. Nothing will be written to the debug output window, and nothing will be written to the debug.log file.

> **NOTE**
>
> A command-line executable called dbmon.exe ships with the MSDN Platform SDK. This monitor tool enables you to see any and all debug messages issued by any application running on the local machine. This can be a quick and easy way to intercept and view trace messages sent out through the `DefaultTraceListener`.

Controlling the Level of Tracing

Provisions also exist in the `System.Diagnostics` namespace for controlling exactly which `Debug` and `Trace` commands get processed. Through two classes, `BooleanSwitch` and `TraceSwitch`, you can set up an independent indicator (which can be changed outside the compiled code) that can be used to control the level of debugging information that is generated. For instance, you may implement a `BooleanSwitch`—or a group of them—that is checked at certain areas of an application. If the switch is enabled, tracing information is broadcast to the listeners. Toward this end, the `BooleanSwitch` class exposes exactly one property, `Enabled`, which is a Boolean value representing the current state of the switch.

The `TraceSwitch` class is used to provide a more granular level of control. Instead of just working against an "on" or "off" position, a `TraceSwitch` can be set to a number of levels. `TraceSwitches` are useful when you want to control the level of debugging from off to verbose and steps in between. The `TraceSwitch.Level` property is used to indicate the current value of the `TraceSwitch` object. This returns a `TraceLevel` enumeration value (see Table 20.3), which indicates the current state of the switch.

TABLE 20.3 The `TraceLevel` Enumeration

Member	Description
Error	Send trace messages dealing with errors
Info	Send informational trace messages, along with errors and warnings
Off	Disable all tracing messages
Verbose	Turn on all tracing messages
Warning	Send warning and error trace messages

The `TraceSwitch` class also lets you check individual Boolean properties to indicate a level of tracing by exposing a separate Boolean property for each `TraceLevel` enumeration value. Thus we have `TraceSwitch.TraceError`, `TraceSwitch.TraceInfo`, `TraceSwitch.TraceOff`, `TraceSwitch.TraceVerbose`, and `TraceSwitch.TraceWarning`.

> **NOTE**
>
> Note that the `Level` property operates on a continuum; if you look at the `TraceLevel` enumeration values, you can see that they represent a cumulative level of tracing that follows this order:
>
> `Off -> Error -> Warning -> Info -> Verbose`
>
> A level of `Info` will enable trace messages for warnings and errors, as well.

Creating Switches

To create a switch, you simply dimension an instance of a particular switch class, assigning it some initial values. In the following, we are creating both a trace and a Boolean switch:

```
Dim dataSwitch As New BooleanSwitch("appDebug", "Application level")
Dim generalSwitch as New TraceSwitch("dbAccess", "All database access")
```

Notice that the constructors for both a BooleanSwitch and a TraceSwitch take two parameters:
The first one is the display name of the switch, and the second is the description of the switch.

Leveraging Switches in Code

The Debug and Trace classes have specialized versions of their Write methods that are used in
conjunction with switch objects. The WriteIf and WriteLineIf methods accept a Boolean
expression that determines whether the trace message actually gets sent to the configured listeners, with the intent that this Boolean expression be evaluated from a switch value.

For example, the following code sets up a BooleanSwitch object and then uses it to determine
whether the application should generate trace messages.

```
Dim debugSwitch As New BooleanSwitch("debugSwitch", "Global debug switch")
 .
 .
 .
Trace.WriteLineIf(debugSwitch.Enabled, "Entering recursion routine")
```

In a similar fashion, we can use a TraceSwitch instance to determine the level of trace messages that are sent out.

```
Dim debugSwitch As New TraceSwitch("debugSwitch", "Global debug switch")

Trace.WriteLineIf(debugSwitch.TraceInfo, "Entering recursion routine")

Try
    'Do work here

Catch appErr As System.Exception
    'An error has occurred
    Trace.WriteLineIf(debugSwitch.TraceError, appErr.Message)

End Try
```

Setting a Switch's Value

The real power of a tracing switch is its capability to be set outside of the executing code. This
allows for situations in which users can be instructed on how to facilitate tracing in an application to enable a help desk to better troubleshoot the problem. It also allows for testing departments to alter switch values and levels between application runs without bothering the
development department with code changes to effect the change.

The .NET Framework enables you to specify switch values through an application's configuration file. To set a switch's value in the configuration file, you add statements into the
<switches> section. The following snippet from a configuration file takes care of
adding one TraceSwitch to a program and setting its current level.

```
<configuration>
        <system.diagnostics>
            <switches>
                    <add name="debugSwitch" value="4" />
            </switches>
    </system.diagnostics>
</configuration>
```

The numeric values for the `TraceSwitch.Level` property follow in sequence from the `TraceLevel` enumeration values, which are

0 = Off

1 = Error

2 = Warning

3 = Info

4 = Verbose

Using Assertions

Peripherally related to tracing is the concept of assertions. The `Debug` and `Trace` classes have a method, `Assert`, which enables you to test for a specific condition in your code. `Assert` statements are typically used to test assumptions in your code and are particularly useful during the active debugging process. The most common version of the `Assert` method takes a Boolean expression and a `string` parameter; if the expression evaluates to `True`, the program will immediately enter break mode and the string will be raised to the screen.

A common example used to illustrate the case for assertions is a block of code that performs division, such as

```
Private Function DivideSomeNumbers(ByVal num1 As Integer, _
    ByVal num2 As Integer) As Double
        Try
            DivideSomeNumbers = num1 \ num2

        Catch
            'error code goes here

        End Try

End Function
```

Even though an error handler is present, an assertion in this function will help to heavily underscore the assumption that `num2` must be nonzero.

```
Private Function DivideSomeNumbers(ByVal num1 As Integer, _
    ByVal num2 As Integer) As Double
```

20

```
    Try
        Debug.Assert(num2 <> 0, _
            "!!!num2 parameter is unexpectedly equal to 0")
        DivideSomeNumbers = num1 \ num2

    Catch
        'error code goes here

    End Try


End Function
```

Assertions are a good form of defensive programming. They can highlight brittle areas of code and point out areas of an application that need to have more safeguards implemented so that assumptions always hold true.

NOTE

Assertion messages are actually raised using the `Fail` method (on either the `Debug` or `Trace` class). This has the subsequent effect of calling the `Fail` method on each listener in the listeners collection. If you want to change how and where assertions are displayed to the screen, you can simply alter the listeners collection or write your own listener that implements the `Fail` method in the fashion you desire.

Like the other debugging mechanisms we have discussed, assertions can also be set up in an applications configuration file like the following (for more information on the exact syntax requirements, see the MSDN documentation):

```
<configuration>
    <system.diagnostics>
        <assert assertuienabled="true" logfilename=".\TraceLog.txt"/>
    </system.diagnostics>
</configuration>
```

Profiling Applications

Profiling is nothing more than the analysis of performance data collected from an application while it is running. Profiling is a useful technique for pinpointing the slowest performing areas of code so that they can be targeted for code improvements. Microsoft has a tool designed to view and track performance data: the Performance Monitor MMC snap-in. This can be launched from a command prompt by just typing "perfmon." The Performance Monitor application feeds off objects called performance counters. These are individual, instrumented pieces of the core operating system that expose a numerical value representing some dimension of performance.

Because the .NET Framework ships with a comprehensive set of performance counters, the first step in profiling a .NET application can start with the default set of performance counters. A set of performance counter classes in the `Systems.Diagnostics` namespace also allows you to define your own performance counter.

The .NET Runtime Performance Counters

Figure 20.6 shows a dialog box from perfmon showing all the installed groups of .NET performance counters.

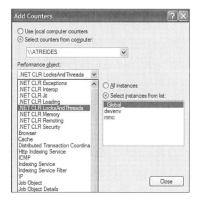

FIGURE 20.6

.NET runtime performance counters.

Each of these can be used to trap historical, benchmark data across a variety of different .NET operations. Using perfmon in conjunction with specific, carefully identified counters is probably the quickest and easiest way to profile an application. But this may not yield the exact information that you are looking for at an application level. In some cases, you may need to create your own performance counters.

Creating Your Own Performance Counter

The `PerformanceCounter` class encapsulates a discrete instance of a performance counter. You can create your own performance counter by instancing an object of this class and then assigning it your own object, counter, and instance information.

Figure 20.7 shows another view of the Add Counters dialog box from the perfmon utility.

FIGURE 20.7

.NET runtime performance counters.

Notice that there are three discrete identifiers for a performance counter: the object (set to Processor in this example), the actual counter (set to % Processor Time), and the instance (set to _Total). The object can be thought of as the category for a performance counter. The counter is the actual dimension being measured, and the instance represents what application or referenced unit the dimension applies to (_Total is often used to represent the sum or average of all available instances).

Following is a short example of the creation of a custom performance counter. We are using the PerformanceCounterCategory.Create method to do two things at once: It will create a new category for our counter and create the counter itself.

```
PerformanceCounterCategory.Create("myApp", "myApp Description", _
    "lingerCounter", "lingerCounter Description")
```

After creating the performance category and the counter, we can bind to it by creating a PerformanceCounter object and passing in the counter name, and so on, to the constructor:

```
Dim compCounter As PerformanceCounter = new PerformanceCounter("myApp", _
    "lingerCounter")
```

After the counter is created, you can write values to the counter using its RawValue property. The PerformanceCounter class also has methods for incrementing and decrementing the raw value by a set amount (IncrementBy and DecrementBy) and for incrementing or decrementing the RawValue by 1 (Increment and Decrement). Before attempting to write to the counter, you first need to set its ReadOnly property to False.

Performance counters may contain calculated values instead of a raw value. This can be determined or set through the PerformanceCounter.CounterType property. This property returns or accepts a PerformanceCounterType enumeration (see Table 20.4) that indicates the exact behavior of the counters value.

TABLE 20.4 The `PerformanceCounterType` Enumeration

Member	Description
AverageBase	The performance counter holds calculated time or count averages.
AverageCount64	The performance counter holds the bytes per operation divided by the number of operations.
AverageTimer32	The performance counter holds a value derived from a timer, specifically for use with time per operation divided by number of operations values.
CounterDelta32	The performance counter holds a value that is the difference between two other counters.
CounterDelta64	The performance counter holds a value that is the difference between two other counters.
CounterMultiBase	The performance counter holds a value equal to the number of items sampled.
CounterMultiTimer	The performance counter holds a value equal to timing information from multiple but similar timed objects.
CounterMultiTimer100Ns	The performance counter holds a value equal to timing information (in 100-nanosecond units) from multiple but similar timed objects.
CounterMultiTimer100NsInverse	The performance counter holds a value equal to the inverse of a `CounterMultiTimer100Ns` counter.
CounterMultiTimerInverse	The performance counter holds a value equal to the inverse of a `CounterMultiTimer` counter.
CounterTimer	The performance counter holds a value from a timer.
CounterTimerInverse	The performance counter holds a value equal to the inverse of a `CounterTimer` counter.
CountPerTimeInterval32	The performance counter holds a value equal to a count-per-time interval.
CountPerTimeInterval64	The performance counter holds a value equal to a count-per-time interval.
ElapsedTime	The performance counter holds a calculated value equal to the results of an elapsed-time calculation.
NumberOfItems32	The performance counter holds a raw value (will return the most recently updated value).
NumberOfItems64	The performance counter holds a raw value (will return the most recently updated value).

20

PROFILING,
DEBUGGING, AND
EXCEPTION
HANDLING

TABLE 20.4   Continued

Member	Description
NumberOfItemsHEX32	The performance counter holds a raw value (will return the most recently updated value in hexadecimal format).
NumberOfItemsHEX64	The performance counter holds a raw value (will return the most recently updated value in hexadecimal format).
RateOfCountsPerSecond32	The performance counter holds a calculated value that equals the number of operations per second.
RateOfCountsPerSecond64	The performance counter holds a calculated value that equals the number of operations per second.
RawBase	The performance counter holds the denominator of a another counter, in which the other counter represents a fractional number.
RawFraction	The performance counter holds a value that is to be divided by a RawBase counter.
SampleBase	The performance counter holds a denominator for use with SampleCounter and SampleFraction counters.
SampleCounter	The performance counter holds a calculated value equal to a count of the sampling interrupts that returned a 1.
SampleFraction	The performance counter holds a calculated value equal to a count of the sampling interrupts that returned a 1.
Timer100Ns	The performance counter holds a calculated value that equals a time of object usage.
Timer100NsInverse	The performance counter holds a value equal to the inverse of a Timer100Ns counter.

Using a Custom Performance Counter

Custom performance counters can be useful for profiling specific sections of an application. For instance, you might choose to use timer objects to calculate the amount of time spent in a specific loop. By stressing the application over time, you should be able to see a trend in the loop linger time if you are updating a performance counter with the information. Beyond raw performance numbers, you might want to write more prosaic data to a performance counter, such as the number of logins for your application over time or the number of files, orders, parts, and so on processed over time. All these clues can help to determine whether any performance problems exist in a project and exactly what body of code is responsible.

Summary

The .NET Framework supplies developers with an adequate stock of components and technologies aimed squarely at improving the quality of applications. In this chapter, we have looked at a few of these items that are focused on the task of debugging applications. We covered

- Implementing structured exception handlers
- Instrumenting applications using the `Debug` and `Trace` classes
- Controlling the actions of the `Debug` and `Trace` classes through switches
- Leveraging stock and custom performance counters for general application performance profiling

Globalization and Localization Techniques

IN THIS CHAPTER

Distributed applications built today often transcend one language or one culture. More and more developers and architects are being presented with the task of creating interfaces that are multilingual and with translating data across cultural and regional boundaries. In fact, it is typical that architects of a system are unsure regarding all the specific cultures a language may need to support. These applications have to be developed with a global perspective—that is, they must assume the need to support as many languages and cultures as possible. In the past, this has meant either multiple versions of the same application (and thus multiple support and extension teams) or bulky and slow code that is difficult to extend. .NET intends to make the task of building a global application easy and manageable.

This chapter is focused on teaching you how to create applications with VB .NET and the FCL that supports multiple cultures. The chapter discusses classes in the `System.Globalization` and `System.Resource` namespaces. We start by defining the process of globalization and localization. We then move through the specifics of working with data and creating and accessing resource files. We end the chapter by creating a multicultural form application.

After reading this chapter, you should

- Understand the process of designing an international application
- Be able to work with dates, currencies, and the like across cultures
- Be able to create and access a resource file
- Be able to create and deploy a global application

Globalization and Localization

The process of creating applications to be used by people of different cultures is referred to as globalization and localization. *Globalization*, in software development, refers to the tasks of separating your core logic from its surrounding data and making that core function language and culture neutral. That is, your code should not presuppose a culture, but expect to work with many cultures. *Localization* is considered the actual process of translating the data that your users need to a given culture and language. This section presents the key points to consider when designing for a multicultural application and details the key classes within `System.Globalization`.

Culture

When we refer to *culture*, we are talking about a set of predefined preferences based on a language, country, and possibly a region. Language is not enough to define a user's preferences. For example, both the U.S. and Great Britain have a default language of English. However, when formatting a currency value, the U.S. uses dollars ($), whereas the U.K. uses pounds (£) or even Euros (€). A user's culture signifies how currencies, dates, time, and the like should be displayed, compared, and sorted.

Globalization and Localization Techniques

CHAPTER 21

927

21

GLOBALIZATION
AND
LOCALIZATION
TECHNIQUES

A specific culture is one that defines both a language and a country or region. A standard exists (RFC 1766) that defines a culture by a two-letter language code, a dash, and a two-letter country/region code that is associated with a specific country or region. Table 21.1 demonstrates a number of specific culture codes (for a complete list, see MSDN, `CultureInfo` Class).

TABLE 21.1 Common Culture Codes

Culture Code	Language–Country/Region
de-DE	German–Germany
en-AU	English–Australia
en-CA	English–Canada
en-GB	English–Great Britain
en-IE	English–Ireland
en-NZ	English–New Zealand
en-US	English–United States
es-Mx	Spanish-Mexico
fr-CA	French–Canada
fr-FR	French–France
he-IL	Hebrew–Israel
hi-IN	Hindi–India
ja-JP	Japanese–Japan

Culture codes are used by your application to determine how to represent dates, currency, numbers, and the like. They are also used to look up resources for your application. Resources are files that contain cultural and language-specific translation of items inside your application. For example, your user interface might have a button that reads Cancel. A resource file would contain information on how to translate the word cancel for a given language and culture (resources are covered more fully later in the chapter).

A *neutral* culture is defined by only a language code. For example, "en" and "fr" refer to English and French, respectively. Your application can use neutral rather than specific culture codes when no need exists to communicate data down to the region or country. Additionally, you can create both a neutral and specific culture for your application to implement. This way, your application can fall back to a neutral culture when a specific one does not exist. For example, if your application defines resources for en-CA (English-Canada), en-GB (English-Great Britain), and a user with a setting of en-US (English-United States), your application will first try to find the U.S. version of your resource. After failing, it will search for a neutral culture definition (en in our case).

There also exists the concept of an invariant culture. An *invariant culture* is said to be culture insensitive, neither neutral nor specific. It is a culture based on English. The invariant culture ensures a known format when data is read or written by users of varying cultures. For instance, a date value stored in the format of the invariant culture can be read by the system, translated to the appropriate format, modified by the user, and then retranslated back to the invariant culture before the underlying value is updated. Another good use for invariant cultures is system services because they typically can run independently of language or culture.

Design Considerations

Now that you understand the concept of culture, you can start to appreciate how different the architecture of an international application will look. In .NET, the typical global application has a core assembly that contains resources based on a default or neutral culture. The code in the application understands how to manage culture and language. The default cultural resources are compiled with the assembly and used as the fallback culture. Additionally, the application links to a number of satellite assemblies (made up of resource files) for specific culture translation. This model is illustrated by Figure 21.1.

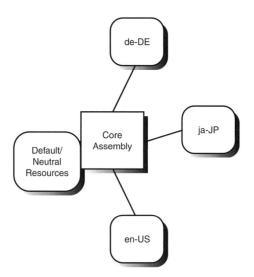

FIGURE 21.1
Satellite assemblies.

If you are in the midst of creating a new application and have an indication that you might need to support more than one culture, you should consider the benefits of switching to this model sooner rather than later. It is relatively straightforward to design new applications using this model; however, retrofitting existing applications (even those originally created with .NET)

Globalization and Localization Techniques

CHAPTER 21

929

21

GLOBALIZATION
AND
LOCALIZATION
TECHNIQUES

can be a much bigger challenge. In addition, the costs to convert an application are far greater than the extra dollars spent at the time of the application's inception.

When designing your application, it's important that you determine cultural support. It is not imperative that you define all the cultures you want to support, but you should at least be able to define a default or neutral culture. A default culture represents the primary culture of the majority of your users. It is also the fallback option when a user's specific culture cannot be found.

After an application has been built to support more than one culture, the process of adding support for additional cultures is rather simple and requires little, if any, actual coding changes (and no architectural changes). You simply create a new resource file for the target culture and deploy it accordingly. Users who now prefer the newly added culture will see your application localized for their needs.

CultureInfo

A user's preferred cultural setting is represented by the `CultureInfo` class in .NET. This class represents everything about a culture: its writing system, calendar, currency formats, and so on. To create an instance of the class, you can pass a culture code to it on the constructor. For example:

```
Dim myCulture As New System.Globalization.CultureInfo(name:="en-GB")
```

To use the `CultureInfo` class to influence the behavior of your code, you change the `CurrentCulture` property on the executing thread, as in the following:

```
Threading.Thread.CurrentThread.CurrentCulture = myCulture
```

Using this example and writing out the value of a call to `Now` prior to setting the thread's culture produces "9/23/2001 9:18:52 PM." After changing the culture to the U.K., you get the date in the format of month/day/year and the time in 24-hour format: 23/09/2001 21:18:52.

This example demonstrates the result of explicitly setting your application's culture. This may be useful only when testing your application or when users are allowed to change their culture on-the-fly. More than likely, your application will implicitly change cultures based on the user's machine settings as set by the Regional Options control panel. This dialog box allows users to override specific regional settings for their given culture. These overrides might cause unexpected results for your application. Therefore, you might consider creating a `CultureInfo` object based on the user's settings, but choose not to use the cultural overrides. The following code demonstrates this concept:

```
myCulture = New CultureInfo(name:= _
    Threading.Thread.CurrentThread.CurrentCulture.Name(), _
    useUserOverride:=False)

Threading.Thread.CurrentThread.CurrentCulture = myCulture
```

Explicitly defining culture is also useful in ASP.NET applications in which it is unlikely that a user's culture will match that of the server that is executing your code. In this case, it is best to use the user's Web browser language setting to initially set the culture by which your code will execute. This setting is available from the Request object. The CultureInfo class exposes a CreateSpecificCulture method that returns a CultureInfo object based on a culture name. The following is an example:

```
Threading.Thread.CurrentThread.CurrentCulture = _
  CultureInfo.CreateSpecificCulture(Request.UserLanguages[0])
```

CultureInfo is a class that you will undoubtedly need time and again. For that reason, we've listed a number of additional key properties and methods of the class in Table 21.2.

TABLE 21.2 CultureInfo Key Properties and Methods

Property	Description
Calendar	The Calendar property is used to return the default calendar used by the culture. The property is of the type Calendar class.
CompareInfo	The CompareInfo property returns the CompareInfo object that defines how strings are compared within the current culture.
CurrentCulture	The CurrentCulture property returns a CultureInfo object that represents the culture the current thread is using.
CurrentUICulture	The CurrentUICulture property returns a CultureInfo object that represents the culture used by the Resource Manager.
DateTimeFormat	The DateTimeFormat property returns or sets the culture-specific format for displaying dates and times. The property is of the type DateTimeFormatInfo.
DisplayName	The DisplayName property returns the culture name in the format [language]<country/region>. For example, en-US returns "English <United States>."
EnglishName	The EnglishName property is the same as DisplayName but always returns in English.
InstalledUICulture	The InstalledUICulture property returns a CultureInfo object that represents the culture of the operating system at the time of installation.
InvariantCulture	The InvariantCulture property returns a CultureInfo object that is culture insensitive.
IsNeutralCulture	The IsNeutralCulture property returns True if the instance represents a neutral culture. For example, "en" for English.

Globalization and Localization Techniques

CHAPTER 21

931

21

GLOBALIZATION
AND
LOCALIZATION
TECHNIQUES

TABLE 21.2 Continued

Property	Description
LCID	The LCID property returns the instance's culture identifier value.
Name	The Name property is used to return the name of the culture in the format language code, dash, country/region code (en-US).
NativeName	The NativeName property returns the name of the culture in the language that the instance is set to display.
NumberFormat	The NumberFormat is used to return or set a value indicating how numbers, currency, and percentages are formatted for display.
OptionalCalendars	The OptionalCalendars property returns a list of optional calendars a given culture can use.
Parent	The Parent property returns a CultureInfo object that represents the current, specific culture's parent. For example, "en-US" has the parent (also called neutral) culture of "en."
TextInfo	The TextInfo property is used to return the TextInfo object that defines the writing system for a given culture. TextInfo defines things such as case and other behaviors.
UseUserOverride	The UseUserOverride property returns True if the CultureInfo instance uses the user-overridden culture settings.
Method	
ClearCachedData	The ClearCachedData method is used to refresh the culture object. Data is loaded when the object is created. The information can change during the object's lifetime based on user settings.
CreateSpecificCulture	CreateSpecificCulture is a shared method that returns a CultureInfo instance from a culture code.
GetCultures	GetCultures is a shared method that returns a collection of CultureInfo objects based on a CultureTypes filter. CultureTypes can be AllCultures, InstalledWin32Cultures, NeutralCultures, and SpecificCultures.

RegionInfo

Additional information about a culture's region, such as measurement system or currency code, can be gathered using the RegionInfo class. To create a RegionInfo instance, you can pass either a two-letter region code (as defined by ISO 3166 standard) or a culture identifier gained by calling the `CultureInfo`'s LCID property. The following are two examples:

```
'create a region object based on a region code (Zimbabwe)
myRegion = New RegionInfo(name:="ZW")

'create a region object from an LCID
myRegion = New RegionInfo(culture:= _
  Threading.Thread.CurrentThread.CurrentCulture.LCID)
```

After you've created a valid `RegionInfo` instance, you have access to a number of important properties. For example, `CurrencySymbol` returns the symbol used to denote currency within the local region, and an `ISOCurrencySymbol` property returns the three-letter ISO standard (4217) for a region's currency. The United States' ISO currency symbol, for example, is USD. The property `IsMetric` is a `Boolean` value that returns `True` if the region uses the metric system for measurement.

Working with Regional Data

Understanding how to work with and display data for various cultures is another key step to developing global applications. Different cultures have different number formats, currency symbols, ways of sorting data—even different calendars. In this section we'll detail how to work with data in a cross-cultural application.

Numbers and Currency

Fortunately, after a user's culture has been set, things such as decimal separators and numeric symbols work according to the rules of a given culture. These rules are defined by an instance of the `NumberFormatInfo` class. To obtain an instance of `NumberFormatInfo` based on the current executing thread, you call the `CurrentCulture.NumberFormat` property, as in the following:

```
myNumInfo = Threading.Thread.CurrentThread.CurrentCulture.NumberFormat
```

You can also set the same property from the `CultureInfo` object when working with custom culture objects.

To function with a given culture, the `NumberFormatInfo` class is not required by your application. Instead, it provides finite control over and access to how numbers get formatted. Let's use the following example: Suppose we have to display the price of our product in both yen and dollars. We can simply switch our application's culture and write out the price. The formatting is done for us automatically. Or suppose that the user's current culture is English-United States, but your requirement is to always display both dollars and yen. We can create a custom `CultureInfo` object and pass it as a provider to the `ToString` method when outputting our price. The following illustrates this example:

Globalization and Localization Techniques

CHAPTER 21

933

21

GLOBALIZATION
AND
LOCALIZATION
TECHNIQUES

```vb
Imports System.Globalization

Module Module1

  Sub Main()

    Dim myPrice As Decimal = 38.99

    'set the current culture to English-United States
    Threading.Thread.CurrentThread.CurrentCulture = _
      New CultureInfo(name:="en-US")

    'display the price in dollars
    Console.WriteLine(myPrice.ToString(Format:="c"))

    'create a cultureInfo object for Japanese-Japan
    Dim myJapan As New CultureInfo(name:="ja-JP")

    'display the price in yen
    Console.WriteLine(myPrice.ToString(Format:="c", provider:=myJapan))

  End Sub

End Module
```

The result of this routine is the values $38.99 and ¥39 written to the console window. The value c passed as the first parameter to the ToString method is a format character that denotes currency. Some other common format characters include: d for decimal, e for exponential, f for fixed-point, and x for hexadecimal.

Of course, you can override the default behavior of the NumberFormatInfo class for a given culture. What if, for instance, you wanted to show the yen price from the preceding example using two digits after the decimal (¥38.99)? You would add the following line:

```vb
myJapan.NumberFormat.CurrencyDecimalDigits = 2
```

Other NumberFormatInfo properties include CurrencySymbol, NegativeSign, and PercentDecimalDigits, to name a few. The NumberFormatInfo class provides more than 25 properties that you can use to change the way in which a culture's numbers are formatted.

Dates and Times

Date and time formats are also defined by the current culture. The DateTimeFormat property of the CultureInfo class is of the type DateTimeFormatInfo class. This class defines the various patterns used to display dates and times based on a user's preferred culture. This class is primarily used for overriding or accessing these values to determine a given culture's specific default format.

The following is an example of the result of simply switching cultures and displaying the current date and time.

```
'set the current culture to English-US
Threading.Thread.CurrentThread.CurrentCulture = _
  New CultureInfo(name:="en-US")

'write out the date value
Console.WriteLine(Now)

'change the current culture to Japanese-Japan
Threading.Thread.CurrentThread.CurrentCulture = _
  New CultureInfo(name:="ja-JP")

'write out the date value
Console.WriteLine(Now)
```

The code outputs the English date of 9/24/2001 9:27:44 a.m. followed by the Japanese version of the same date and time of 2001/09/24 9:27:44. However, suppose you want to override the default date separate for the English-United States culture ("/"). You would do so using the DateSeparator property, as in the following:

```
Threading.Thread.CurrentThread. _
  CurrentCulture.DateTimeFormat.DateSeparator = "."
```

The DateFormatInfo class also enables you to return dates in various formats or patterns. These properties include LongDatePattern, LongTimePattern, MonthDayPattern, ShortDatePattern, ShortTimePattern, YearMonthPattern. Other notable properties of the DateFormatInfo class include the following:

- AMDesignator—Used to return or set a string value that indicates time that is "ante meridiem" (before noon).
- CalendarWeekRule—Specifies the rule to use (of type CalendarWeekRule enumeration) to determine the first calendar week of the year.
- DayNames—Used to return or set an array that indicates the culture's names for the days of the week.
- FirstDayOfWeek—Used to return or set the culture's accepted day that a week starts. The property is of the type DateTime.DayOfWeek enumeration.
- MonthNames—Used to return or set an array that indicates the culture's names for the months in a year.
- PMDesignator—Used to return or set a string value that indicates time that is "post meridiem" (after noon).

Calendars

A culture's calendar is another important item to consider when creating applications of a global scale. Calendar classes in .NET are used to divide time into a culture's recognized units. For instance, a year can be divided into a number of months, a month into days, and so on. Each calendar can represent these items differently. .NET provides the base class `Calendar` for creating classes that define a culture's calendar. The Framework Class Library defines the calendars listed in Table 21.3.

TABLE 21.3   Calendar Classes

Class	Description
GregorianCalendar	The GregorianCalendar class recognizes the era A.D. (Latin "Anno Domini," which means "in the year of the Lord") or C.E. (common era). The Gregorian calendar has 12 months with 28 to 31 days each.
HebrewCalendar	The HebrewCalendar class recognizes the era A.M. (Latin "Anno Mundi", which means "the year of the world") and the Hebrew years 5343 to 6000 (1582 to 2240 in the Gregorian calendar). The Hebrew calendar has 12 months during common years and 13 months during leap years.
HijriCalendar	The HijriCalendar class recognizes the era A.H. (Latin "Anno Hegirae," which means "the year of the migration," in reference to the migration of Muhammad from Mecca). The Hijri calendar has 12 months with 29 to 30 days each.
JapaneseCalendar	The JapaneseCalendar class works like the Gregorian calendar, except that the year and era are different. The Japanese calendar recognizes one era for every emperor's reign. The current era is the Heisei era, which began in the Gregorian calendar year 1989.
KoreanCalendar	The KoreanCalendar class works like the Gregorian calendar, except that the year and era are different. The KoreanCalendar class recognizes only the current era. The year 2001 A.D. in the Gregorian calendar is equivalent to the year 4334 of the current era in the Korean calendar.
TaiwanCalendar	The TaiwanCalendar class works like the Gregorian calendar, except that the year and era are different. The TaiwanCalendar class recognizes only the current era. The year 2001 A.D. in the Gregorian calendar is equivalent to the year 90 of the current era in the Taiwan calendar.

Table 21.3   Continued

Class	Description
ThaiBuddhistCalendar	The ThaiBuddhistCalendar class works like the Gregorian calendar, except that the year and era are different. The year 2001 A.D. in the Gregorian calendar is equivalent to the year 2544 of the current era in the Thai Buddhist calendar.

To access a given culture's calendar, you can use the Calendar property of the CultureInfo class. This will return its default calendar class. Some cultures, however, support multiple calendars. Access to these calendars can be gained through the CultureInfo class's OptionalCalendars property. As an example, the following code outputs the calendars used in the culture Hebrew-Israel. The output is HebrewCalendar followed by GregorianCalendar.

```
Dim myCulture As CultureInfo
Dim i As Short

'create new culture (Hebrew-Israel)
myCulture = New CultureInfo("he-IL")

'display optional calendars
For i = 0 To myCulture.OptionalCalendars.Length - 1
  Console.WriteLine(myCulture.OptionalCalendars(i).ToString)
Next
```

The calendar classes contain a number of methods for getting information about how a specific time is represented by a given calendar. These methods primarily use the DateTime class as a parameter. The methods of the DateTime class always use the Gregorian calendar to perform calculations. However, the results can be mapped directly to an instance of another calendar. For example, the GetDayOfWeek method returns a value of the type DayOfWeek enumeration for a given DateTime value. Other key methods include AddMonths, AddWeeks, AddYears, GetDayOfMonth, GetDayOfYear, GetDaysInMonth, GetDaysInYear, GetMonth, IsLeapDay, IsLeapMonth, and IsLeapYear.

Suggestions for Further Exploration

➲ If you need to format currency for countries supporting the Euro, check out: MSDN/Visual Studio .NET/.NET Framework/Programming with the .NET Framework/Developing World-Ready Applications/Formatting Numeric Data for a Specific Culture.

➲ Use the DateTime.ToUniversalTime method, the DateTimeStyles enumeration, and the System.TimeZone class to work with different time zones.

Globalization and Localization Techniques

CHAPTER 21

937

21

GLOBALIZATION
AND
LOCALIZATION
TECHNIQUES

⊃ Check out the `System.Globalization.DaylightTime` class for managing daylight saving time.

⊃ The .NET Framework uses the Unicode Transformation Format with 16-bit encoding (Unicode UTF-16) to represent characters. Unicode is the universal standard for encoding characters and text. For more information, check out `www.unicode.org`.

⊃ If you need to work with Unicode surrogate pairs and combining characters to represent characters from other languages, try the `StringInfo` class.

Resource Files

Resource files enable you to separate your core application from its resources. A *resource file* is data (not code) that gets deployed with your application. A global application will typically define one resource file for every culture it needs to support. The data in a resource file includes things such as application help text, form text, and image files all translated for the target culture. This section details creating and using resource files in your application using the `System.Resources` namespace and associated VS .NET utilities.

Creation

The process of creating resource files involves the following steps:

1. Define your application's cultural support—This is a requirements step in which you decide which cultures your application will support and what the default or fallback culture will be. Of course, you can easily add support for additional cultures at a later time, but understanding the primary cultures will help you make decisions about deployment and design.

2. Identify which items in your user interface require translation—This step is part of building your core application to understand and use resources. It is not sufficient to hard-code the word "cancel" on a button or write the instruction text in English on your Web page. You must pull this information directly from resource files for a user's selected culture.

3. Translate your resource—In this step, you will typically pass a file containing all your application's resources off to a translator. Remember, resources can include text and images.

4. Convert translated values into resource files—Finally, you must take the resources for a given culture and define a resource file for your application. The remainder of this section is focused on this step.

Resource files, at their most basic level, are composed of name/value pairs grouped for a specific culture. The name is used as a key to retrieve a value. Names are case sensitive and are followed by an equals (=) sign to denote the name's value, as in `Name = Value`. At least three file types are used for resource files.

Text files can be used to create a resource file that contains only string values. In this case, you can define comments in the text file by preceding the line with a semicolon (;). The following is an example of a simple text-only resource file:

```
;define names and values
CommandCancel = Cancel
WindowTitle = MyApplication
```

You can also create an XML-based resource file. These files have the extension .resx and can be created with a resource editing tool embedded within VS .NET. The preceding resource file is represented as the following using XML inside a .resx file:

```
<?xml version="1.0" encoding="utf-8" ?>
<root>
    <xsd:schema ... > ... </xsd:schema>
    <resheader name="ResMimeType">
        <value>text/microsoft-resx</value>
    </resheader>
    <resheader name="Version">
        <value>1.0.0.0</value>
    </resheader>
    <resheader name="Reader">
        <value>System.Resources.ResXResourceReader</value>
    </resheader>
    <resheader name="Writer">
        <value>System.Resources.ResXResourceWriter</value>
    </resheader>
    <data name="CommandCancel">
        <value>Cancel</value>
    </data>
    <data name="WindowTitle">
        <value>MyApplication</value>
    </data>
</root>
```

Note that we omitted the xsd information in the preceding example for clarity and brevity.

Before you use a resource file, it must be converted into a .resource file. These are binary files used by .NET to embed within assemblies and to create satellite assemblies (see packaging).

Files of type .resources can be created in at least two ways. One is to use the utility, Resource File Generator (ResGen.exe). This utility takes a text (.txt extension) or an XML-based resource file (.resx extension) and outputs a .resource file. The utility can also work in the other direction. That is, create a .txt or .resx file from a .resource file.

Note that if you work with XML resource files, you will want to use the .resx file type. Files of type .txt will not be translated as XML by the utility regardless of content.

Globalization and Localization Techniques

CHAPTER 21

939

21

GLOBALIZATION
AND
LOCALIZATION
TECHNIQUES

The `ResGen` utility is used from a command prompt. For example, to output the text file from the preceding example, we would enter the following command:

```
Resgen myRes.txt myRes.resources
```

This command used the text file `myRes.txt` to output the binary `myRes.resources`.

You can also create resource files using the .NET Framework Class Library. The class `ResourceWriter` inside the `System.Resources` namespace is used to write resource values to a file or stream. For example, the following code creates a resource file called `myRes.resources`. It then adds two items to the resource file using the `AddResource` method and passing a name/value pair as parameters.

```
Imports System.Resources

Module Module1

  Sub Main()

    'purpose: write resources to a .resource file

    'local scope
    Dim myResWriter As ResourceWriter

    'create new ResourceWriter class
    myResWriter = New ResourceWriter(fileName:="myRes.resources")

    'add resources
    myResWriter.AddResource(name:="ApplicationName", value:="Res Example")
    myResWriter.AddResource(name:="HelpButton", value:="Help")

    'close the resource file
    myResWriter.Close()

  End Sub

End Module
```

The counterpart to the `ResourceWriter` class is `ResourceReader`. This class can be used to iterate through the contents of a .resource file. In the following example, we create a `ResourceReader` instance based on our `myRes.resources` file. We then call the method `GetEnumerator`, which returns a dictionary-style collection. We iterate this collection and output the name/value pairs to the console.

```
Imports System.Resources

Module Module1

  Sub Main()
```

```
'purpose: read resources from a .resource file

Dim myResReader As ResourceReader
Dim myEnumerator As IDictionaryEnumerator

'create ResourceReader class
myResReader = New ResourceReader(fileName:="myRes.resources")

'return the resources as a collection
myEnumerator = myResReader.GetEnumerator()

'iterate resource and write to console
While myEnumerator.MoveNext

    Console.WriteLine(myEnumerator.Key.ToString & " = " & _
        myEnumerator.Value.ToString)

End While

'close the reader
myResReader.Close()

'pause
Do While Not Console.ReadLine = "s" : Loop

  End Sub

End Module
```

The ResourceReader class can be handy at times, especially when you're debugging or coding a tool whose purpose is to read .resource files. For your global-ready application, however, you should use the ResourceManager class to access your resources. This class is covered in the following section.

Accessing

The classes ResourceManager and ResourceSet are most often used when accessing resource files for use inside your application. The code to use both classes is very similar. For example, to access string values, you call the GetString method. For images and other binary information, you call GetObject. The key differences lie in how the objects are created.

The ResourceSet object is created against a specific resource file. For this reason, it has no support for "falling back" to a neutral culture; it works only with the file you specify. Additionally, the ResourceSet object caches the entire resource file's contents when it is created. This provides faster access to resources but consumes memory regardless of whether you access the resource items.

Globalization and Localization Techniques

CHAPTER 21

941

21

GLOBALIZATION
AND
LOCALIZATION
TECHNIQUES

The `ResourceManager` class, on the other hand, determines which culture's resource file or associated satellite assembly to access based on a user's current culture setting. If it does not find the requested culture, it can process a set of fallback rules that determine what culture to access (the `ResourceSet` class throws an exception when it cannot find a specified culture-resource file). Falling back typically involves switching your application to a neutral culture you've defined during packaging and deployment. In addition, the `ResourceManager` class loads only a resource file's keys at the time of instantiation. This consumes less memory, especially if users don't typically access all your resources in one session. It has the effect of seeming faster initially; however, the time to access resources is spread over the lifetime of your application. Every time a new resource is requested, the `ResourceManager` must retrieve it from your file. After the initial retrieval, however, the item is cached for the next use. For these reasons, the `ResourceManager` class is the preferred solution when creating global applications.

Deploying

Deploying resource files that are of the type .txt, .resx, or .resources is called *loose deployment*. This type of deployment is contrasted with compiled satellite assemblies that contain your resources (more on these in a minute). Loose resource files are somewhat easier to manage; however, they do not provide the versioning and signature support of a satellite assembly. Nor can they be deployed into the Global Assembly Cache.

Typically, you deploy these loose resource files into a subdirectory within your application. Each file has what is referred to as a base name, followed by the culture the resource file represents and the .resource extension. Figure 21.2 represents the deployment of three resource files into a folder called Resources.

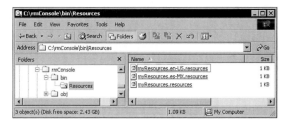

FIGURE 21.2
Loose deployment.

Notice that the previous figure has two culture resource files (`en-US` and `es-MX`) and another file that did not indicate culture (`myResources.resources`). In this deployment, this file will act as the fallback set of resources. When a user's cultural preferences dictate something other than these two cultures, the `ResourceManager` object will fall back to the file with the base name. This is better illustrated with some code.

In Listing 21.1, we use these three resource files to output text based on a given culture. The text items we are going to output in this example are named GoodMorning and Hello in each resource file. To simulate different user culture settings, we are going to cheat and simply set the CurrentUICulture of the executing thread to a new culture. This enables us to switch cultures on-the-fly and watch as the ResourceManager object reacts accordingly.

To create a ResourceManager instance based on a .resource file, we use the shared method CreateFileBasedResourceManager. In this function call, we indicate the base name of our resource files (myResources) and the directory in which they are located (./resources). We then simply call the GetString method of the class, passing it the key (as the name parameter) of our name/value pair.

LISTING 21.1   ResourceManager Loose Access

```
Imports System.Resources
Imports System.Globalization

Module Module1

  Sub Main()

    'purpose: demonstrate the resource manager class

    'local scope
    Dim myRm As ResourceManager

    'set the current thread to English-US
    Threading.Thread.CurrentThread.CurrentUICulture = _
      New CultureInfo(name:="en-US")

    'create new resource manager class to access .resource files
    myRm = ResourceManager.CreateFileBasedResourceManager( _
      baseName:="myResources", _
      resourceDir:="./resources", _
      usingResourceSet:=Nothing)

    'access resources and write to console
    Console.WriteLine(myRm.GetString(name:="GoodMorning"))
    Console.WriteLine(myRm.GetString(name:="Hello"))

    'set the current thread to Spanish-Mexico
    Threading.Thread.CurrentThread.CurrentUICulture = _
      New CultureInfo(name:="es-MX")
```

Globalization and Localization Techniques
CHAPTER 21

943

21

GLOBALIZATION
AND
LOCALIZATION
TECHNIQUES

LISTING 21.1   Continued

```
    'access resources and write to console
    Console.WriteLine(myRm.GetString(name:="GoodMorning"))
    Console.WriteLine(myRm.GetString(name:="Hello"))

    'set the current thread to Japanese-Japan
    Threading.Thread.CurrentThread.CurrentUICulture = _
      New CultureInfo(name:="ja-JP")

    'access resources and write to console
    Console.WriteLine(myRm.GetString(name:="GoodMorning"))
    Console.WriteLine(myRm.GetString(name:="Hello"))

    'pause
    Do While Console.ReadLine <> "s" : Loop

  End Sub

End Module
```

Notice that as we switched cultures, the ResourceManager understood how to find the appropriate resource file without our interaction. This would be the same for users. Your application need not respond to events when users change their regional settings. Instead, the CLR and the class manage this for you.

Also notice that our last culture switch was to ja-JP. We did not define a resource file for this culture. However, we did define a fallback option. The ResourceManager class picked up our base name file and used it to respond to ja-JP. This is illustrated in the console's output as rendered in Figure 21.3.

FIGURE 21.3

ResourceManager *loose access output.*

Note that the only thing required to support an additional culture in this case is to create an additional resource file. No code changes nor recompiling are necessary!

Using Satellite Assemblies

Resource files can be bound into assemblies for versioning, signature, and deployment. These assemblies are compiled into either the main executable or a separate DLL file. In a typical deployment, you will bind the default or fallback assembly to your core executable. Each culture-specific assembly will be deployed into a separate DLL. These resource assemblies are called *satellite assemblies*.

A satellite assembly is created directly from a .resource file. To do so, you use the Assembly Linker (Al.exe) utility provided with VS .NET. For example, the following commands create assembly files for our culture-specific resource files:

```
'create en-US satellite assembly
al /out:en-US/myResources.dll /v:1.0.0.0 /c:en-US
  /embed:myResources.en-US.resources,myResources.en-US.resources,private

'create es-MX satellite assembly
al /out:es-MX/myResources.dll /v:1.0.0.0 /c:es-MX
  /embed:myResources.es-MX.resources,myResources.es-MX.resources,private
```

Notice that we output each file with the same name (myResources.dll). This is possible for two reasons: first, we indicated culture when we created the assembly (c:en-US), and second, the files are actually deployed in different directories. Private satellite assemblies are deployed into a directory structure within your application. This allows the CLR and the ResourceManager class to locate these files. Each directory gets its name from the culture that it represents. For example, the English-United States directory would be called en-US. Public satellite assemblies get deployed into the Global Assembly Cache. When doing so, you must strongly name your assembly.

The next step is to embed our default resource file into our executable. Before we do this, however, we are going to create a separate class file that wraps the ResourceManager access to our name/value pairs. Listing 21.2 presents this code.

LISTING 21.2   Satellite Assembly Class Example

```
Imports System.Resources

Public Class SatelliteTestClass

  'class level scope
  Private myRm As ResourceManager

  Public Sub New()
```

LISTING 21.2 Continued

```
    'create new resource manager class
    myRm = New ResourceManager(baseName:="myResources", _
       assembly:=Me.GetType().Assembly)

  End Sub

  Public ReadOnly Property Hello()
    Get
       Return myRm.GetString(name:="Hello")
    End Get
  End Property

  Public ReadOnly Property GoodMorning()
    Get
       Return myRm.GetString(name:="GoodMorning")
    End Get
  End Property

End Class
```

This class file is compiled from the command line using the following switches. The switch, "/resource" indicates that the compiler is to embed our default resource file as part of the executable.

```
vbc /target:library /out:satClass.dll /r:system.dll
   /resource:myResources.resources Class1.vb
```

Next, we create a client to access our newly created library. This client switches cultures and accesses resources accordingly. To make this work, we must deploy our class and its associated resource files into the client application's directory (bin). This code is presented in Listing 21.3.

LISTING 21.3 Satellite Assembly Client Example

```
Imports System.Resources
Imports System.Globalization

Module Module1

  Sub Main()

    'purpose: demonstrate satellite assemblies

    'local scope
    Dim mySatClass As SatelliteTestClass
```

LISTING 21.3   Continued

```
    'switch cultures to Spanish-Mexico
    Threading.Thread.CurrentThread.CurrentUICulture = _
      New CultureInfo(name:="es-MX")

    'create a new instance of SatelliteTestClass
    mySatClass = New SatelliteTestClass()

    'write values to console
    Console.WriteLine((mySatClass.Hello & ", " & mySatClass.GoodMorning))

    'set the current thread to English-United States
    Threading.Thread.CurrentThread.CurrentUICulture = _
      New CultureInfo(name:="en-US")

    'write values to console
    Console.WriteLine(mySatClass.Hello & ", " & mySatClass.GoodMorning)

    'switch cultures to Japanese-Japan
    Threading.Thread.CurrentThread.CurrentUICulture = _
        New CultureInfo(name:="ja-JP")

    'write values to console
    Console.WriteLine(mySatClass.Hello & ", " & mySatClass.GoodMorning)

    'pause
    Do While Console.ReadLine <> "s" : Loop

  End Sub

End Module
```

 ## Suggestions for Further Exploration

For specific details on working with resource files in ASP.NET applications, check out MSDN/Visual Studio .NET/.NET Framework/Programming with the .NET Framework/Developing World Ready Applications/Resources in Applications/Resources in ASP.NET Applications.

Summary

In this chapter, we've covered the basic steps for creating global applications with the .NET Framework Class Library. This seemingly daunting task now should seem well within your reach.

The following lists the key points presented in this chapter:

- It is often far easier and cheaper to bake globalization into your application at the time of inception rather than retrofitting your application at a later date.
- When designing for the global scale, it is important to partition your application's data into what is core and what is translated.
- The `System.Globalization` namespace defines key classes for writing global-ready applications.
- To define a culture, you use the language-country/region syntax (en-US for example).
- The `CultureInfo` class represents a culture in .NET.
- The `RegionInfo` class is used to get more information about a culture's region.
- The `NumberFormatInfo` class defines how to format numbers for a given culture.
- The `DateTimeFormatInfo` class is used to work with dates and times in a given culture's format.
- A number of `Calendar` derived classes enable you to manage dates for the current culture.
- You store your application's localized resources in resource files (.txt, .resx, and .resources).
- You can deploy your resource files loosely or as satellite assemblies.

Deploying, Configuring, and Licensing .NET Components

IN THIS CHAPTER

A developer's job is not over after an application is written. After spending countless hours trying to craft a software solution that addresses a business problem, developers now face what is sometimes the most complex task in the development cycle: making sure that the application can be installed and used by its intended audience. A smooth application deployment requires extensive research and insight into both the computing environment on which the software was written and the environment in which it will run.

With .NET, developers certainly are not relieved of this responsibility, but, considerable inroads have been made with respect to removing technical complexity and issues arising from the convoluted interactions of software on any particular machine.

In this chapter, we will show you how to successfully deploy applications written for the .NET Framework. We'll discuss the problems inherent with deploying traditional COM components, and then look at how .NET components have been structured to eliminate or drastically reduce these problems. We will also investigate how to license applications to ensure that only valid, authenticated users can run a given application.

By the end of this chapter, you should be able to:

- Explain the physical structure of assemblies and their role in application deployment
- Understand how the .NET runtime handles component versioning
- Deploy an application inside the Global Assembly Cache
- Enforce licensing restrictions on components

The Deployment Dilemma

To fully appreciate the deployment architecture of the .NET runtime, you must first understand the problems that it was built to resolve. In this section, we briefly visit the issues with deploying COM-based components outside of .NET. Then we focus on what .NET brings to the table in terms of easing the burden of physical deployments, including versioning.

DLL Hell

"DLL Hell" is a term that has developed over the years to describe the near misery experienced by developers while trying to distribute and register their applications into a Microsoft Windows environment. Registering a component with the operating system and COM involves touching the registry; this complicates the whole install process by forcing installers to physically touch the registry, introducing the potential for system-wide errors and security problems that can prevent the install from taking place. To understand what DLL Hell is all about, you really need to understand how Windows and COM deal with applications.

Let's take a simple scenario: A word-processor application is being developed by a hardworking team of software engineers. It will leverage a pre-existing COM DLL for its spell-checking capabilities. This spell-checking DLL is in use by many other applications as well. As the developers progress through their design, they discover that they really need the latest and greatest version of this DLL to achieve their design goals. After grabbing the latest version of the spell-checker component, they include it in their install script, master their discs, and start sending their software to those who have purchased it.

Unfortunately, they immediately start hearing about problems from their tech support staff. Users of the word processor are finding that, although it performs as advertised, their spreadsheet applications and email applications have started having problems. Eventually, the problems are traced back to the spell-checker component that, as we have stated, is used not just by one application, but by many on any given machine. It seems that the latest revision of the spell-checker component is not backward-compatible with the previous versions; any application developed against one of the previous versions fails on any call into the new component.

This scenario outlines a typical issue that developers who reuse components face. On the one hand, leveraging a common, shared component is a great way to speed development and avoid reinventing the wheel every time a piece of software is written. Doing so, however, exposes you to some risk. If another application comes along that does something to that shared component, it has the potential to break your application. What's more, you have no way of preventing it!

So, why does this happen? The key is in the way that Windows and COM identify components.

Component Identification

Windows and COM use the registry to describe components. That means that the Windows registry is used to tell COM certain things about a component, such as where it is located and what interfaces it supports. Deploying a COM component onto a machine was usually a two-step process: The DLL was copied to the Windows System32 directory (or some other global directory), and the registry was updated with its information. Although this seems like an easy way to approach things, it is fraught with danger (as we have shown). For one thing, versioning the component is not enforced by anyone or anything. If application A was specifically written to use Version 2.0 of the spell-checker component and the component was then revised to Version 3.0, there is no way for that application to realize that a potentially disastrous "upgrade" has been done to the component. Simply put, component identification with COM meant a few registry entries that matched up a physical file with its interfaces. This can be a brittle mechanism: COM does not actively police its registry entries, registries can become corrupt, and access to certain areas of a registry force developers to deal with obscure security issues as well.

Preserving Backward Compatibility

For COM developers, the solution for this problem seemed to lie with the concept of preserving *backward compatibility*. This means that the interfaces defined by the COM component are not allowed to change. If you had a method that defines four parameters, you were forever bound to using just these four parameters if you wanted to ensure that the component remained compatible with the current crop of applications that use it. Typically, development environments have been good at alerting programmers about changes that would break this backward compatibility, so it would seem that this "solution" makes everyone happy: It protects against new versions of the component from breaking all the applications that used downstream versions.

But what happens when the component simply outgrows its compatibility contract? This might not happen for a few years, but it is almost inevitable that features necessary to drive a component forward in terms of functionality and market competitiveness will force a break in compatibility. Enter the concept of side-by-side components.

Component Locks

The scenario just presented didn't even deal with another common issue facing deployment efforts: that of replacing components that are currently in use by a process running on the target machine. This has been the bane of Web developers for quite some time. As long as a single process is using the component that you want to replace, the component will be locked: The file system physically won't allow it to be replaced. The solution is usually to hunt down and kill or stop any processes that might attach to the component. This whole procedure needs to be done at a time when no one can access the application, or another lock could be generated on the component at any time!

Even stopping the offending process is sometimes not enough, necessitating a reboot of the machine. This tends to be a pain on client machines—in a server environment where operations are expected to continue 24×7, it is anathema.

In summary:

- Registering a component with the operating system and COM involves touching the registry; this complicates the whole install process by forcing installers to physically touch the registry, introducing the potential for system-wide errors and security problems that can prevent the install from taking place.

- Shared component replacement has the potential to break applications. Applications have no way of knowing that a shared component has been replaced, and they might have specific calling code that is affected by a change in a globally shared component.

- Versioning is not enforced. Newer or older versions of components can be installed over the top of current components. Applications have no good way to specify which version of the DLL they were developed against. What's more, no central authority monitors component versioning for the system as a whole.

- Backward compatibility is not a valid approach in the long term. Development teams must keep extending their applications to deal with new business problems and remain competitive in the market place. This can continue only for so long under the requirement to retain backward compatibility.

- Process locks on components must be handled before replacing the targeted component. This could mean anything from shutting down the currently running processes to rebooting the server or PC.

The Deployment Solution?

Before the arrival of .NET, there have been some preliminary steps take to combat DLL Hell (primarily arriving on the scene with Windows 2000). .NET builds on the efforts of Windows 2000 to ease the complexities of component deployment.

Side-by-Side Component Sharing

Microsoft Windows 2000 (and Microsoft Windows 98 Second Edition) introduced new technology that enables something called side-by-side component sharing. In this scenario, limited versioning support is thrown into the mix so that multiple versions of the same DLL can be hosted on one machine. If one application uses Version 1.0 of the spell-checker DLL and another uses Version 2.0, both applications have these DLLs running in isolation from one another. That is, the runtime will load both the 1.0 and the 2.0 versions into memory at the same time. The runtime is then responsible for directing the DLL calls to the appropriate instance. Figure 22.1 shows a side-by-side component scenario.

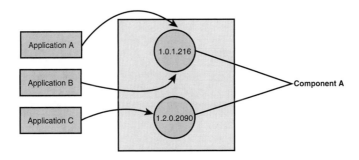

FIGURE 22.1

Side-by-side components.

Windows File Protection

Windows File Protection (WFP) also was introduced with Microsoft Windows 2000. WFP enables the operating system to keep a cache of a number of DLLs (currently, just less than 3000) that it recognizes as crucial, system-wide components. Replacing one of these components would have such far-reaching repercussions that WFP simply doesn't allow it. If a DLL file is written to the file system that replaces one of these protected DLLs, the operating system receives a notification of this and simply copies the old one back in (all this without even raising an error!). This is yet another mechanism that helps to alleviate the DLL Hell problems.

The .NET Answer

Although they are incapable of reducing deployment problems to nothing, the mechanisms put into place by the .NET runtime significantly decrease the complexity of deployment operations. This section gives an overview of the different portions of .NET related to application deployment. From here, we will examine each one in depth and illustrate how they all come together to enable you to distribute the code that you have worked so hard to write.

Self-Describing Components

Components deployed in the .NET runtime do not rely on the registry any longer. Instead, they are said to be *self-describing*: Each component carries its own information around as baggage that uniquely describes itself, including its version number. Components do not rely on any other mechanism to indicate their identity, nor can any other system entity affect their functioning. In this way, components are said to be isolated within the .NET runtime. Changing component A should have absolutely no effect on component B.

Version Control

The .NET runtime also provides a gatekeeper that monitors and records version information for each component. This also provides the side benefit of allowing newer versions of components to be introduced without breaking other applications: Each application is inherently aware of the specific versions of components that it needs to run. When a component is encountered that does not match this reference, it is up to the developer how to handle this situation. These settings can be controlled universally per machine, or on a per-application or per-component basis.

The runtime also keeps track of the last known set of components (and their versions) that actually worked for a given application. This allows developers or administrators to roll back components to a point in time that everything was still working, and then work out the issues from there.

So, how does .NET do all of this? A discussion of component deployment with .NET starts with assemblies.

Assemblies: The Basic Unit of Deployment

An assembly is roughly equivalent to a DLL in the COM world: It wraps up one or more pieces of an application into a self-contained package. When we talk about deploying applications and components in .NET, we are really talking about deploying assemblies. As an example, if you compile a simple forms application, the resulting .exe file is the assembly.

The Parts of an Assembly

An assembly is constructed with a few different pieces of information. Figure 22.2 shows a rough schema for the different pieces of an assembly.

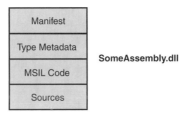

FIGURE 22.2
Anatomy of an assembly.

An assembly can span multiple files or can be entirely contained in a single file. If the assembly spans more than one file, each file could contain one or more of the four different parts of the assembly. It could be, for instance, that the resources for an assembly are placed into a separate file to ease globalization of the application. Figure 22.3 shows an example of the same assembly with its graphics resources contained in a separate file.

The Manifest

The manifest section is what makes the assembly self-describing. It contains information about the assembly's identity, the list of all the physical files that are within it, a list of any other assemblies that need to be referenced by the compiled code, any types or resources "exported" by the assembly, and, finally, any code access security attributes that have been applied to the assembly.

> **NOTE**
>
> The identity of an assembly consists of three different parts: a name (required), a version (also required), and a culture (optional). Each is used together to provide a way to reference the specific assembly.

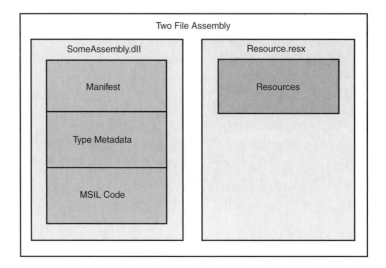

FIGURE 22.3

Multiple files in an assembly.

Type Metadata

Type metadata is information that identifies the various types used in the assembly (such as classes).

MSIL Code

MSIL code provides the instructions that will get parsed by the MSIL engine when the application is truly compiled during runtime.

Resources

These are the actual resources compiled into the assembly. String or image resources could be included for easy extension or localization, if the need arises.

Examining an Assembly

Ildasm.exe is a tool provided with the .NET Framework that enables you to decompile an assembly and view its contents. This tool is useful in terms of studying the composition of assemblies, in particular their manifest and type metadata information.

After launching the Ildasm utility, you can open an assembly using the File Open command. Figure 22.4 shows the Ildasm utility with an assembly loaded into it. It presents you with a tree view of the different constituents of the loaded assembly.

FIGURE 22.4

Ildasm.exe in action.

To check out the manifest information, double-click on the Manifest node. You should get a
new window that looks something like Figure 22.5.

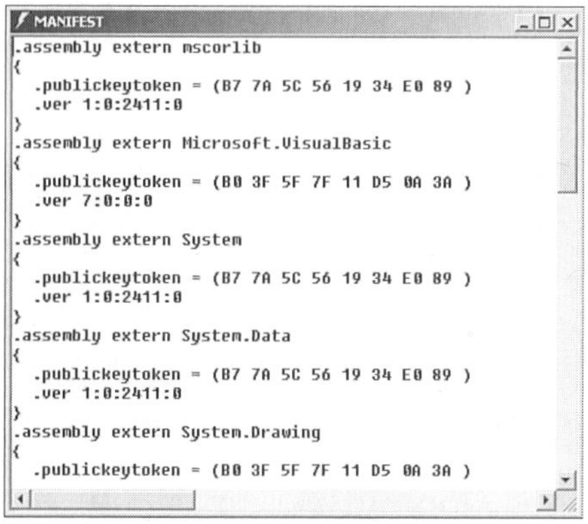

FIGURE 22.5

Examining the manifest.

Visible in this example are all the external assemblies that the loaded assembly depends on.
They are prefaced with the .assembly extern keywords, like this:

```
.assembly extern mscorlib
{
  .publickeytoken = (B7 7A 5C 56 19 34 E0 89 )
  .ver 1:0:2411:0
}
```

The actual reference contains three distinct pieces of information about the assembly dependency. It shows the name of the assembly—in this case, mscorlib. It also shows its version (1.0.2411.0). The third nugget of information that is evident is a public key token. (We'll get more into the reason for identifying a public key later in the chapter when we talk about the concept of strong names. For now, just know that this is a way for the runtime to identify that the referenced assembly really is what it says it is.)

If you scroll down farther, you should see the actual assembly definition.

```
.assembly AssemblyTest
{
  .custom instance void _
[mscorlib]System.Runtime.InteropServices.GuidAttribute::.ctor(string) = _
( 01 00 24 46 44 37 42 39 42 30 35 2D 45 39 36 43
2D 34 34 38 36 2D 42 42 30 34 2D 41 33 46 39 30 _
46 37 45 42 34 36 37 00 00 )
  .custom instance void [mscorlib]System.CLSCompliantAttribute::.ctor(bool) = _
( 01 00 01 00 00 )
  .custom instance void _
[mscorlib]System.Reflection.AssemblyTrademarkAttribute::.ctor(string) = _
( 01 00 00 00 00 )
  .custom instance void _
[mscorlib]System.Reflection.AssemblyCopyrightAttribute::.ctor(string) = _
( 01 00 00 00 00 )
  .custom instance void _
[mscorlib]System.Reflection.AssemblyProductAttribute::.ctor(string) = _
( 01 00 00 00 00 )
  .custom instance void _
[mscorlib]System.Reflection.AssemblyCompanyAttribute::.ctor(string) = _
( 01 00 00 00 00 )
  .custom instance void _
[mscorlib]System.Reflection.AssemblyDescriptionAttribute::.ctor(string) = _
( 01 00 00 00 00 )
  .custom instance void _
[mscorlib]System.Reflection.AssemblyTitleAttribute::.ctor(string) = _
( 01 00 00 00 00 )
  .hash algorithm 0x00008004
  .ver 1:0:602:29468
}
```

Here, there is evidence of some attributes that have been applied to the assembly (such as `InteropServices.GuidAttribute` and `Reflection.AssemblyProductAttribute`). The last line of the assembly definition shows its version number: `1.0.602.29468`.

The last thing that you see in the assembly manifest is a list of the files and resources that belong to the assembly.

```
.mresource public AssemblyTest.Resource1.resources
{
}
.mresource public AssemblyTest.Form1.resources
{
}
.mresource public AssemblyTest.exe.licenses
{
}
.module AssemblyTest.exe
// MVID: {0D0F2EE1-A719-4729-BFB5-5424F124E5AD}
.imagebase 0x11000000
.subsystem 0x00000002
.file alignment 512
.corflags 0x00000001
// Image base: 0x03680000
```

Versioning

As you might have noticed in the previous manifest examples, each assembly has a version number. The version number actually consists of four parts, arranged like this:

```
major.minor.build.revision
```

The runtime treats major and minor version differences as entirely different assemblies. This is necessary to implement the concepts that we have talked about related to side-by-side shared components. In other words, changes to an assembly's major or minor version number cause that assembly to not be compatible with applications that were using the older version. This is an important behavior to understand. Let's walk through a possible deployment scenario:

1. A developer deploys two different applications (WordEditor.exe and FinanceEditor.exe).

2. As part of the deployment, the developer also installs a shared component into the GAC that both the WordEditor and the FinanceEditor executables use (CommonFuncs.dll). The shared component is installed as Version 1.0.92.106.

3. Over time, the developer comes up with some optimizations and feature enhancements to the CommonFuncs.dll component. After revising the component, it is now at 1.1.0.1028.

4. The developer deploys the new component and tests the WordEditor and FinanceEditor applications to verify the added functionality.

5. Neither application appears to have changed at all, even though the use of the new component should be immediately obvious!

What happened here? The answer is simple if you understand how the versioning policy works. Because the new component was considered to be an entirely new component by .NET (due to the fact that its minor version number had changed), it is being served up side by side with the older component. The default version policy resolves assembly references at runtime and does so based on the version of the assembly registered at the time the application was installed. This means that both WordEditor.exe and FinanceEditor.exe actually have hard-coded into their metadata a reference to the CommonFuncs.dll version 1.0.92.106. Installing the new version has done nothing to their functionality because they are still loading the old version. Had the new component possessed a version number of 1.0.93.0, the link would happen automatically because .NET does not recognize a build number change as an incompatible change.

> **NOTE**
>
> Why are build and revision number changes not treated as new assemblies by .NET? The default version policy was implemented in this manner to allow for hot fixes and patches to be applied to a system without worrying about applications still referencing the older components. A build or revision number change equals a hot fix or patch in .NET's eyes.

You can use application configuration files to override or change the default version policies maintained by the runtime. We discuss configuration files in general later in the chapter (see the section "Using Application Configuration Files").

Deploying Private and Shared Components

Now that you know that assemblies are the base unit for deployment and you know how they are built and what they contain, we can start examining the specifics related to pushing an application or component to its intended audience.

Distribution

Distribution is the process of placing executable code onto the end user's machine, and it is really the first step in the installation process. With .NET, all the traditional methods of delivering an application still exist. For instance, you can use CAB files to compress the install components to significantly shorten download or transmission time. You also can build Windows Installer packages; Version 2.0 of this technology is .NET-aware and is capable of deploying both private and shared components (more on these in a minute).

But the real attraction with .NET deployment is its treatment of self-contained components. .NET components truly are self-contained and don't rely on the registry or any other external apparatus to work. As a result, you can simply copy an executable along with its attendant DLLs from a disc into a directory, and it will run with no other required effort.

If you want to deploy a local copy of a component or an entire application, all you have to do is copy it to the application's intended directory. These are referred to as XCopy deployments because you can simply XCopy an entire application's files and directory structure over to the target machine, with no additional effort required.

This begs the question, "What is the difference between a local and a global install?" The answer lies in the intended use of the component—specifically, whether your component is intended for use by multiple applications (a global install) or by only one application (a local install). The decision of whether to deploy locally or globally is one that is left to the developer based on the design and installation requirements of a particular application.

22

DEPLOYING,
CONFIGURING, AND
LICENSING .NET
COMPONENTS

> **NOTE**
>
> We are using the terms "global components" and "shared components" interchangeably; both refer to pieces of an application that also are used by other applications (and thus are subject to special treatment by the .NET runtime). Likewise, when we say "local," "private," or "isolated," we are referring to applications and components being deployed inside a "local" application directory.

Local Components

Local components are isolated from other applications because they physically sit inside the calling applications directory. When the application is started, the runtime automatically "probes" for its components in the application directory (if it doesn't find one in the global cache).

There is no need for the runtime to perform any other type of policing for locally installed components because they are meant to be consumed by only one application. In general, deploying components as private components is the easiest and the least technically challenging means of deploying applications in the .NET environment.

Shared Components

Because of the dangers previously discussed with using shared components, .NET treats these differently and imposes some additional requirements (and thus overhead) on the deployment process of shared components.

Shared components are written into a special area of the file system called the *Global Assembly Cache* (GAC). The GAC functions much like the System32 directory did under native Windows. It provides a central repository for components that will be used across many applications and users. Because of the process overhead involved, the decision to deploy a component into the GAC is not one that should come lightly. Only if you are absolutely certain that your particular component needs the benefits of the GAC should you continue with a GAC install.

> **NOTE**
>
> It is important to note that although the deployment process is different for local and shared components in .NET, there is no actual physical difference between a local assembly and a shared assembly.

The GAC builds on the same side-by-side component sharing supported by Windows 2000 and Windows 98 SE: It allows multiple versions of an assembly to coexist peacefully. Because one assembly that calls another explicitly records the version number and name of the referenced assembly, the runtime is capable of reaching the correct version in the GAC and completing the reference call.

The GAC also provides you with a central store for code so that system administrators and developers can apply patches and quick fixes in one location and have them affect the system as a whole. This works to substantially lower administrative efforts with respect to application updates.

> **NOTE**
>
> The GAC, by default, is restricted to administrative user level access only. This means that you must be an administrator, or must have your administrator grant you permission, to publish code there.

The safety and features of the GAC come with some overhead, in that you cannot simply copy an assembly into the GAC as you could copy DLLs into the System32 directory. Placing an assembly into the GAC requires the use of one of the .NET tools designed just for this: Windows Installer 2.0 or a .NET Framework SDK utility called gacutil.exe. Before that can be done, however, the assembly must be given a *strong name*.

Strong names are .NET's mechanism for ensuring a unique name for each assembly in the GAC. Remember that the name must be unique to prevent another component developer from interfering with your components, in case they are named alike. Unlike previous Microsoft platforms, the .NET platform actively seeks to protect assembly names, preventing another author's components from overwriting your components.

Probing for Assemblies

As you might guess, the .NET runtime follows a pre-established process, called *probing*, when trying to locate a reference assembly. Figure 22.6 shows the sequence of events that is kicked off when an application calls into an assembly.

Strong Names and Signing Assemblies

A strong name is constructed of an assembly's text name (called its *simple* name, to contrast with its strong name), a public key, and a digital signature.

> **NOTE**
>
> Strong named assemblies can reference only other strong named assemblies. If a strong named assembly referenced an assembly with a simple name, it would open itself up to DLL Hell all over again. This is the "chain is only as strong as its weakest link" analogy in action.

Strong names actually rely on public key cryptography to secure and protect the operations of assemblies both inside and outside the GAC (you *can* have an assembly with a strong name outside the GAC). Although we don't have the time or the space to get into a discussion of public key cryptography here, we can summarize its usefulness with a few statements:

- Public key cryptography relies on the concept of key pairs. There is a public key, which is distributed freely, and a private key, which is held close and is not released outside its owning organization.

- As part of its strong name, an assembly exposes both the public key and a signature that was created using the private key.

- By comparing the keys stored in an assembly's manifest, the runtime can figure out whether the assembly is valid and ensure that it has not been tampered with.

- Because assemblies leverage the public-private key pair, you are guaranteed that no one can spoof the assembly's strong name because the public-private key pair is unique and can't be duplicated.

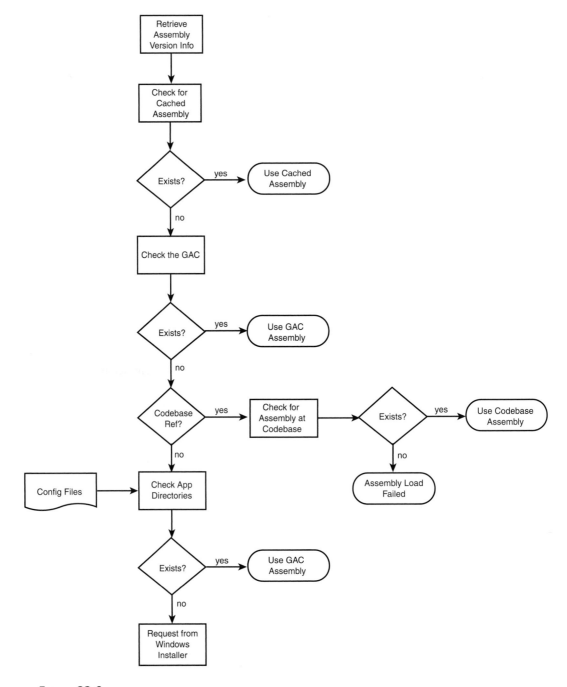

FIGURE 22.6
Locating assemblies.

By using cryptographic keys in this fashion, the .NET runtime can assure itself of an assembly's purported identity every time it is called during execution.

There are two ways that .NET currently supports the signing of assemblies with strong names. One involves the use of another .NET Framework command-line utility (sn.exe). The other uses the Visual Studio .NET IDE (or any other .NET compiler).

Using the Strong Name Utility

The Strong Name utility (sn.exe) is capable of signing a target assembly; you provide it with a key pair, and it does the rest. If you don't have a key pair, don't worry: It can generate those as well.

Let's look at the syntax for using this command-line utility:

Usage: SN [-q(uiet)] <option> [<parameters>]

Options:

-c [<csp>]	Sets or resets the name of the cryptographic service provider (CSP) to use for signing assemblies with strong names.
-d <container>	Deletes the key container with the name <container>.
-D <assembly1> <assembly2>	Verifies that the assemblies identified by <assembly1> and <assembly2> differ only by signature.
-e <assembly> <outfile>	Extracts the public key from the assembly identified by <assembly> and writes it to the file identified by <outfile>.
-I <infile> <container>	Installs a key pair (contained in the <infile>) into the container <container>.
-k <outfile>	Generates a key pair and writes it into the file identified by <outfile>.
-m [y | n]	Enables, disables, or returns an indication of whether key containers are machine-specific instead of user-specific.
-o <infile> [<outfile>]	Converts the public key in the file <infile> to a comma-separated list of decimal byte values, written to the output file <outfile>. If no output file is specified, the data is written to the Clipboard.
-p <infile> <outfile>	Extracts the public key from the key pair in the input file <infile> and writes it to the output file <outfile>.

`-pc <container> <outfile>`	Extracts the public key from the key pair in the container `<container>`, and writes it to an output file `<outfile>`.
`-q`	When used as the first parameter on the command line, forces the utility into quiet mode, which suppresses all messages other than error messages.
`-R <assembly> <infile>`	Re-signs a previously signed or partially signed assembly `<assembly>` with the key pair in the input file `<infile>`.
`-Rc <assembly> <container>`	Re-signs a previously signed or partially signed assembly `<assembly>` with the key pair in the container `<container>`.
`-t[p] <infile>`	Displays the token for the public key in the input file `<infile>`. If the p parameter is specified, also displays the entire public key itself.
`-T[p] <assembly>`	Displays the token for the public key in the assembly `<assembly>`. If the p parameter is specified, also displays the entire public key itself.
`-v[f] <assembly>`	Verifies the assembly `<assembly>` for strong name consistency. If the f parameter is used, this verification is forced even if turned off in the registry.
`-Vl`	Displays a list of the current strong name verification settings.
`-Vr <assembly> [<userlist>]`	Registers the assembly `<assembly>` for verification skipping; can apply to specific usernames if provided in the `<userlist>`.
`-Vu <assembly>`	Unregisters the assembly `<assembly>` for verification skipping.
`-Vx`	Removes all previously registered verification-skipping entries.
`-?`	Displays the command-line syntax help.
`-h`	Displays the command-line syntax help.

Using the Compiler

The `System.Reflection` namespace contains a few attribute classes that can be used to supply the needed crypto key information for strong named assemblies. By attaching these attributes to an assembly, you don't have to call the separate command-line tool to sign the assembly.

The `AssemblyKeyFileAttribute` class is used to specify the name of a file that contains the key pair to be used when signing the assembly. To specify this in the IDE, you simply include the attribute tag in your code:

```
<Assembly:AssemblyKeyFileAttribute("KeyPair.snk")>
```

When the application or component is compiled, the compiler uses this attribute to build the assembly manifest data and associate a strong name with the assembly. You alternatively can use the `AssemblyKeyNameAttribute` class in the same way:

```
<Assembly:AssemblyKeyNameAttribute("KeyPairContainer")>
```

The `AssemblyKeyNameAttribute` class performs the same function as the `AssemblyKeyFileAttribute` class, but instead of specifying a file with the key pairs, it specifies a cryptographic service provider container that holds the key pairs.

> **NOTE**
>
> The decision of whether to give an assembly a strong name should come early in the game: Strong names cannot be associated with assemblies that already have been created with only simple names.

Delayed Signing

When dealing with public-private key pairs, developers might encounter a situation in which they do not have ready access to the private key half of the key pair. Because the private key is the key to the kingdom, so to speak, access to private keys often is limited to very few people. In other words, development teams just might not be trusted with an organization's private keys. The dilemma here is how a developer can create a strong named assembly if he does not know the private key. The answer is with *delayed signing*.

Delayed signing allows assemblies to be created that you intend to be strongly named. A public key must be provided, but the private key can wait until later in the deployment process.

To make the delayed signing work, the developer must do the following:

1. Obtain the public key for the public-private key pair.
2. Place that public key inside of a key file. This file can be created using the sn.exe utility.
3. Mark the assembly with the appropriate attribute tags. You use the `AssemblyKeyFileAttribute` class, as outlined previously, to provide the public key file. You also use the `AssemblyDelaySignAttribute` class, passing it a value of `True`, as shown in this code:

```
<Assembly:AssemblyDelaySignAttribute(true)>
```

Now, when the assembly is created by the compiler, it places the public key into the manifest just as it normally would. Because it can't generate the digital signature without the private key, it just reserves space in the assembly's manifest for where the signature eventually will go (after the private key has been provided). Because the .NET runtime expects to see the signature in the assembly, you must turn off strong name verification for that assembly by using the -Vr switch with the sn.exe utility.

The development team can continue to develop the assemblies in this manner until just before the assembly must be shipped to the end user(s). At this point, the actual persons who have access to the private key step in and complete the signing by again running the sn.exe program with the -R switch, feeding it the private key container or file.

Deploying Assemblies into the GAC

When you possess an assembly with a strong name, you can deploy that assembly inside of the Global Assembly Cache. There are three ways to accomplish the actual deployment:

1. You can build an install package and run it through the Microsoft Windows Installer 2.0. Because this version of the Windows Installer is aware of the GAC, it has the capability to publish components into it.

2. You can manually or programmatically push an assembly into the GAC by using the command-line tool Gacutil.exe.

3. You can manually copy an assembly into the GAC by using Windows Explorer and the shell extension called the Assembly Cache Viewer.

Let's walk through the last two options (for more information on creating installation packages that can be deployed with the Microsoft Windows Installer, see the MSDN Platform SDK documentation).

> **Note**
>
> You actually can create an installation package inside Visual Studio .NET. In the New Project dialog box, select a project type of Setup and Deployment Projects' and then select Setup Project. These Visual Studio .NET projects will generate .msi files to be installed with the Microsoft Windows Installer. For more information, consult the Visual Studio documentation.

Using Gacutil.exe

Gacutil.exe is a standalone command-line executable that has the capability to both add and remove assemblies from the Global Assembly Cache.

Let's review its syntax:

Usage: Gacutil <option> [<parameters>]

Options:

/i <manifestfile>	Installs an assembly into the GAC. You must provide it with the assembly file that contains the assembly manifest information.
/u <assembly>	Uninstalls an assembly from the GAC. The <assembly> can identify strong names by using commas to separate their parts: componentA ,Version=2.0.3.2406, PublicKeyToken=394b78ae90878ab.
/ungen <assembly>	Removes the indicated assembly <assembly> from the .NET native image cache.
/l	Displays all the assemblies in the GAC.
/cdl	Deletes the contents of the download cache.
/ldl	Displays the assemblies in the download cache.
/nologo	Suppresses display of the logo banner.
/silent	Suppresses display of all output.
/?	Displays the command-line syntax help.

After you have compiled an assembly, making sure that it has been signed with a strong name, you can install it into the GAC quite easily:

```
gacutil /i testAssembly.dll
```

Most of the options are self-explanatory, but a few require further details.

For example, the /ungen switch might be confusing with its reference to the ".NET native image cache." Specifically, the documentation says that it "removes the indicated assembly <assembly> from the .NET native image cache"—but what is the .NET native image cache? Put simply, it's a cache that holds a precompiled "image" of assemblies; it is meant to speed up loading times of assemblies because their types and structure don't have to be constituted from the manifest or MSIL information in the assembly. They are stored and ready to go in the cache. You can even explicitly "compile" an assembly into the native image cache by using the Native Image Generator tool (Ngen.exe). For more information, consult the MSDN .NET Framework documentation.

There are also two switches, /cdl and /ldl, that make reference to a download cache. The download cache is a special storage area designed to contain components that have been downloaded from the Internet.

Using the Assembly Cache Viewer

The Assembly Cache Viewer is a Windows shell extension installed with the .NET Framework SDK. It allows you to interact with the GAC inside Windows Explorer, essentially treating it as if it is just another folder in the file store—just navigate to the c:\WINNT\assembly directory. Figure 22.7 shows how assemblies show up as "files" in the Assembly Cache Viewer.

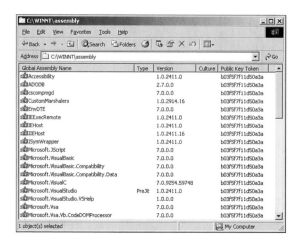

FIGURE 22.7

The Assembly Cache Viewer.

You can display information about an assembly by right-clicking on it and selecting Properties. Notice in Figure 22.8 that the assembly Properties dialog box shows some very basic information about the selected component, including its name, its version number, the date it was last modified, and its public key token.

FIGURE 22.8

Assembly properties.

You also can deploy assemblies into the GAC by dragging and dropping them into the Assembly Cache window. Deleting assemblies is just as easy: Simply select the assembly and press Delete.

Using Application Configuration Files

Application configuration files are XML-formatted documents that sit in the root of an application's directory; they have the capability to affect the behavior of each particular application. They are of interest from a deployment perspective because they allow you to change certain operations related to assemblies.

> **NOTE**
>
> An application configuration file is called app.config and sits in the root of the application directory. There is actually a Visual Studio .NET template that you can add to your project, to allow you to easily create one of these configuration files. Just select the Project menu inside the IDE and then select Add New Item. When the dialog box of possible items appears, scroll down until you see the application configuration item.

Configuration File Content

Each application configuration file has one root node (or document element) that can contain child elements to hold six different groups of settings:

- Startup settings
- Runtime settings
- Remoting settings
- Cryptographic settings
- Security settings

Each of these settings has a set of XML elements that are valid. We will examine only the runtime settings in this chapter. To affect the way that assemblies are bound for your application, you would manipulate the XML content of the Runtime Settings grouping of nodes.

Runtime Settings

A total of nine different XML tags are allowed in the runtime settings section of the configuration file. Each of them is described in Table 22.1.

Table 22.1   Runtime Settings Tags

Name	Description
`<assemblyBinding>`	Affects assembly version redirection and explicitly defines the locations of assemblies.
`<assemblyIdentity>`	Encapsulates the different parts of an assembly's identity.
`<bindingRedirect>`	Redirects one assembly version to another.
`<codeBase>`	Directs the runtime to an alternate location for a shared assembly if it cannot be located on the current machine.
`<dependentAssembly>`	Contains binding policies and locations for each assembly in the application.
`<gcCurrent>`	Specifies whether the runtime should run garbage collection concurrently.
`<probing>`	Lists which subdirectories, if any, the runtime should search for assemblies.
`<publisherPolicy>`	Indicates to the runtime whether it should apply a publisher policy to the application.
`<runtime>`	The `ResultPropertyValueCollection` class holds all the property values for each property in a `ResultPropertyCollection` instance.

As an example, Listing 22.1 shows a configuration file making use of the `assemblyBinding` element and child elements.

Listing 22.1   Application Configuration File

```xml
<?xml version="1.0" encoding="utf-8" ?>
<configuration>
   <runtime>
      <assemblyBinding xmlns="urn:schemas-microsoft-com:asm.v1">
         <dependentAssembly>
            <assemblyIdentity name="AssemblyTest"
                              publickeytoken="66a12b2304e0a45ba7"
                              culture="en-us" />
            <bindingRedirect oldVersion="1.0.0.0" newVersion="2.0.0.0"/>
            <codeBase version="2.0.0.0"
                      href="http://www.brilliantstorm.com/AssemblyTest.dll"/>
         </dependentAssembly>
         <probing privatePath="bin;bin\components;bin\exe " />

      </assemblyBinding>
   </runtime>
</configuration>
```

We can tell a few things from looking at this configuration file:

- It defines one dependent assembly (AssemblyTest—note that it identifies it by its strong name, including the public key token and culture).

- It overrides the default version policy by specifying that the application should load, if available, Version 2.0.0.0 of the AssemblyTest component instead of Version 1.0.0.0. If this redirect was not present, the runtime would instead reference the old version of the AssemblyTest component in a side-by-side scenario.

- It specifies, with the codeBase tag, a location to find the AssemblyTest component if it is not available on the local machine.

- It defines a specific path that the runtime should search when trying to resolve any local/private assemblies.

Using the application configuration file allows you to control a vast variety of settings on a per-application basis. For machine-wide settings, there is also a machine configuration file (machine.config) that you will find in the .NET Framework deployment directory. It is an XML document as well, but it has a different schema. (Consult the Framework reference documentation for more information on machine configuration files. Better yet, open one in Notepad or your favorite XML editor and examine the contents.)

Licensing Your Application

The .NET Framework supports a component licensing model that works identically regardless of the application: UI control, Web control, application, component, and so on.

Enabling Licensing

Licenses are meant to provide some proof that the entity running the component is authorized by the component author to do so. The most obvious example comes in the form of companies protecting their copyrights and sales by ensuring that only valid, paid-for copies of their software can be executed.

If you are going to develop components that need to be licensed, the steps to do so are straightforward: First, you apply an attribute to the class that identifies a license provider that will dispense the license for the component. Then, inside the component's code, you validate the dispensed license, releasing it when the component expires. All Framework code that makes this happen is in the System.ComponentModel namespace.

The License Provider

The licenses supported out of the box by .NET are simply text files and work just as they did with ActiveX controls. Support for these license files is implemented with the LicFileLicenseProvider class. It is this license provider, or a custom one that you create by inheriting the `LicenseProvider` base class, that must be "attached" to the licensed component using an attribute class: `LicenserProviderAttribute`. This attribute class takes the type of license provider into its constructor, like this:

```
<LicenseProviderAttribute(GetType(LicFileLicenseProvider))>
```

This declaratively marks the component for licensing enforcement. From there, you must implement code using an instance of the `LicenseManager` class to determine whether the license dispensed was valid.

The License Manager and License Instance

License management is provided by the `LicenseManager` class. It exposes a `Validate` method and an `IsValid` method, both of which can be used to make sure that a valid license exists for the component. If the license is not valid, a `LicenseException` is raised.

Some housekeeping also needs to be performed beyond checking the validity of the component; the license must be released as a resource when the component is released. This is done in the component's `Dispose` method.

Listing 22.2 pulls all of this together with some sample code. Note that a class-scoped variable, `compLicense`, holds the license instance.

LISTING 22.2   Implementing a License

```
Imports System.ComponentModel

<LicenseProviderAttribute(GetType(LicFileLicenseProvider))> Public Class _
    SomeComponent

    'Holds the license instance; initially nulled.
    Private compLicense As License = Nothing

    Public Sub New()
        Try
            'During component construction, check to see if the license
            'dispensed is valid
            compLicense = LicenseManager.Validate(GetType(SomeComponent), Me)

        Catch licErr As LicenseException
            'invalid license! probably want to kill the component, etc.

        Catch appErr As Exception
            'generic app error occurred
```

LISTING 22.2   Continued

```
        End Try

    End Sub

    Public Overloads Sub Dispose()
        If Not (compLicense Is Nothing) Then
            compLicense.Dispose()
            compLicense = Nothing
        End If
    End Sub
End Class
```

Summary

.NET provides the developer with a host of tools that make application packaging, configuration, deployment, and licensing almost easy. From its support for XCopy deployment to its robust mechanisms for coping with shared component problems, the deployment system offered for managed code sits fully exposed for Visual Basic developers to use as needed for a wide variety of deployment scenarios.

In this chapter, we touched on

- The deployment problems that .NET has focused on eliminating
- Distributing private versus shared assemblies
- Signing assemblies with strong names
- The various methods for publishing components into the Global Assembly Cache
- Implementing custom application configuration through application configuration files
- Checking for valid licenses during component instantiation

Calling the Win32 API from Managed Code

IN THIS APPENDIX

Windows' new API, the Framework Class Library, replaces many of the Win32 API functions and wraps others. However, you will find that some API functions are not to be found inside the class library, and some class library methods will not work exactly the same as their equivalent API functions. Not to worry, you can still access the Win32 API from .NET code. In fact, for VB developers, .NET makes it easier to access this massive library.

This appendix focuses on writing VB .NET code to access the Win32 API. Accessing the Win32 API will be the most common reason for using this type of interoperability, but of course the content of the appendix can be applied to access other legacy APIs.

(For .NET equivalents to specific Win32 API functions, please read Appendix B, "Win32 API-to-Namespace Cross-Reference.")

Platform Invoke

Platform Invoke is a service provided by .NET that allows you to call functions inside of unmanaged code directly from managed code. Unmanaged code is any code that is not running under the service of the Common Language Runtime (CLR). The entire Win32 API is unmanaged code because it predates .NET. Managed code is code that executes under, and conforms to, the confines of the CLR. As you might imagine, there is a boundary between code that is managed and code that exists outside of the CLR. To cross this boundary you must rely on the services of Platform Invoke.

Platform Invoke provides a number of services to your managed code. First, it locates an unmanaged function on the machine and inside a Windows' DLL. Next, it invokes that function for your application. Additionally, it marshals data (parameters and return values) between the boundaries of the CLR and the given API. Finally, it returns exceptions raised by the unmanaged function call directly to your .NET code. Platform Invoke relies on metadata to operate. It uses this metadata to locate functions and perform marshalling at runtime. Figure A.1 illustrates how Platform Invoke is used to interoperate with unmanaged code.

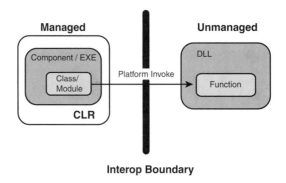

FIGURE A.1

Platform Invoke—managed to unmanaged.

Consuming API Functions

The process of accessing and using unmanaged code inside the Win32 API is straightforward. First, you must identify the DLL function and the library containing that function. Common Win32 API libraries include the following:

- `GDI32.dll` provides Graphics Device Interface (GDI) functions for drawing, printing, and font manipulation.

- `Kernel32.dll` provides functions to access low-level OS features like memory management.

- `User32.dll` provides functions for menus, timers, and Windows message handling.

> **NOTE**
>
> If you are unfamiliar with what the API has to offer, we suggest perusing the MSDN SDK documentation or taking a look at the title from which this book derives its name, *Visual Basic Programmer's Guide to the Win32 API*.

The next step in accessing the Win32 API from managed code is to declare the API function inside a class or module. We suggest you wrap your API functions with a class. This provides easier access from other managed code and is often easier to maintain. Finally, you call the function directly, passing it the necessary parameters.

The code in Listing A.1 illustrates three simple API calls from managed code. We first create a class called `EventLog`. Inside this class we declare the functions `OpenEventLog`, `ClearEventLog`, and `CloseEventLog`. We then simply call the API functions from inside the sub `Main` of a module.

LISTING A.1 Event Log API Functions

```
Imports System.Runtime.InteropServices

Public Class EventLog

    'purpose: exposes event log api functions

    'opens the specified log (sourceName) for the specified
    '   server (serverName) and returns a handle to it
    Declare Auto Function OpenEventLog Lib "Advapi32.dll" _
        (ByVal serverName As String, ByVal sourceName As String) _
        As Integer
```

LISTING A.1 Continued

```
    'clears the specified event log  (hEventLog) and optionally
    '   backs it up to a file (backupFileName)
    Declare Auto Function ClearEventLog Lib "Advapi32.dll" _
        (ByVal hEventLog As Integer, ByVal backupFileName As String) _
        As Integer

    'closes the specified event log (hEventLog)
    Declare Auto Function CloseEventLog Lib "Advapi32.dll" _
        (ByVal hEventLog As Integer) As Integer

End Class

Module Module1

    Sub Main()

        'purpose: call event log api functions

        'local scope
        Dim handleLog As Integer

        'return a handle to the event log on the local box
        handleLog = EventLog.OpenEventLog( _
            serverName:=vbNullString, sourceName:="Application")

        'clear the event log
        EventLog.ClearEventLog( _
            hEventLog:=handleLog, backupFileName:=vbNullString)

        'close the event log
        EventLog.CloseEventLog(hEventLog:=handleLog)

    End Sub

End Module
```

Note that these API functions have equivalents within the Framework Class Library inside of the System.Diagnostics namespace. Also notice that each function declared inside the class actually becomes a method of that class.

Of course, there are a number of additional settings available to you when using Platform Invoke. The rest of this section details those settings.

Declaring Unmanaged Functions

Visual Basic .NET developers have two options available when declaring a function. The first option uses the traditional declare syntax to which VB developers of old have become accustomed. The second option uses attribute classes to define a function as an unmanaged declaration to be passed to Platform Invoke. Most of the time, you can get away with the old style of declaration. However, many of the Platform Invoke settings that .NET provides are not available to this style of declaration.

The following code declares the Beep function inside a module using the typical declare syntax.

```
Module Module1

    'beep function (frequency and duration)
    Declare Unicode Function Beep Lib "Kernel32.dll" _
        (ByVal dwFreq As Integer, ByVal dwDuration As Integer)

    Sub Main()

        'call function
        Beep(300, 1000)

    End Sub

End Module
```

Platform Invoke has a set of default values that indicate how the service operates. These values are available for you to override and tweak to your needs. For declarations that require additional settings, use the DllImportAttribute class available to you through the System.Runtime.InteropServices namespace. This class allows you to mark a method as being handled by Platform Invoke and passed to an unmanaged API.

The following code declares the same function as the preceding but using the DllImportAttribute class.

```
Imports System.Runtime.InteropServices

Module Module1

    'beep function (frequency and duration)
    <DllImport("Kernel32.dll", CharSet:=CharSet.Unicode)> _
    Public Function Beep(ByVal dwFreq As Integer, _
        ByVal dwDuration As Integer)

        'passes to Kernel32 through Platform Invoke
```

A

CALLING THE
WIN32 API FROM
MANAGED CODE

```
    End Function

    Sub Main()

        'call function
        Beep(300, 1000)

    End Sub

End Module
```

The functionality of the two code blocks is identical. For the majority of function declarations it comes down to personal preference. Some will like the better readability and .NET-like code written with the attribute class while others will want to stick with the old VB-looking declarations.

Sometimes, however, you will need to access specific settings inside of Platform Invoke. Tweaking these settings can only be done via the attribute class. For this reason, we suggest always using the attribute class syntax.

EntryPoint

The `EntryPoint` object field inside of the `DllImportAttribute` class allows you to set the functions alias. This is equivalent to using the `Alias` keyword inside a standard `Declare` statement. An *alias* is simply an alternate name for your function outside of the Win32 API's name. Aliases are useful when your code needs to comply with a specific naming standard or you wish to declare multiple versions of the same DLL function with different names.

The following are examples of setting aliases. The first creates an alias using the `Declare` syntax and the `Alias` keyword for a Unicode version of the `Beep` function. Note that the alias is a string literal.

```
Declare Unicode Function BeepUnicode Lib "Kernel32.dll" Alias "Beep" _
    (ByVal dwFreq As Integer, ByVal dwDuration As Integer)
```

The second example uses the `DllImportAttributeClass` to create an ANSI version of our `Beep` function. Notice that we set the field `EntryPoint` this time, rather than using the `Alias` keyword.

```
<DllImport("Kernel32.dll", CharSet:=CharSet.Ansi, EntryPoint:="Beep")> _
Public Function BeepAnsi(ByVal dwFreq As Integer, _
    ByVal dwDuration As Integer)
    'passes to Kernel32 through Platform Invoke
End Function
```

CharSet

The CharSet enumeration inside of DllImportAttribute controls how the Platform Invoke service marshals strings and finds function names inside an unmanaged DLL.

As you saw with the beep function, many libraries export both a Unicode and an ANSI version of the same function. The ANSI version typically carries the letter A at its end (MessageBoxA). The Unicode usually carries the letter W as a suffix (MessageBoxW). CharSet allows you to specify which function you are trying to access. The enumeration has the following three values: ANSI, Unicode, and Auto. The first two are self-explanatory while the last simply passes the job of determining to the Platform Invoke service. If you do not specify CharSet inside of VB, the default is ANSI.

> **NOTE**
>
> ANSI is a 1-byte character set that is typically used for operating systems running Windows 95/98. Unicode applies to Windows NT/2000/XP and uses a 2-byte character set.

Like EntryPoint, CharSet allows you to set its value either using a keyword or by using the enumeration. The following are examples of setting CharSet. The first uses the keyword Auto and the Declare syntax.

```
Declare Auto Function Beep Lib "Kernel32.dll" _
    (ByVal dwFreq As Integer, ByVal dwDuration As Integer)
```

The second example uses the DllImportAttributeClass and the CharSet enumeration to create a Unicode version of our Beep function.

```
<DllImport("Kernel32.dll", CharSet:=CharSet.Unicode)> _
Public Function Beep(ByVal dwFreq As Integer, _
    ByVal dwDuration As Integer)
    'passes to Kernel32 through Platform Invoke
End Function
```

ExactSpelling

The ExactSpelling field of DllImportAttribute works directly with the CharSet enumeration to manage how the compiler and Platform Invoke interprets your request for a given function name. The following are possible combinations and their descriptions:

- CharSet.Ansi and ExactSpelling = True—Platform Invoke only searches for the exact name you specify.

- CharSet.Unicode and ExactSpelling = True—Platform Invoke only searches for the exact name you specify.

- `CharSet.Ansi` and `ExactSpelling = False`—Platform Invoke searches for the unmangled name first (`MessageBox`) and ANSI-mangled name second (`MessageBoxA`).

- `CharSet.Unicode` and `ExactSpelling = False`—Platform Invoke searches for the unmangled name first (`MessageBox`) and Unicode-mangled name second (`MessageBoxW`).

Note that `ExactSpelling` is set to `True` by default when using VB .NET. Also, note that you cannot override this value to `False` unless you use the attribute-like syntax. The following is an example where we force ourselves to call the version of the function tagged with the letter "A" as in `MessageBoxA`.

```
<DllImport("user32.dll", ExactSpelling:=True, charSet:=CharSet.Ansi)> _
Public Function MessageBoxA(ByVal hWnd As Integer, _
    ByVal messageText As String, ByVal dialogCaption As String, _
    ByVal type As Integer) As Integer

    'passes to user32.dll through Platform Invoke

End Function
```

CallingConventions

The `CallingConventions` enumeration inside of the `DllImportAttribute` class allows you to specify the conventions used when calling the function. The default value of this enumeration is `WinAPI`. As calling the Win32 API from managed code is the focus of this chapter, we will leave it to the readers to peruse the other values of this enumeration should they require their use. Setting this enumeration is only possible using the attribute-like syntax for function declarations.

PreserveSig

The `PreserveSig` object field is used to indicate whether the `HRESULT` or `Retval` should be suppressed. The default value for `PreserveSig` is `True`; that is, the signature transformations are preserved. Setting this value to `False` indicates that you wish the `HRESULT` to be transformed into the `Retval` and thus discarded. This field is only accessible via the `DllImportAttribute` class and the attribute-like syntax for function declarations.

SetLastError

The `SetLastError` object field is used to indicate that the API should allow you to call the `GetLastError` API call after a given API call. This was common practice for VB developers. The `GetLastError` API allowed you to determine whether an error occurred while executing a given API call. For this reason, inside of VB, the default value of the field is `True`. This field is only available to those using the attribute-like syntax for function declarations.

Passing Structures and Classes

A number of unmanaged DLL functions require you to pass structures of data. Structures are similar to VB's UDTs of old. When passing these structures/classes it is usually necessary to define additional information about the sequence of the members of a given structure. To do so, you use the `StructLayoutAttribute` class. This class is of the type `LayoutKind` enumeration. This enumeration has the following three values:

- `Auto` indicates that the runtime can reorder the members in the structure. This option is *not* meant for calling unmanaged DLL functions and should not be used.

- `Explicit` indicates that the members should be ordered explicitly as set using the `FieldOffset` attribute applied to each item in the structure. The `FieldOffset` attribute indicates a physical position.

- `Sequential` orders the items of the given structure as they appear in the type definition.

Listing A.2 provides an example of passing a data structure, represented by the class `SystemTime`, to a DLL function. We first set the system time by calling `SetSystemTime` and passing it an instance of the `SystemTime` class. Notice that `SystemTime` is tagged as a `StructLayout` with a `LayoutKind` of sequential. We then retrieve the system time by passing another instance of `SystemTime` to the `GetSystemTime` function. Notice that we must make this pass `ByRef`.

LISTING A.2 Passing a Class

```
Imports System.Runtime.InteropServices

'declare a structured class with properties
<StructLayout(LayoutKind.Sequential)> _
Public Structure SystemTime
  Public wYear As Short
  Public wMonth As Short
  Public wDayOfWeek As Short
  Public wDay As Short
  Public wHour As Short
  Public wMinute As Short
  Public wSecond As Short
  Public wMiliseconds As Short
End Structure

Public Class SysTime

  'declare the set system time function
  Declare Auto Sub SetSystemTime Lib "Kernel32.dll" _
    (ByRef sysTime As SystemTime)
```

LISTING A.2 Continued

```
'declare the get system time function
Declare Auto Sub GetSystemTime Lib "Kernel32.dll" _
    (ByRef sysTime As SystemTime)

End Class

Public Class SetGetTime

  Public Shared Sub Main()

    'local scope
    Dim sTimeSet As New SystemTime()
    Dim sTimeGet As New SystemTime()

    'set the properties of our set time instance
    sTimeSet.wYear = 2001
    sTimeSet.wMonth = 8
    sTimeSet.wDayOfWeek = 7
    sTimeSet.wDay = 26
    sTimeSet.wHour = 10
    sTimeSet.wMinute = 30
    sTimeSet.wSecond = 0
    sTimeSet.wMiliseconds = 0

    'call set time
    SysTime.SetSystemTime(sysTime:=sTimeSet)

    'call get time
    SysTime.GetSystemTime(sysTime:=sTimeGet)

    'write time to screen
    Console.WriteLine(sTimeGet.wHour & ":" & sTimeGet.wMinute)

  End Sub

End Class
```

Callback Functions

Creating callback functions is a typical task of the Win32 API developer. Callback functions work directly with the unmanaged code to execute a given task. For example, suppose that you needed to execute the same task on a group of objects. The API call would find the first object and return it to your callback function. Your callback function would execute another task and the API would then find the next object. This is illustrated by Figure A.2.

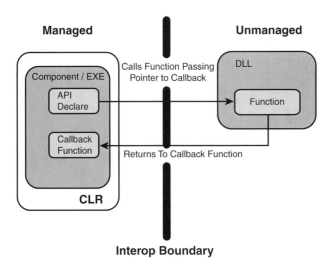

FIGURE A.2

Callback functions.

As you can see, callbacks are implemented by passing the DLL function a pointer to the callback function. You must first determine if your DLL function requires callbacks prior to your using them. To do so, you can often check the argument of a given parameter. An argument whose prefix is lp and whose suffix is Func usually indicates a callback. The prefix stands for Long Pointer and the suffix, Function.

After you've identified a need for a callback function, you implement it via delegates. Platform Invoke converts a given delegate to a familiar callback format for you.

Listing A.3 represents a DLL function that makes a callback to a managed function. We initially create a delegate (CallBack) that has a Windows handle as its first parameter. Note that EnumWindowsProc defines the proper format for our delegate used with the DLL function EnumWindows. Next, we declare the EnumWindows function and set its first parameter to a type of our delegate, CallBack. We then define the class that will actually receive the delegate calls, ReceiveCallBack. This function takes the Windows handle and writes it to the console. Finally, create a simple Main in our module to call the EnumWindows API. We then pass the AddressOf ReceiveCallBack to it. This is standard for delegates in VB. Note that the ReceiveCallBack function automatically returns True. This indicates to the API function that we wish to continue. Returning False would halt the callbacks.

The result of this code is a list of all the top-level Windows handles displayed inside the console.

LISTING A.3 Callback

```
Imports System.Runtime.InteropServices

'create a delegate for callback
Public Delegate Function CallBack( _
    ByVal hwnd As Integer, _
    ByVal lParam As Integer) As Boolean

Module Module1

    'declare the dll function that enumerates all windows
    '   and returns them to the callback
    Declare Function EnumWindows Lib "user32" ( _
        ByVal lpEnumFunc As CallBack, _
        ByVal lParam As Integer) As Integer

    Public Function ReceiveCallBack(ByVal hwnd As Integer, _
        ByVal lParam As Integer) As Boolean

        'write the windows handle out
        Console.WriteLine(hwnd)

        'indicate to API that we wish to continue
        Return True

    End Function

    Sub Main()

        'call the api and pass the pointer
        EnumWindows(AddressOf ReceiveCallBack, 0)

        'pause
        Do While Not Console.ReadLine = "s" : Loop

    End Sub

End Module
```

Win32 API-to-Namespace Cross-Reference

The Win32 API-to-Framework Class Library Namespace Cross-Reference is intended to provide readers who are familiar with the API a place to look up API calls for a managed code equivalent. This is in no way intended to be a complete cross-reference. Instead, it is another tool to help you as you transition your coding practice to .NET. In some cases, we are able only to point you to a similar namespace or function because not all Win32 functions have a one-to-one FCL equivalent. We've placed a dash next to those Win32 APIs for which we could not find FCL equivalents. That does not mean there isn't one—we simply didn't find it.

Win32 API Function Call	Class Library Equivalent (Italics Represent Peripherally Related Items)
AbnormalTermination	—

AbortDoc	*System.Drawing.Printing Namespace*
	     PrintDocument Class
	     PrintPageEventArgs Class

AbortPath	*System.Drawing.Drawing2D Namespace* *GraphicsPath Class*
AbortPrinter	*System.Drawing.Printing Namespace*
AbortProc	*See SetAbortProc Namespace*
AbortSystemShutdown	—
ActivateKeyboardLayout	—
AddAtom	—

AddFontMemResourceEx	*System.Drawing.Text Namespace*
	     PrivateFontCollection Class
	         AddMemoryFont Method

AddFontResource	*System.Drawing.Text Namespace*
	     PrivateFontCollection Class
	         AddFontFile Method

AddFontResourceEx	System.Drawing.Text Namespace
	     PrivateFontCollection Class
	         AddFontFile Method

AddForm	*System.Drawing.Printing Namespace*
AddJob	*System.Drawing.Printing Namespace*
AddMonitor	—
AddPort	—
AddPrinter	*System.Drawing.Printing Namespace*

Win32 API Function Call	Class Library Equivalent (Italics Represent Peripherally Related Items)
AddPrinterConnection	*System.Drawing.Printing Namespace*
AddPrinterDriver	*System.Drawing.Printing Namespace*
AddPrinterDriverEx	*System.Drawing.Printing Namespace*
AddPrintProcessor	*System.Drawing.Printing Namespace*
AddPrintProvider	*System.Drawing.Printing Namespace*
AddUsersToEncryptedFile	—
AddVectoredExceptionHandler	—
AdjustWindowRect	—
AdjustWindowRectEx	—
AdvancedDocumentProperties	*System.Windows.Forms Namespace* *PrintDialog Class*
AlertSamplesAvail	—
AllocateUserPhysicalPages	—
AllocConsole	System Namespace *Console Class*
AllowSetForegroundWindow	—
AlphaBlend	System.Drawing Namespace Bitmap Class Graphics Class CompositingMode Property
AngleArc	System.Drawing Namespace Graphics Class DrawArc Method
AnimatePalette	—
AnimateWindow	—
AnyPopup	—
APCProc	—
AppendMenu	System.Windows.Forms Namespace MenuItem Class MenuItems Property Menu.MenuItemCollection Class Add Method

Win32 API Function Call	Class Library Equivalent (Italics Represent Peripherally Related Items)
Arc	System.Drawing Namespace
	Graphics Class
	DrawArc Method
ArcTo	System.Drawing Namespace
	Graphics Class
	DrawArc Method
AreFileApisANSI	—
ArrangeIconicWindows	System.Windows.Forms Namespace
	Form Class
	LayoutMdi Method
	MdiLayout Enumeration
	ArrangeIcons Member
AssignProcessToJobObject	—
AttachThreadInput	—
BackupEventLog	*System.Diagnostics Namespace*
	EventLog Class
BackupRead	*System.IO Namespace*
	FileStream Class
	Read Method
BackupSeek	*System.IO Namespace*
	FileStream Class
	Seek Method
BackupWrite	*System.IO Namespace*
	FileStream Class
	Write Method
Beep	—
BeginDeferWindowPos	—
BeginPaint	—
BeginPath	System.Drawing.Drawing2D Namespace
GraphicsPath Class	
Constructor	
BeginUpdateResource	—

Win32 API Function Call	Class Library Equivalent (Italics Represent Peripherally Related Items)
BindIoCompletionCallback	—
BitBlt	*System.Drawing Namespace*
BlockInput	—
BringWindowToTop	System.Windows.Forms Namespace Form Class BringToFront Method
BroadcastSystemMessage	—
BroadcastSystemMessageEx	—
BuildCommDCB	—
BuildCommDCBAndTimeouts	—
CallMsgFilter	—
CallNamedPipe	—
CallNextHookEx	—
CallWindowProc	—
CallWndProc	—
CallWndRetProc	—
CancelDC	*System.Drawing Namespace*
CancelIo	*System.IO Namespace*
CancelWaitableTimer	System.Threading Namespace *Timer Class* *Dispose Method*
CascadeWindows	System.Windows.Forms Namespace Form Class LayoutMdi Method
CBTProc	—
CCHookProc	—
CFHookProc	—
ChangeClipboardChain	*System.Windows.Forms Namespace* *Clipboard Class*
ChangeDisplaySettings	—
ChangeDisplaySettingsEx	—

Win32 API Function Call	Class Library Equivalent *(Italics Represent Peripherally Related Items)*
ChangeServiceConfig	System.ServiceProcess Namespace
	ServiceController Class
	DisplayName Property
	ServicesDependedOn Property
	ServiceName Property
	ServiceType Property
	ServiceInstaller Class
	DisplayName Property
	ServicesDependedOn Property
	ServiceName Property
	StartType Property
	ServiceProcessInstaller Class
	Account Property
	Password Property
	UserName Property
	ServiceStartMode Enumeration
	ServiceType Enumeration
ChangeTimerQueueTimer	System.Threading Namespace
	Timer Class
	Change Method
CharLower	System Namespace
	Char Structure
	ToLower Method
CharLowerBuff	System Namespace
	Char Structure
	ToLower Method
CharNext	—
CharNextExA	—
CharPrev	—
CharPrevExA	—
CharToOem	—
CharToOemBuff	—

Win32 API Function Call	Class Library Equivalent (Italics Represent Peripherally Related Items)

CharUpper	System Namespace
	   Char Structure
	      ToUpper Method

CharUpperBuff	System Namespace
	   Char Structure
	      ToUpper Method

CheckDlgButton	—

CheckMenuItem	System.Windows.Forms Namespace
	   MenuItem Class
	      Checked Property

CheckMenuRadioItem	System.Windows.Forms Namespace
	   MenuItem Class
	      Checked Property
	      RadioChecked Property

CheckRadioButton	System.Windows.Forms Namespace
	   RadioButton Class
	      Checked Property

ChildWindowFromPoint	—
ChildWindowFromPointEx	—

ChooseColor	System.Windows.Forms Namespace
	   ColorDialog Class
	      ShowDialog Method

ChooseFont	System.Windows.Forms Namespace
	   FontDialog Class
	      ShowDialog Method

Chord	*System.Drawing.Imaging*
	   Graphics Class
	      DrawEllipse Method

ClearCommBreak	—
ClearCommError	—

ClearEventLog	System.Diagnostics Namespace
	   EventLog Class
	      Clear Method

Win32 API Function Call	Class Library Equivalent (Italics Represent Peripherally Related Items)
ClientToScreen	*System.Drawing Namespace*
	PointConverter Class
ClipCursor	System.Windows.Form Namespace
	Cursor Class
	Clip Property
CloseClipboard	System.Windows.Forms Namespace
	Clipboard Class
CloseDesktop	—
CloseEnhMetaFile	—
CloseEventLog	System.Diagnostics Namespace
	EventLog Class
CloseFigure	System.Drawing.Drawing2D Namespace
	GraphicsPath Class
	CloseFigure Method
CloseHandle	—
CloseMetaFile	—
ClosePrinter	*System.Drawing.Printing Namespace*
CloseServiceHandle	—
CloseWindow	System.Windows.Forms Namespace
	Form Class
	WindowState Property
	FormWindowState Enumeration
	Minimized Member
CloseWindowStation	—
CombineRgn	System.Drawing Namespace
	Graphics Class
	SetClip Method
	CombineMode Enumeration
CombineTransform	*System.Drawing Namespace*
	Graphics Class
	TranslateTransform Method

Win32 API Function Call	Class Library Equivalent (Italics Represent Peripherally Related Items)

CommandLineToArgvW	System Namespace
	    Environment Class
	        GetCommandLineArgs Method

CommConfigDialog	—
CommDlgExtendedError	—
CompareFileTime	—

CompareString	System Namespace
	    String Class
	        Compare Method
	        CompareOrdinal Method
	        CompareTo Method

ConfigurePort	—
ConnectNamedPipe	—

ConnectToPrinterDlg	System.Windows.Forms Namespace
	    PrintDialog Class
	        ShowNetwork Property
	        ShowDialog Method

ContinueDebugEvent	—

ControlService	System.ServiceProcess Namespace
	    ServiceController Class
	        Continue Method
	        Pause Method
	        Stop Method

ConvertDefaultLocale	—
ConvertThreadToFiber	—
CopyAcceleratorTable	—

CopyCursor	*System.Windows.Forms Namespace*
	    Cursor Class
	        CopyHandle Method

CopyEnhMetaFile	—

CopyFile	System.IO Namespace
	    File Class
	        Copy Method

Win32 API Function Call	Class Library Equivalent (Italics Represent Peripherally Related Items)
CopyFileEx	*System.IO Namespace*
	File Class
	Copy Method
CopyIcon	—
CopyImage	System.Drawing Namespace
	Image Class
	Clone Method
CopyMemory	*System Namespace*
	Buffer Class
CopyMetaFile	—
CopyProgressRoutine	—
CopyRect	*System.Drawing Namespace*
	Graphics Class
	DrawRectangle Method
CountClipboardFormats	System.Windows.Forms Namespace
	DataFormats Class
CounterPathCallBack	—
CreateAcceleratorTable	—
CreateBitmap	System.Drawing Namespace
	Bitmap Class
	Constructor
CreateBitmapIndirect	System.Drawing Namespace
	Bitmap Class
	Constructor
CreateBrushIndirect	System.Drawing Namespace
	Bitmap Class
	Constructor
CreateCaret	—
CreateCompatibleBitmap	System.Drawing Namespace
	Bitmap Class
	Constructor

Win32 API Function Call	Class Library Equivalent (Italics Represent Peripherally Related Items)
CreateCompatibleDC	*System.Drawing*
	Graphics Class
CreateConsoleScreenBuffer	—
CreateCursor	System.Windows.Forms
	Cursor Class
	Constructor
CreateDC	*System.Drawing Namespace*
	Graphics Class
CreateDesktop	—
CreateDialog	System.Windows.Forms Namespace
	CommonDialog Class
	Constructor
	HookProc Method
CreateDialogIndirect	System.Windows.Forms Namespace
	CommonDialog Class
	Constructor
	HookProc Method
CreateDialogIndirectParam	—
CreateDialogParam	—
CreateDIBitmap	System.Drawing Namespace
	Bitmap Class
	Constructors
CreateDIBPatternBrush	System.Drawing Namespace
	TextureBrush Class
	Constructors
CreateDIBPatternBrushPt	System.Drawing Namespace
	TextureBrush Class
	Constructors
CreateDIBSection	—
CreateDirectory	System.IO Namespace
	Directory Class
	CreateDirectory Method

Win32 API Function Call	Class Library Equivalent (Italics Represent Peripherally Related Items)
CreateDirectoryEx	*System.IO Namespace*
	Directory Class
	CreateDirectory Method
CreateDiscardableBitmap	—
CreateEllipticRgn	*System.Drawing Namespace*
	Graphics Class
	DrawEllipse Method
	Region Class
CreateEllipticRgnIndirect	—
CreateEnhMetaFile	—
CreateEnvironmentBlock	—
CreateEvent	System.Threading Namespace
	AutoResetEvent Class
	Constructor
	ManualResetEvent Class
	Constructor
CreateFiber	—
CreateFile	System.IO Namespace
	File Class
	Create Method
CreateFileMapping	—
CreateFont	*System.Drawing*
	Font Class
	FromLogFont Method
CreateFontIndirect	*System.Drawing*
	Font Class
	FromLogFont Method
CreateFontIndirectEx	*System.Drawing*
	Font Class
	FromLogFont Method
CreateHalftonePalette	*System.Drawing.Imaging*
CreateHardLink	—

Win32 API Function Call	Class Library Equivalent (Italics Represent Peripherally Related Items)
CreateHatchBrush	System.Drawing.Drawing2D
	HatchBrush Class
	Constructor
CreateIC	—
CreateIcon	System.Drawing
	Icon Class
	Constructor
CreateIconFromResource	System.Drawing
	Icon Class
	Constructor
CreateIconFromResourceEx	System.Drawing
	Icon Class
	Constructor
CreateIconIndirect	System.Drawing
	Icon Class
	Constructor
CreateIoCompletionPort	—
CreateJobObject	—
CreateMailslot	—
CreateMDIWindow	System.Windows.Forms
	Form Class
	Constructor
	IsMdiContainer Property
CreateMenu	System.Windows.Forms
	MenuItem Class
	Constructor
CreateMetaFile	—
CreateMutex	System.Threading Namespace
	Mutex Class
	Constructor
CreateNamedPipe	—
CreatePalette	—

Win32 API Function Call	Class Library Equivalent (Italics Represent Peripherally Related Items)
CreatePatternBrush	*System.Drawing.Drawing2D*
	Texture Class
	Constructor
CreatePen	System.Drawing Namespace
	Pen Class
	Constructor
CreatePenIndirect	*System.Drawing Namespace*
	Pen Class
	Constructor
CreatePipe	—
CreatePolygonRgn	System.Drawing Namespace
	Graphics Class
	DrawPolygon Method
CreatePolyPolygonRgn	System.Drawing Namespace
	Graphics Class
	DrawPolygon Method
	Region Class
CreatePopupMenu	System.Windows.Forms Namespace
	ContextMenu Class
	Constructor
	Show Method
CreateProcess	System.Diagnostics Namespace
	Process Class
	Constructor
	Start Method
CreateProcessAsUser	System.Diagnostics Namespace
	Process Class
	Constructor
	Start Method
CreateProcessWithLogonW	System.Diagnostics Namespace
	Process Class
	Constructor
	Start Method

Win32 API Function Call	Class Library Equivalent (Italics Represent Peripherally Related Items)
CreateRectRgn	System.Drawing Namespace
	Graphics Class
	DrawRectangle Method
	Region Class
CreateRectRgnIndirect	System.Drawing Namespace
	Graphics Class
	DrawRectangle Method
	Region Class
CreateRemoteThread	—
CreateRoundRectRgn	System.Drawing Namespace
	Graphics Class
	DrawRectangle Method
	Region Class
	Pen Class
	LineJoin Property
CreateScalableFontResource	—
CreateSemaphore	—
CreateService	*System.ServiceProcess Namespace*
	ServiceInstaller Class
CreateSolidBrush	System.Drawing Namespace
	Solid Brush Class
	Constructor
CreateTapePartition	—
CreateThread	System.Threading Namespace
	Thread Class
	Constructor
	Start Method
	ThreadStart Class
CreateTimerQueue	System.Threading Namespace
	Timer Class
CreateTimerQueueTimer	System.Threading Namespace
	Timer Class

Win32 API Function Call	Class Library Equivalent (Italics Represent Peripherally Related Items)
CreateToolhelp32Snapshot	—
CreateWaitableTimer	System.Threading Namespace
	Timer Class
	Constructor
	Start Method
	Enabled Property
CreateWindow	System.Windows.Forms Namespace
	Form Class
	Constructor
	FormBorderStyle Property
	Height Property
	Owner Property
	Show Method
	ShowDialog Method
	StartPosition Property
	Width Property
	Control Class
	Constructor
	Show Method
	Height Property
	Width Property
CreateWindowEx	System.Windows.Forms Namespace
	Form Class
	Constructor
	FormBorderStyle Property
	Height Property
	Owner Property
	Show Method
	ShowDialog Method
	StartPosition Property
	Width Property

Win32 API Function Call	Class Library Equivalent (Italics Represent Peripherally Related Items)
	Control Class
	Constructor
	Show Method
	Height Property
	Width Property
CreateWindowStation	—
DdeAbandonTransaction	—
DdeAccessData	—
DdeAddData	—
DdeCallback	—
DdeClientTransaction	—
DdeCmpStringHandles	—
DdeConnect	—
DdeConnectList	—
DdeCreateDataHandle	—
DdeCreateStringHandle	—
DdeDisconnect	—
DdeDisconnectList	—
DdeEnableCallback	—
DdeFreeDataHandle	—
DdeFreeStringHandle	—
DdeGetData	—
DdeGetLastError	—
DdeImpersonateClient	—
DdeInitialize	—
DdeKeepStringHandle	—
DdeNameService	—
DdePostAdvise	—
DdeQueryConvInfo	—
DdeQueryNextServer	—
DdeQueryString	—
DdeReconnect	—

Win32 API Function Call	Class Library Equivalent (Italics Represent Peripherally Related Items)
DdeSetQualityOfService	—
DdeSetUserHandle	—
DdeUnaccessData	—
DdeUninitialize	—
DebugActiveProcess	—
DebugActiveProcessStop	—
DebugBreak	—
DebugProc	—
DebugSetProcessKillOnExit	—
DecryptFile	System.Security.Cryptography Namespace *RSACryptoServiceProvider Class* *Decrypt Method* *CryptoStream Class*
DefDlgProc	—
DeferWindowPos	—
DefFrameProc	—
DefineDosDevice	—
DefMDIChildProc	—
DefRawInputProc	—
DefWindowProc	—
DeleteAtom	—
DeleteCriticalSection	—
DeleteDC	—
DeleteEnhMetaFile	—
DeleteFiber	—
DeleteFile	System.IO Namespace File Class Delete Method FileInfo Class Delete Method
DeleteForm	—

Win32 API Function Call	Class Library Equivalent (Italics Represent Peripherally Related Items)
DeleteMenu	System.Windows.Forms Namespace
	Menu Class
	MenuItems Property
	Menu.MenuItemCollection Class
	Remove Method
	RemoveAt Method
DeleteMetaFile	—
DeleteMonitor	—
DeleteObject	—
DeletePort	—
DeletePrinter	—
DeletePrinterConnection	—
DeletePrinterData	—
DeletePrinterDataEx	—
DeletePrinterDriver	—
DeletePrinterDriverEx	—
DeletePrinterKey	—
DeletePrintProcessor	—
DeletePrintProvider	—
DeleteProfile	—
DeleteService	System.ServiceProcess Namespace
	ServiceInstaller Class
	RollBack Method
DeleteTimerQueue	—
DeleteTimerQueueEx	—
DeleteTimerQueueTimer	—
DeleteVolumeMountPoint	—
DeregisterEventSource	System.Diagnostics Namespace
	EventLog Class
	DeleteEventSource Method
DestroyAcceleratorTable	—
DestroyCaret	—

Win32 API Function Call	Class Library Equivalent (Italics Represent Peripherally Related Items)
DestroyCursor	—
DestroyEnvironmentBlock	—

DestroyIcon	System.Drawing Namespace
	    Icon Class
	        Dispose Method

DestroyMenu	—
DestroyWindow	—
DeviceCapabilities	—
DeviceIoControl	—

DialogBox	System.Windows.Forms
	    Form Class
	        Constructor
	        ShowDialog Method

DialogBoxIndirect	System.Windows.Forms
	    Form Class
	        Constructor
	        ShowDialog Method

DialogBoxIndirectParam	—
DialogBoxParam	—
DialogProc	—
DisableThreadLibraryCalls	—
DisconnectNamedPipe	—
DispatchMessage	—

DlgDirList	System.Windows.Forms Namespace
	    Form Class
	        OpenFileDialog Method
	        SaveFileDialog Method

DlgDirListComboBox	System.Windows.Forms Namespace
	    Form Class
	        OpenFileDialog Method
	        SaveFileDialog Method

Win32 API Function Call	Class Library Equivalent (Italics Represent Peripherally Related Items)
DlgDirSelectComboBoxEx	System.Windows.Forms Namespace
	Form Class
	OpenFileDialog Method
	SaveFileDialog Method
DlgDirSelectEx	System.Windows.Forms Namespace
	Form Class
	OpenFileDialog Method
	SaveFileDialog Method
DllMain	—
DnsHostnameToComputerName	System.Net Namespace
	Dns Class
	GetHostName Method
	GetHostByName Method
	System.Windows.Forms Namespace
	SystemInformation Class
	ComputerName Property
DocumentProperties	*System.Drawing.Printing Namespace*
	PrintDocument Class
DosDateTimeToFileTime	—
DPtoLP	—
DragDetect	—
DrawAnimatedRects	*System.Drawing Namespace*
	ImageAnimator Class
DrawCaption	—
DrawEdge	*System.Drawing Namespace*
	Graphics Class
	DrawRectangle Method
DrawEscape	—
DrawFocusRect	—
DrawFrameControl	—
DrawIcon	System.Drawing Namespace
	Graphics Class
	DrawIcon Method

Win32 API Function Call	Class Library Equivalent (Italics Represent Peripherally Related Items)

DrawIconEx	System.Drawing Namespace
	    Graphics Class
	        DrawIcon Method

DrawMenuBar	—
DrawState	—
DrawStateProc	—

DrawText	*System.Drawing Namespace*
	    Graphics Class
	        DrawString Method

DrawTextEx	*System.Drawing Namespace*
	    Graphics Class
	        DrawString Method

DuplicateHandle	—

DuplicateIcon	*System.Drawing Namespace*
	    Icon Class
	    Graphics Class
	        DrawIcon Method

EditWordBreakProc	—

Ellipse	System.Drawing Namespace
	    Graphics Class
	        DrawEllipse Method

EmptyClipboard	—
EmptyWorkingSet	—

EnableMenuItem	System.Windows.Forms Namespace
	    MenuItem Class
	        Enabled Property

EnableScrollBar	System.Windows.Forms Namespace
	    ScrollableControl Class
	        HScroll Property
	        VScroll Property

Win32 API Function Call	Class Library Equivalent (Italics Represent Peripherally Related Items)
EnableWindow	System.Windows.Forms Namespace
	Control Class
	Enabled Property
	Form Class
	Enabled Property
EncryptFile	System.Security.Cryptography Namespace
	RSACryptoServiceProvider Class
	Encrypt Method
	CryptoStream Class
EncryptionDisable	—
EndDeferWindowPos	—
EndDialog	—
EndDoc	—
EndDocPrinter	—
EndMenu	—
EndPage	*System.Drawing.Printing Namespace*
	PrintDocument Class
	OnPrintPage Method
EndPagePrinter	*System.Drawing.Printing Namespace*
	PrintDocument Class
	OnEndPrint Method
EndPaint	—
EndPath	*System.Drawing.Drawing2D Namespace*
	GraphicsPath Class
EndUpdateResource	—
EnhMetaFileProc	—
EnterCriticalSection	—
EnumCalendarInfo	—
EnumCalendarInfoEx	—
EnumCalendarInfoProc	—
EnumCalendarInfoProcEx	—
EnumChildProc	—

Win32 API Function Call	Class Library Equivalent (Italics Represent Peripherally Related Items)
EnumChildWindows	System.Windows.Forms Namespace
	Form Class
	MdiChild Property
EnumClipboardFormats	—
EnumCodePagesProc	—
EnumDateFormats	System.Globalization
	DateTimeStyles Enumeration
EnumDateFormatsEx	System.Globalization
	DateTimeStyles Enumeration
EnumDateFormatsProc	System.Globalization
	DateTimeStyles Enumeration
EnumDateFormatsProcEx	System.Globalization
	DateTimeStyles Enumeration
EnumDependentServices	System.ServiceProcess Namespace
	ServiceController Class
	DependentServices Property
EnumDesktopProc	—
EnumDesktops	—
EnumDesktopWindows	—
EnumDeviceDrivers	—
EnumDisplayDevices	—
EnumDisplayMonitors	—
EnumDisplaySettings	—
EnumDisplaySettingsEx	—
EnumEnhMetaFile	—
EnumFontFamExProc	—
EnumFontFamilies	System.Drawing Namespace
	FontFamily Class
	GetFamilies Method
EnumFontFamiliesEx	System.Drawing Namespace
	FontFamily Class
	GetFamilies Method

Win32 API Function Call	Class Library Equivalent (Italics Represent Peripherally Related Items)
EnumFontFamProc	System.Drawing Namespace
	FontStyle Enumeration
EnumFonts	System.Drawing Namespace
	FontFamily Class
	GetFamilies Method
EnumFontsProc	System.Drawing Namespace
	FontFamily Class
	GetFamilies Method
EnumForms	—
EnumGeoInfoProc	—
EnumInputContext	—
EnumJobs	—
EnumLanguageGroupLocales	System.Globalization
	CultureTypes Enumeration
EnumLanguageGroupLocalesProc	System.Globalization
	CultureTypes Enumeration
EnumLanguageGroupsProc	System.Globalization
	CultureTypes Enumeration
EnumLocalesProc	—
EnumMetaFile	—
EnumMetaFileProc	—
EnumMonitors	—
EnumObjects	—
EnumObjectsProc	—
EnumPorts	—
EnumPrinterData	—
EnumPrinterDataEx	—
EnumPrinterDrivers	—
EnumPrinterKey	—
EnumPrinters	—
EnumPrintProcessorDatatypes	—
EnumPrintProcessors	—

Win32 API Function Call	Class Library Equivalent (Italics Represent Peripherally Related Items)
EnumProcesses	—
EnumProcessModules	—
EnumProps	—
EnumPropsEx	—
EnumRegisterWordProc	—
EnumResLangProc	—
EnumResNameProc	—
EnumResourceLanguages	—
EnumResourceNames	—
EnumResourceTypes	—
EnumResTypeProc	—
EnumServicesStatus	—
EnumServicesStatusEx	—
EnumSystemCodePages	—
EnumSystemGeoID	—
EnumSystemLanguageGroups	—
EnumSystemLocales	—
EnumThreadWindows	—
EnumThreadWndProc	—
EnumTimeFormats	System.Globalization Namespace *DateTimeStyles Enumeration*
EnumTimeFormatsProc	System.Globalization Namespace *DateTimeStyles Enumeration*
EnumUILanguages	—
EnumUILanguagesProc	—
EnumWindows	—
EnumWindowsProc	—
EnumWindowStationProc	—
EnumWindowStations	—
EqualRect	System.Drawing Rectangle Structure

Win32 API Function Call	Class Library Equivalent *(Italics Represent Peripherally Related Items)*
EqualRgn	System.Drawing Region Structure
EraseTape	—
Escape	System.Drawing Namespace
EscapeCommFunction	—
ExcludeClipRect	System.Drawing Region Class Graphics Class SetClip Method
ExcludeUpdateRgn	—
ExitProcess	System.Diagnostics Namespace Process Class *Close Method* *CloseMainWindow Method* *WaitForExit Method*
ExitThread	System.Threading Namespace Thread Class Abort Method
ExitWindows	—
ExitWindowsEx	—
ExpandEnvironmentStrings	—
ExpandEnvironmentStringsForUser	—
ExtCreatePen	System.Drawing Namespace Pen Class
ExtCreateRegion	System.Drawing Namespace Region Class
ExtEscape	—
ExtFloodFill	System.Drawing Namespace Graphics Class Fill Region Method
ExtractAssociatedIcon	—
ExtractIcon	—

Win32 API Function Call	Class Library Equivalent (Italics Represent Peripherally Related Items)
ExtractIconEx	—
ExtSelectClipRgn	—
ExtTextOut	—
FatalAppExit	—
FatalExit	—
FiberProc	—
FileEncryptionStatus	—
FileIOCompletionRoutine	—
FileTimeToDosDateTime	—
FileTimeToLocalFileTime	—
FileTimeToSystemTime	—
FillConsoleOutputAttribute	—
FillConsoleOutputCharacter	—
FillMemory	—
FillPath	System.Drawing Namespace 　　Graphics Class 　　　　FillPath Method
FillRect	System.Drawing Namespace 　　Graphics Class 　　　　FillRectangle Method
FillRgn	System.Drawing Namespace 　　Graphics Class 　　　　FillRegion Method
FindAtom	—
FindClose	—
FindCloseChangeNotification	—
FindClosePrinterChangeNotification	—
FindFirstChangeNotification	—
FindFirstFile	*System.IO Namespace* 　　*File Class* 　　　　*Exists Method* 　　*Directory Class* 　　　　*GetFiles Method*

Win32 API Function Call	Class Library Equivalent *(Italics Represent Peripherally Related Items)*
FindFirstFileEx	*System.IO Namespace*
	File Class
	Exists Method
	Directory Class
	GetFiles Method
FindFirstPrinterChangeNotification	—
FindFirstVolume	—
FindFirstVolumeMountPoint	—
FindNextChangeNotification	—
FindNextFile	*System.IO Namespace*
	Directory Class
	GetFiles Method
FindNextPrinterChangeNotification	—
FindNextVolume	—
FindNextVolumeMountPoint	—
FindResource	—
FindResourceEx	—
FindText	—
FindVolumeClose	—
FindVolumeMountPointClose	—
FindWindow	—
FindWindowEx	—
FlashWindow	—
FlashWindowEx	—
FlattenPath	System.Drawing Namespace
	GraphicsPath Class
	Flatten Method
FloodFill	*System.Drawing Namespace*
	Graphics Class
FlushConsoleInputBuffer	—
FlushFileBuffers	System.IO Namespace
	FileStream Class
	Flush Method

Win32 API Function Call	Class Library Equivalent (Italics Represent Peripherally Related Items)
FlushInstructionCache	—
FlushPrinter	—
FlushViewOfFile	—
FoldString	—
ForegroundIdleProc	—
FormatMessage	—
FrameRect	*System.Drawing Namespace*
	Graphics Class
	DrawRectangle Method
	Pen Class
FrameRgn	*System.Drawing Namespace*
	Graphics Class
	DrawRegion Method
	Pen Class
FreeConsole	—
FreeDDElParam	—
FreeEncryptionCertificateHashList	—
FreeEnvironmentStrings	—
FreeLibrary	—
FreeLibraryAndExitThread	—
FreePrinterNotifyInfo	—
FreeUserPhysicalPages	—
FRHookProc	—
GdiComment	—
GdiFlush	—
GdiGetBatchLimit	—
GdiSetBatchLimit	—
GenerateConsoleCtrlEvent	—
GetACP	—
GetActiveWindow	System.Windows.Forms Namespace
	Form Class
	ActiveForm Property

Win32 API Function Call	Class Library Equivalent (Italics Represent Peripherally Related Items)
GetAllUsersProfileDirectory	—
GetAltTabInfo	—
GetAncestor	—
GetArcDirection	—
GetAspectRatioFilterEx	—
GetAsyncKeyState	—
GetAtomName	—
GetBinaryType	—
GetBitmapBits	System.Drawing Namespace Bitmap Class Constructor
GetBitmapDimensionEx	—
GetBkColor	—
GetBkMode	—
GetBoundsRect	—
GetBrushOrgEx	—
GetCalendarInfo	—
GetCapture	—
GetCaretBlinkTime	—
GetCaretPos	—
GetCharABCWidths	—
GetCharABCWidthsFloat	
GetCharABCWidthsI	—
GetCharacterPlacement	—
GetCharWidth	—
GetCharWidth32	—
GetCharWidthFloat	—
GetCharWidthI	—
GetClassInfo	—
GetClassInfoEx	—
GetClassLong	—
GetClassLongPtr	—

Win32 API Function Call	Class Library Equivalent (Italics Represent Peripherally Related Items)
GetClassName	—
GetClassWord	—
GetClientRect	—

GetClipboardData	System.Windows.Forms Namespace
	    Clipboard Class
	        GetDataObject Method

GetClipboardFormatName	System.Windows.Forms Namespace
	    DataFormats.Format Class
	        Name Property

GetClipboardOwner	—
GetClipboardSequenceNumber	—
GetClipboardViewer	—

GetClipBox	System.Drawing Namespace
	    Region Class
	        GetBounds Method

GetClipCursor	System.Windows.Forms Namespace
	    Cursor Class
	        Clip Property

GetClipRgn	System.Drawing Namespace
	    Graphics Class
	        ClipBounds Property

GetColorAdjustment	—
GetComboBoxInfo	System.Windows.Forms Namespace *ComboBox Class*
GetCommandLine	—
GetCommConfig	—
GetCommMask	—
GetCommModemStatus	—
GetCommProperties	—
GetCommState	—
GetCommTimeouts	—

Win32 API Function Call	Class Library Equivalent *(Italics Represent Peripherally Related Items)*

GetCompressedFileSize	*System.IO Namespace*
	    FileInfo Class
	        Length Property
	        FileAttributes Enumeration

GetComputerName	System.Windows.Forms Namespace
	    SystemInformation Class
	        ComputerName Property

GetComputerNameEx	System.Windows.Forms Namespace
	    SystemInformation Class
	        ComputerName Property

GetComputerObjectName	—
GetConsoleCP	—
GetConsoleCursorInfo	—
GetConsoleMode	—
GetConsoleOutputCP	—
GetConsoleScreenBufferInfo	—
GetConsoleTitle	—
GetConsoleWindow	—
GetCPInfo	—
GetCPInfoEx	—

GetCurrencyFormat	System Namespace
	    String Class
	        Format Method

GetCurrentDirectory	System.IO Namespace
	    Directory Class
	        GetCurrentDirectory Class

GetCurrentHwProfile	—
GetCurrentObject	—
GetCurrentPositionEx	System.Drawing

GetCurrentProcess	System.Diagnostics
	    Process Class
	        GetCurrentProcess Property

Win32 API Function Call	Class Library Equivalent (Italics Represent Peripherally Related Items)
GetCurrentProcessId	—
GetCurrentThread	System.Threading
	Thread Class
	CurrentThread Property
GetCurrentThreadId	—
GetCursor	*System.Windows.Forms*
	Cursor Class
	Handle Property
GetCursorInfo	*System.Windows.Forms*
	Cursor Class
GetCursorPos	System.Windows.Forms
	Cursor Class
	Position Property
GetDateFormat	System Namespace
	String Class
	Format Method
GetDC	System.Drawing
	Graphics Class
GetDCBrushColor	—
GetDCEx	System.Drawing
	Graphics Class
GetDCOrgEx	—
GetDCPenColor	—
GetDefaultCommConfig	—
GetDefaultPrinter	System.Drawing.Printing
	PrintDocument Class
GetDefaultUserProfileDirectory	—
GetDesktopWindow	—
GetDeviceCaps	—
GetDeviceDriverBaseName	—
GetDeviceDriverFileName	—
GetDevicePowerState	—

Win32 API Function Call	Class Library Equivalent (Italics Represent Peripherally Related Items)
GetDialogBaseUnits	—
GetDIBColorTable	—
GetDIBits	—
GetDiskFreeSpace	System.Management Namespace
GetDiskFreeSpaceEx	System.Management Namespace
GetDlgCtrlID	—
GetDlgItem	—
GetDlgItemInt	—
GetDlgItemText	—
GetDoubleClickTime	—
GetDriveType	—
GetEnhMetaFile	—
GetEnhMetaFileBits	—
GetEnhMetaFileDescription	—
GetEnhMetaFileHeader	—
GetEnhMetaFilePaletteEntries	—
GetEnvironmentStrings	—
GetEnvironmentVariable	—
GetEventLogInformation	System.Diagnostics Namespace *EventLog Class*
GetExceptionCode	System Namespace *Exception Class*
GetExceptionInformation	System Namespace *Exception Class* *Message Property* *Source Property* *StackTrace Property*
GetExitCodeProcess	System.Diagnostics Namespace Process Class *HasTerminated Property*

Win32 API Function Call	Class Library Equivalent (Italics Represent Peripherally Related Items)
GetExitCodeThread	System.Threading Namespace
	Thread Class
	ThreadState Property
	IsAlive Property
GetExpandedName	—
GetFileAttributes	System.IO Namespace
	File Class
	GetAttributes Method
	FileInfo Class
	Attributes Property
GetFileAttributesEx	System.IO Namespace
	File Class
	GetAttributes Method
	FileInfo Class
	Attributes Property
GetFileInformationByHandle	—
GetFileSize	System.IO Namespace
	FileInfo Class
	Length Property
GetFileSizeEx	System.IO Namespace
	FileInfo Class
	Length Property
GetFileTime	System.IO Namespace
	FileSystemInfo Class
	CreationTime Property
	LastAccessTime Property
	LastWriteTime Property
GetFileTitle	System.IO Namespace
	FileInfo Class
	DirectoryName Property
	Name Property

Win32 API Function Call	*Class Library Equivalent* *(Italics Represent Peripherally Related Items)*
	FileSystemInfo Class
	FullName Property
	Name Property
GetFileType	—
GetFileVersionInfo	System.IO Namespace
	FileVersionInfo Class
	Comments Property
	CompanyName Property
	FileDescription Property
	FileMajorPart Property
	FileMinorPart Property
	FileName Property
	FilePrivatePart Property
	FileVersion Property
	InternalName Property
	LegalCopyright Property
	LegalTrademarks Property
	OriginalFilename Property
	ProductBuildPart Property
	ProductMajorPart Property
	ProductMinorPart Property
	ProductName Property
	ProductPrivatePart Property
	ProductVersion Property
GetFileVersionInfoSize	—
GetFocus	*System.Windows.Forms*
	Control Class
	Focused Property
GetFontData	*System.Drawing*
	Font Class
GetFontLanguageInfo	*System.Drawing*
	Font Class

Win32 API Function Call	Class Library Equivalent (Italics Represent Peripherally Related Items)
GetFontUnicodeRanges	*System.Drawing*
	Font Class
GetForegroundWindow	—
GetForm	—
GetFullPathName	System.IO Namespace
	FileSystemInfo Class
	FullName Property
GetGeoInfo	—
GetGlyphIndices	—
GetGlyphOutline	—
GetGraphicsMode	—
GetGuiResources	—
GetGuiThreadInfo	—
GetHandleInformation	—
GetIconInfo	System.Drawing
	Icon Class
GetInputState	—
GetJob	—
GetKBCodePage	—
GetKerningPairs	—
GetKeyboardLayout	System.Windows.Forms
	InputLanguage Class
	LayoutName Property
GetKeyboardLayoutList	—
GetKeyboardLayoutName	System.Windows.Forms
	InputLanguage Class
	LayoutName Property
GetKeyboardState	—
GetKeyboardType	—
GetKeyNameText	—
GetKeyState	—
GetLargestConsoleWindowSize	—

Win32 API Function Call	Class Library Equivalent (Italics Represent Peripherally Related Items)
GetLastActivePopup	—
GetLastError	System Namespace *Exception Class*
GetLastInputInfo	—
GetLayeredWindowAttributes	—
GetLayout	—
GetListBoxInfo	System.Windows.Forms ListBox Control
GetLocaleInfo	—
GetLocalTime	System Namespace DateTime Class Now Property
GetLogicalDrives	System.IO Namespace Directory Class GetLogicalDrives Method
GetLogicalDriveStrings	System.IO Namespace *Directory Class* *GetLogicalDrives Method*
GetLongPathName	—
GetMailslotInfo	—
GetMapMode	—
GetMappedFileName	—
GetMenu	System.Windows.Forms Namespace Form Class Menu Property
GetMenuBarInfo	—
GetMenuCheckMarkDimensions	—
GetMenuDefaultItem	System.Windows.Forms Namespace MenuItem Class DefaultItem Property
GetMenuInfo	System.Windows.Forms Namespace *Menu Class* *MenuItem Class*

Win32 API Function Call	Class Library Equivalent (Italics Represent Peripherally Related Items)
GetMenuItemCount	System.Windows.Forms Namespace
	Menu.MenuItemCollection Class
	Count Property
GetMenuItemID	System.Windows.Forms Namespace
	MenuItem Class
	MenuID Property
GetMenuItemInfo	System.Windows.Forms Namespace
	MenuItem Class
GetMenuItemRect	—
GetMenuState	System.Windows.Forms Namespace
	MenuItem Class
	BarBreak Property
	Break Property
	Checked Property
	Enabled Property
	OwnerDraw Property
GetMenuString	—
GetMessage	—
GetMessageExtraInfo	—
GetMessagePos	—
GetMessageTime	—
GetMetaFileBitsEx	—
GetMetaRgn	—
GetMiterLimit	*System.Drawing Namespace*
	Pen Class
GetModuleBaseName	—
GetModuleFileName	—
GetModuleFileNameEx	—
GetModuleHandle	—
GetModuleInformation	—
GetMonitorInfo	—
GetMouseMovePointsEx	—

Win32 API Function Call	Class Library Equivalent *(Italics Represent Peripherally Related Items)*
GetMsgProc	—
GetNamedPipeHandleState	—
GetNamedPipeInfo	—
GetNearestColor	*System.Drawing Namespace* *KnownColor Enumeration*
GetNearestPaletteIndex	—
GetNextDlgGroupItem	—
GetNextDlgTabItem	—
GetNextWindow	—
GetNumberFormat	System Namespace String Class Format Method
GetNumberOfConsoleInputEvents	—
GetNumberOfConsoleMouseButtons	—
GetNumberOfEventLogRecords	System.Diagnostics EventLog Class Entries Property EventLogEntryCollection Class Count Property
GetObject	—
GetObjectType	—
GetOEMCP	—
GetOldestEventLogRecord	System.Diagnostics Namespace *EventLog Class* *Entries Property* *EventLogEntryCollection Class*
GetOpenClipboardWindow	—
GetOpenFileName	System.Windows.Forms Namespace FileDialog Class
GetOutlineTextMetrics	—
GetOverlappedResult	—
GetPaletteEntries	—

Win32 API Function Call	Class Library Equivalent (Italics Represent Peripherally Related Items)
GetParent	—
GetPath	System.Drawing.Drawing2D Namespace GraphicsPath Class
GetPixel	—
GetPolyFillMode	—
GetPrinter	—
GetPrinterData	—
GetPrinterDataEx	—
GetPrinterDriver	—
GetPrinterDriverDirectory	—
GetPrintProcessorDirectory	—
GetPriorityClass	System.Diagnostics Namespace Process Class PriorityClass Property
GetPriorityClipboardFormat	—
GetPrivateProfileInt	—
GetPrivateProfileSection	—
GetPrivateProfileSectionNames	—
GetPrivateProfileString	—
GetPrivateProfileStruct	—
GetProcAddress	—
GetProcessAffinityMask	System.Diagnostics Namespace Process Class *ProcessorAffinity Property*
GetProcessDefaultLayout	—
GetProcessHeap	—
GetProcessHeaps	—
GetProcessIoCounters	—
GetProcessMemoryInfo	—
GetProcessPriorityBoost	System.Diagnostics Namespace Process Class PriorityClass Property PriorityBoostEnabled Property

Win32 API Function Call	Class Library Equivalent (Italics Represent Peripherally Related Items)
GetProcessShutdownParameters	—
GetProcessTimes	—
GetProcessVersion	—
GetProcessWindowStation	—
GetProcessWorkingSetSize	—
GetProfileInt	—
GetProfilesDirectory	—
GetProfileSection	—
GetProfileString	—
GetProfileType	—
GetProp	—
GetQueuedCompletionStatus	—
GetQueueStatus	—
GetRandomRgn	—
GetRasterizerCaps	—
GetRawInputBuffer	—
GetRawInputData	—
GetRawInputDeviceInfo	—
GetRawInputDeviceList	—

GetRegionData	System.Drawing Namespace
	    Region Class
	        GetRegionData Method

GetRegisteredRawInputDevices	—

GetRgnBox	System.Drawing Namespace
	    Region Class
	        GetBounds Method

GetROP2	—
GetSaveFileName	—
GetScrollBarInfo	System.Windows.Forms Namespace *ScrollBar Class*
GetScrollInfo	System.Windows.Forms Namespace *ScrollBar Class*

Win32 API Function Call	Class Library Equivalent (Italics Represent Peripherally Related Items)
GetScrollPos	System.Windows.Forms Namespace *ScrollBar Class*
GetScrollRange	System.Windows.Forms Namespace *ScrollBar Class*
GetServiceDisplayName	System.ServiceProcess Namespace ServiceController Class DisplayName Property
GetServiceKeyName	System.ServiceProcess Namespace ServiceController Class ServiceName Property
GetShortPathName	—
GetStartupInfo	—
GetStdHandle	—
GetStockObject	—
GetStretchBltMode	—
GetStringTypeA	—
GetStringTypeEx	—
GetStringTypeW	—
GetSubMenu	System.Windows.Forms Namespace MenuItem Class MenuItems Property
GetSysColor	—
GetSysColorBrush	—
GetSystemDefaultLangID	—
GetSystemDefaultLCID	—
GetSystemDefaultUILanguage	—
GetSystemDirectory	System Namespace Environment Class System.Directory Property
GetSystemInfo	System.Windows.Forms Namespace *SystemInformation Class*

Win32 API Function Call	Class Library Equivalent (Italics Represent Peripherally Related Items)
GetSystemMenu	—
GetSystemMetrics	—
GetSystemPaletteEntries	—
GetSystemPaletteUse	—
GetSystemPowerStatus	—
GetSystemTime	—
GetSystemTimeAdjustment	—
GetSystemTimeAsFileTime	—
GetSystemWindowsDirectory	—
GetSystemWow64Directory	—
GetTabbedTextExtent	—
GetTapeParameters	—
GetTapePosition	—
GetTapeStatus	—
GetTempFileName	—
GetTempPath	—
GetTextAlign	—
GetTextCharacterExtra	—
GetTextCharset	—
GetTextCharsetInfo	—
GetTextColor	—
GetTextExtentExPoint	—
GetTextExtentExPointI	—
GetTextExtentPoint	—
GetTextExtentPoint32	—
GetTextExtentPointI	—
GetTextFace	—
GetTextMetrics	—
GetThreadContext	—
GetThreadDesktop	—
GetThreadLocale	—

Win32 API Function Call	Class Library Equivalent (Italics Represent Peripherally Related Items)
GetThreadPriority	System.Threading Namespace
	Thread Class
	Priority Property
	ThreadPriority Enumeration
GetThreadPriorityBoost	—
GetThreadSelectorEntry	—
GetThreadTimes	—
GetTickCount	—
GetTimeFormat	System Namespace
	String Class
	Format Method
GetTimeSysInfo	—
GetTimeZoneInformation	System Namespace
	TimeZone Class
	CurrentTimeZone Class
	DaylightName Property
	StandardName Property
GetTitleBarInfo	—
GetTopWindow	—
GetUpdateRect	System.Drawing Namespace
GetUpdateRgn	System.Drawing Namespace
GetUserDefaultLangID	—
GetUserDefaultLCID	—
GetUserDefaultUILanguage	—
GetUserGeoID	—
GetUserName	—
GetUserNameEx	—
GetUserObjectInformation	—
GetUserProfileDirectory	—
GetVersion	System Namespace
	OperatingSystem Class
	Version Property

Win32 API Function Call	Class Library Equivalent (Italics Represent Peripherally Related Items)
GetVersionEx	System Namespace
	OperatingSystem Class
	Version Property
GetViewportExtEx	—
GetViewportOrgEx	—
GetVolumeInformation	—
GetVolumeNameForVolumeMountPoint	—
GetVolumePathName	—
GetVolumePathNamesForVolumeName	—
GetWindow	System.Windows.Forms Namespace
	Form Class
	Owner Property
GetWindowDC	—
GetWindowExtEx	—
GetWindowInfo	System.Windows.Forms Namespace
	Form Class
	FormBorderStyle Property
GetWindowLong	—
GetWindowLongPtr	—
GetWindowModuleFileName	—
GetWindowOrgEx	—
GetWindowPlacement	—
GetWindowRect	—
GetWindowRgn	—
GetWindowRgnBox	—
GetWindowsDirectory	System.Management Namespace
GetWindowText	—
GetWindowTextLength	—
GetWindowThreadProcessId	—
GetWinMetaFileBits	—
GetWorldTransform	—
GetWriteWatch	—

Win32 API Function Call	Class Library Equivalent (Italics Represent Peripherally Related Items)
GetWsChanges	—
GlobalAddAtom	—
GlobalAlloc	—
GlobalDeleteAtom	—
GlobalDiscard	—
GlobalFindAtom	—
GlobalFlags	—
GlobalFree	—
GlobalGetAtomName	—
GlobalHandle	—
GlobalLock	—
GlobalMemoryStatus	—
GlobalMemoryStatusEx	—
GlobalReAlloc	—
GlobalSize	—
GlobalUnlock	—
GradientFill	System.Drawing.Drawing2D Namespace LinearGradientBrush Class
GrayString	—
Handler	—
HandlerEx	—
HandlerRoutine	—
Heap32First	—
Heap32ListFirst	—
Heap32ListNext	—
Heap32Next	—
HeapAlloc	—
HeapCompact	—
HeapCreate	—
HeapDestroy	—
HeapFree	—
HeapLock	—

Win32 API Function Call	Class Library Equivalent *(Italics Represent Peripherally Related Items)*
HeapReAlloc	—
HeapSize	—
HeapUnlock	—
HeapValidate	—
HeapWalk	—
HideCaret	—
HiliteMenuItem	System.Windows.Forms Namespace
	MenuItem Class
	PerformSelect Method
ImmAssociateContext	—
ImmAssociateContextEx	—
ImmConfigureIME	—
ImmCreateContext	—
ImmDestroyContext	—
ImmDisableIME	—
ImmEnumInputContext	—
ImmEnumRegisterWord	—
ImmEscape	—
ImmGetCandidateList	—
ImmGetCandidateListCount	—
ImmGetCandidateWindow	—
ImmGetCompositionFont	—
ImmGetCompositionString	—
ImmGetCompositionWindow	—
ImmGetContext	—
ImmGetConversionList	—
ImmGetConversionStatus	—
ImmGetDefaultIMEWnd	—
ImmGetDescription	—
ImmGetGuideLine	—
ImmGetImeFileName	—
ImmGetImeMenuItems	—

Win32 API Function Call	Class Library Equivalent (Italics Represent Peripherally Related Items)
ImmGetOpenStatus	—
ImmGetProperty	—
ImmGetRegisterWordStyle	—
ImmGetStatusWindowPos	—
ImmGetVirtualKey	—
ImmInstallIme	—
ImmIsIme	—
ImmIsUIMessage	—
ImmNotifyIme	—
ImmRegisterWord	—
ImmReleaseContext	—
ImmSetCandidateWindow	—
ImmSetCompositionFont	—
ImmSetCompositionString	—
ImmSetCompositionWindow	—
ImmSetConversionStatus	—
ImmSetOpenStatus	—
ImmSetStatusWindowPos	—
ImmSimulateHotKey	—
ImmUnregisterWord	—
ImpersonateDdeClientWindow	—
InflateRect	System.Drawing Rectangle Class Inflate Method
InitAtomTable	—
InitializeCriticalSection	—
InitializeCriticalSectionAndSpinCount	—
InitializeProcessForWsWatch	—
InitializeSListHead	—
InitiateSystemShutdown	—
InitiateSystemShutdownEx	—
InSendMessage	—

Win32 API Function Call	Class Library Equivalent (Italics Represent Peripherally Related Items)
InSendMessageEx	—
InsertMenu	System.Windows.Forms Namespace
	MenuItem Class
	MenuItems Property
	Menu.MenuItemCollection Class
	Add Method
InsertMenuItem	System.Windows.Forms Namespace
	MenuItem Class
	MenuItems Property
	Menu.MenuItemCollection Class
	Add Method
Int32x32To64	—
Int64ShllMod32	—
Int64ShraMod32	—
Int64ShrlMod32	—
InterlockedCompareExchange	—
InterlockedCompareExchangePointer	—
InterlockedDecrement	System.Threading Namespace
	Interlocked Class
	Decrement Method
InterlockedExchange	—
InterlockedExchangeAdd	—
InterlockedExchangePointer	—
InterlockedFlushSList	—
InterlockedIncrement	System.Threading Namespace
	Interlocked Class
	Increment Method
InterlockedPopEntrySList	—
InterlockedPushEntrySList	—
IntersectClipRect	System.Drawing Namespace
IntersectRect	System.Drawing Namespace
	Region Class
	Intersect Method

Win32 API Function Call	Class Library Equivalent (Italics Represent Peripherally Related Items)
InvalidateRect	—
InvalidateRgn	—
InvertRect	—
InvertRgn	—
IsBadCodePtr	—
IsBadReadPtr	—
IsBadStringPtr	—
IsBadWritePtr	—

IsCharAlpha	System Namespace
	    Char Structure
	        IsLetter Method

IsCharAlphaNumeric	System Namespace
	    Char Structure
	        IsLetterOrDigit Method

IsCharLower	System Namespace
	    Char Structure
	        IsLower Method

IsCharUpper	System Namespace
	    Char Structure
	        IsUpper Method

IsChild	—
IsClipboardFormatAvailable	—
IsDBCSLeadByte	—
IsDBCSLeadByteEx	—
IsDebuggerPresent	—
IsDialogMessage	—
IsDlgButtonChecked	—
IsGUIThread	—
IsIconic	—
IsMenu	—
IsProcessInJob	—
IsProcessorFeaturePresent	—

Win32 API Function Call	Class Library Equivalent (Italics Represent Peripherally Related Items)
IsRectEmpty	—
IsSystemResumeAutomatic	—
IsTextUnicode	—
IsValidCodePage	—
IsValidLanguageGroup	—
IsValidLocale	—
IsWindow	—
IsWindowEnabled	—
IsWindowUnicode	—
IsWindowVisible	—
IsZoomed	—
JournalPlaybackProc	—
JournalRecordProc	—
keybd_event	—
KeyboardProc	—
KillTimer	System.Threading Namespace Timer Class Dispose Method
LCMapString	—
LeaveCriticalSection	—
LineDDA	—
LineDDAProc	—
LineTo	System.Drawing Namespace Graphics Class DrawLine Method
LoadAccelerators	—
LoadBitmap	System.Drawing Namespace Bitmap Class Constructor
LoadCursor	—
LoadCursorFromFile	—

Win32 API Function Call	Class Library Equivalent *(Italics Represent Peripherally Related Items)*
LoadIcon	System.Windows.Forms Cursor Class Constructor
LoadImage	—
LoadKeyboardLayout	—
LoadLibrary	—
LoadLibraryEx	—
LoadMenu	—
LoadMenuIndirect	—
LoadModule	—
LoadResource	—
LoadString	—
LoadUserProfile	—
LocalAlloc	—
LocalDiscard	—
LocalFileTimeToFileTime	—
LocalFlags	—
LocalFree	—
LocalHandle	—
LocalLock	—
LocalReAlloc	—
LocalSize	—
LocalUnlock	—
LockFile	—
LockFileEx	—
LockResource	—
LockServiceDatabase	—
LockSetForegroundWindow	—
LockWindowUpdate	—
LockWorkStation	—
LogTimeProvEvent	—
LookupIconIdFromDirectory	—

Win32 API Function Call	Class Library Equivalent (Italics Represent Peripherally Related Items)
LookupIconIdFromDirectoryEx	—
LowLevelKeyboardProc	—
LowLevelMouseProc	—
LPtoDP	—
lstrcat	System Namespace
	String Class
	Concat Method
	System.Text Namespace
	StringBuilder Class
lstrcmp	System Namespace
	String Class
	Compare Method
lstrcmpi	System Namespace
	String Class
	Compare Method
lstrcpy	System Namespace
	String Class
	Copy Method
lstrcpyn	System Namespace
	String Class
	Copy Method
lstrlen	System Namespace
	String Class
	Length Property
LZClose	System.IO Namespace
	FileInfo Class
LZCopy	System.IO Namespace
	FileInfo Class
LZInit	System.IO Namespace
	FileInfo Class
LZOpenFile	System.IO Namespace
	FileInfo Class

Win32 API Function Call	Class Library Equivalent (Italics Represent Peripherally Related Items)
LZRead	System.IO Namespace
	FileInfo Class
LZSeek	System.IO Namespace
	Stream Class
	Seek Method
MapDialogRect	—
MapUserPhysicalPages	—
MapUserPhysicalPagesScatter	—
MapViewOfFile	—
MapViewOfFileEx	—
MapVirtualKey	—
MapVirtualKeyEx	—
MapWindowPoints	—
MaskBlt	—
MenuItemFromPoint	—
MessageBeep	—
MessageBox	System.Windows.Forms Namespace
	MessageBox Class
	Constructor
MessageBoxEx	System.Windows.Forms Namespace
	MessageBox Class
	Constructor
MessageBoxIndirect	—
MessageProc	—
ModifyMenu	—
ModifyWorldTransform	—
Module32First	—
Module32Next	—
MonitorEnumProc	—
MonitorFromPoint	—
MonitorFromRect	—
MonitorFromWindow	—

Win32 API Function Call	Class Library Equivalent *(Italics Represent Peripherally Related Items)*
mouse_event	—
MouseProc	—

MoveFile	System.IO Namespace
	    FileInfo Class
	        MoveTo Method

MoveFileEx	System.IO Namespace
	    FileInfo Class
	        MoveTo Method

MoveFileWithProgress	System.IO Namespace
	    FileInfo Class
	        MoveTo Method

MoveMemory	—
MoveToEx	—

MoveWindow	System.Windows.Forms Namespace
	    Control Class
	        Height Property
	        Left Property
	        Size Property
	        Top Property
	        Width Property
	    Form Class
	        Height Property
	        Left Property
	        Size Property
	        Top Property
	        Width Property

MsgWaitForMultipleObjects	System.Threading Namespace
	    ThreadPool Class
	        RegisterWaitForSingleObject Method

MsgWaitForMultipleObjectsEx	System.Threading Namespace
	    ThreadPool Class
	        RegisterWaitForSingleObject Method

B

WIN32 API-TO-
NAMESPACE
CROSS-REFERENCE

Win32 API Function Call	Class Library Equivalent (Italics Represent Peripherally Related Items)
MulDiv	—
MultiByteToWideChar	—
NetAccessAdd	—
NetAccessCheck	—
NetAccessDel	—
NetAccessEnum	—
NetAccessGetInfo	—
NetAccessGetUserPerms	—
NetAccessSetInfo	—
NetAlertRaise	—
NetAlertRaiseEx	—
NetApiBufferAllocate	—
NetApiBufferFree	—
NetApiBufferReallocate	—
NetApiBufferSize	—
NetAuditClear	—
NetAuditRead	—
NetAuditWrite	—
NetConfigGet	—
NetConfigGetAll	—
NetConfigSet	—
NetConnectionEnum	—
NetDfsAdd	—
NetDfsAddFtRoot	—
NetDfsAddStdRoot	—
NetDfsAddStdRootForced	—
NetDfsEnum	—
NetDfsGetClientInfo	—
NetDfsGetInfo	—
NetDfsManagerInitialize	—
NetDfsRemove	—
NetDfsRemoveFtRoot	—

Win32 API Function Call	Class Library Equivalent (Italics Represent Peripherally Related Items)
NetDfsRemoveFtRootForced	—
NetDfsRemoveStdRoot	—
NetDfsSetClientInfo	—
NetDfsSetInfo	—
NetErrorLogClear	—
NetErrorLogRead	—
NetErrorLogWrite	—
NetFileClose	—
NetFileClose2	—
NetFileEnum	—
NetFileGetInfo	—
NetGetAnyDCName	—
NetGetDCName	—
NetGetDisplayInformationIndex	—
NetGetJoinableOUs	—
NetGetJoinInformation	—
NetGroupAdd	—
NetGroupAddUser	—
NetGroupDel	—
NetGroupDelUser	—
NetGroupEnum	—
NetGroupGetInfo	—
NetGroupGetUsers	—
NetGroupSetInfo	—
NetGroupSetUsers	—
NetJoinDomain	—
NetLocalGroupAdd	—
NetLocalGroupAddMember	—
NetLocalGroupAddMembers	—
NetLocalGroupDel	—
NetLocalGroupDelMember	—
NetLocalGroupDelMembers	—

Win32 API Function Call	Class Library Equivalent (Italics Represent Peripherally Related Items)
NetLocalGroupEnum	—
NetLocalGroupGetInfo	—
NetLocalGroupGetMembers	—
NetLocalGroupSetInfo	—
NetLocalGroupSetMembers	—
NetMessageBufferSend	—
NetMessageNameAdd	—
NetMessageNameDel	—
NetMessageNameEnum	—
NetMessageNameGetInfo	—
NetQueryDisplayInformation	—
NetRemoteComputerSupports	—
NetRemoteTOD	—
NetRenameMachineInDomain	—
NetReplExportDirAdd	—
NetReplExportDirDel	—
NetReplExportDirEnum	—
NetReplExportDirGetInfo	—
NetReplExportDirLock	—
NetReplExportDirSetInfo	—
NetReplExportDirUnlock	—
NetReplGetInfo	—
NetReplImportDirAdd	—
NetReplImportDirDel	—
NetReplImportDirEnum	—
NetReplImportDirGetInfo	—
NetReplImportDirLock	—
NetReplImportDirUnlock	—
NetReplSetInfo	—
NetScheduleJobAdd	—
NetScheduleJobDel	—
NetScheduleJobEnum	—

Win32 API Function Call	Class Library Equivalent (Italics Represent Peripherally Related Items)
NetScheduleJobGetInfo	—
NetSecurityGetInfo	—
NetServerComputerNameAdd	—
NetServerComputerNameDel	—
NetServerDiskEnum	—
NetServerEnum	—
NetServerGetInfo	—
NetServerSetInfo	—
NetServerTransportAdd	—
NetServerTransportAddEx	—
NetServerTransportDel	—
NetServerTransportEnum	—
NetServiceControl	—
NetServiceEnum	—
NetServiceGetInfo	—
NetServiceInstall	—
NetSessionDel	—
NetSessionEnum	—
NetSessionGetInfo	—
NetShareAdd	—
NetShareCheck	—
NetShareDel	—
NetShareEnum	—
NetShareGetInfo	—
NetShareSetInfo	—
NetStatisticsGet	—
NetUnjoinDomain	—
NetUseAdd	—
NetUseDel	—
NetUseEnum	—
NetUseGetInfo	—
NetUserAdd	—

Win32 API Function Call	Class Library Equivalent (Italics Represent Peripherally Related Items)
NetUserChangePassword	—
NetUserDel	—
NetUserEnum	—
NetUserGetGroups	—
NetUserGetInfo	—
NetUserGetLocalGroups	—
NetUserModalsGet	—
NetUserModalsSet	—
NetUserSetGroups	—
NetUserSetInfo	—
NetValidateName	—
NetWkstaGetInfo	—
NetWkstaSetInfo	—
NetWkstaTransportAdd	—
NetWkstaTransportDel	—
NetWkstaTransportEnum	—
NetWkstaUserEnum	—
NetWkstaUserGetInfo	—
NetWkstaUserSetInfo	—
NotifyBootConfigStatus	—
NotifyChangeEventLog	—
OemKeyScan	—
OemToChar	—
OemToCharBuff	—

OffsetClipRgn	System.Drawing
	    Region Class
	        Translate Method

OffsetRect	System.Drawing
	    Rectangle Structure
	        Offset Method

OffsetRgn	System.Drawing
	    Region Class
	        Translate Method

Win32 API Function Call	Class Library Equivalent *(Italics Represent Peripherally Related Items)*
OffsetViewportOrgEx	—
OffsetWindowOrgEx	—
OFNHookProc	—
OFNHookProcOldStyle	—
OpenBackupEventLog	—
OpenClipboard	System.Windows.Forms Namespace Clipboard Class GetDataObjectMethod
OpenDesktop	—
OpenEvent	—
OpenEventLog	System.Diagnostics Namespace EventLog Class Constructor
OpenFile	System.IO Namespace FileInfo Class Open Method
OpenFileMapping	—
OpenIcon	—
OpenInputDesktop	—
OpenJobObject	—
OpenMutex	System.Threading Namespace *Mutex Class*
OpenPrinter	System.Drawing.Printing Namespace PrintDocument Class
OpenProcess	System.Diagnostics Namespace *Process Class*
OpenSCManager	—
OpenSemaphore	—
OpenService	System.ServiceProcess ServiceController Class
OpenThread	System.Threading Namespace *Thread Class*

Win32 API Function Call	Class Library Equivalent (Italics Represent Peripherally Related Items)
OpenWaitableTimer	System.Threading Namespace
	Timer Class
OpenWindowStation	—
OutputDebugString	—
OutputProc	—
PackDDElParam	—
PagePaintHook	—
PageSetupDlg	—
PageSetupHook	—
PaintDesktop	—
PaintRgn	System.Drawing
	Graphics Class
	FillRegion Method
PatBlt	—
PathToRegion	System.Drawing
	Region Class
	Constructor
PdhAddCounter	—
PdhBrowseCounters	—
PdhCalculateCounterFromRawValue	—
PdhCloseLog	—
PdhCloseQuery	—
PdhCollectQueryData	—
PdhCollectQueryDataEx	—
PdhComputeCounterStatistics	—
PdhConnectMachine	—
PdhEnumMachines	—
PdhEnumObjectItems	—
PdhEnumObjects	—
PdhExpandCounterPath	—
PdhExpandWildCardPath	—
PdhFormatFromRawValue	—

Win32 API Function Call	Class Library Equivalent (Italics Represent Peripherally Related Items)
PdhGetCounterInfo	—
PdhGetCounterTimeBase	—
PdhGetDataSourceTimeRange	—
PdhGetDefaultPerfCounter	—
PdhGetDefaultPerfObject	—
PdhGetDllVersion	—
PdhGetFormattedCounterArray	—
PdhGetFormattedCounterValue	—
PdhGetLogFileSize	—
PdhGetRawCounterArray	—
PdhGetRawCounterValue	—
PdhIsRealTimeQuery	—
PdhLookupPerfIndexByName	—
PdhLookupPerfNameByIndex	—
PdhMakeCounterPath	—
PdhObjectHasInstances	—
PdhOpenLog	—
PdhOpenQuery	—
PdhParseCounterPath	—
PdhParseInstanceName	—
PdhReadRawLogRecord	—
PdhRemoveCounter	—
PdhSelectDataSource	—
PdhSetCounterScaleFactor	—
PdhSetDefaultRealTimeDataSource	—
PdhSetQueryTimeRange	—
PdhUpdateLog	—
PdhUpdateLogFileCatalog	—
PdhValidatePath	—
PeekConsoleInput	—
PeekMessage	—
PeekNamedPipe	—

Win32 API Function Call	Class Library Equivalent (Italics Represent Peripherally Related Items)
Pie	System.Drawing Namespace
	Graphics Class
	DrawPie Method
PlayEnhMetaFile	—
PlayEnhMetaFileRecord	—
PlayMetaFile	—
PlayMetaFileRecord	—
PlgBlt	—
PolyBezier	System.Drawing Namespace
	Graphics Class
	DrawBezier Method
	DrawBeziers Method
PolyBezierTo	System.Drawing Namespace
	Graphics Class
	DrawBezier Method
	DrawBeziers Method
PolyDraw	System.Drawing Namespace
	Graphics Class
	DrawBezier Method
	DrawLine Method
Polygon	System.Drawing Namespace
	Graphics Class
	DrawPolygon Method
Polyline	System.Drawing Namespace
	Graphics Class
	DrawPolygon Method
	DrawLines Method
PolylineTo	System.Drawing Namespace
	Graphics Class
	DrawLine Method
	DrawLines Method

Win32 API Function Call	Class Library Equivalent (Italics Represent Peripherally Related Items)
PolyPolygon	System.Drawing Namespace
	Graphics Class
	DrawPolygon Method
PolyPolyline	System.Drawing Namespace
	Graphics Class
	DrawLines Method
PolyTextOut	System.Drawing Namespace
	Graphics Class
	DrawString Method
PostMessage	System.Messaging Namespace
	MessageQueue Class
	Send Method
PostQueuedCompletionStatus	—
PostQuitMessage	—
PostThreadMessage	—
PrepareTape	—
PrintDlg	System.Windows.Forms
	PrintDialog
PrintDlgEx	System.Windows.Forms
	PrintDialog
PrinterProperties	System.Windows.Forms
	PrintDialog
	PrinterSettings Property
	System.Drawing.Printing
	PrinterSettings Class
PrintHookProc	—
PrintWindow	—
Process32First	—
Process32Next	—
PropEnumProc	—
PropEnumProcEx	—

Win32 API Function Call	Class Library Equivalent (Italics Represent Peripherally Related Items)
PtInRect	System.Drawing Namespace
	Graphics Class
	IsVisible Method
	Rectangle Structure
	Contains Method
PtInRegion	System.Drawing Namespace
	Graphics Class
	IsVisible Method
	Region Class
	IsVisible Method
PtVisible	System.Drawing Namespace
	Graphics Class
	IsVisible Method
	Region Class
	IsVisible Method
PulseEvent	System.Threading
PurgeComm	—
QueryDosDevice	—
QueryInformationJobObject	—
QueryPerformanceCounter	—
QueryPerformanceFrequency	—
QueryRecoveryAgentsOnEncryptedFile	—
QueryServiceConfig	System.ServiceProcess Namespace
	ServiceController Class
QueryServiceConfig2	System.ServiceProcess Namespace
	ServiceController Class
QueryServiceLockStatus	System.ServiceProcess Namespace
	ServiceController Class
QueryServiceStatus	System.ServiceProcess Namespace
	ServiceController Class
	Status Property

Win32 API Function Call	Class Library Equivalent (Italics Represent Peripherally Related Items)
QueryServiceStatusEx	System.ServiceProcess Namespace
	ServiceController Class
	Status Property
QueryUsersOnEncryptedFile	—
QueryWorkingSet	—
QueueUserAPC	—
QueueUserWorkItem	—
RaiseException	System Namespace
	Exception Class
ReadConsole	System Namespace
	Console Class
	Read Method
	ReadLine Method
ReadConsoleInput	System Namespace
	Console Class
	Read Method
	ReadLine Method
ReadConsoleOutput	—
ReadConsoleOutputAttribute	—
ReadConsoleOutputCharacter	—
ReadDirectoryChangesW	*System.IO*
	FileSystemWatcher Class
ReadEventLog	System.Diagnostics Namespace
	EventLog Class
	Entries Property
ReadFile	System.IO Namespace
	FileStream Class
	Read Method
ReadFileEx	System.IO Namespace
	FileStream Class
	Read Method
ReadFileScatter	—

Win32 API Function Call	Class Library Equivalent (Italics Represent Peripherally Related Items)
ReadPrinter	—
ReadProcessMemory	—
RealChildWindowFromPoint	—
RealGetWindowClass	—
RealizePalette	—

Rectangle	System.Drawing Namespace
	    Graphics Class
	        Draw Rectangle

RectInRegion	System.Drawing Namespace
	    Graphics Class
	        IsVisible Method
	    Region Class
	        IsVisible Method

RectVisible	System.Drawing Namespace
	    Graphics Class
	        IsVisible Method
	    Region Class
	        IsVisible Method

RedrawWindow	—

RegCloseKey	Microsoft.Win32 Namespace
	    RegistryKey Class
	        Close Method

RegConnectRegistry	Microsoft.Win32 Namespace *Registry Class*

RegCreateKey	Microsoft.Win32 Namespace
	    RegistryKey Class
	        CreateSubKey Method

RegCreateKeyEx	Microsoft.Win32 Namespace
	    RegistryKey Class
	        CreateSubKey Method

RegDeleteKey	Microsoft.Win32 Namespace
	    RegistryKey Class
	        DeleteSubKey Method

Win32 API Function Call	Class Library Equivalent *(Italics Represent Peripherally Related Items)*
RegDeleteValue	Microsoft.Win32 Namespace
	RegistryKey Class
	DeleteValue Method
RegDisablePredefinedCache	—
RegEnumKey	Microsoft.Win32 Namespace
	RegistryKey Class
	GetSubKeyNames Method
RegEnumKeyEx	Microsoft.Win32 Namespace
	RegistryKey Class
	GetSubKeyNames Method
RegEnumValue	Microsoft.Win32 Namespace
	RegistryKey Class
	GetValues Method
	GetValueNames Method
RegFlushKey	Microsoft.Win32 Namespace
	RegistryKey Class
	SetValue Method
RegisterClass	—
RegisterClassEx	—
RegisterClipboardFormat	—
RegisterDeviceNotification	—
RegisterEventSource	—
RegisterHotKey	—
RegisterRawInputDevices	—
RegisterServiceCtrlHandler	—
RegisterServiceCtrlHandlerEx	—
RegisterWaitForSingleObject	—
RegisterWindowMessage	—
RegLoadKey	Microsoft.Win32 Namespace
	RegistryKey Class
RegNotifyChangeKeyValue	—
RegOpenCurrentUser	—

Win32 API Function Call	Class Library Equivalent (Italics Represent Peripherally Related Items)
RegOpenKey	Microsoft.Win32 Namespace *RegistryKey Class*
RegOpenKeyEx	Microsoft.Win32 Namespace *RegistryKey Class*
RegOpenUserClassesRoot	—
RegOverridePredefKey	—
RegQueryInfoKey	—
RegQueryMultipleValues	—
RegQueryValue	Microsoft.Win32 Namespace *RegistryKey Class* *GetValue Method*
RegQueryValueEx	Microsoft.Win32 Namespace *RegistryKey Class* *GetValue Method*
RegReplaceKey	—
RegRestoreKey	—
RegSaveKey	—
RegSetValue	Microsoft.Win32 Namespace *RegistryKey Class* *SetValue Method*
RegSetValueEx	Microsoft.Win32 Namespace *RegistryKey Class* *SetValue Method*
RegUnLoadKey	—
ReleaseCapture	—
ReleaseDC	—
ReleaseMutex	System.Threading Namespace Mutex Class ReleaseMutex Method
ReleaseSemaphore	—
RemoveDirectory	System.IO Namespace DirectoryInfo Class Delete Method

Win32 API Function Call	Class Library Equivalent (Italics Represent Peripherally Related Items)
RemoveFontMemResourceEx	—
RemoveFontResource	—
RemoveFontResourceEx	—
RemoveMenu	—
RemoveProp	—
RemoveUsersFromEncryptedFile	—
RemoveVectoredExceptionHandler	—
ReplaceFile	System.IO Namespace FileInfo Class
ReplaceText	—
ReplyMessage	—
ReportEvent	—
ReportFault	—
RequestWakeupLatency	—
ResetDC	—

ResetEvent	System.Threading Namespace
	    ManualResetEvent Class
	        Reset Method

ResetPrinter	—
ResetWriteWatch	—
ResizePalette	—
RestoreDC	—

ResumeThread	System.Threading Namespace
	    Thread Class
	        Resume Method

ReuseDDElParam	—

RoundRect	System.Drawing Namespace
	    Graphics Class
	        DrawRectangle Method

Rectangle Structure	
	Pen Class

Win32 API Function Call	Class Library Equivalent (Italics Represent Peripherally Related Items)

SaveDC	System.Drawing
	    Graphics Class
	        Save Method

ScaleViewportExtEx	—
ScaleWindowExtEx	—
ScheduleJob	—
ScreenToClient	—
ScriptApplyDigitSubstitution	—
ScriptApplyLogicalWidth	—
ScriptBreak	—
ScriptCacheGetHeight	—
ScriptCPtoX	—
ScriptFreeCache	—
ScriptGetCMap	—
ScriptGetFontProperties	—
ScriptGetGlyphABCWidth	—
ScriptGetLogicalWidths	—
ScriptGetProperties	—
ScriptIsComplex	—
ScriptItemize	—
ScriptJustify	—
ScriptLayout	—
ScriptPlace	—
ScriptRecordDigitSubstitution	—
ScriptShape	—
ScriptString_pcOutChars	—
ScriptString_pLogAttr	—
ScriptString_pSize	—
ScriptStringAnalyze	—
ScriptStringCPtoX	—
ScriptStringFree	—
ScriptStringGetLogicalWidths	—

Win32 API Function Call	Class Library Equivalent (Italics Represent Peripherally Related Items)
ScriptStringGetOrder	—
ScriptStringOut	—
ScriptStringValidate	—
ScriptStringXtoCP	—
ScriptTextOut	—
ScriptXtoCP	—
ScrollConsoleScreenBuffer	—
ScrollDC	—
ScrollWindow	—
ScrollWindowEx	—
SearchPath	System.IO Namespace Directory Class FileInfo Class Exists Property
SelectClipPath	System.Drawing.Drawing2D CombineMode Enumeration GraphicsPath Class System.Drawing.Namespace Graphics Class SetClip Method
SelectClipRgn	System.Drawing.Drawing2D CombineMode Enumeration GraphicsPath Class System.Drawing.Namespace RegionClass Graphics Class SetClip Method
SelectObject	—
SelectPalette	—
SendAsyncProc	—
SendDlgItemMessage	—
SendInput	—

Win32 API Function Call	Class Library Equivalent (Italics Represent Peripherally Related Items)
SendMessage	—
SendMessageCallback	—
SendMessageTimeout	—
SendNotifyMessage	—
ServiceMain	—
SetAbortProc	System.Drawing.Printing PrintPageEventArgs Class Cancel Property
SetActiveWindow	System.Windows.Forms Namespace Form Class Activate Method
SetArcDirection	—
SetBitmapBits	—
SetBitmapDimensionEx	—
SetBkColor	—
SetBkMode	—
SetBoundsRect	—
SetBrushOrgEx	—
SetCalendarInfo	—
SetCapture	—
SetCaretBlinkTime	—
SetCaretPos	—
SetClassLong	—
SetClassLongPtr	—
SetClassWord	—
SetClipboardData	System.Windows.Forms Namespace Clipboard Class SetDataObject Method
SetClipboardViewer	—
SetColorAdjustment	—
SetCommBreak	—
SetCommConfig	—

Win32 API Function Call	Class Library Equivalent (Italics Represent Peripherally Related Items)
SetCommMask	—
SetCommState	—
SetCommTimeouts	—
SetComputerName	—
SetComputerNameEx	—
SetConsoleActiveScreenBuffer	—
SetConsoleCP	—
SetConsoleCtrlHandler	—
SetConsoleCursorInfo	—
SetConsoleCursorPosition	—
SetConsoleMode	—
SetConsoleOutputCP	—
SetConsoleScreenBufferSize	—
SetConsoleTextAttribute	—
SetConsoleTitle	—
SetConsoleWindowInfo	—
SetCriticalSectionSpinCount	—

SetCurrentDirectory	System.IO Namespace
	    Directory Class
	        SetCurrentDirectory Method

SetCursor	System.Windows.Forms Namespace
	    Cursor Class
	        Current Property
	    Cursors Class

SetCursorPos	System.Windows.Forms Namespace
	    Cursor Class
	        Position Property

SetDCBrushColor	—
SetDCPenColor	—
SetDefaultCommConfig	—
SetDefaultPrinter	—
SetDIBColorTable	—

Win32 API Function Call	Class Library Equivalent (Italics Represent Peripherally Related Items)
SetDIBits	—
SetDIBitsToDevice	—
SetDlgItemInt	—
SetDlgItemText	—
SetDoubleClickTime	—
SetEndOfFile	—
SetEnhMetaFileBits	—
SetEnvironmentVariable	—
SetErrorMode	—

SetEvent	System.Threading Namespace
	    ManualResetEvent Class
	        Constructor
	        Set Method

SetFileApisToANSI	—
SetFileApisToOEM	—

SetFileAttributes	System.IO Namespace
	    File Class
	        SetAttributes Method
	        FileAttributes Enumeration

SetFilePointer	—
SetFilePointerEx	—

SetFileShortName	System.IO Namespace
	    FileInfo Class
	        Name Property

SetFileTime	System.IO Namespace
	    File Class
	        SetCreationTime Method
	        SetLastAccessTime Method
	        SetLastWriteTime Method

SetFileValidData	—

SetFocus	System.Windows.Forms Namespace
	    Form Class
	        Activate Method

Win32 API Function Call	Class Library Equivalent (Italics Represent Peripherally Related Items)
SetForegroundWindow	System.Windows.Forms Namespace
	Form Class
	Activate Method
SetForm	—
SetGraphicsMode	—
SetHandleInformation	—
SetInformationJobObject	—
SetJob	—
SetKeyboardState	—
SetLastError	—
SetLastErrorEx	—
SetLayeredWindowAttributes	—
SetLayout	—
SetLocaleInfo	—
SetLocalTime	—
SetMailslotInfo	—
SetMapMode	—
SetMapperFlags	—
SetMenu	System.Windows.Forms Namespace
	Form Class
	Menu Property
SetMenuDefaultItem	System.Windows.Forms Namespace
	MenuItem Class
	DefaultItem Property
SetMenuInfo	System.Windows.Forms Namespace
	MenuItem Class
SetMenuItemBitmaps	—
SetMenuItemInfo	System.Windows.Forms Namespace
	MenuItem Class
SetMessageExtraInfo	—
SetMetaFileBitsEx	—
SetMetaRgn	—

Win32 API Function Call	Class Library Equivalent *(Italics Represent Peripherally Related Items)*
SetMiterLimit	*System.Drawing Namespace*
	Pen Class
SetNamedPipeHandleState	—
SetPaletteEntries	—
SetParent	System.Windows.Forms Namespace
	Form Class
	Owner Property
SetPixel	System.Drawing Namespace
	Bitmap Class
	SetPixel Method
SetPixelV	—
SetPolyFillMode	—
SetPort	—
SetPrinter	—
SetPrinterData	—
SetPrinterDataEx	—
SetPriorityClass	System.Diagnostics Namespace
	Process Class
	PriorityClass Property
SetProcessAffinityMask	System.Diagnostics.Namespace
	ProcessThread Class
	ProcessAffinity Property
SetProcessDefaultLayout	—
SetProcessPriorityBoost	System.Diagnostics Namespace
	Process Class
	PriorityClass Property
	PriorityBoostEnabled Property
SetProcessShutdownParameters	—
SetProcessWindowStation	—
SetProcessWorkingSetSize	—
SetProp	—

Win32 API Function Call	Class Library Equivalent (Italics Represent Peripherally Related Items)
SetRect	System.Drawing Namespace
	Graphics Class
	DrawRectangle Method
SetRectEmpty	—
SetRectRgn	—
SetROP2	—
SetScrollInfo	—
SetScrollPos	—
SetScrollRange	—
SetServiceBits	—
SetServiceStatus	System.ServiceProcess Namespace
	ServiceController Class
	Status Property
SetStdHandle	—
SetStretchBltMode	—
SetSysColors	—
SetSystemCursor	—
SetSystemPaletteUse	—
SetSystemPowerState	—
SetSystemTime	—
SetSystemTimeAdjustment	—
SetTapeParameters	—
SetTapePosition	—
SetTextAlign	—
SetTextCharacterExtra	—
SetTextColor	—
SetTextJustification	—
SetThreadAffinityMask	—
SetThreadContext	—
SetThreadDesktop	—
SetThreadExecutionState	—

Win32 API Function Call	Class Library Equivalent (Italics Represent Peripherally Related Items)

SetThreadIdealProcessor	System.Diagnostics Namespace
	    ProcessThread Class
	        ResetIdealProcessor Method
	        IdealProcessor Property

SetThreadLocale	—

SetThreadPriority	System.Threading
	    Thread Class
	        Priority Property

SetThreadPriorityBoost	—
SetTimer	—

SetTimeZoneInformation	System Namespace
	    TimeZone Class
	        CurrentTimeZone Property
	        DaylightName Property
	        StandardName Property

SetUnhandledExceptionFilter	—
SetupComm	—
SetupDiCreateDeviceInfoList	—
SetupDiCreateDeviceInfoListEx	—
SetupDiCreateDeviceInterfaceRegKey	—
SetupDiDeleteDeviceInterfaceData	—
SetupDiDeleteDeviceInterfaceRegKey	—
SetupDiDestroyDeviceInfoList	—
SetupDiEnumDeviceInterfaces	—
SetupDiGetClassDevs	—
SetupDiGetClassDevsEx	—
SetupDiGetDeviceInterfaceAlias	—
SetupDiGetDeviceInterfaceDetail	—
SetupDiOpenClassRegKeyEx	—
SetupDiOpenDeviceInterface	—
SetupDiOpenDeviceInterfaceRegKey	—
SetupHookProc	—

Win32 API Function Call	Class Library Equivalent (Italics Represent Peripherally Related Items)
SetUserFileEncryptionKey	—
SetUserGeoID	—
SetUserObjectInformation	—
SetViewportExtEx	—
SetViewportOrgEx	—
SetVolumeLabel	—
SetVolumeMountPoint	—
SetWaitableTimer	—
SetWindowExtEx	—
SetWindowLong	—
SetWindowLongPtr	—
SetWindowOrgEx	—
SetWindowPlacement	—

SetWindowPos	System.Windows.Forms Namespace
	    Form Class
	        Left Property
	        Top Property

SetWindowRgn	—
SetWindowsHookEx	—
SetWindowText	—
SetWinMetaFileBits	—

SetWorldTransform	System.Drawing Namespace
	    Graphics Class
	        RotateTransform Method
	        ScaleTransform Method
	        TranslateTranform Method

ShellProc	—
ShowCaret	—

ShowCursor	System.Windows.Forms Namespace
	    Cursor Class
	        Show Method
	        Hide Method

Win32 API Function Call	Class Library Equivalent (Italics Represent Peripherally Related Items)
ShowOwnedPopups	—
ShowScrollBar	—
ShowWindow	System.Windows.Forms Namespace
	Form Class
	Show Method
	ShowDialog Method
ShowWindowAsync	—
SignalObjectAndWait	—
SizeofResource	—
Sleep	System.Threading Namespace
	Thread Class
	Sleep Method
SleepEx	System.Threading Namespace
	Thread Class
	Sleep Method
StartDoc	System.Drawing.Printing Namespace
	PrintDocument Class
	OnBeginPrint Method
StartDocPrinter	—
StartPage	System.Drawing.Printing Namespace
	PrintController Class
	OnStartPage Method
StartPagePrinter	—
StartService	System.ServiceProcess
	ServiceController Class
	Start Method
StartServiceCtrlDispatcher	—
STM_GETICON	—
STM_GETIMAGE	—
STM_SETICON	—
STM_SETIMAGE	—
STN_CLICKED	—

Win32 API Function Call	Class Library Equivalent (Italics Represent Peripherally Related Items)
STN_DBLCLK	—
STN_DISABLE	—
STN_ENABLE	—
StretchBlt	—
StretchDIBits	—
StrokeAndFillPath	—
StrokePath	—
SubtractRect	—

SuspendThread	System.Threading Namespace
	    Thread Class
	        Suspend Method

SwapMouseButton	—
SwitchDesktop	—
SwitchToFiber	—
SwitchToThread	—
SysMsgProc	—
SystemParametersInfo	—
SystemTimeToFileTime	—
SystemTimeToTzSpecificLocalTime	—
TabbedTextOut	—
TerminateJobObject	—

TerminateProcess	System.Diagnostics Namespace
	    Process Class
	        Close Method

TerminateThread	System.Threading Namespace
	    Thread Class
	        Abort Method

TextOut	—
Thread32First	—
Thread32Next	—
ThreadProc	—

Win32 API Function Call	Class Library Equivalent *(Italics Represent Peripherally Related Items)*

TileWindows	System.Windows.Forms Namespace
	    Form Class
	        LayoutMdi Method

TimeProvClose	—
TimeProvCommand	—
TimeProvOpen	—
TimerAPCProc	—
TimerProc	—

TlsAlloc	System Namespace
	    ThreadStaticAttribute Class
	System.Threading Namespace
	    Thread Class
	        AllocateDataSlot Method
	        AllocateNamedDataSlot Method

TlsFree	System Namespace
	    ThreadStaticAttribute Class
	System.Threading Namespace
	    Thread Class
	        AllocateDataSlot Method
	        AllocateNamedDataSlot Method

TlsGetValue	System Namespace
	    ThreadStaticAttribute Class
	System.Threading Namespace
	    Thread Class
	        GetData Method

TlsSetValue	System Namespace
	    ThreadStaticAttribute Class
	System.Threading Namespace
	    Thread Class
	        SetData Method

ToAscii	—
ToAsciiEx	—

Win32 API Function Call	Class Library Equivalent (Italics Represent Peripherally Related Items)
Toolhelp32ReadProcessMemory	—
ToUnicode	—
ToUnicodeEx	—
TrackMouseEvent	—
TrackPopupMenu	—
TrackPopupMenuEx	—
TransactNamedPipe	—
TranslateAccelerator	—
TranslateCharsetInfo	—
TranslateMDISysAccel	—
TranslateMessage	—
TranslateName	—
TransmitCommChar	—
TransparentBlt	—
TryEnterCriticalSection	—
TzSpecificLocalTimeToSystemTime	—
UInt32x32To64	—
UnhandledExceptionFilter	—
UnhookWindowsHookEx	—
UnionRect	—
UnloadKeyboardLayout	—
UnloadUserProfile	—
UnlockFile	System.IO Namespace FileStream Class Lock Method Unlock Method
UnlockFileEx	System.IO Namespace FileStream Class Lock Method Unlock Method
UnlockServiceDatabase	—
UnmapViewOfFile	—

Win32 API Function Call	Class Library Equivalent (Italics Represent Peripherally Related Items)
UnpackDDElParam	—
UnrealizeObject	—
UnregisterClass	—
UnregisterDeviceNotification	—
UnregisterHotKey	—
UnregisterWait	—
UnregisterWaitEx	—
UpdateColors	—
UpdateLayeredWindow	—
UpdateResource	—
UpdateWindow	—
UserHandleGrantAccess	—
ValidateRect	—
ValidateRgn	—
VectoredHandler	—
VerFindFile	—
VerifyVersionInfo	—
VerInstallFile	—
VerLanguageName	—
VerQueryValue	—
VerSetConditionMask	—
VirtualAlloc	—
VirtualAllocEx	—
VirtualFree	—
VirtualFreeEx	—
VirtualLock	—
VirtualProtect	—
VirtualProtectEx	—
VirtualQuery	—
VirtualQueryEx	—
VirtualUnlock	—
VkKeyScan	—

Win32 API Function Call	Class Library Equivalent (Italics Represent Peripherally Related Items)
VkKeyScanEx	—
WaitCommEvent	—
WaitForDebugEvent	—
WaitForInputIdle	—
WaitForMultipleObjects	—
WaitForMultipleObjectsEx	—
WaitForSingleObject	—
WaitForSingleObjectEx	—
WaitMessage	—
WaitNamedPipe	—
WaitOrTimerCallback	—
WideCharToMultiByte	—
WidenPath	—
WindowFromDC	—
WindowFromPoint	—
WindowProc	—
WinExec	—
WinMain	—
WM_CTLCOLORSTATIC	—

WriteConsole	System Namespace
	    Console Class
	        Write Method
	        WriteLine Method

WriteConsoleInput	—

WriteConsoleOutput	System Namespace
	    Console Class
	        Write Method
	        WriteLine Method

WriteConsoleOutputAttribute	—
WriteConsoleOutputCharacter	—

Win32 API Function Call	Class Library Equivalent (Italics Represent Peripherally Related Items)
WriteFile	System.IO Namespace
	StreamWriter Class
	Write Method
	FileStream Class
	Write Method
WriteFileEx	System.IO
	Stream Class
	BeginWrite Method
	EndWrite Method
WriteFileGather	—
WritePrinter	System.Drawing.Printing
	PrintDocument Class
	Print Method
WritePrivateProfileSection	—
WritePrivateProfileString	—
WritePrivateProfileStruct	—
WriteProcessMemory	—
WriteProfileSection	—
WriteProfileString	—
WriteTapemark	—
wsprintf	—
wvsprintf	—
ZeroMemory	—

.NET Security Models

IN THIS APPENDIX

The .NET Framework provides developers with a multitude of constructs for enforcing application-level security. This appendix describes how security policies work in the Framework and details the two major application security models embraced by the .NET Framework: role-based security and code access security.

Security Policies

When code is loaded into the runtime, the first things the runtime must figure out are "what actions should I allow this code to perform, and what resources should I allow it access to?" This is handled in a straightforward way: Each assembly in .NET exposes a series of characteristics (called *evidence*) that the runtime will examine in order to answer the aforementioned questions. Examples of this evidence include who signed the assembly, where the assembly came from, and so on.

> **NOTE**
>
> Remember that assemblies are units of deployable code.

The supplied evidence is used in conjunction with the established *security policy* to determine which permissions the assembly will be assigned. A security policy is a set of rules that are followed when determining which set of permissions to apply to a specific assembly. In addition to these default permissions applied to the running code, an assembly can also specifically request a set of permissions, usually to indicate that they are needed in order for the assembly to run properly. This request won't cause the runtime to add permissions that aren't covered by a policy, but they can cause the runtime to throw an exception and not load the code if it won't get the permissions it needs to run. To further secure things, the runtime may take away standard permissions from an assembly if it has indicated that it doesn't need them.

The set of default security policies can be altered by administrators through two different tools: the .NET Framework Configuration Tool (an MMC snap-in) and the Code Access Security Policy Tool (a stand-alone executable: caspol.exe). Both of these are shipped with the Framework and are documented in the MSDN framework documentation.

Beyond policies, developers have two ways of further securing their applications: code access security and role-based security.

Code Access Security

Code access security protects managed resources in the runtime from unrestrained code access. In other words, developers can specifically identify which resources can and cannot be accessed by a particular body of code. Code access security can operate at a more granular level than simple security policies in that it can be enforced at the class level or at the class member level, in addition to the assembly level.

Code access security checks are said to happen declaratively or imperatively, and there are two mirrored sets of permission classes that allow this to happen. For imperative security, you would use the core permission class specific to the resource you are interested in. For example, if you want to specify security for file I/O, you would use the `FileIOPermission` class. For declarative security, you would use the permission *attribute* classes. Each permission class has a counterpart permission attribute class for use with declarative security. The declarative counterpart to the `FileIOPermission` class is the `FileIOPermissionAttribute` class.

Declarative Code Access

Declarative security involves placing attributes inside of your code's metadata. As an example, you would use the following syntax to institute file I/O permissions on a class (and all of its members):

```
<FileIOPermissionAttribute(SecurityAction.LinkDemand)> Public Class Test
```

These permission attributes can be applied against assemblies, classes, and class members. Note that the constructor accepts a `SecurityAction` enumeration value. Selecting one security action type over another will affect the results of the code access security check.

Choosing a Security Action

The `SecurityAction` enumeration indicates to the runtime exactly how the specific permission attribute should be evaluated (and when). Table C.1 lists its members.

TABLE C.1 SecurityAction Enumeration

Member	Description
Assert	Instructs the runtime to only examine the current caller of the code to see if he has sufficient privileges to access the indicated resource. Asserts happen at runtime.
Demand	Instructs the runtime to require all callers higher in the call stack to have correct permissions to access the indicated resource. Demands happen at runtime.
Deny	Indicates that no caller can access the specified resource, even if he has the correct permissions.
InheritanceDemand	Indicates that any class which inherits from the current class must have the correct permissions. Inheritance demands happen during the loading of a class or assembly.

TABLE C.1 Continued

Member	Description
LinkDemand	Requires that the immediate caller have the specified resource permission. Link demands happen during the JIT compilation process.
PermitOnly	Specifies that only the resources explicitly identified by the permission class can be accessed. Permit only demands happen during runtime.
RequestMinimum	Requests only the minimum permissions needed for the code to run. This action is only valid for assemblies.
RequestOptional	Requests permissions over and above the baseline needed for the code to run. This action is only valid for assemblies.
RequestRefuse	Requests that the code be denied certain permissions. This action is only valid for assemblies.

The Permission Attribute Classes

Each permission attribute class is designed to protect a specific resource. These classes are all primarily defined inside of the Security.Security.Permissions namespace, although a few of them are defined in other namespaces related to their resource relationship. (For example, the EventLogPermissionAttribute class is defined in the System.Diagnostics namespace, along with the other event log classes.)

Table C.2 itemizes all of the possible permission attribute classes. For the most part, they all support the same methods and properties. See the Framework documentation for more details.

TABLE C.2 Classes for Declarative Code Access Security

Class	Namespace	Description
CodeAccessSecurityAttribute	System.Security.Permissions1	The parent class of all the other attribute classes
DBDataPermissionAttribute	System.Data.Common	Protects access to data exposed by .NET data providers
DirectoryServicesPermissionAttribute	System.DirectoryServices	Protects access to Active Directory resources
DnsPermissionAttribute	System.Net	Protects DNS servers from unauthorized access
EnvironmentPermissionAttribute	System.Security.Permissions	Protects system environment variables from modification and viewing
EventLogPermissionAttribute	System.Diagnostics	Protects read and write operations against event logs
FileDialogPermissionAttribute	System.Security.Permissions	Protects access to common file dialogs
FileIOPermissionAttribute	System.Security.Permissions	Protects files and folders from access
IsolatedStoragePermissionAttribute	System.Security.Permissions	Protects the .NET isolated storage area from unauthorized access
MessageQueuePermissionAttribute	System.Messaging	Protects message queues from unauthorized access
PerformanceCounterPermissionAttribute	System.Diagnostics	Protects the system performance counters from code access
PermissionSetAttribute	System.Security.Permissions	Protects PermissionSet class actions from code access
PrincipalPermissionAttribute	System.Security.Permissions	Protects PrincipalPermissions class actions from code access
PrintingPermissionAttribute	System.Drawing.Printing	Protects printer resources from code access

TABLE C.2 Continued

Class	Namespace	Description
PublisherIdentityPermissionAttribute	System.Security.Permissions	Protects PublisherIdentityPermission class actions from code access
ReflectionPermissionAttribute	System.Security.Permissions	Protects code metadata from code access through the System.Reflection classes
RegistryPermissionAttribute	System.Security.Permissions	Protects the system registries from modificaton
SecurityPermissionAttribute	System.Security.Permissions	Protects SecurityPermission class actions from code access
ServiceControllerPermissionAttribute	System.ServiceProcess	Protects ServiceController class actions from code access
SiteIdentityPermissionAttribute	System.Security.Permissions	Protects manipulation of site evidence
SocketPermissionAttribute	System.Net	Protects sockets from connection attempts
StrongNameIdentityPermissionAttribute	System.Security.Permissions	Protects strong names from manipulation
UIPermissionAttribute	System.Security.Permissions	Protects user interface elements, including the clipboard, from access by unauthorized code
UrlIdentityPermissionAttribute	System.Security.Permissions	Protects URL access and manipulation for an assembly
WebPermissionAttribute	System.Net	Protects access to Internet-based resources
ZoneIdentityPermissionAttribute	System.Security.Permissions	Protects a components zone information from code access

Imperative Code Access

Imperative code access happens at runtime, against a specific class member. This method does not involve the use of attributes. To implement imperative code access security, you simply instantiate an object from one of the permission classes (these resemble the permission attribute classes), and then call one of the object's various security action methods.

The syntax should look more familiar to you than the attribute syntax, because it follows the same code usage patterns as all of the other framework classes. If we were to rewrite our previous declarative example using imperative code access security, it would look like this:

```
Public Sub SomeMethod()
        Dim ioPermission As FileIOPermission

        ioPermission = New FileIOPermission(unrestricted)

        ioPermission.LinkDemand()

        .
        .
        .
End Sub
```

The runtime would throw an exception on the call to LinkDemand if the appropriate permissions were not available; thus, the rest of the code in the method would not run.

The Permission Classes

Table C.3 itemizes the permission classes used for imperative code access security checks.

TABLE C.3 Classes for Imperative Code Access Security

Class	Namespace	Description
CodeAccessPermission	System.Security	The parent class of all the other permission classes
DBDataPermission	System.Data.Common	Protects access to data exposed by .NET data providers
DirectoryServicesPermission	System.DirectoryServices	Protects access to Active Directory resources
DnsPermission	System.Net	Protects DNS servers from unauthorized access
EnvironmentPermission	System.Security.Permissions	Protects system environment variables from modification and viewing
EventLogPermission	System.Diagnostics	Protects read and write operations against event logs
FileDialogPermission	System.Security.Permissions	Protects access to common file dialogs
FileIOPermission	System.Security.Permissions	Protects files and folders from access
IsolatedStoragePermission	System.Security.Permissions	Protects the .NET isolated storage area from unauthorized access
MessageQueuePermission	System.Messaging	Protects message queues from unauthorized access
PerformanceCounterPermission	System.Diagnostics	Protects the system performance counters from code access
PermissionSet	System.Security.Permissions	Protects PermissionSet class actions from code access
PrincipalPermission	System.Security.Permissions	Protects PrincipalPermissions class actions from code access
PrintingPermission	System.Drawing.Printing	Protects printer resources from code access
PublisherIdentityPermission	System.Security.Permissions	Protects PublisherIdentityPermission class actions from code access

TABLE C.3 Continued

Class	Namespace	Description
ReflectionPermission	System.Security.Permissions	Protects code metadata from code access through the System.Reflection classes
RegistryPermission	System.Security.Permissions	Protects the system registries from modificaton
SecurityPermission	System.Security.Permissions	Protects SecurityPermission class actions from code access
ServiceControllerPermission	System.ServiceProcess	Protects ServiceController class actions from code access
SiteIdentityPermission	System.Security.Permissions	Protects manipulation of site evidence
SocketPermission	System.Net	Protects sockets from connection attempts
StrongNameIdentityPermission	System.Security.Permissions	Protects strong names from manipulation
UIPermission	System.Security.Permissions	Protects user interface elements, including the clipboard, from access by unauthorized code
UrlIdentityPermission	System.Security.Permissions	Protects URL access and manipulation for an assembly
WebPermission	System.Net	Protects access to Internet-based resources
ZoneIdentityPermission	System.Security.Permissions	Protects a components zone information from code access

Role-Based Security

Role-based security is a more traditional security model. Instead of being based on the concept of code accessing a particular resource, it is based on the concept of limiting or allowing actions as determined by a user's identity and his membership in a role group. In .NET, a *principal object* is used to encapsulate a user's identity and indicate to which roles he belongs.

Principals

In a sense, a principal is a sort of proxy that interacts with the security system as a representation of a user. Principals work in conjunction with *identity* objects. Identity objects uniquely identify users to the runtime.

There are three types of principals:

- Generic—These apply to users and roles that exist outside of the concept of Windows users and roles. In the .NET Framework, these are represented by the `GenericPrincipal` class in the `System.Security.Principal` namespace.
- Windows—These are a one-to-one map with Windows users and groups. These are represented by the `WindowsPrincipal` class—also in the `System.Security.Principal` namespace.
- Custom—These are defined by an application. They have no default representation in the class library, and need to be created and defined by each application that uses them.

Creating and Assigning Identities and Principals

Principal objects are used to retrieve and establish the security context of a particular user. A security context includes both the actual identity of the user and her roles. Each principal object is based around the `IPrincipal` interface; this is the base interface used to provide security context awareness to classes.

A common programming task in role-based applications is determining who the current user is and which roles she belongs to. There are two ways to do this in .NET. The first way revolves around the `Thread.CurrentPrincipal` property. This property will return a principal object for the current user. The second uses the `WindowsIdentity` class and its `GetCurrent` method. This will return an identity object, which can be passed into the constructor of a `WindowsPrincipal` object to create the desired principal.

After creating the principal object, it is easy to leverage it to secure functions in an application. Just like code access security, you can perform role-based security checks in either a declarative fashion or an imperative fashion.

Declarative Role-Based Security Checks

The `PrincipalPermissionAttribute` class is used to establish declarative principal and identity checks in your code's metadata. You can check whether the user matches a specific name, whether he is in a group, or you can simply verify that he has been authenticated by the operating system.

The following code verifies that the user is 'Johnathan', and that he belongs in the 'User' group.

```
<PrincipalPermissionAttribute(SecurityAction.Demand, _
    Name := "Johnathan", Role := "User")> Public Sub Test
```

Imperative Role-Based Security Checks

Imperative role checks use the `PrincipalPermission` class. Again, just like the code access model we described previously, this imperative design pattern involves the instantiation of a permission object and the use of its methods.

The following code accomplishes the same basic thing as our declarative code did:

```
Public Sub Test
        Dim pPermit As New PrincipalPermission("Johnathan", " User")

        pPermit.Demand()

        .
        .
        .

End Sub
```

Joining Permissions

If your code needs to check for a blend of identities or roles, you can use the `PrincipalPermission.Union` method to combine one permission object with another:

```
pPermit.Union(otherPermit).Demand
```

.NET Framework Base Data Types

Base Data Type Class		VB.NET Data Type	Description
Boolean	Boolean		Specification: Boolean value
			Value Range: true or false
Byte	Byte		Specification: 8-bit unsigned integer
			Value Range: 0 to 255
Char	Char		Specification: 16-bit, Unicode, character
			Value Range: 0x0000 to 0xFFFF (hex character codes)
Decimal	Decimal		Specification: 96-bit decimal
			Value Range: +79,228,162,514,264,337,593,543,950,335 to -79,228,162,514,264,337,593,543,950,335
Double	Double		Specification: 64-bit, double precision, float
			Value Range: -1.79769313486232e308 to +1.79769313486232e308
Int16	Short		Specification: 16-bit signed integer
			Value Range: -32768 through +32767
Int32	Integer		Specification: 32-bit signed integer
			Value Range: -2,147,483,648 to +2,147,483,647
Int64	Long		Specification: 64-bit signed integer
			Value Range: -9,223,372,036,854,775,808 to +9,223,372,036,854,775,807
IntPtr	n/a		Specification: signed integer (platform-specific size)
			Value Range: ---
Object	Object		Specification: root class instance
			Value Range: any and all derived classes
Sbyte	n/a		Specification: 8-bit signed integer
			Value Range: ---
Single	Single		Specification: 32-bit, single precision, float
			Value Range: -3.402823e38 to +3.402823e38

Base Data Type Class		VB.NET Data Type	Description
String	String		Specification: string of Unicode characters (fixed member set)
			Value Range: 0 to ~2,000,000,000 characters
UInt16	n/a		Specification: 16-bit unsigned integer
			Value Range: ---
UInt32	n/a		Specification: 32-bit unsigned integer
			Value Range: ---
UInt64	n/a		Specification: 64-bit unsigned integer
			Value Range: ---
UIntPtr	n/a		Specification: unsigned integer (platform specific size)
			Value Range: ---

INDEX

A

abstract classes, 70-71

AccessControlEntry class, 649

AccessControlEntryType enumeration, 649

AccessControlList class, 600, 650

accessing, 217-223

    COM+ services, 810-812

    directories, 216-223

    files, 216, 227-228

    objects in directories, 783-785

    Win32 API, 978-984

Active Directory (AD)

    accessing objects, 783-785

    additional resources, 789

    ADSI (Active Directory Services Interface), 778

    attributes, 780-781, 785-788

    capabilities, 778

    classes, 779-781

    Directory Information Tree (DIT), 781

    DirectoryBrowser application, 791-802

    LDAP (Lightweight Directory Access Protocol), 778

    object identities, 782-783

    overview, 776

    password protection, 788

    schemas, 779

    searching, 789-791

    security, 788

    sorting search results, 790

    structure, 778-779

    System.DirectoryServices namespace, 776

Active Directory Services Interface (ADSI), 778

Active Server Pages (ASP), ASP.NET, 692

ActiveX controls, 131-132

ActiveXMessengerFormatter class, 600

AD (Active Directory). *See* Active Directory

ADO.NET, 722

    Command object, 727-728

    Connection object, 726-727

    data providers, 725-730

    DataAdapter object, 729-730

    database connections, 731-732

    database inserts, 736-741

    database queries, 732-734

    database resultsets, 734-735

    database transactions, 742-744

    database updates, 736-741

    DataReader object, 728-729

    overview, 725

ADSI (Active Directory Services Interface), 778

algorithms, hash algorithms, 654

aliases, functions, 982

app.config, 971-973

AppendText method, 238

Application Center 2000, 13

applications

    COM applications, .NET Interop with COM applications, 850-866

    configuration files, 971-973